Durham's

Place-Names
of

California's Central Coast

Durham's Place-Names of California Series

- Fourteen volumes cover the state of California by region
- The most complete California place-name series

- *Durham's Place-Names of California's Gold Country Including Yosemite National Park:* **Includes Mariposa, Tuolumne, Calaveras, Amador, El Dorado, Placer, Sierra & Nevada Counties** ISBN 1-884995-25-X

- *Durham's Place-Names of the California North Coast:* **Includes Del Norte, Humbolt, Lake, Mendocino & Trinity Counties** ISBN 1-884995-26-8

- *Durham's Place-Names of California's Old Wine Country:* **Includes Napa & Sonoma Counties** ISBN 1-884995-27-6

- *Durham's Place-Names of Greater Los Angeles:* **Includes Los Angeles, Orange & Ventura Counties** ISBN 1-884995-28-4

- *Durham's Place-Names of California's Central Coast:* **Includes Santa Barbara, San Luis Obispo, San Benito, Monterey & Santa Cruz Counties** ISBN 1-884995-29-2

- *Durham's Place-Names of California's Eastern Sierra:* **Includes Alpine, Inyo & Mono Counties** ISBN 1-884995-30-6

- *Durham's Place-Names of California's Desert Counties:* **Includes Imperial, Riverside & San Bernadino Counties** ISBN 1-884995-31-4

- *Durham's Place-Names of* **San Diego County** ISBN 1-884995-32-2

- *Durham's Place-Names of Central California:* **Includes Madera, Fresno, Tulare, Kings & Kern Counties** ISBN 1-884995-33-0

- *Durham's Place-Names of California's North Sacramento Valley:* **Includes Butte, Glenn, Shasta, Siskiyou & Tehama Counties** ISBN 1-884995-34-9

- *Durham's Place-Names of The San Francisco Bay Area:* **Includes Marin, San Francisco, San Mateo, Contra Costa, Alameda , Solano & Santa Clara Counties** ISBN 1-884995-35-7

- *Durham's Place-Names of California's South Sacramento Valley:* **Includes Colusa, Sacramento, Sutter, Yuba & Yolo Counties** ISBN 1-884995-36-5

- *Durham's Place-Names of California's North San Joaquin Valley:* **Includes San Joaquin, Stanislaus & Merced Counties** ISBN 1-884995-37-3

- *Durham's Place-Names of Northeastern California:* **Includes Lassen, Modoc & Plumas Counties** ISBN 1-884995-38-1

The above titles are available at better bookstores, online bookstores or by calling 1-800-497-4909

Durham's

Place-Names
of

California's Central Coast

Includes Santa Barbara, San Luis Obispo,
San Benito, Monterey & Santa Cruz Counties

David L. Durham

Word Dancer Press

Clovis, California

Printed in the United States of America
Published by
Quill Driver Books/Word Dancer Press, Inc.
8386 N. Madsen
Clovis, CA 93611
559-322-5917
800-497-4909

Word Dancer Press books may be purchased at special prices for educational, fund-raising, business or promotional use. Please contact Special Markets, Quill Driver Books/Word Dancer Press, Inc. at the above address or phone number.

To order another copy of this book or another book in the Durham's Place-Names of California series, please call 1-800-497-4909.

Quill Driver Books/Word Dancer Press, Inc. project cadre:
Doris Hall, Dave Marion, Stephen Blake Mettee

ISBN 1-884995-29-2

Library of Congress Cataloging-in-Publication Data

Durham, David L., 1925-
    Durham's place names of California's Central Coast : includes Santa Barbara, San Luis Obispo, San Benito, Monterey & Santa Cruz counties / David L. Durham.
    p. cm.
    Includes bibliographical references (p.).
    ISBN 1-884995-29-2
    1. Names, Geographical--California. 2. California--History, Local. 3. Santa Barbara County (Calif.)--History, Local. 4. San Luis Obispo County (Calif.)--History, Local. 5. San Benito County (Calif.)--History, Local. 6. Monterey County (Calif.)--History, Local. 7. Santa Cruz County (Calif.)--History, Local. I. Title: Place names of California's Central Coast. II. Title.

F859 .D875 2001
917.94'7'003--dc21

                                                                00-054633

Cover photo: "Point Lobos" by Martin Brown, courtesy of the Monterey County Convention & Visitor's Bureau. Website: gomonterey.org. Hotline: (831)-649-1770.

CONTENTS

CALIFORNIA
CENTRAL COAST COUNTIES
SHADED

INTRODUCTION

Purpose, organization and scope

This gazetteer, which lists geographic features of Santa Barbara, San Luis Obispo, San Benito, Monterey, and Santa Cruz counties, California, is one of a series of fourteen books that cover the whole state. This series is derived from *California's Geographic Names: A Gazetteer of Historic and Modern Names of the State,* David L. Durham's definitive gazetteer of California. Each book contains all the entries for the counties covered that are included in the larger volume. United States government quadrangle maps, which are detailed, somewhat authoritative, and generally available, are the primary source of information. Included are features that are named on quadrangle maps, or that can be related to features named on the maps. The books list relief features, water features, and most kinds of cultural features, but omit names of streets, parks, schools, churches, cemeteries, dams and the like. Some names simply identify a person or family living at a site because such places are landmarks in sparsely settled parts of the state.

The listing of names is alphabetical, and multiword names are alphabetized as one word. Terms abbreviated on maps are given in full in the alphabetical list, and numerals in names are listed in alphabetical order rather than in numerical order. In addition to the principal entries, the list includes cross references to variant names, obsolete names and key words in multiword English-language names. For each principal entry, the name is followed by the name of the county or counties in which the feature lies, a classifying term, general and specific locations, identification of one or more quadrangle maps that show the name and other information. All features named in an entry generally belong to the same county. The classifying terms are defined under the heading "Geographic Terms" beginning on page *xi.*

Locations and measurements are from quadrangle maps, distances and directions are approximate, and latitude and longitude generally are to the nearest five seconds. Distances between post offices are measured by road, as the mail would be carried. Other distances are measured in a straight line unless the measurement is given with a qualifying expression such as "downstream" or "by road." For streams, the location given generally is the place that the stream joins another stream, enters the sea or a lake, or debouches into a canyon or valley. For features of considerable areal extent, the location given ordinarily is near the center, except for cities and towns, for which the location given is near the center of the downtown part, or at the city hall or civic center. Measurements to or from areal features usually are to or from the center. Specific locations are omitted for some very large or poorly defined places. Books, articles, and miscellaneous maps are listed under "References Cited." The references identify sources of data and provide leads to additional information. If a name applies to more than one feature in a county, the features are numbered and identified elsewhere in the list by that number in parentheses following the name.

REGIONAL SETTING

General.—This book concerns geographic features in five counties—Monterey, San Benito, San Luis Obispo, Santa Barbara, and Santa Cruz—that lie near the coast of California from Monterey Bay south to Santa Barbara Channel; all but San Benito County front on the sea. Townships (T) South refer to Mount Diablo Base and Meridian; Townships North refer to San Bernardino Base and Meridian. The region generally is mountainous and includes islands on the south side of Santa Barbara Channel. The map on page *vi* shows the location of the counties included in this book.

Monterey County.—Monterey County covers the north part of the valley of Salinas River and highlands east and west of the valley. The first state legislature created the county in 1850. Officials changed the boundary between Monterey and San Luis Obispo Counties several times before they fixed it at its present position in 1863; Monterey County lost part of its original territory when San Benito County was organized in 1874 (Coy, p. 184-186). The city of Monterey was the county seat until the county government moved to Salinas in 1873 (Hoover, Rensch, and Rensch, p. 216). The name "Monterey" in the region dates from 1602, when Vizcaino gave his anchorage near present Monterey the designation "Puerto de Monterey" to honor the Conde de Monterey, Viceroy of New Spain (Wagner, H.R., p. 398).

San Benito.—San Benito County is mostly mountainous; extensive lowlands occur only in the north part. The state legislature created the county in 1874 from part of Monterey County, and added territory in 1887 at the expense of Fresno County (Coy, p. 213-214). Hollister is and always has been the county seat; the county name is from San Benito River, which flows nearly the entire length of the county (Hoover, Rensch, and Rensch, p. 309, 315).

San Luis Obispo.—San Luis Obispo County includes part or all of several mountain ranges as well as lowlands along the coast, near Santa Maria River, and along part of Salinas River. The state legislature created the county in

1850; the original boundaries of the county have been modified only slightly (Coy, p. 233-237). The city of San Luis Obispo has been the county seat from the beginning; the name "San Luis Obispo" for city and county is from San Luis Obispo de Tolusa mission, founded in 1772 (Hoover, Rensch, and Rensch, p. 378-380).

Santa Barbara.—Santa Barbara County lies along the coast where the general south-southeast trend of the coastline turns eastward at Point Conception, and includes offshore islands. It is one of the original counties that the first state legislature created in 1850. Officials modified Santa Barbara-San Luis Obispo County line several times before 1872, when they fixed the present boundary; the east part of the original territory of Santa Barbara County was lost in 1872 with the formation of Ventura County (Coy, p. 242-244). The county name is from Santa Barbara Channel, which Vizcaino named; the city of Santa Barbara has always been the county seat (Hoover, Rensch, and Rensch, p. 413).

Santa Cruz.—Santa Cruz County extends inland from the coast to the crest of Santa Cruz Mountains. It is one of the counties that the state legislature created in 1850 when California achieved statehood; the north part of the original territory of the county was lost to San Mateo County in 1868, but otherwise the county boundaries differ little from those of 1850—the county was called Branciforte for a brief time before the name was changed to Santa Cruz (Coy, p. 248). The city of Santa Cruz is the first and only county seat; the county name is from Santa Cruz mission, founded in 1891 (Hoover, Rensch, and Rensch, p. 464).

GEOGRAPHIC TERMS

Anchorage —A somewhat protected place where ships anchor.

Area —A tract of land, either precisely or indefinitely defined.

Bay —A body of water connected to a larger body of water and nearly surrounded by land.

Beach —An expanse of sandy or pebbly material that borders a body of water.

Bend —A pronounced curve in the course of a stream, and the land partly enclosed therein.

Canyon —A narrow elongate depression in the land surface, generally confined between steep sides and usually drained by a stream.

Cave —A naturally formed subterranean chamber.

City —An inhabited place that has a population greater than about 25,000 in an urban setting.

District —Part of an inhabited place, either precisely or indefinitely defined.

Embayment —An indentation in the shoreline of a body of water.

Escarpment —A cliff or a nearly continuous line of steep slopes.

Hill —A prominent elevation on the land surface that has a well-defined outline on a map, and that rises less than 1000 feet above its surroundings.

Intermittent lake —A lake that ordinarily contains water only part of the time.

Island —A tract of normally dry land, or of marsh, that is surrounded by water.

Lake —A body of standing water, either natural or artificial.

Land grant —A gift of land made by Spanish or Mexican authority and eventually confirmed by the United States government.

Locality —A place that has past or present cultural associations.

Marsh —A poorly drained wet area.

Military installation —Land or facility used for military purposes.

Mountain —A prominent elevation on the land surface that has a well-defined outline on a map, and that rises more than 1000 feet above its surroundings.

Narrows —The constricted part of a channel, river, canyon, valley, or pass.

Pass —A saddle or natural depression that affords passage across a range or between peaks.

Peak —A prominent high point on a larger elevated land surface.

Promontory —A conspicuous, but not necessarily hihg, elevation of the land surface that protrudes into a body of water or into a lowland.

Range —An elevated land surface of ridges and peaks.

Relief feature —A general term for a recognizable form of the land surface produced by natural causes.

Ridge —A prominent elongate elevation on the land surface; occurs either independently or as part of a larger elevation.

Rock —A rocky mass that lies near or projects above the surface of a body of water.

Settlement —An informal inhabited place.

Shoal —A shallow place in a body of water.

Spring —A natural flow of water from the ground.

Stream —A body of water that moves under gravity in a depression on the land surface; includes watercourses that have intermittent flow and watercourses that are modified by man.

Town —An inhabited place that has a population of about 500 to 25,000 in an urban setting.

Valley —A broad depression in the land surface, or a wide place in an otherwise narrow depression.

Village —An inhabited place that has a compact cluster of buildings and a population less than about 500.

Waterfall —A perpendicular or very steep descent of the water in a stream.

Water feature —A general term for something or some place involving water.

Well —A hole sunk into the ground to obtain water.

DURHAM'S
PLACE-NAMES OF
CALIFORNIA'S CENTRAL COAST

– A –

Abalone Point: see **Carmel Beach** [MONTEREY]; **Point Alones** [MONTEREY].

Abbott Canyon [SAN LUIS OBISPO]: *canyon,* drained by a stream that flows 3.5 miles to Carrizo Plain 25 miles southeast of Simmler (lat. 35°03'50" N, long. 119°42'50" W; sec. 1, T 11 N, R 27 W). Named on Caliente Mountain (1959) and Wells Ranch (1954) 7.5' quadrangles.

Abel Canyon [SANTA BARBARA]: *canyon,* drained by a stream that flows 6.5 miles to Sisquoc River 6.25 miles west of Montgomery Potrero (lat. 34°49'25" N, long. 119°51'45" W). Named on Hurricane Deck (1964) and Peak Mountain (1964) 7.5' quadrangles.

Abel Canyon Campground [SANTA BARBARA]: *locality,* 6.25 miles west of Montgomery Potrero along Sisquoc River (lat. 34°49'20" N, long. 119°51'40" W); the place is near the mouth of Abel Canyon. Named on Hurricane Deck (1964) 7.5' quadrangle.

Abel Canyon Spring [SANTA BARBARA]: *spring,* 4.25 miles northwest of Montgomery Potrero (lat. 34°52'15" N, long. 119°48'50" W); the spring is in a branch of Abel Canyon. Named on Hurricane Deck (1964) 7.5' quadrangle.

Adams Cove [SANTA BARBARA]: *embayment,* 0.5 mile east of Point Bennett on the south side of San Miguel Island (lat. 34°01'50" N, long. 120°26'25" W). Named on San Miguel Island West (1950) 7.5' quadrangle.

Adelaida [SAN LUIS OBISPO]: *locality,* 10 miles west of Paso Robes (lat. 35°38'45" N, long. 120°52'20" W; near NE cor. sec. 27, T 26 S, R 10 E). Named on Adelaida (1948) 7.5' quadrangle. The place was the site of a Mennonite settlement (Lee and others, p. 8). Called Adelaide on California Mining Bureau's (1909b) map, and Crawford (1894, p. 394) referred to Adelaide P.O. Postal authorities established Adelaida post office in 1877 when they moved Josephine post office to the place; they moved Adelaida post office 1 mile northeast in 1880 and discontinued it in 1936—the name "Adelaida" was for the daughter of the postmaster (Salley, p. 1). They established Josephine post office in 1873, discontinued it for a time in 1877, and discontinued it finally in 1883; the name

"Josephine" was for the first white child born at the site, which was 14 miles west of Paso Robles (Salley, p. 108). Josephine post office may have been at Josephine mine, a quicksilver mine discovered in 1862 about 5 miles southwest of present Adelaida (Logan, p. 711). California Mining Bureau's (1909b) map shows a place called Gibbons located 7.5 miles by stage line northwest of Adelaide (present Adelaida); postal authorities established Gibbons post office in 1894 and discontinued it in 1909 (Frickstad, p. 164).

Adelaide: see **Adelaida** [SAN LUIS OBISPO].

Adobe Canyon [SAN LUIS OBISPO]:

(1) *canyon,* drained by a stream that flows 1.5 miles to Rocky Canyon 6 miles north of Santa Margarita (lat. 35°28'35" N, long. 120°36'30" W; sec. 19, T 28 S, R 13 E). Named on Santa Margarita (1965) 7.5' quadrangle.

(2) *canyon,* drained by a stream that flows 2 miles to Los Berros Canyon 5 miles east-southeast of the town of Arroyo Grande (lat. 35°05'40" N, long. 120°30'05" W; sec. 32, T 32 S, R 14 E). Named on Oceano (1965) 7.5' quadrangle.

Adobe Canyon [SANTA BARBARA]: *canyon,* drained by a stream that flows 4 miles to Santa Ynez River 2.5 miles southeast of Buellton (lat. 34°35'30" N, long. 120°01'50" W). Named on Solvang (1959) and Zaca Creek (1959) 7.5' quadrangles.

Adobe Creek [SAN LUIS OBISPO]: *stream,* flows 2 miles to the sea nearly 2 miles west-northwest of the village of San Simeon (lat. 35°39'05" N, long. 121°13'20" W). Named on San Simeon (1958) 7.5' quadrangle.

Adobe Springs [SAN LUIS OBISPO]: *spring,* 4 miles west of Cholame (2) in McMillan Canyon (lat. 35°44' N, long. 120°21'55" W; sec. 21, T 25 S, R 15 E). Named on Cholame (1961) 7.5' quadrangle.

Agenda: see **Buena Vista** [MONTEREY] (2).

Agua Caliente Canyon [SANTA BARBARA]: *canyon,* drained by a stream that flows 14 miles to Santa Ynez River 6.5 miles south-southwest of Hildreth Peak (lat. 34°30'30" N, long. 119°34'45" W). Named on Hildreth Peak (1964) and Old Man Mountain (1943) 7.5' quadrangles.

Agua Caliente Spring [SANTA BARBARA]: *spring,* 4.5 miles south of Hildreth Peak (lat. 34°32'25" N, long. 119°33'45" W); the spring is in Agua Caliente Canyon. Named on Hildreth Peak (1964) 7.5' quadrangle.

Agua del Gavilan: see **Gabilan Creek** [MONTEREY] (2).

Aguadulce Spring [SANTA BARBARA]: *spring,* 2 miles east of Salisbury Potrero (lat. 34°49'10" N, long. 119°39'50" W). Named on Salisbury Potrero (1964) 7.5' quadrangle.

Agua Escondida Spring [SAN LUIS OBISPO]: *spring,* 7.5 miles west of Branch Mountain near the head of Arroyo Seco (lat. 35°10'55" N, long. 120°13'40" W; sec. 35, T 31 S, R 16 E). Named on Branch Mountain (1952) 15' quadrangle. Called Aqua Escondida Spr. on Branch Mountain (1942) 15' quadrangle.

Agua Escondido Campground [SAN LUIS OBISPO]: *locality,* 7.5 miles west of Branch Mountain (lat. 35°10'45" N, long. 120°13'40" W; on N line sec. 2, T 32 S, R 16 E). Named on Los Machos Hills (1967) 7.5' quadrangle. Branch Mountain (1952) 15' quadrangle shows Agua Escondida Spring near the site.

Agua Fria Creek [MONTEREY]: *stream,* flows nearly 3 miles to Gabilan Creek (2) 6 miles south-southwest of Jolon (lat. 35°53'40" N, long. 121°13'35" W). Named on Jolon (1949) 7.5' quadrangle.

Agua Grande Canyon [MONTEREY]: *canyon,* flows 6.25 miles to lowlands 5 miles east-southeast of Greenfield (lat. 36°18'10" N, long. 121°09'15" W). Named on Greenfield (1956) and Pinalito Canyon (1969) 7.5' quadrangles.

Aguajita [SANTA CRUZ]: *land grant,* 2.25 miles north-northwest of Soquel Point at the east edge of Santa Cruz. Named on Soquel (1954) 7.5' quadrangle. Miguel Villagrana received the land in 1837; 40 acres were patented to Villagrana or his son (Rowland, p. 41; Rowland used the form "Aguajito" for the name).

Aguajito [MONTEREY]: *land grant,* south and southeast of Monterey. Named on Monterey (1947) and Seaside (1947) 7.5' quadrangles. Gregorio Tapia received 0.5 league in 1835 and claimed 3323 acres patented in 1868 (Cowan, p. 13). Gudde (1949, p. 5) noted that *aguajito* is the diminutive of *aguaje,* which means "reservoir," "spring," or "watering place" in Spanish.

Aguajito: see **Aguajita** [SANTA CRUZ].

Aguajito Canyon [SANTA BARBARA]: *canyon,* drained by a stream that flows 2.5 miles to Cañada del Refugio 8.5 miles east of Gaviota (lat. 34°28'35" N, long. 120°04'05" W). Named on Santa Ynez (1959) and Tajiguas (1953) 7.5' quadrangles.

Agua Mala Creek [MONTEREY]: *stream,* flows 6.25 miles to Rana Creek 6.5 miles east-southeast of the town of Carmel Valley (lat. 36°26'20" N, long. 121°37'35" W). Named on Rana Creek (1956) 7.5' quadrangle.

Agua Puerca y las Trancas [SANTA CRUZ]: *land grant,* 4 miles north-northwest of Davenport along the coast at El Jarro Point. Named on Año Nuevo (1955) and Davenport (1955) 7.5' quadrangles. Ramon Rodriguez and Francisco Alviso received 1 league in 1843; their heirs claimed 4421 acres patented

in 1867—the grant also was called El Jarro (Cowan, p. 13).

Airbase [SANTA BARBARA]: *locality,* 3 miles south of Santa Maria along Santa Maria Valley Railroad (lat. 34°54'25" N, long. 120°26'40" W; near N line sec. 34, T 10 N, R 34 W). Named on Santa Maria (1959) 7.5' quadrangle.

Airstrip Pond [SAN BENITO]: *intermittent lake,* 450 feet long, 12.5 miles east-southeast of Bitterwater (lat. 36°18'35" N, long. 120°47'50" W; sec. 5, T 19 S, R 11 E); the feature is near a landing strip situated along upper reaches of Laguna Creek. Named on Hepsedam Peak (1969) 7.5' quadrangle.

Ajax: see **Surf** [SANTA BARBARA].

Ajax Mountain: see **Alder Peak** [MONTEREY].

Alamar Campground: see **Lower Alamar Campground** [SANTA BARBARA].

Alamar Canyon [SANTA BARBARA]: *canyon,* drained by a stream that flows 9 miles to Mono Creek 2 miles northwest of Hildreth Peak (lat. 34°37'05" N, long. 119°34'20" W). Named on Hildreth Peak (1964) and Madulce Peak (1964) 7.5' quadrangles. Called Roble Canyon on Santa Ynez (1905) 30' quadrangle. Strawberry Peak (1944) 7.5' quadrangle shows Alamar Canyon as a branch of Roble Canyon.

Alamar Hill [SANTA BARBARA]: *ridge,* southeast-trending, less than 1 mile long, about 4 miles south of Madulce Peak (lat. 34°37'50" N, long. 119°35'25" W); the ridge is west of Alamar Canyon. Named on Madulce Peak (1964) 7.5' quadrangle.

Alamo Canyon [SANTA BARBARA]: *canyon,* drained by a stream that flows 4.5 miles to Santa Barbara Canyon 3 miles south-southeast of Fox Mountain (lat. 34°46'30" N, long. 119°34'20" W). Named on Fox Mountain (1964) and Strawberry Peak (1944) 7.5' quadrangles.

Alamo Creek [SAN LUIS OBISPO]:

(1) *stream,* flows 5.5 miles to Santa Margarita Lake 4 miles west-northwest of Pozo (lat. 35°19'40" N, long. 120°26'20" W; sec. 11, T 30 S, R 14 E). Named on Santa Margarita Lake (1967) 7.5' quadrangle.

(2) *stream,* flows 23 miles to Cuyama River 2.5 miles southeast of Huasna Peak (lat. 35°00'30" N, long. 120°18'50" W). Named on Chimney Canyon (1967), Huasna Peak (1967), and Los Machos Hills (1967) 7.5' quadrangles. Called Alamos Creek on Nipomo (1922) 15' quadrangle. The stream now joins Cuyama River in Twitchell Reservoir. California Mining Bureau's (1909b) map shows a place called Avenal located 14.5 miles by stage line southeast of Pozo, probably along Alamo Creek (2) at or near the place that Los Machos Hills (1967) 7.5' quadrangle shows Avenales ranch (lat. 35°12'20" N, long. 120°11'25" W). Postal authorities established Avenal post office in 1887 and discontinued

it in 1905 (Frickstad, p. 163).

Alamo Creek [SANTA BARBARA]: *stream,* flows 2.5 miles to El Jaro Creek 12 miles southeast of the city of Lompoc (lat. 34°31'05" N, long. 120°18'20" W). Named on Santa Rosa Hills (1959) 7.5' quadrangle.

Alamo Pintado: see **Ballard** [SANTA BARBARA].

Alamo Pintado Creek [SANTA BARBARA]: *stream,* flows 18 miles to Santa Ynez River 3.5 miles southeast of Buellton near Solvang (lat. 34°35' N, long. 120°08'15" W). Named on Los Olivos (1959), Santa Ynez (1959), and Solvang (1959) 7.5' quadrangles.

Alamos Anchorage [SANTA BARBARA]: *anchorage,* 2.5 miles east of Punta Arena on the south side of Santa Cruz Island (lat. 33°57'40" N, long. 119°46'10" W). Named on Santa Cruz Island B (1943) 7.5' quadrangle. Bremner's (1932) map has the name "Cñ. del Alamo" for a canyon that opens to the sea 0.5 mile west of present Alamos Anchorage.

Alamos Creek: see **Alamo Creek** [SAN LUIS OBISPO] (2).

Alba Creek [SANTA CRUZ]: *stream,* flows 1.25 miles to San Lorenzo River 2 miles south-southeast of the town of Boulder Creek (lat. 37°06'10" N, long. 122°06'10" W; sec. 32, T 9 S, R 2 W). Named on Felton (1955) 7.5' quadrangle.

Albañez Spring [SAN BENITO]: *spring,* 7.5 miles west of Panoche (lat. 36°35'40" N, long. 120°58'05" W; sec. 27, T 15 S, R 9 E). Named on Llanada (1969) 7.5' quadrangle.

Albert Anchorage [SANTA BARBARA]: *embayment,* 3.5 miles south of Prisoners Harbor on the south side of Santa Cruz Island (lat. 33° 58'10" N, long. 119°41'50" W). Named on Santa Cruz Island C (1943) 7.5' quadrangle.

Alcatraz [SANTA BARBARA]: *locality,* less than 1 mile east of Gaviota (lat. 34°28'15" N, long. 120°12'15" W); the place is near the mouth of present Cañada Alcatraz. Named on Lompoc (1905) 30' quadrangle. Postal authorities established Alcatraz Landing post office at the site in 1898 and discontinued it in 1901—the landing was a shipping point for oil (Salley, p. 4).

Alcatraz Landing: see **Alcatraz** [SANTA BARBARA].

Alder Creek [MONTEREY]: *stream,* flows 4.5 miles to the sea 3.5 miles southeast of Cape San Martin (lat. 35°51'30" N, long. 121° 25' W; sec. 10, T 14 S, R 5 E); the stream heads near Alder Peak. Named on Villa Creek (1949) 7.5' quadrangle. Irelan (p. 406) mentioned a mining town called Alder Creek—Cape San Martin (1921) 15' quadrangle shows mines situated 1 to 1.5 miles west and southwest of Alder Peak on the upper reaches of Alder Creek. Reinstedt (1973, p. 13-14) noted that the community of Alder Creek later was called Manchester for a blacksmith who lived there in the early days; when a post office opened,

the name of the place was changed to Mansfield for the Mansfield family of Gorda, the earliest residents in the neighborhood. Postal authorities established Mansfield post office in 1889 and discontinued it in 1897 (Frickstad, p. 107). Davis (p. 696) noted that an old townsite called Los Burros was situated "upon a fairly level piece of ground sloping into a gulch opening into Alder creek . . . just below the old Last Chance mine (now the Buclimo)." This site is about 2.5 miles from the mouth of Alder Creek (sec. 2, T 24 S, R 5 E).

Alder Creek [SANTA BARBARA]: *stream,* flows 3 miles to Santa Ynez River 6.25 miles north of Carpinteria (lat. 34°29'15" N, long. 119°31'10" W; sec. 29, T 5 N, R 25 W). Named on Carpinteria (1952) and White Ledge Peak (1952) 7.5' quadrangles.

Alder Creek Mountain: see **Alder Peak** [MONTEREY].

Alder Peak [MONTEREY]: *peak,* 5.5 miles east of Cape San Martin (lat. 35°53'05" N, long. 121°22'05" W; at E line sec. 36, T 23 S, R 5 E); the peak is near the head of Alder Creek. Altitude 3744 feet. Named on Alder Peak (1949) 7.5' quadrangle. The feature also was known as Alder Creek Mountain, and perhaps as Ajax Mountain (Clark, 1991, p. 5).

Alegria Canyon: see **Cañada de Alegria** [SANTA BARBARA].

Alejandro Campground [SANTA BARBARA]: *locality,* 1.25 miles east-southeast of Tepusquet Peak (lat. 34°54'20" N, long. 120°09'45" W); the place is in Alejandro Canyon. Named on Tepusquet Canyon (1964) 7.5' quadrangle. The name commemorates Alejandro Ontiveras, head of the Spanish family that held land in the vicinity (Gagnon, p. 65).

Alejandro Canyon [SANTA BARBARA]: *canyon,* drained by a stream that flows 5.5 miles to La Brea Creek 3.5 miles south-southeast of Tepusquet Peak (lat. 34°51'35" N, long. 120°09'55" W). Named on Foxen Canyon (1964) and Tepusquet Canyon (1964) 7.5' quadrangles. Called Alejandra Canyon on Tepusquet Peak (1943) 15' quadrangle, but United States Board on Geographic Names (1965c, p. 10) rejected this form for the name.

Alexander Canyon: see **Powell Canyon** [MONTEREY].

Alexander Peak [SANTA BARBARA]: *peak,* 7 miles north-northeast of San Marcos Pass (lat. 34°35'55" N, long. 119°45'45" W). Altitude 4107 feet. Named on San Marcos Pass (1959) 7.5' quadrangle.

Alisal [MONTEREY]: *district,* east of downtown Salinas (lat. 36°40'45" N, long. 121°36'45" W); the district is on and near El Alisal (1) grant. Named on Natividad (1947) and Salinas (1947) 7.5' quadrangles. Unnamed and shown as part of Salinas on Natividad (1947, photorevised 1968) and Salinas (1947, photorevised 1968 and 1975) 7.5' quadrangles. Alisal became part of Salinas in

1963 (Clark, 1991, p. 6). Postal authorities established Alisal post office in 1866 and discontinued it in 1869, when they moved it and changed the name to Gabilan; they discontinued Gabilan post office in 1883, reestablished it in 1898, discontinued it in 1900, and reestablished it in 1950; they established East Salinas post office in 1940 and discontinued it in 1947, when they changed the name to Alisal—they changed the name back to East Salinas in 1949, and changed it to Alisal again in 1950 (Salley, p. 4, 64, 82).

Alisal Creek [MONTEREY]: *stream,* flows 5.5 miles to lowlands 5 miles east of Salinas (lat. 36°41'30" N, long. 121°34'05" W). Named on Mount Harlan (1968) and Natividad (1947) 7.5' quadrangles.

Alisal Creek [SANTA BARBARA]: *stream,* flows 8 miles to Santa Ynez River 3.5 miles southeast of Buellton (lat. 34°35'05" N, long. 120°08'35" W). Named on Santa Ynez (1959) and Solvang (1959) 7.5' quadrangles.

Alisal Slough [MONTEREY]: *stream* and *dry wash,* branches north from Salinas River 5 miles southeast of Salinas (lat. 36°37'15" N, long. 121°36'20" W) and meanders for 20 miles toward the coast. Named on Chualar (1947), Natividad (1947), and Salinas (1947) 7.5' quadrangles.

Aliso Campground [SANTA BARBARA]: *locality,* 3 miles east-northeast of McPherson Peak (lat. 34°54'30" N, long. 119°46'05" W); the place is in Aliso Canyon (1). Named on Peak Mountain (1964) 7.5' quadrangle.

Aliso Canyon [SAN LUIS OBISPO]: *canyon,* drained by a stream that flows 2.5 miles to Alamo Creek (2) 8 miles west-northwest of Branch Mountain (lat. 35°13'25" N, long. 120°12'25" W). Named on La Panza (1967) and Los Machos Hills (1967) 7.5' quadrangles.

Aliso Canyon [SANTA BARBARA]:
(1) *canyon,* drained by a stream that flows 9.5 miles to Cuyama River 7 miles north-northeast of McPherson Peak (lat. 34°59'15" N, long. 119°46'40" W). Named on Peak Mountain (1964) 7.5' quadrangle.
(2) *canyon,* drained by a stream that flows nearly 2 miles to Santa Ynez River 3 miles northeast of San Marcos Pass (lat. 34°32'40" N, long. 119°47'20" W). Named on San Marcos Pass (1959) 7.5' quadrangle.

Aliso Creek [SANTA BARBARA]: *stream,* flows 7.25 miles to Cuyama River 9 miles west of Miranda Pine Mountain (lat. 35°01'55" N, long. 120°11'15" W). Named on Chimney Canyon (1967) and Miranda Pine Mountain (1967) 7.5' quadrangles.

Aliso Creek: see **Carrie Creek** [SAN LUIS OBISPO].

Alkali Canyon [SANTA BARBARA]: *canyon,* drained by a stream that flows 4 miles to Sisquoc River 5.25 miles north-northwest of Zaca Lake (lat. 34°51'05" N, long. 120°04'05" W). Named on Manzanita Mountain (1964) and Zaca Lake (1964) 7.5' quadrangles.

Alley Camp [SAN LUIS OBISPO]: *locality,* 9.5 miles south-southwest of Shandon on the east side of present Camatta Canyon (lat. 35°31'25" N, long. 120°19'15" W). Named on Commatti Canyon (1943) 7.5' quadrangle.

Allison Creek [MONTEREY]: *stream,* flows 1 mile to an unnamed stream 4 miles west-northwest of Fremont Peak (lat. 36°47'20" N, long. 121°34' W). Named on San Juan Bautista (1917) 15' quadrangle.

Almaden Flats [SAN LUIS OBISPO]: *area,* 7 miles east-northeast of the village of San Simeon (lat. 35°41'05" N, long. 121°04'50" W; sec. 11, T 26 S, R 8 E). Named on Pebblestone Shut-in (1959) 7.5' quadrangle, which shows Alamden mine at the place.

Almeja: see **Point Almeja,** under **Mussel Point** [MONTEREY].

Alones: see **Point Alones** [MONTEREY].

Alta Peak [SAN BENITO]: *peak,* 4 miles south of Idria (lat. 36°21'30" N, long. 120°39'40" W; sec. 16, T 18 S, R 12 E). Altitude 4709 feet. Named on San Benito Mountain (1969) 7.5' quadrangle.

Alva Paul Creek: see **Morro Bay** [SAN LUIS OBISPO] (2).

Alvarez Creek: see **Tully Creek** [SAN BENITO].

Alvisa Canyon [SAN BENITO]: *canyon,* drained by a stream that flows 1.25 miles to Three Troughs Canyon 6 miles south of Paicines (lat. 36°38'25" N, long. 121°17'15" W; sec. 11, T 15 S, R 6 E). Named on Paicines (1968) 7.5' quadrangle.

Amaya Creek [SANTA CRUZ]: *stream,* flows 2.5 miles to Soquel Creek 6.5 miles north-northeast of Soquel (lat. 37°04'30" N, long. 121°55'30" W). Named on Laurel (1955) 7.5' quadrangle. The name commemorates Casimero Amaya and Dario Amaya, brothers who owned land along the stream as early as 1860 (Clark, 1986, p. 4).

Amaya Lagoon: see **Brush Lagoon** [SANTA CRUZ].

American Canyon [SAN LUIS OBISPO]: *canyon,* drained by a stream that flows nearly 7 miles to Salinas River 6 miles east-southeast of Pozo (lat. 35°15'45" N, long. 120°17' W). Named on La Panza (1967) and Pozo Summit (1967) 7.5' quadrangles.

American Canyon Campground [SAN LUIS OBISPO]: *locality,* 6.25 miles east-southeast of Pozo (lat. 35°17' N, long. 120°15'55" W); the place is in American Canyon. Named on Pozo Summit (1967) 7.5' quadrangle.

American Canyon Spring [SAN LUIS OBISPO]: *spring,* 7 miles east of Pozo (lat. 35°17'30" N, long. 120°15'05" W); the spring is in a branch of American Canyon. Named on Pozo Summit (1967) 7.5' quadrangle.

Anacapa: see **Gato** [SANTA BARBARA].

Anacapa Passage [SANTA BARBARA]: *water feature,* strait between Santa Cruz Island and Anacapa Island (Anacapa Island is in

Ventura County); the islands are only 4.5 miles apart where they are closest. Named on Santa Cruz Island D (1943) 7.5' quadrangle.

Anastasia Canyon [MONTEREY]: *canyon,* drained by a stream that flows 3.25 miles to Finch Creek nearly 3 miles east-southeast of Jamesburg (lat. 36°21'05" N, long. 121°32'35" W; sec. 21, T 18 S, R 4 E). Named on Chews Ridge (1956) 7.5' quadrangle.

Andersen Canyon [MONTEREY]: *canyon,* drained by a stream that flows nearly 3 miles to the sea less than 2.5 miles southeast of Partington Point (lat. 36°09'10" N, long. 121°39'55" W; sec. 32, T 20 N, R 13 E). Named on Partington Ridge (1956) 7.5' quadrangle. Called Anderson Canyon on Lucia (1921) 15' quadrangle, and United States Board on Geographic Names (1960c, p. 16) approved this form of the name. According to Fink (p. 209), Jim Anderson homesteaded near the canyon; according to Lussier (p. 33), the name is for Peter Andersen, a homesteader of 1883.

Andersen Landing [MONTEREY]: *locality,* nearly 1 mile southeast of the mouth of Andersen Canyon (present Anderson Canyon) along the coast (lat. 36°08'40" N, long. 121°39'25" W; sec. 32, T 20 S, R 3 E). The abandoned site is named on Partington Ridge (1956) 7.5' quadrangle. Called Anderson Landing on Lucia (1921) 15' quadrangle. The place also was known as Hot Springs Landing (Clark, 1991, p. 12-13).

Andersen Peak [MONTEREY]: *peak,* 3.25 miles east of Partington Point (lat. 36°10'50" N, long. 121°38'30" W; sec. 21, T 20 S, R 3 E). Altitude 4099 feet. Named on Partington Ridge (1956) 7.5' quadrangle. Called Anderson Peak on Lucia (1921) 15' quadrangle, and United States Board on Geographic Names (1960c, p. 16) approved this form of the name.

Anderson Canyon [SAN LUIS OBISPO]: *canyon,* drained by a stream that flows 3.25 miles to San Juan Creek 3 miles west-northwest of Freeborn Mountain (lat. 35°17'55" N, long. 120°06'05" W; sec. 24, T 30 S, R 17 E). Named on California Valley (1966) 7.5' quadrangle.

Anderson Canyon: see **Andersen Canyon** [MONTEREY].

Anderson Landing: see **Andersen Landing** [MONTEREY].

Anderson Peak: see **Andersen Peak** [MONTEREY].

Andrews Peak [MONTEREY]: *peak,* 3.5 miles southeast of Smith Mountain (lat. 36°02'20" N, long. 120°33'10" W; sec. 3, T 22 S, R 13 E). Altitude 3502 feet. Named on Smith Mountain (1969) 7.5' quadrangle. The name commemorates the family of George Leslie Andrews; the family moved to Stone Canyon below the peak in 1878 (Clark, 1991, p. 14).

Angle Canyon [SANTA BARBARA]: *canyon,* drained by a stream that flows 1 mile to Windmill Canyon 4 miles southwest of New

Cuyama (lat. 34°54'35" N, long. 119°44'35" W; near W line sec. 35, T 10 N, R 27 W). Named on New Cuyama (1964) and Peak Mountain (1964) 7.5' quadrangles.

Angostura Pass [SANTA BARBARA]: *pass,* 5 miles north of downtown Santa Barbara (lat. 34°29'45" N, long. 119°41'55" W; sec. 22, T 5 N, R 27 W). Named on Santa Barbara (1952) 7.5' quadrangle.

Año Nuevo Creek [SANTA CRUZ]: *stream,* flows 3.25 miles to San Mateo County 2.5 miles north-northwest of the mouth of Waddell Creek (lat. 37°07'40" N, long. 122°17'50" W; sec. 28, T 9 S, R 4 W); the stream reaches the sea 1.5 miles east of Año Nuevo Point, which is in San Mateo County. Named on Franklin Point (1955) 7.5' quadrangle. United States Board on Geographic Names (1933, p. 97) rejected the name "New Year Creek" for the stream, and (1962a, p. 4) the form "Ano Nuevo Creek" for the name. According to Brown (p. 61), the name "New Year's Creek" is proper, and the name "Año Nuevo Creek" has never been used; the stream was called arroyo de Lucía in the 1840's and 1850's from an incident involving Lucia Bolcof of Santa Cruz—earlier the stream had the name "arroyo de los Lobos."

Antelope Creek [SAN BENITO]: *stream,* flows 3.5 miles to Tres Pinos Creek 1.5 miles north-northwest of Panoche Pass (lat. 36° 38'45" N, long. 121°01'55" W; at N line sec. 7, T 15 S, R 9 E); the stream joins Tres Pinos Creek near the northwest end of Antelope Valley. Named on Panoche Pass (1968) 7.5' quadrangle.

Antelope Valley [SAN BENITO]: *valley,* nearly 1 mile northwest of Panoche Pass along Payne Creek (lat. 36°38'15" N, long. 121°01'15" W). Named on Panoche Pass (1968) 7.5' quadrangle.

Anthony Creek [MONTEREY]: *stream,* flows nearly 3.5 miles to San Miguel Creek 8.5 miles east-northeast of Cape San Martin (lat. 35°56'40" N, long. 121°20' W; near E line sec. 8, T 23 S, R 6 E). Named on Alder Peak (1949) 7.5' quadrangle. The stream had the early name "Potrancas Creek"—*potrancas* means "little mares" in Spanish (Clark, 1991, p. 16).

Antimony Mountain: see **Antimony Peak** [SAN BENITO].

Antimony Peak [SAN BENITO]: *peak,* 2.25 miles southwest of Mariposa Peak on San Benito-Merced county line (lat. 36°55'50" N, long. 121°13'55" W; sec. 32, T 11 S, R 7 E). Altitude 3297 feet. Named on Mariposa Peak (1969) 7.5' quadrangle. Angel (1890b, p. 516) called the feature Antimony Mountain, and noted that "As its name implies the mountain is characterized by its many veins of antimony." Irelan (p. 351) mentioned that Antimony Mountain was known locally as Gipsy Peak—Gipsy Mining Company had a mine there.

Antone Canyon [MONTEREY]: *canyon,* drained by a stream that flows 4 miles to

Lynch Canyon 3.5 miles east-southeast of San Ardo (lat. 36°00'30" N, long. 120°50'20" W; at S line sec. 13, T 22 S, R 10 E). Named on Pancho Rico Valley (1967) 7.5' quadrangle.

Antonio [SANTA BARBARA]: *locality,* 2.25 miles west of the village of Casmalia along Southern Pacific Railroad (lat. 34°50'05" N, long. 120°34'05" W). Named on Casmalia (1959) 7.5' quadrangle.

Anzar Lake [SAN BENITO]: *lake,* 1100 feet long, 4.5 miles northwest of San Juan Bautista (lat. 36°53'20" N, long. 121°36' W); the lake is on Las Aromitas y Agua Caliente grant, received by Juan M. Ansar, or Anzar. Named on Chittenden (1955) 7.5' quadrangle.

Apple Camp: see **Chalk Peak Camp** [MONTEREY].

Apple Tree Camp: see **Chalk Peak Camp** [MONTEREY]; **Turner Creek Camp** [MONTEREY].

Apricot: see **Vineyard Canyon** [MONTEREY-SAN LUIS OBISPO].

Aptos [SANTA CRUZ]:
(1) *land grant,* at and inland from the town of Aptos. Named on Laurel (1955), Soquel (1954), and Watsonville West (1954) 7.5' quadrangles. Rafael Castro received 1 league in 1833 and claimed 6686 acres patented in 1860 (Cowan, p. 16). The word "Aptos" is from the name of an Indian community (Rowland, p. 61).
(2) *town,* 4.5 miles east-northeast of Soquel Point (lat. 36°58'35" N, long. 121°53'55" W); the place is along Aptos Creek on Aptos grant. Named on Soquel (1954) 7.5' quadrangle. Postal authorities established Aptos post office in 1870 (Frickstad, p. 176). They established Glenecho post office 3.5 miles east of Aptos in 1894 and discontinued it in 1897; they established Rancho del Mar post office, named for a real estate development, 1 mile south of Aptos in 1962 and discontinued it in 1963 (Salley, p. 86, 181).

Aptos Creek [SANTA CRUZ]: *stream,* flows 9.5 miles to the sea 4 miles east-northeast of Soquel Point (lat. 36°58'10" N, long. 121° 54'20" W). Named on Laurel (1955), Loma Prieta (1955), and Soquel (1954) 7.5' quadrangles. Hamman's (1980a) map shows a tributary called Spring Creek that joins Aptos Creek 0.5 mile east-northeast of the confluence of Aptos Creek and Bridge Creek. The same map shows several named branches of the canyon of Aptos Creek: Long Gulch, which enters 1.5 miles north of Aptos; Love Gulch, which enters 3450 feet south-south-west of the confluence of Aptos Creek and Bridge Creek; Porter Gulch, which enters just west of the confluence of Aptos Creek and Bridge Creek; and Bassett Gulch, which enters near the head of Aptos Creek about 1 mile south of Santa Rosalita Mountain. Hamman's (1980a) map also has the name "Hell's Gate" for narrows in the canyon of Aptos Creek 1.25 miles east-northeast of the confluence of Aptos Creek and Bridge Creek, and shows several localities situated along Aptos Creek: a railroad siding called Hihn Spur or Ready, located 1 mile north of Aptos on land purchased from Mrs. Ruth Ready (Hamman, p. 78); Molino, located along the railroad nearly 1 mile south-southwest of the confluence of Aptos Creek and Bridge Creek, where a spur line ran to a lumber mill (Hamman, p. 43)—*molino* means "mill" in Spanish; Loma Prieta, located along the railroad 0.25 mile south-southwest of the confluence of Aptos Creek and Bridge Creek, where Loma Prieta Lumber Company had a mill (Hamman, p. 50); Camp Number 1, located 0.5 mile northeast of the confluence of Aptos Creek and Bridge Creek; and two places called Monte Vista, the first located 1 mile east of the confluence of Aptos Creek and Bridge Creek, and the second located nearly 2 miles northeast of the first—both along the railroad. Postal authorities established Loma Prieta post office in 1884, discontinued it in 1885, reestablished it in 1887, and discontinued it in 1901 (Frickstad, p. 177). The lumber mill at Loma Prieta was torn down in 1899 (Hamman, p. 56). The settlement of Schillings Camp, situated about 1 mile below Loma Prieta along Aptos Creek, was run by the Schilling family, who hauled out shingle bolts, pickets, posts, ties, and cordwood by pack train (Hamman, p. 78). A place called The Island was located just below the confluence of Aptos Creek and Valencia Creek; it now is called Treasure Island, although it no longer is surrounded by water (Hoover, Rensch, and Rensch, p. 469).

Aqua Buena Spring [SAN BENITO]: *spring,* 6.5 miles southeast of Idria (lat. 36°20'45" N, long. 120°35'50" W; near E line sec. 24, T 18 S, R 12 E). Named on Santa Rita Peak (1969) 7.5' quadrangle.

Aqua Escondida Spring: see **Agua Escondida Spring** [SAN LUIS OBISPO].

Arana Gulch [SANTA CRUZ]: *canyon,* drained by a stream that flows nearly 4 miles to Woods Lagoon 2 miles northwest of Soquel Point (lat. 36°58'30" N, long. 121°59'50" W). Named on Laurel (1955) and Soquel (1954) 7.5' quadrangles. The name commemorates Jose Arana (Gudde, 1949, p. 13), who received Potreros y Rincon de San Pedro de Reglado grant

Arbolado: see **Big Sur** [MONTEREY].

Archibald Creek [SANTA CRUZ]: *stream,* flows nearly 1 mile to Scott Creek 3.5 miles north-northwest of Davenport (lat. 37°03'25" N, long. 122°13'35" W). Named on Davenport (1955) 7.5' quadrangle. The name recalls James Archibald, who purchased Agua Puerca y las Trancas grant, which includes the mouth of the stream (Hoover, Rensch, and Rensch, p. 473). On Hamman's (1980c) map, this stream has the name "Winter Creek" and the name "Archibald Creek" applies to the next tributary of Scott Creek to the south.

Arch Point [SANTA BARBARA]: *promontory,* at the north end of Santa Barbara Island (lat. 33°29'15" N, long. 119°01'40" W). Named on United States Geological Survey's (1973) map.

Arch Rock [SANTA BARBARA]: *rock,* 2.5 miles west of Diablo Point on the north side of Santa Cruz Island, and 700 feet offshore (lat. 34°03'25" N, long. 119°48' W). Named on Santa Cruz Island B (1943) 7.5' quadrangle. United States Board on Geographic Names (1978a, p. 3) rejected the form "Arch Rocks" for the name.

Arguelia: see **Point Arguelia**, under **Point Arguello** [SANTA BARBARA].

Arguello [SANTA BARBARA]:
(1) *locality,* less than 0.5 mile east of Point Arguello (lat. 34°34'40" N, long. 120°38'35" W). Named on Point Arguello (1959) 7.5' quadrangle.
(2) *locality,* 2.5 miles east-southeast of Point Arguello along Southern Pacific Railroad (lat. 34°33'30" N, long. 120°36'45" W). Named on Guadalupe (1905) 30' quadrangle.

Arguello: see **Point Arguello** [SANTA BARBARA]; **Tranquillon Mountain** [SANTA BARBARA].

Arguello Mountain: see **Tranquillon Mountain** [SANTA BARBARA].

Argyle Creek: see **Murry Creek** [MONTEREY].

Argyle District: see **Jolon Valley** [MONTEREY].

Arlight [SANTA BARBARA]: *locality,* 0.5 mile east of Point Arguello along Southern Pacific Railroad (lat. 34°34'40" N, long. 120°38'20" W). Named on Point Arguello (1959) 7.5' quadrangle. Postal authorities established Arlight post office in 1917 and discontinued it in 1951; the coined name was from the words "<u>Ar</u>guello <u>Light</u>house" (Salley, p. 9).

Arlington Canyon [SANTA BARBARA]: *canyon,* drained by a stream that flows 6 miles to the sea 4.25 miles east of Sandy Point on Santa Rosa Island (lat. 34°00'20" N, long. 120°10'35" W). Named on Santa Rosa Island North (1943) and Santa Rosa Island West (1943) 7.5' quadrangles. Called Cañada Corral on Kew's (1927) map.

Aromas [MONTEREY-SAN BENITO]: *village,* 6.5 miles west-northwest of San Juan Bautista on Monterey-San Benito county line (lat. 36°53'20" N, long. 121°38'30" W); the village is at the edge of Las Aromitas y Agua Caliente grant. Named on Watsonville East (1955) 7.5' quadrangle. The place first was known as Sand Cut because of a tunnel built there in the 1870's by workmen for Southern Pacific Railroad (Gudde, 1949, p. 15). Postal authorities established Aromas post office in Monterey County in 1894, moved it 100 rods into San Benito County in 1897, and returned it to Monterey County in 1924 (Salley, p. 10).

Arrowhead Island [SANTA BARBARA]: *island,* 100 feet long, 4.5 miles northeast of Santa Ynez Peak in Lake Cachuma (lat. 34°33'50" N, long. 119°54'40" W). Named on Lake Cachuma (1959) 7.5' quadrangle.

Arrowhead Point [MONTEREY]: *promontory,* 3500 feet east of Pescadero Point on the north side of Carmel Bay (lat. 36°33'40" N, long. 121°56'20" W). Named on Monterey (1947) 7.5' quadrangle. Called Sunium Pt. on Lawson's (1893) map. The name "Arrowhead" is from the shape of the promontory (Clark, 1991, p. 20).

Arroyo Burro [SANTA BARBARA]:
(1) *canyon,* drained by a stream that flows 2.5 miles to Santa Ynez River 4 miles east-northeast of San Marcos Pass (lat. 34°32'20" N, long. 119°45'50" W). Named on San Marcos Pass (1959) 7.5' quadrangle.
(2) *stream,* flows 1.5 miles to San Antonio Creek 4.25 miles northeast of present downtown Goleta (lat. 34°28'15" N, long. 119° 46' W). Named on Goleta (1903) 30' quadrangle.
(3) *stream,* flows nearly 6 miles to the sea 3 miles west-southwest of downtown Santa Barbara (lat. 34°24'10" N, long. 119°44'30" W); the stream drains Barger Canyon.. Named on Santa Barbara (1952) 7.5' quadrangle. Called San Roque Cr. on Santa Barbara (1903) 15' quadrangle, but United States Board on Geographic Names (1961b, p. 9) rejected the names "San Roque Creek," "Arroyo Burro Creek," and "Barger Canyon" for the feature.

Arroyo Burro: see **Barger Canyon** [SANTA BARBARA].

Arroyo Burro Creek: see **Arroyo Burro** [SANTA BARBARA] (3).

Arroyo Center [MONTEREY]: *settlement,* 14 miles west-southwest of Greenfield (lat. 36°14' N, long. 121°28'05" W; in and near sec. 31, T 19 S, R 5 E); the place is along Arroyo Seco (1). Named on Junipero Serra (1961) 15' quadrangle.

Arroyo de Agalia: see **Eagle Canyon** [SANTA BARBARA].

Arroyo de la Casa Blanca: see **Whitehouse Creek** [SANTA CRUZ].

Arroyo de la Cruz [SAN LUIS OBISPO]: *stream,* formed by the confluence of Burnett Creek and Marmolejo Creek, flows 10 miles to the sea 3.5 miles north-northwest of Piedras Blancas Point (lat. 35°42'35" N, long. 121°18'35" W). Named on Piedras Blancas (1959) and San Simeon (1958) 7.5' quadrangles. On San Simeon (1919) 15' quadrangle, Marmolejo Creek is shown as a tributary of Arroyo de la Cruz.

Arroyo de la Laguna [SANTA CRUZ]: *land grant,* 8 miles west-northwest of Point Santa Cruz along the coast and inland. Named on Davenport (1955) and Santa Cruz (1954) 7.5' quadrangles. Gil Sanchez received the land in 1840; James Williams and Squire Williams claimed 4418 acres patented in 1882 (Cowan, p. 16; Rowland, p. 42). Perez (p. 53) gave the date of the grant as 1839, and gave the date of the patent as 1881.

Arroyo de la Laguna: see **Laguna Creek** [SANTA CRUZ].

Arroyo de las Garrapatas: see **Garrapata Creek** [MONTEREY].

Arroyo de las Ortegas: see **Romero Creek** [SANTA BARBARA].

Arroyo de las Piedras: see **Stony Creek** [MONTEREY].

Arroyo de las Viboras [SAN BENITO]: *stream,* flows 14 miles to join Arroyo Dos Picachos and form Tequisquita Slough 4.5 miles north of Hollister (lat. 36°55' N, long. 121°23'20" W). Named on Mariposa Peak (1969), San Felipe (1955), and Three Sisters (1954) 7.5' quadrangles. According to Gudde (1949, p. 379), the stream is called Viboras Creek—*las viboras* means "the rattlesnakes" in Spanish.

Arroyo del Corral [SAN LUIS OBISPO]: *stream,* flows 2.5 miles to the sea 1.5 miles north of Piedras Blancas Point (lat. 35°41'05" N, long. 121°17'10" W). Named on Piedras Blancas (1959) 7.5' quadrangle.

Arroyo del Huasna: see **Huasna River** [SAN LUIS OBISPO].

Arroyo del Molino: see **Molino Creek** [SANTA CRUZ].

Arroyo del Montecito: see **Montecito Creek** [SANTA BARBARA].

Arroyo de los Alamos: see **San Antonio Creek** [SANTA BARBARA] (1).

Arroyo de los Chinos [SAN LUIS OBISPO]: *stream,* flows 3.5 miles to the sea 4.5 miles north-northwest of Piedras Point (lat. 35°43'30" N, long. 121°18'55" W). Named on Piedras Blancas (1959) 7.5' quadrangle.

Arroyo de los Lobos: see **Año Nuevo Creek** [SANTA CRUZ].

Arroyo del Oso [SAN LUIS OBISPO]: *stream,* flows 1.5 miles to the sea nearly 2 miles north-northwest of Piedras Blancas Point (lat. 35°41'30" N, long. 121°17'20" W). Named on Piedras Blancas (1959) 7.5' quadrangle.

Arroyo del Padre Juan [SAN LUIS OBISPO]: *stream,* flows 2.5 miles to the sea 3.25 miles southeast of the village of San Simeon (lat. 35°36'40" N, long. 121°08'45" W). Named on Cambria (1959), Pebblestone Shut-in (1959), and Pico Creek (1959) 7.5' quadrangles.

Arroyo del Palo Colorado: see **Palo Colorado Canyon** [MONTEREY].

Arroyo del Pecho: see **Pecho Creek** [SAN LUIS OBISPO].

Arroyo del Pedregoso: see **Mission Creek** [SANTA BARBARA].

Arroyo del Pino: see **Pine Canyon** [MONTEREY] (2).

Arroyo del Puerto [SAN LUIS OBISPO]: *stream,* flows 4 miles to San Simeon Bay at the village of San Simeon (lat. 35°38'35" N, long. 121°11'15" W). Named on San Simeon (1958) 7.5' quadrangle.

Arroyo del Puerto del Rosario: see **Tres Pinos Creek** [SAN BENITO].

Arroyo del Rodeo [SANTA CRUZ]: *land grant,* at and inland from Soquel Point east of Rodeo Creek Gulch. Named on Soquel (1954) 7.5' quadrangle. Francisco Rodriguez received 1.25 leagues in 1834; John Hames and John Daubenbis claimed 1473 acres patented in 1882 (Cowan, p. 69). The name alludes to cattle roundups, or rodeos, held at the place in the early days (Hoover, Rensch, and Rensch, p. 471).

Arroyo del Rosario: see **Tres Pinos Creek** [SAN BENITO].

Arroyo del Tulare: see **Oak Creek** [SANTA BARBARA].

Arroyo de Lucía: see **Año Nuevo Creek** [SANTA CRUZ].

Arroyo de Salispuedes: see **Corralitos Creek** [SANTA CRUZ].

Arroyo de San Augustin: see **Arroyo San Augustin** [SANTA BARBARA].

Arroyo de San Felipe: see **Pacheco Creek** [SAN BENITO].

Arroyo de San Joaquin y Santana: see **Arroyo Dos Picachos** [SAN BENITO].

Arroyo de San Nicolas: see **San Simeon Creek** [SAN LUIS OBISPO].

Arroyo de San Vicente: see **Arroyo Laguna** [SAN LUIS OBISPO]; **San Vicente Creek** [SANTA CRUZ].

Arroyo de Soto: see **Whitehouse Creek** [SANTA CRUZ].

Arroyo de Tepusque: see **Tepusquet Canyon** [SANTA BARBARA].

Arroyo de Villa: see **Branciforte Creek** [SANTA CRUZ].

Arroyo Dos Picachos [SAN BENITO]: *stream,* flows 12 miles to join Arroyo de las Viboras and form Tequisquita Slough 4.5 miles north of Hollister (lat. 36°55' N, long. 121°23'20" W). Named on Mariposa Peak (1969), San Felipe (1955), and Three Sisters (1954) 7.5' quadrangles. Called Arroyo de San Joaquin y Santana on a diseño of San Joaquin grant made in 1836 (Becker, 1964).

Arroyo El Bulito [SANTA BARBARA]: *canyon,* drained by a stream that flows 3.5 miles to the sea 8 miles east of Point Conception (lat. 34°27'45" N, long. 120°19'25" W). Named on Sacate (1953) 7.5' quadrangle. According to Bolton (p. 240), the name should have the form "Bullillo."

Arroyo Grande [SAN LUIS OBISPO]:
(1) *land grant,* 10 miles east-northeast of the town of Arroyo Grande along Arroyo Grande Creek. Named on Tar Spring Ridge (1967) 7.5' quadrangle. Seferino Carlon received the land in 1841; Francis Branch claimed 4437 acres patented in 1867 (Cowan, p. 16; Cowan gave the name "San Ramon" as an alternate). According to Perez (p. 54), Carlon received the grant in 1842. Angel (1883, p. 215) noted that the grant commonly was known as the Ranchita.
(2) *town,* 12 miles south-southeast of San Luis Obispo near the coast (lat. 35°07'15" N, long. 120°35' W); the town is along Arroyo Grande

Creek. Named on Arroyo Grande NE (1965) and Oceano (1965) 7.5' quadrangles. The community began about 1867 with a schoolhouse and a blacksmith shop (Angel, 1883, p. 351). Postal authorities established Arroyo Grande post office in 1869 (Frickstad, p. 163), and the town incorporated in 1911.

Arroyo Grande Creek [SAN LUIS OBISPO]: *stream,* flows 22 miles to the sea 3 miles west-southwest of downtown Arroyo Grande (lat. 35°06'05" N, long. 120°37'50" W). Named on Arroyo Grande NE (1965), Oceano (1965), and Tar Spring Ridge (1967) 7.5' quadrangles. Called Rio Grande on Goddard's (1857) map.

Arroyo Grande Station [SAN LUIS OBISPO]: *locality,* 11 miles north-northeast of the town of Nipomo (lat. 35°11'35" N, long. 120°25'55" W); the place is along Arroyo Grande Creek. Named on Tar Spring Ridge (1967) 7.5' quadrangle.

Arroyo Grande Valley [SAN LUIS OBISPO]: *valley,* opens into lowlands near the sea 2 miles south-southeast of downtown Arroyo Grande (lat. 35°05'45" N, long. 120°36' W); Arroyo Grande Creek drains the valley. Named on Arroyo Grande NE (1965) and Oceano (1965) 7.5' quadrangles.

Arroyo Hondo [SAN BENITO]:
(1) *canyon,* drained by a stream that flows 3 miles to Tres Pinos Creek 1 mile south-southeast of Tres Pinos (lat. 36°46'35" N, long. 121°18'35" W). Named on Tres Pinos (1955) 7.5' quadrangle.
(2) *stream,* flows 1.5 miles to Fresno County 4.5 miles east-northeast of Idria (lat. 36°26' N, long. 120°35'45" W; at E line sec. 24, T 17 S, R 12 E). Named on Ciervo Mountain (1969) 7.5' quadrangle.

Arroyo Hondo [SAN LUIS OBISPO]: *stream,* flows nearly 2.5 miles to the sea 6 miles north-northwest of Piedras Blancas Point (lat. 35°45' N, long. 121°18'50" W). Named on Piedras Blancas (1959) 7.5' quadrangle.

Arroyo Hondo [SANTA BARBARA]: *stream,* flows 3.5 miles to the sea 4.5 miles east of Gaviota (lat. 34°28'25" N, long. 120°08'25" W). Named on Gaviota (1953) 7.5' quadrangle. On Solvang (1959) 7.5' quadrangle, the name applies to the canyon of the stream.

Arroyo Hondo: see **Arroyo Laguna** [SAN LUIS OBISPO].

Arroyo Joaquin Soto: see **Tres Pinos Creek** [SAN BENITO].

Arroyo Laguna [SAN LUIS OBISPO]: *stream,* flows nearly 3 miles to Oak Knoll Creek 1.5 miles northwest of the village of San Simeon (lat. 35°39'50" N, long. 121°12'40" W). Named on San Simeon (1958) 7.5' quadrangle. According to H.R. Wagner (p. 462, 508), Crespi gave the name "Arroyo de San Vicente" to the stream in 1769, but other members of the Portola expedition called it Arroyo Hondo.

Arroyo la Mission: see **Mission Creek** [MONTEREY].

Arroyo las Trancas [SANTA CRUZ]: *stream,* flows nearly 1 mile to the sea 0.5 mile southsoutheast of the mouth of Waddell Creek (lat. 37°05'10" N, long. 122°16'15" W; sec. 2, T 10 S, R 4 W); the stream is near the northwest boundary of Agua Puerca y las Trancas grant. Named on Año Nuevo (1955) 7.5' quadrangle. United States Board on Geographic Names (1978c, p. 5) approved the name "Laguna de las Trancas" for a lake, 0.1 mile long, that is located less than 1 mile east of the mouth of Arroyo las Trancas on Agua Puerca y las Trancas grant. A stage station called Seaside was situated on the bluff at the mouth of Las Trancas Creek in 1872 (Hoover, Rensch, and Rensch, p. 478). Postal authorities established Sea Side post office in 1873 and discontinued it in 1881 (Frickstad, p. 177). Rowland (p. 131) reported that a village and post office known as Seaside were at a saw mill that William W. Waddell built along Waddell Creek. A place called China Ladder, located at the sea cliff about 1.5 miles southeast of the mouth of Arroyo las Trancas, received its name because Chinese abalone gatherers used a ladder there to reach the rocks at the base of the cliff (Hoover, Rensch, and Rensch, p. 474).

Arroyo Paredon [SANTA BARBARA]: *stream,* flows 5.25 miles to the sea 2.5 miles west-southwest of Carpinteria (lat. 34°24'45" N, long. 119°33'25" W). Named on Carpinteria (1952) 7.5' quadrangle. Called Arroyo Parida on Santa Barbara (1903) 15' quadrangle, but United States Board on Geographic Names (1961b, p. 13) rejected the names "Arroyo Parida," "Arroyo Parida Creek," and "Parida Creek" for the stream.

Arroyo Parida: see **Arroyo Paredon** [SANTA BARBARA].

Arroyo Parida Creek: see **Arroyo Paredon** [SANTA BARBARA].

Arroyo Quemado [SANTA BARBARA]: *stream,* flows 3 miles to the sea 5.25 miles east of Gaviota (lat. 34°28'10" N, long. 120°07'05" W). Named on Tajiguas (1953) 7.5' quadrangle. On Santa Ynez (1959) 7.5' quadrangle, the name applies to the canyon of the stream.

Arroyo San Agustin: see **Arroyo San Augustin** [SANTA BARBARA].

Arroyo San Augustin [SANTA BARBARA]: *stream,* flows 2.5 miles to the sea nearly 7 miles east of Point Conception (lat. 34°27'30" N, long. 120°21'10" W). Named on Sacate (1953) 7.5' quadrangle. Called Arroyo de San Augustin on Lompoc (1905) 30' quadrangle. United States Board on Geographic Names (1978b, p. 5) approved the form "Arroyo San Agustin" for the name, and rejected the names "Arroyo de San Augustin," "Arroyo San Augustin," and "Arroyo San Augustine" for the stream.

Arroyo San Carpoforo: see **San Carpoforo Creek** [MONTEREY-SAN LUIS OBISPO].

9

Arroyo San Carpojo: see **San Carpoforo Creek** [MONTEREY-SAN LUIS OBISPO].

Arroyo San Miguel: see **Mission Creek** [MONTEREY].

Arroyo San Ysidro: see **San Ysidro Creek** [SANTA BARBARA].

Arroyo Seco [MONTEREY]:

(1) *stream,* flows 44 miles to Salinas River 1 mile south-southwest of Soledad (lat. 36°24'45" N, long. 121°20'15" W). Named on Cone Peak (1949), Junipero Serra Peak (1949), Paraiso Springs (1956), Soledad (1955), Sycamore Flat (1956), and Tassajara Hot Springs (1956) 7.5' quadrangles.

(2) *land grant,* near Greenfield; includes the lowermost course of Arroyo Seco (1). Named on Greenfield (1956), Paraiso Springs (1956), and Soledad (1955) 7.5' quadrangles. Joaquin de la Torre received 4 leagues in 1840 and claimed 16,523 acres patented in 1859 (Cowan, p. 17). Soon after 1900 some promoters began a real-estate development that they called Clark Colony after one of the promoters; the development was on the grant near the mouth of the canyon of Arroyo Seco (1) at a place called Three Mile Flat (Fink, p. 164).

Arroyo Seco [SAN LUIS OBISPO]: *stream,* flows 10.5 miles to Huasna River 9.5 miles northeast of Nipomo (lat. 35°08'30" N, long. 120°21'30" W). Named on Caldwell Mesa (1967) and Los Machos Hills (1967) 7.5' quadrangles.

Arsenic Springs: see **Hot Springs** [SANTA BARBARA] (2).

Artillery Hill [MONTEREY]: *hill,* 3.5 miles south of Marina (lat. 36° 38'10" N, long. 121°47'20" W); the hill is on Fort Ord Military Reservation. Named on Marina (1947) 7.5' quadrangle.

Asbury Creek [SAN LUIS OBISPO]: *stream,* flows 3 miles to Nacimiento Reservoir 12 miles northeast of the village of San Simeon (lat. 35°45'40" N, long. 121°02'10" W; near N line sec. 18, T 25 S, R 9 E). Named on Bryson (1949, photorevised 1979) 7.5' quadrangle.

Ascension: see **Asuncion** [SAN LUIS OBISPO] (1) and (2).

Ashbury Gulch [SANTA CRUZ]: *canyon,* drained by a stream that flows 1.25 miles to Soquel Creek 8 miles north-northeast of Soquel (lat. 37°05'35" N, long. 121°53'30" W). Named on Laurel (1955) 7.5' quadrangle. According to Clark (1986, p. 13), the word "Ashbury" is a misspelling of the name "Asbury."

Ashurst Spring [SAN BENITO]: *spring,* 12 miles east-northeast of Bitterwater (lat. 36°27'05" N, long. 120°48'35" W; sec. 18, T 17 S, R 11 E). Named on Hernandez Reservoir (1969) 7.5' quadrangle. Called Henry Ashurst Spr. on Hernandez Valley (1943) 15' quadrangle.

Asilomar [MONTEREY]: *locality,* 1.25 miles south of Point Pinos (lat. 36°37'15" N, long.

121°56'10" W). Named on Monterey (1947) 7.5' quadrangle. The place began in 1913 as a campground for Young Women's Christian Association; the name is a contraction of *asilo del mar,* which means "refuge by the sea" in Spanish (Fink, p. 176). Postal authorities established Asilomar post office in 1914 and discontinued it in 1935 (Frickstad, p. 106).

Asilomar Beach: see **Moss Beach** [MONTEREY].

Asphaltea: see **Sisquoc** [SANTA BARBARA] (3).

Asphaltum Creek [SANTA BARBARA]: *stream,* flows 5.25 miles to join the stream in Foxen Canyon 7.5 miles south of Tepusquet Peak (lat. 34°48' N, long. 120°11'40" W). Named on Foxen Canyon (1964) and Zaca Lake (1964) 7.5' quadrangles. Zaca Lake (1964) 7.5' quadrangle shows an asphaltum mine near the head of the creek.

Asuncion [SAN LUIS OBISPO]:

(1) *land grant,* mainly west of Atascadero. Named on Atascadero (1965), Creston (1948), Morro Bay North (1965), Santa Margarita (1965), Templeton (1948), and York Mountain (1948) 7.5' quadrangles. Pedro Estrada received the land in 1845 and claimed 39,225 acres patented in 1866 (Cowan, p. 17). The name refers to the Ascension of the Virgin Mary; the form "Ascension" also has been used for the name (Gudde, 1949, p. 17).

(2) *locality,* nearly 2 miles north of Atascadero along Southern Pacific Railroad (lat. 35°30'50" N, long. 120°40'35" W); the place is on Asuncion grant. Named on Templeton (1948) 7.5' quadrangle. Postal authorities established Ascension post office in 1879 and discontinued it in 1881 (Frickstad, p. 163).

Atascadero [SAN LUIS OBISPO]:

(1) *land grant,* along Salinas River at the town of Atascadero. Named on Atascadero (1965), Santa Margarita (1965), and Templeton (1948) 7.5' quadrangles. Trifon Garcia received 1 league in 1842; Henry Haight claimed 4348 acres patented in 1860 (Cowan, p. 17). According to Hanna (p. 19), *atascadero* means "boggy ground" in Spanish.

(2) *town,* 10 miles south of Paso Robles (lat. 35°29'20" N, long. 120°40'05" W); the town is on and near Atascadero grant. Named on Atascadero (1965) and Templeton (1948) 7.5' quadrangles. San Luis Obispo (1897) 15' quadrangle shows a place called Atascadero located along Southern Pacific Railroad where later maps have the name "Henry." Postal authorities established Atascadero post office in 1914 (Frickstad, p. 163), and the town incorporated in 1979. Edward Gardner Lewis bought 23,000 acres in 1913 and began promoting a model community called Atascadero Colony, but financial problems and a jail term for Lewis ended the development as he proposed it (Lee and others, p. 17).

Atascadero Creek [SAN LUIS OBISPO]: *stream,* flows 10 miles to Salinas River 1.25

miles north-northeast of downtown Atascadero (lat. 35°30'20" N, long. 120°39'35" W). Named on Atascadero (1965) 7.5' quadrangle.

Atascadero Creek [SANTA BARBARA]: *stream,* flows 6.25 miles to San Pedro Creek 1 mile south of downtown Goleta (lat. 34°25'10" N, long. 119°49'45" W). Named on Goleta (1950) 7.5' quadrangle.

Atascadero Lake [SAN LUIS OBISPO]: *lake,* 0.5 mile long, 1.5 miles south of downtown Atascadero (lat. 35°27'50" N, long. 120°39'55" W). Named on Atascadero (1965) 7.5' quadrangle.

Atascoso Creek [SANTA BARBARA]: *stream,* flows 1.25 miles to El Jaro Creek 12 miles southeast of the city of Lompoc (lat. 34°31'05" N, long. 120°18'45" W). Named on Santa Rosa Hills (1959) 7.5' quadrangle.

Atherton Peak [SANTA CRUZ]: *peak,* 6 miles east-northeast of Watsonville on Santa Cruz-Santa Clara county line (lat. 36°56'15" N, long. 121°38'50" W). Altitude 1616 feet. Named on Watsonville East (1955) 7.5' quadrangle. The name commemorates Faxon Dean Atherton; the feature was called Vanoni Peak on a map of 1913 (Clark, 1986, p. 13-14).

Augustine Creek [SAN BENITO]: *stream,* flows 3 miles to San Benito River 14 miles east of Bitterwater (lat. 36°20'45" N, long. 120°45'20" W; sec. 22, T 18 S, R 11 E). Named on Hepsedam Peak (1969) 7.5' quadrangle.

Aulon: see **Point Aulon,** under **Lovers Point** [MONTEREY].

Aumentos Rock [MONTEREY]: *rock,* less than 1 mile east-southeast of Point Pinos, and 700 feet offshore (lat. 36°38'05" N, long. 121°55'10" W). Named on Monterey (1913) 15' quadrangle. United States Coast Survey officials applied the name in 1856 and 1857; the feature probably first had the name "Armenta's," for Jose Maria Armenta, who received Punta de Pinos grant where the rock is situated (Gudde, 1949, p. 18).

Ausaymas y San Felipe [SAN BENITO]: *land grant,* 8 miles north-northeast of Hollister on San Benito-Santa Clara county line. Named on San Felipe (1955) and Three Sisters (1954) 7.5' quadrangles. Francisco Perez Pacheco received 2 leagues in 1836 and claimed 35,504 acres patented in 1859 (Cowan, p. 17). According to Kroeber (1916, p. 35), the name "Ausaymas" came from the designation of Indians who lived near San Juan Bautista mission.

Austin Peak [MONTEREY]: *peak,* 16 miles north-northeast of San Ardo on Mustang Ridge (lat. 36°14'50" N, long. 120°50'25" W; sec. 25, T 19 S, R 10 E). Altitude 2594 feet. Named on Monarch Peak (1967) 7.5' quadrangle.

Avenal: see **Alamo Creek** [SAN LUIS OBISPO] (2).

Avenal's Station [SAN LUIS OBISPO]: *local-*ity, 19 miles northeast of the town of Nipomo along Salinas River (lat. 35°14'50" N, long. 120°15'55" W). Named on Caldwell Mesa (1967) 7.5' quadrangle.

Avila: see **Avila Beach** [SAN LUIS OBISPO].

Avila Beach [SAN LUIS OBISPO]: *village,* 8 miles south-southwest of downtown San Luis Obispo along the coast (lat. 35°10'45" N, long. 120°43'50" W). Named on Pismo Beach (1965) 7.5' quadrangle. Called Avila on Arroyo Grande (1942) 15' quadrangle, but United States Board on Geographic Names (1967a, p. 8) rejected this designation for the place. Postal authorities established Avila post office in 1907 and changed the name to Avila Beach in 1955 (Salley, p. 12). The name commemorates Miguel Avila, who received San Miguelito grant (Hoover, Rensch, and Rensch, p. 385). The community developed around a place called People's Wharf that John Harford built in 1869; when Harford built another wharf in 1872 at Port Harford, shipping activity transferred to that place (Angel, 1883, p. 322, 350). Postal authorities established Laplaya post office in 1876 at or near present Avila Beach; they changed the name to La Playa the same year, and discontinued it in 1878 (Salley, p. 117-118).

Avila Rock [SAN LUIS OBISPO]: *rock,* 100 feet long, nearly 1 mile southeast of Avila Beach, and 0.25 mile offshore (lat. 35°10'25" N, long. 120°43'25" W). Named on Pismo Beach (1965) 7.5' quadrangle.

Azalea Canyon [SAN BENITO]: *canyon,* drained by a stream that flows 2 miles to Bird Creek nearly 6.5 miles south-southwest of Hollister (lat. 36°46' N, long. 121°26'35" W). Named on Hollister (1955) 7.5' quadrangle.

– B –

Babies Gulch [SAN BENITO]: *canyon,* drained by a stream that flows 2 miles to Pimental Creek nearly 6 miles south of Panoche (lat. 36°30'45" N, long. 120°50'40" W; sec. 26, T 16 S, R 10 E). Named on Hernandez Reservoir (1969) and Panoche (1969) 7.5' quadrangles.

Bachelder Gulch: see **Granite Creek** [SANTA CRUZ].

Badger Spring [SANTA CRUZ]: *spring,* 6.5 miles north-northeast of Soquel (lat. 37°04'35" N, long. 121°55'05" W). Named on Laurel (1955) 7.5' quadrangle.

Bad Gulch [MONTEREY]: *canyon,* drained by a stream that flows nearly 1 mile to Big Sur River 9 miles east-southeast of Point Sur (lat. 36°15'05" N, long. 121°45'05" W; sec. 28, T 19 S, R 2 E). Named on Partington Ridge (1956) 15' quadrangle. The name reportedly is from conditions at the place during construction of a trail there in 1916 (Clark, 1991, p. 26).

Badlands [SAN BENITO]: *area,* 14 miles east-southeast of Bitterwater (lat. 36°17'10" N, long. 120°46'35" W; sec. 9, T 19 S, R 11 E). Named on Hepsedam Peak (1969) 7.5' quadrangle.

Bahia de los Pinos: see **Monterey Bay** [MONTEREY].

Bahia de San Pedro: see **Monterey Bay** [MONTEREY].

Baker Canyon [SAN BENITO]: *canyon,* drained by a stream that flows nearly 4 miles to Hernandez Reservoir 11 miles east of Bitterwater (lat. 36°22'50" N, long. 120°48'40" W; sec. 7, T 18 S, R 11 E). Named on Hernandez Reservoir (1969) 7.5' quadrangle. Called Cane Canyon on Hernandez Valley (1943) 15' quadrangle.

Balconies [SAN BENITO]: *relief feature,* 7 miles west of San Benito (lat. 36°30'15" N, long. 121°12'15" W; near SE cor. sec. 28, T 16 S, R 7 E). Named on Bickmore Canyon (1968) 7.5' quadrangle.

Bald Hill [SAN LUIS OBISPO]: *peak,* 2 miles south of Lopez Mountain (lat. 35°16'35" N, long. 120°34'35" W; near E line sec. 33, T 30 S, R 13 E). Named on Lopez Mountain (1965) 7.5' quadrangle.

Bald Knob [SAN LUIS OBISPO]: *peak,* 2.5 miles north-northwest of Point San Luis (lat. 35°11'50" N, long. 120°46'10" W). Altitude 1186 feet. Named on Port San Luis (1965) 7.5' quadrangle.

Bald Mountain [MONTEREY]:
(1) *ridge,* north-northwest-trending, nearly 1 mile long, 5 miles north-northeast of Charley Mountain on Monterey-Fresno county line (lat. 36°12'25" N, long. 120°37'40" W; sec. 12, T 20 S, R 12 E). Named on Priest Valley (1969) 7.5' quadrangle.
(2) *peak,* 8 miles south-southeast of Jolon (lat. 35°51'50" N, long. 121°07'25" W; sec. 8, T 24 S, R 8 E). Altitude 2132 feet. Named on Bryson (1949) and Burnett Peak (1949) 7.5' quadrangles.

Bald Mountain [SAN BENITO]: *peak,* 4.25 miles north of San Benito (lat. 36°34'15" N, long. 121°05'20" W). Altitude 2923 feet. Named on San Benito (1968) 7.5' quadrangle.

Bald Mountain [SAN LUIS OBISPO]:
(1) *peak,* 6.5 miles east-northeast of Edna (lat. 35°14'25" N, long. 120°30'10" W; near W line sec. 8, T 31 S, R 14 E). Altitude 2834 feet. Named on Arroyo Grande NE (1965) 7.5' quadrangle.
(2) *ridge,* northeast-trending, 1.25 miles long, 12 miles northeast of the town of Nipomo (lat. 35°09' N, long. 120°18'30" W). Named on Caldwell Mesa (1967) 7.5' quadrangle.

Bald Mountain [SANTA BARBARA]:
(1) *peak,* 8.5 miles southwest of McPherson Peak (lat. 34°48'45" N, long. 119°56'05" W). Altitude 4087 feet. Named on Bald Mountain (1964) 7.5' quadrangle.
(2) *peak,* 5.5 miles south of Santa Ynez (lat. 34°31'50" N, long. 120°05'25" W; sec. 11, T 5 N, R 31 W). Altitude 2614 feet. Named on

Santa Ynez (1959) 7.5' quadrangle.

Bald Mountain [SANTA CRUZ]: *peak,* 3 miles east-northeast of Davenport (lat. 37°01'30" N, long. 122°08'20" W; near N line sec. 36, T 10 S, R 3 W). Altitude 1296 feet. Named on Davenport (1955) 7.5' quadrangle.

Bald Mountain Canyon [SANTA BARBARA]: *canyon,* drained by a stream that flows nearly 3 miles to Sisquoc River 2.25 miles west-northwest of Bald Mountain (1) (lat. 34°49'40" N, long. 119°58'15" W); the canyon heads near Bald Mountain (1). Named on Bald Mountain (1964) 7.5' quadrangle.

Bald Peak [MONTEREY-SAN BENITO]: *peak,* 9.5 miles north-northwest of Charley Mountain on Monterey-San Benito county line. 36°16'40" N, long. 120°41'40" W; sec. 17, T 19 S, R 12 E). Altitude 3676 feet. Named on San Benito Mountain (1969) 7.5' quadrangle.

Bald Ridge [SANTA CRUZ]: *ridge,* west-south-west-trending, 1.5 miles long, 5 miles north-east of Watsonville (lat. 36°57'30" N, long. 121°40'45" W). Named on Watsonville East (1955) 7.5' quadrangle.

Bald Top [SAN LUIS OBISPO]: *peak,* nearly 2 miles east-northeast of the mouth of San Carpoforo Creek (lat. 35°46'35" N, long. 121°17'45" W; sec. 11, T 25 S, R 6 E). Named on Burro Mountain (1949) 7.5' quadrangle.

Baldwin Creek [SANTA CRUZ]: *stream,* flows 4 miles to the sea 5.5 miles west-northwest of Point Santa Cruz (lat. 36°58' N, long. 122°07'20" W). Named on Felton (1955) and Santa Cruz (1954) 7.5' quadrangles.

Ballard [SANTA BARBARA]: *village,* 2 miles south of Los Olivos (lat. 34°38'10" N, long. 120°06'50" W; on S line sec. 35, T 7 N, R 31 W); the place is along Alamo Pintado Creek. Named on Los Olivos (1959) 7.5' quadrangle. The name commemorates W.N. Ballard, who from 1862 until 1870 had a stage station at the site, which then was called Alamo Pintado; George W. Lewis, who married Ballard's widow, gave the name "Ballard" to the place (Gudde, 1949, p. 21). Postal authorities established Ballards post office in 1870, discontinued it in 1872, reestablished it with the name "Ballard" in 1881, and discontinued it in 1918 (Salley, p. 14).

Ballard Campground [SANTA BARBARA]: *locality,* 2.5 miles southeast of Zaca Lake (lat. 34°45'05" N, long. 120°00'40" W). Named on Zaca Lake (1964) 7.5' quadrangle.

Ballard Canyon [SANTA BARBARA]: *canyon,* drained by a stream that flows 6 miles to low-lands 2 miles east-southeast of Buellton (lat. 34°36'15" N, long. 120°09'30" W). Named on Los Olivos (1959), Solvang (1959), and Zaca Creek (1959) 7.5' quadrangles.

Ballard Canyon: see **Birabent Canyon** [SANTA BARBARA].

Ballard Creek [SANTA BARBARA]: *stream,* flows 0.5 mile to Birbent Canyon (present Birabent Canyon) 8 miles northeast of Los Olivos (lat. 34°45' N, long. 120°01'05" W; at

NW cor. sec. 25, T 8 N, R 30 W). Named on Los Olivos (1959) 7.5' quadrangle.

Ballard Creek: see **Quiota Creek** [SANTA BARBARA].

Ballards: see **Ballard** [SANTA BARBARA].

Ballinger Canyon [SANTA BARBARA]: *canyon,* drained by a stream that heads in Ventura and Kern Counties, and flows 3 miles in Santa Barbara County to Cuyama Valley 8.5 miles east-southeast of the village of Cuyama (lat. 34°53' N, long. 119°29'15" W). Named on Ballinger Canyon (1943) 7.5' quadrangle.

Ballinger Canyon Wash [SANTA BARBARA]: *stream,* flows 1.25 miles from the mouth of Ballinger Canyon to Cuyama River 7 miles east-southeast of the village of Cuyama (lat. 34°52'45" N, long. 119°30'25" W). Named on Cuyama (1964) 7.5' quadrangle.

Balloon Spring [SAN LUIS OBISPO]: *spring,* 6.25 miles north of Pozo (lat. 35°23'30" N, long. 120°21'35" W; near SW cor. sec. 15, T 29 S, R 15 E). Named on Camatta Ranch (1966) 7.5' quadrangle.

Balm of Gilead Campground [SAN LUIS OBISPO]: *locality,* 4.5 miles southeast of Pozo (lat. 35°15'25" N, long. 120°18'55" W; near NE cor. sec. 1, T 31 S, R 15 E). Named on Pozo Summit (1967) 7.5' quadrangle.

Banchero Rock [MONTEREY]: *peak,* 0.5 mile east-northeast of Monarch Peak on Mustang Ridge (lat. 36°13'10" N, long. 120°47'35" W; sec. 4, T 20 S, R 11 E). Named on Monarch Peak (1967) 7.5' quadrangle. The name is for the Banchero family; the feature has been mistakenly called Ranchero Rock (Clark, 1991, p. 27).

Banks Canyon [SANTA CRUZ]: *canyon,* nearly 2 miles long, drained by Casserly Creek above a point 5.25 miles north-northeast of Watsonville (lat. 36°59'25" N, long. 121°44'05" W). Named on Mount Madonna (1955) and Watsonville East (1955) 7.5' quadrangles.

Bardin [MONTEREY]: *locality,* 3 miles south-southeast of the mouth of Salinas River along Southern Pacific Railroad (lat. 36°42'25" N, long. 121°47'20" W). Named on Monterey (1913) 15' quadrangle.

Barger Canyon [SANTA BARBARA]: *canyon,* nearly 2 miles long, along Arroyo Burro (3) above a point 3.5 miles northwest of downtown Santa Barbara (lat. 34°27'15" N, long. 119°44'40" W). Named on Santa Barbara (1952) 7.5' quadrangle. United States Board on Geographic Names (1961b, p. 7) rejected the name "Arroyo Burro" for the feature.

Barger Canyon: see **Arroyo Burro** [SANTA BARBARA] (3).

Barka Slough [SANTA BARBARA]: *marsh,* 6.5 miles south of Orcutt in San Antonio Valley (lat. 34°46'15" N, long. 120°28' W). Named on Orcutt (1959) 7.5' quadrangle.

Barlow Flat Camp [MONTEREY]: *locality,* 5 miles north of Partington Point along the upper reaches of Big Sur River (lat. 36°14'50"

N, long. 121°42'40" W; sec. 26, T 19 S, R 2 E). Named on Partington Ridge (1956) 7.5' quadrangle.

Barloy Canyon [MONTEREY]: *canyon,* drained by a stream that flows 2.25 miles to an unnamed stream 5 miles west of Spreckels (lat. 36°37'30" N, long. 121°44'20" W). Named on Spreckels (1947) 7.5' quadrangle.

Barn Springs: see **Lower Barn Springs,** under **Hot Springs** [SANTA BARBARA] (2); **Upper Barn Springs,** under **Hot Springs** [SANTA BARBARA] (2).

Baroda [SANTA BARBARA]: *locality,* less than 1 mile east-northeast of Surf along Southern Pacific Railroad (lat. 34°41'10" N, long. 120°35'25" W). Named on Surf (1959) 7.5' quadrangle.

Barranca Honda [SANTA BARBARA]: *canyon,* drained by a stream that flows 2.25 miles to the sea 5 miles east of Point Conception (lat. 34°27'25" N, long. 120°22'55" W). Named on Point Conception (1953) 7.5' quadrangle. Called Canada del Gato on Lompoc (1905) 30' quadrangle, but United States Board on Geographic Names (1962a, p. 5) rejected the names "Canada del Gato" and "Cañada del Gato" for the feature.

Barr Canyon [MONTEREY]: *canyon,* nearly 3 miles long, opens into lowlands 3.5 miles northeast of Jolon (lat. 36°00'30" N, long. 121° 08' W; near NW cor. sec. 20, T 22 S, R 8 E). Named on Cosio Knob (1949) and Espinosa Canyon (1949) 7.5' quadrangles. The name commemorates Harry Barr, who homesteaded about 2 miles east of the mouth of the canyon (NE quarter sec. 23, T 22 S, R 8 E) (Clark, 1991, p. 29).

Barrell Canyon [MONTEREY]: *canyon,* drained by a stream that flows nearly 5 miles to lowlands 5 miles west-northwest of San Ardo (lat. 36°03' N, long. 120°59'20" W). Named on Espinosa Canyon (1949) and San Ardo (1967) 7.5' quadrangles.

Barrel Springs [SANTA BARBARA]: *spring,* 2.5 miles east-southeast of Tepusquet Peak (lat. 34°54'05" N, long. 120°08'40" W). Named on Tepusquet Canyon (1964) 7.5' quadrangle.

Barrett Creek [SAN LUIS OBISPO]: *stream,* flows 11.5 miles to San Juan Creek 3.5 miles northeast of Branch Mountain (lat. 35°13'40" N, long. 120°02'40" W; sec. 16, T 31 S, R 18 E). Named on Branch Mountain (1967) and Chimineas Ranch (1959) 7.5' quadrangles.

Barsug [SANTA BARBARA]: *locality,* at the south edge of the town of Guadalupe, where Southern Pacific Railroad and Santa Maria Valley Railroad cross (lat. 34°57'25" N, long. 120°34'20" W). Named on Guadalupe (1959) 7.5' quadrangle.

Bartlett Canyon [SANTA BARBARA]: *canyon,* 4 miles long, along Carneros Creek above a point 2 miles west-northwest of downtown Goleta (lat. 34°26'45" N, long. 119°51'20" W). Named on Goleta (1950) 7.5' quadrangle.

Basin: see **The Basin** [MONTEREY].
Basin Creek [MONTEREY]: *stream,* flows nearly 5 miles to Sand Creek 11.5 miles south-southwest of Soledad (lat. 36°17' N, long. 121°25'45" W; sec. 16, T 19 S, R 5 E); the stream goes through The Basin. Named on Sycamore Flat (1956) 7.5' quadrangle.
Basket Spring [MONTEREY]: *spring,* 6 miles east-northeast of Cape San Martin (lat. 35°54'35" N, long. 121°21'40" W; sec. 30, T 23 S, R 6 E). Named on Alder Peak (1949) 7.5' quadrangle.
Basquez Creek: see **Vasquez Creek** [SAN LUIS OBISPO].
Bassett Gulch: see **Aptos Creek** [SANTA CRUZ].
Bates Canyon [SANTA BARBARA]: *canyon,* drained by a stream that flows nearly 4.5 miles to Cottonwood Canyon 7.25 miles northwest of McPherson Peak (lat. 34°58'15" N, long. 119°53'05" W; near NW cor. sec. 9, T 10 N, R 28 W). Named on Bates Canyon (1964) 7.5' quadrangle.
Bates Canyon Campground [SANTA BARBARA]: *locality,* 7.25 miles northwest of McPherson Peak (lat. 34°57'15" N, long. 119°54'25" W); the place is in Bates Canyon. Named on Bates Canyon (1964) 7.5' quadrangle.
Bates Creek [SANTA CRUZ]: *stream,* flows 3 miles to Soquel Creek 3 miles north-northeast of Soquel Point (lat. 36°59'45" N, long. 121°57'15" W). Named on Laurel (1955) and Soquel (1954) 7.5' quadrangles. The name commemorates Joel Bates, who settled in the neighborhood as early as 1853; the feature also was called Picnic Gulch Creek (Clark, 1986, p. 18).
Bat Rock [SANTA BARBARA]: *rock,* 4.25 miles northwest of Cardwell Point, and 50 feet offshore on the north side of San Miguel Island (lat. 34°03'35" N, long. 120°21'15" W). Named on San Miguel Island East (1950) 7.5' quadrangle.
Battles [SANTA BARBARA]: *locality,* 2.25 miles southeast of Santa Maria along Santa Maria Valley Railroad (lat. 34°55'50" N, long. 120°24'20" W). Named on Santa Maria (1959) 7.5' quadrangle.
Bay de los Esteros: see **Estero Bay** [SAN LUIS OBISPO].
Bay of San Luis: see **San Luis Obispo Bay** [SAN LUIS OBISPO].
Bay-Osos: see **Los Osos** [SAN LUIS OBISPO].
Bay Point [SANTA BARBARA]: *promontory,* 2 miles northwest of Cardwell Point on the north side of San Miguel Island (lat. 34°02'30" N, long. 120°19'05" W). Named on San Miguel Island East (1950) 7.5' quadrangle. Bremner's (1933) map shows a feature called Eagle Cliff located along the coast less than 0.5 mile west-northwest of present Bay Point.
Baywood Park [SAN LUIS OBISPO]: *town,* 3.5 miles south-southeast of Morro Rock on the southeast side of Morro Bay (1) (lat.

35°19'35" N, long. 120°50'10" W). Named on Morro Bay South (1965) 7.5' quadrangle. Lots in a subdivision called El Moro were sold at the place in 1894 (Nicholson, p. 168). Walter Redfield resumed development of the subdivision in 1919, and changed the name from El Moro to Baywood Park; the community later was combined with Los Osos for census and postal purposes (Lee and others, p. 21). Postal authorities established Baywood Park post office in 1948 and discontinued it in 1967 (Salley, p. 16).
Beacon Reef: see **Carrington Point** [SANTA BARBARA].
Beam Flat [SAN LUIS OBISPO]: *area,* 36 miles southeast of Simmler near the southeast end of Elkhorn Plain (lat. 35°01'15" N, long. 119°29'25" W; near SE cor. sec. 24, T 11 N, R 25 W). Named on Maricopa (1951) 7.5' quadrangle.
Bean Canyon [SAN LUIS OBISPO]: *canyon,* drained by a stream that flows 3 miles to Pozo Creek 2.25 miles east-northeast of Pozo (lat. 35°18'45" N, long. 120°20'15" W; sec. 14, T 30 S, R 15 E). Named on Pozo Summit (1967) 7.5' quadrangle. Called Fraser Canyon on Pozo (1922) 15' quadrangle, but United States Board on Geographic Names (1968b, p. 5) rejected this name.
Bean Creek [SANTA CRUZ]: *stream,* flows 9 miles to Zayante Creek 6 miles southeast of the town of Boulder Creek (lat. 37°03'05" N, long. 122°03'35" W). Named on Felton (1955), Laurel (1955), and Los Gatos (1953) 7.5' quadrangles. John Bean settled along the stream in 1853 (Young, p. 10).
Bean Hill [SANTA CRUZ]: *peak,* 3.25 miles northwest of Corralitos (lat. 37°01'25" N, long. 121°50'50" W). Named on Loma Prieta (1955) 7.5' quadrangle.
Bean Hollow: see **Glenwood** [SANTA CRUZ].
Bear Basin [MONTEREY]: *area,* 2 miles east of Ventana Cone (lat. 36°17'10" N, long. 121°38'25" W; on N line sec. 16, T 19 S, R 3 E). Named on Ventana Cones (1956) 7.5' quadrangle.
Bear Basin Camp [MONTEREY]: *locality,* 2 miles east of Ventana Cone (lat. 36°17' N, long. 121°38'35" W; sec. 16, T 19 S, R 3 E); the place is on the south side of Bear Basin. Named on Ventana Cones (1956) 7.5' quadrangle.
Bear Basin Creek [MONTEREY]: *stream,* flows nearly 1 mile to Carmel River 2 miles east-northeast of Ventana Cone (lat. 36°17'50" N, long. 121°38'55" W; sec. 9, T 19 S, R 3 E); the stream heads in Bear Basin. Named on Ventana Cones (1956) 7.5' quadrangle.
Bear Campground [SANTA BARBARA]: *locality,* 1.25 miles east-northeast of Big Pine Mountain along Sisquoc River (lat. 34°42'15" N, long. 119°38' W). Named on Big Pine Mountain (1964) 7.5' quadrangle.
Bear Campground: see **Lower Bear Campground** [SANTA BARBARA].

Bear Canyon [MONTEREY]:
(1) *canyon*, drained by a stream that flows nearly 4 miles to Robertson Creek 4 miles east of Jamesburg (lat. 36°22'05" N, long. 121°31'20" W; near E line sec. 15, T 18 S, R 4 E). Named on Chews Ridge (1956) and Rana Creek (1956) 7.5' quadrangles.
(2) *canyon*, drained by a stream that flows 7.5 miles to San Antonio River 10 miles northwest of Jolon (lat. 36°04' N, long. 121°19'15" W); the canyon heads near Bear Mountain. Named on Bear Canyon (1949) and Reliz Canyon (1949) 7.5' quadrangles.
Bear Canyon [SAN BENITO]:
(1) *canyon*, drained by a stream that flows 3.25 miles to Stone Canyon 6 miles south of Paicines (lat. 36°38'25" N, long. 121°15'30" W; sec. 12, T 15 S, R 6 E). Named on Mount Johnson (1968) and Paicines (1968) 7.5' quadrangles.
(2) *canyon*, drained by a stream that flows 1 mile to Payne Creek 4 miles northeast of San Benito (lat. 36°33'25" N, long. 121°02'15" W). Named on San Benito (1968) 7.5' quadrangle.
Bear Canyon [SANTA BARBARA]: *canyon*, drained by a stream that flows 5.5 miles to North Fork La Brea Creek 2.5 miles east-northeast of Tepusquet Peak (lat. 34°55'10" N, long. 120°08'20" W). Named on Tepusquet Canyon (1964) 7.5' quadrangle.
Bear Canyon: see **Deer Canyon** [SAN LUIS OBISPO] (3); **De Vaul Canyon** [SANTA BARBARA].
Bear Creek [SAN BENITO]: *stream*, flows 3.25 miles to Chalone Creek 3 miles north-north-east of North Chalone Peak (lat. 36°29'05" N, long. 121°09'50" W; sec. 1, T 17 S, R 7 E); the stream drains Bear Gulch (1). Named on North Chalone Peak (1969) 7.5' quadrangle.
Bear Creek [SANTA BARBARA]:
(1) *stream*, flows 3.25 miles to lowlands along the coast 2.5 miles south of Surf (lat. 34°38'50" N, long. 120°36' W). Named on Surf (1959) and Tranquillon Mountain (1959) 7.5' quadrangles.
(2) *stream*, flows 2.5 miles to Kelly Creek 2.5 miles northwest of San Marcos Pass (lat. 34°32'30" N, long. 119°51'15" W). Named on San Marcos Pass (1959) 7.5' quadrangle.
Bear Creek [SANTA CRUZ]: *stream*, flows 8 miles to San Lorenzo River at the town of Boulder Creek (lat. 37°07'40" N, long. 122°07'15" W; near N line sec. 30, T 9 S, R 2 W). Named on Castle Rock Ridge (1955) 7.5' quadrangle.
Bear Creek: see **Rancho Nuevo Creek** [SANTA BARBARA].
Bear Gulch [SAN BENITO]:
(1) *canyon*, drained by Bear Creek, which flows 3.25 miles to Chalone Creek 3 miles north-northeast of North Chalone Peak (lat. 36°29'05" N, long. 121°09'50" W; sec. 1, T 17 S, R 7 E). Named on North Chalone Peak (1969) 7.5' quadrangle.

(2) *canyon*, drained by a stream that flows 1.5 miles to Rock Springs Creek 7.5 miles north-northeast of Bitterwater (lat. 36°28'20" N, long. 120°55'45" W; near N line sec. 7, T 17 S, R 10 E). Named on Rock Spring Peak (1969) 7.5' quadrangle.
Bear Gulch Reservoir [SAN BENITO]: *lake*, 1200 feet long, behind a dam in Bear Gulch (1) nearly 2 miles north-northeast of North Chalone Peak (lat. 36°28'20" N, long. 121°11'10" W; near NW cor. sec. 11, T 17 S, R 7 E). Named on North Chalone Peak (1969) 7.5' quadrangle.
Bear Mountain [MONTEREY]: *peak*, 14 miles west-southwest of King City (lat. 36°09'30" N, long. 121°22'30" W; sec. 25, T 20 S, R 5 E). Altitude 4771 feet. Named on Junipero Serra Peak (1949) and Reliz Canyon (1949) 7.5' quadrangles.
Bear Spring [MONTEREY]: *spring*, 7.5 miles north of Charley Mountain (lat. 36°14'50" N, long. 120°41'05" W; sec. 28, T 19 S, R 12 E). Named on Priest Valley (1969) 7.5' quadrangle.
Bear Trap: see **Little Bear Trap** [MONTEREY]; **The Bear Trap** [MONTEREY].
Bear Trap Canyon [MONTEREY]: *canyon*, drained by a stream that flows nearly 1 mile to Anastasia Canyon 3 miles south-southeast of Jamesburg (lat. 36°20' N, long. 121°33'55" W; sec. 29, T 18 S, R 4 E); the canyon is southwest of The Bear Trap. Named on Chews Ridge (1956) 7.5' quadrangle.
Beartrap Canyon [MONTEREY]: *canyon*, drained by a stream that flows 1 mile to Bixby Creek 5 miles north-northeast of Point Sur (lat. 36°22'10" N, long. 121°51'40" W; sec. 16, T 18 S, R 1 E). Named on Big Sur (1956) 7.5' quadrangle.
Beartrap Creek [SAN LUIS OBISPO]: *stream*, flows 5.5 miles to San Juan Creek 4 miles east-northeast of Castle Crags (lat. 35°20'05" N, long. 120°08'25" W; sec. 10, T 30 S, R 17 E). Named on La Panza (1967) 7.5' quadrangle.
Beartrap Flat [MONTEREY]: *area*, 7.5 miles south-southeast of Jolon (lat. 35°51'50" N, long. 121°08'30" W; sec. 6, 7, T 24 S, R 8 E). Named on Burnett Peak (1949) 7.5' quadrangle.
Bear Trap Gulch: see **San Vicente Creek** [SANTA CRUZ].
Bear Trap Spring [MONTEREY]: *spring*, 1 mile west-northwest of Charley Mountain (lat. 36°08'50" N, long. 120°40'50" W; sec. 33, T 20 S, R 12 E). Named on Priest Valley (1969) 7.5' quadrangle.
Beartrap Spring [SAN LUIS OBISPO]: *spring*, 2 miles east-northeast of Castle Crags (lat. 35°19'10" N, long. 120°10'10" W); the spring is along Beartrap Creek. Named on La Panza (1967) 7.5' quadrangle.
Beartree Canyon [MONTEREY]: *canyon*, drained by a stream that flows nearly 1.5 miles to Gabilan Creek 10 miles east-northeast of

Salinas (lat. 36°44' N, long. 121°28'50" W). Named on Mount Harlan (1968) 7.5' quadrangle.

Bear Valley [SAN BENITO]: *valley,* opens into the canyon of Chalone Creek 3 miles northeast of North Chalone Peak (lat. 36° 28'50" N, long. 121°09'20" W; sec. 1, T 17 S, R 7 E). Named on Bickmore Canyon (1968) and North Chalone Peak (1969) 7.5' quadrangles.

Bear Valley [SANTA CRUZ]: *canyon,* nearly 1 mile long, opens into lowlands 3.25 miles west-northwest of Corralitos (lat. 37°00'30" N, long. 121°51'35" W). Named on Loma Prieta (1955) 7.5' quadrangle.

Beasley Flat [SAN LUIS OBISPO]: *area,* 11 miles northeast of the village of San Simeon (lat. 35°46'10" N, long. 121°04'20" W; near E line sec. 11, T 25 S, R 8 E). Named on Bryson (1949) 7.5' quadrangle.

Beatty Ridge [SANTA CRUZ]: *ridge,* south- to south-southeast-trending, 1.5 miles long, 6 miles north-northeast of the town of Boulder Creek (lat. 37°12' N, long. 122°03'55" W). Named on Castle Rock Ridge (1955) 7.5' quadrangle. The name is for G.W. Beatty and W.J. Beatty, brothers who settled in the neighborhood about 1905 and had a ranch on the ridge (Clark, 1986, p. 23).

Beatty Slide [SANTA CRUZ]: *relief feature,* nearly 6 miles north-northeast of the town of Boulder Creek (lat. 37°11'55" N, long. 122°04'10" W; near N line sec. 34, T 8 S, R 2 W); the slide is on the west side of Beatty Ridge. Named on Castle Rock Ridge (1955) 7.5' quadrangle. The feature is a landslide caused by the 1906 earthquake (Clark, 1986, p. 23).

Beauty Spring [SAN LUIS OBISPO]: *spring,* 9 miles northeast of the mouth of Morro Creek (lat. 35°28'55" N, long. 120°46'10" W). Named on Morro Bay North (1965) 7.5' quadrangle.

Bechers Bay: see **Beechers Bay** [SANTA BARBARA].

Becker Valley [SAN BENITO]: *canyon,* drained by a stream that flows nearly 5 miles to an unnamed canyon at Monterey-San Benito county line 5.25 miles south-southwest of Bitterwater (lat. 36°18'35" N, long. 121°02'20" W; sec. 6, T 19 S, R 9 E). Named on Lonoak (1969) and Pinalito Canyon (1969) 7.5' quadrangles.

Beckett: see **Emmett Station** [SAN BENITO].

Beck Lake [SAN LUIS OBISPO]: *intermittent lake,* 350 feet long, 8 miles north-northeast of Santa Margarita (lat. 35°29'30" N, long. 120°32' W). Named on Santa Margarita (1965) 7.5' quadrangle.

Bee Camp [MONTEREY]: *locality,* 3 miles east-northeast of Slates Hot Springs (lat. 36°08'10" N, long. 121°35'05" W; sec. 1, T 21 S, R 3 E). Named on Tassajara Hot Springs (1956) 7.5' quadrangle. The place also was called Upper Bee Camp to distinguish it from Lower Bee Camp (Clark, 1991, p. 32).

Bee Camp: see **Lower Bee Camp** [MONTEREY].

Bee Canyon [SAN LUIS OBISPO]: *canyon,* drained by a stream that flows nearly 0.5 mile to Corbit Canyon 4.5 miles southeast of Edna (lat. 35°09'25" N, long. 120°33'25" W). Named on Arroyo Grande NE (1965) 7.5' quadrangle. Called Deer Canyon on Arroyo Grande (1897) 15' quadrangle, where present Deer Canyon (2) is called Bee Canyon.

Bee Cave Canyon [MONTEREY]: *canyon,* drained by a stream that flows nearly 1 mile to Loeber Canyon 8.5 miles east of Jolon (lat. 35°57'35" N, long. 121°01'45" W; sec. 5, T 32 S, R 9 E). Named on Williams Hill (1949) 7.5' quadrangle.

Beechers Bay [SANTA BARBARA]: *embayment,* 5.5 miles northwest of East Point on the north side of Santa Rosa Island (lat. 34°00' N, long. 120°02'15" W). Named on Santa Rosa Island East (1943) and Santa Rosa Island North (1943) 7.5' quadrangles. United States Board on Geographic Names (1995, p. 5) approved the name "Bechers Bay" for the feature.

Beehive [SANTA CRUZ]: *peak,* 2.25 miles northwest of Laurel (lat. 37°08'30" N, long. 121°59'30" W; on N line sec. 20, T 9 S, R 1 W). Named on Los Gatos (1919) 15' quadrangle. The name is from the resemblance of the feature to a beehive (Gudde, 1949, p. 27).

Beeman Canyon [MONTEREY]: *canyon,* drained by a stream that flows 3.5 miles to Peachtree Valley (lat. 36°13'45" N, long. 120°53' W). Named on Hepsedam Peak (1969), Monarch Peak (1967), and Nattrass Valley (1967) 7.5' quadrangles.

Bee Rock [SAN LUIS OBISPO]: *locality,* nearly 3 miles east-northeast of Tierra Redonda Mountain (lat. 35°47'15" N, long. 120°56'20" W; sec. 6, T 25 S, R 10 E); the place is in the upper part of Bee Rock Canyon (1). Named on Tierra Redonda Mountain (1949) 7.5' quadrangle.

Bee Rock [SANTA BARBARA]:
(1) *relief feature,* 5.5 miles northwest of Zaca Lake along Sisquoc River (lat. 34°50' N, long. 120°06'15" W). Named on Zaca Lake (1964) 7.5' quadrangle.
(2) *peak,* 2 miles north of Santa Ynez Peak (lat. 34°33'20" N, long. 119°58'40" W). Altitude 2091 feet. Named on Lake Cachuma (1959) 7.5' quadrangle.
(3) *rock,* 4 miles south-southeast of Sandy Point on the west side of Santa Rosa Island, and 4400 feet offshore (lat. 33°57' N, long. 120°12'45" W). Named on Santa Rosa Island West (1943) 7.5' quadrangle.

Bee Rock Canyon [MONTEREY-SAN LUIS OBISPO]: *canyon,* drained by a stream that heads in San Luis Obispo County and flows 4.5 miles to San Antonio River 6.5 miles southwest of Bradley in Monterey County (lat. 35°48'05" N, long. 120°53'25" W; sec. 33, T 24 S, R 10 E). Named on Tierra Redonda

Mountain (1949) 7.5' quadrangle. The stream in the canyon is called Lynch's Creek on an unpublished map used about 1915. Water of San Antonio Reservoir (present Lake San Antonio) now floods the lower part of the canyon.

Bee Rock Canyon [SAN LUIS OBISPO]: *canyon,* drained by a stream that flows 3 miles to Cuyama Valley 2.5 miles northwest of New Cuyama [SANTA BARBARA] (lat. 34°58'30" N, long. 119°42'35" W). Named on New Cuyama (1964) 7.5' quadrangle.

Bee Rock Canyon [SANTA BARBARA]: *canyon,* drained by a stream that flows 2.25 miles to Sisquoc River 0.5 mile east of Bee Rock (1) (lat. 34°50'05" N, long. 120°05'45" W). Named on Zaca Lake (1964) 7.5' quadrangle.

Beeswax Canyon [MONTEREY]: *canyon,* drained by a stream that flows 1 mile to lowlands 5 miles west-southwest of Greenfield (lat. 36°18'05" N, long. 121°19'30" W). Named on Paraiso Springs (1956) 7.5' quadrangle.

Bee Tree Spring [SAN LUIS OBISPO]: *spring,* 2 miles west of Cholame (lat. 35°43'05" N, long. 120°19'50" W; sec. 26, T 25 S, R 15 E). Named on Cholame (1961) 7.5' quadrangle.

Bell Canyon [SANTA BARBARA]:
(1) *canyon,* drained by a stream that flows 2.25 miles to Zaca Creek 3 miles west of Zaca Lake (lat. 34°46'45" N, long. 120°05'25" W). Named on Zaca Lake (1964) 7.5' quadrangle.
(2) *canyon,* 1.25 miles long, opens to the sea 2.5 miles northwest of Coal Oil Point (lat. 34°25'45" N, long. 119°54'45" W). Named on Dos Pueblos Canyon (1951) 7.5' quadrangle.

Bello Spring [SAN LUIS OBISPO]: *spring,* 8.5 miles north-northwest of San Luis Obispo (lat. 35°23'25" N, long. 120°43'45" W; sec. 19, T 29 S, R 12 E). Named on Atascadero (1965) 7.5' quadrangle.

Bellyache Spring [SAN LUIS OBISPO]: *spring,* 14 miles southeast of Shandon (lat. 35°30'30" N, long. 120°11'40" W; sec. 12, T 28 S, R 16 E). Named on Holland Canyon (1961) 7.5' quadrangle.

Ben Graves Canyon [MONTEREY]: *canyon,* drained by a stream that flows 2.25 miles to McCoy Canyon 6 miles east-northeast of Gonzales (lat. 36°33' N, long. 121°21'05" W; sec. 7, T 16 S, R 6 E). Named on Mount Johnson (1968) 7.5' quadrangle. The name commemorates Benjamin Graves, who owned land in and near the canyon (Clark, 1991, p. 33).

Benham: see **Carpinteria** [SANTA BARBARA].

Ben Lomond [SANTA CRUZ]: *town,* 3.25 miles southeast of the town of Boulder Creek along San Lorenzo River (lat. 37°05'20" N, long. 122°05'15" W; in and near sec. 4, T 10 S, R 2 W). Named on Felton (1955) 7.5' quadrangle. Postal authorities established Ben Lomond post office in 1887 (Frickstad, p. 176). James

J. Pierce, owner of timber operations in the neighborhood, laid out the town in the 1880's (Hoover, Rensch, and Rensch, p. 479-480). The community first was called Pacific Mills, but when postal authorities objected to this name, the place was renamed Ben Lomond for nearby Ben Lomond Mountain (Rowland, p. 173). Hamman's (1980b) map shows a place called Shingle Springs located along the railroad just south of Ben Lomond, and north of the confluence of Newell Creek and San Lorenzo River. Rowland (p. 172) mentioned two places situated along San Lorenzo River near Ben Lomond: Hicks' ford near the south edge of the present town, named for Napoleon Bonaparte Hicks, who settled there in 1868; and Priest's ford near the north end of the present town, named for James Priest, who had a sawmill nearby.

Ben Lomond: see **Camp Ben Lomond** [SANTA CRUZ].

Ben Lomond Mountain [SANTA CRUZ]: *ridge,* north-northwest-trending, 9 miles long, 11 miles northwest of Santa Cruz (lat. 37°06' N, long. 122°08'30" W). Named on Big Basin (1955), Davenport (1955), and Felton (1955) 7.5' quadrangles. John Burns, a native of Scotland, took up land on the ridge in 1850, planted a vineyard, and named the ridge after the Scotch wine-grape district of Ben Lomond (Rowland, p. 173).

Bennett: see **Point Bennett** [SANTA BARBARA].

Bennett Creek [SANTA CRUZ]: *stream,* flows nearly 2 miles to Fall Creek 5.5 miles southsoutheast of the town of Boulder Creek (lat. 37°03'05" N, long. 122°05' W; sec. 21, T 10 S, R 2 W). Named on Felton (1955) 7.5' quadrangle. The name commemorates Eben Bennett, who came to Santa Cruz in 1866 and operated lime kilns near the stream (Clark, 1986, p. 26).

Bennett Slough [MONTEREY]: *water feature,* nearly 2 miles long, joins Elkhorn Slough at Moss Landing (lat. 36°48'35" N, long. 121°47'10" W). Named on Moss Landing (1954) 7.5' quadrangle.

Ben Willow Spring [SAN LUIS OBISPO]: *spring,* 4.25 miles southwest of Wilson Corner (lat. 35°25'15" N, long. 120°25'40" W; sec. 12, T 29 S, R 14 E). Named on Wilson Corner (1966) 7.5' quadrangle.

Bern [SAN LUIS OBISPO]: *locality,* 9.5 miles east-northeast of Paso Robles near Estrella Creek (lat. 35°41'20" N, long. 120°32'15" W; near S line sec. 2, T 26 S, R 13 E). Named on Paso Robles (1919) 15' quadrangle. Postal authorities established Bern post office in 1904 and discontinued it in 1932 (Frickstad, p. 164).

Bernard's Bay: see **Morro Bay** [SAN LUIS OBISPO] (1).

Berros [SAN LUIS OBISPO]: *settlement,* 4 miles southeast of downtown Arroyo Grande (lat. 35°04'40" N, long. 120°32'20" W); the place is along Los Berros Creek. Named on Oceano (1965) 7.5' quadrangle. Called Los Berros on Arroyo Grande (1897) 15' quadrangle, which shows the place located along Pacific Coast Railroad, and United States Board on Geographic Names (1991, p. 5) approved this name for the settlement. Postal authorities established Berros Creek post office in 1870 and discontinued it in 1872; they established Los Berros post office in 1888, changed the name to Berros in 1901, discontinued it in 1920, reestablished it in 1921, and discontinued it in 1940 (Salley, p. 19). *Berros* means "watercress" in Spanish (Gudde, 1949, p. 29).

Berros Creek: see **Berros** [SAN LUIS OBISPO].

Berry Creek [SANTA CRUZ]:

(1) *stream,* heads just inside San Mateo County and flows nearly 2 miles to West Waddell Creek 5 miles north of the mouth of Waddell Creek (lat. 37°10'05" N, long. 122°15'50" W; sec. 11, T 9 S, R 4 W). Named on Franklin Point (1955) 7.5' quadrangle. T.G. Berry homesteaded along the stream in 1878 (Brown, p. 7).

(2) *stream,* flows 1.25 miles to Big Creek nearly 5 miles north-northwest of Davenport (lat. 37°04'40" N, long. 122°13'05" W; sec. 8, T 10 S, R 3 W). Named on Davenport (1955) 7.5' quadrangle. The name is for Andrew Warren Berry, who homesteaded and had a cabin along the stream in the 1850's (Clark, 1986, p. 27).

Berry Creek Falls [SANTA CRUZ]: *waterfall,* 5 miles north of the mouth of Waddell Creek (lat. 37°10'10" N, long. 122°15'50" W; sec. 11, T 9 S, R 4 W); the waterfall is along Berry Creek (1). Named on Franklin Point (1955) 7.5' quadrangle. The feature also is called Lower Berry Creek Falls to distinguish it from other waterfalls on Berry Creek (Clark, 1986, p. 27).

Berry Falls: see **Davenport Landing** [SANTA CRUZ].

Berta Canyon [MONTEREY]: *canyon,* drained by a stream that flows 1 mile to an unnamed canyon nearly 1 mile north-northeast of Prunedale (lat. 36°47'15" N, long. 121°39'50" W). Named on Prunedale (1954) 7.5' quadrangle.

Berwick Canyon [MONTEREY]: *canyon,* drained by a stream that flows 2 miles to Carmel Valley (1) 6.5 miles east of the mouth of Carmel River (lat. 36°31'25" N, long. 121°48'35" W). Named on Seaside (1947) 7.5' quadrangle. The name commemorates Edward Berwick, who bought land in Carmel Valley (1) in 1867 (Clark, 1991, p. 34).

Bethany Park [SANTA CRUZ]: *settlement,* 6.5 miles north-northwest of Soquel (lat. 37°04'35" N, long. 121°59'35" W). Named on Laurel (1955) 7.5' quadrangle. The name is from Bethany Bible College (Clark, 1986, p. 28).

Bethel District: see **Templeton** [SAN LUIS OBISPO].

Betteravia [SANTA BARBARA]: *village,* 5 miles southeast of Guadalupe (lat. 34°55' N, long. 120°31' W). Named on Guadalupe (1959) 7.5' quadrangle. Postal authorities established Betteravia post office in 1900 and discontinued it in 1970 (Salley, p. 20). *Betterave* means "beet" in French; a sugar-beet processing plant opened at the site in 1897 (Gudde, 1949, p. 30).

Betteravia Junction [SANTA BARBARA]: *locality,* 4 miles southeast of the town of Guadalupe along Santa Maria Valley Railroad (lat. 34°55'40" N, long. 120°31'55" W); the place is 1 mile northwest of Betteravia. Named on Guadalupe (1959) 7.5' quadrangle.

Betteravia Stockyards [SANTA BARBARA]: *locality,* 4.25 miles southeast of the town of Guadalupe along Santa Maria Valley Railroad (lat. 34°55'45" N, long. 120°31' W); the place is nearly 1 mile north of Betteravia. Named on Guadalupe (1959) 7.5' quadrangle. California Division of Highways' (1934) map has the name "Springer" for a place situated along the railroad at or near present Betteravia Stockyards.

Betteravia Storage [SANTA BARBARA]: *locality,* 4 miles southeast of the town of Guadalupe along Santa Maria Valley Railroad (lat. 34°55'40" N, long. 120°31'35" W); the place is 1 mile northwest of Betteravia. Named on Guadalupe (1959) 7.5' quadrangle.

Beulah Park [SANTA CRUZ]: *settlement,* 9.5 miles southeast of the town of Boulder Creek (lat. 37°00'40" N, long. 122°01'15" W). Named on Felton (1955) 7.5' quadrangle. The place grew around Beulah Park Conference Grounds, a church summer camp (Clark, 1986, p. 28).

Bickmore Canyon [SAN BENITO]: *canyon,* 5 miles long, opens into Bear Valley nearly 6 miles west-northwest of San Benito (lat. 36° 03'05" N, long. 121°10' W; near E line sec. 11, T 16 S, R 7 E). Named on Bickmore Canyon (1968) 7.5' quadrangle.

Bicknell [SANTA BARBARA]:

(1) *locality,* 4.25 miles southeast of Orcutt (lat. 34°49' N, long. 120° 23'30" W). Named on Orcutt (1959) 7.5' quadrangle. Postal authorities established Bicknell post office in 1909 and discontinued it in 1940 (Frickstad, p. 170). The name commemorates John Dustin Bicknell, a pioneer in the development of oil in Santa Maria Valley (Hanna, p. 31).

(2) *locality,* 10.5 miles south of Santa Maria along Pacific Coast Railroad in Harris Canyon (lat. 34°47'45" N, long. 120°26'25" W). Named on Lompoc (1905) 30' quadrangle.

Bielawski Mountain [SANTA CRUZ]: *peak,* 7 miles north-northeast of the town of Boulder Creek on Santa Cruz-Santa Clara county line (lat. 37°13'25" N, long. 122°05'30" W; sec. 21, T 8 S, R 2 W). Altitude 3231 feet. Named on Castle Rock Ridge (1955) 7.5' quadrangle.

Whitney (p. 70) called the feature Mount Bielawski to honor C. Bielawski, chief draughtsman of the Surveyor-General's Office. United States Board on Geographic Names (1960c, p. 16) approved the name "Mount Bielawski" for the peak, and rejected the names "Bielawski Mountain," "Bielwaski Mountain," and "Mount McPherson."

Big Baldy [SAN LUIS OBISPO]: *peak*, 14 miles north-northeast of the town of Nipomo (lat. 35°13'40" N, long. 120°23'50" W; sec. 17, T 31 S, R 15 E). Altitude 2686 feet. Named on Tar Spring Ridge (1967) 7.5' quadrangle. Angel (1883, p. 354-355) called the feature Mount Hasbrouck for a landowner in the vicinity.

Big Basin [SANTA CRUZ]: *valley*, 6.5 miles west-northwest of the town of Boulder Creek (lat. 37°10'05" N, long. 122°13'15" W; sec. 7, 8, T 9 S, R 3 W). Named on Big Basin (1955) 7.5' quadrangle. On Ben Lomond (1946) 15' quadrangle, the name "Big Basin" applies to a group of buildings that represent the headquarters of Big Basin Redwoods State Park. Big Basin (1955) 7.5' quadrangle shows Big Basin P.O. at park headquarters in Big Basin. Postal authorities established Redwood Park post office in 1907 and changed the name to Big Basin in 1928 (Frickstad, p. 177).

Big Bend Canyon [SANTA BARBARA]: *canyon*, drained by a stream that flows 3.5 miles to Sisquoc River 5 miles west-southwest of Montgomery Potrero (lat. 34°48'40" N, long. 19°50'05" W). Named on Bald Mountain (1964) and Hurricane Deck (1964) 7.5' quadrangles.

Big Cone Spruce Camp [SANTA BARBARA]: *locality*, 2 miles west-northwest of San Rafael Mountain along Manzana Creek (lat. 34°43'35" N, long. 119°50'45" W; near E line sec. 5, T 7 N, R 28 W). Named on San Rafael Mountain (1959) 7.5' quadrangle.

Big Creek [MONTEREY]:
(1) *stream*, flows 5 miles to Finch Creek 1.5 miles east of Jamesburg (lat. 36°22'45" N, long. 121°33'50" W; sec. 8, T 18 S, R 4 E). Named on Rana Creek (1956) 7.5' quadrangle.
(2) *stream*, flows 6.25 miles to the sea 1.5 miles north-northwest of Gamboa Point (lat. 36°04'10" N, long. 121°36' W; sec. 26, T 21 S, R 3 E). Named on Lopez Point (1956) 7.5' quadrangle. North Fork enters from the north nearly 3 miles upstream from the mouth of the creek; it is 4 miles long and is named on Lopez Point (1956) and Tassajara Hot Springs (1956) 7.5' quadrangles. G.A. Waring (p. 57) described a spring called Dolans Hot Spring located along North Fork Big Creek—actually along Big Creek—about 1.5 miles from the coast. Crawford (1894, p. 340) mentioned Dolan's Hot Sulphur Spring, and Berkstresser (p. A-9) listed Dolans Hot Springs (sec. 24, T 21 S, R 3 E). The feature was called Hollins Hot Springs in the early 1930's, for Marion Hollins, who owned the land at the site; it also

had the local name "Big Creek Hot Springs" (Clark, 1991, p. 142).

Big Creek [SANTA CRUZ]: *stream*, flows 7 miles to Scott Creek 4.5 miles north-northwest of Davenport (lat. 37°04' N, long. 122°13'45" W). Named on Big Basin (1955) and Davenport (1955) 7.5' quadrangles.

Big Creek Hot Springs: see **Dolans Hot Spring**, under **Big Creek** [MONTEREY] (2).

Big Dome: see **Big Dome Cove** [MONTEREY].

Big Dome Cove [MONTEREY]: *embayment*, 1000 feet east of Point Lobos on the south shore of Carmel Bay (lat. 36°31'20" N, long. 121°56'50" W). Named on Monterey (1947) 7.5' quadrangle. California Department of Parks and Recreation's map has the name "Big Dome" for the promontory just east of the cove, and has the name "Terminal Rock" for a small island northeast of Big Dome.

Big Falls Canyon [SAN LUIS OBISPO]: *canyon*, drained by a stream that flows 3 miles to Lopez Canyon 4.5 miles southeast of Lopez Mountain (lat. 35°15'35" N, long. 120°30'45" W; near N line sec. 6, T 31 S, R 14 E). Named on Lopez Mountain (1965) 7.5' quadrangle. Called Little Falls Canyon on San Luis Obispo (1897) 15' quadrangle.

Big Gulch: see **Waddell Creek** [SANTA CRUZ].

Big Meadow [MONTEREY]: *area*, 0.5 mile east-southeast of Point Lobos (lat. 36°31'05" N, long. 121°56'35" W). Named on Monterey (1947) 7.5' quadrangle.

Big Mountain [SAN BENITO]: *peak*, 6.5 miles north-northeast of San Benito (lat. 36°35'30" N, long. 121°01'30" W; sec. 30, T 15 S, R 9 E). Altitude 3992 feet. Named on San Benito (1968) 7.5' quadrangle.

Big Oak Flat [SAN BENITO]: *area*, 4 miles northeast of San Benito (lat. 36°32'45" N, long. 121°01'45" W; near SE cor. sec. 7, T 16 S, R 9 E). Named on San Benito (1968) 7.5' quadrangle.

Big Panoche Creek: see **Panoche Creek** [SAN BENITO].

Big Pine Campground [SANTA BARBARA]: *locality*, 0.25 mile west of Big Pine Mountain (lat. 34°41'50" N, long. 119°39'35" W). Named on Big Pine Mountain (1964) 7.5' quadrangle.

Big Pine Canyon [SANTA BARBARA]: *canyon*, drained by a stream that flows 2.5 miles to Sisquoc River 2.5 miles north-northwest of Big Pine Mountain (lat. 34°43'50" N, long. 119°40'25" W); the canyon heads at Big Pine Mountain. Named on Big Pine Mountain (1964) 7.5' quadrangle.

Big Pine Mountain [SANTA BARBARA]: *ridge*, west-trending, 1 mile long, 8 miles northeast of Little Pine Mountain (lat. 34°41'50" N, long. 119°39'10" W). Named on Big Pine Mountain (1964) 7.5' quadrangle.

Big Pines [MONTEREY]: *locality*, 3 miles northwest of Uncle Sam Mountain (lat. 36°22'15" N, long. 121°45' W). Named on Big

Sur (1956) and Ventana Cones (1956) 7.5' quadrangles.

Big Pocket Lake [SAN LUIS OBISPO]: *intermittent lake,* 1750 feet long, 3.25 miles south-southwest of downtown Arroyo Grande near the coast (lat. 35°04'55" N, long. 120°36'50" W). Named on Oceano (1965) 7.5' quadrangle

Big Rocks [SAN LUIS OBISPO]: *peak,* 4 miles south-southwest of Branch Mountain (lat. 35°07'50" N, long. 120°07' W). Named on Branch Mountain (1967) 7.5' quadrangle.

Big Sand Creek [MONTEREY]: *stream,* flows 4 miles to Paloma Creek 14 miles west of Greenfield (lat. 36°19'30" N, long. 121°29'20" W; sec. 36, T 18 S, R 4 E). Named on Sycamore Flat (1956) 7.5' quadrangle. Called Little Sand Creek on Soledad (1915) 15' quadrangle.

Big Sandy Creek [MONTEREY]: *stream,* flows 28 miles to Salinas River 6.5 miles southeast of Bradley (lat. 35°47'30" N, long. 120° 43'30" W; near SW cor. sec. 31, T 24 S, R 12 E). Named on San Miguel (1948), Smith Mountain (1969), Stockdale Mountain (1948), and Valleton (1948) 7.5' quadrangles. The lower part of the stream flows through Indian Valley (3) for 15 miles. A map of Monterey County used about 1900 has the name "Nelson's Cr." for present Big Sandy Creek above Indian Valley (3). The stream in Indian Valley (3) is called Indian Valley Cr. on California Mining Bureau's (1917b) map, which fails to name the valley itself; the same map shows a locality called Oak Flat situated along Stone Canyon Railroad by present Big Sandy Creek between places called Pope and Hill that also are along the railroad.

Big Spring [SAN LUIS OBISPO]:
(1) *spring,* 2 miles southeast of Pozo (lat. 35°16'50" N, long. 120° 21'10" W; sec. 27, T 30 S, R 15 E). Named on Pozo Summit (1967) 7.5' quadrangle.
(2) *spring,* 8.5 miles south of Simmler (lat. 35°14' N, long. 119°59'50" W; near N line sec. 13, T 31 S, R 18 E). Named on Chimineas Ranch (1959) 7.5' quadrangle.

Big Spring [SANTA BARBARA]:
(1) *spring,* 5 miles northwest of McPherson Peak (lat. 34°55'40" N, long. 119°52'45" W); the feature is in Big Spring Canyon 850 feet south of Little Spring. Named on Bates Canyon (1964) 7.5' quadrangle.
(2) *spring,* 8.5 miles south of the city of Lompoc along Escondido Creek (lat. 34°31'30" N, long. 120°27'20" W). Named on Lompoc Hills (1959) 7.5' quadrangle.

Big Spring Canyon [SANTA BARBARA]: *canyon,* drained by a stream that flows 1 mile to Schoolhouse Canyon (1) 5 miles northwest of McPherson Peak (lat. 34°55'50" N, long. 119°52'30" W); Big Spring (1) is in the canyon. Named on Bates Canyon (1964) 7.5' quadrangle.

Big Sur [MONTEREY]: *settlement,* 5.5 miles east-southeast of Point Sur (lat. 36°16'10" N,

long. 121°48'25" W; sec. 24, T 19 S, R 1 E); the place is by Big Sur River. Named on Big Sur (1956) 7.5' quadrangle. Postal authorities established Arbolado post office in 1910 and changed the name to Big Sur in 1915; they established Rainbow Lodge post office at a vacation resort along Bixby Creek 11 miles northwest of Big Sur in 1922 and discontinued it in 1925 (Salley, p. 9, 180).

Big Sur Hot Springs: see **Slates Hot Springs** [MONTEREY].

Big Sur River [MONTEREY]: *stream,* formed by the confluence of North Fork and South Fork, flows 15 miles to the sea 3 miles southeast of Point Sur (lat. 36°16'50" N, long. 121°51'30" W); the mouth of the stream is on El Sur grant. Named on Big Sur (1956), Partington Ridge (1956), Pfeiffer Point (1956), and Ventana Cones (1956) 7.5' quadrangles. Called Sur River on Point Sur (1925) 15' quadrangle. United States Board on Geographic Names (1943, p. 14) decided in favor of the name "Sur River," and later (1960b, p. 6) reversed the decision in favor of the name "Big Sur River." According to Lussier (p. 4), the early Spaniards at Carmel mission called the wilderness south of the mission *El Pais Grande del Sur*, which means "The Big Country to the South" in Spanish, and called the largest river there *El Rio Grande del Sur*, which means "The Big River to the South"—eventually the name of the stream became the partial translation "Big Sur River." North Fork is nearly 6.5 miles long and South Fork is 6.25 miles long; both forks are named on Partington Ridge (1956) and Tassajara Hot Springs (1956) 7.5' quadrangles.

Big Tree Gulch: see **Bridge Creek** [SANTA CRUZ].

Big Trees [SANTA CRUZ]: *locality,* 1.5 miles southeast of Felton along Southern Pacific Railroad (lat. 37°02'10" N, long. 122°03'30" W). Named on Santa Cruz (1902) 30' quadrangle.

Big Twin Lake [SAN LUIS OBISPO]: *lake,* 2100 feet long, nearly 4 miles south-southwest of downtown Arroyo Grande near the coast (lat. 35°04'10" N, long. 120°36'30" W); the lake is west of Small Twin Lake. Named on Oceano (1965) 7.5' quadrangle.

Bill Faris Campground [SANTA BARBARA]: *locality,* less than 1 mile south-southwest of Madulce Peak in Alamar Canyon (lat. 34° 40'50" N, long. 119°35'50" W). Named on Madulce Peak (1964) 7.5' quadrangle. The name commemorates a Boy Scout leader of Santa Barbara (Gagnon, p. 69).

Billiard Flats [SANTA BARBARA]: *area,* 8 miles north of Rincon Point along Santa Ynez River (lat. 34°29'20" N, long. 119°29' W; sec. 27, T 5 N, R 25 W). Named on White Ledge Peak (1952) 7.5' quadrangle. On Ventura (1904) 15' quadrangle, the name applies to a place located 1 mile farther west at a site that water of Jamesan Lake now covers.

Birabent Canyon [SANTA BARBARA]: *canyon,* 5 miles long, along Alamo Pinto Creek above a point 6 miles north-northeast of Los Olivos (lat. 34°44'30" N, long. 120°03'40" W). Named on Zaca Lake (1964) 7.5' quadrangle. Called Birbent Canyon on Tepusquet Peak (1943) 15' quadrangle, and on Figueroa Mountain (1959) and Los Olivos (1959) 7.5' quadrangles, but United States Board on Geographic Names (1965d, p. 7) rejected the names "Birbent Canyon" and "Ballard Canyon" for the feature.

Birbent Canyon: see **Birabent Canyon** [SANTA BARBARA].

Bird Creek [SAN BENITO]: *stream,* flows 7.5 miles to San Benito River 5 miles south-south-east of Hollister (lat. 36°47' N, long. 121° 22'15" W). Named on Hollister (1955), Mount Harlan (1968), and Tres Pinos (1955) 7.5' quadrangles. Left Fork enters nearly 5 miles upstream from the mouth of the main stream; it is 2.5 miles long and is named on Hollister (1955) and Mount Harlan (1968) 7.5' quadrangles. Jesse Whitton, who was in the neighborhood with Fremont in 1846, named the stream (Pierce, p. 69).

Bird Island [MONTEREY]: *island,* 500 feet long, 1 mile south-southeast of Point Lobos and 300 feet offshore (lat. 36°30'25" N, long. 121°56'35" W). Named on Monterey (1947) 7.5' quadrangle. The feature has a colony of sea birds in the spring and summer (Clark, 1991, p. 41).

Bird Rock [MONTEREY]:
(1) *rock,* 300 feet long, 1 mile northeast of Cypress Point and 400 feet offshore (lat. 36°35'30" N, long. 121°58' W). Named on Monterey (1947) 7.5' quadrangle.
(2) *rock,* 100 feet long, 1.25 miles southeast of Cape San Martin, and 1050 feet offshore (lat. 35°52'35" N, long. 121°27'10" W). Named on Cape San Martin (1949) 7.5' quadrangle. United States Coast and Geodetic Survey (p. 117) described Whaleboat Rock, which is near Bird Rock (2).

Bird Rock [SAN LUIS OBISPO]: *rock,* 75 feet long, 0.5 mile offshore at Shell Beach (lat. 35°08'55" N, long. 120°41' W). Named on Pismo Beach (1965) 7.5' quadrangle.

Bird Spring [MONTEREY]: *spring,* 12 miles east of San Ardo (lat. 36°02'05" N, long. 120°41'15" W; sec. 9, T 22 S, R 12 E). Named on Slack Canyon (1969) 7.5' quadrangle.

Bishop Peak [SAN LUIS OBISPO]: *peak,* nearly 2.5 miles northwest of downtown San Luis Obispo (lat. 35°18'10" N, long. 120°41'50" W; sec. 21, T 30 S, R 12 E). Altitude 1546 feet. Named on San Luis Obispo (1965) 7.5' quadrangle. Goodyear (1888, p. 99) called the feature Obispo Peak—*obispo* means "bishop" in Spanish.

Bitter Creek [SANTA BARBARA]: *stream,* formed by the confluence of the streams in Central Canyon and East Canyon, flows 4 miles to Cuyama River 2.25 miles northwest of New Cuyama (lat. 34°58'15" N, long. 119°43' W). Named on New Cuyama (1964) 7.5' quadrangle.

Bitter Creek Spring [SANTA BARBARA]: *spring,* 3.5 miles east of McPherson Peak (lat. 34°53'20" N, long. 119°45'05" W). Named on Peak Mountain (1964) 7.5' quadrangle.

Bitterwater [SAN BENITO]: *settlement,* 10 miles south-southeast of San Benito (lat. 36°22'50" N, long. 121°00' W; sec. 9, T 18 S, R 9 E); the place is in Bitterwater Valley. Named on Topo Valley (1969) 7.5' quadrangle. Postal authorities established Bitterwater post office in 1878, discontinued it in 1888, reestablished it in the same year with the name "Bitter Water," changed the name back to Bitterwater in 1894, changed it again to Bitter Water in 1905, and discontinued the post office in 1907 (Salley, p. 22).

Bitterwater Canyon [SAN BENITO]: *canyon,* drained by a stream that flows 8 miles to Panoche Valley nearly 5 miles west of Panoche at Llanada (lat. 36°36'35" N, long. 120°54'55" W; sec. 19, T 15 S, R 10 E). Named on Llanada (1969) and San Benito (1968) 7.5' quadrangles.

Bitterwater Canyon [SAN LUIS OBISPO]: *canyon,* 5 miles long, 20 miles east-southeast of Shandon on San Luis Obispo-Kern county line (lat. 35°30'30" N, long. 120°03'30" W); the canyon is along upper reaches of Bitterwater Creek. Named on La Panza NE (1966) and Packwood Creek (1961) 7.5' quadrangles.

Bitterwater Canyon: see **Little Bitterwater Canyon** [MONTEREY].

Bitterwater Creek [SAN BENITO]: *stream,* flows 6.5 miles to Lewis Creek 6.5 miles southeast of Bitterwater (lat. 36°18'35" N, long. 120°55'20" W; sec. 6, T 19 S, R 10 E); the stream drains the southeast part of Bitterwater Valley. Named on Lonoak (1969) 7.5' quadrangle.

Bitterwater Creek [SAN LUIS OBISPO]: *stream,* formed by the confluence of Walnut Creek and Yeguas Creek, flows 6.25 miles in and out of Kern County to enter Kern County finally 19 miles east-southeast of Shandon (lat. 35°31'35" N, long. 120°04'20" W; at S line sec. 31, T 27 S, R 18 E). Named on La Panza NE (1966) and Packwood Creek (1961) 7.5' quadrangles.

Bitterwater Lake [SAN BENITO]: *intermittent lake,* 3300 feet long, 1 mile southeast of Bitterwater (lat. 36°22'20" N, long. 120°59'10" W; sec. 10, 15, T 18 S, R 9 E); the feature is in the northwest part of Bitterwater Valley. Named on Lonoak (1969) and Rock Spring Peak (1969) 7.5' quadrangles.

Bitterwater Spring: see **Little Bitterwater Spring** [MONTEREY].

Bitterwater Valley [SAN BENITO]: *valley,* around Bitterwater (lat. 36°21'45" N, long. 120°58'15" W); the southeast part of the valley is drained by Bitterwater Creek. Named on Lonoak (1969), Rock Spring Peak (1969), and Topo Valley (1969) 7.5' quadrangles.

Bixby Creek [MONTEREY]: *stream,* formed by the confluence of Turner Creek and Mill Creek (1), flows 4.5 miles to the sea 4.5 miles north of Point Sur (lat. 36°22'20" N, long. 121°54'10" W; sec. 18, T 18 S, R 1 E). Named on Big Sur (1956) and Point Sur (1956) 7.5' quadrangles. Present Mill Creek (1) is called Bixby Creek on Point Sur (1925) 15' quadrangle. The name "Bixby" commemorates Charles Bixby, who filed for a homestead along the creek; the stream originally was called Mill Creek (Fink, p. 208).

Bixby Landing [MONTEREY]: *locality,* 0.25 mile west of the mouth of Bixby Creek along the coast (lat. 36°22'20" N, long. 121°54'20" W; sec. 18, T 18 S, R 1 E). Site named on Point Sur (1956) 7.5' quadrangle.

Bixby Mountain [MONTEREY]: *peak,* 4.5 miles northeast of Point Sur (lat. 36°21'15" N, long. 121°50'20" W; sec. 23, T 18 S, R 1 E). Altitude 2920 feet. Named on Big Sur (1956) 7.5' quadrangle.

Bixby's Mill: see **Point Sur** [MONTEREY].

Blackburn Gulch [SANTA CRUZ]: *canyon,* 2.25 miles long, on upper reaches of Branciforte Creek above a point 5 miles north-northwest of Soquel (lat. 37°03'25" N, long. 121°58'45" W; sec. 16, T 10 S, R 1 W). Named on Laurel (1955) 7.5' quadrangle. The name commemorates William F. Blackburn, who arrived in the neighborhood in the 1840's (Clark, 1986, p. 32).

Black Butte [MONTEREY]: *peak,* 7.5 miles south-southeast of Jamesburg (lat. 36°16' N, long. 121°32'25" W; sec. 21, T 19 S, R 4 E). Altitude 4941 feet. Named on Chews Ridge (1956) 7.5' quadrangle.

Black Butte [SAN LUIS OBISPO]:*peak,* 1 mile northwest of Lopez Mountain (lat. 35°18'45" N, long. 120°35'30" W; sec. 16, T 30 S, R 13 E). Altitude 2749 feet. Named on Lopez Mountain (1965) 7.5' quadrangle.

Black Canyon [SAN BENITO]: *canyon,* drained by a stream that flows 6 miles to San Lorenzo Creek 7.5 miles south-southwest of Bitterwater (lat. 36°16'30" N, long. 121°02'05" W; sec. 18, T 19 S, R 9 E). Named on Lonoak (1969) and Pinalito Canyon (1969) 7.5' quadrangles.

Black Canyon [SANTA BARBARA]:
(1) *canyon,* drained by a stream that flows 3.5 miles to Santa Cruz Creek 6 miles south-southeast of San Rafael Mountain (lat. 34°37'55" N, long. 119°45'55" W; at N line sec. 6, T 6 N, R 27 W). Named on San Rafael Mountain (1959) 7.5' quadrangle.
(2) *canyon,* drained by a stream that flows 2.5 miles to the sea 1.5 miles north of Point Conception (lat. 34°28'25" N, long. 120°28'30" W). Named on Point Conception (1953) 7.5' quadrangle. On Point Conception (1942) 15' quadrangle, the stream in the canyon has the name "Las Animas Creek."

Black Cone [MONTEREY]: *peak,* 6.5 miles east-northeast of Partington Point (lat. 36°12'50" N, long. 121°35'30" W; near S line sec. 1, T 20 S, R 3 E). Altitude 4535 feet. Named on Tassajara Hot Springs (1956) 7.5' quadrangle.

Black Hill [SAN LUIS OBISPO]: *hill,* 2.25 miles east-southeast of Morro Rock (lat. 35°21'30" N, long. 120°49'50" W; sec. 31, T 29 S, R 11 E). Altitude 661 feet. Named on Morro Bay South (1965) 7.5' quadrangle.

Black Lake [SAN LUIS OBISPO]: *lake,* 1300 feet long, 4.5 miles south-southwest of downtown Arroyo Grande near the coast (lat. 35°03'25" N, long. 120°36'10" W). Named on Oceano (1965) 7.5' quadrangle.

Black Lake Canyon [SAN LUIS OBISPO]: *canyon,* 3.5 miles long, opens into lowlands near the coast 4.5 miles south of the town of Arroyo Grande (lat. 35°03'25" N, long. 120°35'40" W); a stream flows for 0.25 mile from the mouth of the canyon to Black Lake. Named on Oceano (1965) 7.5' quadrangle.

Black Mountain [SAN BENITO]: *ridge,* northwest-trending, 1.5 miles long, 7.5 miles east of Bitterwater (lat. 36°23'15" N, long. 120°51'30" W). Named on Hernandez Reservoir (1969) 7.5' quadrangle.

Black Mountain [SAN LUIS OBISPO]:
(1) *ridge,* northwest-trending, 1.5 miles long, 4 miles southeast of Cypress Mountain (lat. 35°33'20" N, long. 120°54'20" W). Named on Cypress Mountain (1948) 7.5' quadrangle.
(2) *peak,* 6.25 miles north-northeast of Pozo (lat. 35°23'35" N, long. 120°21'05" W; sec. 15, T 29 S, R 15 E). Altitude 3622 feet. Named on Camatta Ranch (1966) 7.5' quadrangle.

Black Mountain: see **Castle Mountain** [MONTEREY].

Black Oak Mountain [SAN LUIS OBISPO]: *peak,* nearly 5 miles east-northeast of the village of San Simeon (lat. 35°40'25" N, long. 121°06'55" W). Altitude 2266 feet. Named on Pebblestone Shut-in (1959) 7.5' quadrangle.

Black Point [SANTA BARBARA]: *promontory,* 3 miles east-southeast of Fraser Point on Santa Cruz Island (lat. 34°02'15" N, long. 119°53'05" W). Named on Santa Cruz Island A (1943) 7.5' quadrangle. Called Punta Negra on Rand's (1931) map.

Black Point [SANTA CRUZ]: *promontory,* 1 mile west-northwest of Soquel Point on the coast at the west end of Santa Cruz Harbor (lat. 36°57'30" N, long. 121°59'30" W). Named on Soquel (1954) 7.5' quadrangle. The feature also had the names "Prieta Point" and "Santa Maria Point" (Clark, 1986, p. 33).

Black Rock [SAN LUIS OBISPO]: *rocks,* 1 mile east of Cayucos Point, and 1100 feet offshore (lat. 35°26'50" N, long. 120°55'25" W). Named on Cayucos (1965) 7.5' quadrangle.

Black Rock Creek [MONTEREY]: *stream,* flows 5 miles to San Clemente Creek 4 miles south of the town of Carmel Valley (lat. 36°25'20" N, long. 121°44'15" W; sec. 27, T

17 S, R 2 E). Named on Carmel Valley (1956) and Mount Carmel (1956) 7.5' quadrangles. South Fork enters from the south 0.5 mile upstream from the mouth of the main creek; it is 3.5 miles long and is named on Carmel Valley (1956) and Mount Carmel (1956) 7.5' quadrangles.

Black Rock Ridge [MONTEREY]: *ridge*, east-northeast-trending, 1.5 miles long, 5 miles south of the town of Carmel Valley (lat. 36° 24'35" N, long. 121°45'15" W); the ridge is between Black Rock Creek and South Fork Black Rock Creek. Named on Carmel Valley (1956) and Mount Carmel (1956) 7.5' quadrangles.

Black Spring [SAN LUIS OBISPO]: *spring*, 9.5 miles southeast of Shandon in Hughes Canyon (lat. 35°33'50" N, long. 120°14'45" W; near W line sec. 22, T 27 S, R 16 E). Named on Holland Canyon (1961) 7.5' quadrangle.

Black Sulphur Spring [SAN LUIS OBISPO]: *spring*, 5 miles north-northwest of Caliente Mountain (lat. 35°06'10" N, long. 119°48'05" W; near S line sec. 26, T 32 S, R 20 E). Named on Caliente Mountain (1959) 7.5' quadrangle.

Black Willow Spring [SANTA BARBARA]: *spring*, at Montgomery Potrero (lat. 34°49'50" N, long. 119°45'50" W). Named on Hurricane Deck (1964) 7.5' quadrangle.

Blair Canyon [MONTEREY]: *canyon*, 3 miles long, opens into the canyon of Pine Creek (3) 8 miles north-northeast of San Ardo (lat. 36°08'30" N, long. 120°51'45" W; sec. 35, T 20 S, R 10 E). Named on Monarch Peak (1967) 7.5' quadrangle. The name commemorates Robert A. Blair, who patented land in the neighborhood in the 1880's (Clark, 1991, p. 44).

Blanco [MONTEREY]: *locality*, 4.5 miles west of Salinas on the northeast side of Salinas River (lat. 36°40'40" N, long. 121°44'15" W). Named on Salinas (1947) 7.5' quadrangle. On Salinas (1912) 15' quadrangle, the name applies to a place situated 0.5 mile farther east along Pajaro Valley Consolidated Railroad. According to Gudde (1949, p. 33), the name is from Tom White, a sailor who deserted ship at Monterey in 1840, and who was known as Tomas Blanco—*blanco* means "white" in Spanish; White's place along Salinas River was known as Blanco Crossing. Postal authorities established Blanco post office in 1873, discontinued it for a time in 1878, discontinued it again in 1917, reestablished it in 1930, and discontinued it finally in 1941 (Frickstad, p. 106).

Blanco: see **Ernest Blanco Spring** [SANTA BARBARA].

Blanco Crossing: see **Blanco** [MONTEREY].

Blas Creek: see **San Vicente Creek** [SANTA CRUZ].

Blinn Spring [SAN LUIS OBISPO]: *spring*, 6.5 miles north-northeast of Pozo (lat. 35°23'25" N, long. 120°20'10" W; near S line sec. 14, T 29 S, R 15 E). Named on Camatta Ranch

(1966) 7.5' quadrangle.

Blooms Creek [SANTA CRUZ]: *stream*, flows 3 miles to join Opal Creek and form East Waddell Creek at the south end of Big Basin (lat. 37°09'55" N, long. 122°13'25" W; near E line sec. 7, T 9 S, R 3 W). Named on Big Basin (1955) 7.5' quadrangle. The name is for Irvin T. Bloom, who acquired land along the stream in 1897 (Clark, 1986, p. 34).

Blooms Mill [SANTA CRUZ]: *locality*, 5.25 miles northwest of the town of Boulder Creek (lat 37°09'50" N, long. 122°11'55" W; sec. 9, T 9 S, R 3 W); the place is along Blooms Creek. Named on Santa Cruz (1902) 30' quadrangle. The locality also was called Old Park Mill and Park Mills (Clark, 1986, p. 34).

Blue Bank: see **Valley Anchorage** [SANTA BARBARA].

Blue Canyon [MONTEREY]: *canyon*, drained by a stream that flows 2.5 miles to Priest Valley nearly 4 miles north of Charley Mountain (lat. 36°11'15" N, long. 120°39'35" W; sec. 15, T 20 S, R 12 E). Named on Priest Valley (1969) 7.5' quadrangle.

Blue Canyon [SANTA BARBARA]: *canyon*, 5.25 miles long, opens into the canyon of Santa Ynez River 7.5 miles south-southwest of Hildreth Peak (lat. 34°30'15" N, long. 119°36'30" W). Named on Carpinteria (1952) and Hildreth Peak (1964) 7.5' quadrangles.

Blue Canyon Pass [SANTA BARBARA]: *pass*, 6.5 miles north-northwest of Carpinteria (lat. 34°29'10" N, long. 119°33'20" W; sec. 25, T 5 N, R 26 W); the pass is near the head of Blue Canyon. Named on Carpinteria (1952) 7.5' quadrangle.

Blue Canyon Pass: see **Romero Saddle** [SANTA BARBARA].

Blue Creek [MONTEREY]: *stream*, flows nearly 2 miles to Carmel River 1.5 miles north-northeast of Ventana Cone (lat. 36°18'10" N, long. 121°39'55" W; sec. 5, T 19 S, R 3 E). Named on Ventana Cones (1956) 7.5' quadrangle.

Bluefish Cove [MONTEREY]: *embayment*, 0.5 mile east of Point Lobos on the south side of Carmelo Bay (lat. 36°31'15" N, long. 121°56'35" W). Named on Monterey (1947) 7.5' quadrangle. According to Clark (1991, p. 46), the name is from blue rockfish found at the place. California Department of Parks and Recreation's map has the name "Viscaino Hill" on the east side of the cove, and has the name "Guillemot Island" for a small island at the northwest corner of the cove.

Blue Jay Splash [SAN BENITO]: *water feature*, 4 miles east-northeast of Bitterwater along San Benito River (lat. 36°24'10" N, long. 120°56'10" W; near SW cor. sec. 31, T 17 S, R 10 E). Named on Rock Spring Peak (1969) 7.5' quadrangle.

Blue Oak Spring [SAN LUIS OBISPO]: *spring*, 6.25 miles north-northeast of Pozo (lat. 35°22'50" N, long. 120°19'25" W; near W line sec. 24, T 29 S, R 15 E). Named on Camatta

Ranch (1966) 7.5' quadrangle.

Blue Point [SAN LUIS OBISPO]: *peak,* 12 miles northeast of Shandon (lat. 35°46'35" N, long. 120°12'55" W; sec. 11, T 25 S, R 16 E). Named on Tent Hills (1942) 7.5' quadrangle.

Bluerock Mountain [MONTEREY]: *peak,* 12 miles north of Gonzales (lat. 36°40'55" N, long. 121°29'10" W). Altitude 2556 feet. Named on Mount Harlan (1968) 7.5' quadrangle.

Blue Rock Ridge [MONTEREY]: *ridge,* northeast-trending, 2.5 miles long, 7 miles southsoutheast of the town of Carmel Valley (lat. 36°23'15" N, long. 121°41'05" W). Named on Carmel Valley (1956) 7.5' quadrangle.

Bluff: see **The Bluff** [SAN BENITO].

Bluff Campground [SANTA BARBARA]: *locality,* 2 miles south-southwest of Big Pine Mountain by Indian Creek (lat. 34°40'25" N, long. 119°39'55" W). Named on Big Pine Mountain (1964) 7.5' quadrangle. Called Bluff Camp on Big Pine Mountain (1944) 7.5' quadrangle.

Bluff Spring [SAN LUIS OBISPO]: *spring,* 4 miles west-northwest of Branch Mountain (lat. 35°12'35" N, long. 120°08'45" W). Named on Los Machos Hills (1967) 7.5' quadrangle.

Boar Peak [SAN LUIS OBISPO]: *peak,* nearly 1 mile north-northeast of Huasna Peak (lat. 35°02'50" N, long. 120°21'15" W; sec. 9, T 11 N, R 33 W). Altitude 1871 feet. Named on Huasna Peak (1967) 7.5' quadrangle.

Boat Landing: see **Ladys Harbor** [SANTA BARBARA].

Bolcoff Creek: see **Wilder Creek** [SANTA CRUZ].

Bolsa [SAN BENITO]: *valley,* the southeasternmost extension of Santa Clara Valley north and northeast of Hollister. Named on Chittenden (1955) and San Felipe (1955) 7.5' quadrangles.

Bolsa Chica Lake [SAN LUIS OBISPO]: *lake,* 1100 feet long, 4 miles south-southwest of downtown Arroyo Grande near the coast (lat. 35°04'05" N, long. 120°36'10" W). Named on Oceano (1965) 7.5' quadrangle. Called Bolsa Chico Lake on Arroyo Grande (1942) 15' quadrangle.

Bolsa de Chamisal [SAN LUIS OBISPO]: *land grant,* south of Arroyo Grande Creek along the coast. Named on Arroyo Grande NE (1965) and Oceano (1965) 7.5' quadrangles. Francisco Quijada received the land in 1837; Lewis T. Burton claimed 14,335 acres patented in 1867 (Cowan, p. 26; Cowan used the form "Bolsa de Chamizal" for the name). Angel (1883, p. 215) used the name "Bolsa de Chemisal," for the grant, but United States Board on Geographic Names (1933, p. 155) rejected the names "Bolsa de Chemisal" and "Chemisal" for it.

Bolsa de las Escorpinas [MONTEREY]: *land grant,* 6 miles north of Salinas. Named on Prunedale (1954), Salinas (1947), and San Juan Bautista (1955) 7.5' quadrangles. Salvador Espinosa received 2 leagues before 1828, and again in 1837; he claimed 6416 acres patented in 1876 (Cowan, p. 34; Cowan listed the grant under the designation "Escarpines, (or Escorpinas, or Escarpiones), Bolsa de, (or) San Miguel").

Bolsa del Moro Cojo: see **Bolsa Nueva y Moro Cojo** [MONTEREY].

Bolsa del Pajaro [SANTA CRUZ]: *land grant,* at and southwest of Watsonville in Pajaro Valley. Named on Moss Landing (1954), Watsonville East (1955), and Watsonville West (1954) 7.5' quadrangles. Sebastian Rodriguez received 2 leagues in 1837 and claimed 5497 acres patented in 1860 (Cowan, p. 56).

Bolsa del Potrero y Moro Cojo [MONTEREY]: *land grant,* 6 miles northwest of Salinas. Named on Marina (1947), Moss Landing (1954), Prunedale (1954), and Salinas (1947) 7.5' quadrangles; the maps have the name "La Sagrada Familia" as an alternate title for the grant. Jose Joaquin de la Torre received 2 leagues in 1822 and sold the land to John B.R. Cooper in 1829; Cooper claimed 6916 acres patented in 1859 (Cowan, p. 35-36).

Bolsa de San Cayetano [MONTEREY]: *land grant,* 15 miles northwest of Salinas near the coast. Named on Moss Landing (1954), Prunedale (1954), Watsonville East (1955), and Watsonville West (1954) 7.5' quadrangles. Ignacio Vincente Ferrer Vallejo received 2 leagues in 1824; Jose de Jesus Vallejo claimed 8866 acres patented in 1865 (Cowan, p. 74). According to Perez (p. 56), Jose Ignacio Vallejo was the grantee in 1834.

Bolsa de San Felipe [SAN BENITO]: *land grant,* north of Hollister. Named on San Felipe (1955) and Three Sisters (1954) 7.5' quadrangles. Francisco Perez Pacheco received 2 leagues in 1836 and 1840; he claimed 6795 acres patented in 1871 (Cowan, p. 75). *Bolsa* means "pocket" in Spanish, and this term was applied because a swamp, a willow grove, and a ravine almost enclosed the grant (Hoover, Rensch, and Rensch, p. 312).

Bolsa Knolls [MONTEREY]: *settlement,* 4 miles north-northeast of Salinas (lat. 36°44' N, long. 121°38'15" W). Named on Salinas (1947, photorevised 1968 and 1975) 7.5' quadrangle.

Bolsa Nueva y Moro Cojo [MONTEREY]: *land grant,* near Prunedale. Named on Moss Landing (1954), Prunedale (1954), and San Juan Bautista (1955) 7.5' quadrangles. According to Cowan (p. 49-50, 53), this feature is a combination of two grants: Francisco Soto received Bolsa Nueva (listed by Cowan under the name "Nueva Bolsa") in 1829 and 1836; Simeon Castro received 2 leagues, called Bolsa del Moro Cojo, in 1825, 1836-1837, and 1844, and added Bolsa Nueva to it; M. Antonia Pico de Castro and others claimed 30,901 acres patented in 1873. There is a tradition that the name "Moro Cojo" is from a lame black horse—*cojo* means "lame" in Spanish, and *moro* here has the meaning "black" rather that the more common meaning "Moor" (Hoover, Rensch, and Rensch, p. 224).

Bonanza Gulch [SAN BENITO]: *canyon,* 1.5 miles long, opens into the canyon of Bird Creek 5.5 miles south of Hollister (lat. 36°46'15" N, long. 121°24'40" W). Named on Hollister (1955) 7.5' quadrangle.

Bone Mountain [SANTA BARBARA]: *peak,* 4.5 miles southeast of Tepusquet Peak (lat. 34°51'45" N, long. 120°07'55" W). Altitude 2822 feet. Named on Foxen Canyon (1964) 7.5' quadrangle.

Bonnet Rock [SAN LUIS OBISPO]: *relief feature,* 16 miles northeast of the town of Nipomo (lat. 35°13'10" N, long. 120°18'15" W). Named on Caldwell Mesa (1967) 7.5' quadrangle.

Bonnie Doon [SANTA CRUZ]: *settlement,* 3.25 miles northeast of Davenport (lat. 37°02'30" N, long. 122°09' W). Named on Davenport (1955) 7.5' quadrangle. United States Board on Geographic Names (1933, p. 157) first rejected the form "Bonny Doon" for the name, but later (1995, p. 5) approved it. Postal authorities established Bonny Doon post office in 1887 and discontinued it in 1930; they established Waddell post office in 1890 and discontinued it in 1891, when they moved the service to Bonny Doon (Frickstad, p. 176, 177).

Bonny Brae: see **Felton** [SANTA CRUZ].

Bonny Doon: see **Bonnie Doon** [SANTA CRUZ].

Boot Canyon [SANTA BARBARA]: *canyon,* drained by a stream that flows 2.5 miles to Horse Canyon (3) 5.5 miles east-northeast of Santa Ynez Peak (lat. 34°34'05" N, long. 119°53'25" W). Named on Lake Cachuma (1959) 7.5' quadrangle.

Bootleg Spring [MONTEREY]: *spring,* 5 miles east of Lonoak (lat. 36°16'30" N, long. 120°51'15" W; sec. 14, T 19 S, R 10 E). Named on Hepsedam Peak (1969) 7.5' quadrangle.

Boronda Creek [MONTEREY]: *stream,* flows 3.25 miles to Cachagua Creek 8.5 miles southeast of the town of Carmel Valley (lat. 36°23'30" N, long. 121°37'45" W; sec. 3, T 18 S, R 3 E). Named on Carmel Valley (1956), Chews Ridge (1956), and Ventana Cones (1956) 7.5' quadrangles. The name commemorates a family of early settlers in the neighborhood (Gudde, 1949, p. 37). Clark (1991, p. 48) noted use of the name "Percys Creek" for the stream.

Borregas Creek [SANTA CRUZ]: *stream,* flows nearly 1.5 miles to the sea 3 miles east-north-east of Soquel Point (lat. 36°58'40" N, long. 121°55'40" W). Named on Soquel (1954) 7.5' quadrangle. Clark (1986, p. 39) referred to Borregas Gulch, and noted that the feature had

the name "Sanjon de Borregas" or "Zanjon de Borregas" in Spanish days—*borregas* means "lamb" in Spanish

Borregas Gulch: see **Borregas Creek** [SANTA CRUZ].

Bosworth Canyon [SAN BENITO]: *canyon,* drained by a stream that flows nearly 2 miles to San Benito River 3 miles north-northwest of San Benito (lat. 36°32'50" N, long. 121°06'20" W). Named on San Benito (1968) 7.5' quadrangle.

Bottchers Gap: see **Bouchers Gap** [MONTEREY].

Bouchers Gap [MONTEREY]: *pass,* 6 miles northeast of Point Sur (lat. 36°21'15" N, long. 121°48'45" W; sec. 24, T 18 S, R 1 E). Named on Big Sur (1956) 7.5' quadrangle. United States Board on Geographic Names (1961b, p. 8) approved the name "Bottchers Gap" for the feature. Clark (1991, p. 49) noted that John Bottcher patented land in the vicinity in the 1880's.

Boulder Creek [SAN BENITO]: *stream,* flows 2 miles to Tres Pinos Creek 4.25 miles west-northwest of Panoche Pass (lat. 36°39'10" N, long. 121°04'55" W; sec. 3, T 15 S, R 8 E). Named on Panoche Pass (1968) 7.5' quadrangle.

Boulder Creek [SANTA CRUZ]:
(1) *stream,* flows 7.5 miles to San Lorenzo River in the town of Boulder Creek (lat. 37°07'35" N, long. 122°07'15" W). Named on Big Basin (1955) and Castle Rock Ridge (1955) 7.5' quadrangles.
(2) *town,* 12 miles north-northwest of Santa Cruz where Boulder Creek (1), Bear Creek, and San Lorenzo River meet (lat. 37°07'30" N, long. 122°07'15" W). Named on Castle Rock Ridge (1955), Davenport (1955), and Felton (1955) 7.5' quadrangles. The place where the three streams meet was known in the early days as the Turkey Foot (Hamman, p. 84). It was the base of operations for bull-team logging in the 1850's, and the camp there was called Boulder Creek long before 1875 (MacGregor, p. 131). A lumber mill began operations a couple of miles south of Boulder Creek (2) in 1868, and a town called Lorenzo was started near the mill in 1875 (Rowland, p. 175)—the site of the old community of Lorenzo is in the present town of Boulder Creek. Postal authorities established Boulder Creek post office in 1872, changed the name to Lorenzo in 1875, and changed it back to Boulder Creek 1877 (Frickstad, p. 176). A place called Filbert was situated along the railroad about 1 mile south of the town of Boulder Creek (MacGregor, p. 175).

Boulder Creek: see **Little Boulder Creek** [SANTA CRUZ].

Boulder Mountain: see **Mount Carmel** [MONTEREY].

Bourdieu Valley [MONTEREY]: *valley,* 1 mile west of Smith Mountain along the uppermost part of Pancho Rico Creek (lat. 36° 04'45" N, long. 120°36'30" W). Named on Smith Mountain (1969) 7.5' quadrangle. The name commemorates Ed Bourdieu, who raised cattle and sheep in the valley after 1900 (Clark, 1991, p. 50).

Bowen Point [SANTA BARBARA]: *promontory,* 5.5 miles east of Punta Arena on the south side of Santa Cruz Island (lat. 33°57'35" N, long. 119°43'15" W). Named on Santa Cruz Island B (1943) 7.5' quadrangle.

Bowman Spring [SAN LUIS OBISPO]: *spring,* 1.25 miles north-northwest of Castle Crags near the head of South Fork Willow Canyon (lat. 35°19'20" N, long. 120°12'25" W). Named on La Panza (1967) 7.5' quadrangle.

Box Spring: see **Hepsedam Spring** [SAN BENITO].

Boyer Creek [SANTA CRUZ]: *stream,* flows 3 miles to Big Creek nearly 6 miles north of Davenport (lat. 37°05'40" N, long. 122°12'20" W; near E line sec. 5, T 10 S, R 3 W). Named on Big Basin (1955) and Davenport (1955) 7.5' quadrangles. The name is for Armenia Boyea and Oliver Boyea (or Boyer), early landholders in the neighborhood (Clark, 1986, p. 41).

Bracken Brae Creek [SANTA CRUZ]: *stream,* flows 0.5 mile to Boulder Creek (1) 4.5 miles east-southeast of Big Basin (lat. 37°08'20" N, long. 122°08'40" W; sec. 24, T 9 S, R 3 W). Named on Big Basin (1955) 7.5' quadrangle. The name is from a subdivision laid out in 1904; the feature also is known as Sand Creek (Clark, 1986, p. 42).

Brackney [SANTA CRUZ]: *settlement,* 4.5 miles south-southeast of the town of Boulder Creek along San Lorenzo River (lat. 37°04'10" N, long. 122°04'50" W; near S line sec. 9, T 10 S, R 2 W). Named on Felton (1955) 7.5' quadrangle. The name commemorates Alonzo L. Brackney, an early landholder in the neighborhood (Clark, 1986, p. 42).

Bradley [MONTEREY]: *village,* 12 miles south-southeast of San Ardo along Salinas River (lat. 35°51'50" N, long. 120°48'05" W; at N line sec. 8, T 24 S, R 11 E). Named on Bradley (1949) 7.5' quadrangle. When Southern Pacific Railroad reached the site in 1886, the station there was named for Bradley V. Sargent, who owned the land (Gudde, 1949, p. 39). Postal authorities established Bradley post office in 1886 (Frickstad, p. 106). They established Nasimento post office 8 miles southwest of Bradley in 1887, changed the name to Veratina in 1888, and discontinued it in 1895 (Salley, p. 150, 230).

Bradley Canyon [SANTA BARBARA]: *canyon,* drained by a stream that flows 5 miles to Santa Maria Valley 5.5 miles east-southeast of Santa Maria (lat. 34°54'40" N, long. 120°21'10" W; sec. 28, T 10 N, R 33 W). Named on Sisquoc (1959) and Twitchell Dam (1959) 7.5' quadrangles

Bragur [SANTA BARBARA]: *locality,* 3 miles

south-southeast of the town of Guadalupe along Santa Maria Valley Railroad (lat 34°56'10" N, long. 120°32'50" W). Named on Guadalupe (1959) 7.5' quadrangle.

Branch Canyon [SANTA BARBARA]: *canyon,* 8 miles long, opens into Cuyama Valley 2.25 miles south of New Cuyama (lat. 34° 55' N, long. 119°41'30" W). Named on Hurricane Deck (1964), New Cuyama (1964), and Salisbury Potrero (1964) 7.5' quadrangles.

Branch Canyon Campground [SANTA BARBARA]: *locality,* nearly 4 miles south of New Cuyama in Newsome Canyon (lat. 34°53'35" N, long. 119°42' W; sec. 6, T 9 N, R 26 W); the place is near Branch Canyon. Named on New Cuyama (1964) 7.5' quadrangle.

Branch Canyon Spring: see **Upper Branch Canyon Spring** [SANTA BARBARA].

Branch Canyon Wash [SANTA BARBARA]: *stream,* flows 4.5 miles from the mouth of Branch Canyon to Cuyama River 2.25 miles northwest of New Cuyama (lat. 34°58'25" N, long. 119°42'40" W). Named on New Cuyama (1964) 7.5' quadrangle.

Branch Creek [SAN LUIS OBISPO]: *stream,* flows 8 miles to Alamo Creek (2) 6.25 miles west-southwest of Branch Mountain (lat. 35° 08'40" N, long. 120°10'50" W); the stream heads at Branch Mountain. Named on Branch Mountain (1967) and Los Machos Hills (1967) 7.5' quadrangles

Branch Mountain [SAN LUIS OBISPO]: *peak,* 33 miles east-southeast of San Luis Obispo (lat. 35°11'05" N, long. 120°05' W; sec. 31, T 31 S, R 18 E). Altitude 3770 feet. Named on Branch Mountain (1967) 7.5' quadrangle.

Branciforte: see **Santa Cruz** [SANTA CRUZ].

Branciforte Creek [SANTA CRUZ]: *stream,* flows 9 miles to San Lorenzo River 1.5 miles north of Point Santa Cruz in Santa Cruz (lat. 36°58'25" N, long. 122°01'20" W). Named on Felton (1955), Laurel (1955), and Santa Cruz (1954) 7.5' quadrangles. The stream also has been called Arroyo de Villa and Brown's Creek (Clark, 1986, p. 44). Present Carbonera Creek has been called West Branch Branciforte Creek, West Fork Branciforte Creek, and West Branciforte Creek (Clark, 1986, p. 64-65).

Branstetter Canyon [MONTEREY]: *canyon,* drained by a stream that flows 2.5 miles to Salinas River nearly 2 miles west of King City (lat. 36°12'40" N, long. 121°09'35" W). Named on Thompson Canyon (1949) 7.5' quadrangle. The Branstetter family owned land in the canyon (Clark, 1991, p. 51).

Breaker Point [SAN LUIS OBISPO]: *promontory,* nearly 6 miles north-northwest of Piedras Blancas Point along the coast (lat. 35° 44'35" N, long. 121°19'05" W). Named on Piedras Blancas (1959) 7.5' quadrangle.

Brennans Landing: see **Pajaro River** [SANTA CRUZ].

Bridge Canyon [SAN LUIS OBISPO]: *canyon,* drained by a stream that flows nearly 2 miles to Salinas River 1 mile south of San Miguel (lat. 35°44'05" N, long. 120°41'55" W; sec. 20, T 25 S, R 12 E). Named on Paso Robles (1948) 7.5' quadrangle.

Bridge Creek [SANTA CRUZ]: *stream,* flows 2.25 miles to Aptos Creek 4.25 miles northeast of Soquel (lat. 37°01'45" N, long. 121° 54' W). Named on Laurel (1955) 7.5' quadrangle. Hamman's (1980a) map has the name "Big Tree Gulch" for a canyon that branches west from the canyon of Bridge Creek 0.5 mile north-northwest of the mouth of Bridge Creek, and shows a place called Camp No. 5 located nearly 1 mile north-northwest of the confluence of Bridge Creek and Aptos Creek at the end of a railroad spur; Camp No. 5 also was called Hoffman's Camp for the lumber company superintendent there (Hamman, p. 78). Hamman's (1980a) map shows a place called Camp No. 4 located along upper reaches of Bridge Creek between China Ridge and Hinckley Ridge—Camp No. 4 also was called Chalk Point (Hamman, p. 74).

Brinan Spring [MONTEREY]: *spring,* 7.25 miles east-northeast of San Ardo (lat. 36°04'35" N, long. 120°47'50" W; sec. 29, T 21 S, R 11 E). Named on Pancho Rico Valley (1967) 7.5' quadrangle. Called Brinnan Springs on San Ardo (1943) 15' quadrangle. The name commemorates Thomas Brinan, Sr., who settled in the neighborhood in 1886 (Clark, 1991, p. 52).

Brinnan Springs: see **Brinan Spring** [MONTEREY].

Brizziolari Creek [SAN LUIS OBISPO]: *stream,* flows 3.25 miles to Stenner Creek 1 mile north-northwest of downtown San Luis Obispo (lat. 35°17'45" N, long. 120°40' W; near SW cor. sec. 23, T 30 S, R 12 E). Named on San Luis Obispo (1965) 7.5' quadrangle.

Broadcast Peak [SANTA BARBARA]: *peak,* 1 mile east of Santa Ynez Peak (lat. 34°31'30" N, long. 119°57'30" W; sec. 7, T 5 N, R 29 W). Altitude 4028 feet. Named on Lake Cachuma (1959) 7.5' quadrangle.

Broadhurst Canyon [MONTEREY]: *canyon,* drained by a stream that flows 2 miles to lowlands 4.5 miles south of San Lucas (lat. 36°03'50" N, long. 121°01'05" W). Named on Espinosa Canyon (1949) 7.5' quadrangle.

Brock Springs [MONTEREY]: *springs,* 13 miles east of San Ardo near the head of Indian Valley (3) (lat. 36°02'50" N, long. 120°40'15" W; sec. 3, T 22 S, R 12 E). Named on Slack Canyon (1969) 7.5' quadrangle.

Brockway Point [SANTA BARBARA]: *promontory,* 6 miles west of Carrington Point on the north side of Santa Rosa Island (lat. 34°01'30" N, long. 120°08'50" W). Named on Santa Rosa Island North (1943) 7.5' quadrangle. Sunken rocks called Rodes Reef lie 1.2 miles east-northeast of Brockway Point, and 0.8 mile offshore (United States Coast and Geodetic Survey, p. 111).

Broken Bridge Creek [SAN LUIS OBISPO]:

stream, flows 2.5 miles to San Simeon Bay 0.5 mile east of the village of San Simeon (lat. 35°38'30" N, long. 121°10'55" W). Named on San Simeon (1958) 7.5' quadrangle.

Bromela [SAN LUIS OBISPO]: *locality,* 7 miles south of the town of Arroyo Grande along Southern Pacific Railroad (lat. 35°01'05" N, long. 120°35' W). Named on Oceano (1965) 7.5' quadrangle.

Brookdale [SANTA CRUZ]: *settlement,* 1.5 miles southeast of the town of Boulder Creek along San Lorenzo River (lat. 37°06'30" N, long. 122°06'20" W; sec. 32, T 9 S, R 2 W). Named on Felton (1955) 7.5' quadrangle. John H. Logan laid out the place in 1900 at what had been known as Reed's Spur; the settlement was called Clear Creek until 1902 (Rowland, p. 186)—it is at the mouth of Clear Creek. Postal authorities established Brookdale post office in 1902, discontinued it in 1944, and reestablished it in 1945 (Frickstad, p. 176). Hamman's (1980b) map shows a place called Harris located along the railroad about 0.5 mile northwest of Brookdale

Brookshire Campground [SANTA BARBARA]: *locality,* 4.5 miles west-southwest of Miranda Pine Mountain in Pine Canyon (1) (lat. 35°01'15" N, long. 120°06'50" W). Named on Miranda Pine Mountain (1967) 7.5' quadrangle. Branch Mountain (1942) 15' quadrangle shows Plowshare Spr. at the place.

Brown: see **Davey Brown Campground** [SANTA BARBARA]; **Davey Brown Creek** [SANTA BARBARA]; **Davy Brown Canyon**, under **Fir Canyon** [SANTA BARBARA].

Brown Canyon [MONTEREY]: *canyon,* drained by a stream that flows 8 miles to Pine Creek (3) 5 miles north-northeast of San Ardo (lat. 36°05'30" N, long. 120°53'05" W; near E line sec. 21, T 21 S, R 10 E). Named on Monarch Peak (1967) and Pancho Rico Valley (1967) 7.5' quadrangles. The name is for the Brown family, early residents in the neighborhood (Clark, 1991, p. 52-53).

Brown Canyon [SAN LUIS OBISPO]: *canyon,* drained by a stream that flows 4.5 miles to Cuyama River 5 miles south of Branch Mountain (lat. 35°06'45" N, long. 120°05'40" W; sec. 30, T 32 S, R 18 E). Named on Branch Mountain (1967) and Miranda Pine Mountain (1967) 7.5' quadrangles. East Fork branches east 1.5 miles upstream from the mouth of the main canyon; it is 3.25 miles long and is named on Branch Mountain (1967) 7.5' quadrangle.

Brown Creek: see **Browns Creek** [SANTA CRUZ].

Brown Mountain [SAN LUIS OBISPO]: *peak,* nearly 5 miles south-southwest of Branch Mountain (lat. 35°07'25" N, long. 120°07'15" W). Altitude 2514 feet. Named on Miranda Pine Mountain (1967) 7.5' quadrangle.

Browns Canyon [SAN LUIS OBISPO]: *canyon,* 1.5 miles long, 9.5 miles northwest of Midway Peak on San Luis Obispo-Kern county line (lat. 35°16' N, long. 119°43' W; at N line sec. 4, T 31 S, R 21 E). Named on Reward (1951) 7.5' quadrangle.

Browns Creek [SANTA CRUZ]: *stream,* flows 4.5 miles to Corralitos Creek 0.5 mile north-northeast of Corralitos (lat. 36°59'40" N, long. 121°48'05" W). Named on Loma Prieta (1955) 7.5' quadrangle. Called Brown Creek on Watsonville West (1954) 7.5' quadrangle. The name is for Isaiah Brown, who settled in the neighborhood by 1862 (Clark, 1986, p. 48).

Brown's Creek: see **Branciforte Creek** [SANTA CRUZ].

Browns Creek: see **West Browns Creek**, under **Carbonera Creek** [SANTA CRUZ].

Browns Valley [SAN BENITO]: *valley,* 4 miles northwest of Cherry Peak along a branch of Los Muertos Creek (lat. 36°43'55" N, long. 121°11'30" W). Named on Cherry Peak (1968) 7.5' quadrangle. Henderson Brown owned land in the valley (Elliott and Moore, p. 153).

Browns Valley [SANTA CRUZ]: *valley,* 1 mile north-northeast of Corralitos (lat. 37°00'15" N, long. 121°47'45" W); the valley is drained by Browns Creek. Named on Loma Prieta (1955) and Watsonville West (1954) 7.5' quadrangles.

Brubaker Canyon [SANTA BARBARA]: *canyon,* drained by a stream that flows 1.5 miles to Ventura County 16 miles southeast of the village of Cuyama (lat. 34°44'45" N, long. 119°26'35" W). Named on Rancho Nuevo Creek (1943) 7.5' quadrangle.

Bruce Fork: see **Carmel River** [MONTEREY].

Bruce Spring [SAN LUIS OBISPO]: *spring,* 2.5 miles south-southeast of Cholame (lat. 35°41'20" N, long. 120°16'50" W; near SW cor. sec. 5, T 26 S, R 16 E). Named on Cholame (1961) 7.5' quadrangle.

Brush Lagoon [SANTA CRUZ]: *lake,* 300 feet long, 3 miles southeast of Laurel (lat. 37°04'50" N, long. 121°55'55" W). Named on Los Gatos (1919) 15' quadrangle. Called Amaya Lagoon on a map of 1881 (Clark, 1986, p. 49).

Brush Peak [SANTA BARBARA]: *ridge,* east-northeast-trending, 0.5 mile long, 2 miles west of San Marcos Pass (lat. 34°30'30" N, long. 119°51'25" W; on N line sec. 19, T 5 N, R 28 E). Named on San Marcos Pass (1959) 7.5' quadrangle.

Bryan Canyon [MONTEREY]: *canyon,* drained by a stream that flows 4 miles to Pine Creek (3) nearly 7 miles north-northeast of San Ardo (lat. 36°06'50" N, long. 120°52'25" W; sec. 10, T 21 S, R 10 E). Named on Monarch Peak (1967) and Pancho Rico Valley (1967) 7.5' quadrangles.

Bryant Canyon [MONTEREY]: *canyon,* drained by a stream that flows nearly 5 miles to lowlands 2 miles northeast of Soledad (lat. 36°26'45" N, long. 121°17'55" W; sec. 15, T

17 S, R 6 E). Named on Soledad (1955) 7.5' quadrangle.

Bryson [MONTEREY]: *settlement,* 12 miles south-southeast of Jolon (lat. 35°48'30" N, long. 121°05'15" W; near S line sec. 27, T 24 S, R 8 E). Named on Bryson (1949) 7.5' quadrangle. Postal authorities established Bryson post office in 1887, moved it 1 mile southwest in 1889, moved it 1.5 miles south in 1898, moved it 1 mile northwest in 1899, moved it 1.5 mile east in 1905, moved it 1.25 miles west in 1906, and discontinued it in 1937 (Salley, p. 28). The name is for an early settler who had a store at the site; the place first was called Sapaque (Clark, 1991, p. 54). Postal authorities established Gem post office 3 miles east of Bryson (sec. 25, T 24 S, R 8 E) in 1894 and discontinued it in 1899—the name was for the postmaster's wife (Salley, p. 83).

Buchon: see **Mount Buchon**, under **Irish Hills** [SAN LUIS OBISPO]; **Point Buchon** [SAN LUIS OBISPO].

Buchon Range: see **Irish Hills** [SAN LUIS OBISPO].

Buck Cove Spring [SANTA BARBARA]: *spring,* 6 miles west of Miranda Pine Mountain (lat. 35°02'10" N, long. 120°08'20" W). Named on Chimney Canyon (1967) 7.5' quadrangle.

Buck Creek [MONTEREY]: *stream,* flows about 2 miles to the sea 10 miles southeast of Partington Point (lat. 36°08'05" N, long. 121°38'55" W; sec. 5, T 21 S, R 3 E). Named on Partington Ridge (1956) 7.5' quadrangle.

Buckeye Camp [SAN LUIS OBISPO]: *locality,* 16 miles north-northeast of the town of Nipomo (lat. 35°14'50" N, long. 120°20'40" W; sec. 11, T 31 S, R 15 E). Named on Caldwell Mesa (1967) 7.5' quadrangle. The name is from a lone buckeye tree at the place (Clark, 1991, p. 55).

Buckeye Canyon [MONTEREY]: *canyon,* drained by a stream that flows 3.25 miles to Carmel Valley (1) 7 miles east of the mouth of the Carmel River (lat. 36°31'20" N, long. 121°48'20" W). Named on Seaside (1947) 7.5' quadrangle.

Buckeye Hill [MONTEREY]: *peak,* 3 miles east-northeast of Jamesburg (lat. 36°23'20" N, long. 121°32'20" W; on W line sec. 3, T 18 S, R 4 E). Altitude 2541 feet. Named on Rana Creek (1956) 7.5' quadrangle.

Buckeye Ridge [MONTEREY]: *ridge,* west-trending, 3.5 miles long, 5.5 miles east of the town of Carmel Valley (lat. 36°28'30" N, long. 121°38' W). Named on Carmel Valley (1956) and Rana Creek (1956) 7.5' quadrangles.

Buckeye Spring [MONTEREY]:
(1) *spring,* 4.25 miles west-northwest of Charley Mountain (lat. 36° 09'45" N, long. 120°44'15" W). Named on Priest Valley (1969) 7.5' quadrangle.
(2) *spring,* 12 miles east-northeast of San Ardo (lat. 36°03'15" N, long. 120°41'20" W; sec.

32, T 21 S, R 12 E). Named on Slack Canyon (1969) 7.5' quadrangle.

(3) *spring,* 6 miles southeast of Cape San Martin (lat. 35°50'25" N, long. 121°22'35" W; near S line sec. 13, T 24 S, R 5 E). Named on Cape San Martin (1921) 15' quadrangle.

Buckhorn Canyon [SAN LUIS OBISPO]: *canyon,* 2.5 miles long, opens into the canyon of San Juan Creek 2.25 miles west-southwest of Freeborn Mountain (lat. 35°16'20" N, long. 120°05'30" W; sec. 31, T 30 S, R 18 E). Named on Branch Mountain (1967) and California Valley (1966) 7.5' quadrangles. Rogers Creek drains the canyon.

Buckhorn Canyon [SANTA BARBARA]: *canyon,* drained by a stream that flows 6 miles to Cuyama River 10 miles west of Miranda Pine Mountain (lat. 35°01'20" N, long. 120°12'35" W); the canyon is west of Buckhorn ridge. Named on Chimney Canyon (1967) and Tepusquet Canyon (1964) 7.5' quadrangles.

Buckhorn Creek [SANTA BARBARA]: *stream,* flows 5 miles to Indian Creek 4 miles east-southeast of Little Pine Mountain (lat. 34°34'40" N, long. 119°40'10" W). Named on Little Pine Mountain (1964) 7.5' quadrangle.

Buckhorn Ridge [SANTA BARBARA]: *ridge,* west-northwest-trending, 6 miles long, 6.5 miles north-northeast of Tepusquet Peak (lat. 35°00' N, long. 120°09'10" W). Named on Chimney Canyon (1967), Manzanita Mountain (1964), and Tepusquet Canyon (1964) 7.5' quadrangles.

Buck Opening Spring [SANTA BARBARA]: *spring,* 1.25 miles east of McPherson Peak (lat. 34°53'25" N, long. 119°47'20" W). Named on Peak Mountain (1964) 7.5' quadrangle.

Buck Peak [SAN BENITO]: *peak,* 4.25 miles south-southwest of Panoche (lat. 36°32'40" N, long. 120°52'20" W; near NW cor. sec. 15, T 16 S, R 10 E). Altitude 3535 feet. Named on Panoche (1969) 7.5' quadrangle.

Buck Ridge [SAN BENITO]: *ridge,* northwest-trending, 7.5 miles long, 5 miles north of Bitterwater (lat. 36°27'15" N, long. 121°00'45" W). Named on Rock Spring Peak (1969) and Topo Valley (1969) 7.5' quadrangles.

Buckskin Flat Camp [MONTEREY]: *locality,* 2 miles east-southeast of Uncle Sam Mountain along Carmel River (lat. 36°19'55" N, long. 121°40'20" W; sec. 29, T 18 S, R 3 E). Named on Ventana Cones (1956) 7.5' quadrangle.

Bucks Peak [SAN BENITO]: *ridge,* northwest-trending, 0.5 mile long, 11.5 miles east-north-east of Bitterwater (lat. 36°27'30" N, long. 120°49'15" W; near SW cor. sec. 7, T 17 S, R 11 E). Named on Hernandez Reservoir (1969) 7.5' quadrangle.

Bucks Peak Spring [SAN BENITO]: *spring,* 11 miles east-northeast of Bitterwater (lat. 36°27'15" N, long. 120°49'30" W; near NE

cor. sec. 13, T 17 S, R 10 E); the spring is on the southwest side of Bucks Peak. Named on Hernandez Reservoir (1969) 7.5' quadrangle.

Buck Spring [SAN BENITO]: *spring,* nearly 5 miles west-southwest of Panoche (lat. 36°34'20" N, long. 120°54'45" W; near NE cor. sec. 6, T 16 S, R 10 E). Named on Llanada (1969) 7.5' quadrangle.

Buck Spring [SAN LUIS OBISPO]: *spring,* nearly 3 miles south-southwest of Branch Mountain (lat. 35°08'50" N, long. 120°06'15" W). Named on Branch Mountain (1967) 7.5' quadrangle.

Budan Spring: see **Ontario Hot Springs** [SAN LUIS OBISPO].

Bud Canyon [SAN LUIS OBISPO]: *canyon,* drained by a stream that flows 7 miles to McMillan Canyon 2.25 miles northwest of Shandon (lat. 35°40'25" N, long. 120°24'25" W; near SW cor. sec. 7, T 26 S, R 15 E). Named on Cholame Valley (1961) and Shandon (1961) 7.5' quadrangles. Called Budd Canyon on Cholame (1917) 30' quadrangle, but United States Board on Geographic Names (1963b, p. 13) rejected the names "Budd Canyon" and "McMillan Canyon" for the feature.

Budd Canyon: see **Bud Canyon** [SAN LUIS OBISPO].

Buell: see **Buellton** [SANTA BARBARA].

Buell Reservoir [SANTA BARBARA]: *lake,* 650 feet long, 4.25 miles northwest of Carpinteria (lat. 34°26'40" N, long. 119°34'05" W). Named on Carpinteria (1952) 7.5' quadrangle.

Buellton [SANTA BARBARA]: *town,* 27 miles south-southeast of Santa Maria along Santa Ynez River (lat. 34°36'50" N, long. 120°11'35" W); the town is on San Carlos de Jonata grant. Named on Solvang (1959) 7.5' quadrangle. Postal authorities established Buell post office in 1897, discontinued it in 1900, and reestablished it in 1920 with the name "Buellton" (Salley, p. 29). The name is from Rufus Thompson Buell and his brother Alonzo Buell, who bought San Carlos de Jonata grant in 1867 (Rife, p. 90).

Buenaventura River: see **Salinas River** [MONTEREY-SAN LUIS OBISPO].

Buena Vista [MONTEREY]:

(1) *land grant,* 6 miles south-southeast of Salinas. Named on Chualar (1947), Salinas (1947), and Spreckels (1947) 7.5' quadrangles. Jose Maria Soberanes and Joaquin Castro held the land in 1795; Santiago and Jose Mariano Estrada received 2 leagues in 1822-1823, and Mariano Malarin claimed 7726 acres patented in 1869 (Cowan, p. 20). According to Perez (p. 56), Jose S. Estrada was the grantee in 1822, and the patentee in 1869.

(2) *locality,* 8 miles south-southeast of Salinas along Pajaro Valley Consolidated Railroad (lat. 36°34'35" N, long. 121°35'10" W); the place is on Buena Vista grant. Named on Sali-

nas (1912) 15' quadrangle. Postal authorities established Buena Vista post office for a brief time in 1959 (Salley, p. 29). California Mining Bureau's (1917b) map shows a place called Agenda along the railroad between Buena Vista (2) and Spreckels; postal authorities established Agenda post office in 1896 and discontinued it in 1907 (Frickstad, p. 106).

Buena Vista: see **San Vicente Creek** [SANTA CRUZ].

Bull Canyon [MONTEREY]:

(1) *canyon,* 5 miles long; the lower is part drained by a stream that enters Sweetwater Canyon 4.5 miles east-northeast of King City (lat. 36°14' N, long. 121°03' W; sec. 36, T 19 S, R 8 E). Named on Lonoak (1969), Nattrass Valley (1967), and San Lucas (1949) 7.5' quadrangles. A tributary to San Lorenzo Creek drains the upper part of the feature.

(2) *canyon,* drained by a stream that flows 2 miles to Nacimiento River 11 miles south-southeast of Jolon (lat. 35°48'45" N, long. 121°07'55" W; sec. 29, T 24 S, R 8 E). Named on Burnett Peak (1949) 7.5' quadrangle.

Bull Creek [SANTA CRUZ]: *stream,* flows 2 miles to San Lorenzo River 3.5 miles south-southeast of the town of Boulder Creek at Felton (lat. 37°03'10" N, long. 122°04'15"W). Named on Felton (1955) 7.5' quadrangle. The name commemorates Thomas Bull, who was in the neighborhood in the 1860's (Clark, 1986, p. 50).

Bull Ridge [SANTA BARBARA]: *ridge,* north-trending, 2.5 miles long, 2.25 miles north-northeast of Salisbury Potrero (lat. 34°51'15" N, long. 119°41'25" W). Named on Salisbury Potrero (1964) 7.5' quadrangle.

Burned Mountain [MONTEREY]: *peak,* 5.5 miles north of Jamesburg (lat. 36°27'05" N, long. 121°35'30" W). Altitude 2846 feet. Named on Rana Creek (1956) 7.5' quadrangle.

Burnett Camp [SAN LUIS OBISPO]: *locality,* 6.5 miles north of the village of San Simeon (lat. 35°44'25" N, long. 121°11'40" W); the place is along Burnett Creek. Named on San Simeon (1958) 7.5' quadrangle.

Burnett Creek [SAN LUIS OBISPO]: *stream,* flows 7.5 miles to join Marmolejo Creek and form Arroyo de la Cruz 4 miles north-north-east of the village of San Simeon (lat. 35°41'55" N, long. 121°10'15" W); the stream heads at Burnett Peak. Named on Burnett Peak (1949) and San Simeon (1958) 7.5' quadrangles. West Fork enters from the northwest 4 miles upstream from the mouth of the main creek; it is 3.25 miles long and is named on Burnett Peak (1949) and San Simeon (1958) 7.5' quadrangles.

Burnett Creek: see **Little Burnett Creek** [SAN LUIS OBISPO].

Burnett Peak [SAN LUIS OBISPO]: *peak,* 8 miles north of the village of San Simeon (lat. 35°45'25" N, long. 121°09'35" W; near E line sec. 13, T 25 S, R 7 E). Named on Burnett Peak (1949) 7.5' quadrangle.

Burns Creek [MONTEREY]: *stream,* flows nearly 1 mile to the sea 3.5 miles southeast of Partington Point (lat. 36°08'30" N, long. 121°39'15" W; at S line sec. 32, T 20 S, R 3 E). Named on Partington Ridge (1956) 7.5' quadrangle. The name commemorates John B. Burns, who settled in the neighborhood in the 1860's (Clark, 1991, p. 57).

Burns Creek [SANTA CRUZ]: *stream,* flows 2.5 miles to join Laurel Creek and form West Branch Soquel Creek at Laurel (lat. 37°07'10" N, long. 121°57'35" W). Named on Laurel (1955) and Los Gatos (1953) 7.5' quadrangles.

Burrell Creek: see **Laurel Creek** [SANTA CRUZ].

Burrito Creek [SAN LUIS OBISPO]: *stream,* flows 2 miles to Rinconada Creek 3.5 miles northeast of Lopez Mountain (lat. 35°20'15" N, long. 120°31'55" W). Named on Lopez Mountain (1965) 7.5' quadrangle.

Burro Canyon [SANTA BARBARA]: *canyon,* drained by a stream that flows 3 miles to Sisquoc River 3.25 miles west-northwest of Bald Mountain (1) (lat. 34°49'40" N, long. 119°59'25" W). Named on Bald Mountain (1964) 7.5' quadrangle.

Burro Mountain [MONTEREY]: *peak,* 11 miles east of Cape San Martin (lat. 35°52'15" N, long. 121°16'20" W; sec. 1, T 24 S, R 6 E). Altitude 2827 feet. Named on Burro Mountain (1949) 7.5' quadrangle.

Burros Creek: see **Little Burros Creek** [MONTEREY].

Burton Mesa [SANTA BARBARA]: *area,* 4.5 miles north-northeast of Surf (lat. 34°44'15" N, long. 120°34'30" W); the place is on Jesus Maria grant, for which Luis T. Burton was a claimant. Named on Casmalia (1959) and Surf (1959) 7.5' quadrangles.

Burton Mound: see **Mission Creek** [SANTA BARBARA].

Burton Mount Sulphur Springs: see **Mission Creek** [SANTA BARBARA].

Bush Gulch [SANTA CRUZ]: *canyon,* drained by a stream that flows 1.25 miles to the sea 5.25 miles east of Soquel Point (lat. 36°57'05" N, long. 121°52'50" W). Named on Soquel (1954) and Watsonville West (1954) 7.5' quadrangles. The name commemorates Conrad Bush, who bought land in the canyon in 1866 (Clark, 1986, p. 52).

Butterfly Canyon [SAN BENITO]: *canyon,* drained by a stream that flows nearly 2 miles to Johnson Canyon 8.5 miles northeast of Bitterwater (lat. 36°27'40" N, long. 120°52'55" W; sec. 9, T 17 S, R 10 E). Named on Rock Spring Peak (1969) 7.5' quadrangle.

Buttle Canyon [MONTEREY]: *canyon,* drained by a stream that flows nearly 2 miles to Hames Valley 3.5 miles west-southwest of Bradley (lat. 35°51'05" N, long. 120°51'55" W; sec. 11, T 24 S, R 10 E). Named on Bradley (1949) and Tierra Redonda Mountain (1949) 7.5' quadrangles. Members of the Buttle family owned land at the place (Clark, 1991, p. 58).

Buzzard Canyon [MONTEREY]: *canyon,* drained by a stream that flows 4.25 miles to Big Sandy Creek 13 miles northeast of Bradley (lat. 35°59'35" N, long. 120°36'20" W; sec. 30, T 22 S, R 13 E). Named on Smith Mountain (1969) 7.5' quadrangle.

Buzzard Lagoon [SANTA CRUZ]: *lake,* 175 feet long, 4.25 miles north-northwest of Corralitos (lat. 37°02'50" N, long. 121°50' W; sec. 23, T 10 S, R 1 E). Named on Loma Prieta (1955) 7.5' quadrangle.

Byles Canyon [SAN BENITO]: *canyon,* drained by a stream that flows 4 miles to Hernandez Valley 10.5 miles east of Bitterwater (lat. 36°22'10" N, long. 120°47'30" W; near S line sec. 8, T 18 S, R 11 E). Named on Hepsedam Peak (1969) and Hernandez Reservoir (1969) 7.5' quadrangles.

Bythenia Springs: see **Veronica Springs** [SANTA BARBARA].

– C –

Caballada Creek [SAN LUIS OBISPO]: *stream,* flows 1.25 miles to Little Burnett Creek 9 miles northeast of the village of San Simeon (lat. 35°44'40" N, long. 121°05'40" W; sec. 22, T 25 S, R 8 E). Named on Bryson (1949) and Pebblestone Shut-in (1959) 7.5' quadrangles.

Cabeza de Milligan: see **Mulligan Hill** [MONTEREY].

Cabezo Prieto [MONTEREY]: *ridge,* west-northwest-trending, 1 mile long, 7 miles east-southeast of Point Sur (lat. 36°17'10" N, long. 121°46'55" W; near N line sec. 18, T 19 S, R 2 E). Named on Big Sur (1956) 7.5' quadrangle.

Cable Corral Spring [SAN LUIS OBISPO]: *spring,* nearly 7 miles west-southwest of Branch Mountain along Alamo Creek (2) (lat. 35°08'20" N, long. 120°11'10" W). Named on Los Machos Hills (1967) 7.5' quadrangle.

Cabo de Galera: see **Point Conception** [SANTA BARBARA].

Cabo de Nieve: see **Cypress Point** [MONTEREY].

Cabrillo: see **Point Cabrillo**, under **Mussel Point** [MONTEREY].

Cachagua Creek [MONTEREY]: *stream,* formed by the confluence of Finch Creek and James Creek, flows 4.5 miles to Carmel River 7 miles southeast of the town of Carmel Valley (lat. 36°24'05" N, long. 121°39'30" W; near S line sec. 32, T 17 S, R 3 E). Named on Carmel Valley (1956) and Rana Creek (1956) 7.5' quadrangles. On Jamesburg (1921) 15' quadrangle, the name "Cachagua Creek" applies to present Finch Creek.

Cache Creek: see **Coche Creek** [SANTA BARBARA].

Cachuma: see **Cachuma Village** [SANTA BARBARA].

Cachuma Bay [SANTA BARBARA]: *embayment,* 5 miles north-northeast of Santa Ynez Peak (lat. 34°35'40" N, long. 119°56'30" W); the feature is along the north side of Lake Cachuma at the mouth of Cachuma Creek. Named on Lake Cachuma (1959) 7.5' quadrangle.

Cachuma Camp [SANTA BARBARA]: *locality,* 5 miles southeast of Figueroa Mountain (lat. 34°41'50" N, long. 119°54'45" W); the place is along Cachuma Creek. Named on Figueroa Mountain (1959) 7.5' quadrangle.

Cachuma Cañon: see **Cachuma Creek** [SANTA BARBARA].

Cachuma Creek [SANTA BARBARA]: *stream,* flows 9.5 miles to Lake Cachuma 6 miles north-northeast of Santa Ynez Peak (lat. 34°36'20" N, long. 119°56'10" W). Named on Figueroa Mountain (1959) and Lake Cachuma (1959) 7.5' quadrangles. Irelan (p. 537) referred to Cuchamma River, and Fairbanks (1894, p. 504) described Cachuma Cañon. The name apparently is of Indian origin (Gudde, 1949, p. 48).

Cachuma Lake: see **Lake Cachuma** [SANTA BARBARA].

Cachuma Mountain [SANTA BARBARA]: *peak,* 5 miles east-southeast of Figueroa Mountain (lat. 34°43'35" N, long. 119°54' W; sec. 35, T 8 N, R 29 W). Altitude 4696 feet. Named on Figueroa Mountain (1959) 7.5' quadrangle.

Cachuma Point [SANTA BARBARA]: *promontory,* 4.5 miles north-northeast of Santa Ynez Peak (lat. 34°35'15" N, long. 119°56'55" W); the feature is on the north side of Lake Cachuma at the mouth of Cachuma Bay. Named on Lake Cachuma (1959) 7.5' quadrangle.

Cachuma Reservoir: see **Lake Cachuma** [SANTA BARBARA].

Cachuma Village [SANTA BARBARA]: *locality,* 4 miles north of Santa Ynez Peak (lat. 34°35'10" N, long. 119°59'20" W); the place is just below the dam that forms Lake Cachuma. Named on Lake Cachuma (1959) 7.5' quadrangle. United States Board on Geographic Names (1962a, p. 6) rejected the name "Cachuma" for the place.

Cahoon Spring [MONTEREY]: *spring,* about 4 miles south-southeast of Jamesburg (lat. 36°19'40" N, long. 121°33'25" W; near SE cor. sec. 29, T 18 S, R 4 E). Named on Chews Ridge (1956) 7.5' quadrangle.

Calabazal Creek [SANTA BARBARA]: *stream,* flows 4.25 miles to Santa Ynez River 3 miles southeast of Santa Ynez (lat. 34°35'20" N, long. 120°02'20" W). Named on Santa Ynez (1959) 7.5' quadrangle. Called San Lucas Creek on Lompoc (1905) 30' quadrangle, but United States Board on Geographic Names (1961b, p. 9) rejected this name for the stream.

Calaboose Creek [MONTEREY]: *stream,* flows nearly 5 miles to Piney Creek 13 miles southwest of Soledad (lat. 36°17'45" N, long.

121°29'35" W; near E line sec. 11, T 19 S, R 4 E). Named on Chews Ridge (1956) and Sycamore Flat (1956) 7.5' quadrangles.

Caldwell Canyon [MONTEREY]: *canyon,* drained by a stream that flows 3.25 miles to Chualar Canyon 9 miles north-northeast of Gonzales (lat. 36°37'20" N, long. 121°22'05" W; sec. 13, T 15 S, R 5 E). Named on Mount Harlan (1968) and Paicines (1968) 7.5' quadrangles.

Caldwell Gulch [SANTA CRUZ]: *canyon,* drained by a stream that flows 0.5 mile to Hester Creek 3 miles south-southeast of Laurel (lat. 37°04'35" N, long. 121°56'20" W). Named on Laurel (1955) 7.5' quadrangle.

Caldwell Mesa [SAN LUIS OBISPO]: *area,* 16 miles northeast of the town of Nipomo (lat. 35°13'20" N, long. 120°18' W). Named on Caldwell Mesa (1967) 7.5' quadrangle.

Caldwell Mountain [SAN LUIS OBISPO]: *peak,* 12 miles northeast of the town of Nipomo (lat. 35°10'25" N, long. 120°20' W; sec. 2, T 32 S, R 15 E). Altitude 1812 feet. Named on Caldwell Mesa (1967) 7.5' quadrangle.

Calera Canyon [MONTEREY]: *canyon,* 6 miles long, on the upper reaches of El Toro Creek above the confluence with Watson Creek 9.5 miles south-southwest of Salinas (lat. 36°33' N, long. 121°43'55" W). Named on Spreckels (1947) 7.5' quadrangle.

Calf Canyon [SAN LUIS OBISPO]: *canyon,* drained by a stream that flows nearly 4 miles to Salinas River 3 miles northeast of Santa Margarita (lat. 35°25'15" N, long. 120°34'10" W; sec. 10, T 29 S, R 13 E). Named on Santa Margarita (1965) 7.5' quadrangle.

Caliente Canyon: see **Little Caliente Canyon** [SANTA BARBARA].

Caliente Mountain [SAN LUIS OBISPO]: *peak,* 25 miles south-southeast of Simmler (lat. 35°02'10" N, long. 119°45'35" W; sec. 16, T 11 N, R 27 W); the peak is in Caliente Range. Altitude 5106 feet. Named on Caliente Mountain (1959) 7.5' quadrangle. According to Gudde (1949, p. 50), the name "Caliente" comes from a hot spring located south of the peak in Cuyama Valley—*caliente* means "hot" in Spanish.

Caliente Range [SAN LUIS OBISPO]: *range,* between Carrizo Plain and Cuyama Valley. Named on Caliente Mountain (1959), Chimineas Ranch (1959), Cuyama (1964), Elkhorn Hills (1954), Painted Rock (1959), Taylor Canyon (1959), and Wells Ranch (1954) 7.5' quadrangles.

Caliente Spring: see **Little Caliente Spring** [SANTA BARBARA].

California Flats [MONTEREY]: *valley,* 6 miles southeast of Parkfield (lat. 35°50'45" N, long. 120°20'45" W). Named on Cholame Valley (1961) 7.5' quadrangle.

California Flats Canyon [MONTEREY]: *canyon,* drained by a stream that flows nearly 2 miles to California Flats 6 miles southeast of Parkfield (lat. 35°50'55" N, long. 120°20'55" W). Named on Cholame Valley (1961) 7.5' quadrangle.

California Valley [SAN LUIS OBISPO]: *settlement,* 3.5 miles northeast of Freeborn Mountain in Carrizo Plain (lat. 35°19'10" N, long. 120°00'20" W; near NE cor. sec. 14, T 30 S, R 18 E). Named on California Valley (1966) 7.5' quadrangle. Postal authorities established California Valley post office in 1963 and discontinued it in 1974 (Salley, p. 32). Development of the place began in 1960 (Lee and others, p. 30).

Callender [SAN LUIS OBISPO]: *locality,* nearly 5 miles south of the town of Arroyo Grande along Southern Pacific Railroad (lat. 35° 03'10" N, long. 120°35'45" W). Named on Oceano (1965) 7.5' quadrangle.

Call Mountains [SAN BENITO]: *ridge,* west-northwest- to north-northwest-trending, 5 miles long, 4 miles west of Panoche Pass (lat. 36°37'30" N, long. 121°05' W). Named on Panoche Pass (1968) and San Benito (1968) 7.5' quadrangles.

Calpaco: see **Port Watsonville** [SANTA CRUZ].

Camatta Canyon [SAN LUIS OBISPO]: *canyon,* drained by Camatta Creek, which flows 17 miles to lowlands 4.5 miles south-southeast of Shandon (lat. 35°35'50" N, long. 120°20'20" W; sec. 10, T 27 S, R 15 E). Named on Camatta Canyon (1961) and Camatta Ranch (1966) 7.5' quadrangles. Called Commatti Canyon on Cholame (1917) 30' quadrangle. Anderson and Martin (p. 49) referred to Cammatti Canyon. United States Board on Geographic Names (1962a, p. 7) rejected the names "Cammatta Canyon," "Cammatti Canyon," "Commatri Canyon," "Commatta Canyon," and "Commatti Canyon" for the feature. G.A. Waring (p. 77) listed Cameta Warm Spring, which from his description probably was in or near Camatta Canyon.

Camatta Creek [SAN LUIS OBISPO]: *stream* and *dry wash,* extends for 17 miles to lowlands 4.5 miles south-southeast of Shandon (lat. 35°35'50" N, long. 120°20'20" W; sec. 10, T 27 S, R 15 E); the feature drains Camatta Canyon. Named on Camatta Ranch (1966) 7.5' quadrangle. Called Cammatti Creek on Pozo (1922) 15' quadrangle. United States Board on Geographic Names (1962a, p. 7) rejected the names "Cammatta Creek," "Cammatti Creek," "Commatri Creek," "Commatta Creek," and "Commatti Creek" for the feature.

Cambria [SAN LUIS OBISPO]: *town,* 8.5 miles southeast of the village of San Simeon (lat. 35°33'50" N, long. 121°04'50" W). Named on Cambria (1959) 7.5' quadrangle. The place was settled in the 1860's and called Slabtown (Gudde, 1949, p. 52). Names proposed for the community included Rosaville, Santa Rosa, and San Simeon (Angel, 1883, p. 337). Postal authorities established San Simeon post office in 1864, discontinued it in 1865, reestablished it in 1867, and changed the name to Cambria in 1870 (Frickstad, p. 166). Although the townsfolk first agreed on the name "Santa Rosa" for their community—for the stream that runs by the town—postal authorities gave the name "San Simeon" to the post office there (Hamilton, p. 7). Finally the name was changed to Cambria, from the Latin name for Wales, because of the urgings of a single Welsh resident (Stewart, p. 73).

Cambria Pines [SAN LUIS OBISPO]: *district,* 7 miles southeast of San Simeon at the mouth of Santa Rosa Creek (lat. 35°34' N, long. 121°06'15" W). Named on San Simeon (1942) 15' quadrangle.

Cambria Rock [SAN LUIS OBISPO]: *rock,* 2.25 miles west of Cambria, and 2750 feet offshore (lat. 35°34'15" N, long. 121°07'20" W). Named on Cambria (1959) 7.5' quadrangle.

Camelback Hill [SANTA BARBARA]: *peak,* 4.5 miles southeast of Orcutt (lat. 34°48'55" N, long. 120°23'20" W). Named on Orcutt (1959) 7.5' quadrangle.

Camerus Valley Creek: see **Carneros Creek** [SANTA BARBARA].

Cameta Warm Spring: see **Camatta Canyon** [SAN LUIS OBISPO].

Cammatta Canyon: see **Camatta Canyon** [SAN LUIS OBISPO].

Cammatta Creek: see **Camatta Creek** [SAN LUIS OBISPO].

Cammatti Canyon: see **Camatta Canyon** [SAN LUIS OBISPO].

Cammatti Creek: see **Camatta Creek** [SAN LUIS OBISPO].

Campbell: see **Camp Campbell** [SANTA CRUZ].

Camp Ben Lomond [SANTA CRUZ]: *locality,* 4 miles southeast of Big Basin (lat. 37°07'50" N, long. 122°10'05" W); the place is on Ben Lomond Mountain. Named on Big Basin (1955) 7.5' quadrangle.

Camp Campbell [SANTA CRUZ]: *locality,* 4.5 miles east of Big Basin near San Lorenzo River (lat. 37°09'45" N, long. 122°08'10" W; sec. 12, T 9 S, R 3 W). Named on Big Basin (1955) 7.5' quadrangle. The place is a YMCA camp started in 1934 and named for George Campbell, a principal donor (Clark, 1986, p. 56).

Camp Capitola: see **Capitola** [SANTA CRUZ].

Camp Cawatre Campground [MONTEREY]: *locality,* 1.25 miles southwest of Arroyo Center (lat. 36°13'20" N, long. 121°29'15" W; sec. 1, T 20 S, R 4 E). Named on Junipero Serra (1961) 15' quadrangle. Junipero Serra (1930) 15' quadrangle has the name "Santa Lucia Ranger Sta." at the place. The name recalls Camp Cawatre, a Girl Scout facility that was abandoned in 1984; the word "Cawatre" was coined from the words "camp" (or "cabin"), "water," and "trees" (Clark, 1991, p. 66).

Camp Clayton Military Reservation: see **Fort Ord Military Reservation** [MONTEREY].

Camp Cooke Military Reservation: see **Vandenberg Air Force Base** [SANTA BARBARA].

Camp Creek [MONTEREY]: *stream,* flows 1.5 miles to Zigzag Creek 7 miles east-northeast of Partington Point (lat. 36°11'50" N, long. 121°34'35" W; sec. 18, T 20 S, R 4 E). Named on Tassajara Hot Springs (1956) 7.5' quadrangle.

Camp Drake [SANTA BARBARA]: *locality,* 2 miles northeast of Santa Ynez Peak (lat. 34°33'05" N, long. 119°57'20" W; at S line sec. 32, T 6 N, R 29 W). Named on Lake Cachuma (1959) 7.5' quadrangle.

Camp Evers [SANTA CRUZ]: *locality,* 7.5 miles southeast of the town of Boulder Creek (lat. 37°02'35" N, long. 122°01'25" W). Named on Felton (1955) 7.5' quadrangle. Postal authorities established Camp Evers post office in 1947 and discontinued it in 1951; the name "Evers" is for the proprietor of a store and lodging place (Salley, p. 34).

Camp Four: see **Camphora** [MONTEREY].

Camp Goodall: see **Palm Beach** [SANTA CRUZ].

Camp Hill [SAN LUIS OBISPO]: *peak,* at Pismo Beach 0.5 mile inland from the coast (lat. 35°38'35" N, long. 120°38'15" W). Named on Pismo Beach (1965) 7.5' quadrangle.

Camphora [MONTEREY]: *locality,* 3 miles northwest of Soledad along Southern Pacific Railroad (lat. 36°27'15" N, long. 121°22'15" W). Named on Palo Escrito Peak (1956) and Soledad (1955) 7.5' quadrangles. A railroad construction camp at the place in 1873 was called Camp Four; Mexican workers referred to the place as Camphora, and railroad officials adopted this name for their station there (Gudde, 1949, p. 53).

Camp Huffman [MONTEREY]: *locality,* 4.5 miles east of Seaside on Fort Ord Military Reservation (lat. 36°37'15" N, long. 121°46'15" W). Named on Seaside (1947) 7.5' quadrangle.

Camp Hunter Liggett Military Reservation: see **Hunter Liggett Military Reservation** [MONTEREY].

Camp Low: see **San Juan Bautista** [SAN BENITO].

Camp McCallum [MONTEREY]: *locality,* 7 miles east-southeast of Salinas (lat. 36°38'35" N, long. 121°32' W). Named on Natividad (1947) 7.5' quadrangle. Postal authorities established Camp McCallum post office in 1942 and discontinued it in 1961 (Salley, p. 35). The place began in 1942 as housing for a project sponsored by the federal government to produce rubber from guayule plants—the name was for Dr. William B. McCallum, a pioneer of guayule farming; farm workers lived at the site later (Clark, 1991, p. 67).

Camp McQuaide: see **San Andres** [SANTA CRUZ].

Camp Merriam: see **Camp San Luis Obispo** [SAN LUIS OBISPO].

Camp Nacimiento [MONTEREY]: *locality,* 9 miles north-northeast of Cape San Martin (lat. 35°59'50" N, long. 121°22'55" W; sec. 24, T 22 S, R 5 E); the place is along Nacimiento River. Named on Cape San Martin (1949) 7.5 quadrangle.

Camp Natoma [SAN LUIS OBISPO]: *locality,* 4 miles east-southeast of Lime Mountain (lat. 35°38'35" N, long. 120°56' W; sec. 30, T 26 S, R 10 E). Named on Lime Mountain (1948) 7.5' quadrangle.

Camp Number 5: see **Bridge Creek** [SANTA CRUZ].

Camp Number 4: see **Bridge Creek** [SANTA CRUZ].

Camp Number 1: see **Aptos Creek** [SANTA CRUZ].

Camp Number 3: see **Santa Rosalia Mountain** [SANTA CRUZ].

Camp Ord: see **Fort Ord Military Reservation** [MONTEREY].

Camp Ord Military Reservation: see **Fort Ord Military Reservation** [MONTEREY].

Camp Pacific [MONTEREY]: *locality,* on Fort Ord Military Reservation south of Main Garrison (lat. 36°38'55" N, long. 121°48'05" W). Named on Marina (1947) 7.5' quadrangle.

Camp Roberts: see **Camp Roberts Military Reservation** [MONTEREY-SAN LUIS OBISPO].

Camp Roberts Military Reservation [MONTEREY-SAN LUIS OBISPO]: *military installation,* on both sides of Salinas River on Monterey-San Luis Obispo county line. Named on Adelaida (1948), Bradley (1949), Paso Robles (1948), San Miguel (1948), and Valleton (1948) 7.5' quadrangles. On San Miguel (1947) 15' quadrangle, the barracks area near Salinas River has the name "Camp Roberts," and the barracks area east of the river has the name "East Garrison." The installation was established in 1940 and named for Corporal Harold W. Roberts, a World War I tank driver who received the Medal of Honor posthumously (Clark, 1991, p. 68).

Camp San Luis Obispo [SAN LUIS OBISPO]: *military installation,* 5.5 miles northwest of San Luis Obispo (lat. 35°19'30" N, long. 120°44'15" W). Named on San Luis Obispo (1965) 7.5' quadrangle. The area in which the camp sets is called Camp San Luis Obispo Military Reservation on Morro Bay South (1965) and San Luis Obispo (1965) 7.5' quadrangles, although it is called Camp San Luis Obispo on Atascadero (1965) 7.5' quadrangle. The place originally was called Camp Merriam, but it was renamed in 1940 (Lee and others, p. 33). Postal authorities established Camp San Luis Obispo post office in 1940, discontinued it in 1948, reestablished it in 1952, and discontinued it in 1957 (Salley, p. 35).

Camp San Luis Obispo Military Reservation:

see **Camp San Luis Obispo** [SAN LUIS OBISPO].

Camp Stephani [MONTEREY]: *locality,* 1 mile southeast of the town of Carmel Valley along Carmel River (lat. 36°28'15" N, long. 121° 43' W). Named on Carmel Valley (1956) 7.5' quadrangle. The name commemorates Joseph Steffani, who settled at the site about 1888 and later subdivided part of his ranch for summer homes; the place also was called Eagle Camp (Clark, 1991, p. 68-69).

Camp Talaki [SAN LUIS OBISPO]: *locality,* 12 miles north of the town of Nipomo in Lopez Canyon (lat. 35°12'45" N, long. 120°28'50" W; sec. 21, T 31 S, R 14 E). Named on Tar Spring Ridge (1967) 7.5' quadrangle.

Camp Wasibo [SANTA CRUZ]: *locality,* 5.5 miles east of the town of Boulder Creek along Zayante Creek (lat. 37°07'15" N, long. 122°00'55" W; sec. 30, T 9 S, R 1 W). Named on Felton (1955) 7.5' quadrangle.

Camuesa Canyon: see **Camuesa Creek** [SANTA BARBARA].

Camuesa Creek [SANTA BARBARA]: *stream,* flows 6 miles to Gibraltar Reservoir 6.25 miles southeast of Little Pine Mountain (lat. 34°32' N, long. 119°39'50" W; sec. 12, T 5 N, R 27 W). Named on Little Pine Mountain (1964) 7.5' quadrangle. On Santa Ynez (1905) 30' quadrangle, the canyon of the stream has the name "Camuesa Canyon."

Camuesa Peak [SANTA BARBARA]: *peak,* 4.5 miles southeast of Little Pine Mountain (lat. 34°32'50" N, long. 119°41'25" W; near NE cor. sec. 3, T 5 N, R 27 W); the peak is south of Camuesa Creek. Altitude 3180 feet. Named on Little Pine Mountain (1964) 7.5' quadrangle.

Cañada Agua Vina: see **Cañada Agua Viva** [SANTA BARBARA].

Cañada Agua Viva [SANTA BARBARA]: *canyon,* drained by a stream that flows 2.5 miles to the sea 2.5 miles southwest of Tranquillon Mountain (lat. 34°33'25" N, long. 120°35'35" W). Named on Tranquillon Mountain (1959) 7.5' quadrangle. Called Canada Agua Vina on Guadalupe (1905) 30' quadrangle, but United States Board on Geographic Names (1962a, p. 7) rejected the forms "Canada Agua Vina," "Cañada Agua Vina," "Cañada Agua Viña," "Cañada Agua Vino," and "Cañada Aqua Vina" for the name.

Cañada Alcatraz [SANTA BARBARA]: *canyon,* drained by a stream that flows 1.25 miles to the sea 0.5 mile east of Gaviota (lat. 34°28'15" N, long. 120°12'15" W). Named on Gaviota (1953) 7.5' quadrangle.

Cañada Angosta: see **San Luis Obispo Creek** [SAN LUIS OBISPO].

Cañada Aqua Vina: see **Cañada Agua Viva** [SANTA BARBARA].

Cañada Arena [SANTA BARBARA]: *canyon,* drained by a stream that flows 2 miles to Cañada de los Coches 10.5 miles south of

Tepusquet Peak (lat. 34°45'45" W, long. 120°13'35" W). Named on Foxen Canyon (1964) 7.5' quadrangle.

Cañada Arena: see **Cañada de los Coches** [SANTA BARBARA] (2).

Cañada Azul [SAN BENITO]: *canyon,* 2.5 miles long, along Cantua Creek 4 miles east-southeast of Idria near San Benito-Fresno county line (lat. 36°23'15" N, long. 120°36'20" W). Named on Ciervo Mountain (1969) 7.5' quadrangle.

Cañada Benito: see **San Benito River** [SAN BENITO].

Cañada Botella [SANTA BARBARA]: *canyon,* drained by a stream that flows 1.5 miles to Zaca Creek nearly 3 miles north of Buellton (lat. 34°39'15" N, long. 120°11' W). Named on Zaca Creek (1959) 7.5' quadrangle.

Cañada Cervada [SANTA BARBARA]: *canyon,* drained by a stream that flows 4.5 miles to the sea 4 miles southeast of Fraser Point on Santa Cruz Island (lat. 34°01'25" N, long. 119°52'35" W). Named on Santa Cruz Island A (1943) 7.5' quadrangle, which shows Christi ranch situated near the mouth of the canyon. Called Christy Cñ. on Bremner's (1932) map. Goodyear (1890, p. 156) stated that the name should have the form "Cañon de Cebada."

Cañada Coches Prietos: see **Coches Prietos Anchorage** [SANTA BARBARA].

Cañada Corral: see **Arlington Canyon** [SANTA BARBARA].

Cañada de Alegria [SANTA BARBARA]: *canyon,* drained by a stream that flows 3 miles to the sea 11.5 miles east of Point Conception (lat. 34°28'05" N, long. 120°16'15" W). Named on Sacate (1953) and Santa Rosa Hills (1959) 7.5' quadrangles. Called Alegria Canyon on Point Conception (1942) 15' quadrangle.

Cañada de Guillermo [SANTA BARBARA]: *canyon,* drained by a stream that flows 1.25 miles to the sea 3.5 miles east of Gaviota (lat. 34°28'25" N, long. 120°09'05" W). Named on Gaviota (1953) 7.5' quadrangle.

Cañada de Jolon: see **Jolon Valley** [MONTEREY].

Canada de la Brea: see **Cañada de las Panochas** [SANTA BARBARA].

Cañada de la Carpinteria [MONTEREY]: *land grant,* 12 miles north of Salinas. Named on Prunedale (1954) and San Juan Bautista (1955) 7.5' quadrangles. Joaquin Soto received 0.5 league in 1845 and his heirs claimed 2236 acres patented in 1873 (Cowan, p. 25). According to Perez (p. 58), the grant was made in 1835.

Cañada de la Cuarta [SANTA BARBARA]: *canyon,* drained by a stream that flows nearly 3 miles to the sea 10.5 miles east of Point Conception (lat. 34°28'10" N, long. 120°17'20" W). Named on Sacate (1953) and Santa Rosa Hills (1959) 7.5' quadrangles. Called Cuarta Canyon on Lompoc (1905) 30' quadrangle.

Cañada de la Destiladera [SANTA BARBARA]: *canyon,* drained by a stream that flows 1.5 miles to the sea 12 miles east of Gaviota (lat. 34°27'40" N, long. 120°00'25" W). Named on Tajiguas (1953) 7.5' quadrangle.

Cañada de la Gallina [SANTA BARBARA]: *canyon,* drained by a stream that flows 0.5 mile to the sea 4 miles east of Gaviota (lat. 34°28'25" N, long. 120°08'40" W). Named on Gaviota (1953) 7.5' quadrangle.

Cañada de la Gaviota [SANTA BARBARA]: *canyon,* drained by a stream that flows 6.5 miles to the sea 0.5 mile west of Gaviota (lat. 34°28'15" N, long. 120°13'30" W). Named on Gaviota (1953) and Solvang (1959) 7.5' quadrangles. Called Gaviota Canyon on Lompoc (1905) 30' quadrangle, but United States Board on Geographic Names (1978b, p. 4) rejected this name for the feature. Soldiers of the Portola expedition gave the name "Gaviota" to an Indian village at the mouth of the canyon in 1769, when they killed a seagull there—*gaviota* means "seagull" in Spanish (Wagner, H.R., p. 389). Parke (p. 16) referred to Gaviote creek.

Cañada del Agua [SANTA BARBARA]: *canyon,* drained by a stream that flows 2.25 miles to the sea 9 miles east of Point Conception (lat. 34°27'55" N, long. 120°18'50" W). Named on Sacate (1953) 7.5' quadrangle.

Cañada del Agua Amarga [SANTA BARBARA]: *canyon,* drained by a stream that flows 1.5 miles to Cañada de los Coches 10.5 miles south-southwest of Tepusquet Peak (lat. 34°45'55" N, long. 120° 13'50" W). Named on Foxen Canyon (1964) 7.5' quadrangle.

Cañada del Agua Caliente [SANTA BARBARA]: *canyon,* drained by a stream that flows 3.25 miles to the sea 13 miles east of Point Conception (lat. 34°28'05" N, long. 120°15'05" W). Named on Sacate (1953) and Santa Rosa Hills (1959) 7.5' quadrangles.

Cañada de la Huerta [SANTA BARBARA]: *canyon,* drained by a stream that flows 0.5 mile to the sea 4.5 miles east of Gaviota (lat. 34°28'25" N, long. 120°08'50" W). Named on Gaviota (1953) 7.5' quadrangle.

Cañada de la Laguna [SANTA BARBARA]: *canyon,* drained by a stream that flows 3.5 miles to lowlands nearly 2 miles west-north-west of Buellton (lat. 34°37'30" N, long. 120°13'20" W). Named on Zaca Creek (1959) 7.5' quadrangle.

Cañada del Alamo: see **Alamos Anchorage** [SANTA BARBARA].

Cañada de la Llegua [SANTA BARBARA]: *canyon,* drained by a stream that flows 2.25 miles to the sea nearly 6 miles east of Point Conception (lat. 34°27'25" N, long. 120°22'10" W). Named on Sacate (1953) 7.5' quadrangle.

Cañada de la Ordena [MONTEREY]: *canyon,* drained by a stream that flows 1.5 miles to Carmel Valley (1) 6 miles east of the mouth of Carmel River (lat. 36°32' N, long. 121°49'15" W). Named on Seaside (1947, photorevised 1968) 7.5' quadrangle.

Cañada de la Pila [SANTA BARBARA]: *canyon,* drained by a stream that flows 1.5 miles to the sea 5 miles east of Gaviota (lat. 34°28'20" N, long. 120°07'35" W). Named on Gaviota (1953) 7.5' quadrangle.

Cañada de la Posta [SANTA BARBARA]: *canyon,* drained by a stream that flows 2 miles to the sea 3.25 miles east of Gaviota (lat. 34°28'20" N, long. 120°09'35" W). Named on Gaviota (1953) 7.5' quadrangle.

Cañada de la Puente [SANTA BARBARA]: *canyon,* drained by a stream that flows 2 miles to San Antonio Creek (1) 7 miles northwest of Los Olivos (lat. 34°43'30" N, long. 120°12'55" W). Named on Zaca Creek (1959) 7.5' quadrangle. Called Cañada de la Puenta on Los Olivos (1943) 15' quadrangle.

Cañada de las Agujas [SANTA BARBARA]: *canyon,* drained by a stream that flows 2.5 miles to the sea 7.5 miles east of Point Conception (lat. 34°27'35" N, long. 120°20'20" W). Named on Sacate (1953) 7.5' quadrangle.

Cañada de la Salud: see **Waddell Creek** [SANTA CRUZ].

Cañada de las Calaveras [SANTA BARBARA]: *canyon,* drained by a stream that flows 2 miles to Los Alamos Valley at the town of Los Alamos (lat. 34°44'15" N, long. 120°16'40" W). Named on Los Alamos (1959) 7.5' quadrangle.

Cañada de las Cruces [SANTA BARBARA]: *canyon,* drained by a stream that flows 4 miles to Cañada de la Gaviota 7.5 miles south-south-west of Buellton at Las Cruces (lat. 34°30'35" N, long. 120° 13'35" W). Named on Solvang (1959) 7.5' quadrangle.

Cañada de la Segunda [MONTEREY]: *land grant,* east of Carmel By The Sea and north of Carmel River. Named on Monterey (1947) and Seaside (1947, photorevised 1968) 7.5' quadrangles. Lazaro Soto received 1 league in 1839; F.M. Haight claimed 4367 acres patented in 1859 (Cowan, p. 97).

Cañada de las Encinas [SANTA BARBARA]: *canyon,* drained by a stream that flows 2.5 miles to Santa Maria Valley nearly 4 miles southwest of Tepusquet Peak (lat. 34°51'55" N, long. 120°13'40" W). Named on Lompoc (1905) 30' quadrangle. The lower part of the canyon corresponds to present Kelly Canyon (2).

Cañada de las Flores [SANTA BARBARA]: *canyon,* drained by a stream that flows 3.5 miles to San Antonio Creek (1) 8 miles south-southwest of the village of Sisquoc (lat. 34°45'25" N, long. 120°21'20" W). Named on Sisquoc (1959) 7.5' quadrangle. Called Careaga Canyon on Lompoc (1905) 30' quadrangle, which has the name "Canada de las Flores" for present Careaga Canyon. United States Board on Geographic Names (1962a, p. 7) rejected the name "Careaga Canyon" for

the feature, and rejected the form "Canada de las Flores" for the name.

Canada de las Llagas: see **Cañada del Capitan** [SANTA BARBARA].

Cañada de las Panochas [SANTA BARBARA]: *canyon,* drained by a stream that flows 2.25 miles to Cañada del Agua 9 miles east of Point Conception (lat. 34°27'55" N, long. 120°18'50" W). Named on Sacate (1953) 7.5' quadrangle. Called Canada de la Brea on Lompoc (1905) 30' quadrangle.

Cañada de las Zorrillas [SANTA BARBARA]: *canyon,* drained by a stream that flows nearly 1 mile to the sea 2 miles east of Gaviota (lat. 34°28'15" N, long. 120°10'40" W). Named on Gaviota (1953) 7.5' quadrangle.

Cañada de la Vina [SANTA BARBARA]: *canyon,* drained by a stream that flows 3 miles to lowlands 6.5 miles east-southeast of the city of Lompoc (lat. 34°36'15" N, long. 120°20'55" W). Named on Santa Rosa Hills (1959) 7.5' quadrangle.

Cañada del Barro [SANTA BARBARA]: *canyon,* drained by a stream that flows nearly 1 mile to the sea at Gaviota (lat. 34°28'15" N, long. 120°13'05" W). Named on Gaviota (1953) 7.5' quadrangle.

Cañada del Capitan [SANTA BARBARA]: *canyon,* drained by a stream that flows 5.5 miles to the sea 11 miles east of Gaviota (lat. 34°27'30" N, long. 120°01'15" W). Named on Lake Cachuma (1959) and Tajiguas (1953) 7.5' quadrangles. Called Canada de las Llagas on Lompoc (1905) 30' quadrangle, which has the name "Canada del Capitan" for present Cañada del Corral (1).

Cañada del Cementerio [SANTA BARBARA]: (1) *canyon,* drained by a stream that flows nearly 2 miles to Cañada del Cojo 3.5 miles east-northeast of Point Conception (lat. 34°27'35" N, long. 120°24'45" W). Named on Point Conception (1953) 7.5' quadrangle. (2) *canyon,* drained by a stream that flows 1.25 miles to the sea 0.5 mile east of Gaviota (lat. 34°28'15" N, long. 120°12'20" W). Named on Gaviota (1953) 7.5' quadrangle. Members of Anza's expedition saw an Indian burial ground at the place in 1776—*cementerio* means "graveyard" in Spanish (Bolton, p. 238).

Cañada del Chiclan [SANTA BARBARA]: *canyon,* drained by a stream that flows 1.25 miles to Arroyo San Augustin 6.5 miles east of Point Conception (lat. 34°27'50" N, long. 120°21'30" W). Named on Sacate (1953) 7.5' quadrangle.

Cañada del Chorro: see **El Chorro** [SAN LUIS OBISPO].

Cañada del Cojo [SANTA BARBARA]: *canyon,* drained by a stream that flows 2.5 miles to the sea 3.25 miles east of Point Conception (lat. 34°27'10" N, long. 120°24'55" W); the mouth of the canyon is east of Cojo Bay. Named on Point Conception (1953) 7.5' quadrangle. Members of the Portola expedition camped at the place in 1769 and called the Indian village there Rancheria del Cojo because the village chief was lame—*cojo* means "lame" or "lame man" in Spanish; A.M. Harrison of United States Coast Survey gave the name "Valley of the Coxo" to the feature in 1850 (Gudde, 1949, p. 73).

Cañada del Comasa [SANTA BARBARA]: *canyon,* drained by a stream that flows 7.5 miles to San Antonio Creek (1) 7.5 miles northwest of Los Olivos (lat. 34°43'40" N, long. 120°13'10" W). Named on Foxen Canyon (1964), Zaca Creek (1959), and Zaca Lake (1964) 7.5' quadrangles.

Cañada del Corral [SANTA BARBARA]:
(1) *canyon,* drained by a stream that flows 5.5 miles to the sea 10 miles east of Gaviota (lat. 34°27'45" N, long. 120°02'40" W). Named on Santa Ynez (1959) and Tajiguas (1953) 7.5' quadrangles. Called Canada del Capitan on Lompoc (1905) 30' quadrangle, where present Cañada del Venadito is called Canada del Corral.
(2) *land grant,* at Capitan; Cañada del Corral (1) is on the grant. Named on Dos Pueblos Canyon (1951), Santa Ynez (1959), and Tajiguas (1953) 7.5' quadrangles. Jose D. Ortega received 2 leagues in 1841 and claimed 8876 acres patented in 1866 (Cowan, p. 29).

Canada del Corral: see **Cañada del Venadito** [SANTA BARBARA].

Cañada del Coyote [SANTA BARBARA]: *canyon,* drained by a stream that flows 1.5 miles to the sea 10 miles east of Point Conception (lat. 34°28'10" N, long. 120°17'50" W). Named on Sacate (1953) 7.5' quadrangle. Called Sacate Canyon on Lompoc (1905) 30' quadrangle.

Cañada del Gato [SANTA BARBARA]: *canyon,* drained by a stream that flows nearly 2 miles to Barranca Honda 5 miles east of Point Conception at the coast (lat. 34°27'25" N, long. 120°22'55" W). Named on Point Conception (1953) 7.5' quadrangle. On Lompoc (1905) 30' quadrangle, the name applies to present Barranca Honda.

Cañada del Gato: see **Cat Canyon** [SANTA BARBARA].

Cañada del Jolloru [SANTA BARBARA]: *canyon,* drained by a stream that flows 3 miles to the sea 3.5 miles south-southeast of Tranquillon Mountain (lat. 34°32'10" N, long. 120°32'05" W). Named on Tranquillon Mountain (1959) 7.5' quadrangle. Called Canada El Jolloru on Guadalupe (1905) 30' quadrangle.

Cañada del Leon [SANTA BARBARA]: *canyon,* drained by a stream that flows 1 mile to the sea 1 mile east of Gaviota (lat. 34°28'15" N, long. 120°11'45" W). Named on Gaviota (1953) 7.5' quadrangle.

Cañada del Medio: see **Central Valley** [SANTA BARBARA].

Cañada del Molino [SANTA BARBARA]: *canyon,* drained by a stream that flows 2.5 miles to the sea nearly 3 miles east of Gaviota (lat. 34°28'10" N, long. 120°10'05" W). Named on Gaviota (1953) and Solvang (1959) 7.5' quadrangles. Called Cañada de Molino on Gaviota (1943) 15' quadrangle.

Cañada del Morida [SANTA BARBARA]: *canyon,* drained by a stream that flows 2.5 miles to the sea 2.5 miles south of Tranquillon Mountain (lat. 34°32'35" N, long. 120°33'20" W). Named on Tranquillon Mountain (1959) 7.5' quadrangle. Called Canada El Morida on Guadalupe (1905) 30' quadrangle.

Cañada de los Alisos [SANTA BARBARA]: *canyon,* drained by a stream that flows 6.25 miles to Los Alamos Valley 8.5 miles northwest of Los Olivos (lat. 34°44'20" N, long. 120°13'55" W). Named on Foxen Canyon (1964) and Zaca Creek (1959) 7.5' quadrangles.

Cañada de los Alisos: see **Clark Valley** [SAN LUIS OBISPO].

Cañada de los Coches [SANTA BARBARA]:
(1) *canyon,* drained by a stream that flows 3.5 miles to Cuyama River 8 miles east of Santa Maria (lat. 34°56'55" N, long. 120°17'35" W); the canyon heads near Los Coches Mountain. Named on Twitchell Dam (1959) 7.5' quadrangle.
(2) *canyon,* drained by a stream that flows 3.5 miles to Los Alamos Valley 8.5 miles northwest of Los Olivos (lat. 34°44'20" N, long. 120°13'55" W). Named on Foxen Canyon (1964) and Zaca Creek (1959) 7.5' quadrangles. United States Board on Geographic Names (1962a, p. 8) rejected the names "Cañada Arena," "Canada Arena," and "Canada de los Coches" for the feature, and pointed out that *Cañada de los Coches* reportedly is a Mexican provincial term meaning "Valley of the Hogs."

Cañada del Osito: see **Santa Rosa Creek** [SAN LUIS OBISPO].

Cañada de los Ladrones [SANTA BARBARA]: *canyon,* drained by a stream that flows 2 miles to the sea nearly 2 miles south-southwest of Tranquillon Mountain (lat. 34°33'10" N, long. 120°34'20" W). Named on Tranquillon Mountain (1959) 7.5' quadrangle.

Cañada de los Laureles: see **Los Laurelles** [MONTEREY] (2).

Cañada de Los Osos: see **Los Osos Valley** [SAN LUIS OBISPO].

Cañada de los Osos y Pecho y Islay [SAN LUIS OBISPO]: *land grant,* covers the west part of Los Osos Valley and the west coast of Irish Hills. Named on Morro Bay South (1965), Port San Luis (1965), and San Luis Obispo (1965) 7.5' quadrangles. Victor Linares and others received 11 leagues in 1842, 1843, and 1845; John Wilson claimed 32,430 acres patented in 1869 (Cowan, p. 55). According to Perez (p. 59), the grantees were James Scott and John Wilson in 1845.

Cañada de los Palos Blancos [SANTA BAR-

BARA]: *canyon,* 4.5 miles long, opens into lowlands 3 miles west-northwest of Buellton (lat. 34°37'30" N, long. 120°14'35" W). Named on Los Alamos (1959) and Zaca Creek (1959) 7.5' quadrangles.

Cañada de los Pinos or College Rancho [SANTA BARBARA]: *land grant,* at and northeast of Santa Ynez. Named on Figueroa Mountain (1959), Lake Cachuma (1959), Los Olivos (1959), and Santa Ynez (1959) 7.5' quadrangles. The Catholic Church received 6 leagues in 1844 and claimed 35,499 acres patented in 1861 (Cowan, p. 92-93; Cowan listed the grant under the designation "Santa Inez (or) Cañada de los Pinos, (or) College").

Cañada de los Sauces [SANTA BARBARA]:
(1) *canyon,* drained by a stream that flows 2 miles to the sea 2.25 miles south of Tranquillon Mountain (lat. 34°33'05" N, long. 120° 34'05" W). Named on Tranquillon Mountain (1959) 7.5' quadrangle.
(2) *canyon,* drained by a stream that flows 4.5 miles to the sea 4.25 miles southeast of Fraser Point on Santa Cruz Island (lat. 34°00'45" N, long. 119°52'55" W). Named on Santa Cruz Island A (1943) 7.5' quadrangle. Called Cñ. los Sauces del Oeste on Bremner's (1932) map.

Cañada del Pecho: see **Pecho Creek** [SAN LUIS OBISPO].

Cañada del Pescado [SANTA BARBARA]: *canyon,* drained by a stream that flows 1.5 miles to Arroyo San Augustin nearly 7 miles east of Point Conception (lat. 34°27'40" N, long. 120°21'20" W). Named on Sacate (1953) 7.5' quadrangle.

Cañada del Portezuelo: see **Central Valley** [SANTA BARBARA].

Cañada del Poso: see **Cañada Posa** [SANTA BARBARA].

Canada del Puerto: see **Prisoners Harbor** [SANTA BARBARA].

Cañada del Refugio [SANTA BARBARA]: *canyon,* drained by a stream that flows 6 miles to the sea 8.5 miles east of Gaviota (lat. 34°27'45" N, long. 120°04'05" W). Named on Santa Ynez (1959) and Tajiguas (1953) 7.5' quadrangles.

Cañada del Rincon en El Rio San Lorenzo de Santa Cruz [SANTA CRUZ]: *land grant,* between Santa Cruz and Felton. Named on Felton (1955) and Santa Cruz (1954) 7.5' quadrangles. Pierre Sainsevain received 2 leagues in 1843 and claimed 5827 acres patented in 1858 (Cowan, p. 92). According to Perez (p. 60), the grant was made in 1846.

Cañada del Rodeo [SANTA BARBARA]: *canyon,* drained by a stream that flows nearly 2 miles to the sea 2 miles south-southwest of Tranquillon Mountain (lat. 34°33'25" N, long. 120°34'50" W). Named on Tranquillon Mountain (1959) 7.5' quadrangle.

Cañada del Sacate [SANTA BARBARA]: *canyon,* drained by a stream that flows 2.5 miles to the sea 10.5 miles east of Point Conception

(lat. 34°28'15" N, long. 120°17'35" W). Named on Sacate (1953) and Santa Rosa Hills (1959) 7.5' quadrangles.

Cañada del Venadito [SANTA BARBARA]: *canyon,* drained by a stream that flows 3.5 miles to the sea 9.5 miles east of Gaviota (lat. 34°27'40" N, long. 120°03'10" W). Named on Santa Ynez (1959) and Tajiguas (1953) 7.5' quadrangles. Called Canada del Corral on Lompoc (1905) 30' quadrangle.

Cañada de Na-joa-ui: see **Nojoqui Creek** [SANTA BARBARA].

Cañada de Salispuedes [SANTA BARBARA]: *land grant,* southeast of the city of Lompoc; Salispuedes Creek crosses the grant. Named on Lompoc (1959), Lompoc Hills (1959), and Santa Rosa Hills (1959) 7.5' quadrangles. Pedro Cordero received 1.5 leagues in 1844; John Keyes claimed 6656 acres patented in 1874 (Cowan, p. 71).

Cañada de San Benancio: see **San Benancio Gulch** [MONTEREY].

Cañada de Santa Anita [SANTA BARBARA]: *canyon,* drained by a stream that flows 5 miles to the sea 9.5 miles east of Point Conception (lat. 39°28' N, long. 120°18'20" W). Named on Sacate (1953) and Santa Rosa Hills (1959) 7.5' quadrangles.

Cañada de Santa Rosa [SANTA BARBARA]: *canyon,* drained by a stream that flows 2.25 miles to Los Alamos Valley 1.5 miles west of the town of Los Alamos (lat. 34°44'30" N, long. 120°18'20" W). Named on Los Alamos (1959) 7.5' quadrangle.

Cañada de Santa Rosalia: see **Surf** [SANTA BARBARA].

Cañada de Santa Ynez [SANTA BARBARA]: *canyon,* drained by a stream that flows 3.5 miles to Los Alamos Valley 1.5 miles southeast of Los Alamos (lat. 34°43'45" N, long. 120°15'30" W). Named on Los Alamos (1959) and Zaca Creek (1959) 7.5' quadrangles.

Cañada de Tequepis: see **Tequipis Canyon** [SANTA BARBARA].

Canada El Jolloru: see **Cañada del Jolloru** [SANTA BARBARA].

Canada El Morida: see **Cañada del Morida** [SANTA BARBARA].

Canada Gallion: see **Cañada Tecolote** [SANTA BARBARA].

Canada Garanon: see **Cañada Tecolote** [SANTA BARBARA].

Cañada Honda Creek [SANTA BARBARA]: *stream,* flows 9 miles to the sea 2.25 miles north-northeast of Point Arguello (lat. 34°36'30" N, long. 120°35'10" W); the stream drains La Honda Canyon. Named on Point Arguello (1959) and Tranquillon Mountain (1959) 7.5' quadrangles.

Cañada Laguna: see **Laguna Canyon** [SANTA BARBARA].

Cañada Laguna Seca [SANTA BARBARA]: *canyon,* drained by a stream that flows nearly 4 miles to Los Alamos Valley 2.5 miles west of the town of Los Alamos (lat. 34°44'50" N, long. 120°19'20" W). Named on Los Alamos (1959) 7.5' quadrangle.

Cañada La Jolla: see **Wreck Canyon** [SANTA BARBARA].

Cañada Las Sauces de los Colorados: see **Willows Anchorage** [SANTA BARBARA].

Cañada Lobos [SANTA BARBARA]: *canyon,* drained by a stream that flows 3.25 miles to the sea 3.25 miles west-southwest of Carrington Point on Santa Rosa Island (lat. 34°01'10" N, long. 120°05'45" W). Named on Santa Rosa Island North (1943) 7.5' quadrangle.

Cañada los Sauces del Oeste: see **Cañada de los Sauces** [SANTA BARBARA] (2).

Cañada Malvareal: see **Malva Real Anchorage** [SANTA BARBARA].

Canada Montosa: see **Canada Montuosa** [MONTEREY].

Canada Montuosa [MONTEREY]: *canyon,* drained by a stream that flows 3.5 miles to Powell Canyon nearly 6.5 miles north-north-east of Bradley (lat. 35°57' N, long. 120°44'50" W; near N line sec. 11, T 23 S, R 11 E). Named on Valleton (1948) 7.5' quadrangle. Called Canada Montosa on San Miguel (1919) 15' quadrangle.

Cañada Pomona: see **Valley Anchorage** [SANTA BARBARA].

Cañada Posa [SANTA BARBARA]: *canyon,* drained by a stream that flows 3 miles to the sea 6.5 miles southeast of Frazer Point on Santa Cruz Island (lat. 33°58'40" N, long. 119°51'50" W). Named on Santa Cruz Island A (1943) 7.5' quadrangle. Called Cñ. del Poso on Bremner's (1932) map.

Cañada San Onofre [SANTA BARBARA]: *canyon,* drained by a stream that flows 2.5 miles to the sea 1.5 miles east of Gaviota (lat. 34°28'10" N, long. 120°11'10" W). Named on Gaviota (1953) and Solvang (1959) 7.5' quadrangles.

Cañada Seca: see **Surf** [SANTA BARBARA].

Cañada Soledad [SANTA BARBARA]: *canyon,* drained by a stream that flows 6.5 miles to the sea 6.5 miles west of Carrington Point on Santa Rosa Island (lat. 34°01' N, long. 120°09'15" W). Named on Santa Rosa Island North (1943) 7.5' quadrangle.

Canada Tecolokita: see **Cañada Tecolote** [SANTA BARBARA].

Cañada Tecolote [SANTA BARBARA]: *canyon,* drained by a stream that flows 5 miles to the sea 3.25 miles east of Sandy Point on Santa Rosa Island (lat. 34°00'20" N, long. 120°11'35" W). Named on Santa Rosa Island North (1943) and Santa Rosa Island West (1943) 7.5' quadrangles. Orr (map on back cover) used the name "Canada Tecolokita" for a tributary that branches south near the mouth of Cañada Tecolote, used the name "Skull Gulch" for a canyon that opens to the sea 900 feet west-southwest of the mouth of Cañada Tecolote, used the name "Fox Gulch" for a canyon that opens to the sea 1500 feet west-

southwest of the mouth of Cañada Tecolote, and used the name "Canada Garanon" for a canyon that opens to the sea 3000 feet west of the mouth of Cañada Tecolote. Orr's Canada Garanon is called C. Gallion on Kew's (1927) map.

Cañada Tortuga [SANTA BARBARA]: *canyon,* drained by a stream that flows 2 miles to the sea nearly 2 miles north of Surf (lat. 34° 42'35" N, long. 120°36'05" W). Named on Surf (1959) 7.5' quadrangle.

Cañada Verde [SAN BENITO]: *canyon,* drained by a stream that flows 5.25 miles to Quien Sabe Creek 7 miles south of Potrero Peak (lat. 36°45'30" N, long. 121°09'20" W). Named on Quien Sabe Valley (1968) 7.5' quadrangle. On Quien Sabe (1922) 15' quadrangle, the name "Cañada Verde" applies also to part of the canyon of present Quien Sabe Creek.

Cañada Verde [SAN LUIS OBISPO]: *canyon,* drained by a stream that flows nearly 3 miles to Pismo Creek 1.25 miles south of Edna (lat. 35°11'05" N, long. 120°36'50" W). Named on Arroyo Grande NE (1965) 7.5' quadrangle.

Cañada Verde [SANTA BARBARA]: *canyon,* drained by a stream that flows 6.25 miles to the sea 5.25 miles west of Carrington Point on Santa Rosa Island (lat. 34°01'30" N, long. 120°08' W). Named on Santa Rosa Island North (1943) 7.5' quadrangle.

Cañada Verde: see **Green Valley** [SANTA CRUZ].

Cañada y arroyo del Pecho: see **Pecho Creek** [SAN LUIS OBISPO].

Cañadita: see **Laguna Seca** [MONTEREY] (2).

Canal de Santa Barbara: see **Santa Barbara Channel** [SANTA BARBARA].

Cane Canyon [SAN BENITO]: *canyon,* drained by a stream that flows 3.25 miles to Hernandez Reservoir 10 miles east of Bitterwater (lat. 36°24' N, long. 120°49'35" W; near E line sec. 36, T 17 S, R 10 E). Named on Hernandez Reservoir (1969) 7.5' quadrangle.

Cane Canyon: see **Baker Canyon** [SAN BENITO].

Cane Mountain: see **Tucker Mountain** [SAN BENITO].

Canfield: see **San Juan Bautista** [SAN BENITO].

Cannery Point: see **Carmel Cove** [MONTEREY].

Cañon de Cebada: see **Cañada Cervada** [SANTA BARBARA].

Cañon de las Piedras: see **Stony Valley** [MONTEREY].

Canovas Canyon [SANTA BARBARA]: *canyon,* drained by a stream that flows 2.25 miles to South Fork La Brea Creek 2.25 miles west-southwest of Manzanita Mountain (lat. 34°53'05" N, long. 120°07'05" W). Named on Manzanita Mountain (1964) 7.5' quadrangle.

Can Rock [SANTA BARBARA]: *rock,* 3.5 miles northwest of Cardwell Point, and 2350 feet offshore on the north side of San Miguel

Island (lat. 34°03'15" N, long. 120°20'25" W). Named on San Miguel Island East (1950) 7.5' quadrangle.

Cantinas: see **The Cantinas** [SAN LUIS OBISPO].

Cantinas Creek [SAN LUIS OBISPO]: *stream,* flows 3 miles to Nacimiento Reservoir 13 miles northeast of the village of San Simeon (lat. 35°45'40" N, long. 121°00'40" W; near S line sec. 9, T 25 S, R 9 E); the stream flows past the feature called The Cantinas. Named on Bryson (1949, photorevised 1979) 7.5' quadrangle.

Cantua Creek [SAN BENITO]: *stream,* flows nearly 4 miles to Fresno County 5 miles east-southeast of Idria (lat. 36°23'30" N, long. 120°35'50" W; at E line sec. 1, T 18 S, R 12 E). Named on Ciervo Mountain (1969) and Santa Rita Peak (1969) 7.5' quadrangles. The name commemorates a member of the Cantua family (Gudde, 1949, p. 55).

Canyon de los Alisos [SAN LUIS OBISPO]: *canyon,* drained by a stream that flows 3 miles to Tar Spring Creek 7 miles southeast of Edna (lat. 35°08'10" N, long. 120°30'50" W). Named on Arroyo Grande NE (1965) and Tar Spring Ridge (1967) 7.5' quadrangles.

Canyon del Rey [MONTEREY]: *canyons,* extend end to end for 8 miles from Seaside to an unnamed canyon 8 miles south-southwest of Salinas (lat. 36°34'45" N, long. 121°43'38" W). Named on Seaside (1947) and Spreckels (1947) 7.5' quadrangles. The stream in the eastern canyon flows to Torro Creek, and the stream in the western canyon flows toward the sea.

Canyon Number 1 [SAN LUIS OBISPO]: *canyon,* drained by a stream that flows 1.5 miles to Canyon Number 2 about 4.5 miles south of Edna (lat. 35°08'30" N, long. 120°35'55" W). Named on Arroyo Grande NE (1965) 7.5' quadrangle.

Canyon Number 2 [SAN LUIS OBISPO]: *canyon,* drained by a stream that flows 1.5 miles to Canyon Number 1 about 4.5 miles south of Edna (lat. 35°08'30" N, long. 120°35'55" W). Named on Arroyo Grande NE (1965) 7.5' quadrangle.

Canyon Secundo [MONTEREY]: *canyon,* drained by a stream that flows 2.5 miles to Carmel Valley (1) 4.25 miles east of the mouth of Carmel River (lat. 36°32'05" N, long. 121°51' W). Named on Monterey (1913) 15' quadrangle.

Canyon Spring [SAN LUIS OBISPO]: *spring,* 5 miles south of Atascadero along Hale Creek (lat. 35°25'05" N, long. 120°41'05" W; near E line sec. 9, T 29 S, R 12 E). Named on Atascadero (1965) 7.5' quadrangle.

Cape San Martin [MONTEREY]: *promontory,* 37 miles southeast of Point Sur along the coast (lat. 39°53'20" N, long. 121°27'50" W; sec. 31, T 23 S, R 5 E). Named on Cape San Martin (1949) 7.5' quadrangle. Called Punta Gorda on Blake's (1857) map, and called Pt.

Gorda on Parke's (1854-1855) map. According to H.R. Wagner (p. 411), members of United States Coast Survey applied the name to the feature because they thought that Cabrillo had given it the name "San Martin." The feature is identified by three rocks, called San Martin Rocks, that lie from 100 yards to 0.5 mile offshore; a rock 4 miles north of Cape San Martin, and 0.7 mile offshore, is called Tide Rock (United States Coast and Geodetic Survey, p. 117).

Capital Hill [SAN LUIS OBISPO]: *district,* east of Salinas River opposite Paso Robles (lat. 35°37'40" N, long. 120°40'45" W). Named on Paso Robles (1948) 7.5' quadrangle.

Capitan [SANTA BARBARA]: *locality,* 10 miles east of Gaviota along Southern Pacific Railroad (lat. 34°27'50" N, long. 120°02'40" W); the place is near the mouth of Cañada del Corral (1), which has the name "Canon del Capitan" on Lompoc (1905) 30' quadrangle. Named on Tajiguas (1953) 7.5' quadrangle.

Capitola [SANTA CRUZ]: *town,* 2 miles northeast of Soquel Point along the coast (lat. 36°58'30" N, long. 121°57' W). Named on Soquel (1954) 7.5' quadrangle. In 1869 F.A. Hihn established a campground for vacationers on flat land east of the mouth of Soquel Creek; the place was called Camp Capitola, and in 1883 Hihn began selling lots there (Lyndon and Swift, p. 21, 36). In 1868 residents of Soquel invited the State of California to move the state capitol to their community; and Hihn created the name "Capitola" from that incident (Hanna, p. 55). The name "Camp Capitola" gave way to the name "Capitola-by-the-Sea," and this finally became the name "Capitola" (Clark, 1986, p. 61). Postal authorities established Capitola post office in 1889 (Frickstad, p. 176). Soquel Landing, which was at present Capitola, had a small wharf before 1857 (Rowland, p. 130). Michael Lodge hauled lumber in the early days to the beach at Capitola, which then was known as Lodge's Beach (Burgess, p. 240).

Capitola-by-the-Sea: see **Capitola** [SANTA CRUZ].

Carbonera Creek [SANTA CRUZ]: *stream,* flows 9 miles to Branciforte Creek 2.5 miles north-northeast of Point Santa Cruz in Santa Cruz (lat. 36°59'10" N, long. 122°00'50" W). Named on Felton (1955), Laurel (1955), and Santa Cruz (1954) 7.5' quadrangles. The stream was called West Browns Creek on a map of 1881; it also was called West Branch Branciforte Creek, West Fork Branciforte Creek, and West Branciforte Creek (Clark, 1986, p. 48, 64-65).

Cardwell Point [SANTA BARBARA]: *promontory,* at the easternmost tip of San Miguel Island (lat. 34°01'20" N, long. 120°17'40" W). Named on San Miguel Island East (1950) 7.5' quadrangle.

Careaga [SANTA BARBARA]: *locality,* 5 miles

west of Los Alamos along Pacific Coast Railroad (lat. 34°45'15" N, long. 120°22' W); the place is near the mouth of Careaga Canyon. Named on Lompoc (1905) 30' quadrangle. Postal authorities established Careaga post office in 1902, discontinued it in 1903, reestablished it in 1904, and discontinued it in 1909 (Salley, p. 37). The name commemorates Juan B. Careaga of the firm of Careaga and Harris, a farming enterprise that operated near Los Alamos in the early 1880's (Gudde, 1949, p. 56).

Careaga Canyon [SANTA BARBARA]: *canyon,* drained by a stream that flows 4.5 miles to San Antonio Creek (1) 8.5 miles south-southwest of the village of Sisquoc (lat. 34°45'25" N, long. 120°21'45" W). Named on Orcutt (1959) and Sisquoc (1959) 7.5' quadrangles. Called Canada de las Flores on Lompoc (1905) 30' quadrangle, which has the name "Careaga Canyon" for present Cañada de las Flores. United States Board on Geographic Names (1962a, p. 8) rejected the name "Cañada de las Flores" for present Careaga Canyon.

Carisa: see **Painted Rock** [SAN LUIS OBISPO].

Carisa Plain: see **Carrizo Plain** [SAN LUIS OBISPO].

Carisa Valley: see **Carrizo Plain** [SAN LUIS OBISPO].

Carmel: see **Carmel By The Sea** [MONTEREY]; **Carmel Valley** [MONTEREY] (2); **Mount Carmel** [MONTEREY]; **Point Carmel**, under **Pinnacle Point** [MONTEREY].

Carmel Bay [MONTEREY]: *embayment,* along the coast between Pescadero Point on the north and Carmel Point on the south (lat. 35°32'30" N, long. 121°57'15" W). Named on Monterey (1947) 7.5' quadrangle. According to Davidson (1907, p. 29), a Spanish chart made before Spanish settlement of California has the name "po de Pinos" for the bay. Forbes' (1839) map has the name "Carmel Cove" for the feature. Whitney (p. 158) referred to Carmelo Bay, and Farnham (p. 111) mentioned the bay of San Carmelo.

Carmel Beach [MONTEREY]: *beach,* on the east side of Carmel Bay at Carmel By The Sea (lat. 36°33' N, long. 121°55'40" W). Named on Monterey (1947) 7.5' quadrangle. Lawson's (1893) map has the name "Abalone Pt." for a promontory near the south end of the beach.

Carmel By The Sea [MONTEREY]: *town,* north of the mouth of Carmel River along Carmel Bay (lat. 36°33'15" N, long. 121°55'15" W). Named on Monterey (1947) 7.5' quadrangle. Called Carmel on Santa Cruz (1956) 1°x 2° quadrangle. The place began in 1903 as an artist colony (Lewis, 1977, p. 1). Postal authorities established Carmel post office in 1903 (Frickstad, p. 106), and the town incorporated in 1916. United States Board on

Geographic Names (1960c, p. 16) approved the hyphenated form "Carmel-by-the-Sea" for the name.

Carmel Cove [MONTEREY]: *embayment,* less than 1 mile east of Point Lobos along the coast (lat. 36°31'15" N, long. 121°56'15" W); the embayment is on the south side of Carmel Bay. Named on Monterey (1947) 7.5' quadrangle. United States Board on Geographic Names (1974b, p. 3) decided in favor of the name "Whalers Cove" for the feature, and gave the name "Carmel Cove" as a variant. California Department of Parks and Recreation's map has the name "Coal Chute Point" for a promontory on the east side of the cove, and the name "Cannery Point" for a promontory on the west side. According to Mosier (p. 5), a coal bunker was built in 1879 at the tip of Coal Chute Point, where coal was loaded on ships; a railroad brought the coal from a mine 5 miles south of the loading place. Cannery Point was the site of an abalone cannery that ceased operation in 1928 (Clark, 1991, p. 69-70).

Carmel Cove: see **Carmel Bay** [MONTEREY].

Carmel Highlands [MONTEREY]: *settlement,* 3.5 miles south of present Carmel-by-the-Sea (lat. 36°30' N, long. 121°56' W). Named on Monterey (1947) and Soberanes Point (1956) 7.5' quadrangles. Franklin Devendorf and Frank Powers began development of the place in 1916 (Clark, 1991, p. 76). California Mining Bureau's (1917b) map shows a place called Carmelito situated along the road just north of present Carmel Highlands; the name recalls a failed land development attempt in the late nineteenth century (Clark, 1991, p. 77).

Carmelito: see **Carmel Highlands** [MONTEREY].

Carmelo: see **Point Carmelo**, under **Pinnacle Point** [MONTEREY]; **Point Carmelo**, under **Point Lobos** [MONTEREY].

Carmelo Bay: see **Carmel Bay** [MONTEREY].

Carmelo River: see **Carmel River** [MONTEREY].

Carmelo Valley: see **Carmel Valley** [MONTEREY] (1).

Carmel Point: see **Pinnacle Point** [MONTEREY].

Carmel River [MONTEREY]: *stream,* flows 38 miles to the sea at Carmel Bay (lat. 36°32'10" N, long. 121°55'40" W); the stream drains Carmel Valley (1). Named on Carmel Valley (1956), Monterey (1947), Mount Carmel (1956), Seaside (1947), and Ventana Cones (1956) 7.5' quadrangles. Vizcaino named the river in 1603, probably for three Carmelite friars who accompanied him (Wagner, H.R., p. 379). Greenhow (p. 16) mentioned River San Carmelo in 1844, Townsend (p. 98) called the stream San Carlos River in 1855, and Whitney (p. 152) referred to Carmelo River in 1865. Miller Fork enters from the east 28 miles upstream from the mouth of the river;

it is 7.25 miles long and is named on Chews Ridge (1956) and Ventana Cones (1956) 7.5' quadrangles. Bruce Fork enters from the southeast 29 miles upstream from the mouth of the river; it is 2.5 miles long and is named on Ventana Cones (1956) 7.5' quadrangle. The name "Bruce Fork" commemorates members of the Bruce family, early residents in the vicinity (Clark, 1991, p. 53)

Carmel River Camp [MONTEREY]: *locality,* 3.25 miles east-northeast of Uncle Sam Mountain (lat. 36°21'05" N, long. 121°29' W; sec. 21, T 18 S, R 3 E); the place is along Carmel River. Named on Ventana Cones (1956) 7.5' quadrangle.

Carmel Valley [MONTEREY]:
(1) *valley,* extends for 12 miles inland from the coast along Carmel River. Named on Carmel Valley (1956), Monterey (1947), Mount Carmel (1956), and Seaside (1947) 7.5' quadrangles. Whitney (p. 152) referred to Carmelo Valley.
(2) *town,* 12 miles from the coast near the east end of Carmel Valley (1) (lat. 36°28'45" N, long. 121°43'45" W). Named on Carmel Valley (1956) 7.5' quadrangle. Postal authorities established Robles del Rio post office in 1941 and changed the name to Carmel Valley in 1952 (Frickstad, p. 109). California Mining Bureau's (1917b) map shows a place called Carmel located 13 miles east-southeast of Carmel by the Sea on the north side of Carmelo River. Postal authorities established Carmel post office in 1889, discontinued it in 1890, reestablished it in 1893, moved it 1 mile east in 1902, and discontinued it in 1903 (Salley, p. 38).

Carmel Woods [MONTEREY]: *district,* at the north edge of present Carmel-by-the-Sea (lat. 36°34'05" N, long. 121°54'55" W). Named on Monterey (1947) 7.5' quadrangle.

Carnasa Creek: see **Carnaza Creek** [SAN LUIS OBISPO].

Carnaza Creek [SAN LUIS OBISPO]: *stream,* flows 7.5 miles to the valley of San Juan Creek 15 miles northeast of Pozo (lat. 35°25'20" N, long. 120°09'45" W; near W line sec. 9, T 29 S, R 17 E). Named on La Panza NE (1966) and La Panza Ranch (1966) 7.5' quadrangles. United States Board on Geographic Names (1933, p. 196) rejected the form "Carnasa Creek" for the name.

Carnaza Spring [SAN LUIS OBISPO]: *spring,* 16 miles east-northeast of Pozo (lat. 35°26' N, long. 120°07'30" W; sec. 2, T 29 S, R 17 E); the spring is along Carnaza Creek. Named on La Panza NE (1966) 7.5' quadrangle.

Carneros Canyon [SAN LUIS OBISPO]: *canyon,* drained by a stream that flows 3.5 miles to Kern County 8 miles northeast of Simmler (lat. 35°25'45" N, long. 119°52'45" W; at E line sec. 1, T 29 S, R 19 E). Named on Las Yeguas Ranch (1959) 7.5' quadrangle.

Carneros Creek [SANTA BARBARA]: *stream,* flows nearly 6 miles to Goleta Slough 1.5

miles west-southwest of downtown Goleta (lat. 34°25'35" N, long. 119°50'55" W). Named on Goleta (1950) 7.5' quadrangle. The stream drains Bartlett Canyon. Goleta (1903) 15' quadrangle has the name "Carneros Valley" for the canyon of the creek below Bartlett Canyon. United States Board on Geographic Names (1961b, p. 9) rejected the name "Camerus Valley Creek" for the stream.

Carneros Valley: see **Carneros Creek** [SANTA BARBARA].

Carpenter Canyon [SAN LUIS OBISPO]: *canyon,* drained by a stream that flows nearly 2 miles to Corbit Canyon 5 miles south-southeast of Edna (lat. 35°08'20" N, long. 120°33'55" W). Named on Arroyo Grande NE (1965) 7.5' quadrangle.

Carpenteria: see **Carpinteria** [SANTA BARBARA].

Carpenteria Creek: see **Carpinteria Creek** [SANTA BARBARA].

Carpinteria [SANTA BARBARA]: *town,* 10 miles east of Santa Barbara (lat. 34°23'50" N, long. 119°31'05" W). Named on Carpinteria (1952) 7.5' quadrangle. Postal authorities established Carpenteria post office in 1867, discontinued it in 1869, reestablished it in 1870, moved it 1 mile west to the railroad depot in 1889, and changed the name to Carpinteria in 1900 (Salley, p. 38). The town incorporated in 1965. United States Board on Geographic Names (1933, p. 197) rejected the form "Carpenteria" for the name. Members of the Portola expedition found an Indian village at or near the place in 1769 and called it La Carpinteria because an Indian was building a canoe there—*carpinteria* means "carpenter shop" in Spanish (Wagner, H.R., p. 379). California Mining Bureau's (1917c) map shows a place called Benham located along the railroad about halfway between Carpinteria and Santa Barbara-Ventura county line.

Carpinteria Creek [SANTA BARBARA]: *stream,* flows 7.5 miles to the sea at Carpinteria (lat. 34°23'25" N, long. 119°31'10" W). Named on Carpinteria (1952) and White Ledge Peak (1952) 7.5' quadrangles. United States Board on Geographic Names (1933, p. 197) rejected the form "Carpenteria Creek" for the name.

Carpinteria Lagoon: see **El Estero** [SANTA BARBARA].

Carpinteria Landing: see **Serena** [SANTA BARBARA].

Carpinteria Slough: see **El Estero** [SANTA BARBARA].

Carr [SANTA BARBARA]: *locality,* 4.5 miles southeast of the town of Guadalupe along Santa Maria Valley Railroad (lat. 34°55'50" N, long. 120°30'35" W). Named on Guadalupe (1959) 7.5' quadrangle.

Carrals Spring [MONTEREY]: *spring,* 4 miles southeast of Cone Peak (lat. 36°00'35" N, long. 121°26'30" W, sec. 20, T 22 S, R 5 E).

Named on Cone Peak (1949) 7.5' quadrangle. The misspelled name is from corrals at the place (Clark, 1991, p. 88).

Carrie Creek [SAN LUIS OBISPO]: *stream,* flows 8 miles to Huasna River 4 miles north of Huasna Peak (lat. 35°05'45" N, long. 120° 21'05" W). Named on Caldwell Mesa (1967) and Huasna Peak (1967) 7.5' quadrangles. Called Aliso Creek on Nipomo (1922) 15' quadrangle, but United States Board on Geographic Names (1963b, p. 13) rejected this name.

Carrington Point [SANTA BARBARA]: *promontory,* 12 miles east-northeast of Sandy Point on the north side of Santa Rosa Island (lat. 34°02'10" N, long. 120°02'30" W). Named on Santa Rosa Island North (1943) 7.5' quadrangle. A shoal called Beacon Reef lies 0.3 mile north of Carrington Point (United States Coast and Geodetic Survey, p. 111).

Carrisa Plains: see **Carrizo Plain** [SAN LUIS OBISPO].

Carriso Plain: see **Carrizo Plain** [SAN LUIS OBISPO].

Carrizo Canyon [SAN LUIS OBISPO]: *canyon,* drained by a stream that flows 7.25 miles to Cuyama River 13 miles west of Caliente Mountain (lat. 35°04'10" N, long. 119°59'50" W). Named on Chimineas Ranch (1959) and Taylor Canyon (1959) 7.5' quadrangles.

Carrizo Creek: see **Garrizo Creek** [MONTEREY]; **San Juan Creek** [SAN LUIS OBISPO].

Carrizo Plain [SAN LUIS OBISPO]: *valley,* southwest of Temblor Range, and northeast of La Panza Range and Caliente Range. Named on Bakersfield (1962) and San Luis Obispo (1956) 1°x 2° quadrangles. The valley was called the Estero in Spanish times (Angel, 1890c, p. 568). Parke's (1854-1855) map has the name "Llano Estero" for the feature, and Hamlin's (1904) map has the name Carriso Plain. Other names applied to the valley include: Estero plain (Antisell, 1856, p. 54), Carrisa Plains (Angel, 1890c, p. 568), Carisa Plain (Fairbanks, 1895, p. 274), Carisa Valley (Anderson, F.M., p. 168), Carrizo Valley (Anderson and Martin, p. 35), and Carrizo Plains (Anderson and Martin, p. 50). California Mining Bureau's (1909b) map shows a place called Goodwin located near the southeast end of Carrizo Plain, 40 miles by stage line southeast of Simmler. Postal authorities established Goodwin post office in 1889, discontinued it in 1891, reestablished it in 1892, and discontinued it in 1899; they established Carissa Plains post office in 1916 and discontinued it the same year (Frickstad, p. 164).

Carrizo Valley: see **Carrizo Plain** [SAN LUIS OBISPO].

Carrol Canyon [SAN LUIS OBISPO]: *canyon,* drained by a stream that flows 3 miles to Town Creek 10 miles east-northeast of the village of San Simeon (lat. 35°40'35" N, long.

121°00'40" W; sec. 16, T 26 S, R 9 E). Named on Pebblestone Shut-in (1959) 7.5' quadrangle. Called Carroll Canyon on San Simeon (1959) 15' quadrangle.

Carter Spring [SANTA BARBARA]: *spring,* 1.5 miles east-southeast of Salisbury Potrero (lat. 34°48'35" N, long. 119°40'40" W). Named on Salisbury Potrero (1964) 7.5' quadrangle.

Cascade Creek [SANTA CRUZ]: *stream,* flows 1.25 miles to San Mateo County 3.5 miles north-northwest of the mouth of Waddell Creek (lat. 37°08'35" N, long. 122°18'30" W; sec. 21, T 9 S, R 4 W). Named on Franklin Point (1955) 7.5' quadrangle. The name goes back to 1863, when Cascade dairy began operating along the stream (Brown, p. 17).

Casey Gulch [MONTEREY]: *canyon,* drained by a stream that flows 1 mile to lowlands nearly 3.5 miles northwest of San Ardo (lat. 36° 03'20" N, long. 120°56'45" W). Named on San Ardo (1967) 7.5' quadrangle.

Casmale: see **Casmalia** [SANTA BARBARA] (2).

Casmalia [SANTA BARBARA]:

(1) *land grant,* mainly northwest of the village of Casmalia. Named on Casmalia (1959), Guadalupe (1959), and Point Sal (1958) 7.5' quadrangles. Antonio Olivera received 2 leagues in 1840 and claimed 8841 acres patented in 1863 (Cowan, p. 25).

(2) *village,* 9.5 miles south-southwest of Santa Maria (lat. 34°50'15" N, long. 120°31'50" W); the place is on Casmalia grant. Named on Casmalia (1959) 7.5' quadrangle. Called Casmale on Goddard's (1857) map. Postal authorities established Casmalia post office in 1896 (Frickstad, p. 170).

Casmalia Canyon [SANTA BARBARA]: *canyon,* drained by a stream that flows nearly 6 miles to Shuman Canyon less than 1 mile west-southwest of the village of Casmalia (lat. 34°49'55" N, long. 120° 32'35" W). Named on Casmalia (1959) and Guadalupe (1959) 7.5' quadrangles.

Casmalia Hills [SANTA BARBARA]: *range,* south of Santa Maria Valley between Graciosa Canyon and Point Sal. Named on Casmalia (1959), Guadalupe (1959), Orcutt (1959), and Point Sal (1958) 7.5' quadrangles.

Casserly Creek [SANTA CRUZ]: *stream,* flows 3 miles to Pajaro Valley 4.25 miles north of Watsonville (lat. 36°58'30" N, long. 121°44'30" W). Named on Watsonville East (1955) 7.5' quadrangle. The name is for Eugene Casserly, a settler of 1853 (Clark, 1986, p. 66).

Casserly Ridge [SANTA CRUZ]: *ridge,* southwest-trending, 1.5 miles long, 5 miles northeast of Watsonville (lat. 36°57'40" N, long. 121°41'05" W). Named on Watsonville East (1955) 7.5' quadrangle.

Cass' Wharf: see **Cayucos** [SAN LUIS OBISPO].

Castillo: see **Point Castillo** [SANTA BARBARA].

Castle Crags [SAN LUIS OBISPO]: *peak,* 10 miles east of Pozo (lat. 35°18'20" N, long. 120°12'05" W). Altitude 2677 feet. Named on La Panza (1967) 7.5' quadrangle.

Castle Mountain [MONTEREY]: *peak,* 6 miles east-northeast of Parkfield on Monterey-Fresno county line (lat. 35°56'20" N, long. 120°20'20" W; sec. 10, T 23 S, R 15 E). Altitude 4343 feet. Named on The Dark Hole (1961) 7.5' quadrangle. The feature also has been called Black Mountain and Castle Peak (Clark, 1991, p. 91).

Castle Peak: see **Castle Mountain** [MONTEREY].

Castle Rock [MONTEREY]: *rock,* 250 feet long, nearly 5 miles north of Point Sur, and 850 feet offshore (lat. 36°22'30" N, long. 121°54'25" W). Named on Point Sur (1956) and Soberanes Point (1956) 7.5' quadrangles.

Castle Rock [SAN BENITO]: *relief feature,* 11 miles northeast of Bitterwater (lat. 36°29'05" N, long. 120°50'55" W; sec. 2, T 17 S, R 10 E). Named on Hernandez Reservoir (1969) 7.5' quadrangle.

Castle Rock [SANTA BARBARA]: *island,* 0.25 mile long, 2 miles north-northeast of Point Bennett and 3100 feet offshore on the north side of San Miguel Island (lat. 34°03'20" N, long. 120°26'10" W). Named on San Miguel Island West (1950) 7.5' quadrangle. The feature had the local name "Flea Island" (Doran, p. 213). Bremner's (1933) map shows a place called Wescott Shoal situated less than 1 mile north of Castle Rock.

Castle Rock [SANTA CRUZ]: *relief feature,* 7.25 miles north of the town of Boulder Creek on Santa Cruz-Santa Clara county line (lat. 37°13'40" N, long. 122°05'40" W; near NE cor. sec. 20, T 8 S, R 2 W). Named on Castle Rock Ridge (1955) 7.5' quadrangle.

Castle Rock Falls [SANTA CRUZ]: *waterfall,* 7 miles north of the town of Boulder Creek (lat. 37°13'35" N, long. 122°06'20" W; sec. 20, T 8 S, R 2 W); the feature is 0.5 mile west-southwest of Castle Rock. Named on Castle Rock Ridge (1955) 7.5' quadrangle.

Castle Rock Ridge [SANTA CRUZ]: *ridge,* northwest-trending, 7 miles long, 7 miles north-northeast of the town of Boulder Creek on Santa Cruz-Santa Clara county line (lat. 37°13'30" N, long. 122°05'30" W); Castle Rock is on the ridge. Named on Castle Rock Ridge (1955) and Cupertino (1961) 7.5' quadrangles.

Castro Canyon [MONTEREY]: *canyon,* drained by a stream that flows 1.5 miles to the sea nearly 4 miles east-southeast of Pfeiffer Point (lat. 36°12'45" N, long. 121°45'15" W; sec. 9, T 20 S, R 2 E). Named on Partington Ridge (1956) and Pfeiffer Point (1956) 7.5' quadrangles. The name commemorates David Antonio Castro, who received a patent to land at the mouth of the canyon in 1883 (Clark, 1991, p. 91).

Castro Canyon [SAN LUIS OBISPO]: *canyon,* drained by a stream that flows 2.25 miles to San Luis Obispo Creek nearly 3 miles northeast of Avila Beach (lat. 35°12'25" N, long. 120°41'40" W). Named on Pismo Beach (1965) 7.5' quadrangle.

Castro Canyon [SANTA BARBARA]: *canyon,* drained by a stream that flows 6.25 miles to Cuyama Valley 3 miles south of the village of Cuyama (lat. 34°53'30" N, long. 119°37'05" W; sec. 1, T 9 N, R 26 W). Named on Cuyama (1964), Fox Mountain (1964), and Salisbury Potrero (1964) 7.5' quadrangles.

Castroville [MONTEREY]: *town,* 9 miles northwest of Salinas (lat. 36°46' N, long. 121°45' W). Named on Moss Landing (1954) and Prunedale (1954) 7.5' quadrangles. Juan B. Castro founded the town in 1864 and named it for his father, Simeon Nepomuceno Castro, owner of Bolsa Nuevo y Moro Cojo grant, where the town lies (Hanna, p. 59). Postal authorities established Castroville post office in 1867 (Frickstad, p. 106).

Cat Canyon [SAN LUIS OBISPO]: *canyon,* drained by a stream that flows 1.25 miles to Huasna River 4 miles north-northwest of Huasna Peak (lat. 35°05'30" N, long. 120°22' W). Named on Huasna Peak (1967) and Nipomo (1965) 7.5' quadrangles.

Cat Canyon [SANTA BARBARA]: *canyon,* drained by a stream that flows 10.5 miles to Santa Maria Valley at the village of Sisquoc (lat. 34°51'50" N, long. 120°17'30" W; near SW cor. sec. 7, T 9 N, R 32 W); the upper part of the canyon is north of Gato Ridge. Named on Foxen Canyon (1964) and Sisquoc (1959) 7.5' quadrangles. Called Canada del Gato on Santa Maria (1947) 15' quadrangle, but United States Board on Geographic Names (1962a, p. 9) rejected the names "Canada del Gato" and "Cañada del Gato" for the feature.

Catfish Lake [MONTEREY]: *intermittent lake,* 300 feet long, 4.5 miles north of Parkfield (lat. 35°57'50" N, long. 120°26'45" W; sec. 3, T 23 S, R 14 E). Named on Parkfield (1961) 7.5' quadrangle.

Cathedral Peak [SANTA BARBARA]: *peak,* 4.5 miles north-northwest of downtown Santa Barbara (lat. 34°29'10" N, long. 119°42'55" W; sec. 28, T 5 N, R 27 W). Altitude 3333 feet. Named on Santa Barbara (1952) 7.5' quadrangle.

Cavalry Bluff [MONTEREY]: *escarpment,* 4 miles west-southwest of Salinas (lat. 36°39'20" N, long. 121°43'45" W); the feature is at the boundary of Fort Ord Military Reservation. Named on Salinas (1947, photorevised 1968 and 1975) 7.5' quadrangle. The name is for the 11th Cavalry, stationed at Presidio of Monterey from 1919 until 1940 (Clark, 1991, p. 93).

Cave Gulch [SANTA CRUZ]: *canyon,* drained by a stream that flows 2 miles to Wilder Creek 3.5 miles northwest of Point Santa Cruz (lat. 36°59'05" N, long. 122°04'15" W). Named on Felton (1955) and Santa Cruz (1954) 7.5' quadrangles.

Cave Landing: see **Mallagh Landing** [SAN LUIS OBISPO].

Cavern Point [SANTA BARBARA]: *promontory,* 3 miles west-northwest of San Pedro Point on the north side of Santa Cruz Island (lat. 34°03'20" N, long. 119°33'45" W). Named on Santa Cruz Island D (1943) 7.5' quadrangle. Called Palo Parado on Rand's (1931) map.

Caves: see **The Caves** [MONTEREY].

Cawatre: see **Camp Cawatre Campground** [MONTEREY].

Cayucas: see **Cayucos** [SAN LUIS OBISPO].

Cayucos [SAN LUIS OBISPO]: *town,* 18 miles northwest of San Luis Obispo near the north end of Estero Bay (lat. 35°26'45" N, long. 120°53'45" W). Named on Cayucos (1965) 7.5' quadrangle. *Cayucos* means "boats" or "skiffs" in South-American Spanish (Kroeber, 1916, p. 38). The name probably came from the small boats used by Indians, and was applied first to Moro y Cayucos grant, and then to the town (Hanna, p. 59). Angel (1883, p. 323, 341-342) referred to a landing called Cayucos, where James Cass built Cass' Wharf in 1873. Present Cayucos is near the mouth of Old Creek; postal authorities established Old Creek post office in 1868, moved it 1 mile northwest and changed the name to Cayucas in 1879, and changed the name again to Cayucos in 1883 (Salley, p. 40, 160).

Cayucos Creek [SAN LUIS OBISPO]: *stream,* flows 6.5 miles to Estero Bay at Cayucos (lat. 35°26'55" N, long. 120°54'25" W). Named on Cayucos (1965) and Cypress Mountain (1948) 7.5' quadrangles. United States Board on Geographic Names (1938, p. 11) rejected the name "Estero River" for the stream. H.R. Wagner (p. 513) believed that a lagoon at the mouth of the creek might be the one that members of the Portola expedition called Estero de Santa Serafina in 1769, although he pointed out that Bolton identified present Ellysly Creek as Portola's Estero de Santa Serafina. Hamilton (p. 106-107) placed El Estero de Santa Serafina at the mouth of present Villa Creek.

Cayucos Creek: see **Little Cayucos Creek** [SAN LUIS OBISPO].

Cayucos Point [SAN LUIS OBISPO]: *promontory,* 20 miles northwest of San Luis Obispo along the coast (lat. 35°26'45" N, long. 120°56'20" W); the feature is 2 miles west of the mouth of Cayucos Creek. Named on Cayucos (1965) 7.5' quadrangle.

Cebada Canyon [SANTA BARBARA]: *canyon,* drained by a stream that flows 5.25 miles to lowlands 3.25 miles northeast of the city of Lompoc (lat. 34°39'55" N, long. 120°24'20" W). Named on Lompoc (1959) and Los Alamos (1959) 7.5' quadrangles.

Cebola Canyon: see **Chavoya Canyon** [MONTEREY].

Cedar Canyon [SAN LUIS OBISPO]: *canyon,* drained by a stream that flows nearly 2 miles to the valley of San Juan Creek 15 miles northeast of Pozo (lat. 35°27'25" N, long. 120°10'05" W; sec. 29, T 28 S, R 17 E). Named on La Panza Ranch (1966) 7.5' quadrangle. On La Panza (1935) 15' quadrangle, the stream in the canyon is called Cedar Creek.

Cedar Creek: see **Cedar Canyon** [SAN LUIS OBISPO].

Cedar Flat [SAN BENITO]: *valley,* 7.25 miles south-southeast of Panoche (lat. 36°30'35" N, long. 120°45'40" W; on E line sec. 28, T 16 S, R 11 E). Named on Panoche (1969) 7.5' quadrangle.

Cedar Flat Canyon [SAN BENITO]: *canyon,* drained by a stream that flows 7.25 miles to Panoche Creek 3.25 miles east of Panoche (lat. 36°35'25" N, long. 120°46'15" W; sec. 28, T 15 S, R 11 E); the canyon heads at Cedar Flat. Named on Panoche (1969) 7.5' quadrangle.

Cedar Spring [SAN BENITO]: *spring,* 13 miles east-southeast of Bitterwater (lat. 36°18'50" N, long. 120°46'20" W; near S line sec. 33, T 18 S, R 11 E). Named on Hepsedam Peak (1969) 7.5' quadrangle.

Cedar Spring [SAN LUIS OBISPO]: *spring,* 15 miles northeast of Pozo (lat. 35°27'30" N, long. 120°09'30" W; near E line sec. 29, T 28 S, R 17 E); the spring is in Cedar Canyon. Named on La Panza Ranch (1966) 7.5' quadrangle.

Celery Lake [SAN LUIS OBISPO]: *lake,* 0.5 mile long, 3.5 miles south-southwest of downtown Arroyo Grande near the coast (lat. 35°04'20" N, long. 120°36'10" W). Named on Oceano (1965) 7.5' quadrangle, which shows marshy places in the lake. Arroyo Grande (1952) 15' quadrangle shows an unnamed marsh instead of a lake.

Cement Trough Spring [SAN LUIS OBISPO]: *spring,* 4 miles west-southwest of Cholame (lat. 35°42'20" N, long. 120°22' W; sec. 33, T 25 S, R 15 E). Named on Cholame (1961) 7.5' quadrangle.

Centerville: see **Idria** [SAN BENITO].

Central Canyon [SANTA BARBARA]: *canyon,* drained by a stream that flows nearly 3 miles to join the stream in East Canyon and form Bitter Creek 4 miles southwest of New Cuyama (lat. 34°54'25" N, long. 119°44'10" W; sec. 35, T 10 N, R 27 W). Named on New Cuyama (1964) and Peak Mountain (1964) 7.5' quadrangles.

Central City: see **Santa Maria** [SANTA BARBARA].

Central Valley [SANTA BARBARA]: *canyon,* 7 miles long, center 4 miles south of Diablo Point in the middle of Santa Cruz Island (lat. 34°00'15" N, long. 119°44'45" W). Named on Santa Cruz Island B (1943) 7.5' quadrangle, which shows Stanton ranch near the east end of the canyon. Called Cñ. del Medio on Bremner's (1932) map, which has the name "Main Rch." for present Stanton ranch. Postal authorities established Laplaya post office at Main ranch in 1895 and discontinued it in 1903 (Salley, p. 117; Doran, p. 154). Bremner's (1932) map has the name "Cñ. del Portezuelo" for the west part of present Central Valley, and shows a place called Portezuelo there.

Cerro Alto [SAN LUIS OBISPO]: *peak,* 6.25 miles southwest of Atascadero (lat. 35°24'50" N, long. 120°44' W; sec. 7, T 29 S, R 12 E). Altitude 2624 feet. Named on Atascadero (1965) 7.5' quadrangle.

Cerro Alto: see **Hollister Peak** [SAN LUIS OBISPO].

Cerro Alto Campground [SAN LUIS OBISPO]: *locality,* 6 miles southwest of Atascadero (lat. 35°25'30" N, long. 120°44'20" W; near NE cor. sec. 12, T 29 S, R 11 E); the place is less than 1 mile north-northwest of Cerro Alto. Named on Atascadero (1965) 7.5' quadrangle.

Cerro Bonito [SAN BENITO]: *ridge,* west-northwest-trending, 3 miles long, 5.5 miles west-southwest of Panoche (lat. 36°34'15" N, long. 120°56' W). Named on Llanada (1969) 7.5' quadrangle. Called Cerros Bonito on Santa Cruz (1956) 1°x 2° quadrangle. Anderson and Pack (p. 17) referred to Cerro Bonito Ridge.

Cerro Bonito Ridge: see **Cerro Bonito** [SAN BENITO].

Cerro Cabrillo [SAN LUIS OBISPO]: *hill,* 3 miles east-southeast of Morro Rock (lat. 35°21'10" N, long. 120°49' W; near N line sec. 5, T 30 S, R 11 E). Named on Morro Bay South (1965) 7.5' quadrangle. The name honors Juan Rodriguez Cabrillo, commander of the first expedition to sail along the California coast (United States Board on Geographic Names, 1965a, p. 9).

Cerro Colorado [SAN BENITO]: *peak,* 11 miles northwest of Panoche (lat. 36°43'05" N, long. 120°57'20" W; sec. 14, T 14 S, R 9 E). Altitude 3656 feet. Named on Cerro Colorado (1969) 7.5' quadrangle.

Cerro del Venado: see **Sugarloaf** [SAN BENITO].

Cerro Romaldo: see **Cerro Romualdo** [SAN LUIS OBISPO].

Cerro Romauldo: see **Cerro Romualdo** [SAN LUIS OBISPO].

Cerro Romualdo [SAN LUIS OBISPO]: *peak,* 4.5 miles west-northwest of San Luis Obispo (lat. 35°18'50" N, long. 120°43'35" W); the peak is south of Huerta de Romualdo grant. Altitude 1307 feet. Named on San Luis Obispo (1965) 7.5' quadrangle. Called Cerro Romauldo on San Luis Obispo (1897) 15' quadrangle. Goodyear (1888, p. 99) called the peak Picacho de Romualdo. United States Board on Geographic Names (1964, p. 15) rejected the names "Cerro Romaldo" and "Cerro Romauldo" for the feature. The name commemorates Romualdo, the Indian who received Huerta Romualdo grant (Gudde, 1949, p. 62-63).

Cerro San Luis Obispo [SAN LUIS OBISPO]: *peak,* 1 mile west of downtown San Luis Obispo (lat. 35°17' N, long. 120°40'45" W; sec. 27, T 30 S, R 12 E). Altitude 1292 feet. Named on San Luis Obispo (1965) 7.5' quadrangle. Goodyear (1888, p. 99) called the feature San Luis Peak, but United States Board on Geographic Names (1961b, p. 9) rejected this name.

Cerros Bonito: see **Cerro Bonito** [SAN BENITO].

Chalk Hill [SAN LUIS OBISPO]: *hill,* 1 mile northeast of Santa Margarita (lat. 35°24' N, long. 120°35'30" W). Named on Santa Margarita (1965) 7.5' quadrangle.

Chalk Hill [SANTA BARBARA]: *peak,* 2.5 miles east of Buellton (lat. 34°36'50" N, long. 120°08'45" W). Named on Solvang (1959) 7.5' quadrangle.

Chalk Mountain [SAN LUIS OBISPO]: *peak,* 4 miles west-southwest of Caliente Mountain at the edge of Cuyama Valley (lat. 35°01' N, long. 119°49'35" W; on W line sec. 25, T 11 N, R 28 W). Named on Caliente Mountain (1959) 7.5' quadrangle.

Chalk Mountain [SANTA CRUZ]: *peak,* 4.5 miles north of the mouth of Waddell Creek (lat. 37°09'40" N, long. 122°17'20" W); the peak is at the south end of The Chalks. Altitude 1609 feet. Named on Franklin Point (1955) 7.5' quadrangle.

Chalk Peak [MONTEREY]:
(1) *peak,* 13 miles northeast of San Ardo (lat. 36°10'35" N, long. 120°46'05" W). Altitude 2456 feet. Named on Monarch Peak (1967) 7.5' quadrangle.
(2) *peak,* 7 miles north-northeast of Cape San Martin (lat. 35°59'15" N, long. 121°25'50" W; sec. 28, T 22 S, R 5 E). Altitude 3590 feet. Named on Cape San Martin (1949) 7.5' quadrangle.

Chalk Peak Camp [MONTEREY]: *locality,* 7.5 miles north-northeast of Cape San Martin (lat. 35°59'40" N, long. 121°25'50" W; sec. 28, T 22 S, R 5 E); the site is 0.5 mile north of Chalk Peak (2). Named on Cape San Martin (1949) 7.5' quadrangle. The place also was called Apple Camp and Apple Tree Camp (Clark, 1991, p. 94). On Cape San Martin (1961) 15' quadrangle, Chalk Peak Camp is shown 0.5 mile south-southwest of Chalk Peak (2).

Chalk Point: see **Camp No. 4**, under **Bridge Creek** [SANTA CRUZ].

Chalks: see **The Chalks** [SANTA CRUZ].

Chalone: see **Metz** [MONTEREY].

Chalone Creek [MONTEREY-SAN BENITO]: *stream,* heads in San Benito County and flows 27 miles to Salinas River 2.5 miles northeast of Greenfield in Monterey County (lat. 36°20'50" N, long. 121°12'35" W; sec. 21, T 18 S, R 7 E). Named on Bickmore Canyon (1968), Greenfield (1956), Mount Johnson (1968), and North Chalone Peak (1969) 7.5' quadrangles. Whitney (p. 159) referred to Chelone Creek.

Chalone Creek Campground [SAN BENITO]: *locality,* 3.25 miles north-northeast of North Chalone Peak (lat. 36°29'30" N, long. 121°10'10" W; sec. 35, T 16 S, R 7 E); the place is along Chalone Creek. Named on North Chalone Peak (1969) 7.5' quadrangle.

Chalone Mountain: see **North Chalone Peak** [MONTEREY-SAN BENITO].

Chalone Peak: see **North Chalone Peak** [MONTEREY-SAN BENITO]; **South Chalone Peak** [MONTEREY].

Chamisal Ridge [MONTEREY]: *ridge,* northwest- to west-northwest-trending, 3.5 miles long, 5.5 miles east-northeast of Soberanes Point (lat. 36°28'45" N, long. 121°50' W). Named on Mount Carmel (1956) 7.5' quadrangle.

Chandler Lake: see **Corralitos Lagoon** [SANTA CRUZ].

Channel Islands: see **Santa Barbara Channel** [SANTA BARBARA].

Chanslor: see **McKay** [SAN LUIS OBISPO].

Chaparral Campground [SAN BENITO]: *locality,* 3.25 miles north-northwest of North Chalone Peak (lat. 36°29'35" N, long. 121°12'35" W; sec. 33, T 16 S, R 7 E). Named on North Chalone Peak (1969) 7.5' quadrangle.

Chaparral Overlook [SAN BENITO]: *locality,* 3 miles north-northwest of North Chalone Peak (lat. 36°29'20" N, long. 121°12'45" W; at S line sec. 33, T 16 S, R 7 E). Named on North Chalone Peak (1969) 7.5' quadrangle.

Charles McFadden: see **One Suerte** [MONTEREY].

Charley Creek [MONTEREY]: *stream,* flows 4.5 miles to San Lorenzo Creek 2.5 miles west-southwest of Charley Mountain (lat. 36°07'55" N, long. 120°42'35" W; sec. 6, T 21 S, R 12 E); the stream heads at Charley Valley. Named on Priest Valley (1969) and Slack Canyon (1969) 7.5' quadrangles.

Charley Mountain [MONTEREY]: *peak,* 15 miles east-northeast of San Ardo on Monterey-Fresno county line (lat. 36°08'25" N, long. 120°39'50" W; sec. 34, T 20 S, R 12 E). Altitude 3885 feet. Named on Priest Valley (1969) 7.5' quadrangle.

Charley Valley [MONTEREY]: *valley,* 1.5 miles south of Charley Mountain (lat. 36°07'15" N, long. 120°39'50" W). Named on Priest Valley (1969) and Slack Canyon (1969) 7.5' quadrangles.

Charlie Valley [SAN LUIS OBISPO]: *valley,* 10.5 miles southwest of Branch Mountain (lat. 35°03'50" N, long. 120°11'55" W; on S line sec. 36, T 12 N, R 32 W). Named on Chimney Canyon (1967) 7.5' quadrangle.

Chase's Corners: see **Dunneville** [SAN BENITO].

Chavoya Canyon [MONTEREY]: *canyon,* drained by a stream that flows 3.25 miles to Pancho Rico Valley 8 miles east-northeast of San Ardo (lat. 36°04'10" N, long. 120°46'30" W; sec. 27, T 21 S, R 11 E). Named on Pancho

Rico Valley (1967) 7.5' quadrangle. Called Cebolla Canyon on San Ardo (1943) 15' quadrangle. The name recalls the Chavoya family, early settlers in the neighborhood (Clark, 1991, p. 97-98).

Chelame Pass: see **Cholame Creek** [MONTEREY-SAN LUIS OBISPO].

Chelone: see **Mount Chelone**, under **North Chalone Peak** [MONTEREY-SAN BENITO].

Chelone Creek: see **Chalone Creek** [MONTEREY-SAN BENITO].

Chemisal: see **Bolsa de Chamisal** [SAN LUIS OBISPO].

Chemise Ridge [SAN BENITO]: *ridge,* north- to northwest-trending, 2 miles long, 3.25 miles east of Panoche Pass (lat. 36°37'45" N, long. 121°04'15" W). Named on Panoche Pass (1968) and San Benito (1968) 7.5' quadrangles.

Cherokee Spring [SANTA BARBARA]: *spring,* 3 miles east of Tepusquet Peak (lat. 34°54'25" N, long. 120°07'50" W). Named on Tepusquet Canyon (1964) 7.5' quadrangle.

Cherry Canyon [MONTEREY]:
(1) *canyon,* drained by a stream that flows 4.5 miles to San Carlos Canyon 4.5 miles east-northeast of Greenfield (lat. 36°20'15" N, long. 121°09'55" W). Named on Greenfield (1956) and Pinalito Canyon (1969) 7.5' quadrangles.
(2) *canyon,* drained by a stream that flows nearly 4 miles to Quinado Canyon 5.5 miles south of King City (lat. 36°08'05" N, long. 121°07'45" W; sec. 5, T 21 S, R 8 E). Named on Thompson Canyon (1949) 7.5' quadrangle.

Cherry Canyon [SAN BENITO]: *canyon,* drained by a stream that flows 1.25 miles to Chalone Creek 2.5 miles east-southeast of North Chalone Peak (lat. 36°25'35" N, long. 121°09'15" W; sec. 25, T 17 S, R 7 E). Named on North Chalone Peak (1969) 7.5' quadrangle.

Cherry Orchard Spring [SANTA BARBARA]: *spring,* 1 mile west-southwest of Salisbury Potrero (lat. 34°49'05" N, long. 119°42'55" W). Named on Salisbury Potrero (1964) 7.5' quadrangle.

Cherry Peak [SAN BENITO]: *peak,* 8 miles east-southeast of Paicines (lat. 36°41'35" N, long. 121°08'35" W; near NW cor. sec. 30, T 14 S, R 8 E). Altitude 2916 feet. Named on Cherry Peak (1968) 7.5' quadrangle.

Cherry Ridge [SANTA BARBARA]: *ridge,* south- to south-southwest-trending, 2 miles long, 7.5 miles south-southwest of the city of Lompoc (lat. 34°32'15" N, long. 120°29'40" W). Named on Lompoc Hills (1959) and Tranquillon Mountain (1959) 7.5' quadrangles.

Cherry Thicket [MONTEREY]: *locality,* 2.5 miles south-southeast of Jamesburg (lat. 36°20'25" N, long. 121°36' W; near N line sec. 25, T 18 S, R 3 E). Named on Chews Ridge (1956) 7.5' quadrangle.

Cherry Tree Ridge [MONTEREY]: *ridge,* north-northwest-trending, 1.5 miles long, 2.5 miles west-northwest of Fremont Peak (lat. 36° 46'10" N, long. 121°32'40" W). Named on San Juan Bautista (1955) 7.5' quadrangle.

Chester Spring [SAN LUIS OBISPO]: *spring,* 3 miles north-northwest of Castle Crags (lat. 35°20'25" N, long. 120°13'45" W). Named on La Panza (1967) 7.5' quadrangle.

Chews Creek: see Kincannon Canyon [MONTEREY].

Chews Ridge [MONTEREY]: *ridge,* northwest-trending, 4 miles long, 5 miles south-south-east of Jamesburg (lat. 36°19'15" N, long. 121°34'45" W). Named on Chews Ridge (1956) 7.5' quadrangle. The name commemo-rates Constantine Marcus Chew, who patented land on the west side of the ridge in the 1890's (Clark, 1991, p. 98).

Chibo Peak: see Cibo Peak [SAN BENITO].

Chicken Springs: see Goat Rock [SANTA BARBARA].

Childs: see Santa Ynez [SANTA BARBARA].

Chileno Camp [SAN LUIS OBISPO]: *locality,* 5 miles north-northwest of the village of San Simeon (lat. 35°42'20" N, long. 121°14'10" W). Named on San Simeon (1958) 7.5' quad-rangle.

Chimney Canyon [SAN LUIS OBISPO]: *can-yon,* 3.5 miles long, opens into the canyon of Cuyama River 14 miles southwest of Branch Mountain (lat. 35°01'30" N, long. 120°13'50" W). Named on Chimney Canyon (1967) 7.5' quadrangle.

Chimney Rock [SAN LUIS OBISPO]: *relief feature,* 5.25 miles east-northeast of Adelaida on the south side of San Marcos Creek (lat. 35°41'20" N, long. 120°47'35" W; near N line sec. 9, T 26 S, R 11 E). Named on Adelaida (1948) 7.5' quadrangle.

China Camp [MONTEREY]: *locality,* 5.5 miles south-southeast of Jamesburg (lat. 36°17'45" N, long. 121°34' W; sec. 7, T 19 S, R 4 E). Named on Chews Ridge (1956) 7.5' quad-rangle. A labor camp for Chinese workers was at the site (Clark, 1991, p. 99).

China Cove [MONTEREY]: *embayment,* 1 mile southeast of Point Lobos along the coast (lat. 36°30'30" N, long. 121°56'25" W). Named on Monterey (1947) 7.5' quadrangle. Califor-nia Department of Parks and Recreation's map shows a place called Hidden Beach situated on the coast about 750 feet north of China Cove.

China Gulch [MONTEREY]:

(1) *canyon,* drained by a stream that flows nearly 1.5 miles to San Antonio River 8.5 miles southeast of Junipero Serra Peak (lat. 36° 03'40" N, long. 121°18'30" W). Named on Bear Canyon (1949) 7.5' quadrangle.

(2) *canyon,* drained by a stream that flows nearly 2 miles to lowlands 4 miles south-southeast of Jolon (lat. 35°55' N, long. 121°08'45" W). Named on Jolon (1949) 7.5' quadrangle.

China Harbor [SAN LUIS OBISPO]: *embayment,* 0.5 mile east-northeast of Point Estero (lat. 35°27'45" N, long. 120°59'30" W; sec. 34, T 28 S, R 9 E). Named on Cayucos (1965) 7.5' quadrangle.

China Harbor: see Chinese Harbor [SANTA BARBARA].

China Ladder: see Arroyo las Trancas [SANTA CRUZ].

China Point: see Mussel Point [MONTEREY].

China Ridge [SANTA CRUZ]: *ridge,* south- to southwest-trending, 2 miles long, 6 miles northeast of Soquel (lat. 37°02'55" N, long. 121°52'50" W). Named on Laurel (1955) 7.5' quadrangle. The name is from the Chinese railroad workers who built a broad-gauge line up the canyon of Aptos Creek about 1890 (Lydon, p. 105).

Chinese Harbor [SANTA BARBARA]: *embayment,* 4.25 miles east of Prisoners Har-bor on the north side of Santa Cruz Island (lat. 34° 01'35" N, long. 119°36'30" W). Named on Santa Cruz Island C (1943) 7.5' quadrangle. Called China Harbor on Bremner's (1932) map. Yankee skippers landed Chinese coolies at the place while awaiting an opportunity to smuggle them to the mainland (Gleason, p. 49).

Chittenden [SANTA CRUZ]: *settlement,* 8 miles west of Watsonville along Pajaro River (lat. 36°54'10" N, long. 121°36'20" W). Named on Chittenden (1955) 7.5' quadrangle. Postal authorities established Chittenden post office in 1893 and discontinued it in 1923; the name is for W.W. Chittenden, who purchased the site 1852 (Salley, p. 43). Chittenden's Sulphur Springs, known locally for their medicinal properties, were near the settlement (Crawford, 1896, p. 519). The springs also were known as Shale Sulphur Springs, El Pajaro Springs (Waring, G.A., p. 274-275), Chittenden Springs, and Saint Francis Springs—the last name when they were owned by the Franciscan order (Laizure, 1926, p. 89). One of the springs was called Rail-road Spring because it was a favorite of rail-road men; two nearby springs were called White Sulphur Springs—the water of these became milky and deposited natural sulphur after flowing for a few yards (Waring, G.A., p. 274).

Chittenden Pass [SAN BENITO-SANTA CRUZ]: *canyon,* nearly 2 miles north-north-east of Aromas along Pajaro River on San Benito-Santa Cruz county line (lat. 36°54'40" N, long. 121° 37'30" W). Named on Chittenden (1955) and Watsonville East (1955) 7.5' quadrangles. The narrow part of the canyon is called Pajaro Gap.

Chittenden Springs: see Chittenden's Sulphur Springs, under Chittenden [SANTA CRUZ].

Chittenden's Sulphur Springs: see Chittenden [SANTA CRUZ].

Choice Valley [SAN LUIS OBISPO]: *valley,* 11 miles east-southeast of Shandon on San Luis

Obispo-Kern county line (lat. 35°37'40" N, long. 120°11'30" W). Named on Orchard Peak (1961) 7.5' quadrangle.

Chokecherry Canyon [SANTA BARBARA]: *canyon,* drained by a stream that flows 3.5 miles to Santa Barbara Canyon 3 miles north-northeast of Madulce Peak (lat. 34°44' N, long. 119°34'15" W). Named on Madulce Peak (1964) 7.5' quadrangle.

Chokecherry Spring [SANTA BARBARA]: *spring,* 2.5 miles northeast of Big Pine Mountain (lat. 34°43'30" N, long. 119°37'35" W); the spring is near the head of Chokecherry Canyon. Named on Big Pine Mountain (1964) 7.5' quadrangle.

Cholame [MONTEREY-SAN LUIS OBISPO]: *land grant,* north of the village of Cholame on Monterey-San Luis Obispo county line; the grant covers most of Cholame Valley. Named on Cholame (1961), Cholame Hills (1961), Cholame Valley (1961), Orchard Peak (1961), and Tent Hills (1942) 7.5' quadrangles. Mauricio Gonzales received 6 leagues in 1844; Ellen E. White claimed 26,622 acres patented in 1865 (Cowan, p. 27; Perez, p. 62). The name is from an Indian village located near San Miguel mission (Kroeber, 1916, p. 38). Angel (1883, p. 215) used the form "Cholamie," and Gudde (1949, p. 67) mentioned early use of the name "Cholan."

Cholame [SAN LUIS OBISPO]: *village,* 23 miles east-northeast of Paso Robles (lat. 35°43'25" N, long. 120°17'45" W; sec. 30, T 25 S, R 16 E); the place is in Cholame Valley. Named on Cholame (1961) 7.5' quadrangle. Postal authorities established Cholame post office in 1873, discontinued it in 1908, and reestablished it the same year (Salley, p. 43).

Cholame Creek [MONTEREY-SAN LUIS OBISPO]: *stream,* heads in Monterey County and flows 35 miles to join San Juan Creek and form Estrella River at Shandon in San Luis Obispo County (lat. 35°39'35" N, long. 120°22'10" W; near NW cor. sec. 21, T 26 S, R 15 E). Named on Cholame (1961), Cholame Hills (1961), Cholame Valley (1961), Parkfield (1961), and Stockdale Mountain (1948) 7.5' quadrangles. Gudde (1949, p, 67) noted that a Land Office map of 1859 has the name "Choloma Creek." Parke's (1854-1855) map has the name "Chelame Pass" for the valley of Cholame Creek between present Shandon and Cholame. On a county map of 1877, the lower part of present Cholame Creek is called Russells Creek (Clark, 1991, p. 103).

Cholame Creek: see **Little Cholame Creek** [MONTEREY].

Cholame Hills [MONTEREY-SAN LUIS OBISPO]: *range,* southwest of Cholame Valley on Monterey-San Luis Obispo county line—mainly in Monterey County. Named on Cholame (1961), Cholame Hills (1961), Cholame Valley (1961), Parkfield (1961), and Stockdale Mountain (1948) 7.5' quadrangles.

Cholame Valley [MONTEREY-SAN LUIS

OBISPO]: *valley,* mainly northwest of the village of Cholame on Monterey-San Luis Obispo county line; Cholame Creek drains the valley. Named on Cholame (1961), Cholame Hills (1961) and Cholame Valley (1961) 7.5' quadrangles.

Cholame Valley: see **Little Cholame Valley**, under **Little Cholame Creek** [MONTEREY].

Cholamie: see **Cholame** [MONTEREY-SAN LUIS OBISPO].

Cholan: see **Cholame** [MONTEREY-SAN LUIS OBISPO].

Cholla Creek [SAN BENITO]: *stream,* flows nearly 4 miles to Bitterwater Creek 4.5 miles southeast of Bitterwater (lat. 36°20' N, long. 120°56'25" W; sec. 25, T 18 S, R 9 E). Named on Lonoak (1969) 7.5' quadrangle.

Choloma Creek: see **Cholame Creek** [MONTEREY-SAN LUIS OBISPO].

Chorro [SAN LUIS OBISPO]: *locality,* 3.25 miles north-northwest of downtown San Luis Obispo along Southern Pacific Railroad (lat. 35°19'35" N, long. 120°40'35" W). Named on San Luis Obispo (1965) 7.5' quadrangle.

Chorro: see **Huerta de Romualdo** [SAN LUIS OBISPO].

Chorro Creek [SAN LUIS OBISPO]: *stream,* flows 14 miles to Morro Bay 3 miles southeast of Morro Rock (lat. 35°20'25" N, long. 120° 50'25" W); the stream is partly on El Chorro grant. Named on Morro Bay South (1965) and San Luis Obispo (1965) 7.5' quadrangles. United States Board on Geographic Names (1933, p. 219) rejected the name "San Luisito Creek" for the stream.

Chorro Reservoir [SAN LUIS OBISPO]: *lake,* 1000 feet long, 4.25 miles north-northwest of San Luis Obispo (lat. 35°20'15" N, long. 120°41'10" W); the lake is along Chorro Creek. Named on San Luis Obispo (1965) 7.5' quadrangle.

Chris Flood Creek [MONTEREY-SAN LUIS OBISPO]: *stream,* heads in Monterey County and flows nearly 6 miles to San Carpoforo Creek 3.25 miles east-northeast of the mouth of that creek in San Luis Obispo County (lat. 35°47'05" N, long. 121°16'15" W; sec. 1, T 25 S, R 6 E). Named on Burnett Peak (1949) and Burro Mountain (1949) 7.5' quadrangles.

Christy Cañada: see **Cañada Cervada** [SANTA BARBARA].

Chualar [MONTEREY]:

(1) *land grant,* 11 miles southeast of Salinas around the village of Chualar. Named on Chualar (1947) and Gonzales (1955) 7.5' quadrangles. Juan Malarin received 2 leagues in 1839; Mariano Malarin, executor, claimed 8890 acres patented in 1872 (Cowan, p. 27; Cowan listed the grant under the name "Santa Rosa de Chualar"). *Chual* is an Indian word for the plant commonly called pigweed; the name "Chualar" apparently is a Spanish adaptation of the Indian word and means "place where chual grows" (Stewart, p. 97).

(2) *village,* 10 miles southeast of Salinas (lat.

49

36°34'15" N, long. 121°31' W); the place is on Chualar grant. Named on Chualar (1947) 7.5' quadrangle. Postal authorities established Chualar post office in 1871, discontinued it in 1873, and reestablished it in 1874 (Frickstad, p. 106).

Chualar Canyon [MONTEREY]: *canyon,* drained by a stream that flows 7.5 miles to lowlands 5 miles east-northeast of the village of Chualar (lat. 36°35'30" N, long. 121°27'30" W). Named on Gonzales (1955), Mount Johnson (1968), and Paicines (1968) 7.5' quadrangles.

Chualar Creek [MONTEREY]: *stream,* flows 5 miles from the mouth of Chualar Canyon to a point 0.5 mile south-southwest of the village of Chualar (lat. 36°33'40" N, long. 121°31'20" W). Named on Gonzales (1955) 7.5' quadrangle.

Chumash Peak [SAN LUIS OBISPO]: *peak,* 3.25 miles northwest of San Luis Obispo (lat. 35°18'25" N, long. 120°42'20" W; near N line sec. 20, T 30 S, R 12 E). Altitude 1268 feet. Named on San Luis Obispo (1965) 7.5' quadrangle. The name is for a linguistic family of California Indians (United States Board on Geographic Names, 1965a, p. 9).

Chupines Creek [MONTEREY]: *stream,* flows 8 miles to Tularcitos Creek 3 miles southeast of the town of Carmel Valley (lat. 36°27'10" N, long. 121°41'45" W). Named on Carmel Valley (1956) and Rana Creek (1956) 7.5' quadrangles.

Church Creek [MONTEREY]: *stream,* flows 4.5 miles to Tassajara Creek 1.25 miles west-northwest of Tassajara Hot Springs (lat. 36° 14'35" N, long. 121°34'35" W; near N line sec. 31, T 19 S, R 4 E). Named on Chews Ridge (1956) and Tassajara Hot Springs (1956) 7.5' quadrangles. The name commemorates the Church family, first settlers near the stream (Gudde, 1949, p. 68).

Church Creek Divide [MONTEREY]: *pass,* 6 miles south-southwest of Jamesburg (lat. 36°17'25" N, long. 121°36'40" W; sec. 11, T 19 S, R 3 E); the feature is at the head of Church Creek. Named on Chews Ridge (1956) 7.5' quadrangle.

Church Creek Rockshelter: see **The Caves** [MONTEREY].

Cibo Peak [MONTEREY]: *peak,* 4.25 miles west-southwest of Potrero Peak (lat. 36°49'40" N, long. 121°13'05" W). Altitude 2845 feet. Named on Quien Sabe Valley (1968) 7.5' quadrangle. Called Chibo Peak on California Mining Bureau's (1917b) map.

Cienega: see **Thompson Creek** [SAN BENITO].

Cienega Camp [MONTEREY]: *locality,* 5.5 miles north-northeast of Partington Point (lat. 36°14'50" N, long. 121°39'10" W; sec. 29, T 19 S, R 3 E); the place is along Cienega Creek. Named on Partington Ridge (1956) 7.5' quadrangle.

Cienega Creek [MONTEREY]: *stream,* flows

2 miles to North Fork Big Sur River 5.25 miles north-northeast of Partington Point (lat. 36°14'35" N, long. 121°39'20" W; at N line sec. 32, T 19 S, R 3 E). Named on Partington Ridge (1956) and Ventana Cones (1956) 7.5' quadrangles. The name is from marsh located 0.5 mile north of the mouth of the stream—*cienega* means "marsh" or "swamp" in Spanish (Clark, 1991, p. 105).

Cienega Creek [SAN LUIS OBISPO]: *stream,* flows nearly 4 miles to Santa Rita Creek 2 miles southwest of York Mountain (lat. 35°31'25" N, long. 120°51'05" W). Named on Cypress Mountain (1948) and York Mountain (1948) 7.5' quadrangles.

Cienega del Gabilan [MONTEREY-SAN BENITO]: *land grant,* 10 miles east-northeast of Salinas on Monterey-San Benito county line. Named on Hollister (1955), Mount Harlan (1968), Natividad (1947), Paicines (1968), San Juan Bautista (1955), and Tres Pinos (1955) 7.5' quadrangles. Antonio Chavis received the grant in 1843; Jessie D. Carr claimed 48,781 acres patented in 1867 (Cowan, p. 37—Cowan listed the grant under the designation "Cienega del Gavilan (or Gabilan)"; Perez, p. 62). United States Board on Geographic Names (1933, p. 221) rejected the form "Sienega del Gabilan" for the name.

Cienega de los Paicines [SAN BENITO]: *land grant,* around Paicines along and west of Tres Pinos Creek. Named on Paicines (1968) and Tres Pinos (1955) 7.5' quadrangles. Angel Castro and Jose Rodroguez received 2 leagues in 1842; Castro claimed 8918 acres patented in 1869 (Cowan, p. 56—Cowan listed the grant under the designation "Cienege de los Paicines (or Pajines, or Paycines)"; Perez, p. 62). According to Kroeber (1916, p. 53), the name "Paicines," or "Pajines," probably is from the designation of an Indian tribe.

Cienega Valley [SAN BENITO]: *valley,* 4 miles west-southwest of Paicines along Pescadero Creek (lat. 36°43' N, long. 121°20'50" W). Named on Paicines (1968) 7.5' quadrangle.

Cienega Valley [SAN LUIS OBISPO]: *area,* 3 miles south-southwest of downtown Arroyo Grande near the coast (lat. 35°05'10" N, long. 120°36'20" W). Named on Oceano (1965) 7.5' quadrangle.

Cieneguitas Creek [SANTA BARBARA]: *stream,* flows 3 miles to Atascadero Creek 3 miles east of downtown Goleta (lat. 34°26'05" N, long. 119°46'30" W). Named on Goleta (1950) 7.5' quadrangle.

Cierro Chalon: see **North Chalone Peak** [MONTEREY-SAN BENITO].

Ciervo Hills [SAN BENITO]: *range,* east of Tumey Gulch on San Benito-Fresno county line, mainly in Fresno County. Named on Ciervo Mountain (1969), Idria (1969), and Tumey Hills (1956) 7.5' quadrangles.

Cigarette Spring [SANTA BARBARA]: *spring,* 5 miles north-northwest of Tepusquet Peak (lat. 34°58'50" N, long. 120°12'30" W).

Named on Tepusquet Canyon (1964) 7.5' quadrangle.

Cinco Canoas Canyon [MONTEREY-SAN BENITO]: *canyon,* drained by a stream that heads in San Benito County and flows nearly 8.5 miles to San Carlos Canyon 4.5 miles east-northeast of Greenfield in Monterey County (lat. 36°20'15" N, long. 121°09'55" W). Named on Greenfield (1956) and Pinalito Canyon (1969) 7.5' quadrangles.

Cinnabar: see **San Benito River** [SAN BENITO].

City of King: see **The City of King**, under **King City** [MONTEREY].

Clapboard Canyon [SAN LUIS OBISPO]: *canyon,* drained by a stream that flows 3.25 miles to Arroyo Grande Creek 10 miles north of the town of Nipomo (lat. 35°11'15" N, long. 120°27'35" W; sec. 34, T 31 S, R 14 E). Named on Tar Spring Ridge (1967) 7.5' quadrangle.

Clark Canyon [SANTA BARBARA]: *canyon,* 1.5 miles long, opens into Lake Cachuma 4.5 miles north of Santa Ynez Peak (lat. 34°35'30" N, long. 119°58'30" W). Named on Lake Cachuma (1959) 7.5' quadrangle. Water of Lake Cachuma now floods the lower part of the canyon.

Clark Colony: see **Arroyo Seco** [MONTEREY] (2).

Clarke Canyon [SAN LUIS OBISPO]: *canyon,* drained by a stream that flows 5.5 miles to lowlands along Estrella Creek 11 miles east-northeast of Paso Robles (lat. 35°40'40" N, long. 120°30'05" W; sec. 7, T 26 S, R 14 E). Named on Shandon (1961) 7.5' quadrangle.

Clarke City: see **Greenfield** [MONTEREY].

Clark Valley [SAN LUIS OBISPO]: *valley,* 7.5 miles southeast of Morro Rock along the upper part of Los Osos Creek (lat. 35°16'45" N, long. 120°47' W). Named on Morro Bay South (1965) 7.5' quadrangle. Called Cañada de los Alisos on a diseño made in 1842 of Cañada de los Osos grant (Becker, 1969).

Clayton: see **Camp Clayton Military Reservation**, under **Fort Ord Military Reservation** [MONTEREY].

Clear Creek [SAN BENITO]: *stream,* flows 8.5 miles to San Benito River 12.5 miles east of Bitterwater (lat. 36°21'20" N, long. 120° 47' W; near SE cor. sec. 17, T 18 S, R 11 E). Named on Hepsedam Peak (1969), Idria (1969), and San Benito Mountain (1969) 7.5' quadrangles.

Clear Creek [SANTA BARBARA]: *stream,* flows 4.25 miles to Cuyama River 6.5 miles northwest of Miranda Pine Mountain (lat. 35°05'50" N, long. 120°07'25" W). Named on Miranda Pine Mountain (1967) 7.5' quadrangle.

Clear Creek [SANTA CRUZ]: *stream,* flows 2.25 miles to San Lorenzo River 1.25 miles southeast of the town of Boulder Creek (lat. 37°06'35" N, long. 122°06'25" W; sec. 32, T 9 S, R 2 W). Named on Davenport (1955) and Felton (1955) 7.5' quadrangles.

Clear Creek: see **Brookdale** [SANTA CRUZ].

Clear Lake [SAN LUIS OBISPO]: *intermittent lake,* 350 feet long, 7.5 miles northeast of Santa Margarita (lat. 35°28'30" N, long. 120°31'15" W). Named on Santa Margarita (1965) 7.5' quadrangle.

Clear Ridge: see **Pfeiffer Ridge** [MONTEREY].

Clems [SANTA CRUZ]: *locality,* 2.25 miles southwest of Laurel along Southern Pacific Railroad (lat. 37°05'55" N, long. 121°59'50" W; near N line sec. 5, T 10 S, R 1 W). Named on Los Gatos (1919) 15' quadrangle. Hamman's (1980b) map shows a place called Tank Siding located nearly 1 mile northwest of Clems along the railroad.

Cleveland Rock [MONTEREY]: *peak,* 16 miles north-northeast of San Ardo on Mustang Ridge (lat. 36°14'45" N, long. 120°49'20" W; sec. 30, T 19 S, R 11 E). Altitude 2494 feet. Named on Monarch Peak (1967) 7.5' quadrangle. The name is for early settlers who owned land near the peak (Clark, 1991, p. 108).

Cliff Canyon [SANTA BARBARA]: *canyon,* drained by a stream that flows 4.5 miles to Sisquoc River 5.25 miles south-southwest of Salisbury Potrero (lat. 34°45'10" N, long. 119°44'25" W). Named on Salisbury Potrero (1964) 7.5' quadrangle.

Cliff Springs: see **Hot Springs** [SANTA BARBARA] (2).

Clipper Gulch [SANTA CRUZ]: *canyon,* drained by a stream that flows nearly 1 mile to Eureka Canyon 3 miles north-northwest of Corralitos (lat. 37°01'50" N, long. 121°49'05" W; at W line sec. 25, T 10 S, R 1 E). Named on Loma Prieta (1955) 7.5' quadrangle.

Clough Canyon [SAN BENITO]: *canyon,* drained by a stream that flows nearly 6.5 miles to Panoche Valley 1 mile west-northwest of Panoche (lat. 36°36' N, long. 120°50'55" W; sec. 26, T 15 S, R 10 E). Named on Llanada (1969) 7.5' quadrangle.

Clover Basin Camp [MONTEREY]: *locality,* 4.25 miles east of Uncle Sam Mountain (lat. 36°20'35" N, long. 121°37'45" W; near SE cor. sec. 22, T 18 S, R 3 E). Named on Ventana Cones (1956) 7.5' quadrangle.

Cluster Point [SANTA BARBARA]: *promontory,* 6.5 miles southeast of Sandy Point on the south side of Santa Rosa Island (lat. 33°55'30" N, long. 120°10'45" W). Named on Santa Rosa Island West (1943) 7.5' quadrangle.

Coal Chute Point: see **Carmel Cove** [MONTEREY].

Coal Oil Point [SANTA BARBARA]: *promontory,* 3.5 miles southwest of Goleta along the coast (lat. 34°24'25" N, long. 119°52'40" W). Named on Dos Pueblos Canyon (1951) 7.5' quadrangle. H.R. Wagner (p. 519) noted the Spanish name "Punta de Tobar" for present Coal Oil Point. Goodyear (1888, p. 91) called the feature Salinas Point, and noted that a large petroleum spring is beneath the sea about 0.5 mile off the point.

Coast: see **Santa Cruz** [SANTA CRUZ].

Coati Point [SANTA BARBARA]: *promontory,* 0.5 mile south of Carrington Point on the north side of Santa Rosa Island (lat. 34°01'40" N, long. 120°02'35" W). Named on Santa Rosa Island North (1943) 7.5' quadrangle.

Cobblestone Creek: see **Steve Creek** [MONTEREY].

Coburn [MONTEREY]: *locality,* 5.5 miles east-southeast of Greenfield along Southern Pacific Railroad (lat. 36°17'20" N, long. 121°09'05" W). Named on Greenfield (1956) 7.5' quadrangle The name commemorates Loren Coburn, who deeded right of way at the place to the railroad in 1883 (Clark, 1991, p. 111).

Coche Campground [SANTA BARBARA]: *locality,* 4.5 miles west-southwest of Big Pine Mountain (lat. 34°40'50" N, long. 119° 44' W); the place is along Coche Creek. Named on Big Pine Mountain (1964) 7.5' quadrangle.

Coche Creek [SANTA BARBARA]: *stream,* flows 4.5 miles to West Fork Santa Cruz Creek 4.25 miles southeast of San Rafael Mountain (lat. 34°39'50" N, long. 119°45'50" W). Named on Big Pine Mountain (1964) and San Rafael Mountain (1959) 7.5' quadrangles. Called Grapevine Cr. on San Rafael Mountain (1943) 15' quadrangle, and called Cache Cr. on San Rafael Mountain (1959) 15' quadrangle.

Coche Point [SANTA BARBARA]: *promontory,* 4.5 miles east-northeast of Prisoners Harbor on the north side of Santa Cruz Island (lat. 34°02'15" N, long. 119°36'30" W). Named on Santa Cruz Island C (1943) 7.5' quadrangle.

Coches Prietos Anchorage [SANTA BARBARA]: *embayment,* nearly 4 miles south-southwest of Prisoners Harbor on the south side of Santa Cruz Island (lat. 33°58'05" N, long. 119°42'15" W). Named on Santa Cruz Island C (1943) 7.5' quadrangle. United States Board on Geographic Names (1936b, p. 18) rejected the forms "Cochies Prietos Anchorage" and "Coche Prietos Anchorage" for the name, and noted that *coches prietos* means "dark barges" or "black barges" in Spanish. Bremner's (1932) map has the name "Cñ. Coches Prietos" for the canyon that opens to the sea at present Coches Prietos Anchorage.

Cochies Prietos Anchorage: see **Coches Prietos Anchorage** [SANTA BARBARA].

Cocks: see **Henry Cocks** [MONTEREY].

Cocks'Station: see **San Bernabe** [MONTEREY].

Coja Creek: see **Majors Creek** [SANTA CRUZ].

Cojo Anchorage: see **Cojo Bay** [SANTA BARBARA].

Cojo Bay [SANTA BARBARA]: *embayment,* 1.5 miles east of Point Conception along the coast (lat. 34°26'50" N, long. 120°26'30" W);

the embayment is west of the mouth of Cañada del Cojo. Named on Point Conception (1953) 7.5' quadrangle. Cabrillo called the place Puerto de Todos Santos in 1542, and Esteban Jose Martinez called it Ensenada de la Purisima Concepcion in 1782 (Wagner, H.R., p. 487, 519). United States Board on Geographic Names (1978b, p. 4) approved the name "Cojo Anchorage" for the place, and rejected the name "Cojo Bay." United States Coast and Geodetic Survey (p. 104) noted that a cove 1.7 miles east of Cojo Anchorage is known as Little Cojo or Old Cojo. Parke's (1854-1855) map has the name "Rcho. Coxo" at present Cojo Anchorage, and Eddy's (1854) map shows a place called Coxo there. The Spaniards used the name "Punta de Sanchez" for the promontory situated east of Cojo Anchorage (Wagner, H.R., p. 509). Cojo Anchorage was an important refuge that the Spaniards preferred to Santa Barbara; some nineteenth-century whaling vessels processed their catches on the beach there (Fagan, p. 96).

Cojo Creek [SANTA BARBARA]: *stream,* flows 2.5 miles to the sea 1.5 miles east of Point Conception at present Cojo Anchorage (lat. 34°27' N, long. 120°26'30" W). Named on Point Conception (1942) 15' quadrangle.

Cold Spring [MONTEREY]: *spring,* nearly 3 miles north-northeast of Partington Point (lat. 36°12'45" N, long. 121°40'45" W; sec. 7, T 20 S, R 3 E). Named on Lucia (1921) 15' quadrangle.

Cold Spring [SAN LUIS OBISPO]: *spring,* 8 miles north-northeast of the town of Nipomo (lat. 35°08'40" N, long. 120°24'50" W). Named on Tar Spring Ridge (1967) 7.5' quadrangle.

Cold Spring [SANTA BARBARA]:
(1) *spring,* 2 miles west of San Rafael Mountain (lat. 34°42'25" N, long. 119°50'40" W; near SE cor. sec. 5, T 7 N, R 28 W). Named on San Rafael Mountain (1959) 7.5' quadrangle.
(2) *locality,* 1 mile northwest of San Marcos Pass (lat. 34°31'15" N, long. 119°50'20" W); the place is in Cold Spring Canyon (1). Named on San Marcos Pass (1959) 7.5' quadrangle. San Rafael Mountain (1943) 15' quadrangle shows Cold Spring Tavern at the site, but United States Board on Geographic Names (1962a, p. 9) rejected this name for the locality.

Cold Spring Camp [MONTEREY]: *locality,* nearly 3 miles north-northeast of Partington Point (lat. 36°12'45" N, long. 121°40'45" W; sec. 7, T 20 S, R 3 E); Cold Spring is at the place. Named on Partington Ridge (1956) 7.5' quadrangle.

Cold Spring Canyon [SANTA BARBARA]:
(1) *canyon,* drained by a stream that flows 2 miles to Los Laureles Canyon 1 mile north-northwest of San Marcos Pass (lat. 34°31'40" N, long. 119°49'45" W; sec. 8, T 5 N, R 28 W); Cold Spring (2) is in the canyon. Named

on San Marcos Pass (1959) 7.5' quadrangle.
(2) *canyon,* 2.5 miles long, along Montecito
Creek above a point 3.25 miles northeast of
downtown Santa Barbara (lat. 34°27' N, long.
119°39'10" W; at SE cor. sec. 1, T 4 N, R 27
W). Named on Santa Barbara (1952) 7.5'
quadrangle. East Fork branches northeast 0.5
mile upstream from the mouth of the main
canyon and is 2 miles long. West Fork
branches northwest 1 mile upstream from the
mouth of the main canyon and is 1.5 miles
long. Both forks are named on Santa Barbara
(1952) 7.5' quadrangle. United States Board
on Geographic Names (1961b, p. 9) rejected
the form "Cold Springs Canyon" for the name.
Cold Spring Saddle [SANTA BARBARA]:
pass, 5.5 miles northeast of downtown Santa
Barbara (lat. 34°29' N, long. 119°38'15" W;
at E line sec. 30, T 5 N, R 26 W); the pass is
near the head of East Fork Cold Spring Canyon (2). Named on Santa Barbara (1952) 7.5'
quadrangle.
Cold Spring Tavern: see **Cold Spring** [SANTA
BARBARA] (2).
Coldwater Campground [SANTA BAR-
BARA]: *locality,* 2.5 miles south-southwest
of Bald Mountain (1) along Manzana Creek
(lat. 34°46'45" N, long. 119°57'25" W).
Named on Bald Mountain (1964) 7.5' quadrangle.
Coleman Canyon [MONTEREY]: *canyon,*
drained by a stream that flows 4.5 miles to an
unnamed valley 9 miles east-southeast of
Junipero Serra Peak (lat. 36°04'45" N, long.
121°16'45" W). Named on Bear Canyon
(1949) 7.5' quadrangle. The name commemorates John W. Coleman, who received
a patent to land near the canyon in 1891
(Clark, 1991, p. 112).
Cole Spring [SANTA BARBARA]: *spring,* 6
miles west-northwest of McPherson Peak (lat.
34°55'20" N, long. 119°54'30" W). Named
on Bates Canyon (1964) 7.5' quadrangle.
Cole Spring Campground [SANTA BAR-
BARA]: *locality,* 6 miles west-northwest of
McPherson Peak (lat. 34°55'30" N, long. 119°
54'30" W); the place is 1100 feet north of Cole
Spring. Named on Bates Canyon (1964) 7.5'
quadrangle.
College Lake [SANTA CRUZ]: *intermittent
lake,* about 1.25 miles long, 2.25 miles north
of Watsonville (lat. 36°56'50" N, long. 121°
44'50" W). Named on Watsonville East (1955)
and Watsonville West (1954) 7.5' quadrangles.
The feature is shown as a permanent lake on
San Juan Bautista (1917) 15' quadrangle. It
first was called Laguna Grande and took the
name "College Lake" after a Roman Catholic orphanage, known as the college, was built
nearby in 1869 (Clark, 1986, p. 81).
College Rancho: see **Cañada de los Pinos or
College Rancho** [SANTA BARBARA].
Colson Canyon [SANTA BARBARA]: *canyon,*
drained by a stream that flows nearly 5 miles
to Tepusquet Canyon 2 miles west-northwest

of Tepusquet Peak (lat. 34°55'25" N, long.
120°13'10" W). Named on Tepusquet Canyon
(1964) 7.5' quadrangle.
Colson Canyon Campgrounds [SANTA BAR-
BARA]: *localities,* 2.25 miles north-northeast
of Tepusquet Peak (lat. 34°56'20" N, long.
120°10'05" W); the campgrounds are in
Colson Canyon. Named on Tepusquet Can-
yon (1964) 7.5' quadrangle.
Comings Creek: see **Pine Creek**
[MONTEREY] (2).
Commatri Canyon: see **Camatta Canyon**
[SAN LUIS OBISPO].
Commatri Creek: see **Camatta Creek** [SAN
LUIS OBISPO].
Commatta Canyon: see **Camatta Canyon**
[SAN LUIS OBISPO].
Commatta Creek: see **Camatta Creek** [SAN
LUIS OBISPO].
Commatti Canyon: see **Camatta Canyon**
[SAN LUIS OBISPO].
Commatti Creek: see **Camatta Creek** [SAN
LUIS OBISPO].
Concepcion [SANTA BARBARA]: *locality,* 1
mile east-northeast of Point Conception along
Southern Pacific Railroad (lat. 34°27'10" N,
long. 120°27'15" W). Named on Point Con-
ception (1953) 7.5' quadrangle. Postal authori-
ties established Concepcion post office in
1902 and discontinued it in 1953 (Frickstad,
p. 170).
Concepcion: see **Point Concepcion**, under **Point
Conception** [SANTA BARBARA].
Conception: see **Point Conception** [SANTA
BARBARA].
Condor Point [SANTA BARBARA]: *peak,* 3.5
miles east-southeast of Santa Ynez Peak (lat.
34°30'20" N, long. 119°55'25" W; sec. 21, T
5 N, R 29 W). Named on Lake Cachuma
(1959) 7.5' quadrangle.
Conejo Creek [MONTEREY]: *stream,* flows 5
miles to Finch Creek 1.5 miles north of Jamesburg (lat. 36°23'20" N, long. 121°35'35" W;
sec. 1, T 18 S, R 3 E). Named on Rana Creek
(1956) 7.5' quadrangle.
Cone Peak [MONTEREY]: *peak,* nearly 8 miles
southwest of Junipero Serra Peak (lat.
36°03'05" N, long. 121°29'45" W; sec. 2, T
22 S, R 4 E). Altitude 5155 feet. Named on
Cone Peak (1949) 7.5' quadrangle. The name
is from the shape of the peak (Clark, 1991, p.
114).
Confederate Corners [MONTEREY]: *locality,*
2 miles south-southwest of Salinas (lat.
36°38'40" N, long. 121°39'45" W). Named
on Salinas (1947) 7.5' quadrangle. The name
is from the Southerners who settled at the site
in the late 1860's; place also was known as
Springtown, or Spring Town (Clark, 1991, p.
115).
Conne Gulch [SANTA CRUZ]: *canyon,* 2 miles
long, along Bear Creek above a point 5.5 miles
northeast of the town of Boulder Creek (lat.
37°11'05" N, long. 122°03'20" W; at N line
sec. 2, T 9 S, R 2 W). Named on Castle Rock

Ridge (1955) 7.5' quadrangle. The misspelled name is for A.B. Conley, an early settler (Clark, 1986, p. 81).

Conroy Spring [SAN LUIS OBISPO]: *spring,* 3 miles west-southwest of Cholame (lat. 35°42'50" N, long. 120°21'05" W; sec. 34, T 25 S, R 15 E). Named on Cholame (1961) 7.5' quadrangle.

Constantine Rock [SAN LUIS OBISPO]: *rock,* 3.5 miles east-southeast of Point Estero, and 0.5 mile offshore (lat. 35°26'20" N, long. 120°56'40" W). Named on Cayucos (1965) 7.5' quadrangle.

Cook: see **Pinnacles** [SAN BENITO].

Cooke: see **Camp Cooke Military Reservation,** under **Vandenberg Air Force Base** [SANTA BARBARA].

Cookhouse Gulch [SANTA CRUZ]: *canyon,* drained by a stream that flows nearly 0.5 mile to Eureka Canyon 3.5 miles north of Corralitos (lat. 37°02'20" N, long. 121°49' W; near NW cor. sec. 25, T 10 S, R 1 E). Named on Loma Prieta (1955) 7.5' quadrangle.

Coon Creek [SAN LUIS OBISPO]: *stream,* flows 9 miles to the sea less than 0.5 mile northeast of Point Buchon (lat. 35°15'35" N, long. 120°53'35" W). Named on Morro Bay South (1965) and Port San Luis (1965) 7.5' quadrangles. United States Board on Geographic Names (1936b, p. 19) rejected the name "Valencia Creek" for the stream.

Cooper [MONTEREY]: *locality,* 4.5 miles northwest of Salinas along Southern Pacific Railroad (lat. 36°42'50" N, long. 121°43' W). Named on Salinas (1947, photorevised 1968 and 1975) 7.5' quadrangle. Called Coopers on Salinas (1947) 7.5' quadrangle.

Cooper Point [MONTEREY]: *promontory,* 1.5 miles northwest of Pfeiffer Point along the coast (lat. 36°14'55" N, long. 121°50'10" W; sec. 27, T 19 S, R 1 E). Named on Pfeiffer Point (1956) 7.5' quadrangle. The promontory is near the south end of El Sur grant, which J.B.R. Cooper owned.

Cooper Slough: see **Tembladero Slough** [MONTEREY].

Copperhead Canyon Creek: see **Copperhead Creek** [MONTEREY].

Copperhead Creek [MONTEREY]: *stream,* flows 5 miles to San Antonio River 11 miles southeast of Jolon (lat. 35°52'10" N, long. 121°00'25" W). Named on Bryson (1949) 7.5' quadrangle. Laizure (1925, p. 35) used the name "Copperhead Canyon Creek." The stream now enters San Antonio Reservoir.

Corbett Canyon: see **Corbit Canyon** [SAN LUIS OBISPO].

Corbit Canyon [SAN LUIS OBISPO]: *canyon,* drained by a stream that flows 4.5 miles to Arroyo Grande Creek nearly 6 miles south-southeast of Edna (lat. 35°07'25" N, long. 120°34'30" W). Named on Arroyo Grande NE (1965) 7.5' quadrangle. United States Board on Geographic Names (1967b, p. 7) rejected the form "Corbett Canyon" for the name.

Corcoran Lagoon [SANTA CRUZ]: *lake,* 1500 feet long, 0.5 mile northwest of Soquel Point near the coast (lat. 36°57'40" N, long. 121°58'50" W; sec. 20, 21, T 11 S, R 1 W). Named on Soquel (1954) 7.5' quadrangle. The name commemorates James Corcoran, a farmer in the neighborhood in the 1850's (Clark, 1986, p. 82).

Cormack Canyon [SAN LUIS OBISPO]: *canyon,* drained by a stream that flows nearly 6.5 miles to San Juan Creek 1 mile south-south-east of Shandon (lat. 35°38'25" N, long. 120°22'05" W; sec. 28, T 26 S, R 15 E). Named on Cholame (1917) 30' quadrangle. The lowermost part of the canyon is called Pfost Gulch on Cholame (1961) 7.5' quadrangle.

Corncob Canyon [MONTEREY]: *canyon,* drained by a stream that flows 1.25 miles to an unnamed canyon 2.25 miles southeast of Watsonville (lat. 36°53'05" N, long. 121°43'30" W). Named on Watsonville East (1955) 7.5' quadrangle. The name allegedly is from piles of corn cobs left from whiskey production at the place during Prohibition time (Clark, 1991, p. 118)

Coromar [SANTA BARBARA]: *locality,* 2.25 miles west of downtown Goleta along Southern Pacific Railroad (lat. 34°26'05" N, long. 119°52' W). Named on Goleta (1950) 7.5' quadrangle.

Corral Canyon [MONTEREY]: *canyon,* drained by a stream that flows 1.5 miles to Paloma Creek 12 miles southwest of Soledad (lat. 36°17'10" N, long. 121°27'30" W; near NE cor. sec. 18, T 19 S, R 5 E). Named on Sycamore Flat (1956) 7.5' quadrangle.

Corral Creek [SAN LUIS OBISPO]: *stream,* flows 2.5 miles to Alamo Creek (2) 10.5 miles southwest of Branch Mountain (lat. 35°05'50" N, long. 120°14'05" W; sec. 35, T 32 S, R 16 E). Named on Chimney Canyon (1967) 7.5' quadrangle.

Corral de Cuati: see **Corral de Quati** [SANTA BARBARA].

Corral de Piedra [SAN LUIS OBISPO]: *land grant,* southeast of San Luis Obispo around Edna. Named on Arroyo Grande NE (1965), Lopez Mountain (1965), and Pismo Beach (1965) 7.5' quadrangles. Jose Maria Villavicencio received 2 leagues in 1841 and 1846; he claimed 30,911 acres patented in 1867 (Cowan, p. 60).

Corral de Piedra Creek: see **East Corral de Piedra Creek** [SAN LUIS OBISPO]; **West Corral de Piedra Creek** [SAN LUIS OBISPO].

Corral de Quati [SANTA BARBARA]: *land grant,* north of Los Olivos. Named on Los Olivos (1959) and Zaca Creek (1959) 7.5' quadrangles. Agustin Davila received 3 leagues in 1845; Maria Antonia de la Guerra de Lataillade claimed 13,322 acres patented in 1876 (Cowan, p. 31; Cowan listed the grant under the designation "Cuati, (or Quate), Corral de").

Corral de Tierra [MONTEREY]: *land grant,* 11 miles south-southwest of Salinas. Named on Seaside (1947) and Spreckels (1947) 7.5' quadrangles. Guadalupe Figueroa received the land in 1836; H.D. McCobb claimed 4435 acres patented in 1876 (Cowan, p. 103).

Corral de Tierra: see **Corral de Tierra Valley** [MONTEREY].

Corral de Tierra Valley [MONTEREY]: *canyon,* 3 miles long, 10 miles south of Salinas on upper reaches of Watson Creek (lat. 36° 31'30" N, long. 121°41'15" W); the canyon is on and near Corral de Tierra grant. Named on Spreckels (1947) 7.5' quadrangle. Called Corral de Tierra on Salinas (1912) 15' quadrangle, where the name applies to the east part of the valley only. Postal authorities established Corral de Tierra post office in 1912, moved it 1 mile west from its original location (NW quarter sec. 19, T 16 S, R 3 E) in 1918, moved it 2 miles north in 1929, and discontinued it in 1931 (Clark, 1991, p. 119).

Corrales Canyon [SANTA BARBARA]: *canyon,* drained by a stream that flows about 6.5 miles to Santa Agueda Creek 5 miles east of Los Olivos (lat. 34°38'55" N, long. 120°01'30" W). Named on Figueroa Mountain (1959) and Los Olivos (1959) 7.5' quadrangles.

Corralillos Canyon: see **Corralitos Canyon** [SANTA BARBARA].

Corralitos [SANTA CRUZ]: *town,* 6 miles north-northwest of Watsonville (lat. 36°59'20" N, long. 121°48'20" W); the town is along Corralitos Creek on Los Corralitos grant. Named on Watsonville West (1954) 7.5' quadrangle. Postal authorities established Corralitos post office in 1861, discontinued it in 1862, reestablished it in 1876, discontinued it in 1923, and reestablished it in 1957 (Salley, p. 51).

Corralitos Canyon [SANTA BARBARA]: *canyon,* drained by a stream that flows 6 miles to Santa Maria Valley 2.5 miles south of the town of Guadalupe (lat. 34°56' N, long. 120°34'05" W). Named on Guadalupe (1959) 7.5' quadrangle. Called Corralillos Canyon on Point Sal (1947) 15' quadrangle, but United States Board on Geographic Names (1962c, p. 18) rejected this name.

Corralitos Creek [SANTA CRUZ]: *stream,* flows 13 miles to Salsipuedes Creek 1.5 miles north-northeast of Watsonville (lat. 36°56'05" N, long. 121°44'30" W). Named on Loma Prieta (1955), Watsonville East (1955), and Watsonville West (1954) 7.5' quadrangles. On San Juan Bautista (1917) 15' quadrangle, the name "Corralitos Creek" applies to present Salsipuedes Creek all the way to Pajaro River. Gudde (1949, p. 296) suggested that a stream called Arroyo de Salsipuedes on a Mexican map of 1836 is present Corralitos Creek.

Corralitos Lagoon [SANTA CRUZ]: *intermittent lake,* 0.5 mile long, 1.5 miles south-southwest of Corralitos (lat. 36°58' N, long. 121° 48'50" W); the lake is on Los Corralitos grant.

Named on Watsonville West (1954) 7.5' quadrangle. Capitola (1914) 15' quadrangle shows marsh at the place. The feature also was called Chandler Lake for the family that owned it in the 1920's (Clark, 1986, p. 72).

Corralitos Valley [SAN LUIS OBISPO]: *canyon,* drained by a stream that flows 1.25 miles to Arroyo Grande Creek nearly 6 miles southeast of Edna (lat. 35°08'50" N, long. 120°32'05" W). Named on Arroyo Grande NE (1965) 7.5' quadrangle.

Corral Point [SANTA BARBARA]: *promontory,* 1 mile south of Carrington Point on the north side of Santa Rosa Island (lat. 34°01'20" N, long. 120°02'40" W). Named on Santa Rosa Island North (1943) 7.5' quadrangle.

Corral Viejo Canyon [MONTEREY]: *canyon,* 3.5 miles long, along Conejo Creek above a point 2 miles northeast of Jamesburg (lat. 36°23'45" N, long. 121°33'30" W). Named on Rana Creek (1956) 7.5' quadrangle.

Cosio Knob [MONTEREY]: *peak,* 8 miles north-northwest of Jolon (lat. 36°04'50" N, long. 121°14' W; sec. 29, T 21 S, R 7 E). Altitude 2530 feet. Named on Cosio Knob (1949) 7.5' quadrangle. Members of the Cosio family owned land near the feature (Clark, 1991, p. 91). Smith (p. 88-93) described a cave called La Cueva Pintada that is located less than 0.5 mile north of Cosio Knob. Padres from San Antonio mission gave this name to the cave (Clark, 1991, p. 256), which is decorated with Indian pictographs—*la cueva pintada* means "the painted cave" in Spanish.

Cottage Corners [SAN BENITO]: *locality,* 1 mile north of Hollister (lat. 36°52'10" N, long. 121°24' W). Named on Hollister (1955) 7.5' quadrangle.

Cotter Spring [SAN LUIS OBISPO]: *spring,* 3.5 miles southwest of Castle Crags (lat. 35°16'05" N, long. 120°14'40" W). Named on La Panza (1967) 7.5' quadrangle.

Cottontail Creek [SAN LUIS OBISPO]: *stream,* flows 5 miles to Whale Rock Reservoir 6 miles north of the mouth of Morro Creek (lat. 35°27'50" N, long. 120°52'15" W; sec. 26, T 28 S, R 10 E). Named on Cayucos (1965), Cypress Mountain (1948), Morro Bay North (1965), and York Mountain (1948) 7.5' quadrangles.

Cottonwood Camp [MONTEREY]: *locality,* 5 miles south-southwest of Parkfield in Keyes Canyon (lat. 35°50'15" N, long. 120°28'30" W; sec. 16, T 24 S, R 14 E). Named on Cholame Hills (1961) 7.5' quadrangle.

Cottonwood Campground [SANTA BARBARA]: *locality,* 4.25 miles northwest of Big Pine Mountain along Sisquoc River (lat. 34°44'45" N, long. 119°41'50" W). Named on Big Pine Mountain (1964) 7.5' quadrangle.

Cottonwood Canyon [SANTA BARBARA]: *canyon,* drained by a stream that flows 9.5 miles to Cuyama River 9 miles east of Miranda Pine Mountain (lat. 35°02'20" N, long. 119°52'55" W). Named on Bates Canyon (1964) and Taylor Canyon (1959) 7.5' quadrangles.

Cottonwood Creek [MONTEREY]: *stream,* flows 9 miles to Cholame Creek 8 miles southeast of Parkfield (lat. 35°48'15" N, long. 120°20'25" W). Named on Cholame Valley (1961) and The Dark Hole (1961) 7.5' quadrangles. Part of the stream was called Rector Creek when the Rector family lived along it (Clark, 1991, p. 120), but United States Board on Geographic Names (1963a, p. 6) rejected this name.

Cottonwood Gulch [SAN BENITO]: *canyon,* drained by a stream that flows nearly 2 miles to Rock Springs Creek 5.5 miles north-north-east of Bitterwater (lat. 36°27'30" N, long. 120°58' W; near N line sec. 14, T 17 S, R 9 E); the canyon heads near the west end of Cottonwood Ridge. Named on Rock Spring Peak (1969) 7.5' quadrangle.

Cottonwood Pass [SAN LUIS OBISPO]: *pass,* 13 miles northeast of Shandon at the northeasternmost corner of San Luis Obispo County (lat. 35°46'50" N, long. 120°12'25" W; sec. 1, T 25 S, R 16 E). Named on Tent Hills (1942) 7.5' quadrangle. F.M. Anderson (p. 158) noted that the feature also has the name "Estrella Pass."

Cottonwood Ridge [SAN BENITO]: *ridge,* east-to northeast-trending, 1.5 miles long, 8 miles north-northeast of Bitterwater (lat. 36° 29'40" N, long. 120°57'10" W). Named on Rock Spring Peak (1969) 7.5' quadrangle.

Cottonwood Spring [SAN LUIS OBISPO]:
(1) *spring,* 5.5 miles north-northeast of Simmler (lat. 35°26' N, long. 119°57'50" W; sec. 5, T 29 S, R 19 E). Named on Las Yeguas Ranch (1959) 7.5' quadrangle.
(2) *spring,* 3.5 miles north-northwest of Caliente Mountain (lat. 35° 05'15" N, long. 119°46'40" W; near N line sec. 32, T 12 N, R 27 W). Named on Caliente Mountain (1959) 7.5' quadrangle.

Cottonwood Springs [SAN BENITO]: *springs,* 10.5 miles east-southeast of Bitterwatrer (lat. 36°18'40" N, long. 120°49'50" W; near NW cor. sec. 6, T 19 S, R 11 E). Named on Hepsedam Peak (1969) 7.5' quadrangle.

Cottonwood Well [SAN LUIS OBISPO]: *well,* 6 miles southeast of Cholame in Palo Prieto Canyon (lat. 35°40'05" N, long. 120°14'10" W; sec. 15, T 26 S, R 16 E). Named on Orchard Peak (1961) 7.5' quadrangle.

Covington Lake [MONTEREY]: *intermittent lake,* 900 feet long, nearly 3.5 miles south-southeast of Parkfield (lat. 35°51'20" N, long. 120°24'20" W; sec. 12, T 24 S, R 14 E). Named on Cholame Hills (1961) 7.5' quadrangle. The name commemorates the Covington family, who settled in Parkfield in 1883 (Clark, 1991, p. 121).

Coward Creek [SANTA CRUZ]: *stream,* flows 3.25 miles to Pajaro Valley 3.5 miles northeast of Watsonville (lat. 36°56'50" N, long.

121°42'10" W). Named on Watsonville East (1955) 7.5' quadrangle. The name commemorates John Rawson Coward, a farmer in the neighborhood as early as 1868 (Clark, 1986, p. 84).

Cow Canyon [SANTA BARBARA]: *canyon,* drained by a stream that flows 3.25 miles to the sea nearly 4 miles west-southwest of Carrington Point on Santa Rosa Island (lat. 34°01'10" N, long. 120°06'20" W). Named on Santa Rosa Island North (1943) 7.5' quadrangle.

Cowell Beach [SANTA CRUZ]: *beach,* less than 1 mile north of Point Santa Cruz in Santa Cruz (lat. 36°57'40" N, long. 122°01'25" W). Named on Santa Cruz (1954) 7.5' quadrangle. The name recalls the Cowell family, who owned the beach (Clark, 1986, p. 84).

Cox Canyon [SANTA BARBARA]: *canyon,* drained by a stream that flows 3.5 miles to Santa Barbara Canyon 2.5 miles south-southeast of Fox Mountain (lat. 34°46'50" N, long. 119°34'25" W). Named on Fox Mountain (1964) 7.5' quadrangle.

Cox Creek: see **Valencia Creek** [SANTA CRUZ].

Cox Flat [SANTA BARBARA]: *area,* 2.5 miles southeast of Fox Mountain in Santa Barbara Canyon (lat. 34°46'55" N, long. 119° 34'15" W); the place is at the mouth of Cox Canyon. Named on Fox Mountain (1964) 7.5' quadrangle.

Coxo: see **Cojo Bay** [SANTA BARBARA].

Coyote: see **Mesa Coyote** [MONTEREY].

Coyote Canyon [MONTEREY]: *canyon,* drained by a stream that flows 5.5 miles to lowlands 6 miles north-northwest of San Ardo (lat. 36°05'55" N, long. 120°57'10" W; sec. 13, T 21 S, R 9 E). Named on Nattrass Valley (1967) and San Ardo (1967) 7.5' quadrangles. The feature also was called Doig Canyon (Clark, 1991, p. 121).

Coyote Gulch [MONTEREY]: *canyon,* drained by a stream that flows nearly 3 miles to Carmel River 7.5 miles east of the mouth of the river (lat. 36°31'10" N, long. 121°47'40" W). Named on Seaside (1947) 7.5' quadrangle.

Coyote Gulch [SANTA BARBARA]: *canyon,* drained by a stream that flows 4.25 miles to Cuyama River 7 miles north-northeast of McPherson Peak (lat. 34°59'15" N, long. 119°47' W). Named on Peak Mountain (1964) 7.5' quadrangle. United States Board on Geographic Names (1965c, p. 10) rejected the name "Wells Creek" for the feature.

Coyote Hole [SAN LUIS OBISPO]: *relief feature,* 2.5 miles south of Castle Crags at a wide place in an unnamed canyon (lat. 35°16'15" N, long. 120°12'30" W). Named on La Panza (1967) 7.5' quadrangle.

Coyote Peak [SAN BENITO]: *peak,* 6.25 miles east-northeast of Hollister (lat. 36°52'40" N, long. 121°17'45" W). Altitude 1543 feet. Named on Three Sisters (1954) 7.5' quadrangle.

Coyote Point [SAN LUIS OBISPO]: *peak,* 9 miles south-southwest of Atascadero (lat. 35°23' N, long. 120°43'55" W; near SW cor. sec. 19, T 29 S, R 12 E). Altitude 1176 feet. Named on Atascadero (1965) 7.5' quadrangle.

Coyote Valley [SAN BENITO]: *valley,* 8 miles north-northwest of Panoche Pass (lat. 36°44'15" N, long. 121°03' W). Named on Panoche Pass (1968) 7.5' quadrangle.

Crawford Canyon [SANTA BARBARA]: *canyon,* 3 miles long, opens into the canyon of Santa Rosa Creek 7.5 miles southwest of the town of Los Alamos (lat. 34°38'10" N, long. 120°16'45" W). Named on Los Alamos (1959) 7.5' quadrangle.

Crazy Canyon [MONTEREY]: *canyon,* drained by a stream that flows 2 miles to Quinado Canyon 8 miles south-southwest of King City (lat. 36°05'35" N, long. 121°09'40" W; sec. 24, T 21 S, R 7 E). Named on Cosio Knob (1949) 7.5' quadrangle.

Crazy Horse Canyon [MONTEREY]: *canyon,* drained by a stream that flows 3.25 miles to Gabilan Creek 8.5 miles north-northeast of Salinas (lat. 36°46'20" N, long. 121°36'05" W). Named on San Juan Bautista (1955) 7.5' quadrangle. According to legend, the name is from a horse that ate loco weed and was called *caballo loco,* which means "crazy horse" in Spanish (Clark, 1991, p. 122).

Creston [SAN LUIS OBISPO]: *village,* 12 miles southeast of Paso Robles (lat. 35°31'10" N, long. 120°31'20" W). Named on Creston (1948) 7.5' quadrangle. Messers. Adams, Amborse, Webster, and Cressy bought 40,000 acres of Huer Huero grant and laid out the townsite in 1884; they called the place Huer Huero, but the townspeople called it Creston in honor of. Mr. Cressy (Lee and others, p. 47). Postal authorities established Creston post office in 1885 (Frickstad, p. 164).

Cristo: see **Manresa** [SANTA CRUZ].

Crocker: see **Templeton** [SAN LUIS OBISPO].

Crocker Canyon [SAN LUIS OBISPO]: *canyon,* drained by a stream that flows nearly 4.5 miles to Kern County 20 miles east-southeast of Simmler (lat. 35°13'45" N, long. 119°39'55" W; at E line sec. 13, T 31 S, R 21 E). Named on Panorama Hills (1954) and Reward (1951) 7.5' quadrangles.

Crook Point [SANTA BARBARA]: *promontory,* 3.5 miles west of Cardwell Point on the south side of San Miguel Island (lat. 34°00'50" N, long. 120°21'30" W). Named on San Miguel Island East (1950) 7.5' quadrangle. United States Coast and Geodetic Survey (p. 112) listed a shoal called Wyckoff Ledge located 1.4 miles west of Crook Point and 0.5 mile offshore.

Cross Canyon [MONTEREY]: *canyon,* drained by a stream that flows nearly 1 mile to Bixby Creek 4.5 miles north-northeast of Point Sur (lat. 36°22' N, long. 121°52'20" W; sec. 16, T 18 S, R 1 E). Named on Big Sur (1956) 7.5' quadrangle.

Crowbar Canyon [SAN LUIS OBISPO]: *canyon,* 1 mile long, opens into lowlands near the coast 7.5 miles northwest of Point San Luis (lat. 35°13'35" N, long. 120°51'55" W). Named on Port San Luis (1965) 7.5' quadrangle.

Crow Canyon [MONTEREY]: *canyon,* drained by a stream that flows 0.5 mile to Miners Gulch 5.25 miles north-northeast of Greenfield (lat. 36°23'15" N, long. 121°11'45" W; sec. 3, T 18 S, R 7 E). Named on North Chalone Peak (1969) 7.5' quadrangle.

Crows Nest [SAN LUIS OBISPO]: *peak,* 3 miles north-northeast of Cambria (lat. 35°36' N, long. 121°03'30" W; sec. 12, T 27 S, R 8 E). Named on San Simeon (1919) 15' quadrangle.

Cruessville: see **San Miguel** [SAN LUIS OBISPO].

Crystal Creek [SANTA CRUZ]: *stream,* flows nearly 2 miles to Branciforte Creek 3.25 miles north-northwest of Soquel (lat. 37°01'40" N, long. 121°59'10" W; sec. 29, T 10 S, R 1 W). Named on Laurel (1955) 7.5' quadrangle.

Crystal Knob [MONTEREY]: *peak,* 11 miles south of Jolon (lat. 35° 48'35" N, long. 121°09'45" W; sec. 25, T 24 S, R 7 E). Named on Burnett Peak (1949) 7.5' quadrangle. The name is from crystalline rocks that crop out on the feature (Clark, 1991, p. 124).

Cuarta Canyon: see **Cañada de la Cuarta** [SANTA BARBARA].

Cuaslui Creek [SANTA BARBARA]: *stream,* flows nearly 4 miles to Cañada de los Alisos 11 miles south of Tepusquet Peak (lat. 34°44'55" N, long. 120°12'15" W). Named on Foxen Canyon (1964) 7.5' quadrangle. The name is of Indian origin (Gudde, 1949, p. 85).

Cuchamma River: see **Cachuma Creek** [SANTA BARBARA].

Cuchudas Canyon [SANTA BARBARA]: *canyon,* drained by a stream that flows 1 mile to South Fork La Brea Creek 3 miles east-northeast of Manzanita Mountain (lat. 34°54'20" N, long. 120°01'50" W). Named on Manzanita Mountain (1964) 7.5' quadrangle.

Cuesta [SAN LUIS OBISPO]: *locality,* 5.5 miles north-northeast of San Luis Obispo along Southern Pacific Railroad (lat. 35°21'25" N, long. 120°38'05" W; sec. 36, T 29 S, R 12 E); the place is 0.5 mile north-northwest of Cuesta Pass. Named on San Luis Obispo (1965) 7.5' quadrangle.

Cuesta-by-the-Sea [SAN LUIS OBISPO]: *village,* 2.5 miles south-southeast of Morro Rock at the south edge of Morro Bay (lat. 35° 19'05" N, long. 120°50'45" W; sec. 13, T 30 S, R 10 E). Named on Morro Bay South (1965) 7.5' quadrangle. Cayucos (1951) 15' quadrangle has the form "Cuesta-By-The-Sea" for the name. The community is called Redfield Woods on Cayucos (1943) 15' quadrangle. The place now is part of Los Osos.

Cuesta de Los Gatos: see **Santa Cruz Mountains** [SANTA CRUZ].

Cuesta Pass [SAN LUIS OBISPO]: *pass,* 5 miles north-northeast of San Luis Obispo between the head of San Luis Obispo Creek and the head of Santa Margarita Creek (lat. 35°20'55" N, long. 120°37'50" W; near W line sec. 6, T 30 S, R 13 E). Named on San Luis Obispo (1965) 7.5' quadrangle. Called Cuesto Pass on Hamlin's (1904) map. Parke (p. 2, 16) used the names "San Luis Pass" and "San Louis Pass" for the feature.

Cueva Pintada: see **La Cueva Pintada**, under **Cosio Knob** [MONTEREY]; **Painted Cave** [SANTA BARBARA] (2).

Cueva Valdaze [SANTA BARBARA]: *cave,* 3.5 miles west of Diablo Point on Santa Cruz Island (lat. 34°03'05" N, long. 119°49'05" W). Named on Santa Cruz Island B (1943) 7.5' quadrangle. Doran (p. 146) called the feature Cueva Valdez, and stated that it is at Valdez Harbor, one of the principal landing places on the island.

Cummings Canyon [SANTA CRUZ]: *canyon,* drained by a stream that flows 1.5 miles to Coward Creek 4 miles northeast of Watsonville (lat. 36°57' N, long. 121°41'50" W). Named on Watsonville East (1955) 7.5' quadrangle.

Cushing [SAN LUIS OBISPO]: *locality,* 2.25 miles north of Santa Margarita along Southern Pacific Railroad (lat. 35°25'35" N, long. 120°36'10" W). Named on Santa Margarita (1965) 7.5' quadrangle.

Cushman Hill [SAN BENITO]: *peak,* 2.5 miles south-southwest of Mount Johnson (lat. 36°34'50" N, long. 121°17'15" W; sec. 35, T 15 S, R 6 E). Altitude 2926 feet. Named on Mount Johnson (1968) 7.5' quadrangle.

Cuyama [SAN LUIS OBISPO-SANTA BARBARA]:

(1) *land grant,* at the west end of Cuyama Valley on San Luis Obispo-Santa Barbara county line. Named on Bates Canyon (1964), Miranda Pine Mountain (1967) and Taylor Canyon (1959) 7.5' quadrangles. Called Cuyama No. 1 on McKittrick (1912) 30' quadrangle and on Branch Mountain (1952) 15' quadrangle. Jose Maria Rojo received 5 leagues in 1843; Maria Antonia de la Guerra de Lataillade claimed 22,193 acres patented in 1877 (Cowan, p. 32).

(2) *land grant,* in the central and east parts of Cuyama Valley on San Luis Obispo-Santa Barbara county line. Named on Ballinger Canyon (1943), Bates Canyon (1964), Caliente Mountain (1959), Cuyama (1964), New Cuyama (1964), Peak Mountain (1964), and Taylor Canyon (1959) 7.5' quadrangles. Called Cuyama No. 2 on McKittrick (1912) 30' quadrangle. Cesario Lataillade received 11 leagues in 1846 and his heirs claimed 48,828 acres patented in 1879 (Cowan, p. 32).

Cuyama [SANTA BARBARA]: *village,* 36 miles north of Santa Barbara in Cuyama Valley (lat. 34°56'05" N, long. 119°36'45" W). Named on Cuyama (1964) 7.5' quadrangle.

Postal authorities established Cuyama post office in 1942 (Salley, p. 54).

Cuyama: see **New Cuyama** [SANTA BARBARA].

Cuyama Hot Springs: see **Hot Spring** [SANTA BARBARA].

Cuyama Mountains: see **Sierra Madre Mountains** [SANTA BARBARA].

Cuyama Peak [SANTA BARBARA]: *peak,* 15 miles southeast of the village of Cuyama (lat. 34°45'15" N, long. 119°28'30" W). Altitude 5875 feet. Named on Cuyama Peak (1943) 7.5' quadrangle.

Cuyama Plain: see **Cuyama Valley** [SAN LUIS OBISPO-SANTA BARBARA].

Cuyama Range: see **Sierra Madre Mountains** [SANTA BARBARA].

Cuyama River [SAN LUIS OBISPO-SANTA BARBARA]: *stream,* heads in Ventura County and flows 92 miles along and near San Luis Obispo-Santa Barbara county line to join Sisquoc River and form Santa Maria River 13 miles southeast of the town of Nipomo (lat. 34°54'10" N, long. 120°18'40" W; sec. 36, T 10 N, R 33 W); the stream flows through Cuyama Valley. Named on Caliente Mountain (1959), Chimney Canyon (1967), Cuyama (1964), Cuyama Peak (1943), Fox Mountain (1964), Huasna Peak (1967), Miranda Pine Mountain (1967), New Cuyama (1964), Peak Mountain (1964), Taylor Canyon (1959), and Twitchell Dam (1959) 7.5' quadrangles. Called Guyamas River on Goddard's (1857) map, Rio S. Maria on Parke's (1854-1855) map, R. Guaymas or Sta. Maria on Colton's (1863) map, and Santa Maria River on California Mining Bureau's (1909c) map. According to Kroeber (1916, p. 41), the term "Cuyama" is from an Indian place name.

Cuyamas Range: see **Sierra Madre Mountains** [SANTA BARBARA].

Cuyamas Valley: see **Cuyama Valley** [SAN LUIS OBISPO-SANTA BARBARA].

Cuyama Valley [SAN LUIS OBISPO-SANTA BARBARA]: *valley,* extends along the upper part of Cuyama River southwest of Caliente Range on San Luis-Obispo-Santa Barbara county line. Named on Ballinger Canyon (1943), Caliente Mountain (1959), Cuyama (1964), Cuyama Peak (1943), Fox Mountain (1964), Miranda Pine Mountain (1967), New Cuyama (1964), Peak Mountain (1964), and Taylor Canyon (1959) 7.5' quadrangles. Parke (p. 6) called the valley Cuyama plain, and Fairbanks (1895, p. 274) called it Cuyamas Valley.

Cuyler Harbor [SANTA BARBARA]: *embayment,* 3.5 miles northwest of Cardwell Point on the north side of San Miguel Island (lat. 34°03' N, long. 120°21' W). Named on San Miguel Island East (1950) 7.5' quadrangle. James Alden of United States Coast Survey named the feature in 1852 for Lieutenant R.M. Cuyler, a member of his surveying party (Gudde, 1949, p. 87).

Cypress Cove [MONTEREY]: *embayment,* east of Point Lobos on the south side of Carmel Bay (lat. 36°31'20" N, long. 121°56'55" W). Named on Monterey (1947) 7.5' quadrangle. California Department of Parks and Recreation's map has the name "North Point" for the promontory situated west of Cypress Cove.

Cypress Mountain [SAN LUIS OBISPO]: *peak,* 7.5 miles east-northeast of Cambria (lat. 35°36'05" N, long. 120°57'15" W; sec. 12, T 27 S, R 9 E). Altitude 2933 feet. Named on Cypress Mountain (1948) 7.5' quadrangle.

Cypress Point [MONTEREY]: *promontory,* 4.5 miles southwest of Point Pinos along the coast (lat. 36°34'50" N, long. 121°58'40" W). Named on Monterey (1947, photorevised 1968) 7.5' quadrangle. Called Point Cypress on Monterey (1947) 7.5' quadrangle, but United States Board on Geographic Names (1967d, p. 4) rejected this form of the name. H.R. Wagner (p. 476) tentatively identified the promontory as probably the one that Cabrillo called Cabo de Nieve in 1542. Gudde (1949, p. 87) noted that the name "La Punta de cipresses" was used in 1774. Taylor (v. 1, p. 172) recorded the name "Punta de los Cipreses" for the feature.

Cypress Point Rock [MONTEREY]: *rock,* 4.5 miles southwest of Point Pinos, and 650 feet offshore (lat. 36°34'50" N, long. 121°58'40" W); the feature is at Cypress Point. Named on Monterey (1947, photorevised 1968) 7.5' quadrangle. Called Point Cypress Rock on Monterey (1947) 7.5' quadrangle.

Cypress Ridge [SANTA BARBARA]: *ridge,* southwest-trending, 2 miles long, 3.25 miles west of Tranquillon Mountain (lat. 34°34'35" N, long. 120°37' W). Named on Point Arguello (1959) and Tranquillon Mountain (1959) 7.5' quadrangles.

– D –

Dairy Creek [SAN LUIS OBISPO]: *stream,* flows 4.5 miles to Chorro Creek 5 miles northwest of San Luis Obispo (lat. 35°19'30" N, long. 120°44' W). Named on San Luis Obispo (1965) 7.5' quadrangle.

Dairy Flat [SAN BENITO]: *valley,* drained by a stream that flows 2.25 miles to Las Aguilas Creek (1) 7 miles north of Panoche Pass (lat. 36°43'40" N, long. 121°02'05" W). Named on Panoche Pass (1968) and Ruby Canyon (1968) 7.5' quadrangles.

Dairy Gulch [MONTEREY]: *canyon,* drained by a stream that flows 0.5 mile to Bixby Creek 4.5 miles north-northeast of Point Sur (lat. 36°22'10" N, long. 121°51'55" W; sec. 16, T 18 S, R 1 E). Named on Big Sur (1956) 7.5' quadrangle.

Damond Ridge [SANTA CRUZ]: *ridge,* south-southeast-trending, 1.25 miles long, 6 miles

north-northeast of the town of Boulder Creek (lat. 37°12'35" N, long. 122°05'20" W; in and near sec. 28, T 8 S, R 2 W). Named on Castle Rock Ridge (1955) 7.5' quadrangle.

Damsite Canyon [SANTA BARBARA]: *canyon,* drained by a stream that flows 3 miles to the sea 2.5 miles east of Point Conception (lat. 34°27' N, long. 120°25'30" W). Named on Point Conception (1953) 7.5' quadrangle.

Danford Canyon [SAN LUIS OBISPO]: *canyon,* drained by a stream that flows 2 miles to Suey Creek nearly 5 miles east of Nipomo (lat. 35°03'15" N, long. 120°23'35" W; near N line sec. 7, T 11 N, R 33 W). Named on Nipomo (1965) 7.5' quadrangle.

Dani Ridge [MONTEREY]: *ridge,* west-trending, 2 miles long, 4 miles east-northeast of Point Sur (lat. 36°19'20" N, long. 121° 50' W). Named on Big Sur (1956) 7.5' quadrangle. The name is for the Dani family, pioneers of the neighborhood (Clark, 1991, p. 128).

Dani Ridge: see **Pfeiffer Ridge** [MONTEREY].

Dani's Beach: see **Pfeffer Beach** [MONTEREY].

Danish Creek [MONTEREY]: *stream,* flows 6.25 miles to Carmel River 3.25 miles northeast of Uncle Sam Mountain (lat. 36°22'20" N, long. 121°39'45" W; near NW cor. sec. 16, T 18 S, R 3 E). Named on Carmel Valley (1956) and Ventana Cones (1956) 7.5' quadrangles.

Dark Range Peak [SAN LUIS OBISPO]: *peak,* 6.5 miles northeast of the mouth of Morro Creek (lat. 35°26'50" N, long. 120°47'20" W; sec. 33, T 28 S, R 11 E). Altitude 2005 feet. Named on Morro Bay North (1965) 7.5' quadrangle.

Davenport [SANTA CRUZ]: *village,* 10 miles west-northwest of Santa Cruz near the coast (lat. 37°00'40" N, long. 122°11'35" W). Named on Davenport (1955) 7.5' quadrangle. The name is from nearby Davenport Landing (Gudde, 1949, p. 89). Postal authorities established Davenport post office in 1906; a previous Davenport post office was located at Davenport Landing (Salley, p. 55). California Mining Bureau's (1917a) map shows a place called Lagos located along the railroad between Davenport and Godola (present Gordola).

Davenport Creek [SAN LUIS OBISPO]: *stream,* flows nearly 6 miles to San Luis Obispo Creek 3.5 miles northeast of Avila Beach (lat. 35°13'20" N, long. 120°41'20" W). Named on Arroyo Grande NE (1965) and Pismo Beach (1965) 7.5' quadrangles.

Davenport Landing [SANTA CRUZ]: *locality,* 1.5 miles northwest of Davenport along the coast (lat. 37°01'30" N, long. 122°12'55" W). Named on Davenport (1955) 7.5' quadrangle. Captain John P. Davenport began a whaling station at the place in the 1850's and built a wharf there 450 feet long; a stage station was at the landing in 1872, and a stage station called Berry Falls was between Davenport

Landing and present Swanton (Hoover, Rensch, and Rensch, p. 475, 478). Postal authorities established Davenport post office at Davenport Landing in 1874 and discontinued it in 1889; they established another Davenport post office later at the village of Davenport (Salley, p. 55).

Davey Brown Campground [SANTA BARBARA]: *locality,* 4 miles south-southwest of Bald Mountain (1) in Munch Canyon (lat. 34° 45'25" N, long. 119°57'05" W); the place is near Davey Brown Creek. Named on Bald Mountain (1964) 7.5' quadrangle.

Davey Brown Creek [SANTA BARBARA]: *stream,* flows 4.5 miles to Manzana Creek nearly 3 miles south of Bald Mountain (1) (lat. 34°46'20" N, long. 119°56'35" W). Named on Bald Mountain (1964) 7.5' quadrangle. The name recalls an early settler who lived near the creek in the 1880's (Rife, p. 119). The stream drains Fir Canyon.

Davis: see **Lonnie Davis Campground** [SANTA BARBARA].

Davis Canyon [MONTEREY]:
(1) *canyon,* 1 mile long, along San Carpoforo Creek above a point 12 miles east-southeast of Cape San Martin (lat. 35°49'10" N, long. 121°16'25" W; sec. 25, T 24 S, R 6 E). Named on Burro Mountain (1949) 7.5' quadrangle. Called Devils Canyon on Cape San Martin (1921) 15' quadrangle.
(2) *canyon,* 3.5 miles long, opens into lowlands 3.5 miles east-northeast of Jolon (lat. 35°59'25" N, long. 121°07'15" W). Named on Espinosa Canyon (1949) 7.5' quadrangle. The name commemorates members of the Davis family who received patents to land in and near the canyon in the 1890's and in 1905 (Clark, 1991, p. 129).

Davis Canyon [SAN LUIS OBISPO]: *canyon,* drained by a stream that flows 3 miles to See Canyon 2.25 miles north of Avila Beach (lat. 35°12'45" N, long. 120°43'25" W; sec. 19, T 31 S, R 12 E). Named on Pismo Beach (1965) and Port San Luis (1965) 7.5' quadrangles.

Davis Canyon [SANTA BARBARA]: *canyon,* drained by a stream that flows nearly 4 miles to Green Canyon 4 miles north of McPherson Peak (lat. 34°56'55" N, long. 119°49'15" W). Named on Peak Mountain (1964) 7.5' quadrangle.

Davy Brown Canyon: see **Fir Canyon** [SANTA BARBARA].

Day Valley [SANTA CRUZ]: *valley,* 2.5 miles west of Corralitos (lat. 36°59'40" N, long. 121°51'15" W). Named on Watsonville West (1954) 7.5' quadrangle. The name is for Darius Washington Day and his wife, who bought land at the place in 1862 (Clark, 1986, p. 92).

Deadman Canyon [SANTA BARBARA]:
(1) *canyon,* drained by a stream that flows 5.25 miles to Cuyama Valley 7.5 miles north of McPherson Peak (lat. 34°59'50" N, long. 119°49'50" W). Named on Peak Mountain (1964) 7.5' quadrangle.

(2) *canyon,* 2 miles long, along San Jose Creek above a point 0.5 mile south-southwest of San Marcos Pass (lat. 34°30'15" N, long. 119°49'45" W; near NE cor. sec. 20, T 5 N, R 28 W). Named on Goleta (1903) 15' quadrangle.

Deadman Flat [SAN LUIS OBISPO]: *area,* 12.5 miles south of Simmler (lat. 35°10'30" N, long. 119°59'30" W; near NE cor. sec. 1, T 32 S, R 18 E). Named on Chimineas Ranch (1959) 7.5' quadrangle.

Deadman Gulch [MONTEREY]: *canyon,* drained by a stream that flows 3.5 miles to Lynch Canyon 8.5 miles north-northwest of Bradley (lat. 35°58'55" N, long. 120°51' W; sec. 25, T 22 S, R 10 E). Named on Wunpost (1949) 7.5' quadrangle, where the name extends into a north branch that is called Dry Gulch on Pancho Rico Valley (1967) 7.5' quadrangle.

Deadman Gulch [SANTA CRUZ]: *canyon,* drained by a stream that flows 2.5 miles to Big Creek 6 miles north of Davenport (lat. 37° 06'05" N, long. 122°11'30" W). Named on Davenport (1955) 7.5' quadrangle.

De Alvarez Creek [SAN BENITO]: *stream,* flows nearly 4 miles to Bitterwater Creek 6 miles southeast of Bitterwater (lat. 36°19' N, long. 120°55'35" W; sec. 31, T 18 S, R 10 E). Named on Lonoak (1969) 7.5' quadrangle.

Dean [MONTEREY]: *locality,* 1.25 miles northwest of Gonzales along Southern Pacific Railroad (lat. 36°31'35" N, long. 121°27'40" W). Named on Gonzales (1921) 15' quadrangle.

Deer Canyon [MONTEREY]: *canyon,* drained by a stream that flows 7.5 miles to Portuguese Canyon (2) 8.5 miles east-southeast of Bradley (lat. 35°50' N, long. 120°39'20" W; near NE cor. sec. 22, T 24 S, R 12 E). Named on San Miguel (1948) and Valleton (1948) 7.5' quadrangles.

Deer Canyon [SAN LUIS OBISPO]:
(1) *canyon,* drained by a stream that flows 1 mile to the sea 3.5 miles northwest of Point San Luis (lat. 35°11'20" N, long. 120°48'40" W). Named on Port San Luis (1965) 7.5' quadrangle. United States Board on Geographic Names (1967c, p. 2) approved the name "Little Irish Canyon" for the feature.
(2) *canyon,* drained by a stream that flows 1 mile to Corbit Canyon 4.25 miles southeast of Edna (lat. 35°09'35" N, long. 120°33'25" W). Named on Arroyo Grande NE (1965) 7.5' quadrangle. Called Bee Canyon on Arroyo Grande (1897) 15' quadrangle, where present Bee Canyon is called Deer Canyon.
(3) *canyon,* drained by a stream that flows 2 miles to Huasna River 4 miles north-north-west of Huasna Peak (lat. 35°05'35" N, long. 120°21'45" W). Named on Huasna Peak (1967) 7.5' quadrangle. Called Bear Canyon on Nipomo (1922) 15' quadrangle, but United States Board on Geographic Names (1963b, p. 14) rejected this name for the feature.

Deer Creek [MONTEREY]: *stream, flows 5*

miles to San Antonio River 8.5 miles southeast of Jolon (lat. 35°53'20" N, long. 121°03'05" W). Named on Bryson (1949) and Williams Hill (1949) 7.5' quadrangles.

Deer Creek [SANTA CRUZ]: *stream,* flows nearly 4 miles to Bear Creek 4 miles northeast of the town of Boulder Creek (lat. 37°10'15" N, long. 122°04'25" W; near SW cor. sec. 3, T 9 S, R 2 W). Named on Castle Rock Ridge (1955) 7.5' quadrangle.

Deer Flat [SAN LUIS OBISPO]: *area,* 11.5 miles east-northeast of the village of San Simeon (lat. 35°41'45" N, long. 121°00'05" W; sec. 4, 9, T 26 S, R 9 E). Named on Pebblestone Shut-in (1959) 7.5' quadrangle.

Deer Park Canyon [SANTA BARBARA]: *canyon,* drained by a stream that heads in Ventura County and flows nearly 5 miles to Cuyama Valley 9.5 miles east-southeast of the village of Cuyama (lat. 34°51'50" N, long. 119°28'45" W; sec. 18, T 9 N, R 25 W). Named on Cuyama Peak (1943) 7.5' quadrangle.

Deer Pasture [MONTEREY]: *area,* 4.25 miles south of Tassajara Hot Springs (lat. 36°10'25" N, long. 121°32'20" W; sec. 21, T 20 S, R 4 E). Named on Tassajara Hot Springs (1956) 7.5' quadrangle.

Deer Ridge [SANTA CRUZ]: *ridge,* south-southwest-trending, 1 mile long, 6.5 miles north-northeast of the town of Boulder Creek (lat. 37°12'50" N, long. 122°04'45" W; sec. 21, 28, T 8 S, R 2 W). Named on Castle Rock Ridge (1955) 7.5' quadrangle.

Deer Spring [SAN LUIS OBISPO]: *spring,* 4 miles south of Wilson Corner (lat. 35°24'40" N, long. 120°23'05" W; sec. 8, T 29 S, R 15 E). Named on Wilson Corner (1966) 7.5' quadrangle.

Deer Spring [SANTA BARBARA]: *spring,* 1200 feet north-northwest of the top of McPherson Peak (lat. 34°53'30" N, long. 119°47'45" W). Named on Peak Mountain (1964) 7.5' quadrangle.

Deer Valley [SANTA CRUZ]: *canyon,* 1 mile long, opens into lowlands 3.25 miles west-northwest of Corralitos (lat. 37°00'30" N, long. 121°51'45" W). Named on Loma Prieta (1955) 7.5' quadrangle.

Defiance: see **Mount Defiance** [SAN BENITO].

De la Guerra Camp [SANTA BARBARA]: *locality,* 5.25 miles southeast of Figueroa Mountain (lat. 34°40'55" N, long. 119°55'30" W; sec. 15, T 7 N, R 29 W). Named on Figueroa Mountain (1959) 7.5' quadrangle.

De la Guerra Gulch: see **Placer Creek** [SAN LUIS OBISPO].

De la Questa Canyon [SANTA BARBARA]: *canyon,* drained by a stream that flows nearly 2 miles to lowlands 1 mile south of Buellton (lat. 34°35'55" N, long. 120°11'40" W). Named on Solvang (1959) 7.5' quadrangle.

Deleissigues Creek [SAN LUIS OBISPO]: *stream,* flows 2.5 miles to Nipomo Creek 0.5 mile west-southwest of the town of Nipomo

(lat. 35°02'25" N, long. 120°28'55" W). Named on Nipomo (1965) 7.5' quadrangle.

Del Mar Heights: see **Morro Bay** [SAN LUIS OBISPO] (2).

Delmonte [MONTEREY]: *locality,* east of Monterey along Southern Pacific Railroad (lat. 36°36'05" N, long. 121°52'10" W). Named on Seaside (1947, photorevised 1968) 7.5' quadrangle. Called Del Monte on Seaside (1947) 7.5' quadrangle. Monterey (1913) 15' quadrangle shows Hotel Del Monte just south of the place. Charles Crocker named the hotel (Gudde, 1949, p. 92). Postal authorities established Delmonte post office in 1882 and discontinued it in 1883; they established Del Monte post office in 1901, discontinued it for a time in 1911, and discontinued it finally in 1952 (Frickstad, p. 106).

Del Monte Heights [MONTEREY]: *district,* 1 mile east of downtown Seaside (lat. 36°36'45" N, long. 121°50' W). Named on Seaside (1947) 7.5' quadrangle. George W. Phelps and F.M. Hilby laid out the place in 1909—now it is a residential district in Seaside (Clark, 1991, p. 133).

Del Monte Junction [MONTEREY]: *locality,* east of Castroville along Southern Pacific Railroad (lat. 38°45'30" N, long. 121°44'30" W). Named on San Juan Bautista (1917) 15' quadrangle. Prunedale (1954) 7.5' quadrangle shows the place as part of Castroville.

Del Monte Lake [MONTEREY]: *lake,* 1150 feet long, at Del Monte (lat. 36°35'55" N, long. 121°52'10" W). Named on Seaside (1947) 7.5' quadrangle.

Del Rey Oaks [MONTEREY]: *town,* southeast of Seaside (lat. 36°35'30" N, long. 121°50' W). Named on Seaside (1947, photorevised 1968) 7.5' quadrangle. The town incorporated in 1953. Before incorporation, the place was known as Del Rey Woods (Clark, 1991, p. 135). Postal authorities established Del Rey Oaks post office in 1968 (Salley, p. 57).

Del Rey Woods: see **Del Rey Oaks** [MONTEREY].

Demesio Spring [SANTA BARBARA]: *spring,* 5.5 miles south of Santa Cruz Mountain (lat. 34°37'50" N, long. 119°49'35" W). Named on San Rafael Mountain (1959) 7.5' quadrangle.

Demijohn Spring [SANTA BARBARA]: *spring,* 2.5 miles south of Salisbury Potrero (lat. 34°47'10" N, long. 119°42'05" W). Named on Salisbury Potrero (1964) 7.5' quadrangle.

De Redwood: see **Redwood Lodge** [SANTA CRUZ].

Destroyer Rock [SANTA BARBARA]: *rock,* nearly 2 miles north of Point Arguello, and 700 feet offshore (lat. 34°36'10" N, long. 120°38'40" W). Named on Point Arguello (1959) 7.5' quadrangle.

De Vaul Canyon [SANTA BARBARA]: *canyon,* drained by a stream that flows 2.5 miles to Lake Cachuma 4 miles northeast of Santa

Ynez Peak (lat. 34°33'35" N, long. 119°55' W). Named on Lake Cachuma (1959) 7.5' quadrangle. Called Bear Canyon on Santa Ynez (1905) 30' quadrangle.

Devil Hill [MONTEREY]: *peak,* 2.5 miles south of Monterey (lat. 36° 34' N, long. 121°53'45" W). Named on Monterey (1947) 7.5' quadrangle. Called Devils Hill on Monterey (1913) 15' quadrangle.

Devils Canyon [MONTEREY]: *canyon,* drained by a stream that flows 2.5 miles to Big Creek (2) 4.5 miles north-northwest of Lopez Point (lat. 36°04'35" N, long. 121°35'40" W; near W line sec. 25, T 21 S, R 3 E). Named on Lopez Point (1956) 7.5' quadrangle. The canyon divides at the head to form Middle Fork and South Fork. Middle Fork is 4 miles long and South Fork is nearly 4 miles long. North Fork branches off less than 2 miles from the mouth of the main canyon and is 2.5 miles long. All the forks are named on Lopez Point (1956) 7.5' quadrangle.

Devils Canyon [SAN BENITO]: *canyon,* drained by a stream that flows nearly 4 miles to San Benito River 3.5 miles north-northeast of Bitterwater (lat. 36°25'35" N, long. 120°58'05" W). Named on Rock Spring Peak (1969) 7.5' quadrangle.

Devils Canyon [SANTA BARBARA]: *canyon,* drained by a stream that flows 2.5 miles to Santa Ynez River 6 miles south-southeast of Little Pine Mountain (lat. 34°31'20" N, long. 119°41'15" W; at SE cor. sec. 10, T 5 N, R 27 W). Named on Little Pine Mountain (1964) 7.5' quadrangle.

Devils Canyon: see **Davis Canyon** [MONTEREY] (1).

Devils Caudron [MONTEREY]: *water feature,* rocky place in the sea just south of Point Lobos (lat. 36°31'05" N, long. 121°57'15" W). Named on Monterey (1947) 7.5' quadrangle.

Devils Gap [SAN LUIS OBISPO]: *narrows,* 4.5 miles west-southwest of Atascadero (2) along Morro Creek (lat. 35°27'40" N, long. 120°44'20" W). Named on Atascadero (1965) 7.5' quadrangle.

Devils Hill: see **Devil Hill** [MONTEREY].

Devils Peak [MONTEREY]: *peak,* 8 miles northeast of Point Sur (lat. 36°22'35" N, long. 121°47'05" W). Altitude 4158 feet. Named on Mount Carmel (1956) 7.5' quadrangle.

Devil's Peak: see **Diablo Point** [SANTA BARBARA].

Devon [SANTA BARBARA]: *locality,* less than 1 mile east-northeast of Casmalia (2) along Southern Pacific Railroad (lat. 34°50'30" N, long. 120°31'05" W). Named on Casmalia (1959) 7.5' quadrangle.

Diablo Anchorage [SANTA BARBARA]: *embayment,* less than 0.5 mile west of Diablo Point on the north side of Santa Cruz Island (lat. 34°03'25" N, long. 119°45'50" W). Named on Santa Cruz Island B (1943) 7.5' quadrangle.

Diablo Canyon [SAN LUIS OBISPO]: *canyon,* drained by a stream that flows 5 miles to the sea 6.5 miles northwest of Point San Luis (lat. 35°12'45" N, long. 120°51'25" W). Named on Port San Luis (1965) 7.5' quadrangle.

Diablo Canyon [SANTA BARBARA]: *canyon,* drained by a stream that flows 6.25 miles to Agua Caliente Canyon 3.5 miles south of Hildreth Peak (lat. 34°32'50" N, long. 119°33'30" W). Named on Hildreth Peak (1964) and Old Man Mountain (1943) 7.5' quadrangles. East Fork branches southeast 2 miles upstream from the mouth of the main canyon; it is 2.25 miles long and is named on Hildreth Peak (1964) 7.5' quadrangle.

Diablo Canyon: see **Lauro Canyon** [SANTA BARBARA].

Diablo Gulch [SANTA BARBARA]: *canyon,* drained by a stream that flows 1.5 miles to Corralitos Creek 4.5 miles north of Corralitos (lat. 37°03'05" N, long. 121°49'15" W; sec. 23, T 10 S, R 1 E). Named on Loma Prieta (1955) 7.5' quadrangle.

Diablo Point [SANTA BARBARA]: *promontory,* 10 miles east of Fraser Point on the north side of Santa Cruz Island (lat. 34°03'30" N, long. 119°45'30" W). Named on Santa Cruz Island B (1943) 7.5' quadrangle. The feature is called Punta Diablo on Bremner's (1932) map, which shows a peak called Picacho Diablo located about 2.5 miles southwest of Diablo Point. Goodyear (1890, p. 156) called the same peak Picacho del Diablo, and Loew (p. 215) called it Devil's Peak.

Diablo Range [MONTEREY-SAN BENITO]: *range,* extends from Carquinez Strait in Contra Costa County southeast to Antelope Valley in Kern County; the east part of San Benito County and the southeasternmost part of Monterey County are in the range. Named on Santa Cruz (1956) and San Luis Obispo (1956) 1°x 2° quadrangles. Mount Diablo is near the northwest end of the range in Contra Costa County. Called Sierra del Monte Diablo on Parke's (1854-1855) map. Whitney (p. 2) called it Monte Diablo Range and stated that it "is so called from the conspicuous point of that name." United States Board on Geographic Names (1933, p. 264) rejected the names "Monte Diablo Range," "Mount Diablo Range," and "Sierra del Monte Diablo" for the feature.

Dibblee Hill [SANTA BARBARA]: *peak,* 1 mile south of downtown Santa Barbara and northwest of Punta del Castillo (present Point Castillo) (lat. 34°24'20" N, long. 119°41'50" W). Named on Santa Barbara (1944) 7.5' quadrangle.

Dicks Harbor: see **Platts Harbor** [SANTA BARBARA].

Difficult Spring [SANTA BARBARA]: *spring,* 2.25 miles east-southeast of Tepusquet Peak (lat. 34°54' N, long. 120°08'45" W). Named on Tepusquet Canyon (1964) 7.5' quadrangle.

Dinsmore Canyon: see **San Ysidro Canyon** [SANTA BARBARA].

Dip Creek [SAN LUIS OBISPO]: *stream,* flows 10 miles to Nacimiento River 6.5 miles northeast of Lime Mountain (lat. 35°44'30" N, long. 120°54'35" W; sec. 20, T 25 S, R 10 E). Named on Adelaida (1948) and Lime Mountain (1948) 7.5' quadrangles. The stream now enters an arm of Nacimiento Reservoir

Divide [SANTA BARBARA]: *locality,* 8.5 miles south of Santa Maria along Pacific Coast Railroad (lat. 34°49'40" N, long. 120°27' W); the place is at the divide between Graciosa Canyon and Harris Canyon. Named on Lompoc (1905) 30' quadrangle.

Divide Camp [MONTEREY]: *locality,* 6 miles south-southwest of Jamesburg (lat. 36°17'25" N, long. 121°37' W; near W line sec. 11, T 19 S, R 3 E); the place is less than 0.5 mile west of Church Creek Divide. Named on Chews Ridge (1956) 7.5' quadrangle.

Divide Canyon [MONTEREY]: *canyon,* drained by a stream that flows 3 miles to Miners Gulch 3.25 miles south of North Chalone Peak (lat. 36°24' N, long. 121°12'25" W; near NE cor. sec. 4, T 18 S, R 7 E). Named on North Chalone Peak (1969) 7.5' quadrangle.

Divide Peak [SANTA BARBARA]: *peak,* 7.5 miles north-northeast of Rincon Point (lat. 34°28'35" N, long. 119°26'40" W; sec. 36, T 5 N, R 25 W). Altitude 4690 feet. Named on White Ledge Peak (1952) 7.5' quadrangle.

Division Knoll [MONTEREY]: *peak,* 5 miles north of Point Sur near the coast (lat. 36°22'30" N, long. 121°54'05" W; sec. 7, T 18 S, R 1 E). Named on Point Sur (1956) and Soberanes Point (1956) 7.5' quadrangles.

Dixon Canyon [SAN BENITO]: *canyon,* drained by a stream that flows nearly 4 miles to Tully Creek 3.5 miles southeast of Bitterwater (lat. 36°20'50" N, long. 120°56'55" W; sec. 24, T 18 S, R 9 E). Named on Lonoak (1969) 7.5' quadrangle.

Dixon Spring [SAN BENITO]: *spring,* 15 miles east-northeast of Bitterwater along Los Pinos Creek (lat. 36°28'35" N, long. 120°46'20" W; sec. 4, T 17 S, R 11 E). Named on Hernandez Reservoir (1969) 7.5' quadrangle, where a windmill symbol marks the feature.

Docas [MONTEREY]: *locality,* 5 miles northnorthwest of San Ardo along Southern Pacific Railroad (lat. 36°05' N, long. 120°56'50" W; sec. 24, T 21 S, R 9 E). Named on San Ardo (1956) 15' quadrangle. Docas is between San Ardo and San Lucas; the name was coined from the last letters of the names of these two places (Gudde, 1949, p. 96).

Docs Spring Campground [SANTA BARBARA]: *locality,* 7 miles west-northwest of McPherson Peak (lat. 34°56'05" N, long. 119° 54'50" W). Named on Bates Canyon (1964) 7.5' quadrangle.

Doig Canyon: see **Coyote Canyon** [MONTEREY].

Dolan Canyon [MONTEREY]: *canyon,* drained by a stream that flows nearly 2 miles to the sea 6.25 miles southeast of Partington Point

(lat. 36°06'20" N, long. 121°37'30" W; sec. 15, T 21 S, R 3 E). Named on Lopez Point (1956) 7.5' quadrangle. Fink (p. 209) associated the name with Phil Dolan, an early settler in the neighborhood.

Dolan Rock [MONTEREY]: *rock,* 150 feet long, 8 miles southeast of Partington Point, and 75 feet offshore (lat. 36°05'05" N, long. 121° 37' W); the feature is 1.5 miles south-southeast of the mouth of Dolan Canyon. Named on Lopez Point (1956) 7.5' quadrangle.

Dolans Hot Spring: see **Big Creek** [MONTEREY] (2).

Dolan's Hot Sulphur Spring: see **Big Creek** [MONTEREY] (2).

Dolores Creek [MONTEREY]: *stream,* flows nearly 1 mile to Big Sur River 1.5 miles southsouthwest of Ventana Cone (lat. 36°15'05" N, long. 121°41'35" W; sec. 25, T 19 S, R 2 E). Named on Partington Ridge (1956) 7.5' quadrangle.

Don Victor Campground [SANTA BARBARA]: *locality,* 4.25 miles east-southeast of Madulce Peak along Mono Creek (lat. 34°40'10" N, long. 119°31' W); the place is in Don Victor Valley. Named on Madulce Peak (1964) 7.5' quadrangle.

Don Victor Canyon [SANTA BARBARA]: *canyon,* 4 miles long, along Mono Creek above a point 4.25 miles east-southeast of Madulce Peak (lat. 34°40'20" N, long. 119°31'15" W). Named on Madulce Peak (1964) 7.5' quadrangle.

Don Victor Valley [SANTA BARBARA]: *valley,* 4.25 miles east-southeast of Madulce Peak along Mono Creek (lat. 34°40'20" N, long. 119°31'05" W); the valley is at the mouth of Don Victor Canyon. Named on Madulce Peak (1964) 7.5' quadrangle. The name commemorates Don Victor, a tuberculosis sufferer who homesteaded at the place early in the 1900's and lived a long life (Gagnon, p. 77).

Doolans Hole Creek [MONTEREY]: *stream,* flows 1.5 miles to Ventana Creek (2) 4 miles west-southwest of Ventana Cone (lat. 36°15'55" N, long. 121°44'35" W; sec. 21, T 19 S, R 2 E). Named on Big Sur (1956) and Ventana Cones (1956) 7.5' quadrangles.

Dos Pueblos Canyon [SANTA BARBARA]: *canyon,* drained by a stream that flows nearly 7 miles to the sea 5.5 miles west-northwest of Coal Oil Point (lat. 34°26'25" N, long. 119°57'50" W). Named on Dos Pueblos Canyon (1951) and Lake Cachuma (1959) 7.5' quadrangles. The name is from two Indian villages situated at the mouth of the canyon— *dos pueblos* means "two towns" in Spanish (Gudde, 1949, p. 98).

Double Corral Canyon [SAN LUIS OBISPO]: *canyon,* 4 miles long, opens into the canyon of Carrie Creek 12.5 miles northeast of the town of Nipomo (lat. 35°38'30" N, long. 120°17'30" W; sec. 17, T 32 S, R 16 E). Named on Caldwell Mesa (1967) and Los Machos Hills (1967) 7.5' quadrangles.

Double Rock [SAN LUIS OBISPO]: *rock,* 100 feet long, 3.5 miles west-northwest of Point San Luis, and 550 feet offshore (lat. 35°11'15" N, long. 120°48'50" W). Named on Port San Luis (1965) 7.5' quadrangle.

Double Springs [SAN LUIS OBISPO]: *springs,* two, nearly 6 miles southwest of Branch Mountain (lat. 35°07'35" N, long. 120°09'05" W). Named on Los Machos Hills (1967) 7.5' quadrangle.

Double Summit: see **Ventana Double Cone** [MONTEREY].

Doud Creek [MONTEREY]: *stream,* flows 4 miles to the sea 8 miles north of Point Sur (lat. 36°25'20" N, long. 121°54'50" W). Named on Mount Carmel (1956) and Soberanes Point (1956) 7.5' quadrangles. The name is for Francis Doud, who had extensive land holdings in Monterey County; on some old maps the stream has the name "Sozers Creek" (Clark, 1991, p. 144).

Dougherty's Mill Number 2: see **Riverside Grove** [SANTA CRUZ].

Douglas Canyon [SAN LUIS OBISPO]: *canyon,* drained by a stream that flows 3 miles to the Salinas River 4.5 miles east-southeast of Pozo (lat. 35°16'35" N, long. 120°17'55" W). Named on Pozo Summit (1967) 7.5' quadrangle.

Douglas Spring [SAN LUIS OBISPO]: *spring,* 5 miles east of Pozo (lat. 35°17'25" N, long. 120°17'10" W); the spring is in Douglas Canyon. Named on Pozo Summit (1967) 7.5' quadrangle.

Douty: see **Point Douty**, under **Sunset Point** [MONTEREY].

Dove [SAN LUIS OBISPO]: *locality,* 3.25 miles southeast of present downtown Atascadero (lat. 35°27' N, long. 120°38' W). Named on San Luis Obispo (1897) 15' quadrangle. Postal authorities established Dove post office in 1889 and discontinued it in 1915 (Frickstad, p. 164).

Dove Canyon [SAN LUIS OBISPO]: *canyon,* 1.5 miles long, drained by a stream that joins a branch of Jack Creek nearly 3 miles north-northwest of York Mountain (lat. 35°34'55" N, long. 120°50'20" W). Named on York Mountain (1948) 7.5' quadrangle.

Doyle Gulch: see **Rodeo Creek Gulch** [SANTA CRUZ].

Drake [SANTA BARBARA]: *locality,* 9.5 miles east of Point Conception along Southern Pacific Railroad (lat. 34°28'15" N, long. 120°18'10" W); the place is near the mouth of Cañada de Santa Anita. Named on Sacate (1953) 7.5' quadrangle. Called Santa Anita on Lompoc (1905) 30' quadrangle.

Drake: see **Camp Drake** [SANTA BARBARA].

Drew Lake [SANTA CRUZ]: *lake,* 0.5 mile long, 2 miles northeast of Watsonville in Pajaro Valley (lat. 36°56'10" N, long. 121°43'50" W). Named on Watsonville East (1955) 7.5' quadrangle.

Dripping Spring [SANTA BARBARA]: *spring,*
9.5 miles northwest of McPherson Peak (lat. 34°59'25" N, long. 119°55'20" W). Named on McPherson Peak (1943) 15' quadrangle.

Drum Canyon [SANTA BARBARA]: *canyon,* 5.25 miles long, along Santa Rosa Creek above a point 7.5 miles south of the town of Los Alamos (lat. 34°38'10" N, long. 120°17' W). Named on Los Alamos (1959) 7.5' quadrangle.

Dry Canyon [SAN LUIS OBISPO]:
(1) *canyon,* nearly 2 miles long, 8 miles southwest of Shandon (lat. 35°35'20" N, long. 120°29'15" W). Named on Shedd Canyon (1961) 7.5' quadrangle.
(2) *canyon,* drained by a stream that flows 1.25 miles to Railpen Canyon 1.5 miles north-northeast of Huasna Peak (lat. 35°04' N, long. 120°19'30" W). Named on Huasna Peak (1967) 7.5' quadrangle.

Dry Canyon [SANTA BARBARA]:
(1) *canyon,* drained by a stream that flows 4.5 miles to Santa Barbara Canyon 2.5 miles southeast of Fox Mountain (lat. 34°47'10" N, long. 119°34'05" W). Named on Fox Mountain (1964) 7.5' quadrangle.
(2) *canyon,* drained by a stream that flows 4 miles to the sea 6.25 miles west of Carrington Point on Santa Rosa Island (lat. 34°01'05" N, long. 120°09' W). Named on Santa Rosa Island North (1943) 7.5' quadrangle.

Dry Creek [SAN LUIS OBISPO]:
(1) *stream,* flows 15 miles to Huerhuero Creek 3.5 miles east-northeast of Paso Robles (lat. 35°39'10" N, long. 120°38'20" W; at W line sec. 24, T 26 S, R 12 E). Named on Creston (1948) and Estrella (1948) 7.5' quadrangles. Shedd Canyon (1961) 7.5' quadrangle shows Dry Canyon (1) along the uppermost part of the watercourse.
(2) *stream,* flows nearly 4 miles to Huffs Hole Creek 12 miles north of the town of Nipomo (lat. 35°13'05" N, long. 120°26'35" W; sec. 23, T 31 S, R 14 E). Named on Tar Spring Ridge (1967) 7.5' quadrangle.

Dry Creek [SANTA BARBARA]:
(1) *stream,* flows 2.25 miles to Manzana Creek 2.5 miles northeast of Zaca Lake (lat. 34°48'10" N, long. 120°00'15" W). Named on Zaca Lake (1964) 7.5' quadrangle.
(2) *stream* and *dry wash,* flows 4.25 miles to Zaca Creek nearly 2 miles north-northeast of Buellton (lat. 34°38'15" N, long. 120° 11' W). Named on Zaca Creek (1959) 7.5' quadrangle.
(3) *stream,* flows 1 mile to Bartlett Canyon nearly 3 miles northwest of downtown Goleta (lat. 34°28'05" N, long. 119°51'25" W; sec. 31, T 5 N, R 28 W). Named on Goleta (1950) 7.5' quadrangle.

Dry Gulch [MONTEREY]: *canyon,* drained by a stream that flows nearly 6 miles to Deadman Gulch 8.5 miles north of Bradley (lat. 35°59'10" N, long. 120°50' W; near E line sec. 25, T 22 S, R 10 E). Named on Bradley (1961) 15' quadrangle, and on Pancho Rico Valley (1967) 7.5' quadrangle. Shown as part of

Deadman Gulch on San Ardo (1956) 15' quadrangle, and on Wunpost (1949) 7.5' quadrangle.

Dry Lake [SAN BENITO]:

(1) *intermittent lake,* 1 mile long, 8 miles north-northwest of Bitterwater (lat. 36°28'45" N, long. 121°04'20" W; sec. 2, T 17 S, R 8 E). Named on Topo Valley (1969) 7.5' quadrangle.

(2) *intermittent lake,* 350 feet long, 9.5 miles east-southeast of Bitterwater (lat. 36°19'15" N, long. 120°50'50" W; sec. 36, T 18 S, R 10 E). Named on Hepsedam Peak (1969) 7.5' quadrangle.

Dry Lake: see **Soda Lake** [SAN LUIS OBISPO]; **The Dry Lake** [MONTEREY].

Dry Lake Valley [SAN BENITO]: *valley,* 8 miles north-northwest of Bitterwater (lat. 36°29' N, long. 121°04'15" W); Dry Lake (1) is in the valley. Named on Topo Valley (1969) 7.5' quadrangle.

Dughi Spring [SAN LUIS OBISPO]: *spring,* 6 miles north-northwest of San Luis Obispo (lat. 35°21'50" N, long. 120°41'20" W; sec. 33, T 29 S, R 12 E). Named on San Luis Obispo (1965) 7.5' quadrangle.

Dunbar: see **Dunbarton** [MONTEREY].

Dunbarton [MONTEREY]: *locality,* 2.25 miles south of Aromas (lat. 36°51'25" N, long. 121°39' W). Named on San Juan Bautista (1917) 15' quadrangle. Called Dunbar on California Mining Bureau's (1917b) map. Postal authorities established Dunbarton post office in 1900 and discontinued it in 1909 (Frickstad, p. 107)

Dunham Canyon [SAN BENITO]: *canyon,* drained by a stream that flows 2.5 miles to North Fork Lewis Creek 10 miles south-southwest of Idria (lat. 36°17'05" N, long. 120°44'05" W; near S line sec. 11, T 19 S, R 11 E). Named on Hepsedam Peak (1969) and San Benito Mountain (1969) 7.5' quadrangles.

Dunham Spring [SAN BENITO]: *spring,* 15 miles east-southeast of Bitterwater (lat. 36°18'05" N, long. 120°45'30" W; sec. 3, T 19 S, R 11 E); the spring is in Dunham Canyon. Named on Hepsedam Peak (1969) 7.5' quadrangle.

Dunn Canyon [MONTEREY]: *canyon,* drained by a stream that flows 4.5 miles to an unnamed canyon 7 miles east-northeast of Salinas (lat. 36°42'05" N, long. 121°32'05" W). Named on Mount Harlan (1968) and Natividad (1947, photorevised 1968) 7.5' quadrangles.

Dunne Ridge [SAN BENITO]: *ridge,* north-trending, mainly in Santa Clara County, but extends south into San Benito County 8 miles north-northeast of Hollister (lat. 36°57'30" N, long. 121°21'15" W). Named on Three Sisters (1954) 7.5' quadrangle.

Dunneville [SAN BENITO]: *locality,* 6 miles north of Hollister (lat. 36°56'25" N, long. 121°24'35" W). Named on San Felipe (1955) 7.5' quadrangle. A small community called Dunneville, situated on the ranch of the Dunne

family, failed to develop (Shumate, p. 23-24). Postal authorities established Dunneville post office in 1874 and discontinued it in 1875 (Salley, p. 62). The place also was called Chase's Corners for a man who operated a bar there (Pierce, p. 96).

Duri [SAN BENITO]: *locality,* 1 mile north-northwest of Hollister along Southern Pacific Railroad (lat. 36°52' N, long. 121°24'30" W). Named on Hollister (1921) 15' quadrangle.

Dutch Henry Canyon [MONTEREY]: *canyon,* drained by a stream that flows nearly 4 miles to Portugee Canyon 5.5 miles northeast of San Ardo (lat. 36°05'20" N, long. 120°50'45" W; sec. 24, T 21 S, R 10 E). Named on Pancho Rico Valley (1967) 7.5' quadrangle. On San Ardo (1956) 15' quadrangle, present Redhead Canyon is called Dutch Henry Canyon.

Dutchman Spring [SAN LUIS OBISPO]: *spring,* 2.25 miles south-southeast of Branch Mountain (lat. 35°09'20" N, long. 120°04'05" W). Named on Branch Mountain (1967) 7.5' quadrangle.

Dutch Oven Campground [SANTA BARBARA]: *locality,* 1.5 miles south of Madulce Peak in Alamar Canyon (lat. 34°40'15" N, long. 119°35'35" W). Named on Madulce Peak (1964) 7.5' quadrangle.

Dutra Creek [MONTEREY]: *stream,* flows 3.25 miles to San Carpoforo Creek 11 miles east-southeast of Cape San Martin (lat. 35°48'05" N, long. 121°16'55" W; sec. 35, T 24 S, R 6 E). Named on Burro Mountain (1949) 7.5' quadrangle. The name commemorates Manuel Dutra, who settled by the stream about 1885 (Clark, 1991, p. 146). A place called Pear Orchard is situated along Dutra Creek where an ancient pear tree survived into modern times; the name of the place traditionally dates from mission days, when workers at a silver mine farther up Dutra Creek supposedly lived there (Hoover, Rensch, and Rensch, p. 237-238).

– E –

Eagle: see **Valleton** [MONTEREY].

Eagle Camp: see **Camp Stephani** [MONTEREY].

Eagle Canyon [SANTA BARBARA]: *canyon,* drained by a stream that flows 4.5 miles to the sea 3.5 miles west-northwest of Coal Oil Point (lat. 34°26'05" N, long. 119°55'40" W). Named on Dos Pueblos Canyon (1951) 7.5' quadrangle. The Spaniards called the feature Arroyo de Agalia—*agalia* means "eagle" in Spanish (Gudde, 1949, p. 102).

Eagle Cliff: see **Bay Point** [SANTA BARBARA].

Eagle Creek [SAN LUIS OBISPO]: *stream,* flows 2 miles to Atascadero Creek nearly 4 miles south-southwest of Atascadero (lat. 35°26'15" N, long. 120°41'35" W); the stream heads east of Eagle Peak. Named on

Atascadero (1965) 7.5' quadrangle.

Eagle Dell Peak [SANTA CRUZ]: *peak,* 3.5 miles east-southeast of the town of Boulder Creek (lat. 37°06'20" N, long. 122°03'35" W; sec. 34, T 9 S, R 2 W). Named on Felton (1955) 7.5' quadrangle.

Eagle Hills [SAN LUIS OBISPO]: *range,* 6 miles north of Shandon on the northwest side of McMillan Canyon (lat. 35°44'30" N, long. 120°22' W). Named on Cholame (1943) 7.5' quadrangle. Cholame (1917) 30' quadrangle shows Eagle school located about 1 mile northwest of the range.

Eagle Mountain [SAN BENITO]: *peak,* 5 miles southeast of Bitterwater (lat. 36°19'25" N, long. 120°57' W; sec. 36, T 18 S, R 9 E). Altitude 2494 feet. Named on Lonoak (1969) 7.5' quadrangle.

Eagle Peak [SAN LUIS OBISPO]: *peak,* 4.5 miles south of Atascadero (lat. 35°25'35" N, long. 120°41'10" W; near S line sec. 4, T 29 S, R 12 E). Altitude 2182 feet. Named on Atascadero (1965) 7.5' quadrangle.

Eagle Peak: see **Eagle Rock** [SANTA CRUZ].

Eagle Rock [MONTEREY]: *relief feature,* 2 miles south-southwest of Smith Mountain (lat. 36°03'25" N, long. 120°36'35" W; sec. 31, T 21 S, R 13 E). Named on Smith Mountain (1969) 7.5' quadrangle.

Eagle Rock [SAN LUIS OBISPO]: *peak,* 10.5 miles east of the village of San Simeon (lat. 35°40' N, long. 121°00'25" W; sec. 16, T 26 S, R 9 E). Named on Pebblestone Shut-in (1959) 7.5' quadrangle.

Eagle Rock [SANTA CRUZ]: *peak,* 2 miles southeast of Big Basin (lat. 37°08'50" N, long. 122°11'40" W; sec. 16, T 9 S, R 3 W). Altitude 2488 feet. Named on Big Basin (1955) 7.5' quadrangle. Called Eagle Pk. on California Mining Bureau's (1917a) map.

Eaglet: see **Have** [SAN LUIS OBISPO].

East Beach [SANTA BARBARA]: *beach,* 2 miles east of downtown Santa Barbara along the coast (lat. 34°25' N, long. 119°40' W). Named on Santa Barbara (1952) 7.5' quadrangle.

East Canyon [SANTA BARBARA]: *canyon,* drained by a stream that flows nearly 2 miles to join the stream in Central Canyon and form Bitter Creek 4 miles southwest of New Cuyama (lat. 34°54'25" N, long. 119°44'10" W; sec. 35, T 10 N, R 27 W). Named on New Cuyama (1964) 7.5' quadrangle.

East Corral de Piedra Creek [SAN LUIS OBISPO]: *stream,* flows 6 miles to join West Corral de Piedra Creek and form Pismo Creek nearly 0.5 mile south-southeast of Edna (lat. 35°11'50" N, long. 120°36'35" W); the stream is on Corral de Piedra grant. Named on Arroyo Grande NE (1965) 7.5' quadrangle.

East End Anchorage: see **Scorpion Anchorage** [SANTA BARBARA].

East Garrison: see **Camp Roberts Military Reservation** [MONTEREY-SAN LUIS OBISPO]; **Fort Ord Military Reservation** [MONTEREY].

East Mine Canyon Spring [SANTA BARBARA]: *spring,* 1.5 miles west-northwest of Montgomery Potrero (lat. 34°50'35" N, long. 119°46'35" W); the spring is 1 mile east-southeast of North Mine Canyon Spring in Mine Canyon (3). Named on Hurricane Deck (1964) 7.5' quadrangle.

East Monterey: see **Seaside** [MONTEREY].

Easton Spring [MONTEREY]: *spring,* 7 miles south-southwest of Charlie Mountain (lat. 36°02'20" N, long. 120°42'35" W; near SE cor. sec. 6, T 22 S, R 12 E). Named on Slack Canyon (1969) 7.5' quadrangle.

East Pinery [SANTA BARBARA]: *area,* 2 miles east-southeast of Figueroa Mountain (lat. 34°44' N, long. 119°57'15" W; on S line sec. 29, T 8 N, R 29 W). Named on Figueroa Mountain (1959) 7.5' quadrangle.

East Point [SANTA BARBARA]: *promontory,* at the easternmost tip of Santa Rosa Island (lat. 33°56'35" N, long. 119°58' W). Named on Santa Rosa Island East (1943) 7.5' quadrangle.

East Salinas: see **Alisal** [MONTEREY].

East Tuley Springs [SAN LUIS OBISPO]: *springs,* two, 850 feet apart, 5 miles north-northwest of Shandon (lat. 35°43'05" N, long. 120°25'15" W; sec. 25, T 25 S, R 14 E); the springs are 0.5 mile east of West Tuley Springs. Named on Shandon (1961) 7.5' quadrangle.

East Waddell Creek [SANTA CRUZ]: *stream,* formed by the confluence of Opal Creek and Blooms Creek, flows 3.5 miles to join West Waddell Creek and form Waddell Creek 2.5 miles north-northwest of the mouth of Waddell Creek (lat. 36°08' N, long. 122°16' W; near S line sec. 23, T 9 S, R 4 W). Named on Big Basin (1955) and Franklin Point (1955) 7.5' quadrangles.

Eblen Spring [MONTEREY]: *spring,* 3 miles south-southeast of Charley Mountain (lat. 36°05'45" N, long. 120°39'15" W; near NE cor. sec. 22, T 21 S, R 12 E). Named on Slack Canyon (1969) 7.5' quadrangle.

Eblis: see **Santa Cruz** [SANTA CRUZ].

Eccles [SANTA CRUZ]: *locality,* 5 miles southeast of the town of Boulder Creek along the railroad that extends up Zayante Creek (lat. 37°04'55" N, long. 122°03' W; near N line sec. 11, T 10 S, R 2 W). Named on Santa Cruz (1902) 30' quadrangle. The name commemorates John Sanderson Eccles, who deeded right of way to South Pacific Coast Railroad in 1878 (Clark, 1986, p. 104). Postal authorities established Eccles post office in 1893 and changed the name to Olympia in 1915 (Frickstad, p. 176). Clark (1986, p. 171-172) listed a railroad stop called Kenville that was located between Eccles and Meehan; the name was for Joseph Kenville, who came to Santa Cruz in 1865 and established the first express company there.

Echo Valley [MONTEREY]: *canyon,* drained by

a stream that flows 1.5 miles to San Miguel Canyon 3 miles north of Prunedale (lat. 36°49'15" N, long. 121°40'15" W). Named on Prunedale (1954) 7.5' quadrangle.

Eckart Canyon [SANTA BARBARA]: *canyon,* drained by a stream that flows 3 miles to Moon Canyon 9.5 miles northwest of McPherson Peak (lat. 34°59'10" N, long. 119°55'45" W; at N line sec. 1, T 10 N, R 29 W). Named on Bates Canyon (1964) 7.5' quadrangle.

Eddys Camp [SAN LUIS OBISPO]: *locality,* 8 miles southwest of Shandon (lat. 35°33'40" N, long. 120°27'50" W; near E line sec. 21, T 27 S, R 14 E). Named on Shedd Canyon (1961) 7.5' quadrangle.

Edna [SAN LUIS OBISPO]: *village,* 6 miles south-southeast of San Luis Obispo (lat. 35°12'15" N, long. 120°36'45" W). Named on Arroyo Grande NE (1965) 7.5' quadrangle. Postal authorities established Edna post office in 1887 and discontinued it in 1920 (Frickstad, p. 164).

El Alisal [MONTEREY]:
(1) *land grant,* 4 miles east of Salinas. Named on Natividad (1947) 7.5' quadrangle. Feliciano Soberanes received the land in 1823 and 1834, and Manuel Butron received it in 1828; Basilio Bernal claimed 5941 acres patented in 1866 (Cowan, p. 14).
(2) *land grant,* 6 miles east-southeast of Salinas. Named on Natividad (1947) 7.5' quadrangle. William E. Hartnell received 0.75 league in 1834; Maria Teresa de la Guerra de Hartnell claimed 2971 acres patented in 1882 (Cowan, p. 14-15; Cowan gave the name "Patrocino" as an alternate).

El Arroyo de San Marcos: see **San Marcos Creek** [SAN LUIS OBISPO].

El Cabo de Martin: see **Point Pinos** [MONTEREY].

El Cabo de San Martin: see **Point Pinos** [MONTEREY].

El Callejon Creek [SANTA BARBARA]: *stream,* flows 2.5 miles to El Jaro Creek 12.5 miles southeast of the city of Lompoc (lat. 34° 31'35" N, long. 120°17'20" W). Named on Santa Rosa Hills (1959) 7.5' quadrangle.

El Cantil: see **San Simeon Creek** [SAN LUIS OBISPO].

El Capitan Beach [SANTA BARBARA]: *beach,* 10.5 miles east of Gaviota along the coast (lat. 34°27'30" N, long. 120°01'35" W); the feature is west of the mouth of Cañada del Capitan. Named on Gaviota (1943) 15' quadrangle.

El Capitan Lodge [SANTA BARBARA]: *locality,* 6.25 miles south-southeast of Santa Ynez (lat. 34°32'15" N, long. 120°01'15" W). Named on Los Olivos (1943) 15' quadrangle.

El Chamisal [MONTEREY]: *land grant,* 6 miles southwest of Salinas. Named on Salinas (1947), Seaside (1947), and Spreckels (1947) 7.5' quadrangles. Felipe Vasquez received 1 league in 1835 and his heirs claimed 2737 acres patented in 1877 (Cowan, p. 26;

Cowan gave both the forms "El Chamizal" and "El Chamisal" for the name). According to Gudde (1949, p. 261-262), a place called Pilarcitos was located on the grant.

El Chorro [SAN LUIS OBISPO]: *land grant,* 4 miles northwest of San Luis Obispo; Chorro Creek is a boundary of the grant. Named on San Luis Obispo (1965) 7.5' quadrangle. James Scott and John Wilson received 1 league in 1845; Wilson claimed 3167 acres patented in 1861 (Cowan, p. 27—Cowan used the name "Cañada del Chorro" for the grant; Perez, p. 60).

Elder Spring [SAN LUIS OBISPO]: *spring,* nearly 4 miles west-northwest of Cholame in McMillan Canyon (lat. 35°44'45" N, long. 120°21'30" W; near N line sec. 21, T 25 S, R 15 E). Named on Cholame (1961) 7.5' quadrangle.

Eldorado Creek [SANTA BARBARA]: *stream,* flows 3.5 miles to join Steer Creek and form Gobernador Creek 3.5 miles north of Rincon Point (lat. 34°25'30" N, long. 119°28'25" W; sec. 14, T 4 N, R 25 W). Named on White Ledge Peak (1952) 7.5' quadrangle.

Elephant Mountain [MONTEREY]: *peak,* 1 mile east-northeast of Uncle Sam Mountain (lat. 36°20'55" N, long. 121°41'20" W; sec. 19, T 18 S, R 3 E). Named on Ventana Cones (1956) 7.5' quadrangle.

El Estero [MONTEREY]: *lake,* 4000 feet long, near the coast in Monterey (lat. 36°35'55" N, long. 121°53'05" W). Named on Monterey (1947, photorevised 1968) 7.5' quadrangle. The lake was part of an estuary before 1874, when construction of Monterey and Salinas Valley Railroad separated the lake from the sea (Clark, 1991, p. 153).

El Estero [SANTA BARBARA]: *marsh,* west of Carpinteria along the coast (lat. 34°24' N, long. 119°32' W). Named on Carpinteria (1952) 7.5' quadrangle. United States Board on Geographic Names (1961b, p. 10) rejected the names "Carpinteria Lagoon" and "Carpinteria Slough" for the feature.

El Jarro: see **Agua Puerca y las Trancas** [SANTA CRUZ].

El Jaro Creek [SANTA BARBARA]: *stream,* flows 11.5 miles to Salsipuedes Creek 4.5 miles southeast of the city of Lompoc (lat. 34°35'05" N, long. 120°24'25" W). Named on Lompoc Hills (1959) and Santa Rosa Hills (1959) 7.5' quadrangles.

El Jarro Point [SANTA CRUZ]: *promontory,* 2 miles west-northwest of Davenport along the coast (lat. 37°01'30" N, long. 122°13'20" W). Named on Davenport (1955) 7.5' quadrangle. The promontory is on Agua Puerca y las Trancas grant, which formerly had the name "El Jarro" (Cowan, p. 13).

Elkhorn [MONTEREY]: *locality,* 13 miles northwest of Prunedale along Southern Pacific Railroad (lat. 36°49'25" N, long. 121°44'20" W); the place is on the east side of Elkhorn Slough. Named on Prunedale

(1954) 7.5' quadrangle.

Elkhorn Ferry: see **Pauls Ferry**, under **Pauls Island** [MONTEREY].

Elkhorn Hills [SAN LUIS OBISPO]: *range,* southwest of the southeast end of Temblor Range at the southeast end of Carrizo Plain (lat. 35°02'30" N, long. 119°32'30" W). Named on Elkhorn Hills (1954) and Maricopa (1951) 7.5' quadrangles. Arnold and Johnson (1910, p. 20) proposed the name.

Elkhorn Plain [SAN LUIS OBISPO]: *valley,* between Temblor Range on the northeast and Panorama Hills and Elkhorn Hills on the southwest. Named on Elkhorn Hills (1954), Maricopa (1951), Painted Rock (1959), Panorama Hills (1954), and Wells Ranch (1954) 7.5' quadrangles. Called Elkhorn Valley on Mendenhall's (1908) map.

Elkhorn Scarp [SAN LUIS OBISPO]: *escarpment,* northwest-trending, 18 miles long, on the northeast side of Carrizo Plain southwest of Panorama Hills and Elkhorn Hills. Named on Elkhorn Hills (1954), Panorama Hills (1954), and Wells Ranch (1954) 7.5' quadrangles. Arnold and Johnson (1910, p. 20) proposed the name and noted that the term "scarp" is appropriate because the feature is along San Andreas fault.

Elkhorn Slough [MONTEREY]: *water feature,* 7 miles long, enters the sea at Moss Landing (lat. 36°48'30" N, long. 121°47'15" W). Named on Moss Landing (1954) and Prunedale (1954) 7.5' quadrangles. According to Elliott and Moore (p. 74), the crookedness of the slough inspired the name. The feature also has the names "Estero Grande," "Estero Vallejo" or "Vallejo Slough," "Estero Viejo," and "Roadhouse Slough"—the last for Joseph Truman Roadhouse, who lived near the slough (Clark, 1991, p. 154-155).

Elkhorn Spring [SAN BENITO]: *spring,* 4 miles northwest of present Idria along Larious Creek (lat. 36°27' N, long. 120°43'55" W; sec. 14, T 17 S, R 11 E). Named on New Idria (1943) 15' quadrangle.

Elkhorn Valley: see **Elkhorn Plain** [SAN LUIS OBISPO].

Ellicott [SANTA CRUZ]: *locality,* 4.5 miles west of Watsonville along Southern Pacific Railroad (lat. 36°55'15" N, long. 121°50'10" W). Named on Watsonville West (1954) 7.5' quadrangle.

Elliot Creek [SANTA CRUZ]: *stream,* flows 1.5 miles to San Mateo County 1.5 miles north-northwest of the mouth of Waddell Creek (lat. 37°06'55" N, long. 122°17'25" W; sec. 27, T 9 S, R 4 W). Named on Año Nuevo (1955) and Franklin Point (1955) 7.5' quadrangles.

Elliott Hill [MONTEREY]: *peak,* 6.25 miles west-southwest of Salinas (lat. 36°37'45" N, long. 121°45'15" W). Named on Marina (1947) 7.5' quadrangle. Salinas (1947) 7.5' quadrangle has the form "Elliot Hill" for the name.

Ellis Canyon [MONTEREY]: *canyon,* drained

by a stream that flows 2 miles to Chualar Canyon 9 miles east-northeast of Chualar (lat. 36°37'20" N, long. 121°22' W; sec. 13, T 15 S, R 5 E). Named on Mount Johnson (1968) 7.5' quadrangle. Called Loudon Gulch on Gonzales (1921) 15' quadrangle.

El Llanito de San Francisquito: see **San Francisquito Flat** [MONTEREY].

El Lobo: see **Lion Rock** [SAN LUIS OBISPO].

Ell Peak [MONTEREY]: *peak,* 7.5 miles southwest of Soledad (lat. 36°21'55" N, long. 121°26'05" W; sec. 16, T 18 S, R 5 E). Named on Sycamore Flat (1956) 7.5' quadrangle.

Ellwood [SANTA BARBARA]: *locality,* nearly 2 miles north-northwest of Coal Oil Point along Southern Pacific Railroad (lat. 34°25'55" N, long. 119°53'15" W); the place is near the mouth of Ellwood Canyon. Named on Dos Pueblos Canyon (1951) 7.5' quadrangle. California Mining Bureau's (1917c) map shows a place called Vilo located along the railroad about 2 miles west of Ellwood.

Ellwood Canyon [SANTA BARBARA]: *canyon,* drained by a stream that flows 5.5 miles to Bell Canyon 2.5 miles north-northwest of Coal Oil Point (lat. 34°26'30" N, long. 119°53'50" W). Named on Dos Pueblos Canyon (1951) and Lake Cachuma (1959) 7.5' quadrangles. United States Board on Geographic Names (1962a, p. 11) rejected the form "Elwood Canyon" for the name, which is from Ellwood Cooper, a horticulturist who had a ranch in the canyon (Tompkins and Ruiz, p. 67).

Ellysly Creek [SAN LUIS OBISPO]: *stream,* flows nearly 4 miles to Villa Creek 2.5 miles northwest of Cayucos Point (lat. 35°28'05" N, long. 120°58'35" W; sec. 26, T 28 S, R 9 E). Named on Cayucos (1965) 7.5' quadrangle.

El Moro: see **Baywood Park** [SAN LUIS OBISPO].

El Morro: see **Morro Rock** [SAN LUIS OBISPO].

El Morro Creek: see **Morro Creek** [SAN LUIS OBISPO].

El Morro Rock: see **Morro Rock** [SAN LUIS OBISPO].

El Pajaro Springs: see **Chittenden's Sulphur Springs**, under **Chittenden** [SANTA CRUZ].

El Paso de Robles: see **Paso Robles** [SAN LUIS OBISPO].

El Pescadero [MONTEREY]: *land grant,* north of Carmel Bay. Named on Monterey (1947) 7.5' quadrangle. Fabian Barreto received 1 league in 1836; David Jacks claimed 4426 acres patented in 1868 (Cowan, p. 59). The name is from fishing activities at the site—*el pescadero* means "the place where fishing is done" in Spanish (Hoover, Rensch, and Rensch, p. 231).

El Piojo [MONTEREY]: *land grant,* 5 miles south of Jolon. Named on Alder Peak (1949), Burnett Peak (1949), and Jolon (1949) 7.5' quadrangles. Joaquin Soto received 3 leagues in 1842 and his heirs claimed 13,329 acres patented in 1866 (Cowan, p. 61). Irelan (p. 405) used the name "Pyojo" for the grant.

El Piojo Creek [MONTEREY]: *stream,* flows nearly 7 miles to Nacimiento River 10 miles south of Jolon (lat. 35°49'50" N, long. 121° 08'50" W; sec. 19, T 24 S, R 8 E); the stream is partly on El Piojo grant. Named on Burnett Peak (1949) and Jolon (1949) 7.5' quadrangles.

El Pizmo: see **Pismo Beach** [SAN LUIS OBISPO].

El Potrero de San Carlos [MONTEREY]: *land grant,* south of Carmel River and 2.5 miles from the coast. Named on Monterey (1947), Mount Carmel (1956), and Seaside (1947) 7.5' quadrangles. Fructuso Real received 1 league in 1837; Joaquin Guiterrez, Estefana Guiterrez, and Maria Guiterrez claimed 4307 acres patented in 1862 (Cowan, p. 74; Perez, p. 82).

El Puerto de Monte-Rey: see **Monterey Bay** [MONTEREY].

El Rincon [SANTA BARBARA]: *land grant,* at Rincon Point on Santa Barbara-Ventura county line. Named on Carpinteria (1952) and White Ledge Peak (1952) 7.5' quadrangles. Teodoro Arellanes received 1 league in 1835 and claimed 4460 acres patented in 1872 (Cowan, p. 67-68).

El Rio Grande del Sur: see **Big Sur River** [MONTEREY].

Elsa [MONTEREY]: *locality,* 2.5 miles north-northwest of King City along Southern Pacific Railroad (lat. 36°15' N, long. 121°08'15" W). Named on Greenfield (1956) 7.5' quadrangle.

El Sueno [SANTA BARBARA]: *locality,* 3.25 miles east of downtown Goleta (lat. 34°26'35" N, long. 119°46'10" W). Named on Goleta (1950) 7.5' quadrangle.

El Sur [MONTEREY]: *land grant,* along the coast at Point Sur. Named on Big Sur (1956) and Point Sur (1956) 7.5' quadrangles. Juan Bautista Alvarado received 2 leagues in 1834; John B.R. Cooper claimed 8949 acres patented in 1866 (Cowan, p. 100).

El Toro [MONTEREY]: *land grant,* 6 miles south-southwest of Salinas. Named on Salinas (1947), Seaside (1947), and Spreckels (1947) 7.5' quadrangles. Jose Ramon Estrada received 1.5 leagues in 1835; Charles Wolters claimed 5668 acres patented in 1862 (Cowan, p. 104). According to Clark (1991, p. 158), the grant was named for El Toro Creek.

El Toro Creek [MONTEREY]: *stream,* flows 14 miles to Salinas River 3.5 miles south-southwest of Salinas (lat. 36°37'45" N, long. 121°41'15" W). Named on Spreckels (1947) 7.5' quadrangle. Called Toro Creek on Salinas (1947) 7.5' quadrangle.

El Toro Lake [MONTEREY]: *intermittent lake,* 1150 feet long, 9.5 miles south-southeast of Salinas (lat. 36°33'25" N, long. 121°44'10" W); the feature is on El Toro grant. Named

on Spreckels (1947) 7.5' quadrangle.

El Tranquillon: see **Tranquillon Mountain** [SANTA BARBARA].

El Tranquillon Mountain: see **Tranquillon Mountain** [SANTA BARBARA].

El Tucho [MONTEREY]: *land grant,* 4.5 miles west of Salinas. Named on Salinas (1947) 7.5' quadrangle. Jose Manuel Boronda received the land about 1795; Boronda and Blas Martinez received it in 1835; Simon Castro received 800 varas in 1841 and his heirs claimed 113 acres patented in 1867; David Jacks claimed 400 acres patented in 1876 (Cowan, p. 105).

Elvina: see **Paicines** [SAN BENITO].

Elwood Canyon: see **Ellwood Canyon** [SANTA BARBARA].

Emmett: see **Emmett Station** [SAN BENITO].

Emmett Station [SAN BENITO]: *locality,* 12 miles north-northwest of San Benito along Tres Pinos Creek (lat. 36°39'45" N, long. 121° 10' W; sec. 2, T 15 S, R 7 E). Named on San Benito (1919) 15' quadrangle. Postal authorities established Emmett post office in 1873 and discontinued it in 1908; they established Beckett post office 8 miles east of Emmett in 1886 and discontinued it in 1887—the name was for Thomas J. Beckett, first postmaster (Salley, p. 17, 69).

Encinal y Buena Esperanza [MONTEREY]: *land grant,* 9 miles east-southeast of Salinas. Named on Chualar (1947), Gonzales (1955), Mount Harlan (1968), and Natividad (1947) 7.5' quadrangles. David Spence received 3 leagues in 1834 and 1839; he claimed 13,391 acres patented in 1862 (Cowan, p. 33). Perez (p. 65) gave the size of the grant as 13,351.65 acres.

Enright: see **Majors** [SANTA CRUZ].

Ensenada de Abrigo: see **San Luis Obispo Bay** [SAN LUIS OBISPO].

Ensenada de Buchon: see **San Luis Obispo Bay** [SAN LUIS OBISPO].

Ensenada de la Purisima Concepcion: see **Cojo Bay** [SANTA BARBARA].

Ensenada del Roque: see **Estero Bay** [SAN LUIS OBISPO].

Entrance Rock: see **North Entrance Rock** [SAN LUIS OBISPO].

Erie: see **Hernandez** [SAN BENITO].

Ernest Blanco Spring [SANTA BARBARA]: *spring,* 5.5 miles west-northwest of Montgomery Potrero (lat. 34°52'15" N, long. 119°50'35" W). Named on Hurricane Deck (1964) 7.5' quadrangle.

Esalen Institute: see **Slates Hot Springs** [MONTEREY].

Escalona Gulch [SANTA CRUZ]: *canyon,* drained by a stream that flows 0.5 mile to the sea 2 miles northeast of Soquel Point (lat. 36° 58'35" N, long. 121°56'35" W). Named on Soquel (1954) 7.5' quadrangle.

Escondido Camp Ground [MONTEREY]: *locality,* 4 miles west of Junipero Serra Peak (lat. 36°08'25" N, long. 121°29'35" W; near

NE cor. sec. 2, T 21 S, R 4 E). Named on Junipero Serra Peak (1949) 7.5' quadrangle. Called Escondido Camp on Junipero Serra (1948) 15' quadrangle, and called Escondido Campground on Junipero Serra (1961) 15' quadrangle. Junipero Serra (1930) 15' quadrangle has the name "Rancho Escondido" at or near the site.

Escondido Canyon [SANTA BARBARA]: *canyon,* drained by a stream that flows 2 miles to Blue Canyon nearly 7 miles north-northwest of Carpinteria (lat. 34°29'10" N, long. 119°34' W; near E line sec. 26, T 5 N, R 26 W). Named on Carpinteria (1952) 7.5' quadrangle.

Escondido Creek [SANTA BARBARA]: *stream,* flows 4 miles to Jalama Creek 8.5 miles south of the city of Lompoc (lat. 34°30'50" N, long. 120°27'15" W). Named on Lompoc Hills (1959) 7.5' quadrangle.

Espada: see **The Espada** [SANTA BARBARA].

Espada Bluff [SANTA BARBARA]: *relief feature,* 4.25 miles south-southeast of Tranquillon Mountain along the coast (lat. 34°31'55" N, long. 120°31'20" W); the feature is near The Espada. Named on Tranquillon Mountain (1959) 7.5' quadrangle. The Railway (1903) map shows a place called Espada Ldg. situated along the coast at or near present Espada Bluff.

Espada Creek [SANTA BARBARA]: *stream,* flows 5 miles to Jalama Creek 9 miles south of the city of Lompoc (lat. 34°30'40" N, long. 120°29'25" W). Named on Lompoc Hills (1959) 7.5' quadrangle. Members of the Portola expedition gave the name "Espada" to an Indian village in the neighborhood in 1769 because a soldier recovered a sword there that had been stolen from him—*espada* means "sword" in Spanish (Wagner, H.R., p. 386).

Espada Landing: see **Espada Bluff** [SANTA BARBARA].

Espinosa Canyon [MONTEREY]:
(1) *canyon,* drained by a stream that flows 2.25 miles to Chualar Canyon 8 miles east-north-east of Gonzales (lat. 36°36'55" N, long. 121°23' W; sec. 23, T 15 S, R 5 E). Named on Gonzales (1955) and Mount Harlan (1968) 7.5' quadrangles.
(2) *canyon,* drained by a discontinuous stream that extends for nearly 5 miles to lowlands 4 miles south of San Lucas (lat. 36°04'25" N, long. 121°02' W). Named on Espinosa Canyon (1949) 7.5' quadrangle. The name commemorates Loridon (or Loredan) Espinosa (or Espinoza), who patented land in the canyon in 1892 (Clark, 1991, p. 28, 160).

Espinosa Lake [MONTEREY]: *marsh,* 1.25 miles long, 5.5 miles north-northwest of Salinas (lat. 36°44'30" N, long. 121°42'30" W); the feature is on Bolsa de las Escorpinas grant, which belonged to Salvador Espinosa. Named on Salinas (1947) 7.5' quadrangle. Salinas (1912) 15' quadrangle shows the feature as a lake, which has the designation "Laguna" on

the diseño that accompanied Espinosa's petition for the grant (Becker, 1969). According to H.R. Wagner (p. 460, 509), this probably is the feature that soldiers of the Portola expedition called Laguna de las Grullas in 1769 for the numerous cranes seen there—*grulla* means "crane" in Spanish—and that Crespi at the same time named Laguna Santa Brigida for the saint on whose day the expedition visited the place. This feature and Merritt Lake together are called Lagunas de la Herba de los Mansos on a diseño of Bolsa del Potrero y Moro Cojo grant (Becker, 1964).

Esteras Bay: see **Estero Bay** [SAN LUIS OBISPO].

Estero: see **Carrizo Plain** [SAN LUIS OBISPO]; **Point Estero** [SAN LUIS OBISPO].

Estero Bay [SAN LUIS OBISPO]: *embayment,* on the coast between Point Estero and Point Buchon. Named on Cayucos (1965), Morro Bay North (1965), and Morro Bay South (1965) 7.5' quadrangles. Called Ensenada del Roque on an early Spanish map (Wagner, H.R., p. 386), called Bay de los Esteros on Colton's (1855) map, and called Esteras Bay on Rogers and Johnston's (1857) map. United States Board on Geographic Names (1933, p. 293) rejected the forms "Esteros Bay" and "Estros Bay" for the name.

Estero de Santa Serafina: see **Cayucos Creek** [SAN LUIS OBISPO].

Estero Grande: see **Elkhorn Slough** [MONTEREY].

Estero Plain: see **Carrizo Plain** [SAN LUIS OBISPO].

Estero River: see **Cayucos Creek** [SAN LUIS OBISPO].

Esteros Bay: see **Estero Bay** [SAN LUIS OBISPO].

Estero Valllejo: see **Elkhorn Slough** [MONTEREY].

Estero Viejo: see **Elkhorn Slough** [MONTEREY].

Estrada Creek [SAN LUIS OBISPO]: *stream,* flows 4 miles to San Carpoforo Creek 3 miles east of the mouth of that stream (lat. 35° 46'20" N, long. 121°16'25" W; sec. 12, T 25 S, R 6 E). Named on Burnett Peak (1949) and Burro Mountain (1949) 7.5' quadrangles.

Estrada Ridge [SAN LUIS OBISPO]: *ridge,* north-northwest-trending, 0.5 mile long, nearly 3 miles southeast of Cambria (lat. 35°31'50" N, long. 121°03'05" W). Named on Cambria (1959, photorevised 1979) 7.5' quadrangle. The name is for Julian Estrada, owner of Santa Rosa grant, who built his home on the east slope of the ridge (United States Board on Geographic Names, 1974a, p. 2).

Estrella [SAN LUIS OBISPO]: *village,* 7 miles northeast of Paso Robles (lat. 35°42'20" N, long. 120°36'35" W; sec. 31, T 25 S, R 13 E); the village is north of Estrella Creek. Named on Estrella (1948) 7.5' quadrangle. Derby (p. 5) described a place called Estrella, apparently located a few miles east of present Estrella, where four valleys diverge, and stated: "The peculiarity of the divergence of these four valleys, and their corresponding ridges from this point resembling the rays of a star, has given it its very appropriate name—Estrella." *Estrella* means "star" in Spanish. Postal authorities established Estrella post office in 1886 and discontinued it in 1918 (Frickstad, p. 164).

Estrella Creek [SAN LUIS OBISPO]: *stream,* formed by the confluence of San Juan Creek and Cholame Creek at Shandon, flows 28 miles to Salinas River less than 1 mile south of San Miguel (lat. 35°44'30" N, long. 120°41'30" W; sec. 21, T 25 S, R 12 E). Named on Estrella (1948) and Paso Robles (1948) 7.5' quadrangles. Called Estrella River on Cholame (1961) and Shandon (1961) 7.5' quadrangles; United States Board on Geographic Names (1963b, p. 14) approved this name for the stream. Called Rio de la Estrella on Parke's (1854-1855) map. Antisell (1856, p. 93) considered Estrella Creek and San Juan Creek to be one stream, and referred to "San Juan or Estrella river." Antisell (1855, p. 35) earlier called the stream Rio Estrello and Estrella River. Trask (p. 21) used the name "Estella," Parke (p. 8) mentioned Estrella valley, and Goodyear (1888, p. 87) referred to La Estrella Creek.

Estrella Pass: see **Cottonwood Pass** [SAN LUIS OBISPO].

Estrella River: see **Estrella Creek** [SAN LUIS OBISPO].

Estrella Valley: see **Estrella Creek** [SAN LUIS OBISPO].

Estros Bay: see **Estero Bay** [SAN LUIS OBISPO].

Eto Lake [SAN LUIS OBISPO]: *lakes,* three connected, largest 400 feet long, 5 miles southeast of Morro Rock in Los Osos Valley (lat. 35°19' N, long. 120°48'50" W). Named on Morro Bay South (1965) 7.5' quadrangle.

Eugene Well [SAN BENITO]: *well,* 14 miles east-northeast of Bitterwater in Vallecitos (lat. 36°28'50" N, long. 120°47'05" W; sec. 5, T 17 S, R 11 E). Named on Hernandez Reservoir (1969) 7.5' quadrangle, where a windmill symbol marks the feature. On Priest Valley (1915) 30' quadrangle, a spring symbol marks it.

Eureka Canyon [SANTA CRUZ]: *canyon,* nearly 6 miles long, drained by Corralitos Creek above a point 0.5 mile north-northeast of Corralitos (lat. 36°59'45" N, long. 121°48'10" W). Named on Loma Prieta (1955) and Watsonville West (1954) 7.5' quadrangles.

Eureka Gulch [SANTA CRUZ]: *canyon,* drained by a stream that flows 1.5 miles to Eureka Canyon 3.25 miles north-northwest of Corralitos (lat. 37°02'10" N, long. 121°49'05" W; near E line sec. 26, T 10 S, R 1 E). Named on Loma Prieta (1955) 7.5' quadrangle.

Evers: see **Camp Evers** [SANTA CRUZ].

Ewing: see **Grant Ewing Ridge** [MONTEREY].

Ex Mission Soledad [MONTEREY]: *land grant,* 3 miles west-southwest of Soledad; includes the site of Soledad mission. Named on Palo Escrito Peak (1956), Paraiso Springs (1956), and Soledad (1955) 7.5' quadrangles. Feliciano Soberanes purchased the land in 1846 and claimed 8900 acres patented in 1874; the Catholic Church claimed 34 acres patented in 1859 (Cowan, p. 99; Cowan listed the grant under the name "Mision Nuestra Señora de la Soledad"). According to Perez (p. 66), Feliciano Soberanes was the grantee in 1846.

– F –

Fairbank Point [SAN LUIS OBISPO]: *promontory,* nearly 2 miles southeast of Morro Rock on the east side of Morro Bay (lat. 35°21'05" N, long. 120°50'40" W; sec. 1, T 30 S, R 10 E). Named on Morro Bay South (1965) 7.5' quadrangle. The name commemorates Dr. and Mrs. Charles Oliver Fairbank, who lived near the feature (United States Board on Geographic Names, 1963a, p. 6).

Fairoaks: see **Oaks** [SAN LUIS OBISPO].

Fairview: see **Twin Lakes** [SANTA CRUZ].

Fall Canyon [SANTA BARBARA]: *canyon,* drained by a stream that flows 4 miles to Sisquoc River nearly 6 miles northwest of Big Pine Mountain (lat. 34°45' N, long. 119°43'55" W); Sisquoc Falls is in the canyon. Named on Big Pine Mountain (1964) 7.5' quadrangle.

Fall Creek [SANTA CRUZ]: *stream,* flows 5 miles to San Lorenzo River 5 miles southeast of the town of Boulder Creek (lat. 37°03'35" N, long. 122°04'40" W). Named on Davenport (1955) and Felton (1955) 7.5' quadrangles.

Falls: see **The Falls** [MONTEREY]:

False Point Sur [MONTEREY]: *hill,* 1 mile southeast of Point Sur (lat. 36°17'45" N, long. 121°52'45" W). Altitude 209 feet. Named on Point Sur (1956) 7.5' quadrangle. United States Board on Geographic Names (1960c, p. 16) approved the name "False Sur" for the feature.

False Sur: see **False Point Sur** [MONTEREY].

Fan Shell Beach [MONTEREY]: *beach,* 0.5 mile east of Cypress Point (lat. 36°34'55" N, long. 121°58'05" W). Named on Monterey (1947) 7.5' quadrangle.

Farallon de Lobos: see **Richardson Rock** [SANTA BARBARA].

Faris: see **Bill Faris Campground** [SANTA BARBARA].

Farley [SANTA CRUZ]: *locality,* 0.5 mile southeast of Aptos along Southern Pacific Railroad in present Del Mar (lat. 36°58'10" N, long. 121°53'35" W). Named on Capitola (1914)

15' quadrangle.

Fat Buck Ridge [SANTA CRUZ]: *ridge,* south-to west-trending, nearly 2 miles long, 5 miles north-northeast of the town of Boulder Creek (lat. 37°11'55" N, long. 122°05'45" W). Named on Castle Rock Ridge (1955) 7.5' quadrangle.

Fauntleroy Canyon [SAN LUIS OBISPO]: *canyon,* drained by a stream that flows nearly 1 mile to Danford Canyon 4.5 miles east of the town of Nipomo (lat. 35°03'20" N, long. 120°23'40" W; near S line sec. 6, T 11 N, R 33 W). Named on Nipomo (1965) 7.5' quadrangle.

Fawn Lake [SAN BENITO]: *lake,* 200 feet long, 6 miles south of Idria (lat. 36°20' N, long. 120°40'25" W; near W line sec. 28, T 18 S, R 12 E); the lake is 500 feet south of Fawn Spring. Named on San Benito Mountain (1969) 7.5' quadrangle.

Fawn Spring [SAN BENITO]: *spring,* 6 miles south of Idria (lat. 36°20'05" N, long. 120°40'25" W; sec. 28, T 18 S, R 12 E); the spring is 500 feet north of Fawn Lake. Named on San Benito Mountain (1969) 7.5' quadrangle.

Feeder Creek: see **San Lorenzo Park** [SANTA CRUZ].

Felipe: see **Point Felipe**, under **Santa Barbara Point** [SANTA BARBARA].

Feliz Canyon [MONTEREY]: *canyon,* drained by a stream that flows nearly 4 miles to an unnamed stream 5 miles southwest of San Lucas (lat. 36°04'40" N, long. 121°04'40" W; sec. 26, T 21 S, R 8 E). Named on Espinosa Canyon (1949) 7.5' quadrangle. The name is for Vincente Feliz, who patented land in the canyon in 1892 (Clark, 1991, p. 165).

Felton [SANTA CRUZ]: *town,* 5.5 miles south-southeast of the town of Boulder Creek along San Lorenzo River (lat. 37°03' N, long. 122°04'30" W). Named on Felton (1955) 7.5' quadrangle. Edward Stanley laid out the town in 1868 at a place that had been a lumbering center since 1843, when Isaac Graham moved his mill to San Lorenzo River there opposite Fall Creek; the name commemorates Stanley's attorney, Charles N. Felton, who became a senator from California (Rowland, p. 169). Postal authorities established Felton post office in 1870 (Salley, p. 73). South Pacific Coast Railroad had a depot serving Felton situated 0.5 mile west of the town just south of the rail crossing of Zayante Creek; the depot sometimes was called New Felton and the town was called Old Felton (MacGregor, p. 127, 152). Santa Cruz (1902) 30' quadrangle has the name "Station" at the depot site, which is in present Mount Hermon (lat. 37°02'45" N, long. 122°03'55" W). Hamman's (1980b) map shows a place called Felton Junction located 1.5 miles south-southeast of Felton, where a branch line to Felton left the main rail line, and shows a place called Bonny Brae situated along the branch line on the north-

east side of San Lorenzo River near the north edge of present Felton.

Felton Junction: see **Felton** [SANTA CRUZ].

Fep [SAN BENITO]: *locality,* 9 miles northwest of Hollister along Southern Pacific Railroad (lat. 36°56'45" N, long. 121°30'25" W). Named on San Juan Bautista (1917) 15' quadrangle.

Ferini: see **Orcutt** [SANTA BARBARA].

Fernald Point [SANTA BARBARA]: *promontory,* 6 miles west-northwest of Carpinteria along the coast (lat. 34°25'05" N, long. 119°37'10" W). Named on Carpinteria (1952) 7.5' quadrangle.

Fernandez Creek [SAN LUIS OBISPO]: *stream,* flows 6.5 miles to Shell Creek 2.5 miles east-southeast of Wilson Corner (lat. 35°27'30" N, long. 120°20' W; sec. 26, T 28 S, R 15 E). Named on Camatta Ranch (1966) 7.5' quadrangle. United States Board on Geographic Names (1968b, p. 7) rejected the name "Fernando Creek" for the stream.

Fernandez Spring [SAN LUIS OBISPO]: *spring,* 9.5 miles north of Pozo (lat. 35°26'25" N, long. 120°21'50" W; near NE cor. sec. 4, T 29 S, R 15 E). Named on Camatta Ranch (1966) 7.5' quadrangle.

Fernando Creek: see **Fernandez Creek** [SAN LUIS OBISPO].

Fern Canyon [SAN LUIS OBISPO]:
(1) *canyon,* drained by a stream that flows nearly 2 miles to lowlands at Paso Robles (lat. 35°37'40" N, long. 120°42'05" W). Named on Paso Robles (1948) 7.5' quadrangle.
(2) *canyon,* drained by a stream that flows 1 mile to Lopez Canyon 4.25 miles southeast of Lopez Mountain (lat. 35°15'50" N, long. 120°31'15" W; near SW cor. sec. 31, T 30 S, R 14 E). Named on Lopez Mountain (1965) 7.5' quadrangle.

Fern Canyon [SANTA CRUZ]: *canyon,* drained by a stream that flows nearly 1.5 miles to Coward Creek 4.5 miles east-northeast of Watsonville (lat. 36°56'50" N, long. 121°40'45" W). Named on Watsonville East (1955) 7.5' quadrangle. United States Board on Geographic Names (1992, p. 4) approved the name "Mill Canyon" for the feature.

Fern Gulch [SANTA CRUZ]: *canyon,* nearly 1 mile long, opens into the canyon of Soquel Creek 7 miles north-northeast of Soquel (lat. 37°05' N, long. 121°54'30" W). Named on Laurel (1955) 7.5' quadrangle.

Ficay Creek: see **Picay Creek** [SANTA BARBARA].

Figueroa Camp [SANTA BARBARA]: *locality,* 0.5 mile south-southwest of Figueroa Mountain (lat. 34°44'05" N, long. 119°59'20" W; near S line sec. 25, T 8 N, R 30 W). Named on Figueroa Mountain (1959) 7.5' quadrangle.

Figueroa Creek [SANTA BARBARA]: *stream,* flows 5.5 miles to Santa Agueda Creek nearly 5 miles east of Los Olivos (lat. 34° 40'05" N, long. 120°01'45" W). Named on Los Olivos (1959) 7.5' quadrangle. United States Board on Geographic Names (1961b, p. 10) rejected the form "Figuero Creek" for the name.

Figueroa Mountain [SANTA BARBARA]: *peak,* 10 miles west-northwest of San Rafael Mountain (lat. 34°44'35" N, long. 119° 59' W; at E line sec. 25, T 8 N, R 30 W). Altitude 4528 feet. Named on Figueroa Mountain (1959) 7.5' quadrangle.

Figueroa Station [SANTA BARBARA]: *locality,* 8 miles northeast of Los Olivos (lat. 34°44'10" N, long. 120°00'20" W; at S line sec. 26, T 8 N, R 30 W). Named on Los Olivos (1959) 7.5' quadrangle.

Filbert: see **Boulder Creek** [SANTA CRUZ] (2).

Finch Creek [MONTEREY]: *stream,* flows 8 miles to join James Creek and form Cachagua Creek 1 mile north-northwest of Jamesburg (lat. 36°23'20" N, long. 121°35'35" W; sec. 1, T 18 S, R 3 E). Named on Chews Ridge (1956) and Rana Creek (1956) 7.5' quadrangles. Called Cachagua Creek on Jamesburg (1921) 15' quadrangle. The name is for brothers Charles Finch and James Finch, ranchers in the neighborhood (Clark, 1991, p. 166).

Fine Spring [SANTA BARBARA]: *spring,* less than 1 mile south of Figueroa Mountain (lat. 34°43'55" N, long. 119°59'05" W; near NE cor. sec. 36, T 8 N, R 30 W). Named on Figueroa Mountain (1959) 7.5' quadrangle.

Fingers: see **The Fingers** [SAN BENITO].

Finney Creek [SANTA CRUZ]: *stream,* flows nearly 1 mile to San Mateo County 2 miles north-northeast of the mouth of Waddell Creek (lat. 37°07'10" N, long. 122°17'30" W; sec. 27, T 9 S, R 4 W). Named on Año Nuevo (1955) and Franklin Point (1955) 7.5' quadrangles. Called Finny Creek on Año Nuevo (1948) 15' quadrangle. Seldon J. Finney had a ranch along the stream from the 1860's until the 1880's (Brown, p. 33-34).

Finny Creek: see **Finney Creek** [SANTA CRUZ].

Fir Canyon [SANTA BARBARA]: *canyon,* 4.5 miles long, opens into the canyon of Manzanita Creek nearly 3 miles south of Bald Mountain (1) (lat. 34°46'20" N, long. 119°56'35" W). Named on Bald Mountain (1964) and Figueroa Mountain (1959) 7.5' quadrangles. The canyon is drained by Davy Brown Creek, and is called Davy Brown Canyon on Santa Ynez (1905) 30' quadrangle, but United States Board on Geographic Names (1962b, p. 16) rejected this name for the feature. Davy Brown built a cabin in the canyon in 1884 (Rife, p. 120).

Fiscalini Creek [SAN LUIS OBISPO]: *stream,* flows 1 mile to Perry Creek 2 miles southeast of Cambria (lat. 35°32'30" N, long. 121° 03'15" W). Named on Cambria (1959) 7.5' quadrangle.

Fish Creek [SAN LUIS OBISPO]: *stream,* flows 5.25 miles to Alamo Creek 10 miles southwest of Branch Mountain (lat. 35°05'40" N, long. 120°14'25" W; near SW cor. sec. 35, T 32 S, R 16 E). Named on Chimney Canyon (1967) 7.5' quadrangle.

Fish Creek [SANTA BARBARA]: *stream,* flows 4 miles to Manzana Creek 4 miles south-southeast of Bald Mountain (1) (lat. 34°45'35" N, long. 119°54'05" W). Named on Bald Mountain (1964) and Figueroa Mountain (1959) 7.5' quadrangles. East Fork enters nearly 1 mile upstream from the mouth of the main creek; it is 1.5 miles long and is named on Bald Mountain (1964) and Figueroa Mountain (1959) 7.5' quadrangles. United States Board on Geographic Names (1962a, p. 10) rejected the name "Fish Creek" for present East Fork.

Fish Creek Campground [SANTA BARBARA]: *locality,* nearly 4 miles south-southeast of Bald Mountain (1) along Manzana Creek (lat. 34°45'45" N, long. 119°54'15" W); the place is near the mouth of Fish Creek. Named on Bald Mountain (1964) 7.5' quadrangle.

Fish Head Hill [MONTEREY]: *peak,* nearly 2 miles northeast of Mount Carmel (lat. 36°24'15" N, long. 121°45'55" W; near SW cor. sec. 33, T 17 S, R 2 E). Named on Mount Carmel (1956) 7.5' quadrangle.

Fitzpatrick Spring [SAN BENITO]: *spring,* 6 miles south of Idria (lat. 36°19'50" N, long. 120°40'45" W; sec. 29, T 18 S, R 12 E). Named on San Benito Mountain (1969) 7.5' quadrangle.

Five Willow Spring [SAN LUIS OBISPO]: *spring,* 19 miles southeast of Simmler near the southwest edge of Carrizo Plain (lat. 35°07'45" N, long. 119°50' W; sec. 21, T 32 S, R 20 E). Named on Painted Rock (1959) 7.5' quadrangle. McKittrick (1912) 30' quadrangle shows the spring located about 1 mile farther southeast (near W line sec. 27, T 32 S, R 20 E).

Flea Island: see **Castle Rock** [SANTA BARBARA].

Fletcher Canyon [MONTEREY]: *canyon,* drained by a stream that flows 3.5 miles to lowlands 6 miles west of Chualar (lat. 36°34'30" N, long. 121°36'20" W). Named on Chualar (1947) 7.5' quadrangle.

Flint Hills [SAN BENITO]: *range,* 4 miles west-northwest of Hollister (lat. 35°52'30" N, long. 121°28' W). Named on Hollister (1955) and San Felipe (1955) 7.5' quadrangles. The feature is on San Justo grant; Thomas Flint and Benjamin Flint, along with their cousin Llewelyn Bixby, bought the grant in 1855 (Pierce, p. 49).

Flood: see **Chris Flood Creek** [MONTEREY-SAN LUIS OBISPO].

Flores Camp [SANTA BARBARA]: *locality,* nearly 5 miles southeast of San Rafael Mountain along West Fork Santa Cruz Creek (lat. 34°39'30" N, long. 119°45'30" W; near NE cor. sec. 30, T 7 N, R 27 W). Named on San Rafael Mountain (1959) 7.5' quadrangle. Gagnon (p. 80) called the site Flores Flat, and stated that the name commemorates Jose Flores, who according to local legend built a cabin there at the turn of the century.

Flores Canyon [SANTA BARBARA]: *canyon,* drained by a stream that flows 5 miles to join the stream in Roque Canyon and form North Fork La Brea Creek 5.5 miles north-north-east of Manzanita Mountain (lat. 34°58'10" N, long. 120°03'05" W). Named on Manzanita Mountain (1964) and Miranda Pine Mountain (1967) 7.5' quadrangles.

Flores Flat [SANTA BARBARA]: *area,* 4.5 miles north of downtown Santa Barbara (lat. 34°29' N, long. 119°40'45" W; sec. 26, T 5 N, R 27 W). Named on Santa Barbara (1952) 7.5' quadrangle.

Flores Flat: see **Flores Camp** [SANTA BARBARA].

Folger: see **Swanton** [SANTA CRUZ].

Folger Wye: see **Swanton** [SANTA CRUZ].

Fontenay Villa [SANTA CRUZ]: *locality,* 2.5 miles south of Laurel (lat. 37°04'55" N, long. 121°58'25" W; near N line sec. 9, T 10 S, R 1 W). Named on Los Gatos (1919) 15' quadrangle.

Forbush Canyon [SANTA BARBARA]: *canyon,* drained by a stream that flows 1.5 miles to Blue Canyon 8.5 miles northwest of Carpinteria (lat. 34°29'45" N, long. 119°36'40" W; sec. 21, T 5 N, R 26 W); the canyon heads at Forbush Flat. Named on Carpinteria (1952) and Santa Barbara (1952) 7.5' quadrangles.

Forbush Flat [SANTA BARBARA]: *area,* 6.25 miles north-northeast of downtown Santa Barbara (lat. 34°29'50" N, long. 119°38'15" W; on W line sec. 20, T 5 N, R 26 W). Named on Santa Barbara (1952) 7.5' quadrangle. Fred Forbush, a turn-of-the-century homesteader, lived at the place (Gagnon, p. 81).

Force Canyon [MONTEREY]: *canyon,* drained by a stream that flows 2 miles to lowlands 6 miles west of Greenfield (lat. 36°19'20" N, long. 121°20' W; near E line sec. 32, T 18 S, R 6 E). Named on Paraiso Springs (1956) 7.5' quadrangle.

Ford Point [SANTA BARBARA]: *promontory,* 4 miles east-northeast of South Point on the south side of Santa Rosa Island (lat. 33°54'55" N, long. 120°02'50" W). Named on Santa Rosa Island South (1943) 7.5' quadrangle.

Foreman Creek [SANTA CRUZ]: *stream,* flows 1.25 miles to Boulder Creek (1) 5.5 miles east-southeast of Big Basin (lat. 37° 07'50" N, long. 122°08' W; near SW cor. sec. 19, T 9 S, R 2 W). Named on Big Basin (1955) and Davenport (1955) 7.5' quadrangles.

Forest Creek [MONTEREY]: *stream,* flows nearly 4 miles to San Antonio River 8 miles southeast of Junipero Serra Peak (lat. 36° 04' N, long. 121°18'45" W). Named on Bear Canyon (1949) 7.5' quadrangle.

Foresters Leap Canyon [SANTA BARBARA]: *canyon,* drained by a stream that flows 6 miles to Sisquoc River 4 miles south-southwest of

Montgomery Potrero (lat. 34°47'05" N, long. 119°47'30" W). Named on Hurricane Deck (1964) and Salisbury Potrero (1964) 7.5' quadrangles.

Forest Lake [MONTEREY]: *lake,* 1200 feet long, 3 miles south-southwest of Point Pinos (lat. 36°35'30" N, long. 121°56'30" W). Named on Monterey (1947) 7.5' quadrangle. Pacific Improvement Company created the reservoir in 1888 (Clark, 1991, p. 169).

Forest Park [SANTA CRUZ]: *settlement,* 5 miles east-southeast of Big Basin along Boulder Creek (1) (lat. 37°08'05" N, long. 122°08'20" W; sec. 24, T 9 S, R 3 W). Named on Big Basin (1955) 7.5' quadrangle.

Forest Springs [SANTA CRUZ]: *settlement,* about 4.5 miles east-southeast of Big Basin (lat. 37°08'20" N, long. 122°08'50" W; sec. 24, T 9 S, R 3 W). Named on Big Basin (1955) 7.5' quadrangle.

Forney Cove [SANTA BARBARA]: *embayment,* 0.5 mile east of Fraser Point at the west end of Santa Cruz Island (lat. 34°03'25" N, long. 119°55' W). Named on Santa Cruz Island A (1943) 7.5' quadrangle. Called Forneys Cove on Bremner's (1932) map.

Fort Halleck: see **Presidio of Monterey** [MONTEREY].

Fort Hunter Liggett: see **Hunter Liggett Military Reservation** [MONTEREY].

Fort Mervine: see **Presidio of Monterey** [MONTEREY].

Fort Ord: see **Fort Ord Military Reservation** [MONTEREY].

Fort Ord Military Reservation [MONTEREY]: *military installation,* between Marina and Seaside along the coast, and extends inland nearly to Salinas. Named on Marina (1947), Salinas (1947), Seaside (1947), and Spreckels (1947) 7.5' quadrangles. Marina (1947) 7.5' quadrangle has the name "Main Garrison" for a cluster of buildings located on the installation 1.5 miles south of Marina. Monterey (1940) 15' quadrangle has the name "Camp Clayton Military Reservation" for the same cluster of buildings, and the has name "Camp Ord Military Reservation" for the entire installation. Salinas (1947) 7.5' quadrangle has the names "Fort Ord" and "East Garrison" for a cluster of buildings situated near Salinas River 4.5 miles west-southwest of Salinas. Salinas (1940) 15' quadrangle has the name "Camp Ord" at the same place. The federal government purchased about 15,000 acres from David Jacks Corporation in 1917 near present East Garrison, and used the land for training troops stationed at Presidio of Monterey; the place first was called Gigling Reservation, for the Gigling family, who had lived on a bluff overlooking Salinas River, and in 1933 the name was changed to Camp Ord; the facility was used only as a summer training ground until 1938, when WPA workers started building what eventually became East Garrison; Camp Ord was combined with Camp Clayton in 1940, and the whole was named Fort Ord—the name "Ord" is for Major General Edward Otho Cresap Ord, who as a Lieutenant was stationed at Monterey in 1847 (Clark, 1991, p. 171; *San Jose Mercury-News,* February 7, 1965).

Fort Ord Village [MONTEREY]: *district,* north of Seaside (lat. 36° 37'30" N, long. 121°50' W); the place is on Fort Ord Military Reservation. Named on Marina (1947) and Seaside (1947) 7.5' quadrangles. Postal authorities established Ord Village post office in 1942 and discontinued it in 1954 (Salley, p. 162).

Fort Romie [MONTEREY]: *settlement,* 2 miles south-southwest of Soledad (lat. 36°24' N, long. 121°20'45" W). Named on Soledad (1955) 7.5' quadrangle. Postal authorities established Romie post office in 1898 and discontinued it in 1900 (Frickstad, p. 109). Salvation Army officials started the place in 1898 as an agricultural commune on a 600-acre tract purchased from Charles Romie, but the endeavor was unsuccessful (Fink, p. 163-164).

Fort Stockton: see **Presidio of Monterey** [MONTEREY].

Fossil Point [SAN LUIS OBISPO]: *promontory,* 0.5 mile southeast of Avila Beach along the coast (lat. 35°10'25" N, long. 120°43'25" W). Named on Pismo Beach (1965) 7.5' quadrangle. On Arroyo Grande (1942) 15' quadrangle, the name applies to a promontory located nearly 1 mile farther west-northwest.

Four Corners [SANTA BARBARA]: *locality,* 2.5 miles northeast of the city of Lompoc (lat. 34°39'50" N, long. 120°25'15" W). Named on Lompoc (1959) 7.5' quadrangle.

Four Corners: see **Santa Cruz** [SANTA CRUZ].

Fourth of July Spring [SAN BENITO]: *spring,* 8 miles east-southeast of Bitterwater (lat. 36°18'55" N, long. 120°52'35" W; sec. 34, T 18 S, R 10 E). Named on Lonoak (1969) 7.5' quadrangle.

Foxen: see **Sisquoc** [SANTA BARBARA] (3).

Foxen Canyon [SANTA BARBARA]: *canyon,* 10 miles long, opens into lowlands 5.25 miles south-southwest of Tepusquet Peak (lat. 34°50"55" N, long. 120°14'25" W). Named on Foxen Canyon (1964) and Zaca Lake (1964) 7.5' quadrangles. The name is for Benjamin Foxen, an English sailor who came to California in 1828 and later received Tinaquaic grant (Gudde, 1949, p. 120).

Fox Gulch: see **Cañada Tecolote** [SANTA BARBARA].

Fox Mountain [SANTA BARBARA]: *peak,* 8.5 miles south of the village of Cuyama (lat. 34°48'50" N, long. 119°35'55" W). Altitude 5167 feet. Named on Fox Mountain (1964) 7.5' quadrangle.

Fox Spring [SAN BENITO]: *spring,* 7 miles east-southeast of Bitterwater (lat. 36°21'15" N, long. 120°53'10" W; near E line sec. 21, T 18 S, R 10 E). Named on Lonoak (1969) 7.5' quadrangle.

Fox Spring [SAN LUIS OBISPO]: *spring,* 6 miles north-northeast of Pozo (lat. 35°23'20" N, long. 120°21'05" W; near N line sec. 22, T 29 S, R 15 E). Named on Camatta Ranch (1966) 7.5' quadrangle.

Frames Peak [MONTEREY]: *peak,* 4.25 miles southeast of Smith Mountain (lat. 36°02'10" N, long. 120°32'30" W; sec. 11, T 22 S, R 13 E). Altitude 3602 feet. Named on Smith Mountain (1969) 7.5' quadrangle.

Franciscan Creek [SAN LUIS OBISPO]: *stream,* flows 1.5 miles to Kern County 14 miles east-southeast of Shandon (lat. 35°36'50" N, long. 120°07'30" W; at N line sec. 3, T 27 S, R 17 E). Named on Holland Canyon (1961) 7.5' quadrangle.

Franklin Canyon [SANTA BARBARA]: *canyon,* 1 mile long, along present Franklin Creek above a point 1.5 miles north-northeast of downtown Carpinteria (lat. 34°24'55" N, long. 119°30'30" W). Named on Santa Barbara (1903) 15' quadrangle.

Franklin Creek [SAN LUIS OBISPO]: *stream,* flows 7.25 miles to Las Tablas Creek 3 miles east-northeast of Lime Mountain (lat. 35°41'25" N, long. 120°56'45" W; near NE cor. sec. 12, T 26 S, R 9 E). Named on Lime Mountain (1948) 7.5' quadrangle. The stream now enters Nacimiento Reservoir.

Franklin Creek [SANTA BARBARA]: *stream,* flows 3.25 miles to the sea 0.5 mile west-southwest of downtown Carpinteria (lat. 34° 23'45" N, long. 119°31'40" W). Named on Carpinteria (1952) 7.5' quadrangle.

Fraser Canyon [SAN LUIS OBISPO]: *canyon,* nearly 3.5 miles long, opens into lowlands 3.25 miles east-northeast of Pozo (lat. 35° 19' N, long. 120°19' W; near N line sec. 13, T 30 S, R 15 E). Named on Pozo Summit (1967) 7.5' quadrangle. Pozo (1922) 15' quadrangle shows the canyon 1 mile farther west at present Bean Canyon.

Fraser Point [SANTA BARBARA]: *promontory,* at the west end of Santa Cruz Island (lat. 34°03'35" N, long. 119°55'45" W). Named on Santa Cruz Island A (1943) 7.5' quadrangle.

Freeborn Mountain [SAN LUIS OBISPO]: *peak,* 18 miles east of Pozo (lat. 35°17'05" N, long. 120°03'10" W; sec. 28, T 30 S, R 18 E). Altitude 3312 feet. Named on California Valley (1966) 7.5' quadrangle.

Freedom [SANTA CRUZ]: *town,* 1.5 miles northwest of Watsonville (lat. 36°56'05" N, long. 121°46'20" W). Named on Watsonville West (1954) 7.5' quadrangle. Postal authorities established Freedom post office in 1940 (Salley, p. 80). The name is from a saloon at the site; the saloon displayed an American flag and a sign with the legend "Flag of Freedom" (Stewart, p. 172). The place first was known as Whiskey Hill (Chase, p. 228).

Freeman Canyon: see **Mason Canyon** [SAN LUIS OBISPO].

Fremont Campground [SANTA BARBARA]: *locality,* 2 miles north of San Marcos Pass along Santa Ynez River (lat. 34°32'35" N, long. 119°49'30" W). Named on San Marcos Pass (1959) 7.5' quadrangle.

Fremont Peak [MONTEREY-SAN BENITO]: *peak,* 10 miles northeast of Salinas on Monterey-San Benito county line (lat. 36°45'25" N, long. 121°30'10" W); the peak is near the north end of Gabilan Range. Altitude 3171 feet. Named on San Juan Bautista (1955) 7.5' quadrangle. Called Gabilan Pk. on San Juan Bautista (1917) 15' quadrangle, and called Picacho de Gavilan on Parke's (1854-1855) map. Talbot (p. 41) called the feature La Natividad Mt., and Whitney (p. 159) called it Gavilan Peak—*gabilan* or *gavilan* means "hawk" in Spanish, and the feature sometimes is called Hawks Peak (Hanna, p. 116). United States Board on Geographic Names (1933, p. 315) approved the name "Gabilan Peak" for the feature, and rejected the names "Fremont Peak" and "Gavilan Peak," but later the Board (1960c, p. 16-17) reversed the decision and approved the name "Fremont Peak" while rejecting the names "Gabilan Peak" and "Gavilan Peak." The name "Fremont" commemorates John Charles Fremont, who built a fort near the peak in 1846 (Spence and Jackson, p. 123).

French Camp [SAN LUIS OBISPO]: *locality,* 9 miles east of Wilson Corner near Navajo Creek (lat. 35°29'30" N, long. 120°12'45" W; sec. 14, T 28 S, R 16 E). Named on La Panza Ranch (1966) 7.5' quadrangle. The place was a placer-mining settlement as late as the 1890's (Dillon, 1960, p. 8).

French Canyon [MONTEREY-SAN BENITO]: *canyon,* drained by a stream that heads in San Benito County and flows nearly 1 mile to Towne Creek 4.5 miles northwest of Fremont Peak in Monterey County (lat. 36°48'20" N, long. 121°33'40" W). Named on San Juan Bautista (1955) 7.5' quadrangle.

Frenchs Pass [SAN BENITO]: *pass,* 1.5 miles southwest of Mariposa Peak on San Benito-Merced county line (lat. 36°56'25" N, long. 121°13'40" W; sec. 32, T 11 S, R 7 E). Named on Mariposa Peak (1969) 7.5' quadrangle, which shows French ranch situated 0.5 mile northwest of the pass.

Friar's Harbor: see **Frys Harbor** [SANTA BARBARA].

Friis Campground [SAN LUIS OBISPO]: *locality,* 6 miles north-northeast of Pozo (lat. 35°22'55" N, long. 120°19'40" W; sec. 23, T 29 S, R 15 E). Named on Camatta Ranch (1966) 7.5' quadrangle.

Fritch Creek [SANTA CRUZ]: *stream,* flows 1 mile to Love Creek 2 miles east-southeast of the town of Boulder Creek (lat. 37°06'40" N, long. 122°05'20" W; sec. 33, T 9 S, R 2 W). Named on Felton (1955) 7.5' quadrangle.

Frog Canyon [SAN BENITO]: *canyon,* drained by a stream that flows 3.5 miles to Chalone Creek 3 miles northeast of North Chalone Peak (lat. 36°28'35" N, long. 121°09'20" W; sec. 1, T 17 S, R 7 E). Named on North Chalone Peak (1969) 7.5' quadrangle.

Frog Pond Mountain [SAN LUIS OBISPO]: *ridge,* northwest-trending, 2 miles long, 4 miles southwest of Atascadero (lat. 35°26'45" N, long. 120°43' W). Named on Atascadero (1965) 7.5' quadrangle.

Froom Creek [SAN LUIS OBISPO]: *stream,* flows 3.5 miles to San Luis Obispo Creek 2.5 miles south-southwest of downtown San Luis Obispo (lat. 35°14'30" N, long. 120°40'55" W). Named on Pismo Beach (1965) and San Luis Obispo (1965) 7.5' quadrangles.

Frys Harbor [SANTA BARBARA]: *embayment,* 0.5 mile southeast of Diablo Point on the north side of Santa Cruz Island (lat. 34°03'10" N, long. 119°45'10" W). Named on Santa Cruz Island B (1943) 7.5' quadrangle. The place also is called Friar's Harbor and Fry's Harbor (Doran, p. 147).

Fulger Point [SANTA BARBARA]: *promontory,* 7.5 miles east-southeast of Santa Maria along Santa Maria River opposite the confluence of Cuyama River and Sisquoc River (lat. 34°54'20" N, long. 120°19'05" W; sec. 35, T 10 N, R 33 W). Named on Twitchell Dam (1959) 7.5' quadrangle. Hobson (p. 600) called the feature Fulger's Point.

– G –

Gabilan [MONTEREY]: *locality,* 4 miles northwest of Gonzales along Southern Pacific Railroad (lat. 36°32'45" N, long. 121°29'30" W). Named on Gonzales (1921) 15' quadrangle.

Gabilan: see **Alisal** [MONTEREY].

Gabilan Acres [MONTEREY]: *settlement,* 6.5 miles west of Fremont Peak (lat. 36°45'15" N, long. 121°37' W); the place is along Gabilan Creek (1). Named on San Juan Bautista (1955) 7.5' quadrangle.

Gabilan Creek [MONTEREY]:
(1) *stream,* flows 17 miles to marsh 2.5 miles northeast of Salinas (lat. 36°42'20" N, long. 121°37'15" W); the stream heads in Gabilan Range. Named on Hollister (1955), Mount Harlan (1968), Natividad (1947), and San Juan Bautista (1955) 7.5' quadrangles. Natividad (1947, photorevised 1968) 7.5' quadrangle does not show the marsh, but it does show the end of the stream at about the same place.
(2) *stream,* flows 6 miles to Nacimiento River 6.5 miles southwest of Jolon (lat. 35°53'50" N, long. 121°14'20" W). Named on Jolon (1949) 7.5' quadrangle. Called Agua del Gavilan on a diseño of El Piojo grant (Becker, 1964).

Gabilan Hills: see **Gabilan Range** [MONTEREY-SAN BENITO].

Gabilan Mountains: see **Gabilan Range** [MONTEREY-SAN BENITO].

Gabilan Peak: see **Fremont Peak** [MONTEREY-SAN BENITO].

Gabilan Range [MONTEREY-SAN BENITO]: *range,* east of Salinas River from near Salinas to Greenfield on Monterey-San Benito county line. Named on Santa Cruz (1956) 1°x 2° quadrangle. Called Sierra de Gavilan on Parke's (1854-1855) map. Blake (1856, p. 378) noted that the north part of the feature was called San Juan range, and farther south it sometimes was called Gavilan or Salinas range. Brewer (p. 128) referred to Gabilan hills, and Irelan (p. 483) mentioned Gabilan Mountains. Elliott and Moore (p. 95) described a mining camp called Rootville that was situated 6 miles northeast of Soledad in Gabilan Range; the place was named for Mr. Root, who discovered gold there about 1870.

Gaffey Creek [SANTA CRUZ]: *stream,* flows 1.5 miles to Casserly Creek 5.25 miles north-northeast of Watsonville (lat. 36°59'25" N, long. 121°44'05" W). Named on Watsonville East (1955) 7.5' quadrangle. The name commemorates Judge William Vincent Gaffey, who lived in Watsonville in the 1870's and 1880's (Clark, 1986, p. 128).

Galen Creek: see **Pancho Rico Creek** [MONTEREY].

Gallighan Slough [SANTA CRUZ]: *stream,* flows 3 miles to Harkins Slough 3 miles west-southwest of Watsonville (lat. 36°54'20" N, long. 121°48'15" W). Named on Watsonville West (1954) 7.5' quadrangle. The name commemorates Bartley Gallighan, who had land near the stream (Clark, 1986, p. 128).

Gamboa Point [MONTEREY]: *promontory,* 2.5 miles northwest of Lopez Point along the coast (lat. 36°03' N, long. 121°35'25" W; sec. 1, T 22 S, R 3 E). Named on Lopez Point (1956) 7.5' quadrangle. The Gamboa family homesteaded in the neighborhood (Howard, p. 65).

Gamecock Canyon [SANTA CRUZ]: *canyon,* drained by a stream that flows 2.25 miles to Browns Creek 3 miles northeast of Corralitos (lat. 37°01'30" N, long. 121°46'25" W). Named on Loma Prieta (1955) 7.5' quadrangle. The name is from a sawmill called Gamecock Mill (Clark, 1986, p. 128).

Garcia Creek [SAN BENITO]: *stream,* flows 3 miles to Lewis Creek 11.5 miles southeast of Bitterwater (lat. 36°16'30" N, long. 120°50'20" W; sec. 13, T 19 S, R 10 E). Named on Hepsedam Peak (1969) 7.5' quadrangle. The name commemorates Joaquín García, who settled along Lewis Creek in 1871 (Clark, 1991, p. 181).

Garcia Mountain [SAN LUIS OBISPO]: *ridge,* west-northwest-trending, 10 miles long, 6 miles southeast of Pozo (lat. 35°14'45" N, long. 120°18' W); the ridge is between Salinas River and Trout Creek (2). Named on Caldwell Mesa (1967), Los Machos Hills (1967), Pozo Summit (1967), and Santa Margarita Lake (1967) 7.5' quadrangles.

Garcia Potrero Spring [SAN LUIS OBISPO]: *spring,* 9 miles west of Branch Mountain along Stony Creek (lat. 35°11'55" N, long. 120° 14'30" W). Named on Los Machos Hills (1967) 7.5' quadrangle. Branch Mountain (1952) 15' quadrangle shows the spring located 1.5 miles farther east-southeast (near N line sec. 36, T 31 S, R 16 E).

Garcia Valley: see **Pozo** [SAN LUIS OBISPO].

Garden Farms [SAN LUIS OBISPO]: *settlement,* nearly 2 miles north of Santa Margarita (lat. 35°25'10" N, long. 120°36'20" W). Named on Santa Margarita (1965) 7.5' quadrangle

Garey [SANTA BARBARA]: *village,* 8 miles east-southeast of Santa Maria (lat. 34°53'20" N, long. 120°18'50" W; sec. 2, T 9 N, R 33 W). Named on Twitchell Dam (1959) 7.5' quadrangle. Called Gary on Lompoc (1905) 30' quadrangle. Postal authorities established Garey post office in 1889 and discontinued it in 1902 (Frickstad, p. 170). The name commemorates Thomas A. Garey, a nurseryman and horticulturist whose specialty was citrus fruit (Gudde, 1949, p. 124).

Garrapata Creek [MONTEREY]: *stream,* flows 7.5 miles to the sea 8 miles north of Point Sur (lat. 36°25'05" N, long. 121°54'55" W). Named on Mount Carmel (1956) and Soberanes Point (1956) 7.5' quadrangles. According to Gudde (1949, p. 124), the name "Arroyo de las Garrapatas" appeared on a map as early as 1835. *Garrapata* means "sheep tick" or "cattle tick" in Spanish (Hanna, p. 117).

Garrapata Creek [SANTA BARBARA]: *stream,* flows 0.5 mile to Torro Canyon Creek 4 miles northwest of Carpinteria (lat. 34° 26' N, long. 119°34'15" W). Named on Carpinteria (1952, photorevised 1967) 7.5' quadrangle. On Carpinteria (1952) 7.5' quadrangle, the name applies to present Torro Canyon Creek.

Garrissere Canyon [MONTEREY]: *canyon,* drained by a stream that flows 6 miles to lowlands 2.25 miles west of San Ardo (lat. 36°01'30" N, long. 120°56'35" W). Named on Hames Valley (1949) and San Ardo (1967) 7.5' quadrangles. English (p. 245) used the name "Garrissere Gulch." The Garrissere family owned land in or near the canyon (Clark, 1991, p. 183).

Garrissere Gulch: see **Garrissere Canyon** [MONTEREY].

Garrity Peak [SAN LUIS OBISPO]: *peak,* 5.25 miles north-northwest of San Simeon (lat. 35°43'10" N, long. 121°12'35" W). Altitude 2397 feet. Named on San Simeon (1958) 7.5' quadrangle.

Garrizo Creek [MONTEREY]: *stream,* flows 2.5 miles to North Fork San Antonio River nearly 4 miles south of Junipero Serra Peak (lat. 36°05'30" N, long. 121°26' W). Named on Cone Peak (1949) 7.5' quadrangle. Called Carrizo Creek on Junipero Serra (1930) 15' quadrangle.

Gary: see **Garey** [SANTA BARBARA].

Gasper Creek [SANTA BARBARA]: *stream,* flows 4.25 miles to Jalama Creek 8.5 miles south of the city of Lompoc (lat. 34°30'45" N, long. 120°28'30" W). Named on Lompoc Hills (1959) 7.5' quadrangle.

Gates [SANTA BARBARA]: *locality,* 5 miles east-southeast of Santa Maria along Santa Maria Valley Railroad (lat. 34°55'30" N, long. 120°21'20" W). Named on Twitchell Dam (1959) 7.5' quadrangle.

Gato [SANTA BARBARA]: *locality,* 5.5 miles east of Point Conception along Southern Pacific Railroad (lat. 34°27'25" N, long. 120° 22'30" W); the place is less than 0.5 mile east of the mouth of Cañada del Gato. Named on Point Conception (1953) and Sacate (1953) 7.5' quadrangles. California Division of Highways' (1934) map shows a place called Anacapa located less than 1 mile west of Gato along the railroad.

Gato Canyon [SANTA BARBARA]: *canyon,* drained by a stream that flows 6 miles to the sea 7 miles west-northwest of Coal Oil Point (lat. 34°27' N, long. 119°59'15" W). Named on Dos Pueblos Canyon (1951) and Lake Cachuma (1959) 7.5' quadrangles.

Gato Ridge [MONTEREY]: *ridge,* generally northwest-trending, 2.5 miles long, 9 miles south-southwest of Tepusquet Peak (lat. 34° 47' N, long. 120°14'30" W). Named on Foxen Canyon (1964) and Sisquoc (1959) 7.5' quadrangles.

Gaudalupe: see **Guadalupe** [SAN LUIS OBISPO-SANTA BARBARA]; **Guadalupe** [SANTA BARBARA].

Gavilan House: see **Lagunita Lake** [MONTEREY].

Gavilan Peak: see **Fremont Peak** [MONTEREY-SAN BENITO].

Gavilan Range: see **Gabilan Range** [MONTEREY-SAN BENITO].

Gaviota [SANTA BARBARA]: *village,* 29 miles west of Santa Barbara (lat. 34°28'15" N, long. 120°12'55" W); the place is 0.5 mile east of the mouth of Cañada de la Gaviota. Named on Gaviota (1953) 7.5' quadrangle. Postal authorities established Gaviota post office in 1896, discontinued it for a time in 1901, moved it 0.25 mile west in 1937, discontinued it in 1957, and reestablished it the same year (Salley, p. 83). California Division of Highways' (1934) map shows a place called Seagirt located 1 mile east of Gaviota along Southern Pacific Railroad.

Gaviota Beach [SANTA BARBARA]: *beach,* 0.5 mile west of Gaviota along the coast (lat. 34°28'15" N, long. 120°13'30" W); the feature is at the mouth of Gaviota Canyon (present Cañada de la Gaviota). Named on Gaviota (1943) 15' quadrangle.

Gaviota Canyon: see **Cañada de la Gaviota** [SANTA BARBARA].

Gaviota Creek: see **Pancho Rico Creek** [MONTEREY].

Gaviota Gorge: see **Gaviota Pass** [SANTA BARBARA].

Gaviota Hot Springs: see **Hot Springs** [SANTA BARBARA] (1).

Gaviota Pass [SANTA BARBARA]: *narrows,* 1.25 miles north-northwest of Gaviota in Cañada de la Gaviota (lat. 34°29'20" N, long. 120°13'30" W). Named on Gaviota (1953) 7.5' quadrangle. Called Gaviota Gorge on Gaviota (1943) 15' quadrangle.

Gaviota Pass: see **Nojoqui Summit** [SANTA BARBARA].

Gaviota Peak [SANTA BARBARA]: *peak,* 8 miles south of Buellton (lat. 34°30'05" N, long. 120°11'50" W; sec. 23, T 5 N, R 32 W); the peak is east of Cañada de la Gaviota. Altitude 2458 feet. Named on Solvang (1959) 7.5' quadrangle.

Gaviota Wharf: see **Port Orford** [SANTA BARBARA].

Gaviote Creek: see **Cañada de la Gaviota** [SANTA BARBARA].

Gaviotito Creek [SANTA BARBARA]: *stream,* flows 1.25 miles to El Jaro Creek 12 miles southeast of the town of Lompoc (lat. 34°30'55" N, long. 120°18'55" W). Named on Santa Rosa Hills (1959) 7.5' quadrangle.

Gay Mountain [SAN LUIS OBISPO]: *peak,* 1.25 miles southeast of Lopez Mountain (lat. 35°17'20" N, long. 120°33'45" W; sec. 27, T 30 S, R 13 E). Altitude 2859 feet. Named on Lopez Mountain (1965) 7.5' quadrangle.

Gem: see **Bryson** [MONTEREY].

George Hansen Canyon [SAN BENITO]: *canyon,* drained by a stream that flows nearly 4 miles to Rosas Canyon 3.25 miles east of North Chalone Peak (lat. 36°27'05" N, long. 121°08'05" W; near E line sec. 18, T 17 S, R 8 E). Named on North Chalone Peak (1969) and Topo Valley (1969) 7.5' quadrangles.

Getty: see **Getty Siding** [MONTEREY].

Getty Siding [MONTEREY]: *locality,* 8.5 miles north-northwest of Bradley along Southern Pacific Railroad (lat. 35°58'25" N, long. 120°52'25" W). Named on Wunpost (1949) 7.5' quadrangle. Called Getty on California Mining Bureau's (1917b) map.

Gibbons: see **Adelaida** [SAN LUIS OBISPO].

Gibbs [SANTA CRUZ]: *locality,* 5 miles east-southeast of the town of Boulder Creek along the rail line that follows Zayante Creek (lat. 37°05'30" N, long. 122°02'30" W; near W line sec. 1, T 10 S, R 2 W). Named on Santa Cruz (1902) 30' quadrangle. Postal authorities established Gibbs post office in 1900, discontinued it in 1906, reestablished it in 1907, and discontinued it in 1916; the name is for Albert W.J. Gibbs, a member of a pioneer family (Salley, p. 84).

Gibraltar Reservoir [SANTA BARBARA]: *lake,* behind a dam on Santa Ynez River 6 miles south-southeast of Little Pine Mountain (lat. 34°31'35" N, long. 119°41'10" W; near W line sec. 11, T 5 N, R 27 W). Named on Little Pine Mountain (1964) 7.5' quadrangle, which shows Gibraltar mine located just south of the lake. Called Santa Barbara Reservoir on Little Pine Mountain (1944) 7.5' quadrangle, but United States Board on Geographic Names (1965d, p. 9) rejected this name for the feature.

Gibson Beach: see **Sandy Beach** [MONTEREY].

Gibson Creek [MONTEREY]: *stream,* flows 2.25 miles to the sea 1.25 miles south-south-east of Point Lobos (lat. 36°30'25" N, long. 121°56'15" W). Named on Monterey (1947) and Soberanes Point (1956) 7.5' quadrangles. The name is for George Martin Gibson, a lumberman who took redwood posts from the canyon; earlier the stream was called Redwood Creek, and then Prader Creek for a man who reportedly cut trees near the stream (Clark, 1991, p. 186).

Gidney Creek [SANTA BARBARA]: *stream,* flows 3.5 miles to Gibraltar Reservoir nearly 7 miles southeast of Little Pine Mountain (lat. 34°31'10" N, long. 119°40'10" W). Named on Little Pine Mountain (1964) 7.5' quadrangle.

Gifford Spring [SAN LUIS OBISPO]: *spring,* 5 miles south-southeast of Branch Mountain (lat. 35°07'20" N, long. 120°02'25" W; on N line sec. 27, T 32 S, R 18 E). Named on Miranda Pine Mountain (1967) 7.5' quadrangle, which shows Gifford ranch situated 0.5 mile south-southwest of the spring.

Gigling: see **Gigling Siding** [MONTEREY].

Gigling Reservation: see **Fort Ord Military Reservation** [MONTEREY].

Gigling Siding [MONTEREY]: *locality,* 2.5 miles south-southwest of Marina along Southern Pacific Railroad on Fort Ord Military Reservation (lat. 36°39' N, long. 121°49' W). Named on Marina (1947) 7.5' quadrangle. Called Gigling on Monterey (1913) 15' quadrangle. The name commemorates the Gigling family, who owned land at the place (Gudde, 1949, p. 127).

Gillam Spring [SAN LUIS OBISPO]: *spring,* 4.5 miles southeast of Branch Mountain (lat. 35°08'35" N, long. 120°01'35" W). Named on Branch Mountain (1967) 7.5' quadrangle.

Gillis Canyon [SAN LUIS OBISPO]: *canyon,* drained by a stream that flows nearly 7 miles to San Juan Creek 4.5 miles south-southeast of Shandon (lat. 35°36'05" N, long. 120°19'55" W; near N line sec. 11, T 27 S, R 15 E). Named on Camatta Canyon (1961), Cholame (1961), and Orchard Peak (1961) 7.5' quadrangles.

Gipsy Peak: see **Antimony Peak** [SAN BENITO].

Glau Canyon [MONTEREY]: *canyon,* 3.5 miles long, opens into lowlands nearly 7 miles east of Jolon (lat. 35°57'15" N, long. 121° 03'20" W; sec. 1, T 23 S, R 8 E). Named on Williams Hill (1949) 7.5' quadrangle. The name commemorates the Glau family, who settled in the neighborhood in the late 1880's (Clark, 1991, p. 189).

Glaucophane Ridge [SAN BENITO]: *ridge,* northwest-trending, 6.5 miles long, 5 miles north-northwest of Panoche on the northeast side of Panoche Valley (lat. 36°40' N, long. 120°52' W). Named on Cerro Colorado (1969) and Mercey Hot Springs (1969) 7.5' quadrangles.

Glen Annie Canyon [SANTA BARBARA]: *canyon,* 3.25 miles long, drained by Tecolotito Creek above a point 2.5 miles west of downtown Goleta (lat. 34°26'10" N, long. 119°52'15" W). Named on Dos Pueblos Canyon (1951) and Goleta (1950) 7.5' quadrangles. Called Glen Anne Canyon on Goleta (1903) 15' quadrangle. West Fork branches north-northwest 4 miles north of Coal Oil Point; it is 2 miles long and is named on Dos Pueblos Canyon (1951) 7.5' quadrangle. In 1869 W.W. Hollister bought land that included the canyon, which he renamed for his wife; previously the feature was called Tecolotito Canyon (Tompkins and Ruiz, p. 88).

Glen Annie Reservoir [SANTA BARBARA]: *lake,* 1700 feet long, 4.5 miles north of Coal Oil Point (lat. 34°28'20" N, long. 119°52'50" W); the lake is in West Fork Glen Annie Canyon. Named on Dos Pueblos Canyon (1951) 7.5' quadrangle.

Glen Arbor [SANTA CRUZ]: *settlement,* 4 miles south-southeast of the town of Boulder Creek along San Lorenzo River (lat. 37°04'30" N, long. 122°04'50" W; sec. 9, T 10 S, R 2 W). Named on Felton (1955) 7.5' quadrangle. Postal authorities established Glen Arbor post office in 1914 and discontinued it in 1915 (Frickstad, p. 176).

Glenecho: see **Aptos** [SANTA CRUZ] (2).

Glen Haven: see **Grover Gulch** [SANTA CRUZ].

Glenrose Spring [SAN LUIS OBISPO]: *spring,* 5.25 miles north-northwest of Point San Luis along Coon Creek (lat. 35°14'35" N, long. 120°48'05" W; sec. 9, T 31 S, R 11 E). Named on Port San Luis (1965) 7.5' quadrangle.

Glenwood [SANTA CRUZ]: *settlement,* 8.5 miles north of Soquel along Bean Creek (lat. 37°06'30" N, long. 121°59'10" W; near E line sec. 32, T 9 S, R 1 W). Named on Laurel (1955) 7.5' quadrangle. Postal authorities established Glenwood post office in 1880 and discontinued it in 1954 (Frickstad, p. 176). The place was called Bean Hollow in the 1850's for the Bean family of Bean Creek (Clark, 1986, p. 21).

Glenwood Basin [SANTA CRUZ]: *valley,* 7 miles north of Soquel along West Branch Soquel Creek (lat. 37°05'20" N, long. 121°57'40" W); the feature is 2 miles southeast of Glenwood. Named on Laurel (1955) 7.5' quadrangle.

Glenwood Magnetic Springs: see **Magnetic Spring** [SANTA CRUZ].

Glines Canyon [SANTA BARBARA]: *canyon,* drained by a stream that flows 2 miles to Cuyama River 7 miles west-northwest of

Miranda Pine Mountain (lat. 35°05'25" N, long. 120°08'20" W; near NW cor. sec. 28, T 12 N, R 31 W). Named on Chimney Canyon (1967) 7.5' quadrangle. United States Board on Geographic Names (1968c, p. 5) rejected the form "Gline Canyon" for the name.

Gloria Lake [SAN BENITO]: *intermittent lake*, 0.25 mile long, 7 miles south-southeast of Mount Johnson along Chalone Creek (lat. 36°30'45" N, long. 121°16'40" W; sec. 26, T 16 S, R 6 E); the feature is in Gloria Valley. Named on Mount Johnson (1968) 7.5' quadrangle.

Gloria Valley [SAN BENITO]: *valley*, 7 miles south-southeast of Mount Johnson at the head of Chalone Creek (lat. 36°31' N, long. 121°16'45" W). Named on Mount Johnson (1968) 7.5' quadrangle.

Goat Camp [MONTEREY]: *locality*, about 7 miles south-southwest of San Lucas in Espinosa Canyon (2) (lat. 36°02'30" N, long. 121° 04'50" W; near W line sec. 2, T 22 S, T 8 E). Named on King City (1919) 15' quadrangle.

Goat Camp [SAN LUIS OBISPO]: *locality*, 8.5 miles east of the village of San Simeon (lat. 35°39'30" N, long. 121°02'30" W; sec. 19, T 26 S, R 9 E). Named on San Simeon (1919) 15' quadrangle.

Goat Mountain [SAN BENITO]: *peak*, 5.5 miles southwest of Idria (lat. 36°21'05" N, long. 120°44'05" W); sec. 23, T 18 S, R 11 E). Altitude 4085 feet. Named on San Benito Mountain (1969) 7.5' quadrangle.

Goat Rock [SANTA BARBARA]: *peak*, 4 south-southeast of Figueroa Mountain (lat. 34°41'30" N, long. 119°57'10" W; at N line sec. 17, T 7 N, R 29 W). Named on Figueroa Mountain (1959) 7.5' quadrangle. United States Board on Geographic Names (1981b, p. 3) approved the name "Chicken Springs" for springs located 2 miles southeast of Goat Rock (lat. 34°40'53" N, long. 119°55'05" W; sec. 15, T 7 N, R 29 W), and (p. 4) approved the name "Soldiers Home Spring" for a spring located 1.4 miles north-northwest of Chicken Springs (lat. 34°42'00" N, long. 119°55'32" W; sec. 10, T 7 N, R 29 W)—Soldiers Home Spring was named for Civil War veterans who homesteaded in the neighborhood.

Goat Rock [SANTA CRUZ]: *relief feature*, 7 miles north of the town of Boulder Creek (lat. 37°13'40" N, long. 122°06'25" W; near N line sec. 20, T 8 S, R 2 W). Named on Castle Rock Ridge (1955) 7.5' quadrangle.

Goat Spring [SAN LUIS OBISPO]: *spring*, 3.25 miles north-northwest of Caliente Mountain (lat. 32°04'45" N, long. 119°46'55" W; sec. 32, T 12 N, R 27 W). Named on Caliente Mountain (1959) 7.5' quadrangle.

Gobernador Creek [SANTA BARBARA]: *stream*, formed by the confluence of Eldorado Creek and Steer Creek, flows nearly 3.5 miles to Carpinteria Creek 2 miles north-northwest of Rincon Point (lat. 34°24'05" N, long.

119°29'05" W). Named on White Ledge Peak (1952) 7.5' quadrangle.

Godola: see **Gordola** [SANTA CRUZ].

Golden Hill [SAN LUIS OBISPO]: *peak*, 6.25 miles east of Adelaida (lat. 35°38'15" N, long. 120°45'45" W; sec. 26, T 26 S, R 11 E). Named on Adelaida (1961) 15' quadrangle.

Gold Gulch [SANTA CRUZ]: *canyon*, drained by a stream that flows 2.5 miles to San Lorenzo River 6.5 miles south-southeast of the town of Boulder Creek (lat. 37°02'25" N, long. 122°04'05" W). Named on Felton (1955) 7.5' quadrangle. John Hines discovered gold in the canyon in 1853 (Hamman, p. 83).

Gold Hill [MONTEREY]: *ridge*, northwest-trending, 1 mile long, 6.5 miles southeast of Parkfield on the northeast side of Cholame Valley (lat. 35°49'50" N, long. 120°21' W). Named on Cholame Valley (1961) 7.5' quadrangle.

Goldtree [SAN LUIS OBISPO]: *locality*, 3 miles north-northwest of San Luis Obispo along Southern Pacific Railroad (lat. 35°19'20" N, long. 120°40'55" W). Named on San Luis Obispo (1965) 7.5' quadrangle. According to Gudde (1969, p. 123), the name is an Americanization of the surname of Morris Goldbaum, who settled at the place in the 1890's—*baum* means "tree" in German. California Mining Bureau's (1917c) map has the name "Hathaway" at the place.

Goleta [SANTA BARBARA]: *town*, 8 miles west of Santa Barbara (lat. 34°26'10" N, long. 119°49'35" W). Named on Goleta (1950) 7.5' quadrangle. Postal authorities established Goleta post office in 1875 (Frickstad, p. 170). They established Los Alisos post office less than 2 miles north-northeast of present downtown Goleta (N half sec. 4, T 4 N, R 28 W) in 1870 and discontinued it in 1871 (Salley, p. 126-127). They established Inez post office 11 miles west of Goleta in 1881 and discontinued it the same year (Salley, p. 104).

Goleta Landing [SANTA BARBARA]: *locality*, 1.5 miles southeast of present downtown Goleta along the coast (lat. 34°24'55" N, long. 119°48'50" W). Named on Goleta (1903) 15' quadrangle.

Goleta Point [SANTA BARBARA]: *promontory*, 2.25 miles south-southwest of downtown Goleta along the coast (lat. 34°24'15" N, long. 118°50'35" W). Named on Goleta (1950) 7.5' quadrangle. United States Board on Geographic Names (1933, p. 329) rejected the name "Pelican Point" for the feature. H.R. Wagner (p. 481) noted that the promontory had the name "Punta de Pantoja" in Spanish times.

Goleta Slough [SANTA BARBARA]: *marsh*, 1.25 miles southwest of downtown Goleta (lat. 34°25'15" N, long. 119°50'30" W). Named on Goleta (1950) 7.5' quadrangle.

Gomez's Pass: see **Mud Creek** [MONTEREY].

Gonzales [MONTEREY]: *town*, 16 miles southeast of Salinas (lat. 36°30'30" N, long.

121°26'40" W). Named on Gonzales (1955) 7.5' quadrangle. Postal authorities established Gonzales post office in 1873 (Frickstad, p. 107), and the town incorporated in 1947. The name commemorates the Gonzales family, owner of Ricon de la Puente del Monte grant where the town lies (Hoover, Rensch, and Rensch, p. 229).

Goodall: see **Camp Goodall**, under **Palm Beach** [SANTA BARBARA].

Goode Canyon [SANTA BARBARA]: *canyon,* drained by a stream that flows 3.5 miles to Cuyama Valley 4 miles southeast of the village of Cuyama (lat. 34°53'15" N, long. 119°34'35" W; sec. 5, T 9 N, R 25 W). Named on Cuyama (1964) and Fox Mountain (1964) 7.5' quadrangles.

Goode Spring [SANTA BARBARA]: *spring,* 2.25 miles north of Fox Mountain (lat. 34°50'50" N, long. 119°35'40" W); the spring is near the head of Goode Canyon. Named on Fox Mountain (1964) 7.5' quadrangle.

Goodwin: see **Carrizo Plain** [SAN LUIS OBISPO].

Gorda [MONTEREY]: *locality,* 3 miles north of Cape San Martin near the coast (lat. 35°56' N, long. 121°28' W; sec. 18, T 23 S, R 5 E). Named on Cape San Martin (1949) 7.5' quadrangle. Cape San Martin (1921) 15' quadrangle has the name "Gorda P.O." at the place. Postal authorities established Gorda post office in 1893, moved it 1 mile north in 1910, and discontinued it in 1923 (Salley, p. 87).

Gorda: see **Point Gorda**, under **Cape San Martin** [MONTEREY].

Gordola [SANTA CRUZ]: *locality,* 6.25 miles west-northwest of Point Santa Cruz along Southern Pacific Railroad (lat. 36°58'30" N, long. 122°08' W). Named on Santa Cruz (1954) 7.5' quadrangle. Called Godola on California Mining Bureau's (1917a) map. Pio Scaroni moved to the vicinity in 1868 and named the site for his birthplace in Switzerland (Clark, 1986, p. 137).

Gorge: see **The Gorge** [SAN BENITO].

Gorge Creek [SAN BENITO]: *stream,* flows 2.5 miles to Red Mountain Creek nearly 6 miles east-northeast of Bitterwater (lat. 36°25'15" N, long. 120°54'25" W; sec. 29, T 17 S, R 10 E). Named on Rock Spring Peak (1969) 7.5' quadrangle.

Gould Creek [SAN LUIS OBISPO]: *stream,* flows nearly 5 miles to Little Burnett Creek 9.5 miles northeast of the village of San Simeon (lat. 35°44'50" N, long. 121°04'40" W; at S line sec. 14, T 25 S, R 8 E). Named on Bryson (1949) and Pebblestone Shut-in (1959) 7.5' quadrangles.

Government Point [SANTA BARBARA]: *promontory,* 1 mile east-southeast of Point Conception along the coast (lat. 34°26'30" N, long. 120°27'05" W); the feature is west of Cojo Bay. Named on Point Conception (1953) 7.5' quadrangle. H.R. Wagner (p. 449) noted that Esteban Jose Martinez gave the name

"Punta de Echevarria" to the promontory in 1782 to honor Agustin de Echevarria, the captain of a vessel under the command of Martinez. H.R. Wagner (p. 523) also mentioned that the promontory west of Cojo Bay was called Punta de Villaverde by the Spaniards to honor Jose Villaverde, chaplain of the Martinez expedition in 1782.

Graciosa [SANTA BARBARA]: *locality,* 6.5 miles south of Santa Maria along Pacific Coast Railroad (lat. 34°51'30" N, long. 120°27'05" W); the place is in Graciosa Canyon. Named on Lompoc (1905) 30' quadrangle.

Graciosa Canyon [SANTA BARBARA]: *canyon,* 2 miles long, opens into the canyon of Orcutt Creek 0.25 mile west of Orcutt (lat. 34° 51'50" N, long. 120°27' W); the canyon heads west of Graciosa Ridge. Named on Orcutt (1959) 7.5' quadrangle. The name "Graciosa" in the region dates from the time of the Portola expedition in 1769 (Gudde, 1949, p. 132). Postal authorities established La Graciosa post office 9 miles south of Santa Maria in 1872, moved it 1 mile north in 1880, and discontinued it in 1889—the name was for the canyon (Salley, p. 114).

Graciosa Ridge [SANTA BARBARA]: *ridge,* generally west-trending, 2 miles long, 3 miles southeast of Orcutt (lat. 34°50' N, long. 120°24'20" W); the ridge is east of Graciosa Canyon. Named on Orcutt (1959) 7.5' quadrangle. United States Board on Geographic Names (1978b, p. 4) rejected the form "Gracioso Ridge" for the name.

Gragg Canyon [SAN LUIS OBISPO]: *canyon,* drained by a stream that flows 3 miles to the canyon of San Luis Obispo Creek 1.5 miles east of Avila Beach (lat. 35°10'50" N, long. 120°42'10" W). Named on Pismo Beach (1965) 7.5' quadrangle. United States Board on Geographic Names (1992, p. 4) rejected the form "Gregg Canyon" for the name, and noted that George Gragg settled at the place.

Grahams: see **Zayanta** [SANTA CRUZ].

Grand Central Sulphur Spring: see **Paso Robles** [SAN LUIS OBISPO].

Grande Canyon: see **Llano Grande Canyon** [MONTEREY].

Grandmas Flat [MONTEREY]: *area,* 9 miles west-southwest of Greenfield on the south side of Arroyo Seco (1) (lat. 36°15'40" N, long. 121°23'10" W; sec. 23, 24, T 19 S, R 5 E). Named on Sycamore Flat (1956) 7.5' quadrangle.

Grand Spring [SANTA BARBARA]: *spring,* 4.5 miles southwest of San Rafael Mountain (lat. 34°39'50" N, long. 119°52'05" W; sec. 19, T 7 N, R 28 W). Named on San Rafael Mountain (1959) 7.5' quadrangle.

Granger Spring [SAN LUIS OBISPO]: *spring,* 2.5 miles southwest of Cholame (lat. 35°42'25" N, long. 120°20' W; sec. 35, T 25 S, R 15 E). Named on Cholame (1961) 7.5' quadrangle.

Grangeville: see **Santa Maria** [SANTA BARBARA].

Granite Canyon [MONTEREY]: *canyon,* drained by a stream that flows 3 miles to the sea 9 miles north of Point Sur (lat. 36°26'10" N, long. 121°55'05" W). Named on Soberanes Point (1956) 7.5' quadrangle.

Granite Creek [SANTA CRUZ]: *stream,* flows 2.5 miles to Branciforte Creek 7 miles south-southwest of Laurel (lat. 37°01'05" N, long. 121°59'45" W; sec. 32, T 10 S, R 1 W). Named on Laurel (1955) 7.5' quadrangle. The canyon of the stream has been called both Bachelder Gulch and Waddell Gulch (Clark, 1986, p. 139).

Granite Point [MONTEREY]: *promontory,* 1 mile east of Point Lobos on the south side of Carmel Bay (lat. 36°31'25" N, long. 121°56'10" W). Named on Monterey (1947) 7.5' quadrangle.

Granite Ridge [SAN LUIS OBISPO]: *ridge,* west-northwest-trending, 1.25 miles long, 5 miles north-northeast of Santa Margarita (lat. 35°27'20" N, long. 120°34'10" W). Named on Santa Margarita (1965) 7.5' quadrangle.

Grant Ewing Ridge [MONTEREY]: *ridge,* west-northwest-trending, 0.5 mile long, 4 miles south of Marina (lat. 36°37'45" N, long. 121°47'10" W). Named on Marina (1947) 7.5' quadrangle.

Grant Lake [SAN LUIS OBISPO]: *lake,* 800 feet long, 13 miles east-southeast of Shandon in Palo Prieto Pass (lat. 35°35'45" N, long. 120°09' W; sec. 9, T 27 S, R 17 E). Named on Cholame (1917) 30' quadrangle. Holland Canyon (1961) 7.5' quadrangle does not show the lake.

Grapevine Campground: see **Lower Grapevine Campground** [SANTA BARBARA].

Grapevine Creek [SANTA BARBARA]: *stream,* flows 4 miles to East Fork Santa Cruz Creek 4.5 miles southwest of Big Pine Mountain (lat. 34°39'30" N, long. 119°43'05" W). Named on Big Pine Mountain (1964) 7.5' quadrangle.

Grapevine Creek: see **Coche Creek** [SANTA BARBARA].

Grass Valley [SAN BENITO]: *valley,* 5.5 miles west of Paicines along Pescadero Creek (lat. 36°43'45" N, long. 121°22'30" W). Named on Mount Harlan (1968) and Paicines (1968) 7.5' quadrangles.

Grassy Canyon [SAN BENITO]: *canyon,* drained by a stream that flows nearly 2 miles to Chalone Creek 3 miles northeast of North Chalone Peak (lat. 36°28'30" N, long. 121°09'05" W; near SE cor. sec. 1, T 17 S, R 7 E). Named on North Chalone Peak (1969) 7.5' quadrangle.

Graves [MONTEREY]: *locality,* 2.5 miles west-northwest of Salinas along Southern Pacific Railroad (lat. 36°41'45" N, long. 121°41'50" W). Named on Salinas (1947) 7.5' quadrangle.

Graves: see **Ben Graves Canyon** [MONTEREY].

Graves Canyon [MONTEREY]: *canyon,* drained by a stream that flows 1.5 miles to Mule Canyon Creek 4.25 miles east-southeast of Pfeiffer Point (lat. 36°13'10" N, long. 121°45'30" W; sec. 5, T 20 S, R 2 E). Named on Partington Ridge (1956) and Pfeiffer Point (1956) 7.5' quadrangles. The name is from graves in a small Castro-family cemetery in the canyon (Clark, 1991, p. 195).

Graves Creek [SAN LUIS OBISPO]: *stream,* flows 10.5 miles to Salinas River 7 miles south of Paso Robles (lat. 35°31'50" N, long. 120°42'10" W). Named on Atascadero (1965), Morro Bay North (1965), and Templeton (1948) 7.5' quadrangles.

Green Canyon [SAN LUIS OBISPO]: *canyon,* drained by a stream that flows 3.5 miles to Arroyo de la Cruz nearly 5 miles north-northwest of the village of San Simeon (lat. 35°42'10" N, long. 121°13'55" W). Named on San Simeon (1958) 7.5' quadrangle.

Green Canyon [SANTA BARBARA]: *canyon,* drained by a stream that flows 7 miles to Cuyama Valley 7 miles north of McPherson Peak (lat. 34°59'25" N, long. 119°48'55" W). Named on Peak Mountain (1964) 7.5' quadrangle.

Greenfield [MONTEREY]: *town,* 33 miles southeast of Salinas (lat. 36°19'15" N, long. 121°14'30" W). Named on Greenfield (1956) and Paraiso Springs (1956) 7.5' quadrangles. Promoters laid out the town between 1902 and 1905; first it was called Clarke City for John S. Clarke, one of the promoters, but when postal authorities rejected the name "Clarke City," the town was renamed Greenfield (Gudde, 1949, p. 135). Postal authorities established Greenfield post office in 1905 (Frickstad, p. 107), and the town incorporated in 1947.

Green Mountain [SANTA BARBARA]: *ridge,* south-southeast-trending, 1 mile long, 4 miles east of Point Bennett on San Miguel Island (lat. 34°02'10" N, long. 120°23'05" W). Named on San Miguel Island West (1950) 7.5' quadrangle.

Green Oaks Creek [SANTA CRUZ]: *stream,* flows 1 mile to San Mateo County 3.25 miles north-northwest of the mouth of Waddell Creek (lat. 37°08'20" N, long. 122°18'20" W; sec. 21, T 9 S, R 4 W). Named on Franklin Point (1955) 7.5' quadrangle. Santa Cruz (1902) 30' quadrangle has the form "Greenoaks Cr." for the name, which is from the Green Oaks dairy ranch that was started along the stream in 1863 (Brown, p. 37).

Green Peak [SAN LUIS OBISPO]: *peak,* 5 miles northwest of Point San Luis (lat. 35°12'20" N, long. 120°49'35" W). Altitude 1414 feet. Named on Port San Luis (1965) 7.5' quadrangle.

Greentree Spring [SAN BENITO]: *spring,* 6.25 miles east-southeast of Bitterwater along Cholla Creek (lat. 36°20'15" N, long. 120°54'05" W; near W line sec. 28, T 18 S, R

10 E). Named on Lonoak (1969) 7.5' quadrangle.

Green Valley [MONTEREY]: *canyon,* nearly 3 miles long, opens into Long Valley 9 miles east-northeast of San Lucas (lat. 36°10' N, long. 120°53'10" W; near NE cor. sec. 28, T 20 S, R 10 E). Named on Monarch Peak (1967) and Nattrass Valley (1967) 7.5' quadrangles.

Green Valley [SAN LUIS OBISPO]: *valley,* 2.5 miles long, 4 miles southeast of Cambria (lat. 35°32' N, long. 121°01' W). Named on Cambria (1959) 7.5' quadrangle.

Green Valley [SANTA CRUZ]: *valley,* 1.5 miles east of Corralitos (lat. 36°59'30" N, long. 121°46'35" W). Named on Loma Prieta (1955) and Watsonville West (1954) 7.5' quadrangles. Gudde (1949, p. 134-135) noted that the valley is called Cañada Verde on a Mexican map of 1844. The stream in the valley is called Green Valley Cr. on Alexander's (1953) map.

Green Valley Creek [SAN LUIS OBISPO]: *stream,* flows 7.25 miles to Perry Creek 3 miles southeast of Cambria (lat. 35°31'55" N, long. 121°02'55" W); the stream drains Green Valley. Named on Cambria (1959) and Cypress Mountain (1948, photorevised 1979) 7.5' quadrangles.

Green Valley Creek: see **Green Valley** [SANTA CRUZ].

Gregg Canyon: see **Gragg Canyon** [SAN LUIS OBISPO].

Grey Canyon [SANTA BARBARA]: *canyon,* 2.25 miles long, opens to the sea 1.5 miles north-northeast of Point Arguello (lat. 34°35'40" N, long. 120°38'20" W). Named on Point Arguello (1959) and Tranquillon Mountain (1959) 7.5' quadrangles.

Grey Eagle Terrace: see **Seaside** [MONTEREY].

Greyhound Rock [SANTA CRUZ]: *promontory,* 1.25 miles south-southeast of the mouth of Waddell Creek along the coast (lat. 37° 04'40" N, long. 122°16' W). Named on Año Nuevo (1955) 7.5' quadrangle.

Grimes Canyon [MONTEREY]: *canyon,* drained by a stream that flows nearly 1.5 miles to the sea 3 miles northwest of Point Sur (lat. 36°12'20" N, long. 121°44'20" W; near W line sec. 10, T 20 S, R 2 E). Named on Partington Ridge (1956) 7.5' quadrangle.

Grimes Point [MONTEREY]: *promontory,* 3 miles northwest of Point Sur along the coast (lat. 36°12'20" N, long. 121°44'10" W; at W line sec. 10, T 20 S, R 2 E); the feature is just south of the mouth of Grimes Canyon. Named on Partington Ridge (1956) 7.5' quadrangle.

Griswold: see **San Lucas** [MONTEREY] (2).

Griswold Canyon [MONTEREY]: *canyon,* 2.25 miles long, branches north from Long Valley 9.5 miles east-northeast of San Lucas (lat. 36°10' N, long. 120°52'05" W; near NE cor. sec. 27, T 20 S, R 10 E). Named on Monarch Peak (1967) 7.5' quadrangle. The name is for William E. Griswold, who owned land at and near the mouth of the canyon (Clark, 1991, p. 198).

Griswold Canyon [SAN BENITO]: *canyon,* 3.5 miles long, 3.5 miles south of Panoche between Panoche Valley and Vallecitos (lat. 36° 32'30" N, long. 120°50' W); the canyon is at the west end of Griswold Hills along Griswold Creek. Named on Panoche (1969) 7.5' quadrangle. According to Anderson and Pack (p. 18), "the canyon has been termed variously Griswold, Grizzly, and Lyon Canyon, but Griswold is believed to be the original name." United States Board on Geographic Names (1972a, p. 1) listed the names "Grizzly Canyon" and "Lyon Canyon" as variants.

Griswold Creek [SAN BENITO]: *stream,* formed by the confluence of Vallecitos Creek and Pimental Creek, flows 6.5 miles to Panoche Creek 1.5 miles southeast of Panoche (lat. 36°35' N, long. 120°48'35" W; sec. 31, T 15 S, R 11 E). Named on Panoche (1969) 7.5' quadrangle. The name is for an early rancher (Hoover, Rensch, and Rensch, p. 314).

Griswold Creek: see **Vallecitos Creek** [SAN BENITO].

Griswold Hills [SAN BENITO]: *range,* 4.5 miles south-southeast of Panoche between Panoche Valley on the north, Vallecitos on the south, Griswold Creek on the west, and Silver Creek on the east (lat. 36°32'30" N, long. 120°47'30" W). Named on Idria (1969), Panoche (1969), and Tumey Hills (1956) 7.5' quadrangles.

Griswolds [SAN BENITO]: *locality,* 8 miles northwest of Idria near present Syncline Divide (lat. 36°28'50" N, long. 120°47'15" W; sec. 5, T 17 S, R 11 E). Named on Priest Valley (1915) 30' quadrangle. Whitney (p. 56) referred to Griswold's as a ranch house, and added, "But what the inducements could be to live in such a place it was beyond our power to determine."

Grizzly Bend [SAN LUIS OBISPO]: *bend,* 10 miles northeast of the village of San Simeon along Nacimiento River (lat. 35°45' N, long. 121°03'15" W; near E line sec. 13, 24, T 25 S, R 8 E). Named on Bryson (1949) and Pebblestone Shut-in (1959) 7.5' quadrangles.

Grizzly Bend Creek: see **North Grizzly Bend Creek** [SAN LUIS OBISPO].

Grizzly Canyon: see **Griswold Canyon** [SAN BENITO].

Grizzly Flat [SANTA BARBARA]: *area,* nearly 4 miles north of Corralitos (lat. 37°02'35" N, long. 121°47'40" W; sec. 19, T 10 S, R 2 E). Named on Loma Prieta (1955) 7.5' quadrangle.

Grizzly Mountain: see **Grizzly Rock** [SANTA CRUZ].

Grizzly Rock [SANTA CRUZ]: *relief feature,* 6 miles north-northeast of the town of Boulder Creek (lat. 37°12' N, long. 122°04' W; near S line sec. 27, T 8 S, R 2 W). Altitude 2716 feet. Named on Castle Rock Ridge (1955) 7.5' quadrangle. Called Grizzly Mt. on Hubbard's (1943) map.

Grizzly Spring [SAN LUIS OBISPO]: *spring*, 1 mile east of Branch Mountain (lat. 35°11'05" N, long. 120°03'50" W; sec. 32, T 31 S, R 18 E). Named on Branch Mountain (1967) 7.5' quadrangle.

Grogan: see **Paicines** [SAN BENITO].

Grover: see **Grover City** [SAN LUIS OBISPO].

Grover City [SAN LUIS OBISPO]: *town*, 2 miles west of downtown Arroyo Grande (lat. 35°07'15" N, long. 120°37'15" W). Named on Arroyo Grande NE (1965), Oceano (1965), and Pismo Beach (1965) 7.5' quadrangles. Called Grover on Arroyo Grande (1942) 15' quadrangle. W.A. Grover founded the town in 1890 (Lee and others, p. 64). Postal authorities established Grover City post office in 1947 (Frickstad, p. 164), and the town incorporated in 1959. According to Gudde (1969, p. 129), the town was named Grover in 1892 for Henry Grover; H.V. Bagwell renamed the place Grover City in 1937.

Grover Gulch [SANTA CRUZ]: *canyon*, drained by a stream that flows 2.5 miles to Bates Creek 2 miles northeast of Soquel (lat. 37° 00'35" N, long. 121°56'05" W). Named on Laurel (1955) 7.5' quadrangle. According to Clark (1986, p. 133), the feature now is called Glen Haven.

Gruenhagen Flat [SAN LUIS OBISPO]: *area*, 6.25 miles west of Shandon on the north side of Estrella River (lat. 35°39' N, long. 120°29'15" W). Named on Shandon (1961) 7.5' quadrangle.

Guadaloupe: see **Guadalupe** [SAN LUIS OBISPO-SANTA BARBARA]; **Guadalupe** [SANTA BARBARA].

Guadalupe [SAN LUIS OBISPO-SANTA BARBARA]: *land grant*, at and near the town of Guadalupe on San Luis Obispo-Santa Barbara county line in Santa Maria Valley. Named on Guadalupe (1959), Oceano (1965), Point Sal (1958), and Santa Maria (1959) 7.5' quadrangles. Diego Olivera and Teodoro Arellanes received the land in 1840 and claimed 43,682 acres patented in 1870 (Cowan, p. 38). United States Board on Geographic Names (1933, p. 342) rejected the forms "Gaudalupe," "Guadaloupe," and "Guadelupe" for the name.

Guadalupe [SANTA BARBARA]: *town*, 8 miles west of Santa Maria (lat. 34°58'20" N, long. 120°34'15" W). Named on Guadalupe (1959) 7.5' quadrangle. Postal authorities established Guadaloupe post office in 1873 and changed the name to Guadalupe in 1915 (Frickstad, p. 171). The town incorporated in 1946. United States Board on Geographic Names (1933, p. 342) rejected the forms "Gaudalupe," "Guadaloupe," and "Guadelupe" for the name.

Guadalupe Lake [SANTA BARBARA]: *intermittent lake*, 1.5 miles long, 4.5 miles southeast of the town of Guadalupe (lat. 34° 54'35" N, long. 120°32'05" W). Named on Point Sal (1947) 15' quadrangle. Guadalupe (1905) 30' quadrangle shows a permanent lake. H.R. Wagner (p. 498) identified the lake as the one that members of the Portola expedition called Laguna Grande de San Daniel in 1769, and noted that Portola also called the feature Laguna Larga.

Guadalupe Largo: see **Santa Maria Valley** [SAN LUIS OBISPO-SANTA BARBARA].

Guadalupe y Llanitos de los Correos [MONTEREY]: *land grant*, 2.5 miles southwest of Chualar. Named on Chualar (1947), Gonzales (1955), Palo Escrito Peak (1956), and Rana Creek (1956) 7.5' quadrangles. Juan Malarin received 2 leagues in 1833; Mariano Malarin, executor, claimed 8859 acres patented in 1865 (Cowan, p. 38). Perez (p. 68) gave 1835 as the date of the grant.

Guadelupe: see **Guadalupe** [SAN LUIS OBISPO-SANTA BARBARA]; **Guadalupe** [SANTA BARBARA].

Guaya Canyon [SAN LUIS OBISPO]: *canyon*, 2.5 miles long, opens into Arroyo Grande Valley 1.5 miles east of downtown Arroyo Grande (lat. 35°07'15" N, long. 120°33'25" W). Named on Oceano (1965) 7.5' quadrangles.

Guaymas River: see **San Antonio Creek** [SANTA BARBARA] (1).

Guillemot Island: see **Bluefish Cove** [MONTEREY].

Gulch House Creek [MONTEREY]: *stream*, flows 2.5 miles to Sapaque Creek 13 miles south-southeast of Jolon (lat. 35°47'50" N, long. 121°05'35" W; sec. 34, T 24 S, R 8 E). Named on Bryson (1949) 7.5' quadrangle. The name is from a place called The Gulch House that Job Wood owned in Sapaque Valley (Clark, 1991, p. 198).

Gull Island [SANTA BARBARA]: *island*, 550 feet long, 4000 feet south-southwest of Punta Arena off Santa Cruz Island (lat. 33° 57' N, long. 119°49'30" W). Named on Santa Cruz Island B (1943) 7.5' quadrangle.

Gull Island: see **Sutil Island** [SANTA BARBARA].

Gull Neck Rock [MONTEREY]: *relief feature*, 18 miles north of San Ardo on Mustang Ridge (lat. 36°16'55" N, long. 120°51'50" W; sec. 14, T 19 S, R 10 E). Named on Hepsedam Peak (1969) 7.5' quadrangle.

Gum [SANTA BARBARA]: *locality*, 4.5 miles southeast of the town of Guadalupe along Santa Maria Valley Railroad (lat. 34°55'15" N, long. 120°31'20" W). Named on Guadalupe (1959) 7.5' quadrangle.

Guyamas River: see **Cuyama River** [SAN LUIS OBISPO-SANTA BARBARA].

Gypsum Canyon [SAN LUIS OBISPO]: *canyon*, drained by a stream that flows 3.5 miles to Cuyama River 6.5 miles south of Branch Mountain (lat. 35°05'40" N, long. 120°03'35" W; sec. 33, T 32 S, R 18 E).

Named on Branch Mountain (1967) and Miranda Pine Mountain (1967) 7.5' quadrangles.

– H –

Hadley [SAN LUIS OBISPO]: *locality,* 1 mile south of Etna along Southern Pacific Railroad (lat. 35°11'15" N, long. 120°36'40" W). Named on Arroyo Grande (1952) 15' quadrangle. Called Hadley Tower on Arroyo Grande (1942) 15' quadrangle, which shows Pacific Coast Railroad crossing Southern Pacific Railroad at the place.

Hadley Tower: see **Hadley** [SAN LUIS OBISPO].

Haelleck Canyon [MONTEREY]: *canyon,* drained by a stream that flows 1 mile to James Creek at Jamesburg (lat. 36°22'10" N, long. 121°35'20" W; sec. 18, T 18 S, R 4 E). Named on Chews Ridge (1956) 7.5' quadrangle. Clark (1991, p. 200) associated the name with the Hallock family, who owned land in or near the canyon.

Hains Point [MONTEREY]: *ridge,* east-trending, nearly 0.5 mile long, 4 miles southwest of Salinas (lat. 36°38'15" N, long. 121°42'45" W). Named on Salinas (1947) 7.5' quadrangle.

Halcyon [SAN LUIS OBISPO]: *village,* 1.5 miles south-southwest of downtown Arroyo Grande (lat. 35°06'10" N, long. 120°35'35" W). Named on Oceano (1965) 7.5' quadrangle. In 1904 Dr. William H. Dower and Mrs. Francia A. La Due opened a sanatorium at the place that grew into a cooperative theosophical colony (Hoover, Rensch, and Rensch, p. 386). Postal authorities established Halcyon post office in 1908 (Frickstad, p. 164).

Hale Creek [SAN LUIS OBISPO]: *stream,* flows nearly 3 miles to Atascadero Creek 5 miles south-southwest of Atascadero (lat. 35° 25'25" N, long. 120°41'50" W; sec. 9, T 29 S, R 12 E). Named on Atascadero (1965) 7.5' quadrangle.

Hale McLeod Canyon [SAN LUIS OBISPO]: *canyon,* drained by a stream that flows nearly 3 miles to Kern County 28 miles east-southeast of Simmler (lat. 35°08'55" N, long. 119°33'20" W; at E line sec. 12, T 32 S, R 22 E). Named on Fellows (1951) 7.5' quadrangle. Rintoul (p. 92) noted that Hale-McLeod Oil Company operated in the neighborhood.

Halfway House: see **Salinas** [MONTEREY].

Hall [MONTEREY]: *settlement,* 7 miles north-northwest of Prunedale (lat. 36°51'50" N, long. 121°44' W). Named on Prunedale (1954) 7.5' quadrangle. The name is from a pioneer family (Clark, 1991, p. 200). United States Board on Geographic Names (1994, p. 5) approved the name "Las Lomas" for the place.

Hall Canyon [MONTEREY]: *canyon,* 4.5 miles long, opens into lowlands 3.5 miles east of Jolon (lat. 35°58'45" W, long. 121°06'35" W;

sec. 33, T 22 S, R 8 E). Named on Espinosa Canyon (1949) and Williams Hill (1949) 7.5' quadrangles. The name commemorates Wilson Hall, who lived in the canyon (Clark, 1991, p. 200).

Halleck: see **Fort Halleck**, under **Presidio of Monterey** [MONTEREY].

Hall's Natural Bridge: see **Moore Creek** [SANTA CRUZ].

Hames: see **Hames Valley** [MONTEREY].

Hames Creek [MONTEREY]: *stream,* flows 14 miles to Salinas River 2 miles west-northwest of Bradley (lat. 35°52'40" N, long. 120°50' W; near NE cor. sec. 1, T 24 S, R 10 E); the stream drains Hames Valley. Named on Hames Valley (1949) and Tierra Redonda Mountain (1949) 7.5' quadrangles.

Hames Valley [MONTEREY]: *valley,* 4.5 miles west of Bradley (lat. 35°52'30" N, long. 120°53' W). Named on Bradley (1949), Hames Valley (1949), and Tierra Redonda Mountain (1949) 7.5' quadrangles. California Mining Bureau's (1909a) map shows a place called Hames located 6 miles by stage line west of Bradley. Postal authorities established Hames post office in Hames Valley in 1889, moved it 1.25 miles northeast in 1892, and discontinued it in 1914 (Salley, p. 92). The name is for John Hames, a landowner in the valley (Clark, 1991, p. 201).

Hamilton Canyon [MONTEREY]: *canyon,* drained by a stream that flows 5 miles to lowlands 3.25 miles north-northwest of San Lucas (lat. 36°10'35" N, long. 121°02' W; sec. 19, T 20 S, R 9 E). Named on Nattrass Valley (1967) and San Lucas (1949) 7.5' quadrangles. The name is for Samuel Hamilton, John Steinbeck's maternal grandfather, who patented land in the canyon in 1891 (Clark, 1991, p. 201-202).

Hammond Spring [SAN LUIS OBISPO]: *spring,* 3 miles west-northwest of Cholame (lat. 35°44'15" N, long. 120°20'55" W; sec. 22, T 25 S, R 15 E). Named on Cholame (1961) 7.5' quadrangle.

Hampton Canyon [SAN LUIS OBISPO]: *canyon,* drained by a stream that flows 1.5 miles to Reservoir Canyon 2.25 miles southwest of Lopez Mountain (lat. 35°16'40" N, long. 120°36'15" W; sec. 32, T 30 S, R 13 E). Named on Lopez Mountain (1965) 7.5' quadrangle.

Handley Canyon [MONTEREY]: *canyon,* drained by a stream that flows 0.5 mile to the canyon of Chalone Creek 4 miles northeast of Greenfield (lat. 36°21'50" N, long. 121°11'45" W). Named on Greenfield (1956) 7.5' quadrangle.

Hanlon: see **Jacques Hanlon Creek** [MONTEREY]; **Mount Hanlon**, under **Mount Harlan** [SAN BENITO].

Hansen: see **George Hansen Canyon** [SAN BENITO].

Hanson Slough [SANTA CRUZ]: *stream,* flows 1 mile in an artificial watercourse to

Watsonville Slough 2.5 miles west-southwest of Watsonville (lat. 36°53'50" N, long. 121°47'25" W). Named on Watsonville West (1954) 7.5' quadrangle.

Happy Canyon [SANTA BARBARA]: *canyon,* drained by a stream that flows 9 miles to Santa Agueda Creek 3.5 miles east-southeast of Santa Ynez (lat. 34°36'05" N, long. 120°01'10" W). Named on Figueroa Mountain (1959), Lake Cachuma (1959), and Santa Ynez (1959) 7.5' quadrangles.

Happy Hunting Ground Campground [SANTA BARBARA]: *locality,* 7 miles southwest of Montgomery Potrero (lat. 34°45'05"N, long. 119°49'20" W). Named on Hurricane Deck (1964) 7.5' quadrangle.

Happy Valley [MONTEREY]: *canyon,* drained by a stream that flows 1.5 miles to an unnamed valley 0.5 mile east of Paraiso Springs (lat. 36°20' N, long. 121°21'25" W; sec. 30, T 18 S, R 8 E). Named on Paraiso Springs (1956) 7.5' quadrangle.

Harbor of Saint Simeon: see **San Simeon Bay** [SAN LUIS OBISPO].

Hare Canyon [MONTEREY]:
(1) *canyon,* drained by a stream that flows 3.5 miles to Limekiln Creek nearly 3 miles east-southeast of Lopez Point (lat. 36°00'40" N, long. 121°31' W; near S line sec. 15, T 22 S, R 4 E). Named on Cone Peak (1949) and Lopez Point (1956) 7.5' quadrangles. According to Clark (1991, p. 203), Lou G. Hare, the surveyor who produced the official map of Monterey County in 1898, named the feature for himself.
(2) *canyon,* drained by a stream that flows 6 miles to Salinas River 2 miles east of Bradley (lat. 35°51'30" N, long. 120°46' W; sec. 10, T 24 S, R 11 E). Named on Bradley (1949) and Valleton (1948) 7.5' quadrangles.

Hare Creek [SANTA CRUZ]: *stream,* flows 1.5 miles to Boulder Creek (1) 3.5 miles east-southeast of Big Basin (lat. 37°09'10" N, long. 122°09'40" W; sec. 14, T 9 S, R 3 W). Named on Big Basin (1955) 7.5' quadrangle.

Hare Rock [SANTA BARBARA]: *rock,* 4.5 miles northwest of Cardwell Point, and 600 feet offshore on the north side of San Miguel Island (lat. 34°03'55" N, long. 120°21'15" W). Named on San Miguel Island East (1950) 7.5' quadrangle.

Harford: see **Port Harford**, under **Port San Luis** [SAN LUIS OBISPO].

Harford Canyon [SAN LUIS OBISPO]: *canyon,* drained by a stream that flows 2.5 miles to San Luis Obispo Creek 0.5 mile west-northwest of Avila Beach (lat. 35°10'50" N, long. 120°44'20" W). Named on Pismo Beach (1965) 7.5' quadrangle. Called Hartford Canyon on Arroyo Grande (1942) 15' quadrangle, but United States Board on Geographic Names (1967a, p. 9) rejected this name.

Harkins Slough [SANTA CRUZ]: *stream,* flows 7.25 miles to Watsonville Slough 3 miles west-southwest of Watsonville (lat. 36°53'25" N,

long. 121°48'05" W). Named on Watsonville West (1954) 7.5' quadrangle.

Harlan: see **Mount Harlan** [SAN BENITO].

Harlan Creek [SAN BENITO]: *stream,* flows 2.5 miles to Indian Canyon 5.25 miles west-southwest of Paicines (lat. 36°42'20" N, long. 121°22'05" W; near N line sec. 24, T 14 S, R 5 E); the stream heads near Mount Harlan. Named on Mount Harlan (1968) and Paicines (1968) 7.5' quadrangles.

Harlan Rock [MONTEREY]: *rock,* 100 feet long, 2 miles east of Lopez Point, and 0.25 mile offshore (lat. 36°00'40" N, long. 121° 32'05" W). Named on Lopez Point (1956) 7.5' quadrangle.

Harlan Spring [MONTEREY]: *spring,* 6 miles south of Parkfield (lat. 35°48'50" N, long. 120°26'50" W; sec. 27, T 24 S, R 14 E). Named on Cholame Hills (1961) 7.5' quadrangle. The name is for a member the Harlan family who came to Cholame Valley in 1869 (Clark, 1991, p. 205).

Harlech Castle Rock [SAN LUIS OBISPO]: *rock,* nearly 2 miles north-northwest of Piedras Blancas Point, and 3500 feet offshore (lat. 35°41'10" N, long. 121°18' W). Named on Piedras Blancas (1959) 7.5' quadrangle.

Harlem [MONTEREY]: *locality,* 4.25 miles east-southeast of Soledad along Southern Pacific Railroad (lat. 36°24' N, long. 121°15'15" W; sec. 6, T 18 S, R 7 E). Named on Soledad (1955) 7.5' quadrangle.

Harmony [SAN LUIS OBISPO]: *locality,* 5 miles southeast of Cambria (lat. 35°30'30" N, long. 121°01'20" W). Named on Cambria (1959) 7.5' quadrangle. A Swiss named Salmina started a community at the place about 1910 as a center for a thriving dairy industry (Lee and others, p. 67). Postal authorities established Harmony post office in 1915 (Frickstad, p. 164).

Harmony Valley [SAN LUIS OBISPO]: *valley,* 5 miles southeast of Cambria along Perry Creek (lat. 35°30'45" N, long. 121°01' W); Harmony is in the valley. Named on Cambria (1959) 7.5' quadrangle.

Harper Creek [MONTEREY]: *stream,* flows 3.25 miles to San Benancio Gulch 8 miles south-southwest of Salinas (lat. 36°34'10" N, long. 121°42'25" W). Named on Spreckels (1947) 7.5' quadrangle.

Harris [SANTA BARBARA]: *locality,* 7 miles south of Orcutt (lat. 34°46' N, long. 120°25'25" W); the place is near the mouth of Harris Canyon. Named on Santa Maria (1947) 15' quadrangle. California Mining Bureau's (1917c) map shows a place called Orby located at or near the site of Harris. Postal authorities established Orby post office in 1909, changed the name to Harriston in 1924, and discontinued it in 1934 (Frickstad, p. 171).

Harris: see **Brookdale** [SANTA CRUZ].

Harris Canyon [SANTA BARBARA]: *canyon,* 4.5 miles long, opens into the canyon of San

Antonio Creek (1) 6.5 miles south of Orcutt (lat. 34°46'15" N, long. 120°25'45" W). Named on Orcutt (1959) 7.5' quadrangle.

Harris Creek [MONTEREY]: *stream*, flows 8.5 miles to San Antonio River 8 miles west-southwest of Bradley (lat. 35°48'45" N, long. 120°55'40" W); the stream heads in Harris Valley. Named on Bryson (1949) and Tierra Redonda Mountain (1949) 7.5' quadrangles.

Harris Point [SANTA BARBARA]: *promontory*, 5.5 miles northwest of Cardwell Point at the northernmost tip of San Miguel Island (lat. 34°04'35" N, long. 120°22' W). Named on San Miguel Island East (1950) 7.5' quadrangle. Doran (p. 214) noted that a feature called Wilson Rock, locally known as West Rock, lies 2.25 miles northwest of Point Harris.

Harriston: see **Harris** [SANTA BARBARA].

Harris Valley [MONTEREY]: *valley*, 14 miles southeast of Jolon (lat. 35°49'30" N, long. 121°00'30" W); the valley is along upper reaches of Harris Creek. Named on Bryson (1949) and Tierra Redonda Mountain (1949) 7.5' quadrangles. E.S. Harris farmed in the valley in 1875 (Clark, 1991, p. 207).

Hartford: see **Port Hartford**, under **Port San Luis** [SAN LUIS OBISPO].

Hartford Canyon: see **Harford Canyon** [SAN LUIS OBISPO].

Hasbrouck: see **Mount Hasbrouck**, under **Big Baldy** [SAN LUIS OBISPO].

Hathaway: see **Goldtree** [SAN LUIS OBISPO].

Hatton Canyon [MONTEREY]: *canyon*, drained by a stream that flows 2 miles to Carmel Valley 1.5 miles east-northeast of the mouth of Carmel River (lat. 36°32'35" N, long. 121°54'20" W). Named on Monterey (1947) 7.5' quadrangle. The name is for the Hatton family, who owned land at the place (Clark, 1991, p. 210).

Have [SAN LUIS OBISPO]: *locality*, 3 miles southeast of present Atascadero along Southern Pacific Railroad (lat. 35°27'30" N, long. 120°37'45" W). Named on San Luis Obispo (1897) 15' quadrangle. Diller and others' (1915) map shows a place called Eaglet located along the railroad at or near this place.

Hawkins Lake [SAN BENITO]: *lake*, 0.5 mile long, behind a dam in Little Peak Canyon 9 miles north-northeast of Hollister (lat. 36°57'20" N, long. 121°18'35" W). Named on Three Sisters (1954) 7.5' quadrangle, which shows Hawkins ranch 3.5 miles downstream from the lake.

Hawkins Peak [SAN BENITO]: *peak*, nearly 3 miles north of North Chalone Peak (lat. 36°29'15" N, long. 121°11'45" W; on S line sec. 34, T 16 S, R 7 E). Named on North Chalone Peak (1969) 7.5' quadrangle.

Hawks Peak: see **Fremont Peak** [MONTEREY-SAN BENITO].

Hay Canyon [SAN LUIS OBISPO]: *canyon*, drained by a stream that flows nearly 6 miles to San Juan Creek 4 miles east-northeast of Castle Crags (lat. 35°19'15" N, long. 120°08'

W; near N line sec. 15, T 30 S, R 17 E). Named on La Panza (1967) 7.5' quadrangle. On La Panza (1935) 15' quadrangle, present Willow Canyon and North Fork Willow Canyon are called Hay Canyon, and present Hay Canyon is called Martinez Canyon, but United States Board on Geographic Names (1968c, p. 5) rejected the name "Martinez Canyon" and approved the name "Hay Canyon" for present Hay Canyon. Angel (1883, p, 249) referred to Haystock Cañon. According to Dillon (1960, p. 7), present Hay Canyon was called Haystack Canyon.

Hay Canyon: see **Willow Canyon** [SAN LUIS OBISPO].

Haystack Canyon [SAN LUIS OBISPO]: *canyon*, drained by a stream that flows 6.5 miles to Stephens Canyon 3.5 miles north-northeast of Huasna Peak (lat. 35°05'20" N, long. 120°19'55" W; sec. 27, T 12 N, R 33 E). Named on Caldwell Mesa (1967), Huasna Peak (1967), and Los Machos Hills (1967) 7.5' quadrangles.

Haystack Canyon: see **Hay Canyon** [SAN LUIS OBISPO].

Haystack Hill [MONTEREY]: *peak*, 2 miles northeast of Jamesburg (lat. 36°23'05" N, long. 121°33'40" W; near N line sec. 8, T 18 S, R 4 E). Altitude 2100 feet. Named on Rana Creek (1956) 7.5' quadrangle.

Haystock Cañon: see **Hay Canyon** [SAN LUIS OBISPO].

Hazard Canyon [SAN LUIS OBISPO]: *canyon*, drained by a stream that flows 3 miles to the sea 5.5 miles south of Morro Rock (lat. 35°17'20" N, long. 120°52'55" W; sec. 27, T 30 S, R 10 E). Named on Morro Bay South (1965) 7.5' quadrangle.

Headland Cove [MONTEREY]: *embayment*, 2.5 miles southwest of present Carmel-by-the-Sea along the coast on the south side of Point Lobos (lat. 36°31'10" N, long. 121°57'05" W). Named on Monterey (1947) 7.5' quadrangle. The feature first was called Point Cove after Point Lobos (Clark, 1991, p. 211).

Headland Meadow [MONTEREY]: *area*, 2.5 miles southwest of present Carmel-by-the-Sea (lat. 36°31'05" N, long. 121°56'50" W); the place is less than 0.5 mile southeast of Headland Cove. Named on Monterey (1947) 7.5' quadrangle.

Heath Campground [SANTA BARBARA]: *locality*, 3.25 miles north-northwest of Big Pine Mountain along Sisquoc River (lat. 34°44'15" N, long. 119°40'55" W). Named on Big Pine Mountain (1964) 7.5' quadrangle. The place was a favorite hunting and fishing spot for Jim Heath (Gagnon, p. 84).

Heath Spring [SANTA BARBARA]: *spring*, 3 miles north-northwest of McPherson Peak in Green Canyon (lat. 34°55'30" N, long. 119°50'15" W). Named on Peak Mountain (1964) 7.5' quadrangle.

Hecker Pass [SANTA CRUZ]: *pass*, 6 miles north-northeast of Watsonville on Santa Cruz-

Santa Clara county line (lat. 36°59'45" N, long. 121°43' W). Named on Watsonville East (1955) 7.5' quadrangle. The name honors Henry Hecker, who was a Santa Clara County supervisor when the road over the pass was completed in 1928 (Rambo, p. 36). A change made in the county line in 1971 left the pass entirely in Santa Clara County (Clark, 1986, p. 149).

Heins Lake [MONTEREY]: *lake,* 1 mile long, 3 miles east-southeast of Salinas (lat. 36°39'15" N, long. 121°36'15" W). Named on Salinas (1912) 15' quadrangle. The name commemorates a farmer who settled at the place before 1868 (Gudde, 1949, p. 145).

Hell Hole [SAN BENITO]: *canyon,* drained by a stream that flows nearly 1 mile to Peak Canyon 6.25 miles southwest of Hollister (lat. 36°47'40" N, long. 121°29'20" W). Named on Hollister (1955) 7.5' quadrangle.

Hells Gate: see **Aptos Creek** [SANTA CRUZ].

Hells Half Acre [SANTA BARBARA]: *area,* 6 miles east-southeast of Figueroa Mountain (lat. 34°42'40" N, long. 119°53'05" W; sec. 1, T 7 N, R 29 W). Named on Figueroa Mountain (1959) 7.5' quadrangle.

Hendrys Beach [SANTA BARBARA]: *beach,* 2.5 miles southwest of downtown Santa Barbara along the coast (lat. 34°24'05" N, long. 119°44'20" W). Named on Santa Barbara (1944) 7.5' quadrangle.

Hennicksons Ridge [MONTEREY]: *ridge,* northwest-trending, 2.5 miles long, 4 miles east-northeast of Uncle Sam Mountain (lat. 36° 22'15" N, long. 121°38'30" W). Named on Carmel Valley (1956) and Ventana Cones (1956) 7.5' quadrangles. According to Clark (1991, p. 212), the corrupted name is from the Henningsen family, early settlers in the neighborhood.

Henrietta Peak [SAN BENITO]: *peak,* nearly 4 miles south-southwest of Mariposa Peak (lat. 36°54'15" N, long. 121°13'55" W; sec. 8, T 12 S, R 7 E). Altitude 3626 feet. Named on Mariposa Peak (1969) 7.5' quadrangle.

Henry [SAN LUIS OBISPO]: *locality,* 1.25 miles east of downtown Atascadero along Southern Pacific Railroad (lat. 35°29'20" N, long. 120°38'50" W). Named on Atascadero (1965) 7.5' quadrangle. San Luis Obispo (1897) 15' quadrangle has the name "Atascadero" at this spot, and has the name "Henry" at a place situated 1.5 miles farther northwest.

Henry Ashurst Spring: see **Ashurst Spring** [SAN BENITO].

Henry Cocks [MONTEREY]: *land grant,* 2.5 miles west of Salinas. Named on Salinas (1947) 7.5' quadrangle. Esteban Espinosa received 0.25 league in 1840; Henry Cocks claimed 1106 acres patented in 1870 (Cowan, p. 112).

Henry Creek [SANTA CRUZ]: *stream,* flows 1.25 miles to West Waddell Creek 4.5 miles north of the mouth of Waddell Creek (lat.

37°09'40" N, long. 122°16'20" W; near S line sec. 11, T 9 S, R 4 W). Named on Franklin Point (1955) 7.5' quadrangle. Año Nuevo (1948) 15' quadrangle has the name "Henry Creek" for a stream that joins Berry Creek (1) 0.5 mile northeast of the confluence of present Henry Creek and West Waddell Creek.

Henry Sands Canyon [MONTEREY]: *canyon,* drained by a stream that flows 4.25 miles to lowlands 5 miles east of Gonzales (lat. 36° 30'30" N, long. 121°21'15" W; sec. 30, T 16 S, R 6 E). Named on Mount Johnson (1968) 7.5' quadrangle.

Hepsedam Creek [SAN BENITO]: *stream,* flows 4 miles to Lewis Creek 9.5 miles southeast of Bitterwater (lat. 36°17'35" N, long. 120°52'15" W; sec. 10, T 19 S, R 10 E); the stream is west of Hepsedam Peak. Named on Hepsedam Peak (1969) 7.5' quadrangle.

Hepsedam Peak [SAN BENITO]: *peak,* 11 miles east-southeast of Bitterwater (lat. 36°18'50" N, long. 120°49'25" W; near S line sec. 31, T 18 S, R 11 E). Altitude 4487 feet. Named on Hepsedam Peak (1969) 7.5' quadrangle.

Hepsedam Spring [SAN BENITO]: *spring,* 11.5 miles east-southeast of Bitterwater (lat. 36°18'20" N, long. 120°49'05" W; sec. 6, T 19 S, R 11 E); the spring is 3500 feet southeast of the summit of Hepsedam Peak. Named on Hepsedam Peak (1969) 7.5' quadrangle. Called Box Spring on Hernandez Valley (1943) 15' quadrangle.

Hermon: see **Mount Hermon** [SANTA CRUZ].

Hernandez [SAN BENITO]: *locality,* 11 miles east of Bitterwater (lat. 36°22'30" N, long. 120°48' W; near W line sec. 8, T 18 S, R 11 E); the place is in Hernandez Valley. Named on Priest Valley (1915) 30' quadrangle. Postal authorities established Erie post office in 1874, moved it 1.5 miles northwest and changed the name to Hernandez in 1892; they moved it 1.5 miles southeast in 1896, moved it 1 mile north in 1904, and discontinued it in 1936—the name "Hernandez" commemorates Rafael Hernandez and Jesus Hernandez, farmers in the region in the 1870's (Salley, p. 70, 96). The name "Erie" was from Erie school district, where the post office was situated (Elliott and Moore, p. 153). Postal authorities established Rex post office 11.5 miles northwest of Erie post office in 1892 and discontinued in 1900 (Salley, p. 184).

Hernandez Reservoir [SAN BENITO]: *lake,* behind a dam on San Benito River 9 miles east of Bitterwater (lat. 36°23'45" N, long. 120°50'10" W; near N line sec. 1, T 18 S, R 10 E). Named on Hepsedam Peak (1969) and Hernandez Reservoir (1969) 7.5' quadrangles.

Hernandez Valley [SAN BENITO]: *valley,* 11.5 miles east of Bitterwater along San Benito River (lat. 36°22' N, long. 120°48' W). Named on Hernandez Valley (1957) 15' quadrangle. Water of Hernandez Reservoir now covers most of the valley.

Hester Creek [SANTA CRUZ]: *stream*, flows 4 miles to West Branch Soquel Creek 5 miles north-northeast of Soquel (lat. 37°03'20" N, long. 121°56'25" W; sec. 14, T 10 S, R 1 W). Named on Laurel (1955) 7.5' quadrangle. The name commemorates Craven P. Hester, a landowner in the neighborhood in the 1850's (Clark, 1986, p. 151).

Hewitt Valley [MONTEREY]: *valley*, drained by a stream that flows 1.5 miles to Lynch Canyon 9 miles east-northeast of San Ardo (lat. 36°03' N, long. 120°44'35" W; near W line sec. 1, T 22 S, R 11 E). Named on Slack Canyon (1969) 7.5' quadrangle.

Hiawatha Campground [SANTA BARBARA]: *locality*, 11 miles west-northwest of McPherson Peak along South Fork La Brea Creek (lat. 34°56'15" N, long. 120°00' W). Named on Bates Canyon (1964) 7.5' quadrangle.

Hicks' Ford: see **Ben Lomond** [SANTA CRUZ].

Hidalgo Canyon [MONTEREY]: *canyon*, drained by a stream that flows 2.5 miles to Peachtree Canyon 10 miles east-northeast of San Ardo (lat. 36°05'45" N, long. 120°45'25" W; near S line sec. 14, T 21 S, R 11 E). Named on Monarch Peak (1967) and Pancho Rico Valley (1967) 7.5' quadrangles.

Hidden Beach: see **China Cove** [MONTEREY].

Hidden Potrero [SANTA BARBARA]: *area*, 2.5 miles south of Little Pine Mountain (lat. 34°33'50" N, long. 119°44'30" W). Named on Little Pine Mountain (1964) 7.5' quadrangle.

Hidden Spring [SAN BENITO]: *spring*, 6.5 miles east-southeast of Bitterwater (lat. 36°20'35" N, long. 120°53'25" W; sec. 21, T 18 S, R 10 E). Named on Lonoak (1969) 7.5' quadrangle.

Hidden Spring [SANTA BARBARA]: *spring*, 4.25 miles west of McPherson Peak (lat. 34°54'10" N, long. 119°53'10" W). Named on Bates Canyon (1964) 7.5' quadrangle.

Hidden Valley [MONTEREY]: *valley*, 18 miles east of San Ardo on upper reaches of Wayland Creek (lat. 36°02' N, long. 120°34'45" W). Named on Smith Mountain (1969) 7.5' quadrangle.

Hidden Valley Hot Springs: see **Ontario Hot Springs** [SAN LUIS OBISPO].

Hiding Canyon [MONTEREY]: *canyon*, drained by a stream that flows nearly 2 miles to Carmel River 2 miles north of Ventana Cone (lat. 36°18'50" N, long. 121°40'40" W; near S line sec. 32, T 18 S, R 3 E). Named on Ventana Cones (1956) 7.5' quadrangle.

Hiding Canyon Camp [MONTEREY]: *locality*, 2.5 miles north of Ventana Cone along Carmel River (lat. 36°19'15" N, long. 121°41'05" W; sec. 31, T 18 S, R 3 W); the place is less than 1 mile northwest of the mouth of Hiding Canyon. Named on Ventana Cones (1956) 7.5' quadrangle.

Higgins Camp [MONTEREY]: *locality*, 8 miles southwest of Tassajara Hot Springs (lat. 36°10'45" N, long. 121°36'15" W; sec. 23, T 20 S, R 3 E); the place is along an upper branch of Higgins Creek. Named on Tassajara Hot Springs (1956) 7.5' quadrangle.

Higgins Creek [MONTEREY]: *stream*, flows nearly 5 miles to Lost Valley Creek 5.25 miles south of Tassajara Hot Springs (lat. 36° 09'25" N, long. 121°33'35" W; sec. 29, T 20 S, R 4 E). Named on Tassajara Hot Springs (1956) 7.5' quadrangle.

Highland: see **Laurel** [SANTA CRUZ].

Higuera: see **Juan Higuera Creek** [MONTEREY].

Hihn Mill: see **Logan Creek** [SANTA CRUZ].

Hihn Spur: see **Aptos Creek** [SANTA CRUZ].

Hildreth Peak [SANTA BARBARA]: *peak*, 10.5 miles east of Little Pine Mountain (lat. 34°36' N, long. 119°33'05" W). Altitude 5065 feet. Named on Hildreth Peak (1964) 7.5' quadrangle.

Hill: see **Mary Hill Mineral Well**, under **Paso Robles** [SAN LUIS OBISPO]; **Wayland Creek** [MONTEREY].

Hilltown: see **Old Hilltown** [MONTEREY].

Hilton Canyon [SANTA BARBARA]: *canyon*, drained by a stream that flows 4 miles to Santa Ynez River 4 miles north of Santa Ynez Peak (lat. 34°35'15" N, long. 119°59'10" W). Named on Lake Cachuma (1959) 7.5' quadrangle. Called Rock Canyon on Santa Ynez (1905) 30' quadrangle, but United States Board on Geographic Names (1962a, p. 12) rejected this name for the feature.

Hi Mountain [SAN LUIS OBISPO]: *peak*, 4 miles southwest of Pozo (lat. 35°15'35" N, long. 120°25'25" W; near N line sec. 1, T 31 S, R 14 E). Altitude 3198 feet. Named on Santa Margarita Lake (1967) 7.5' quadrangle.

Hi Mountain Campground [SAN LUIS OBISPO]: *locality*, 3.5 miles southwest of Pozo (lat. 35°15'40" N, long. 120°24'50" W; near S line sec. 31, T 30 S, R 15 E); the place is 0.5 mile east of Hi Mountain. Named on Santa Margarita Lake (1967) 7.5' quadrangle.

Hi Mountain Potrero [SAN LUIS OBISPO]: *area*, 4 miles southwest of Pozo (lat. 35°16'05" N, long. 120°25'45" W; sec. 36, T 30 S, R 14 E); the place is 0.5 mile northnorthwest of Hi Mountain. Named on Santa Margarita Lake (1967) 7.5' quadrangle.

Hi Mountain Spring [SAN LUIS OBISPO]: *spring*, nearly 4 miles southwest of Pozo (lat. 35°15'35" N, long. 120°24'50" W; near N line sec. 6, T 31 S, R 15 E); the spring is 0.5 mile east of Hi Mountain. Named on Santa Margarita Lake (1967) 7.5' quadrangle.

Hinckley Creek [SANTA CRUZ]: *stream*, flows 4 miles to Soquel Creek 5 miles north-northeast of Soquel (lat. 37°03'20" N, long. 121°55'20" W); the stream is north of Hinckley Ridge. Named on Laurel (1955) and Loma Prieta (1955) 7.5' quadrangles. The name commemorates Roger Gibson Hinkley, who settled in the neighborhood about 1854 (Clark, 1986, p. 156-157).

Hinckley Ridge [SANTA CRUZ]: *ridge,* west-to west-southwest-trending, 2.5 miles long, 5.5 miles northeast of Soquel (lat. 37°03'15" N, long. 121°53'45" W); the ridge is south of Hinckley Creek. Named on Laurel (1955) 7.5' quadrangle.

Hinns Sulphur Spring: see **Olive Springs** [SANTA CRUZ].

Hitchcock Canyon [MONTEREY]: *canyon,* drained by a stream that flows 3.5 miles to Carmel River at the town of Carmel Valley (lat. 36°28'25" N, long. 121°43'30" W). Named on Carmel Valley (1956) and Mount Carmel (1956) 7.5' quadrangles. The name commemorates Joe Hitchcock, who lived in the canyon (Fink, p. 199).

Hi Valley [SAN LUIS OBISPO]: *valley,* 5 miles southeast of Pozo (lat. 35°15' N, long. 120°25' W; on E line sec. 1, T 31 S, R 14 E); the valley is less than 1 mile south-southeast of Hi Mountain. Named on Santa Margarita Lake (1967) and Tar Spring Ridge (1967) 7.5' quadrangles.

Hoffman's Camp: see **Camp No. 5**, under **Bridge Creek** [SANTA CRUZ].

Hog Canyon [MONTEREY]:

(1) *canyon,* drained by a stream that flows 5 miles to Paris Valley 3.5 miles west-northwest of San Ardo (lat. 36°02' N, long. 120°58'10" W; sec. 11, T 22 S, R 9 E). Named on San Ardo (1967) 7.5' quadrangle.

(2) *canyon,* drained by a stream that flows 3.25 miles to Sargent Canyon 8 miles east of San Ardo (lat. 36°00'05" N, long. 120°45'30" W; sec. 23, T 22 S, R 11 E). Named on Pancho Rico Valley (1967) and Slack Canyon (1969) 7.5' quadrangles.

Hog Canyon [MONTEREY-SAN LUIS OBISPO]: *canyon,* drained by a stream that heads in Monterey County and flows 15 miles to Estrella Creek 7.5 miles northeast of Paso Robles in San Luis Obispo County (lat. 35°42'10" N long. 120°36'10" W; at NW cor. sec. 5, T 26 S, R 13 E). Named on Cholame Hills (1961) Estrella (1948), and Ranchito Canyon (1948) 7.5' quadrangles. Stanley (map on p. 18) called the feature Pleasant Valley.

Hog Hole [SAN BENITO]: *relief feature,* 14 miles east-southeast of Bitterwater (lat. 36°18'05" N, long. 120°46'25" W; sec. 4, T 19 S, R 11 E). Named on Hepsedam Peak (1969) 7.5' quadrangle, which shows two small intermittent lakes at the place.

Hog Pen Spring [SANTA BARBARA]: *spring,* 1.5 miles east-southeast of McPherson Peak (lat. 34°52'45" N, long. 119°47'10" W). Named on Peak Mountain (1964) 7.5' quadrangle.

Hog Pen Spring: see **Upper Hog Pen Spring** [SANTA BARBARA].

Hog's Back: see **Paradise Park** [SANTA CRUZ].

Hogs Canyon [MONTEREY]: *canyon,* drained

by a stream that flows nearly 1 mile to lowlands 5 miles west of Greenfield (lat. 36°18'55" N, long. 121°19'45" W). Named on Paraiso Springs (1956) 7.5' quadrangle.

Hole: see **The Hole** [SAN BENITO].

Holland Canyon [SAN LUIS OBISPO]: *canyon,* drained by a stream that flows 5 miles to San Juan Valley 10.5 miles southeast of Shandon (lat. 35°32'55" N, long. 120°14'10" W; sec. 27, T 27 S, R 16 E). Named on Holland Canyon (1961) 7.5' quadrangle.

Hollins Hot Springs: see **Dolans Hot Spring**, under **Big Creek** [MONTEREY] (2).

Hollister [SAN BENITO]: *town,* near the northwest end of San Benito County (lat. 36°51'05" N, long. 121°24'05" W). Named on Hollister (1955) 7.5' quadrangle. San Justo Homestead Association bought 21,000 acres of San Justo grant from W.W. Hollister in 1868 and laid out a town that they named for the former owner of the land (Pierce, p. 103). Postal authorities established Hollister post office in 1869 (Frickstad, p. 136), and the town incorporated in 1874.

Hollister Peak [SAN LUIS OBISPO]: *peak,* 5 miles east-southeast of Morro Rock (lat. 35°20'40" N, long. 120°47'10" W). Named on Morro Bay South (1965) 7.5' quadrangle. United States Coast Survey personnel gave the name in 1884 for the Hollister family, ranchers at the base of the peak, which also was known as Cerro Alto and Morro Twin (Gudde, 1949, p. 151).

Honda [SANTA BARBARA]: *locality,* 3 miles north-northeast of Point Arguello along Southern Pacific Railroad (lat. 34°36'55" N, long. 120°37'55" W); the place is 0.5 mile north-northeast of the mouth of La Honda Canyon. Named on Point Arguello (1959) 7.5' quadrangle.

Honda Valley [SANTA BARBARA]: *canyon,* 1.25 miles long, 1 mile south-southwest of downtown Santa Barbara (lat. 34°24'20" N, long. 119°42'20" W). Named on Santa Barbara (1952) 7.5' quadrangle.

Honeymoon Flat [SANTA BARBARA]: *area,* 4 miles west-northwest of Zaca Lake (lat. 34°47'50" N, long. 120°06'30" W). Named on Zaca Lake (1964) 7.5' quadrangle.

Hope Ranch [SANTA BARBARA]:

(1) *locality,* 4 miles east of Goleta along Southern Pacific Railroad (lat. 34°26'15" N, long. 119°45'15" W); the place is at the north edge of Hope Ranch district. Named on Goleta (1950) 7.5' quadrangle. Called Irma on Goleta (1903) 15' quadrangle.

(2) *district,* 4 miles west of downtown Santa Barbara (lat. 34°25'20" N, long. 119°46' W). Named on Goleta (1950) 7.5' quadrangle. Thomas W. Hope bought part of Las Positas y La Calera grant in 1870 and called the property Hope Ranch; Hope's heirs subdivided the land (Gudde, 1949, p. 153).

Hopkins Gulch [SANTA CRUZ]: *canyon,* drained by a stream that flows 1 mile to Bear

Creek 1.5 miles east-northeast of the town of Boulder Creek (lat. 37°08'10" N, long. 122°05'55" W; sec. 20, T 9 S, R 2 W). Named on Castle Rock Ridge (1955) 7.5' quadrangle.

Hopkins Ridge [MONTEREY]: *ridge,* west-southwest-trending, 1 mile long, 7 miles east-southeast of Point Sur (lat. 36°16'05" N, long. 121°46'45" W). Named on Big Sur (1956) 7.5' quadrangle.

Hopper Canyon [SAN LUIS OBISPO]: *canyon,* drained by a stream that flows 2.5 miles to lowlands along Estrella River nearly 1 mile north-northwest of Shandon (lat. 35°40' N, long. 120°22'15" W; near W line sec. 16, T 26 S, R 15 E). Named on Cholame (1961) 7.5' quadrangle.

Horse Canyon [MONTEREY]: *canyon,* drained by Horse Creek, which flows 7.5 miles to Arroyo Seco (1) 11 miles west-southwest of Greenfield (lat. 36°15'10" N, long. 121°24'55" W; sec. 27, T 19 S, R 5 E). Named on Junipero Serra Peak (1949) and Reliz Canyon (1949) 7.5' quadrangles. Clark (1991, p. 222) reported an account that attributed the name to stolen horses left in the canyon by Tiburcio Vasquez, the outlaw.

Horse Canyon [SAN LUIS OBISPO]: *canyon,* drained by a stream that flows 4.25 miles to Cuyama Valley 2.5 miles north of New Cuyama [SANTA BARBARA] (lat. 34°58'55" N, long. 119°41'10" W; sec. 5, T 10 N, R 26 W). Named on New Cuyama (1964) 7.5' quadrangle.

Horse Canyon [SANTA BARBARA]:
(1) *canyon,* drained by a stream that flows 10.5 miles to Sisquoc River 4 miles north-north-east of Zaca Lake (lat. 34°50'05" N, long. 120°01'05" W). Named on Bald Mountain (1964), Bates Canyon (1964), and Zaca Lake (1964) 7.5' quadrangles. Called Horse Gulch on Lompoc (1905) 30' quadrangle.
(2) *canyon,* drained by a stream that flows 2.5 miles to Santa Ynez River 6.25 miles south-southwest of Hildreth Peak (lat. 34°30'50" N, long. 119°35'25" W). Named on Hildreth Peak (1964) 7.5' quadrangle.
(3) *canyon,* drained by a stream that flows nearly 7 miles to Lake Cachuma 5.25 miles east-northeast of Santa Ynez Peak (lat. 34° 33'55" N, long. 119°53'45" W). Named on Lake Cachuma (1959) and San Marcos Pass (1959) 7.5' quadrangles.

Horse Canyon: see **Upper Horse Canyon** [SANTA BARBARA].

Horse Creek [MONTEREY]: *stream,* flows 7.5 miles to Arroyo Seco (1) 11 miles west-south-west of Greenfield (lat. 36°15'10" N, long. 121°24'55" W; sec. 27, T 19 S, R 5 E); the stream drains Horse Canyon. Named on Sycamore Flat (1956) 7.5' quadrangle.

Horse Gulch: see **Horse Canyon** [SANTA BARBARA] (1).

Horse Mesa [SAN LUIS OBISPO]: *area,* 2 miles southwest of Pozo (lat. 35°17'10" N, long. 120°24'10" W; sec. 30, T 30 S, R 15 E).

Named on Santa Margarita Lake (1967) 7.5' quadrangle.

Horse Pasture: see **Horse Pasture Camp** [MONTEREY].

Horse Pasture Camp [MONTEREY]: *locality,* nearly 1 mile northeast of Tassajara Hot Springs (lat. 36°14'25" N, long. 121°32'30" W; sec. 33, T 19 S, R 4 E). Named on Tassajara Hot Springs (1956) 7.5' quadrangle. Lucia (1921) 15' quadrangle has the name "Horse Pasture" at the place. A fenced horse pasture was at the site originally (Clark, 1991, p. 222).

Horse Potrero [SANTA BARBARA]: *area,* 3 miles east of Salisbury Potrero (lat. 34°49'40" N, long. 119°38'40" W). Named on Salisbury Potrero (1964) 7.5' quadrangle.

Horse Run [MONTEREY]: *stream,* flows 2.25 miles to Arroyo Seco (1) 6.25 miles north-northwest of Junipero Serra Peak (lat. 36° 14' N, long. 121°27'10" W; sec. 32, T 19 S, R 5 E). Named on Junipero Serra Peak (1949) 7.5' quadrangle.

Horseshoe Canyon [SANTA BARBARA]: *canyon,* drained by a stream that flows 2.25 miles to Pine Canyon (1) 5.5 miles west-southwest of Miranda Pine Mountain (lat. 35°00'10" N, long. 120° 07'50" W). Named on Manzanita Mountain (1964) 7.5' quadrangle.

Horseshoe Spring [SANTA BARBARA]: *spring,* 7.5 miles north-northwest of Manzanita Mountain (lat. 34°59'50" N, long. 120°07'05" W); the spring is in Horseshoe Canyon. Named on Manzanita Mountain (1964) 7.5' quadrangle.

Hospital Lake [SAN LUIS OBISPO]: *lake,* 1850 feet long, nearly 4 miles south-south-west of downtown Arroyo Grande near the coast (lat. 35°04'20" N, long. 120°36'40" W). Named on Oceano (1965) 7.5' quadrangle.

Hot Spring [SANTA BARBARA]: *spring,* 5.5 miles east of Santa Ynez Peak (lat. 34°32'15" N, long. 119°52'50" W; near SE cor. sec. 2, T 5 N, R 29 W). Named on Lake Cachuma (1959) 7.5' quadrangle. Berkstresser (p. A-16) called the feature San Marcos Hot Springs, and gave the names "Mountain Glen Hot Springs" and "Cuyama Hot Springs" as alternates.

Hot Spring Canyon [SANTA BARBARA]: *canyon,* drained by a stream that flows 3 miles to Santa Ynez River 6 miles east-northeast of Santa Ynez Peak (lat. 34°33'20" N, long. 119°52'45" W); Hot Spring is in the canyon. Named on Lake Cachuma (1959) 7.5' quadrangle.

Hot Spring Canyon: see **Hot Springs Canyon** [SANTA BARBARA].

Hot Springs [SANTA BARBARA]:
(1) *spring,* 8 miles south of Buellton (lat. 34°30'10" N, long. 120° 13'05" W); the feature is 0.5 mile southeast of Las Cruces (2). Named on Solvang (1959) 7.5' quadrangle. Berkstresser (p. A-16) called the feature Gaviota Hot Springs, and gave the names "Las Cruces Hot Springs" and "Las Cruces Sul-

phur Springs" as alternates.

(2) *springs,* 4.5 miles northeast of downtown Santa Barbara (lat. 34°27'45" N, long. 119°38'20" W; near NE cor. sec. 6, T 4 N, R 26 W). Named on Santa Barbara (1952) 7.5' quadrangle. Berkstresser (p. A-15) called the feature Montecito Hot Springs, gave the name "Santa Barbara Hot Springs" as an alternate, and listed the names "Lower Barn Springs," "Upper Barn Springs," "Arsenic Springs," and "Cliff Springs" for elements of the group. Crawford (1896, p. 517) called the place Santa Barbara Hot Sulphur Springs.

Hot Springs: see **Paso Robles** [SAN LUIS OBISPO].

Hot Springs Canyon [MONTEREY]: *canyon,* drained by a stream that flows 3 miles to the sea 8 miles north-northwest of Lopez Point (lat. 36°07'25" N, long. 121°38'20" W; sec. 9, T 21 S, R 3 E); the mouth of the canyon is 850 feet northwest of Slates Hot Springs. Named on Partington Ridge (1956) and Tassajara Hot Springs (1956) 7.5' quadrangles.

Hot Springs Canyon [SANTA BARBARA]: *canyon,* drained by a stream that flows 2 miles to Montecito Creek 3 miles east-northeast of downtown Santa Barbara (lat. 34°26'35" N, long. 119°39' W); Hot Springs (2) are in the canyon. Named on Santa Barbara (1952) 7.5' quadrangle. Called Hot Spring Canyon on Santa Barbara (1903) 15' quadrangle, but United States Board on Geographic Names (1961b, p. 10) rejected this form for the name.

Hot Springs Creek [SANTA BARBARA]: *stream,* flows 1 mile to Las Canovas Creek 7.5 miles south of Buellton (lat. 34°30'20" N, long. 120°13'20" W); Hot Springs (1) is along the stream. Named on Solvang (1959) 7.5' quadrangle.

Hot Springs Landing: see **Andersen Landing** [MONTEREY].

Howard Canyon [SANTA BARBARA]: *canyon,* drained by a stream that flows 3.5 miles to Los Alamos Valley 7 miles south of the village of Sisquoc (lat. 34°45'45" N, long. 120°17'35" W). Named on Sisquoc (1959) 7.5' quadrangle.

Howell Rock [SAN LUIS OBISPO]: *shoal,* 1.5 miles south of Avila Beach in San Luis Obispo Bay (lat. 35°09'30" N, long. 120°43'35" W). Named on Pismo Beach (1965) 7.5' quadrangle.

Huasna [SAN LUIS OBISPO]:

(1) *land grant,* 20 miles southeast of San Luis Obispo; covers Huasna Valley and much of the drainage areas of Huasna River and Huasna Creek. Named on Caldwell Mesa (1967), Huasna Peak (1967), Nipomo (1965), and Tar Spring Ridge (1967) 7.5' quadrangles. Isaac J. Sparks received 5 leagues in 1843 and claimed 22,153 acres patented in 1879 (Cowan, p. 40). The name apparently is from the designation of an Indian village (Kroeber, 1916, p. 43).

(2) *locality,* 7.25 miles northeast of the town of Nipomo (lat. 35°07'20" N, long. 120°23'35" W); the place is along Huasna Creek on Huasna grant. Named on Nipomo (1965) 7.5' quadrangle. Postal authorities established Huasna post office in 1889 and discontinued it in 1910 (Salley, p. 101).

Huasna Creek [SAN LUIS OBISPO]: *stream,* flows 7.5 miles to Huasna River 3 miles north-northwest of Huasna Peak (lat. 35°04'50" N, long. 120°22'15" W). Named on Huasna Peak (1967), Nipomo (1965), and Tar Spring Ridge (1967) 7.5' quadrangles. The stream now enters Twitchell Reservoir.

Huasna Peak [SAN LUIS OBISPO]: *peak,* 7.5 miles east of Nipomo (lat. 35°02'10" N, long. 120°20'50" W; near W line sec. 15, T 11 N, R 33 W). Altitude 1902 feet. Named on Huasna Peak (1967) 7.5' quadrangle.

Huasna River [SAN LUIS OBISPO]: *stream,* formed by the confluence of Trout Creek (2) and Stony Creek, flows 18 miles to Cuyama River 9 miles east of the town of Nipomo (lat. 35° 00'55" N, long. 120°19'40" W). Named on Caldwell Mesa (1967) and Huasna Peak (1967) 7.5' quadrangles. Called Rio Wasna on Parke's (1854-1855) map. Parke (p. 6) also used the name "Wasna creek." Gudde (1949, p. 155) noted that the name "Arroyo del Huasna" appears on an early map. The stream now enters Twitchell Reservoir.

Huasna Valley [SAN LUIS OBISPO]: *valley,* 3 miles north-northwest of Huasna Peak along Huasna Creek and the lower part of Huasna River (lat. 35°05' N, long. 120°22' W). Named on Huasna Peak (1967) and Nipomo (1965) 7.5' quadrangles. Water of Twitchell Reservoir now floods part of the valley.

Hubbard Gulch [SANTA CRUZ]: *canyon,* drained by Marshall Creek, which flows 1.5 miles to San Lorenzo River 2.5 miles south-southeast of the town of Boulder Creek (lat. 37°05'30" N, long. 122°05'35" W; near W line sec. 4, T 10 S, R 2 W). Named on Felton (1955) 7.5' quadrangle.

Hubbard Hill [SAN LUIS OBISPO]: *peak,* nearly 4 miles northwest of Freeborn Mountain (lat. 35°19'30" N, long. 120°06'05" W; sec. 12, T 30 S, R 17 E). Altitude 1966 feet. Named on California Valley (1966) 7.5' quadrangle.

Huckleberry Hill [MONTEREY]:

(1) *hill,* 3.5 miles south of Point Pinos (lat. 36°35'10" N, long. 121° 55'15" W). Named on Monterey (1947) 7.5' quadrangle.

(2) *peak,* 2 miles east-southeast of Point Lobos (lat. 36°30'40" N, long. 121°55'10" W; sec. 25, T 16 S, R 1 W). Altitude 932 feet. Named on Monterey (1947) 7.5' quadrangle.

Hudson Canyon [SANTA BARBARA]: *canyon,* drained by a stream that flows 3 miles to Tepusquet Canyon 2.5 miles west of Tepusquet Peak (lat. 34°54'15" N, long. 120°13'45" W). Named on Tepusquet Canyon (1964) 7.5' quadrangle.

Huerfano: see **Huerhuero** [SAN LUIS OBISPO].

Huer Huero: see **Creston** [SAN LUIS OBISPO]; **Huerhuero** [SAN LUIS OBISPO].

Huerhuero [SAN LUIS OBISPO]: *land grant,* 12 miles southeast of Paso Robles along Huerhuero Creek. Named on Creston (1948), Santa Margarita (1965), Shedd Canyon (1961), and Wilson Corner (1966) 7.5' quadrangles. Jose Mariano Bonilla received 1 league in 1842 and 1844; Francis Z. Branch claimed 15,685 acres patented in 1866 (Cowan, p. 40; Cowan gave the name "Huerfano" as an alternate). Angel (1883, p. 215) used the form "Huer-Huero" for the name, but United States Board on Geographic Names (1933, p. 377) rejected the forms "Huer Huero," "Huer-Huero," and "Huero Huero." According to Gudde (1949, p. 156), the name may be from a place called Huergüero as early as 1843, and may be related to *huero,* which means "putrid," or "rotten," in Mexican Spanish—perhaps referring to the odor of sulphur water.

Huer-Huero Creek: see **Huerhuero Creek** [SAN LUIS OBISPO].

Huerhuero Creek [SAN LUIS OBISPO]: *stream,* formed by the confluence of East Branch and Middle Branch at Creston, flows 21 miles to Salinas River 3 miles north of Paso Robles (lat. 35°40'30" N, long. 120°41'10" W; sec. 9, T 26 S, R 12 E). Named on Creston (1948), Estrella (1948), and Paso Robles (1948) 7.5' quadrangles. Called Rio de la Sta. Isabel on Parke's (1854-1855) map. Franke (p. 457) mentioned Huer-Huero creek. United States Board on Geographic Names (1933, p. 377) rejected the forms "Huer-Huero Creek," "Huer Huero Creek," and "Huero Huero Creek" for the name. East Branch is 10.5 miles long and Middle Branch is 15 miles long; both branches are named on Creston (1948), Santa Margarita (1965), and Wilson Corner (1966) 7.5' quadrangles. West Branch enters 18 miles upstream from the mouth of the main creek; it is 8.5 miles long and is named on Creston (1948) and Santa Margarita (1965) 7.5' quadrangles.

Huer Huero Springs: see **Iron Spring** [SAN LUIS OBISPO] (1)

Huero Huero: see **Huerhuero** [SAN LUIS OBISPO].

Huero Huero Creek: see **Huerhuero Creek** [SAN LUIS OBISPO].

Huerta de la Nacion: see **Noche Buena** [MONTEREY].

Huerta de Romaldo: see **Huerta de Romualdo** [SAN LUIS OBISPO].

Huerta de Romualdo [SAN LUIS OBISPO]: *land grant,* 4.5 miles northwest of downtown San Luis Obispo along Chorro Creek. Named on San Luis Obispo (1965) 7.5' quadrangle. Romaldo, an Indian, received 0.1 league in 1842; John Wilson claimed 117 acres patented in 1871 (Cowan, p. 27; Cowan listed the grant

under the designation "Chorro (or) Huerta de Romaldo"). Perez (p. 69) gave 1846 as the date of the grant.

Huffman: see **Camp Huffman** [MONTEREY].

Huffs Hole [SAN LUIS OBISPO]: *relief feature,* 15 miles north of the town of Nipomo (lat. 35°14'50" N, long. 120°26' W; near NW cor. sec. 12, T 31 S, R 14 E). Named on Tar Spring Ridge (1967) 7.5' quadrangle.

Huffs Hole Creek [SAN LUIS OBISPO]: *stream,* flows nearly 5 miles to Wittenberg Creek 12 miles north of the town of Nipomo (lat. 35°12'50" N, long. 120°27'25" W; sec. 22, T 31 S, R 14 E); one branch of the stream heads at Huffs Hole. Named on Tar Spring Ridge (1967) 7.5' quadrangle.

Hughes Canyon [SAN LUIS OBISPO]: *canyon,* drained by a stream that flows 5.5 miles to San Juan Valley 10 miles southeast of Shandon (lat. 35°33'25" N, long. 120°15'20" W; near N line sec. 28, T 27 S, R 16 E). Named on Camatta Canyon (1961) and Holland Canyon (1961) 7.5' quadrangles.

Hughes Creek [SANTA CRUZ]: *stream,* flows 2.25 miles to Pajaro Valley 4 miles northeast of Watsonville (lat. 36°58'25" N, long. 121°44'05" W). Named on Watsonville East (1955) 7.5' quadrangle.

Hughes Spring [SAN LUIS OBISPO]: *spring,* 8 miles east-southeast of Shandon (lat. 35°37' N, long. 120°14'05" W; sec. 34, T 26 S, R 16 E); the spring is in the upper part of Hughes Canyon. Named on Holland Canyon (1961) 7.5' quadrangle.

Hungry Flats: see **Lockwood** [MONTEREY].

Hungryman Gulch [SANTA BARBARA]: *canyon,* less than 0.5 mile long, 0.5 mile west of San Pedro Point at the east end of Santa Cruz Island (lat. 34°02' N, long. 119°31'35" W). Named on Santa Cruz Island D (1943) 7.5' quadrangle.

Hunter Liggett Military Reservation [MONTEREY]: *military installation,* covers a large area in and near Santa Lucia Range southwest of King City, mainly in the upper San Antonio River drainage area. Named on San Luis Obispo (1956) and Santa Cruz (1956) 1°x 2° quadrangles. Called Camp Hunter Liggett Military Reservation on Bryson (1942) 15' quadrangle. The installation, which started in 1941, now is called Fort Hunter Liggett; the name honors Major General Hunter Liggett, who commanded a corps in World War I (Clark, 1991, p. 170).

Hunter Spring [SAN LUIS OBISPO]: *spring,* 6.25 miles north-northeast of Pozo (lat. 35°23' N, long. 120°19'20" W; sec. 24, T 29 S, R 15 E). Named on Camatta Ranch (1966) 7.5' quadrangle.

Hunter Spring [SANTA BARBARA]: *spring,* 6.5 miles north of Zaca Lake in Alkali Canyon (lat. 34°52'15" N, long. 120°03'45" W). Named on Zaca Lake (1964) 7.5' quadrangle.

Hunt Spring [SAN LUIS OBISPO]: *spring,* 3 miles south-southeast of Branch Mountain

(lat. 39°09'05" N, long. 120°04'05" W).
Named on Branch Mountain (1967) 7.5' quadrangle.

Hurricane Deck [SANTA BARBARA]: *ridge,* west-northwest-trending, 4 miles long, 6 miles southwest of Montgomery Potrero (lat. 34°46' N, long. 119°49' W). Named on Hurricane Deck (1964) 7.5' quadrangle. The name is from high winds that are common on the ridge (Gudde, 1949, p. 157).

Hurricane Point [MONTEREY]: *promontory,* 3.5 miles north of Point Sur along the coast (lat. 36°21'25" N, long. 121°54'20" W; sec. 19, T 18 S, R 1 E). Named on Point Sur (1956) 7.5' quadrangle. The name is from strong winds at the place (Lussier, p. 16).

— I —

Idlewild: see **Little Sur River** [MONTEREY].

Idria [SAN BENITO]: *village,* 18 miles east of Bitterwater along San Carlos Creek (lat. 36°25' N, long. 120°40'20" W; sec. 29, T 17 S, R 12 E); New Idria mine is at the place. Named on Idria (1969) 7.5' quadrangle. New Idria (1943) 15' quadrangle has the names "New Idria" and "Idria P.O." at the site. United States Board on Geographic Names (1964, p. 14) rejected the name "New Idria," but noted that the place was named for New Idria quicksilver mine. Stewart (p. 218) pointed out that the name "Idria" is from the Italian form of the name of a city in former Yugoslavia that is famous for its quicksilver production. Postal authorities established New Idria post office in 1869 and discontinued it in 1894; they established Idria post office in 1894, discontinued it in 1934, reestablished it in 1938, and discontinued it in 1974 (Salley, p. 103). Brewer (p. 138-139) noted that a cluster of miners' tents and cabins called Centerville was situated south of Idria between New Idria mine and San Carlos mine.

Idria Peak [SAN BENITO]: *peak,* 1.5 miles south-southwest of Idria (lat. 36°23'50" N, long. 120°41'15" W; near SE cor. sec. 31, T 17 S, R 12 E). Altitude 4655 feet. Named on Idria (1969) 7.5' quadrangle.

Impossible Canyon [MONTEREY]: *canyon,* 2.5 miles long, 5 miles east of Seaside (lat. 36°36'30" N, long. 121°45'40" W); the canyon is west of Impossible Ridge. Named on Seaside (1947) 7.5' quadrangle.

Impossible Ridge [MONTEREY]: *ridge,* north-to northeast-trending, nearly 1 mile long, 6 miles east of Seaside (lat. 36°36'20" N, long. 121°45'20" W); the ridge is east of Impossible Canyon. Named on Seaside (1947) 7.5' quadrangle.

Imusdale: see **Parkfield** [MONTEREY].

Indian Canyon [SAN BENITO]: *canyon,* drained by a stream that flows 1.5 miles to Grass Valley 5 miles west of Paicines (lat. 36° 43'10" N, long. 121°22' W). Named on

Paicines (1968) 7.5' quadrangle.

Indian Creek [SAN LUIS OBISPO]:
(1) *stream,* flows nearly 3 miles to Estrella River 6 miles west of Shandon (lat. 35°38'45" N, long. 120°28'45" W; near SE cor. sec. 20, T 26 S, R 14 E). Named on Shandon (1961) and Shedd Canyon (1961) 7.5' quadrangles.
(2) *stream,* flows 10 miles to Shedd Canyon 9 miles south of Shandon (lat. 35°31'45" N, long. 120°24'25" W; sec. 31, T 27 S, R 15 E). Named on Shedd Canyon (1961) and Wilson Corner (1966) 7.5' quadrangles.

Indian Creek [SANTA BARBARA]: *stream,* flows 16 miles to Mono Creek 7.5 miles southeast of Little Pine Mountain (lat. 34°32' N, long. 119°37'55" W). Named on Big Pine Mountain (1964) and Little Pine Mountain (1964) 7.5' quadrangles.

Indian Creek: see **San Antonio River, North Fork** [MONTEREY].

Indian Creek Campground [SANTA BARBARA]: *locality,* 3.5 miles east of Little Pine Mountain (lat. 34°36'40" N, long. 119°40'25" W); the place is along Indian Creek. Named on Little Pine Mountain (1964) 7.5' quadrangle.

Indian Head Beach [MONTEREY]: *beach,* between Seaside and Marina along the coast (lat. 36°40' N, long. 121°49'10" W). Named on Marina (1947) 7.5' quadrangle.

Indian Head Rock [SANTA BARBARA]: *rock,* at Point Conception (lat. 34°26'55" N, long. 120°28'10" W). Named on Point Conception (1953) 7.5' quadrangle.

Indian Knob [SAN LUIS OBISPO]: *peak,* 4.25 miles east-northeast of Avila Beach (lat. 35°11'55" N, long. 120°39'30" W). Altitude 887 feet. Named on Pismo Beach (1965) 7.5' quadrangle.

Indians: see **The Indians** [MONTEREY].

Indian Spring [MONTEREY]: *spring,* 1.5 miles east-northeast of the center of Priest Valley (lat. 36°11'50" N, long. 120°40'10" W; near NW cor. sec. 15, T 20 S, R 12 E). Named on Priest Valley (1969) 7.5' quadrangle.

Indian Valley [MONTEREY]:
(1) *area,* 5.25 miles southwest of Tassajara Hot Springs on upper reaches of Higgins Creek (lat. 36°10'50" N, long. 121°37'10" W; sec. 22, T 20 S, R 3 E). Named on Tassajara Hot Springs (1956) 7.5' quadrangle.
(2) *area,* 7 miles west of Greenfield at Paraiso Springs (lat. 36° 20' N, long. 121°22' W; near W line sec. 30, T 18 S, R 6 E). Named on Paraiso Springs (1956) 7.5' quadrangle.
(3) *canyon,* 20 miles long, lower part drained by Big Sandy Creek, which reaches Salinas River 6.5 miles southeast of Bradley (lat. 35°47'30" N, long. 120°43'30" W; near SW cor. sec. 31, T 24 S, R 12 E). Named on San Miguel (1948), Slack Canyon (1969), and Valleton (1948) 7.5' quadrangles. The upper part of the canyon is drained by a tributary of Big Sandy Creek. California Mining Bureau's (1917b) map shows a place called Pope lo-

cated along a railroad about 10 miles northeast of Bradley where Big Sandy Creek enters Indian Valley.

Indian Valley [SAN BENITO]: *valley,* 4 miles northeast of Panoche on San Benito-Fresno county line (lat. 36°37'55" N, long. 120° 47' W; around SE cor. sec. 8, T 15 S, R 4 E). Named on Mercey Hot Springs (1969) 7.5' quadrangle.

Indian Valley Creek: see **Big Sandy Creek** [MONTEREY].

Inez: see **Goleta** [SANTA BARBARA].

Ingalls Station: see **Swanton** [SANTA CRUZ].

Inspiration Point [SANTA CRUZ]: *locality,* 9.5 miles north of Soquel (lat. 37°07'20" N, long. 121°58'20" W). Named on Laurel (1955) 7.5' quadrangle.

Inspiration Point: see **Rincon** [SANTA CRUZ].

Intermediate Point: see **Point Joe** [MONTEREY].

Ionata: see **Solvang** [SANTA BARBARA].

Iremel [SANTA BARBARA]: *locality,* 4.25 miles southeast of the town of Guadalupe along Santa Maria Valley Railroad (lat. 34°55'25" N, long. 120°31'35" W). Named on Guadalupe (1959) 7.5' quadrangle.

Irish Canyon: see **Little Irish Canyon**, under **Deer Canyon** [SAN LUIS OBISPO] (1); **Vineyard Canyon** [SAN LUIS OBISPO].

Irish Hills [SAN LUIS OBISPO]: *range,* west of San Luis Obispo Creek between Los Osos Valley and the sea. Named on Morro Bay South (1965), Pismo Beach (1965), Port San Luis (1965), and San Luis Obispo (1965) 7.5' quadrangles. Called San Luis Range on Cayucos (1897) 15' quadrangle. H.R. Wagner (p. 378) noted the early names "Monte de Buchon" and "Sierra de Buchon" for the range. Vancouver (p. 142) in 1793 referred to Mountain del Buchon and Mount del Buchon. Angel (1883, p. 323) mentioned the names "Monte de Buchon" and "Mount Buchon," and later (1890c, p. 570) considered the name "Buchon Range" as appropriate. Harder (p. 20) referred to "the San Luis Range or Los Osos Mountains." United States Coast and Geodetic Survey (p. 115) called the range Mount Buchon, and described it as "a rugged mountain mass between San Luis Obispo Bay, Estero Bay, and the valley of San Luis Obispo." United States Board on Geographic Names (1995, p. 5) rejected both the names "Mount Buchon" and "San Luis Range" for the feature.

Irma: see **Hope Ranch** [SANTA BARBARA] (1).

Iron Spring [SAN LUIS OBISPO]:
(1) *spring:* 7 miles northeast of Santa Margarita (lat. 35°27'55" N, long. 120°31'20" W; sec. 25, T 28 S, R 13 E). Named on Santa Margarita (1965) 7.5' quadrangle. G.A. Waring (p. 277) described this spring under the name "New Springs," and described another spring located about 2 miles farther north under the name "Old Spring"; he noted that

New Spring was used by campers and that the area around Old Spring was used as a summer campground—Old Spring also was the site of Keunard German settlement. Waring referred to the two springs collectively as Huer Huero Springs.
(2) *spring,* 0.5 mile west-northwest of Branch Mountain (lat. 35° 11'15" N, long. 120°05'35" W; near W line sec. 31, T 31 S, R 18 E). Named on Branch Mountain (1967) 7.5' quadrangle.

Iron Springs [MONTEREY]: *springs,* 8 miles east of San Ardo in Lynch Canyon (lat. 36°02'40" N, long. 120°45'40" W; sec. 3, T 22 S, R 11 E). Named on Pancho Rico Valley (1967) 7.5' quadrangle.

Isla Capitana: see **San Miguel Island** [SANTA BARBARA].

Isla de Baxos: see **Richardson Rock** [SANTA BARBARA].

Isla de Gente Barbudo: see **Santa Cruz Island** [SANTA BARBARA].

Isla de Juan Rodrigues: see **San Miguel Island** [SANTA BARBARA].

Isla de Lobos: see **Richardson Rock** [SANTA BARBARA].

Island: see **The Island**, under **Aptos Creek** [SANTA CRUZ].

Island Mountain [MONTEREY]: *peak,* nearly 3 miles west-southwest of Ventana Cone (lat. 36°15'55" N, long. 121°43'25" W; near E line sec. 22, T 19 S, R 2 E). Named on Ventana Cones (1956) 7.5' quadrangle.

Isla Posesion: see **San Miguel Island** [SANTA BARBARA].

Isla San Ambrosio: see **Santa Rosa Island** [SANTA BARBARA].

Isla San Sebastian: see **Santa Cruz Island** [SANTA BARBARA].

Islas de San Lucas: see **San Miguel Island** [SANTA BARBARA]; **Santa Cruz Island** [SANTA BARBARA]; **Santa Rosa Island** [SANTA BARBARA].

Islay Creek [SAN LUIS OBISPO]: *stream,* flows 7.5 miles to the sea 6.5 miles south of Morro Rock (lat. 35°16'35" N, long. 120°53'15" W). Named on Morro Bay South (1965) 7.5' quadrangle. The name is from an Indian word for the so-called hollyleaf cherry (Gudde, 1949, p. 162). G.A. Waring (p. 69) described Pecho Warm Springs, two springs located in the canyon of Islay Creek about 2 miles from the coast; the warm sulphureted water of the springs was used for drinking and bathing

Islay Hill [SAN LUIS OBISPO]: *hill,* 3 miles north of Edna (lat. 35° 14'45" N, long. 120°37'15" W). Named on Arroyo Grande NE (1965) 7.5' quadrangle.

Italian Flat [MONTEREY]: *area,* 8 miles south-southwest of Jolon (lat. 35°51'10" N, long. 121°13' W; on S line sec. 9, T 24 S, R 7 E). Named on Burnett Peak (1949) 7.5' quadrangle.

– J –

Jackass Canyon [MONTEREY]: *canyon,* drained by a stream that flows 2.25 miles to Divide Canyon 6.25 miles north-northeast of Greenfield (lat. 36°24'40" N, long. 121°12'25" W; near E line sec. 33, T 17 S, R 7 E). Named on North Chalone Peak (1969) 7.5' quadrangle.

Jack Canyon [SAN LUIS OBISPO]: *canyon,* 2 miles long, 5 miles east of Cholame on San Luis Obispo-Kern county line (lat. 35°42'30" N, long. 120°11'45" W). Named on Orchard Peak (1961) 7.5' quadrangle.

Jack Creek [SAN LUIS OBISPO]: *stream,* flows 8 miles to Paso Robles Creek 2.25 miles east of York Mountain (lat. 35°32'55" N, long. 120°47'30" W). Named on York Mountain (1948) 7.5' quadrangle.

Jack Lake [SAN LUIS OBISPO]: *intermittent lake,* 100 feet long, nearly 6 miles south of the town of Arroyo Grande near the coast (lat. 35°02'20" N, long. 120°36'10" W). Named on Oceano (1965) 7.5' quadrangle.

Jackrabbit Flat [SANTA BARBARA]: *area,* 4.5 miles west-southwest of Big Pine Mountain (lat. 34°40'35" N, long. 119°43'35" W). Named on Big Pine Mountain (1964) 7.5' quadrangle. On Big Pine Mountain (1944) 7.5' quadrangle, the name applies to a place located about 1 mile farther south-southeast along lower reaches of Grapevine Creek.

Jacks Hill [SAN BENITO]: *peak,* 2 miles west of Mariposa Peak (lat. 36°57'05" N, long. 121°14'40" W; sec. 30, T 11 S, R 7 E). Altitude 2297 feet. Named on Mariposa Peak (1969) 7.5' quadrangle.

Jackson Camp [MONTEREY]: *locality,* 6.5 miles east of Point Sur along Little Sur River (lat. 36°19'35" N, long. 121°47' W). Named on Big Sur (1956) 7.5' quadrangle.

Jackson Creek: see **Ventana Creek** [MONTEREY] (1).

Jackson Hill [MONTEREY]: *peak,* nearly 7 miles southeast of Jolon (lat. 35°54'40" N, long. 121°04'45" W; sec. 23, T 23 S, R 8 E). Altitude 1283 feet. Named on Williams Hill (1949) 7.5' quadrangle. The name is for Milligan Jackson, who settled in Tule Canyon in the early 1900's (Clark, 1991, p. 235).

Jackson Spring [SANTA BARBARA]: *spring,* 1.25 miles west of Montgomery Potrero (lat. 34°50' N, long. 119°46'35" W). Named on Hurricane Deck (1964) 7.5' quadrangle.

Jack Spring [SAN LUIS OBISPO]: *spring,* 2.5 miles south-southeast of Branch Mountain (lat. 35°09'05" N, long. 120°04'05" W). Named on Branch Mountain (1967) 7.5' quadrangle.

Jacques Hanlon Creek [MONTEREY]: *stream,* flows 3.25 miles to Quail Creek 10 miles north of Gonzales (lat. 36°39' N, long. 121° 27'30" W). Named on Mount Harlan (1968) 7.5' quadrangle.

Jade Cove: see **Plaskett** [MONTEREY].

Jalama [SANTA BARBARA]: *locality,* 3.5 miles north-northwest of Point Conception along Southern Pacific Railroad (lat. 34°29'50" N, long. 120°29'35" W); the place is 1 mile south-southeast of the mouth of Jalama Creek. Named on Point Conception (1953) 7.5' quadrangle.

Jalama Creek [SANTA BARBARA]: *stream,* flows 9.5 miles to the sea 6 miles southeast of Tranquillon Mountain (lat. 34°30'40" N, long. 120°30'05" W). Named on Lompoc Hills (1959) 7.5' quadrangle. The name is from the designation of an Indian village (Kroeber, 1916, p. 44).

Jamesburg [MONTEREY]: *settlement,* 7.5 miles northeast of Ventana Cone (lat. 36°22'10" N, long. 121°35'20" W; sec. 18, T 18 S, R 4 E); the place is along James Creek. Named on Chews Ridge (1956) 7.5' quadrangle. Jamesburg (1921) 15' quadrangle shows the place situated 0.5 mile farther north. The name commemorates John James, who founded the settlement in 1867 (Gudde, 1949, p. 164). Postal authorities established Jamesburgh post office in 1886, changed the name to Jamesburg in 1894, and discontinued it in 1935 (Frickstad, p. 107).

James Canyon [SAN BENITO]: *canyon,* drained by a stream that flows 3 miles to Lewis Creek 13 miles southeast of Bitterwater (lat. 36°15'35" N, long. 120°49'40" W; near W line sec. 19, T 19 S, R 11 E). Named on Hepsedam Peak (1969) 7.5' quadrangle.

James Creek [MONTEREY]: *stream,* flows 4.5 miles to join Finch Creek and form Cachagua Creek 1 mile north-northwest of Jamesburg (lat. 36°23'20" N, long. 121°35'35" W; sec. 1, T 18 S, R 3 E). Named on Chews Ridge (1956) and Rana Creek (1956) 7.5' quadrangles.

James Creek [SAN BENITO]: *stream,* flows 4.5 miles to San Benito River 4 miles east of Bitterwater (lat. 36°23'25" N, long. 120°55'50" W; sec. 6, T 18 S, R 10 E). Named on Rock Spring Peak (1969) 7.5' quadrangle.

James Meadows [MONTEREY]: *land grant,* 6 miles east of the mouth of Carmel River on the north side of Carmel Valley (1). Named on Seaside (1947) 7.5' quadrangle. Called Meadows Tract on Santa Cruz (1956) 1°x 2° quadrangle. Antonio Romero received 1 league in 1840; James Meadows claimed 4592 acres patented in 1866 (Cowan, p. 112).

Jameson Lake [SANTA BARBARA]: *lake,* behind a dam on Santa Ynez River 6.5 miles north of Carpinteria (lat. 34°29'30" N, long. 119°30'25" W; sec. 28, T 5 N, R 25 W). Named on Carpinteria (1952) and White Ledge Peak (1952) 7.5' quadrangles.

James Spring [SANTA BARBARA]: *spring,* 1.5 miles west of Salisbury Potrero (lat. 34°49'20" N, long. 119°43'35" W). Named on Salisbury Potrero (1964) 7.5' quadrangle.

Jamieson Creek [SAN BENITO]: *stream,* flows

2.5 miles to Pescadero Creek 10 miles west of Paicines (lat. 36°41'55" N, long. 121° 26'55" W; sec. 20, T 14 S, R 5 E). Named on Mount Harlan (1968) 7.5' quadrangle.

Jamison Creek [SANTA CRUZ]: *stream,* flows 2.25 mile to Boulder Creek (1) 4 miles east-southeast of Big Basin (lat. 37°08'45" N, long. 122°09'20" W; sec. 14, T 9 S, R 3 W). Named on Big Basin (1955) 7.5' quadrangle.

Jenks Spring [SAN LUIS OBISPO]: *spring,* 20 miles southeast of Shandon (lat. 35°27'50" N, long. 120°05'50" W; sec. 25, T 28 S, R 17 E). Named on La Panza NE (1966) 7.5' quadrangle.

Jespersen Spring [SAN LUIS OBISPO]: *spring,* 0.5 mile north of Cholame (lat. 35°43'55" N, long. 120°17'50" W; sec. 19, T 25 S, R 16 E). Named on Cholame (1961) 7.5' quadrangle.

Jesse Campground [SANTA BARBARA]: *locality,* 4 miles north-northwest of Manzanita Mountain along North Fork La Brea Creek (lat. 34°56'45" N, long. 120°06'20" W). Named on Manzanita Mountain (1964) 7.5' quadrangle.

Jesse Canyon: see **Jesus Canyon** [SANTA BARBARA].

Jesus Canyon [SANTA BARBARA]: *canyon,* drained by a stream that flows 3.25 miles to Foxen Canyon 4 miles west of Zaca Lake (lat. 34°46'30" N, long. 120°06'30" W). Named on Zaca Lake (1964) 7.5' quadrangle. United States Board on Geographic Names (1978b, p. 4) rejected the name "Jesse Canyon" for the feature.

Jesus Maria [SANTA BARBARA]: *land grant,* at and east of Purisima Point. Named on Casmalia (1959), Lompoc (1959), Orcutt (1959), and Surf (1959) 7.5' quadrangles. Lucas Olivera and others received 11 leagues in 1837; Luis T. Burton and others claimed 42,185 acres patented in 1871 (Cowan, p. 42).

Jesus Maria River: see **San Antonio Creek** [SANTA BARBARA] (1).

Jim Lawson Gulch [MONTEREY]: *canyon,* drained by a stream that flows 4.25 miles to lowlands nearly 2 miles north-northwest of San Ardo (lat. 36°02'45" N, long. 120°54'45" W; sec. 5, T 22 S, R 10 E). Named on Pancho Rico Valley (1967) and San Ardo (1967) 7.5' quadrangles.

Jim Lowe's: see **Mansfield Canyon** [MONTEREY].

Joaquin Canyon [MONTEREY]: *canyon,* drained by a stream that flows 9 miles to Little Cholame Creek 1 mile north of Parkfield (lat. 35°55' N, long. 120°26'05" W). Named on Parkfield (1961) and The Dark Hole (1961) 7.5' quadrangles.

Joaquin Canyon [SAN LUIS OBISPO]: *canyon,* drained by a stream that flows 2.5 miles to Huasna River 13 miles northeast of the town of Nipomo (lat. 35°11'30" N, long. 120°20'45" W; near NW cor. sec. 35, T 31 S, R 15 E). Named on Caldwell Mesa (1967) 7.5' quadrangle.

Joaquin's Valley: see **Priest Valley** [MONTEREY-SAN BENITO].

Joe: see **Point Joe** [MONTEREY].

Joe's Point: see **Point Joe** [MONTEREY].

Johnson: see **Mount Johnson** [SAN BENITO].

Johnson Canyon [SAN BENITO]: *canyon,* drained by a stream that flows nearly 4 miles to McCoy Creek 9 miles east-northeast of Bitterwater (lat. 36°26'25" N, long. 120°51'35" W; near NW cor. sec. 23, T 17 S, R 10 E). Named on Hernandez Reservoir (1969) and Rock Spring Peak (1969) 7.5' quadrangles. On Hernandez Valley (1957) 15' quadrangle, the name "Johnson Canyon" applies to a canyon that branches north-northeast from McCoy Creek 0.5 mile upstream from the mouth of present Johnson Canyon

Johnson Canyon [MONTEREY]: *canyon,* 3 miles long, 5.5 miles northeast of Gonzales (lat. 36°34' N, long. 121°23' W). Named on Gonzales (1955) and Mount Johnson (1968) 7.5' quadrangles. The name is from an early settler (Clark, 1991, p. 242).

Johnson Canyon [SANTA BARBARA]: *canyon,* 2 miles long, opens into Lake Cachuma 4 miles north of Santa Ynez Peak (lat. 34°35'35" N, long. 119°57'45" W). Named on Lake Cachuma (1959) 7.5' quadrangle. Water of Lake Cachuma now floods the lower part of the canyon.

Johnson Corner [SANTA CRUZ]: *locality,* nearly 3 miles east-northeast of Watsonville in Pajaro Valley (lat. 36°55'45" N, long. 121°42'20" W). Named on Watsonville East (1955) 7.5' quadrangle.

Johnson Creek [MONTEREY]: *stream,* heads at the mouth of Johnson Canyon and flows 5.5 miles, partly in an artificial watercourse, to a point near Gonzales (lat. 36°31' N, long. 121°26'45" W). Named on Gonzales (1955) 7.5' quadrangle.

Johnsons Lee [SANTA BARBARA]: *anchorage,* 0.5 mile northeast of South Point on Santa Rosa Island (lat. 33°54' N, long. 120°06'25" W). Named on Santa Rosa Island South (1943) 7.5' quadrangle.

Johnson Surprise Spring [SANTA BARBARA]: *spring,* 3 miles west-southwest of Miranda Pine Mountain (lat. 35°01'05" N, long. 120°05'10" W). Named on Miranda Pine Mountain (1967) 7.5' quadrangle.

Johnston Canyon [SANTA BARBARA]: *canyon,* drained by a stream that flows 1.25 miles to the sea 8 miles southeast of Fraser Point on Santa Cruz Island (lat. 33°58'10" N, long. 119°50'35" W). Named on Santa Cruz Island A (1943) 7.5' quadrangle. Bremner's (1932) map shows an anchorage called Johnston Lee situated off the mouth of present Johnston Canyon.

Johnston Lee: see **Johnston Canyon** [SANTA BARBARA].

Johnston Spring [SANTA BARBARA]: *spring,* 1.5 miles east-southeast of McPherson Peak (lat. 34°52'50" N, long. 119°48'45" W).

Named on Peak Mountain (1964) 7.5' quadrangle.

Jolla Vista Canyon [SANTA BARBARA]: *canyon,* drained by a stream that flows nearly 4 miles to the sea 2.5 miles east-northeast of South Point on Santa Rosa Island (lat. 33°54'35" N, long. 120° 04'25" W). Named on Santa Rosa Island South (1943) 7.5' quadrangle.

Jollo Creek [SAN LUIS OBISPO]: *stream,* flows 5 miles to Alamo Creek 4.5 miles east-northeast of Huasna Peak (lat. 35°04'20" N, long. 120°16'50" W; sec. 31, T 12 N, R 32 W). Named on Chimney Canyon (1967) and Huasna Peak (1967) 7.5' quadrangles.

Jollo Creek: see **Little Jolo Creek** [SAN LUIS OBISPO].

Jolon [MONTEREY]: *village,* 17 miles south of King City in the valley of San Antonio River (lat. 35°58'15" N, long. 121°10'30" W). Named on Bryson (1961) 15' quadrangle. Antionio Ramirez built an adobe inn at the site in 1850 (Clark, 1991, p. 242), and postal authorities established Jolon post office in 1872 (Frickstad, p. 107). Kroeber (1925, p. 895) considered the name "Jolon" as probably Indian in origin.

Jolon Creek [MONTEREY]: *stream,* flows 10 miles to San Antonio River 2.25 miles south-southeast of Jolon (lat. 35°56'20" N, long. 121°09'55" W). Named on Cosio Knob (1949) and Jolon (1949) 7.5' quadrangles. The name is from the village of Jolon (Clark, 1991, p. 244).

Jolon Valley [MONTEREY]: *valley,* 4 miles north of Jolon (lat. 36° 01'45" N, long. 121°10'15" W); the valley is along upper reaches of Jolon Creek. Named on Cosio Knob (1949) 7.5' quadrangle. According to Gudde (1949, p. 168), the name "Cañada de Jolon" is recorded as early as 1842. The Jolon Valley neighborhood was called Argyle District, a name given by teacher Allen McLean for his favorite Scottish statesman (Howard, p. 56). King City (1919) 15' quadrangle shows Argyle school in Jolon Valley, and later maps show Argyle Road there.

Jones: see **Sam Jones Canyon** [MONTEREY].

Jones Mountain [MONTEREY]: *peak,* 13 miles east-southeast of Cape San Martin (lat. 35°48'25" N, long. 121°15'15" W; sec. 31, T 24 S, R 7 E). Named on Burro Mountain (1949) 7.5' quadrangle. The name is for homesteaders who lived near the peak (Clark, 1991, p. 245).

Josephine: see **Adelaida** [SAN LUIS OBISPO].

Joshua Creek [MONTEREY]: *stream,* flows nearly 3.5 miles to Garrapata Creek 7.5 miles north of Point Sur (lat. 36°24'55" N, long. 121°54'15" W; sec. 31, T 17 S, R 1 E). Named on Mount Carmel (1956) and Soberanes Point (1956) 7.5' quadrangles.

Juan de Matte Canyon [MONTEREY]: *canyon,* drained by a stream that flows nearly 2 miles to Carmel River 9 miles east of the

mouth of that river (lat. 36°30'35" N, long. 121°45'55" W). Named on Seaside (1947) 7.5' quadrangle. The name is for Juan de Mata Boronda, son of José Manuel Boronda, grantee of Los Laureles grant where the canyon lies (Clark, 1991, p. 245).

Juan Higuera Creek [MONTEREY]: *stream,* flows 2 miles to Big Sur River 3.5 miles east-southeast of the mouth of that river (lat. 36°15'50" N, long. 121°47'55" W; sec. 24, T 19 S, R 1 E). Named on Big Sur (1956) 7.5' quadrangle. The name is for Juan Nepomuceno Higuera, a vaquero who began working on Sur grant in 1866 (Clark, 1991, p. 245).

Juan Spring [SANTA BARBARA]: *spring,* 1.5 miles south of Salisbury Potrero (lat. 34°47'50" N, long. 119°41'55" W). Named on Salisbury Potrero (1964) 7.5' quadrangle.

Judell Canyon [SANTA BARBARA]: *canyon,* drained by a stream that flows 4.25 miles to Sisquoc River 3.5 miles north-northwest of Big Pine Mountain (lat. 34°44'20" N, long. 119°41'05" W). Named on Big Pine Mountain (1964) and Salisbury Potrero (1964) 7.5' quadrangles.

Judge Rock [SANTA BARBARA]: *rock,* 4 miles west-northwest of Cardwell Point, and 450 feet offshore in Cuyler Harbor on the north side of San Miguel Island (lat. 34°03' N, long. 120°21'15" W). Named on San Miguel Island East (1950) 7.5' quadrangle.

Judith Rock [SANTA BARBARA]: *rock,* nearly 2 miles east of Point Bennett, and 100 feet offshore on the south side of San Miguel Island (lat. 34°01'30" N, long. 120°25'15" W). Named on San Miguel Island West (1950) 7.5' quadrangle.

Juncal Campground [SANTA BARBARA]: *locality,* 6.5 miles north of Carpinteria along Santa Ynez River (lat. 34°29'15" N, long. 119°32'15" W; sec. 30, T 5 N, R 25 W). Named on Carpinteria (1952) 7.5' quadrangle.

Juncal Canyon [SANTA BARBARA]: *canyon,* 2.5 miles long, along Santa Ynez River above a point 8 miles north of Rincon Point (lat. 34°29'15" N, long. 119°29'30" W). Named on White Ledge Peak (1952) 7.5' quadrangle.

Juncal Creek, North Fork [SANTA BARBARA]: *stream,* flows 5.25 miles to Jameson Lake nearly 7 miles north of Carpinteria (lat. 34° 29'40" N, long. 119°30'05" W; at N line sec. 28, T 5 N, R 25 W). Named on Carpinteria (1952), Hildreth Peak (1964), and Old Man Mountain (1943) 7.5' quadrangles.

Junction Camp [SANTA BARBARA]: *locality,* nearly 1 mile south-southeast of Figueroa Mountain (lat. 34°43'55" N, long. 119°58'45" W). Named on Figueroa Mountain (1959) 7.5' quadrangle.

Junipero Serra Peak [MONTEREY]: *peak,* 17 miles west-southwest of King City (lat. 36°08'45" N, long. 121°25'05" W; sec. 34, T 20 S, R 5 E). Altitude 5862 feet. Named on Junipero Serra Peak (1949) 7.5' quadrangle. Davidson (1887, p. 210) called the peak Santa

Lucia Mountain. United States Board on Geographic Names (1933, p. 403) rejected the name "Santa Lucia Peak" for the feature.

Juniper Spring [SAN LUIS OBISPO]: *spring,* nearly 3 miles north-northwest of New Cuyama [SANTA BARBARA] (lat. 34°59'05" N, long. 119°42'20" W; sec. 6, T 10 N, R 26 W). Named on New Cuyama (1964) 7.5' quadrangle.

– K –

Kalte Canyon [MONTEREY]: *canyon,* drained by a stream that flows 2 miles to Pine Canyon (1) 6.5 miles south-southeast of Salinas (lat. 36°34'15" N, long. 121°37'35" W; sec. 3, T 16 S, R 3 E). Named on Spreckels (1947) 7.5' quadrangle.

Kasler Point [MONTEREY]: *promontory,* 7.5 miles north of Point Sur along the coast (lat. 36°24'40" N, long. 121°54'55"). Named on Soberanes Point (1956) 7.5' quadrangle. Clark (1991, p. 249) associated the name with Charles Kasler, who lived near the promontory in 1877.

Kathleen Valley [SAN LUIS OBISPO]: *valley,* 5 miles south of the town of Atascadero (lat. 35°24'45" N, long. 120°40'20" W; near S line sec. 10, T 29 S, R 12 E). Named on Atascadero (1965) 7.5' quadrangle.

Kavanaugh Creek [MONTEREY-SAN LUIS OBISPO]: *stream,* heads in Monterey County and flows 6 miles to an arm of Nacimiento Reservoir 4 miles west of Tierra Redonda Mountain in San Luis Obispo County (lat. 35°46'05" N, long. 121°00'15" W; sec. 9, T 25 S, R 9 E). Named on Bryson (1949, photorevised 1979) 7.5' quadrangle. The misspelled name commemorates John Kavanagh, who settled near the stream in the 1880's (Clark, 1991, p. 249).

Kelly Canyon [SANTA BARBARA]:

(1) *canyon,* drained by a stream that flows 6.5 miles to Cuyama Valley 5.25 miles east of Miranda Pine Mountain (lat. 35°02'55" N, long. 119°56'50" W). Named on Bates Canyon (1964) and Taylor Canyon (1959) 7.5' quadrangles.

(2) *canyon,* drained by a stream that flows 3 miles to Sisquoc River 4.5 miles south-southwest of Tepusquet Peak (lat. 34°51'15" N, long. 120°14' W). Named on Foxen Canyon (1964) and Tepusquet Canyon (1964) 7.5' quadrangles.

Kelly Creek [SANTA BARBARA]: *stream,* flows 4 miles to Santa Ynez River 3 miles northwest of San Marcos Pass (lat. 34°32'35" N, long. 119°51'30" W). Named on San Marcos Pass (1959) 7.5' quadrangle. The stream drains Los Laureles Canyon.

Kelly Creek [SANTA CRUZ]: *stream,* flows nearly 1 mile to West Waddell Creek 1.5 miles west of Big Basin (lat. 37°10'20" N, long. 122°15' W; sec. 12, T 9 S, R 4 W). Named on

Big Basin (1955) 7.5' quadrangle. The name commemorates Dr. Thomas Kelly, who took up a timber claim in the neighborhood in the 1870's (Clark, 1986, p. 171).

Kelly Lake [SANTA CRUZ]: *lake,* 0.5 mile long, 2 miles north-northeast of Watsonville in Pajaro Valley (lat. 36°56'25" N, long. 121°44' W). Named on Watsonville East (1955) 7.5' quadrangle. The name is for Edward Kelly, an early landowner in the neighborhood; the feature also was called White Lake for W.F. White, who owned part of it (Clark, 1986, p. 171, 400).

Kelsey Canyon [SANTA BARBARA]: *canyon,* drained by a stream that flows 5 miles to join the stream in Moon Canyon 10 miles northwest of McPherson Peak (lat. 34°59'45" N, long. 119°55'25" W; at W line sec. 31, T 11 N, R 28 W). Named on Bates Canyon (1964) 7.5' quadrangle.

Kemp Canyon [MONTEREY]: *canyon,* 2 miles long, opens into lowlands along San Antonio River 5.5 miles southwest of Bradley (lat. 35°48' N, long. 120°51'45" W; sec. 35, T 24 S, R 10 E). Named on Bradley (1949) and Tierra Redonda Mountain (1949) 7.5' quadrangles.

Kendall Spring [SANTA BARBARA]: *spring,* 2 miles south-southeast of Fox Mountain (lat. 34°47'20" N, long. 119°35'15" W). Named on Fox Mountain (1964) 7.5' quadrangle.

Kennel Creek [SAN LUIS OBISPO]: *stream,* flows 6.5 miles to Aliso Creek 5.25 miles west of Branch Mountain (lat. 35°11' N, long. 120°10'40" W). Named on Branch Mountain (1967) and Los Machos Hills (1967) 7.5' quadrangles.

Kenner Lake [MONTEREY]: *lake,* 600 feet long, 5.25 miles east of Lonoak (lat. 36°16'05" N, long. 120°50'55" W; on W line sec. 24, T 19 S, R 10 E). Named on Hepsedam Peak (1969) 7.5' quadrangle.

Kennolyn Camp [SANTA CRUZ]: *locality,* 3.5 miles north-northeast of Soquel (lat. 37°02'10" N, long. 121°55'50" W). Named on Laurel (1955) 7.5' quadrangle. The name is from syllables in the names of <u>Kenn</u>eth and Car<u>olyn</u>, children of the owners and founders of the private summer camp, which began in 1946 (Clark, 1986, p. 171).

Kent Canyon: see **Quinado Canyon** [MONTEREY].

Kenville: see **Eccles** [SANTA CRUZ].

Kerr Lake [SAN LUIS OBISPO]: *intermittent lake,* 1100 feet long, 8.5 miles north of Shandon in Cholame Hills near the head of White Canyon (lat. 35°46'35" N, long. 120°21'35" W; on S line sec. 4, T 25 S, R 15 E). Named on Cholame Valley (1961) 7.5' quadrangle.

Kerr Spring [SAN LUIS OBISPO]: *spring,* 7.5 miles north of Shandon (lat. 35°45'45" N, long. 120°21'20" W; near SE cor. sec. 9, T 25 S, R 15 E); the spring is 1 mile south of Kerr Lake. Named on Cholame Valley (1961) 7.5' quadrangle.

Kerry Canyon [SANTA BARBARA]: *canyon,* drained by a stream that flows 5.5 miles to North Fork La Brea Creek 5.25 miles north of Manzanita Mountain (lat. 34°58'15" N, long. 120°04'40" W). Named on Manzanita Mountain (1964) and Miranda Pine Mountain (1967) 7.5' quadrangles.

Kerry Canyon Campground [SANTA BARBARA]: *locality,* 7.25 miles north of Manzanita Mountain (lat. 34°59'55" N, long. 120°03'45" W); the place is situated in Kerry Canyon. Named on Manzanita Mountain (1964) 7.5' quadrangle.

Keunard German Settlement: see **Iron Spring** [SAN LUIS OBISPO] (1).

Keyes Canyon [MONTEREY-SAN LUIS OBISPO]: *canyon,* drained by a stream that heads in Monterey County and flows 14 miles to Estrella Creek 8.5 miles northeast of Paso Robles in San Luis Obispo County (lat. 35°41'50" N, long. 120°34'05" W; at W line sec. 3, T 26 S, R 13 E). Named on Cholame Hills (1961), Estrella (1948), and Ranchito Canyon (1948) 7.5' quadrangles. Cholame (1917) 30' quadrangle has the form "Keys Canyon" for the name.

Keys Canyon: see **Keyes Canyon** [MONTEREY-SAN LUIS OBISPO].

Kid Rock [SANTA BARBARA]: *rock,* 100 feet off of Prince Island at the east end of San Miguel Island (lat. 34°03'35" N, long. 120°19'50" W). Named on San Miguel Island East (1950) 7.5' quadrangle.

Kiler Canyon [SAN LUIS OBISPO]: *canyon,* drained by a stream that flows nearly 1 mile to lowlands along Salinas River near the south edge of Paso Robles (lat. 35°36'50" N, long. 120°41'20" W). Named on Templeton (1948) 7.5' quadrangle.

Kincannon Canyon [MONTEREY]: *canyon,* on upper reaches of James Creek above a point 2.25 miles from the head of the creek (lat. 36°20'50" N, long. 121°35'45" W). Named on Chews Ridge (1956) 7.5' quadrangle. The name commemorates Elgin W. Kincannon, who homesteaded in 1913 or 1914 along Chews Creek, an early name for the stream in present Kincannon Canyon (Clark, 1991, p. 250).

King Camp [MONTEREY]: *locality,* 6.5 miles west-southwest of Jolon (lat. 35°55'50" N, long. 121°17' W). Named on Cape San Martin (1921) 15' quadrangle.

King City [MONTEREY]: *town,* 21 miles southeast of Salinas along Salinas River (lat. 36°12'45" N, long. 121°07'30" W). Named on San Lucas (1949) and Thompson Canyon (1949) 7.5' quadrangles. The name commemorates C.H. King, who laid out the town on his San Lorenzo (2) grant when the railroad reached the place in 1886 (Gudde, 1949, p. 174). Postal authorities established King City post office in 1887 (Frickstad, p. 107), and the town incorporated under the name "The City of King" in 1911. Crawford (1894,

p. 29) called the place Kings City.

King David Spring [SAN LUIS OBISPO]: *spring,* 2.5 miles north of Castle Crags in North Fork Willow Canyon (lat. 35°20'25" N, long. 120°12'35" W). Named on La Panza (1967) 7.5' quadrangle.

Kings City: see **King City** [MONTEREY].

Kings Creek [SANTA CRUZ]: *stream,* flows 6.5 miles to San Lorenzo River 5 miles east of Big Basin (lat. 37°09'20" N, long. 122° 08' W; near W line sec. 18, T 9 S, R 2 W). Named on Big Basin (1955) and Castle Rock Ridge (1955) 7.5' quadrangles. The name commemorates James King, who had a ranch near the mouth of the stream (Clark, 1986, p. 172).

Kinky Canyon: see **Mill Canyon** [SANTA CRUZ].

Kinton Point [SANTA BARBARA]: *promontory,* 4.25 miles southeast of Fraser Point on Santa Cruz Island (lat. 34°00'30" N, long. 119° 53'10" W). Named on Santa Cruz Island A (1943) 7.5' quadrangle.

Kirk Canyon [MONTEREY]: *canyon,* drained by a stream that flows 2.5 miles to Jolon Valley 5.5 miles north of Jolon (lat. 36°02'40" N, long. 121°10'25" W; sec. 2, T 22 S, R 7 E). Named on Cosio Knob (1949) 7.5' quadrangle. The name commemorates Edward William Kirk and his family, who lived at the place (Clark, 1991, p. 253).

Kirk Creek [MONTEREY]: *stream,* flows 2.5 miles to the sea 7 miles north-northwest of Cape San Martin (lat. 35°59'15" N, long. 121°29'40" W; sec. 26, T 22 S, R 4 E). Named on Cape San Martin (1949) 7.5' quadrangle.

Klau [SAN LUIS OBISPO]: *locality,* 6.5 miles east-southeast of Lime Mountain (lat. 35°37'30" N, long. 120°53'30" W; near E line sec. 33, T 26 S, R 10 E). Named on Lime Mountain (1948) 7.5' quadrangle. Postal authorities established Klau post office in 1901 and discontinued it in 1924 (Frickstad, p. 165).

Klondike Canyon [MONTEREY]: *canyon,* drained by a stream that flows nearly 3 miles to Carmel River 1 mile southeast of the town of Carmel Valley (lat. 36°28'10" N, long. 121°42'50" W). Named on Carmel Valley (1956) 7.5' quadrangle.

– L –

Laboratory Point: see **Lovers Point** [MONTEREY].

La Brea Creek [SANTA BARBARA]: *stream,* formed by the confluence of North Fork and South Fork, flows 6.25 miles to Sisquoc River 4.25 miles south-southwest of Tepusquet Peak (lat. 34°51' N, long. 120°12' W). Named on Foxen Canyon (1964) and Tepusquet Canyon (1964) 7.5' quadrangles. Called Labrea Creek on Lompoc (1905) 30' quadrangle, but United States Board on Geographic Names (1961b, p. 10) rejected this form of the name. North

Fork is formed by the confluence of streams in Flores Canyon and Roque Canyon; it is 11 miles long and is named on Manzanita Mountain (1964) and Tepusquet Canyon (1964) 7.5' quadrangles. United States Board on Geographic Names (1961b, p. 12) approved the name "North Fork La Brea Creek" and rejected the forms "North Fork Labrea Creek" and "North Fork of La Brea Creek" for the name. South Fork is 15 miles long and is named on Bates Canyon (1964), Manzanita Mountain (1964), and Tepusquet Canyon (1964) 7.5' quadrangles. United States Board on Geographic Names (1961b, p. 16) rejected the names "South Fork Labrea Creek" and "La Brea Creek" for present South Fork La Brea Creek.

La Cañada de San Luis Beltran: see **Waddell Creek** [SANTA CRUZ].

La Carbonera [SANTA CRUZ]: *land grant,* extends north from Santa Cruz into Santa Cruz Mountains. Named on Felton (1955) and Santa Cruz (1954) 7.5' quadrangles. William Buckle received 0.5 league in 1838 and claimed 2225 acres patented in 1873 (Cowan, p. 24). Perez (p. 61) gave the grant date as 1839.

La Carpa Potrero [SANTA BARBARA]: *area,* 6 miles north-northwest of Old Man Mountain (1) (lat. 34°35'55" N, long. 119°29'20" W). Named on Old Man Mountain (1943) 7.5' quadrangle. United States Board on Geographic Names (1981b, p. 4) approved the name "Three Sisters" for a relief feature described as "rocks" located 1.6 miles east-northeast of La Carpa Potrero at the head of Agua Caliente Canyon (lat. 34°36'16" N, long. 119°27'45" W).

La Carpa Spring [SANTA BARBARA]: *spring,* about 6 miles north-northwest of Old Man Mountain (1) (lat. 34°36' N, long. 119°29'25" W); the spring is at La Carpa Potrero. Named on Old Man Mountain (1943) 7.5' quadrangle.

La Corona [SANTA CRUZ]: *peak,* 2.5 miles northwest of Soquel (lat. 37°00'25" N, long. 121°59'45" W; sec. 5, T 11 S, R 1 W). Altitude 456 feet. Named on Laurel (1955) 7.5' quadrangle. Jose Vincent De Laveaga named the peak about 1880—*la corona* means "the crown" in Spanish (Clark, 1986, p. 173).

Lacosca Creek [SANTA BARBARA]: *stream,* flows 4 miles to Mono Creek 6 miles southeast of Madulce Peak (lat. 34°37'50" N, long. 119°30'35" W). Named on Madulce Peak (1964) and Rancho Nuevo Creek (1943) 7.5' quadrangles.

La Cruz Rock [SAN LUIS OBISPO]: *rock,* 550 feet long, nearly 3.5 miles north-northeast of Piedras Blancas Point, and 800 feet offshore (lat. 35°42'25" N, long. 121°18'40" W); the rock is at the mouth of Arroyo de la Cruz. Named on Piedras Blancas (1959) 7.5' quadrangle.

La Cueva Pintada: see **Cosio Knob** [MONTEREY].

La Cumbre Peak [SANTA BARBARA]: *peak,* 5 miles north of downtown Santa Barbara (lat. 34°29'40" N, long. 119°42'40" W; at S line sec. 21, T 5 N, R 27 W). Altitude 3985 feet. Named on Santa Barbara (1952) 7.5' quadrangle. Called simply La Cumbre on California Mining Bureau's (1917c) map.

Ladies Harbor: see **Ladys Harbor** [SANTA BARBARA].

Ladys Harbor [SANTA BARBARA]: *embayment,* 1.5 miles west of Diablo Point on the north side of Santa Cruz Island (lat. 34°03'20" N, long. 119°47'15" W). Named on Santa Cruz Island B (1943) 7.5' quadrangle. Called Ladies Hbr. on Rand's (1931) map. Doran (p. 146) noted that Lady's Harbor also is called Boat Landing.

La Estrella Creek: see **Estrella Creek** [SAN LUIS OBISPO].

Lafler Canyon [MONTEREY]: *canyon,* drained by a stream that flows 1.5 miles to the sea 2.25 miles northwest of Point Sur (lat. 36°12' N, long. 121°43'35" W; sec. 15, T 20 S, R 2 E). Named on Partington Ridge (1956) 7.5' quadrangle. The name commemorates Harry Lafler, poet and editor (Clark, 1991, p. 256).

Lafler Rock [MONTEREY]: *rock,* 100 feet long, 2.25 miles northwest of Point Sur, and 250 feet offshore (lat. 36°11'55" N, long. 121°43'35" W); the feature is opposite the mouth of Lafler Creek. Named on Partington Ridge (1956) 7.5' quadrangle.

La Goleta [SANTA BARBARA]: *land grant,* at Goleta. Named on Goleta (1950) 7.5' quadrangle. Daniel Hill received 1 league in 1846 and claimed 4426 acres patented in 1865 (Cowan, p. 37).

Lagos: see **Davenport** [SANTA CRUZ].

La Graciosa: see **Graciosa Canyon** [SANTA BARBARA].

Laguna [SAN LUIS OBISPO]: *land grant,* 2.5 miles southwest of downtown San Luis Obispo in Los Osos Valley around Laguna Lake. Named on Pismo Beach (1965) and San Luis Obispo (1965) 7.5' quadrangles. The grant originally was part of the mission lands; the Catholic Church claimed 4157 acres patented in 1859 (Cowan, p. 43-44). Angel (1883, p. 215) used the form "La Laguna" for the name.

Laguna: see **Nuga** [SANTA CRUZ].

Laguna Blanca [SANTA BARBARA]: *lake,* 1450 feet long, 4 miles east of Goleta (lat. 34°25'55" N, long. 119°45'30" W). Named on Goleta (1950) 7.5' quadrangle.

Laguna Canyon [MONTEREY]: *canyon,* drained by a stream that flows 1.25 miles to lowlands along San Antonio River 10 miles southeast of Jolon (lat. 35°53'10" N, long. 121°01'35" W). Named on Williams Hill (1949) 7.5' quadrangle. The name is from the Laguna family (Clark, 1991, p. 257).

Laguna Canyon [SANTA BARBARA]: *canyon,* drained by a stream on Santa Cruz Island that flows nearly 4 miles to the sea 1.25

miles east of Punta Arena (lat. 33°57'45" N, long. 119°47'45" W). Named on Santa Cruz Island B (1943) 7.5' quadrangle. Called Cñ. Laguna on Bremner's (1932) map.

Laguna Creek [SAN BENITO]: *stream,* flows 8 miles to Hernandez Reservoir 9.5 miles east of Bitterwater (lat. 36°22'35" N, long. 120°50' W; sec. 12, T 18 S, R 10 E). Named on Hepsedam Peak (1969) and Hernandez Reservoir (1969) 7.5' quadrangles.

Laguna Creek [SANTA CRUZ]: *stream,* flows 8.5 miles to the sea 7.5 miles west-northwest of Point Santa Cruz (lat. 36°58'55" N, long. 122°09'15" W); the stream forms the east boundary of Arroyo de la Laguna grant near the coast. Named on Davenport (1955) and Santa Cruz (1954) 7.5' quadrangles. The Mexicans used the names "Laguna de Pala" and "Arroyo de la Laguna" for the stream (Hoover, Rensch, and Rensch, p. 472, 473).

Laguna de las Calabasas [SANTA CRUZ]: *land grant,* 2 miles southwest of Corralitos. Named on Watsonville West (1954) 7.5' quadrangle. Felipe Hernandez received 2 leagues in 1833; Felipe Hernandez and C. Morse claimed 2305 acres patented in 1868 (Cowan, p. 21-22; Cowan used the form "Laguna de las Calabazas" for the name).

Laguna de las Grullas: see **Espinosa Lake** [MONTEREY].

Laguna de las Trancas: see **Arroyo las Trancas** [SANTA CRUZ].

Laguna del Rey [MONTEREY]: *lake,* 0.5 mile long, in Seaside (lat. 36°36'20" N, long. 121°51'20" W). Named on Seaside (1947) 7.5' quadrangle. The feature is connected to the sea and a highway bisects it.

Laguna de Pala: see **Laguna Creek** [SANTA CRUZ].

Laguna Grande: see **College Lake** [SANTA CRUZ].

Laguna Grande de San Daniel: see **Guadalupe Lake** [SANTA BARBARA].

Laguna Harbor [SANTA BARBARA]: *embayment,* 1.25 miles east of Punta Arena on the south side of Santa Cruz Island (lat. 33°57'40" N, long. 119°47'45" W); the embayment is at the mouth of Laguna Canyon. Named on Santa Cruz Island B (1943) 7.5' quadrangle.

Laguna Lake [SAN BENITO]: *lake,* 400 feet long, 12 miles east-southeast of Bitterwater (lat. 36°18'35" N, long. 120°48'25" W; sec. 6, T 19 S, R 11 E). Named on Hepsedam Peak (1969) 7.5' quadrangle.

Laguna Lake [SAN LUIS OBISPO]: *lake,* 1 mile long, 2 miles west-southwest of downtown San Luis Obispo in Los Osos Valley (lat. 35°15'55" N, long. 120°41'25" W); the lake is on Laguna grant. Named on San Luis Obispo (1965) 7.5' quadrangle.

Laguna Larga: see **Guadalupe Lake** [SANTA BARBARA].

Laguna Mountain [SAN BENITO]: *peak,* 11 miles east-southeast of Bitterwater (lat.

36°20'20" N, long. 120°48'30" W; sec. 30, T 18 S, R 11 E); the peak is east of Laguna Creek. Altitude 4512 feet. Named on Hepsedam Peak (1969) 7.5' quadrangle.

Laguna Santa Bridida: see **Espinosa Lake** [MONTEREY].

Lagunas de la Herba de los Mansos: see **Merritt Lake** [MONTEREY].

Lagua Seca [MONTEREY]:
(1) *intermittent lake,* 1800 feet long, 5.5 miles east-southeast of Seaside (lat. 36°35' N, long. 121°45'15" W); the feature is on Laguna Seca grant. Named on Seaside (1947) 7.5' quadrangle.
(2) *land grant,* 5 miles east-southeast of Seaside. Named on Seaside (1947) 7.5' quadrangle. Catalina Manzaneli de Munras received the land in 1833 and 1834, and claimed 2179 acres patented in 1865 (Cowan, p. 44; Cowan gave the alternate name "Cañadita" for the grant). The name is from Laguna Seca (1).

Lagunita Lake [MONTEREY]: *intermittent lake,* 600 feet long, 8 miles north-northeast of Salinas (lat. 36°46'30" N, long. 121°36'05" W). Named on San Juan Bautista (1955) 7.5' quadrangle. According to Clark (1991, p. 259), both a travelers stop called Gavilan House and the first location of Natividad post office were at the place.

La Honda Canyon [SANTA BARBARA]: *canyon,* drained by Cañada Honda Creek, which flows 9 miles to the sea 2.25 miles northnortheast of Point Arguello (lat. 34°36'30" N, long. 120°38'10" W). Named on Point Arguello (1959) and Tranquillon Mountain (1959) 7.5' quadrangles.

La Hoya Creek [SANTA BARBARA]: *stream,* flows 4.25 miles to Salsipuedes Creek 5 miles southeast of the city of Lompoc (lat. 34° 34'50" N, long. 120°24'30" W). Named on Lompoc Hills (1959) 7.5' quadrangle.

La Jolla Basin [SANTA BARBARA]: *area,* 5 miles southwest of San Rafael Mountain (lat. 34°39'15" N, long. 119°52'15" W). Named on Figueroa Mountain (1959) and San Rafael Mountain (1959) 7.5' quadrangles.

La Jolla Spring [SANTA BARBARA]:
(1) *spring,* 3 miles north-northwest of Salisbury Potrero (lat. 34°51'50" N, long. 119°42'45" W). Named on Salisbury Potero (1964) 7.5' quadrangle.
(2) *spring,* 2 miles southeast of Zaca Lake (lat. 34°45'25" N, long. 120°00'40" W). Named on Zaca Lake (1964) 7.5' quadrangle.

Lake Cachuma [SANTA BARBARA]: *lake,* behind a dam on Santa Ynez River 4 miles north of Santa Ynez Peak (lat. 34°35'15" N, long. 119°58'50" W). Named on Lake Cachuma (1959) 7.5' quadrangle. United States Board on Geographic Names (1961b, p. 9) rejected the names "Cachuma Lake" and "Cachuma Reservoir" for the feature.

Lake Canyon [SANTA BARBARA]: *canyon,* 2.5 miles long, opens into Santa Lucia Canyon 5.25 miles north-northwest of the city of Lompoc (lat. 34°42'30" N, long. 120°29'25" W). Named on Lompoc (1959) and Surf (1959) 7.5' quadrangles.

Lake Nacimiento: see **Nacimiento Reservoir** [SAN LUIS OBISPO].

Lake Pajaro: see **Watsonville** [SANTA CRUZ].

Lakes: see **The Lakes** [MONTEREY].

Lake San Antonio: see **San Antonio Reservoir** [MONTEREY].

Lake Spring [SAN BENITO]: *spring,* 12.5 miles east-southeast of Bitterwater (lat. 36°18'05" N, long. 120°48' W; near E line sec. 6, T 19 S, R 11 E). Named on Hepsedam Peak (1969) 7.5' quadrangle.

Lake Tanganyika [SAN BENITO]: *intermittent lake,* 275 feet long, 6 miles east-southeast of Bitterwater (lat. 36°21'15" N, long. 120°53'50" W; sec. 21, T 18 S, R 10 E). Named on Lonoak (1969) 7.5' quadrangle.

Lake Tynan [SANTA CRUZ]: *lake,* partly intermittent, 0.5 mile long, 1.5 miles east-northeast of Watsonville (lat. 36°55'45" N, long. 121°43'40" W). Named on Watsonville East (1955) 7.5' quadrangle. The name is for James Tynan, who owned land by the lake (Clark, 1986, p. 177).

Lake View [SANTA BARBARA]: *locality,* 4 miles south of Santa Maria along Pacific Coast Railroad (lat. 34°53'40" N, long. 120°26'45" W). Named on Lompoc (1905) 30' quadrangle. Called Lakeview on California Mining Bureau's (1917a) map, which shows a place called Union located along the railroad about 2 miles north of Lakeview.

Lake Watsonville: see **Watsonville** [SANTA CRUZ].

Lake Ysabel [SAN LUIS OBISPO]: *lake,* 200 feet long, 3 miles south-southeast of Paso Robles (lat. 35°35'20" N, long. 120°40'30" W); the lake is on Santa Ysabel grant. Named on Paso Robles (1919) 15' quadrangle.

La Laguna [SANTA BARBARA]: *land grant,* northeast of Los Olivos. Named on Figueroa Mountain (1959), Foxen Canyon (1964), Los Alamos (1959), Los Olivos (1959), Sisquoc (1959), Zaca Creek (1959), and Zaca Lake (1964) 7.5' quadrangles. Octaviano Gutierrez received 4 leagues in 1845 and claimed 48,704 acres patented in 1867 (Cowan, p. 43).

La Laguna: see **Laguna** [SAN LUIS OBISPO].

Lambert Flats [MONTEREY]: *area,* 1 mile east-southeast of Jamesburg (lat. 36°21'50" N, long. 121°34'15" W; sec. 17, T 18 S, R 4 E). Named on Chews Ridge (1956) 7.5' quadrangle. The name is for the Lambert family, early residents of the neighborhood (Clark, 1991, p. 261).

La Mesa [SANTA BARBARA]: *area,* 1.5 miles south-southwest of downtown Santa Barbara (lat. 34°23'55" N, long. 119°42'40" W). Named on Santa Barbara (1952) 7.5' quadrangle.

La Mission Vieja de la Purisima [SANTA BARBARA]: *land grant,* extends south-

southwest from La Purisima Concepcion mission past the city of Lompoc. Named on Lompoc (1959) and Lompoc Hills (1959) 7.5' quadrangles. Joaquin Carrillo and Jose Antonio Carrillo received 1 league in 1845 and claimed 4414 acres patented in 1873 (Cowan, p. 65).

La Natividad [MONTEREY]: *land grant,* 6 miles north-northeast of Salinas. Named on Natividad (1947), Salinas (1947), and San Juan Bautista (1955) 7.5' quadrangles. Manuel Butron and Nicolas Alviso received 2 leagues about 1830 and in 1837; Ramon Butron and others claimed 8642 acres patented in 1874 (Cowan, p. 51).

La Natividad de la Nuestra Señora: see **Los Osos Valley** [SAN LUIS OBISPO].

La Natividad Mountain: see **Fremont Peak** [MONTEREY-SAN BENITO].

Lang Canyon [MONTEREY]:

(1) *canyon,* drained by a stream that flows 2.5 miles to Sargent Canyon 9 miles north of Bradley (lat. 35°59'30" N, long. 120°46'35" W; sec. 27, T 22 S, R 11 E). Named on Pancho Rico Valley (1967) 7.5' quadrangle.

(2) *canyon,* drained by a stream that flows 2.25 miles to Cholame Creek 2.5 miles west of Parkfield (lat. 35°54'25" N, long. 120°28'25" W; near NW cor. sec. 28, T 23 S, R 14 E). Named on Parkfield (1961) 7.5' quadrangle. The name commemorates members of the Lang family, who homesteaded at the place as early as 1887 (Clark, 1991, p. 262).

Langley Canyon [MONTEREY]: *canyon,* 1.5 miles long, opens into San Miguel Canyon 2 miles north of Prunedale (lat. 36°48'15" N, long. 121°40' W). Named on Prunedale (1954) 7.5' quadrangle. The name commemorates Charles F. Langley, who settled in the neighborhood as early as the 1860's (Clark, 1991, p. 262).

Lankford Flat [SAN BENITO]: *valley,* opens into the canyon of Las Aguilas Creek (1) 5.5 miles north-northwest of Panoche Pass (lat. 36°42'15" N, long. 121°02'50" W). Named on Panoche Pass (1968) 7.5' quadrangle.

Lansing Rock [SAN LUIS OBISPO]: *shoal,* east of Point San Luis, and 0.5 mile offshore in San Luis Obispo Bay (lat. 35°09'45" N, long. 120°44'45" W). Named on Pismo Beach (1965) 7.5' quadrangle.

La Olla [SANTA BARBARA]: *canyon,* drained by a stream that flows 1.25 miles to Cañada del Cojo 4.25 miles northeast of Point Conception (lat. 34°28'55" N, long. 120°24'30" W). Named on Point Conception (1953) 7.5' quadrangle.

La Pansa: see **La Panza** [SAN LUIS OBISPO].

La Panza [SAN LUIS OBISPO]: *locality,* 4 miles north of Castle Crags (lat. 35°21'40" N, long. 120°12'50" W; sec. 36, T 29 S, R 16 E); the place is in La Panza Range. Named on La Panza (1967) 7.5' quadrangle. A settlement developed at the place after discovery of gold at nearby Placer Creek in 1878 (Lee

103

and others, p. 81). Postal authorities established Lapanza post office in 1879, changed the name to La Panza in 1905, discontinued it in 1908, reestablished it in 1911, and discontinued it in 1935 (Salley, p. 117). United States Board on Geographic Names (1968c, p. 5) rejected the names "La Pansa" and "McLean" for the place. *La panza* means "the paunch" in Spanish, and recalls the use of the paunch of slaughtered cattle as bait for grizzly bears (Dillon, 1960, p. 4). Gudde (1969, p. 172) noted that the name was used in the neighborhood as early as 1828.

La Panza Campground [SAN LUIS OBISPO]: *locality,* 7.25 miles east-northeast of Pozo (lat. 35°21'15" N, long. 120°15'45" W; near S line sec. 33, T 29 S, R 16 E); the place is in La Panza Range. Named on Pozo Summit (1967) 7.5' quadrangle.

La Panza Canyon [SAN LUIS OBISPO]: *canyon,* drained by a stream that flows 3 miles to San Juan Creek 6 miles northeast of Castle Crags (lat. 35°22'20" N, long. 120°08'30" W; sec. 27, T 29 S, R 17 E); the canyon is in La Panza Range. Named on La Panza (1967) 7.5' quadrangle.

La Panza Range [SAN LUIS OBISPO]: *range,* northeast of Santa Lucia Range and southwest of the northwest end of Carrizo Plain. Named on San Luis Obispo (1956) 1°x 2° quadrangle. Antisell (1855, p. 35) used the name "Panza hills," and later he (1856, p. 47) used the names "Sierra San Jose" and "San Jose mountains" for the range "between the upper waters of the Salinas river and the valley of Panza and Cariso." Fairbanks (1893, p. 72) used the term "San Jose range" for the feature.

La Panza Summit [SAN LUIS OBISPO]: *locality,* 8 miles east-northeast of Pozo (lat. 35°21'20" N, long. 120°15'05" W; sec. 34, T 29 S, R 16 E); the place is in La Panza Range. Named on Pozo Summit (1967) 7.5' quadrangle.

La Patera [SANTA BARBARA]: *locality,* 1 mile west of downtown Goleta along Southern Pacific Railroad (lat. 34°26'15" N, long. 119°50'25" W). Named on Goleta (1950) 7.5' quadrangle.

La Piedra Pintada: see **Painted Rock** [SAN LUIS OBISPO].

Lapis Siding [MONTEREY]: *locality,* 2.25 miles north-northeast of Marina along Southern Pacific Railroad (lat. 36°42'55" N, long. 121°47'30" W). Named on Marina (1947) 7.5' quadrangle.

La Playa: see **Avila Beach** [SAN LUIS OBISPO]

Laplaya: see **Central Valley** [SANTA BARBARA].

La Punta de Cipreses: see **Cypress Point** [MONTEREY].

La Punta de Pinos: see **Point Pinos** [MONTEREY].

La Purisima: see **Lompoc** [SANTA BAR-

BARA] (2); **Mission La Purisima** [SANTA BARBARA].

Larious Canyon [SAN BENITO]: *canyon,* 6.5 miles long, opens into Vallecitos 4 miles northwest of Idria (lat. 36°27'15" N, long. 120° 43'45" W; sec. 14, T 17 S, R 11 E); the canyon is along Larious Creek. Named on Idria (1969) 7.5' quadrangle.

Larious Creek [SAN BENITO]: *stream,* flows 10 miles to join San Carlos Creek and form Silver Creek 3.5 miles north of Idria (lat. 36°28'05" N, long. 120°41'05" W; near W line sec. 8, T 17 S, R 12 E). Named on Idria (1969) 7.5' quadrangle.

Larious Spring [SAN BENITO]: *spring,* 4 miles west-northwest of Idria (lat. 36°26'25" N, long. 120°44'20" W; sec. 23, T 17 S, R 11 E); the spring is along Larious Creek. Named on Idria (1969) 7.5' quadrangle.

Larkins Valley [SANTA CRUZ]: *valley,* 3 miles south-southwest of Corralitos (lat. 36°56'50" N, long. 121°49'15" W). Named on Watsonville West (1954) 7.5' quadrangle. Capitola (1914) 15' quadrangle has the form "Larkin Valley" for the name.

La Saca: see **La Zaca** [SANTA BARBARA].

La Sagrada Familia: see **Bolsa del Potrero y Morro Cojo** [MONTEREY].

Las Aguilas Canyon [SAN BENITO]: *canyon,* drained by Las Aguilas Creek (2), or a branch of that creek, which flows nearly 3.5 miles in the canyon to a point 7 miles west-northwest of Panoche (lat. 36°38'50" N, long. 120°56'15" W; sec. 1, T 15 S, R 9 E). Named on Cerro Colorado (1969) 7.5' quadrangle.

Las Aguilas Creek [SAN BENITO]:
(1) *stream,* flows 12.5 miles to Tres Pinos Creek 5.5 miles west-northwest of Panoche Pass (lat. 36°39'45" N, long. 121°06' W; sec. 4, T 15 S, R 8 E); the stream is largely on Real de las Aguilas grant. Named on Panoche Pass (1968) 7.5' quadrangle.
(2) *stream,* flows 9 miles to Panoche Creek nearly 2 miles north-northwest of Panoche in Panoche Valley (lat. 36°37'10" N, long. 120°50'55" W; sec. 14, T 15 S, R 10 E); the stream heads on a ridge east of Real de las Aguilas grant. Named on Cerro Colorado (1969), Mercey Hot Springs (1969), and Panoche (1969) 7.5' quadrangles.

Las Aguilas Mountains [SAN BENITO]: *ridge,* northeast-trending, 4 miles long, 7.5 miles north of Panoche Pass (lat. 36°44'19" N, long. 121°00'30" W); the feature is southeast of Las Aguilas Valley. Named on Cerro Colorado (1969), Ortigalita Peak (1969), and Panoche Pass (1968) 7.5' quadrangles.

Las Aguilas Valley [SAN BENITO]: *valley,* 7.5 miles north of Panoche Pass (lat. 36°44'30" N, long. 121°01' W); the valley is along upper reaches of Las Aguilas Creek (1). Named on Panoche Pass (1968) and Ruby Canyon (1968) 7.5' quadrangles.

Las Alamos Creek: see **San Antonio Creek** [SANTA BARBARA] (1).

La Salle [SANTA BARBARA]: *locality,* 5 miles east-southeast of Surf along Southern Pacific Railroad (lat. 34°38'50" N, long. 120°31'30" W); the place is near the mouth of La Salle Canyon. Named on Surf (1959) 7.5' quadrangle. California Division of Highways' (1934) map shows a place called Murray located along the railroad 1 mile east-southeast of La Salle.

La Salle Canyon [SANTA BARBARA]: *canyon,* drained by a stream that flows 2.5 miles to lowlands 5.5 miles east-southeast of Surf (lat. 34°38'30" N, long. 120°31'25" W). Named on Surf (1959) and Tranquillon Mountain (1959) 7.5' quadrangles.

Las Animas Creek [SANTA BARBARA]: *stream,* flows 2.5 miles to the sea 1.5 miles north of Point Conception (lat. 34°28'25" N, long. 120°28'30" W). Named on Point Conception (1942) 15' quadrangle. The stream drains present Black Canyon (2).

Las Animas Spring [SANTA BARBARA]: *spring,* 2.5 miles north-northeast of Point Conception (lat. 34°29' N, long. 120°27'10" W). Named on Point Conception (1953) 7.5' quadrangle.

Las Aromitas y Agua Caliente [SAN BENITO]: *land grant,* in the northwesternmost part of San Benito County near Aromas. Named on Chittenden (1955), Prunedale (1954), San Juan Bautista (1955), and Watsonville East (1955) 7.5' quadrangles. Juan M. Ansar received 3 leagues in 1835; F.A. McDougall and others claimed 8660 acres patented in 1862 (Cowan, p. 16).

Las Canovas Creek [SANTA BARBARA]: *stream,* flows 1.25 miles to Cañada de la Gaviota 8 miles south-southwest of Buellton (lat. 34°30'15" N, long. 120°13'35" W). Named on Solvang (1959) 7.5' quadrangle.

Las Chiches [SAN LUIS OBISPO]: *peak,* 5.25 miles northeast of Pozo (lat. 35°21'20" N, long. 120°18'30" W; near E line sec. 36, T 29 S, R 15 E). Altitude 3141 feet. Named on Pozo Summit (1967) 7.5' quadrangle.

Las Cruces [SANTA BARBARA]:
(1) *land grant,* at and north of Las Cruces (2) along Cañada de las Cruces. Named on Gaviota (1953), Santa Rosa Hills (1959), and Solvang (1959) 7.5' quadrangles. Miguel Cordero received the land in 1836 and claimed 8888 acres patented in 1883 (Cowan, p. 31). Perez gave the grant date as 1837, and gave the grant size as 8512.81 acres. The name goes back to the late eighteenth century, when Franciscan missionaries discovered many Indian grave mounds in the neighborhood and marked each with a cross—*las cruces* means "the crosses" in Spanish (Rife, p. 103).
(2) *locality,* 7.5 miles south-southwest of Buellton (lat. 34°30'25" N, long. 120°13'35" W); at the mouth of Cañada de las Cruces on Las Cruces grant. Named on Solvang (1959) 7.5' quadrangle. Postal authorities established Las Cruces post office in 1869 and discon-

tinued it in 1887 (Frickstad, p. 171). They established Nojoqui post office 4 miles north of Las Cruces in 1887 and discontinued it in 1898 (Salley, p. 155).

Las Cruces Hot Springs: see **Hot Springs** [SANTA BARBARA] (1).

Las Cruces Sulphur Springs: see **Hot Springs** [SANTA BARBARA] (1).

La Selva Beach [SANTA CRUZ]: *town,* 6.25 miles west-northwest of Watsonville near the coast (lat. 36°56'15" N, long. 121°51'30" W). Named on Watsonville East (1955) 7.5' quadrangle. Postal authorities established La Selva Beach post office in 1952 (Salley, p. 118). The train station at the place was called Manresa before 1922, when promoters began Rob Roy real-estate development and changed the station name to Rob Roy; the name became La Selva Beach after the development changed hands in 1935 (Hamman, p. 268).

Las Flores Canyon [SANTA BARBARA]: *canyon,* drained by a stream that flows 2.5 miles to Cañada del Corral 10 miles east of Gaviota (lat. 34°28'45" N, long. 120°02'30" W). Named on Santa Ynez (1959) and Tajiguas (1953) 7.5' quadrangles.

Las Gazas Creek [MONTEREY]: *stream,* flows 7.5 miles to Carmel River 2.25 miles northwest of the town of Carmel Valley (lat. 36° 29'30" N, long. 121°45' W). Named on Mount Carmel (1956) 7.5' quadrangle.

Lasher Canyon [MONTEREY]: *canyon,* drained by a stream that flows nearly 1 mile to lowlands 4.25 miles south-southwest of Soledad (lat. 36°21'55" N, long. 121°21'10" W; sec. 18, T 18 S, R 6 E). Named on Paraiso Springs (1956) 7.5' quadrangle.

Las Llagas Canyon [SANTA BARBARA]: *canyon,* drained by a stream that flows nearly 4 miles to the sea 8 miles west-northwest of Coal Oil Point (lat. 34°27'30" N, long. 120°00'05" W). Named on Dos Pueblos Canyon (1951) 7.5' quadrangle. Called Las Yeguas Canyon on Goleta (1903) 15' quadrangle.

Las Lomas: see **Hall** [MONTEREY].

Las Mesas del Potrero [MONTEREY]: *area,* 6.5 miles east-southeast of the mouth of Carmel River (lat. 36°30'10" N, long. 121°49' W; near N line sec. 35, T 16 S, R 1 E). Named on Monterey (1913) 15' quadrangle.

Las Muertas Canyon [MONTEREY-SAN BENITO]: *canyon,* drained by a stream that heads in San Benito County and flows nearly 5 miles to Cinco Canoas Canyon 6.5 miles east of Greenfield in Monterey County (lat. 36°20'20" N, long. 121°07'45" W). Named on Greenfield (1956) and Pinalito Canyon (1969) 7.5' quadrangles.

Las Piedras Canyon [MONTEREY]: *canyon,* drained by Rocky Creek (1), which flows 6 miles to the sea 5 miles north of Point Sur (lat. 36°22'45" N, long. 121°54'05" W; sec. 7, T 18 S, R 1 E). Named on Mount Carmel (1956) and Soberanes Point (1956) 7.5' quadrangles.

Las Positas y la Calera [SANTA BARBARA]: *land grant,* west of Santa Barbara along the coast. Named on Goleta (1950) and Santa Barbara (1952) 7.5' quadrangles. Narcisco Fabregat and Thomas M. Robbins received the land in 1843 and 1846; Manuela Carrillo de Jones and Robbins claimed 3282 acres patented in 1870 (Cowan, p. 22; Perez, p. 82).

Las Pozas: see **San Miguel** [SAN LUIS OBISPO].

Las Salinas [MONTEREY]: *land grant,* 7 miles west-northwest of Salinas. Named on Marina (1947) and Salinas (1947) 7.5' quadrangles. Gabriel Espinosa received 1 league in 1836 and his heirs claimed 4414 acres patented in 1867 (Cowan, p. 70).

Las Sierras de San Martin: see **Santa Lucia Range** [MONTEREY-SAN LUIS OBISPO].

Las Tablas Creek [SAN LUIS OBISPO]: *stream,* flows 20 miles to Nacimiento River 5.25 miles north-northeast of Lime Mountain (lat. 35°44'35" N, long. 120°57'25" W; sec. 24, T 15 S, R 9 E). Named on Adelaida (1948), Cypress Mountain (1948), and Lime Mountain (1948) 7.5' quadrangles. The stream now enters an arm of Nacimiento Reservoir.

Last Chance Creek [SANTA CRUZ]: *stream,* flows 1.25 miles to East Waddell Creek nearly 3 miles north-northeast of the mouth of Waddell Creek (lat. 37°08'20" N, long. 122°15'30" W; sec. 24, T 9 S, R 4 W). Named on Big Basin (1955) and Franklin Point (1955) 7.5' quadrangles.

Las Varas Canyon [SANTA BARBARA]: *canyon,* drained by a stream that flows 4 miles to the sea 6 miles west-northwest of Coal Oil Point (lat. 34°26'40" N, long. 119°58'15" W). Named on Dos Pueblos Canyon (1951) 7.5' quadrangle.

Las Vegas Creek [SANTA BARBARA]: *stream,* flows 3 miles to San Pedro Creek near downtown Goleta (lat. 34°26'10" N, long. 119° 49'50" W). Named on Goleta (1950) 7.5' quadrangle.

Las Yeguas Canyon: see **Las Llagas Canyon** [SANTA BARBARA].

Latigo Canyon [SANTA BARBARA]: *canyon,* 5.5 miles long, along Santa Agueda Creek above a point nearly 5 miles east of Los Olivos (lat. 34°40' N, long. 120°01'45" W). Named on Los Olivos (1959) 7.5' quadrangle.

La Tinta Basin [SANTA BARBARA]: *area,* 6 miles south of the city of Lompoc along Gasper Creek (lat. 34°33'05" N, long. 120° 28' W); the place is 2 miles south-southeast of La Tinta Hill. Named on Lompoc Hills (1959) 7.5' quadrangle.

La Tinta Hill [SANTA BARBARA]: *peak,* 4.5 miles south-southwest of the city of Lompoc (lat. 34°34'45" N, long. 120°29'15" W). Named on Lompoc Hills (1959) 7.5' quadrangle.

Launtz Creek [MONTEREY]: *stream,* flows nearly 1.5 miles to South Fork Little Sur River 6 miles east of Point Sur (lat. 36°18'35" N,

long. 121°47'30" W; at E line sec. 1, T 19 S, R 1 E); the stream is south of Launtz Ridge. Named on Big Sur (1956) 7.5' quadrangle.

Launtz Ridge [MONTEREY]: *ridge,* northwest-to west-trending, 2.5 miles long, 7 miles east of Point Sur (lat. 36°18'55" N, long. 121° 46'30" W). Named on Big Sur (1956) 7.5' quadrangle. The name commemorates the Launtz family (Clark, 1991, p. 265).

Laurel [SANTA CRUZ]: *settlement,* 9 miles north of Soquel (lat. 37° 07'05" N, long. 121°57'45" W). Named on Laurel (1955) 7.5' quadrangle. Postal authorities established Laurel post office in 1882 and discontinued it in 1953 (Frickstad, p. 176). The place first was called Highland, but after it became a construction site for South Pacific Coast Railroad, the name was changed to Laurel (Clark, 1986, p. 180).

Laurel Canyon: see **Lauro Canyon** [SANTA BARBARA].

Laurel Creek [SANTA CRUZ]: *stream,* flows 3 miles to join Burns Creek and form West Branch Soquel Creek 9 miles north of Soquel at Laurel (lat. 37°07'10" N, long. 121°57'35" W). Named on Laurel (1955) 7.5' quadrangle. The stream first was called Burrell Creek; the name "Laurel" is from the settlement of Laurel (Clark, 1986, p. 180).

Laurel Grove: see **Swanton** [SANTA CRUZ].

Laurel Spring [SAN LUIS OBISPO]: *spring,* 9.5 miles north-northeast of the mouth of Morro Creek (lat. 35°29'25" N, long. 120°45'55" W). Named on Morro Bay North (1965) 7.5' quadrangle.

Laurel Springs [SANTA BARBARA]: *springs,* 1.5 miles east of San Marcos Pass (lat. 34°30'40" N, long. 119°47'45" W; sec. 15, T 5 N, R 28 W). Named on San Marcos Pass (1959) 7.5' quadrangle. San Rafael Mountain (1943) 15' quadrangle shows Laurel Springs Lodge at the site.

Lauro Canyon [SANTA BARBARA]: *canyon,* drained by a stream that flows 1.25 miles to lowlands 2.5 miles northwest of downtown Santa Barbara (lat. 34°27' N, long. 119°43'45" W; at S line sec. 5, T 4 N, R 27 W). Named on Santa Barbara (1952) 7.5' quadrangle. Called Diablo Canyon on Santa Barbara (1944) 7.5' quadrangle, but United States Board on Geographic Names (1961b, p. 11) rejected the names "Diablo Canyon" and "Laurel Canyon" for the feature.

Lavega Peak [SAN BENITO]: *peak,* 5 miles south-southeast of Mariposa Peak on San Benito-Merced county line (lat. 36°53'25" N, long. 121°10'35" W; sec. 14, T 12 S, R 7 E). Altitude 3801 feet. Named on Mariposa Peak (1969) 7.5' quadrangle.

Lavigia Hill [SANTA BARBARA]: *peak,* 1.5 miles southwest of downtown Santa Barbara (lat. 34°24'15" N, long. 119°42'50" W). Altitude 459 feet. Named on Santa Barbara (1952) 7.5' quadrangle.

Lawson: see **Jim Lawson Gulch** [MONTEREY].

Lawson Canyon [MONTEREY]: *canyon,* drained by a stream that flows 3 miles to Portugee Canyon 5.5 miles northeast of San Ardo (lat. 36°05'15" N, long. 120°50'45" W; sec. 24, T 21 S, R 10 E). Named on Pancho Rico Valley (1967) 7.5' quadrangle.

Lawson Spring [SAN LUIS OBISPO]: *spring,* 30 miles southeast of Simmler (lat. 35°01' N, long. 119°36'45" W; near NW cor. sec. 25, T 11 N, R 26 W). Named on Elkhorn Hills (1954) 7.5' quadrangle.

La Zaca [SANTA BARBARA]: *land grant, 9* miles east of Los Alamos. Named on Foxen Canyon (1964), Los Olivos (1959), Zaca Creek (1959), and Zaca Lake (1964) 7.5' quadrangles. Antonio, possibly an Indian, received the land in 1838; Maria Antonio de la Guerra de Lataillade claimed 4458 acres patented in 1876 (Cowan, p. 69; Cowan gave the form "La Saca" as an alternate).

La Zaca Creek: see **Zaca Creek** [SANTA BARBARA].

Lazaro Canyon [SANTA BARBARA]: *canyon,* drained by a stream that flows 6.5 miles to Cachuma Creek 7.5 miles south-southeast of Figueroa Mountain (lat. 34°38'50" N, long. 119°55'10" W). Named on Figueroa Mountain (1959) and San Rafael Mountain (1959) 7.5' quadrangles.

Lazy Campground [SANTA BARBARA]: *locality,* 4.5 miles north of Manzanita Mountain along North Fork La Brea Creek (lat. 34°57'45" N, long. 120°05'10" W). Named on Manzanita Mountain (1964) 7.5' quadrangle.

Leaf Spring [SAN LUIS OBISPO]: *spring, 8* miles northeast of Pozo (lat. 35°22'55" N, long. 120°16'10" W; near SW cor. sec. 21, T 29 S, R 16 E). Named on Camatta Ranch (1966) 7.5' quadrangle.

Leary Hill [MONTEREY]: *peak,* 4.5 miles south-southeast of Marina (lat. 36°37'35" N, long. 121°45'25" W). Named on Marina (1947) 7.5' quadrangle.

Lee Canyon [MONTEREY]: *canyon,* drained by a stream that flows 2.25 miles to lowlands along Cholame Creek 1.25 miles southwest of Parkfield (lat. 35°53'20" N, long. 120°26'50" W; sec. 34, T 23 S, R 14 E). Named on Parkfield (1961) 7.5' quadrangle.

Leffingwell Creek [SAN LUIS OBISPO]: *stream,* flows 2 miles to the sea 5 miles west-northwest of Cambria (lat. 35°34'50" N, long. 121°07'05" W; near S line sec. 16, T 27 S, R 8 E). Named on Cambria (1959) 7.5' quadrangle.

Leffingwell Landing [SAN LUIS OBISPO]: *locality,* 2.5 miles west-northwest of Cambria along the coast (lat. 35°34'50" N, long. 121°07'10" W; near S line sec. 16, T 27 S, R 8 E); the place is at the mouth of present Leffingwell Creek. Named on San Simeon (1919) 15' quadrangle. William Leffingwell, Sr., settled in 1858 on the coast between San Simeon and Santa Rosa grants, where he

established a beach landing known as Leffingwell Landing; in 1874 Leffingwell and J.C. Baker purchased land a little farther south at the mouth of present Leffingwell Creek and constructed a pier there that was called Leffingwell Landing, Leffingwell Pier, and Leffingwell Wharf (Hamilton, p. 122, 124-125). The indentation in the coast at the mouth of Leffingwell Creek was known as Rickard's Cove in the early days for Warren C. Rickard and William C. Rickard, who had a store there (Hamilton, p. 182).

Leffingwell Pier: see **Leffingwell Landing** [SAN LUIS OBISPO].

Leffingwell Wharf: see **Leffingwell Landing** [SAN LUIS OBISPO].

Lento [SANTA BARBARA]: *locality,* 3.25 miles east of Gaviota along Southern Pacific Railroad (lat. 34°28'20" N, long. 120°09'35" W). Named on Gaviota (1953) 7.5' quadrangle.

Leonard [SANTA CRUZ]: *locality,* 6.5 miles west-northwest of Watsonville along Southern Pacific Railroad (lat. 36°56'45" N, long. 121°52'15" W). Named on Capitola (1914) 15' quadrangle. Postal authorities established Leonard post office 7 miles west of Watsonville in 1883 and discontinued it that year—the name was for John Leonard, first postmaster (Salley, p. 121).

Leon Canyon [SANTA BARBARA]: *canyon,* drained by a stream that flows 1.5 miles to Tajiguas Creek 7 miles east of Gaviota (lat. 34°28'45" N, long. 120°05'40" W). Named on Tajiguas (1953) 7.5' quadrangle.

Lettuce Lake [SAN LUIS OBISPO]: *lake,* 600 feet long, 6 miles south-southwest of the town of Arroyo Grande near the coast (lat. 35°02'10" N, long. 120°36'30" W). Named on Arroyo Grande (1952) 15' quadrangle. Oceano (1965) 7.5' quadrangle shows a dry lake.

Lewis Canyon [SANTA BARBARA]: *canyon,* drained by a stream that flows 1.5 miles to Santa Ynez River 3 miles northeast of San Marcos Pass (lat. 34°32'35" N, long. 119°47' W). Named on San Marcos Pass (1959) 7.5' quadrangle.

Lewis Creek [MONTEREY-SAN BENITO]: *stream,* heads in Monterey County and flows 29 miles, partly in San Benito County, to San Lorenzo Creek 10 miles east-northeast of King City (lat. 36°16'50" N, long. 120°57'45" W; sec. 14, T 19 S, R 9 E). Named on Hepsedam Peak (1969), Lonoak (1969), Monarch Peak (1967), and Priest Valley (1969) 7.5' quadrangles. Frank De Alvarez and E.C. Tully named the stream for Dutch Lewis, a cattleman in the region; the stream was called Priest Valley Creek on an early survey (Clark, 1991, p. 267). North Fork enters from the north 24 miles upstream from the mouth of the main creek; it is 9 miles long and is named on Priest Valley (1969) and San Benito Mountain (1969) 7.5' quadrangles. East Fork enters

North Fork 4.5 miles upstream from the mouth of North Fork; it is 3.25 miles long and is named on San Benito Mountain (1969) 7.5' quadrangle. Monterey-San Benito county line follows Lewis Creek from San Lorenzo Creek to North Fork, and then follows North Fork.

Lewis Flat [SAN BENITO]: *area,* 7 miles south-southwest of Idria along San Benito River (lat. 36°19'45" N, long. 120°44' W; sec. 26, T 18 S, R 11 E). Named on San Benito Mountain (1969) 7.5' quadrangle.

Liddell Creek [SANTA CRUZ]: *stream,* flows 3 miles to the sea 1 mile southeast of Davenport (lat. 37°00' N, long. 122°10'50" W). Named on Davenport (1955) 7.5' quadrangle. The name commemorates George Liddell, who started a sawmill along the stream in 1851 (Clark, 1986, p. 183). East Branch enters from the east-northeast 1 mile upstream from the mouth of the main creek; it is nearly 2 miles long and is named on Davenport (1955) 7.5' quadrangle.

Liddell Creek: see **West Liddell Creek** [SANTA CRUZ].

Liebe Canyon [SANTA BARBARA]: *canyon,* drained by a stream that flows 1.25 miles to Zaca Creek 2.25 miles west-northwest of Zaca Lake (lat. 34°47'15" N, long. 120°04'35" W). Named on Zaca Lake (1964) 7.5' quadrangle.

Liggett: see **Hunter Liggett Military Reservation** [MONTEREY].

Lighthouse Point: see **Point Pinos** [MONTEREY]; **Point Santa Cruz** [SANTA CRUZ].

Ligs Spring [SAN BENITO]: *spring,* 4.5 miles southeast of Bitterwater (lat. 36°20'35" N, long. 120°56'10" W; near SW cor. sec. 19, T 18 S, R 10 E). Named on Lonoak (1969) 7.5' quadrangle.

Lime Creek [MONTEREY]: *stream,* flows 1.5 miles to the sea 0.25 mile south-southeast of Slates Hot Springs (lat. 36°07'10" N, long. 121°37'55" W; sec. 9, T 21 S, R 3 E). Named on Lopez Point (1956) 7.5' quadrangle.

Limekiln [MONTEREY]: *locality,* nearly 5 miles north-northeast of Point Sur near the junction of Dairy Gulch and Bixby Creek (lat. 36°22'15" N, long. 121°52'05" W; sec. 16, T 18 S, R 1 E). Named on Point Sur (1925) 15' quadrangle. Monterey Lime Company had kilns at the place (Clark, 1991, p. 268).

Limekiln Creek [MONTEREY]:
(1) *stream,* flows 5 miles to Salinas River 3 miles south of Chualar (lat. 36°31'30" N, long. 121°31' W). Named on Chualar (1947) 7.5' quadrangle. A limekiln operated at the place at one time (Hart, E.W., p. 78).
(2) *stream,* flows 2.5 miles to the sea nearly 3 miles east-southeast of Lopez Point at Rockland Landing (lat. 36°00'30" N, long. 121°31'05" W; sec. 22, T 22 S, R 4 E). Named on Lopez Point (1956) 7.5' quadrangle. Rockland Cement Company operated limekilns in the canyon in the 1880's, and

shipped lime from Rockland Landing (Lussier, p. 35). The canyon of the stream was known as Redwood Cañon in the early days (Clark, 1991, p. 268). West Fork enters from the northwest 0.5 mile upstream from the mouth of the main creek; it is 4 miles long and is named on Lopez Point (1956) 7.5' quadrangle.

Lime Mountain [SAN LUIS OBISPO]: *peak,* 17 miles west of Paso Robles (lat. 35°40'20" N, long. 120°59'35" W; sec. 15, T 26 S, R 9 E). Altitude 2230 feet. Named on Lime Mountain (1948) 7.5' quadrangle. A limestone quarry is at the summit of the peak (Hart, E.W., p. 87).

Lime Rock Spring [SANTA BARBARA]: *spring,* 2.5 miles north of Salisbury Potrero (lat. 34°51'35" N, long. 119°41'35" W). Named on Salisbury Potrero (1964) 7.5' quadrangle.

Lingo Canyon [SAN LUIS OBISPO]: *canyon,* drained by a stream that flows 1.25 miles to McGinnis Creek 6 miles northeast of Pozo (lat. 35°22'10" N, long. 120°18'25" W). Named on Pozo Summit (1967) 7.5' quadrangle.

Linne [SAN LUIS OBISPO]: *locality,* 4.5 miles north-northwest of Creston (lat. 35°34'20" N, long. 120°34' W; near SW cor. sec. 15, T 27 S, R 13 E). Named on Creston (1948) 7.5' quadrangle. Postal authorities established Linné post office in 1889 and discontinued it in 1925 (Frickstad, p. 165). The place was a Swedish community (Lee and others, p. 47).

Lion Canyon [SANTA BARBARA]:
(1) *canyon,* drained by a stream that flows 2.25 miles to Cachuma Creek 4.5 miles southeast of Figueroa Mountain (lat. 34°42'10" N, long. 119°55' W; sec. 10, T 7 N, R 29 W). Named on Figueroa Mountain (1959) 7.5' quadrangle.
(2) *canyon,* drained by a stream that flows 3 miles to Sisquoc River 4 miles north-northeast of Zaca Lake (lat. 34°50' N, long. 120°00'35" W). Named on Zaca Lake (1964) 7.5' quadrangle.
(3) *canyon,* drained by a stream that flows 2.5 miles to South Fork La Brea Creek 1.5 miles east-northeast of Manzanita Mountain (lat. 34°54'20" N, long. 120°03'20" W). Named on Manzanita Mountain (1964) 7.5' quadrangle.
(4) *canyon,* drained by a stream that flows 5.5 miles to Newsome Canyon 3.5 miles north of Salisbury Potrero (lat. 34°52'20" N, long. 119°42'30" W; sec. 7, T 9 N, R 26 W). Named on Salisbury Potrero (1964) 7.5' quadrangle.

Lion Creek [MONTEREY]: *stream,* flows 3.25 miles to Big Sur River 2.5 miles south-southwest of Ventana Cone (lat. 36°15'05" N, long. 121°41'40" W; sec. 25, T 19 S, R 2 E). Named on Ventana Cones (1956) 7.5' quadrangle. The name is from the two mountain lions that Joseph William Post, Jr., killed by the creek in 1920 (Clark, 1991, p. 269).

Lion Creek: see **McWay Canyon**

[MONTEREY]; **Rogers Creek** [SANTA CRUZ].

Lion Gulch: see **McWay Canyon** [MONTEREY].

Lion Peak [MONTEREY]: *peak,* 8.5 miles east-southeast of Cape San Martin (lat. 35°51'05" N, long. 121°19'10" W; near NE cor. sec. 16, T 24 S, R 6 E). Altitude 3499 feet. Named on Burro Mountain (1949) 7.5' quadrangle.

Lion Rock [SAN LUIS OBISPO]: *rock,* 600 feet long, 7.5 miles west-northwest of Point San Luis, and 850 feet offshore (lat. 35°13'05" N, long. 120°52'30" W). Named on Port San Luis (1965) 7.5' quadrangle. The name is from the sea lions at the place; in early days the rock was called El Lobo—*el lobo* means "the wolf," or here "the sea wolf," in Spanish (Gudde, 1949, p. 189)

Lion Rock [SANTA BARBARA]: *rock,* 7.5 miles southwest of Guadalupe, 2000 feet southeast of Point Sal, and 600 feet offshore (lat. 34°53'55" N, long. 120°39'55" W). Named on Point Sal (1958) 7.5' quadrangle. Called Seal Rock on Guadalupe (1905) 30' quadrangle, but United States Board on Geographic Names (1960c, p. 17) rejected this name for the feature.

Lions Head [SANTA BARBARA]: *promontory,* 5.25 miles west-northwest of the village of Casmalia (lat. 34°52'15" N, long. 120° 36'50" W). Named on Casmalia (1959) 7.5' quadrangle. Called Lion's Head on Fairbanks' (1896) map, which shows a promontory called Pt. Morrito located nearly 1 mile west-northwest of Lion's Head along the coast. Postal authorities established Morritto post office near Point Morrito in 1881 and discontinued it in 1884 (Salley, p. 146).

Lion Spring: see **Lower Lion Spring** [SANTA BARBARA].

Lisque Creek [SANTA BARBARA]: *stream* and *dry wash,* flows 4 miles to Figueroa Creek 4.5 miles east-northeast of Los Olivos (lat. 34°41'15" N; long. 120°02'10" W). Named on Los Olivos (1959) 7.5' quadrangle.

Little Basin [SANTA CRUZ]: *valley,* 1.25 miles southeast of Big Basin (lat. 37°09'30" N, long. 122°12'10" W; near NW cor. sec. 16, T 9 S, R 3 W). Named on Big Basin (1955) 7.5' quadrangle.

Little Bear Trap [MONTEREY]: *locality,* 4.5 miles east-northeast of Uncle Sam Mountain (lat. 36°21'30" N, long. 121°37'45" W; near SE cor. sec. 15, T 18 S, R 3 E). Named on Ventana Cones (1956) 7.5' quadrangle.

Little Bitterwater Canyon [MONTEREY]: *canyon,* drained by a stream that flows 3.25 miles to Pancho Rico Creek 11 miles east-northeast of San Ardo (lat. 36°04'40" N, long. 120°43'20" W; sec. 30, T 21 S, R 12 E). Named on Slack Canyon (1969) 7.5' quadrangle.

Little Bitterwater Spring [MONTEREY]: *spring,* 12.5 miles east-northeast of San Ardo (lat. 36°04'20" N, long. 120°41'15" W; near

W line sec. 28, T 21 S, R 12 E); the spring is in Little Bitterwater Canyon. Named on Slack Canyon (1969) 7.5' quadrangle.

Little Boulder Creek [SANTA CRUZ]: *stream,* flows nearly 1 mile to San Mateo County 3.5 miles north-northeast of Big Basin (lat. 37°12'55" N, long. 122°11'40" W; at N line sec. 28, T 8 S, R 3 W). Named on Big Basin (1955) 7.5' quadrangle.

Little Burnett Creek [SAN LUIS OBISPO]: *stream,* flows 9 miles to Nacimiento River 10 miles northeast of the village of San Simeon (lat. 35°44'55" N, long. 121°04'10" W; near N line sec. 23, T 25 S, R 8 E); the stream heads near Burnett Peak. Named on Bryson (1949), Burnett Peak (1949), and Pebblestone Shut-in (1959) 7.5' quadrangles.

Little Burros Creek [MONTEREY]: *stream,* flows nearly 3 miles to Los Burros Creek 0.5 mile south-southeast of Burro Mountain (lat. 35°51'50" N, long. 121°16'05" W; sec. 12, T 24 S, R 6 E). Named on Burro Mountain (1949) 7.5' quadrangle.

Little Caliente Canyon [SANTA BARBARA]: *canyon,* drained by a stream that flows 3 miles to Mono Creek 7.5 miles southeast of Little Pine Mountain (lat. 34°32'05" N, long. 119°37'45" W). Named on Hildreth Peak (1964) 7.5' quadrangle.

Little Caliente Spring [SANTA BARBARA]: *spring,* 5.5 miles southwest of Hildreth Peak (lat. 34°32'25" N, long. 119°37'10" W); the spring is in a branch of Little Caliente Canyon. Named on Hildreth Peak (1964) 7.5' quadrangle.

Little Cayucos Creek [SAN LUIS OBISPO]: *stream,* flows 3 miles to Estero Bay 0.25 mile east-southeast of the mouth of Cayucos Creek at Cayucos (lat. 35°26'40" N, long. 120°54'10" W). Named on Cayucos (1965) 7.5' quadrangle. Called Little Creek on San Luis (1903) 30' quadrangle.

Little Cholame Creek [MONTEREY]: *stream,* flows 10 miles to Cholame Creek 1 mile south of Parkfield (lat. 35°53' N, long. 120° 25' W; sec. 35, T 23 S, R 14 E). Named on Parkfield (1961) and Stockdale Mountain (1948) 7.5' quadrangles. Goodyear (1888, p. 87) referred to the valley of the stream as Little Cholame Valley.

Little Cholame Valley: see **Little Cholame Creek** [MONTEREY].

Little Cojo: see **Cojo Bay** [SANTA BARBARA].

Little Creek [SANTA CRUZ]: *stream,* flows 3 miles to Scott Creek 4 miles north-northwest of Davenport (lat. 37°03'50" N, long. 122° 13'40" W). Named on Davenport (1955) 7.5' quadrangle.

Little Creek: see **Little Cayucos Creek** [SAN LUIS OBISPO].

Little Falls Canyon: see **Big Falls Canyon** [SAN LUIS OBISPO].

Little Falls Creek [SAN LUIS OBISPO]: *stream,* flows 2.5 miles to Lopez Canyon 14

miles north of the town of Nipomo (lat. 35°14'45" N, long. 120°29'10" W; near W line sec. 9, T 31 S, R 14 E). Named on Santa Margarita Lake (1967) and Tar Spring Ridge (1967) 7.5' quadrangles.

Little Falls Spring [SAN LUIS OBISPO]: *spring,* 6 miles west-southwest of Pozo (lat. 35°16'35" N, long. 120°28'35" W); the spring is at the head of Little Falls Creek. Named on Santa Margarita Lake (1967) 7.5' quadrangle.

Little Irish Canyon: see **Deer Canyon** [SAN LUIS OBISPO] (1).

Little Jollo Creek [SAN LUIS OBISPO]: *stream,* flows nearly 3 miles to Alamo Creek (2) 8.5 miles west-southwest of Branch Mountain (lat. 35°07'20" N, long. 120°12'40" W; near S line sec. 24, T 32 S, R 16 E). Named on Chimney Canyon (1967) and Los Machos Hills (1967) 7.5' quadrangles.

Little Morro Creek [SAN LUIS OBISPO]: *stream,* flows 7.25 miles to Morro Creek 3700 feet east-northeast of the mouth of that creek (lat. 35°22'45" N, long. 120°51'05" W). Named on Morro Bay North (1965) 7.5' quadrangle.

Little Oak Flat [MONTEREY]: *area,* 9 miles south of Jolon near Nacimiento River (lat. 35°50'35" N, long. 121°10'10" W; near W line sec. 13, T 24 S, R 7 E). Named on Bryson (1929) 15' quadrangle.

Little Oso Flaco Lake [SAN LUIS OBISPO]: *lake,* 0.5 mile long, 6.5 miles south of the town of Arroyo Grande (lat. 35°01'55" N, long. 120°36'30" W); the feature is east of Oso Flaco Lake. Named on Oceano (1965) 7.5' quadrangle.

Little Panoche Creek [SAN BENITO]: *stream,* flows 1.5 miles to Fresno County 7.5 miles north-northwest of Panoche (lat. 36°42'05" N, long. 120°52'05" W; sec. 22, T 14 S, R 10 E). Named on Cerro Colorado (1969) and Mercey Hot Springs (1969) 7.5' quadrangles. United States Board on Geographic Names (1933, p. 466) ruled against the name "Panochita Creek" for the stream. South Fork heads in San Benito County and flows 5 miles to join the main stream in Fresno County; it is named on Mercey Hot Springs (1969) 7.5' quadrangle.

Little Panoche Valley [SAN BENITO]: *valley,* mainly in Fresno County, but extends south into San Benito County 6 miles north of Panoche (lat. 36°41' N, long. 120°51' W); Little Panoche Creek and South Fork Little Panoche Creek drain the valley. Named on Mercey Hot Springs (1969) 7.5' quadrangle. United States Board on Geographic Names (1933, p. 466) ruled against the name "Panochita Valley" for the feature.

Little Peak Canyon [SAN BENITO]: *canyon,* drained by a stream that heads in Santa Clara County and flows nearly 3 miles to Arroyo de las Viboras 8.5 miles north-northeast of Hollister (lat. 36°57'15" N, long. 121°18'55" W. Named on Three Sisters (1954) 7.5' quadrangle.

Little Pico Creek [SAN LUIS OBISPO]: *stream,* flows 5 miles to the sea 1.5 miles east-southeast of the village of San Simeon (lat. 35° 38' N, long. 121°09'45" W); the mouth of the stream is 1.5 miles north-northwest of the mouth of Pico Creek. Named on San Simeon (1958) 7.5' quadrangle.

Little Pine Mountain [SANTA BARBARA]: *peak,* 13 miles north-northwest of Santa Barbara (lat. 34°36' N, long. 119°44'15" W). Named on Little Pine Mountain (1964) 7.5' quadrangle.

Little Pines [MONTEREY]: *locality,* 1.5 miles northwest of Uncle Sam Mountain (lat. 36°21'25" N, long. 121°43'20" W). Named on Ventana Cones (1956) 7.5' quadrangle.

Little Pines Camp [MONTEREY]: *locality,* 1.25 miles northwest of Uncle Sam Mountain (lat. 36°21'10" N, long. 121°43'25" W); the place is 1700 feet south of Little Pines. Named on Ventana Cones (1956) 7.5' quadrangle.

Little Pine Spring [SANTA BARBARA]: *spring,* 8 miles north-northeast of San Marcos Pass (lat. 34°36'30" N, long. 119°45'05" W); the spring is 1 mile northwest of Little Pine Mountain. Named on San Marcos Pass (1959) 7.5' quadrangle.

Little Pinnacles [SAN BENITO]: *relief feature,* 2 miles north-northeast of North Chalone Peak (lat. 36°28'20" N, long. 121°10'40" W); the feature is 1.5 miles southeast of Pinnacle Rocks. Named on North Chalone Peak (1969) 7.5' quadrangle.

Little Quien Sabe Valley [SAN BENITO]: *valley,* 4 miles west-southwest of Potrero Peak (lat. 36°50'30" N, long. 121°13'15" W); the valley is west of the center of Quien Sabe Valley. Named on Quien Sabe Valley (1968) 7.5' quadrangle.

Little Rabbit Valley [SAN BENITO]: *valley,* opens into the north end of Topo Valley 5.25 miles north-northwest of Bitterwater (lat. 36°26'50" N, long. 121°02'45" W); the valley is northwest of Rabbit Valley. Named on Topo Valley (1969) 7.5' quadrangle.

Little Rabbit Valley: see **Rabbit Valley** [SAN BENITO].

Little River: see **Little Sur River** [MONTEREY].

Little River Hill [MONTEREY]: *peak,* nearly 2 miles east-northeast of Point Sur (lat. 36°19' N, long. 121°52'15" W). Altitude 1214 feet. Named on Big Sur (1956) 7.5' quadrangle.

Little Salmon Creek: see **Salmon Creek** [MONTEREY] (2).

Little Sand Creek [MONTEREY]: *stream,* flows nearly 2 miles to Paloma Creek 11.5 miles southeast of Soledad (lat. 36°20'15" N, long. 121°29'50" W; sec. 25, T 18 S, R 4 E). Named on Sycamore Flat (1956) 7.5' quadrangle. The stream is subparallel to and about 1 mile northwest of Big Sand Creek, which is called Little Sand Creek on Soledad (1915) 15' quadrangle.

Little Scorpion: see **Scorpion Anchorage** [SANTA BARBARA].

Little Slate Rock [MONTEREY]: *rock,* 0.5 mile west of Slates Hot Springs, and 1600 feet off-shore (lat. 36°07'25" N, long. 121°38'45" W); the feature is 1400 feet southeast of Slate Rock. Named on Lucia (1921) 15' quadrangle.

Little Spring [SANTA BARBARA]: *spring,* 5 miles northwest of McPherson Peak (lat. 34°55'45" N, long. 119°52'45" W); the feature is 850 feet north of Big Spring (1). Named on Bates Canyon (1964) 7.5' quadrangle.

Little Spring Canyon [SANTA BARBARA]: *canyon,* drained by a stream that flows less than 0.5 mile to Big Spring Canyon 5 miles northwest of McPherson Peak (lat. 34°55'45" N, long. 119°52'40" W); Little Spring is in the čanyon. Named on Bates Canyon (1964) 7.5' quadrangle.

Little Sulphur Spring [SANTA BARBARA]: *spring,* 1.25 miles west of Salisbury Potrero (lat. 34°49'10" N, long. 119°43'15" W). Named on Salisbury Potrero (1964) 7.5' quadrangle.

Little Sur River [MONTEREY]: *stream,* flows 14 miles to the sea 2 miles north of Point Sur (lat. 36°20'05" N, long. 121°53'35" W; sec. 29, T 18 S, R 1 E). Named on Big Sur (1956), Point Sur (1956), and Ventana Cones (1956) 7.5' quadrangles. According to Lussier (p. 4, 16), the early Spaniards at Carmel mission called the wilderness to the south *El Pais Grande del Sur,* which means "the big country to the south" in Spanish, and called the smaller of two major streams there *El Rio Chiquaito del Sur,* which means "the little river to the south"—eventually the stream took the partial translation "Little Sur River" for a name, although early residents called it simply Little River. South Fork enters from the south nearly 2 miles upstream from the mouth of the main river. It is 10.5 miles long and is named on Big Sur (1956) 7.5' quadrangle. A resort town called Idlewild flourished about 1900 along the stream approximately 1 mile above the present highway bridge (Lussier, p. 17).

Little Tiger Spring [MONTEREY]: *spring,* 10 miles east-southeast of Parkfield (lat. 35°51'55" N, long. 120°15'45" W; sec. 5, T 24 S, R 16 E). Named on Cholame Valley (1961) 7.5' quadrangle.

Live Oak Spring [MONTEREY]:
(1) *spring,* 15 miles east-northeast of San Ardo (lat. 36°05'35" N, long. 120°38'15" W; sec. 23, T 21 S, R 12 E). Named on Slack Canyon (1969) 7.5' quadrangle.
(2) *spring,* 10 miles east-northeast of San Ardo (lat. 36°03'45" N, long. 120°43'05" W; sec. 31, T 21 S, R 12 E). Named on Slack Canyon (1969) 7.5' quadrangle.

Live Oak Spring [SAN LUIS OBISPO]: *spring,* about 1 mile east of Branch Mountain (lat. 35°11'15" N, long. 120°03'55" W; sec. 32, T 31 S, R 18 E). Named on Branch Mountain

(1967) 7.5' quadrangle.

Live Oak Spring [SANTA BARBARA]:
(1) *spring,* 6 miles west of Montgomery Potrero (lat. 34°50'15" N, long. 119°51'35" W). Named on Hurricane Deck (1964) 7.5' quadrangle.
(2) *spring,* 5.5 miles south-southwest of San Rafael Mountain (lat. 34°38'20" N, long. 119°51'35" W). Named on San Rafael Mountain (1959) 7.5' quadrangle.

Lizard Head [SANTA BARBARA]: *peak,* 18 miles south-southeast of the village of Cuyama (lat. 34°41'55" N, long. 119°28' W). Named on Rancho Nuevo Creek (1943) 7.5' quadrangle.

Llanada [SAN BENITO]: *locality,* nearly 5 miles west of Panoche in Panoche Valley (lat. 36°36'35" N, long. 120°54'55" W; sec. 19, T 15 S, R 10 E). Named on Llanada (1969) 7.5' quadrangle. Postal authorities established Llanada post office in 1891 and discontinued it in 1929 (Frickstad, p. 136). According to Gudde (1949, p. 190), the name was given because of the wide expanse of Panoche Valley—*llanada* means "plain" or "level ground" in Spanish.

Llanito Creek [SANTA BARBARA]: *stream,* flows 2.25 miles to El Callejon Creek 12.5 miles southeast of the city of Lompoc (lat. 34° 31'55" N, long. 120°17'05" W). Named on Santa Rosa Hills (1959) 7.5' quadrangle.

Llano de Buena Vista [MONTEREY]: *land grant,* 2.5 miles south-southeast of Salinas. Named on Chualar (1947), Natividad (1947), Salinas (1947), and Spreckels (1947) 7.5' quadrangles. Santiago Estrada and Jose Mariano Estrada received 2 leagues in 1822 and 1823; David Spence claimed 8446 acres patented in 1860 (Cowan, p. 20-21).

Llano del Tequisquita [SAN BENITO]: *land grant,* 9 miles northwest of Hollister between Pajaro River and Lomerias Muertas (1); a small part of the grant is in Santa Clara County. Named on Chittenden (1955) and San Felipe (1955) 7.5' quadrangles. Jose Maria Sanchez received the land in 1835; Vincent Sanchez and others claimed 16,016 acres patented in 1871 (Cowan, p. 102; Cowan listed the grant under the name "Tequisquite"). Arbuckle (p. 23) used the name "Llano del Tequesquite" for the grant. The word "tequesquite" is from an Aztec term for the saline or alkaline deposit found at the bed of a dry lake (Becker, 1969).

Llano Estero: see **Carrizo Plain** [SAN LUIS OBISPO].

Llano Grande Canyon [MONTEREY-SAN BENITO]: *canyon,* drained by a stream that heads in San Benito County and flows 8 miles to lowlands 9 miles east-southeast of Greenfield in Monterey County (lat. 36°15'35" N, long. 121°06'20" W). Named on Pinalito Canyon (1969) 7.5' quadrangle. United States Board on Geographic Names (1972b, p. 4) gave the name "Grande Canyon" as a variant.

Llomas Muertas: see **Lomerias Muertas** [SAN BENITO] (1).

Loanoke: see **Lonoak** [MONTEREY].

Lobos: see **Point Lobos** [MONTEREY].

Lobos Rocks [MONTEREY]: *rocks,* largest 250 feet long, 0.5 mile northwest of Soberanes Point, and 2000 feet offshore (lat. 36°27'20" N, long. 121°56'10" W). Named on Soberanes Point (1956) 7.5' quadrangle. The rocks also were known as Piedras de los Lobos, Piedra de Lobos, and Twin Seal Rocks (Clark, 1991, p. 274).

Loch Lomond [SANTA CRUZ]: *lake,* 2.25 miles long, behind a dam on Newell Creek 3 miles east-southeast of the town of Boulder Creek (lat. 37°06'10" N, long. 122°04'20" W; sec. 34, T 9 S, R 2 W); the lake is 1.5 miles upstream from Ben Lomond. Named on Castle Rock Ridge (1955, photorevised 1968) and Felton (1955, photorevised 1980) 7.5' quadrangles. The lake first was called Newell Creek Reservoir and Newell Lake (Clark, 1986, p. 187).

Lockhart Gulch [SANTA CRUZ]: *canyon,* drained by a stream that flows nearly 3 miles to Bean Creek 6.5 miles southeast of the town of Boulder Creek (lat. 37°03'25" N, long. 122°01'55" W). Named on Felton (1955) 7.5' quadrangle. The name commemorates Samuel Lockhart, who lived in the canyon about 1865 (Clark, 1986. p. 188).

Lockwood [MONTEREY]: *settlement,* 6 miles east-southeast of Jolon (lat. 35°56'40" N, long. 121°04'50" W; sec. 10, 11, T 23 S, R 8 E). Named on Williams Hill (1949) 7.5' quadrangle. Postal authorities established Lockwood post office in 1888—the name commemorates Belva Lockwood, Equal Rights Party candidate for president in 1884 and 1888; the place also was known as Hungry Flats (Salley, p. 124). The area around Lockwood has the informal name "Lockwood Valley."

Lockwood Valley: see **Lockwood** [MONTEREY].

Lodge's Beach: see **Capitola** [SANTA CRUZ].

Loeb: see **Point Loeb**, under **Point Alones** [MONTEREY].

Loeber Canyon [MONTEREY]: *canyon,* drained by a stream that flows 3 miles to lowlands 7.5 miles east-southeast of Jolon (lat. 35° 56'40" N, long. 121°02'35" W; sec. 7, T 23 S, R 9 E). Named on Williams Hill (1949) 7.5' quadrangle. The name commemorates Henry F. Loeber, who ran the store at Lockwood (Clark, 1991, p. 275).

Logan [SAN BENITO]: *locality,* 1.5 miles north-northeast of Aromas along Southern Pacific Railroad (lat. 36°54'30" N, long. 121°37'50" W). Named on Watsonville East (1955) 7.5' quadrangle.

Logan Canyon [SANTA BARBARA]: *canyon,* drained by a stream that flows 4 miles to Sisquoc River 4.5 miles northwest of Big Pine Mountain (lat. 34°44'45" N, long. 119°42'10" W). Named on Big Pine Mountain (1964) and Salisbury Potrero (1964) 7.5' quadrangles.,

Logan Creek [SAN LUIS OBISPO]: *stream,* flows 2.25 miles to Branch Creek 5 miles southwest of Branch Mountain (lat. 35°08'25" N, long. 120°09'15" W); the stream is northeast of Logan Ridge. Named on Chimney Canyon (1967) and Los Machos Hills (1967) 7.5' quadrangles.

Logan Creek [SANTA CRUZ]: *stream,* flows 1.5 miles to Kings Creek 4 miles north of the town of Boulder Creek (lat. 37°11'05" N, long. 122°07'20" W; sec. 6, T 9 S, R 2 W). Named on Castle Rock Ridge (1955) 7.5' quadrangle. Hamman's (1980b) map shows a place called Hihn Mill located along Kings Creek just north of the junction with Logan Creek.

Logan Potrero [SANTA BARBARA]: *area,* 4 miles south-southeast of Salisbury Potrero (lat. 34°46'15" N, long. 119°40'10" W); the place is near the head of Logan Canyon. Named on Salisbury Potrero (1964) 7.5' quadrangle.

Logan Ridge [SAN LUIS OBISPO]: *ridge,* northwest-trending, 2.5 miles long, 6 miles southwest of Branch Mountain (lat. 35°07'45" N, long. 120°09'35" W); the ridge is southwest of Logan Creek. Named on Chimney Canyon (1967) and Los Machos Hills (1967) 7.5' quadrangles.

Logan Spring [SANTA BARBARA]: *spring,* 4.25 miles south-southeast of Salisbury Potrero (lat. 34°46'35" N, long. 119°40'30" W); the spring is in Logan Canyon. Named on Salisbury Potrero (1964) 7.5' quadrangle.

Log Cabin Canyon [SAN BENITO]: *canyon,* drained by a stream that flows 2 miles to Pimental Creek 6.25 miles southwest of Panoche (lat. 36°31'20" N, long. 120°53'35" W; near E line sec. 20, T 16 S, R 10 E). Named on Llanada (1969) 7.5' quadrangle.

Log Cabin Spring [MONTEREY]: *spring,* 3.5 miles northwest of Charley Mountain (lat. 36°10'20" N, long. 120°43' W; sec. 19, T 20 S, R 12 E). Named on Priest Valley (1969) 7.5' quadrangle.

Logwood Creek [MONTEREY]: *stream,* flows 4.25 miles to Big Sur River 5.25 miles north-northwest of Partington Point (lat. 36°15' N, long. 121°43' W; sec. 26, T 19 S, R 2 E); the stream is southwest of Logwood Ridge. Named on Partington Ridge (1956) 7.5' quadrangle.

Logwood Ridge [MONTEREY]: *ridge,* north-northwest-trending, 2 miles long, 4 miles north of Partington Point (lat. 36°13'45" N, long. 121°41'30" W). Named on Partington Ridge (1956) 7.5' quadrangle. The name is from an early settler named Logwood (Clark, 1991, p. 276).

Loma Alta [MONTEREY]: *peak,* 3.25 miles east-northeast of the mouth of Carmel River (lat. 36°33'45" N, long. 121°52'30" W). Named on Monterey (1913) 15' quadrangle.

Loma Alta [SANTA BARBARA]: *peak,* nearly 5 miles north of San Marcos Pass (lat. 34°34'50" N, long. 119°49'40" W). Altitude 2758 feet. Named on San Marcos Pass (1959) 7.5' quadrangle.

Loma Alta Spring [SANTA BARBARA]: *spring,* 5.25 miles north-northwest of San Marcos Pass (lat. 34°35'15" N, long. 119°50'40" W); the spring is 1 mile west-northwest of Loma Alta. Named on San Marcos Pass (1959) 7.5' quadrangle.

Loma Pelona [SAN LUIS OBISPO]: *peak,* 4.5 miles north-northeast of the town of Nipomo (lat. 35°06' N, long. 120°26'10" W; sec. 35, T 32 S, R 14 E). Altitude 1784 feet. Named on Nipomo (1965) 7.5' quadrangle.

Loma Pelona [SANTA BARBARA]: *peak,* 3.5 miles south-southwest of Madulce Peak (lat. 34°38'35" N, long. 119°36'55" W). Altitude 4453 feet. Named on Madulce Peak (1964) 7.5' quadrangle.

Loma Prieta: see **Aptos Creek** [SANTA BARBARA].

Lomas de La Purificacion [SANTA BARBARA]: *land grant,* southeast of Santa Ynez. Named on Lake Cachuma (1959) and Santa Ynez (1959) 7.5' quadrangles. Agustin Janssens received 3 leagues in 1844 and claimed 13,341 acres patented in 1871 (Cowan, p. 65).

Lomerias del Espiritu Santo: see **Lomerias Muertas** [SAN BENITO] (2).

Lomerias Muertas [SAN BENITO]:
(1) *range,* 4 miles north of San Juan Bautista between San Juan Valley and Santa Clara Valley (lat. 36°54'20" N, long. 121°31'15" W). Named on Chittenden (1955) and San Felipe (1955) 7.5' quadrangles. Antisell (1856, p. 36) used the form "Llomas Muertas" for the name, which is from the lack of water on the range—*lomerias muertas* means "dead hills" in Spanish (Gudde, 1949, p. 192).
(2) *land grant,* at San Juan Bautista; includes Lomerias Muertas (1). Named on Chittenden (1955), San Felipe (1955), and San Juan Bautista (1955) 7.5' quadrangles. Jose Antonio Castro received 1.5 leagues in 1842; the heirs of Vicente Sanchez claimed 6659 acres patented in 1866 (Cowan, p. 45—Cowan gave the name "Lomerias del Espiritu Santo" as an alternate; Perez, p. 72).

Lomita [SANTA CRUZ]: *peak,* 4 miles east of Laurel on Santa Cruz-Santa Clara county line (lat. 37°06'40" N, long. 121°53'40" W). Named on Laurel (1955) 7.5' quadrangle.

Lompico [SANTA CRUZ]: *settlement,* 4 miles east-southeast of the town of Boulder Creek (lat. 37°06'15" N, long. 122°03' W; sec. 35, T 9 S, R 2 W); the settlement is along Lompico Creek. Named on Felton (1955) 7.5' quadrangle.

Lompico Creek [SANTA CRUZ]: *stream,* flows 4.5 miles to Zayante Creek 5 miles southeast of the town of Boulder Creek (lat. 37°04'55" N, long. 122°03' W; sec. 11, T 10 S, R 2 W).

Named on Castle Rock Ridge (1955) and Felton (1955) 7.5' quadrangles. Hamman's (1980b) map shows a place called Meehan located along the railroad near the mouth of Lompico Creek.

Lompoc [SANTA BARBARA]:
(1) *land grant,* at and near the city of Lompoc. Named on Lompoc (1959), Lompoc Hills (1959), Point Arguello (1959), Surf (1959), and Tranquillon Mountain (1959) 7.5' quadrangles. Joaquin Carrillo and Jose Antonio Carrillo received the land in 1837 and claimed 42,085 acres patented in 1873 (Cowan, p. 46). The name is from an Indian village (Kroeber, 1916, p. 46).
(2) *city,* 21 miles south of Santa Maria (lat. 34°38'20" N, long. 120° 27'25" W); the place is mainly on Lompoc grant. Named on Lompoc (1959) 7.5' quadrangle. Postal authorities established Lompoc post office in 1875 (Frickstad, p. 171), and the city incorporated in 1888. Parke (p. 9) used the name "La Purisima" for the part of the valley of Santa Ynez River around the present city of Lompoc. United States Board on Geographic Names (1988, p. 3) approved the name "Lompoc Valley" for the tract that extends for 19 miles inland along the river from the sea, and that has Lompoc near the center. Postal authorities established Stuart post office 9.5 miles northeast of Lompoc in 1885 and discontinued it in 1902 (Salley, p. 214).

Lompoc Beach: see **Surf** [SANTA BARBARA].

Lompoc Canyon [SANTA BARBARA]: *canyon,* drained by a stream that flows 4.5 miles to the valley of Santa Ynez River 3 miles east-southeast of Surf (lat. 34°40'05" N, long. 120°33'30" W). Named on Surf (1959) 7.5' quadrangle.

Lompoc Hills [SANTA BARBARA]: *range,* 4 miles south of the city of Lompoc (lat. 34°35' N, long. 120°27'30" W). Named on Lompoc Hills (1959) 7.5' quadrangle.

Lompoc Junction: see **Surf** [SANTA BARBARA].

Lompoc Landing [SANTA BARBARA]: *locality,* 2.5 miles north of Surf along the coast (lat. 34°43'15" N, long. 120°36'30" W); the place is 10 miles northwest of the city of Lompoc. Site named on Surf (1959) 7.5' quadrangle.

Lompoc Terrace [SANTA BARBARA]: *area,* 2.5 miles south-southeast of Surf (lat. 34°39' N, long. 120°35'15" W); the place is 7 miles west of the city of Lompoc. Named on Surf (1959) 7.5' quadrangle.

Lompoc Valley: see **Lompoc** [SANTA BARBARA] (2).

Lone Black Rock [SAN LUIS OBISPO]: *shoal,* 0.5 mile west of Point San Luis, and 0.25 mile offshore (lat. 35°09'35" N, long. 120°46'15" W). Named on Port San Luis (1965) 7.5' quadrangle.

Lone Oak: see **Lonoak** [MONTEREY].

Lone Pine Camp [MONTEREY]: *locality,* 1.5

miles south-southwest of Uncle Sam Mountain (lat. 36°19'20" N, long. 121°43' W). Named on Ventana Cones (1956) 7.5' quadrangle.

Lone Rock [SAN LUIS OBISPO]: *rock,* nearly 1 mile southeast of Avila Beach, and 650 feet offshore in San Luis Obispo Bay (lat. 35°10'25" N, long. 120°43'10" W). Named on Pismo Beach (1965) 7.5' quadrangle.

Lone Tree: see **Mariposa Peak** [SAN BENITO].

Lonetree: see **Mariposa Peak** [SAN BENITO].

Lone Tree Creek [SAN BENITO]: *stream,* flows 2.5 miles to Arroyo Dos Picachos nearly 7 miles east-northeast of Hollister (lat. 36° 53'15" N, long. 121°17'15" W; sec. 14, T 12 S, R 6 E). Named on Three Sisters (1954) 7.5' quadrangle.

Lone Tree Hill [SAN LUIS OBISPO]: *peak,* 3 miles north-northeast of the village of San Simeon (lat. 35°41'10" N, long. 121°10'40" W). Named on San Simeon (1958) 7.5' quadrangle.

Long Canyon [MONTEREY]:
(1) *canyon,* drained by a stream that flows nearly 3 miles to marsh along Elkhorn Slough 4.25 miles northwest of Prunedale (lat. 36° 48'50" N, long. 121°43'45" W). Named on Prunedale (1954) 7.5' quadrangle.
(2) *canyon,* drained by a stream that flows nearly 3 miles to Quail Creek 9.5 miles north of Gonzales (lat. 36°38'45" N, long. 121° 28' W). Named on Mount Harlan (1968) 7.5' quadrangle.
(3) *canyon,* nearly 2 miles long, opens into the canyon of Paloma Creek 12 miles west-southwest of Greenfield (lat. 36°16'30" N, long. 121°27' W; sec. 17, T 19 S, R 5 E). Named on Sycamore Flat (1956) 7.5' quadrangle.

Long Canyon [SAN BENITO]: *canyon,* drained by a stream that flows 2 miles to the canyon of San Benito River 5.25 miles east of Bitterwater (lat. 36°23' N, long. 120°54'15" W; near NE cor. sec. 8, T 18 S, R 10 E). Named on Rock Spring Peak (1969) 7.5' quadrangle.

Long Canyon [SAN LUIS OBISPO]:
(1) *canyon,* drained by a stream that flows 3 miles to Arroyo de la Cruz 3.5 miles north of the village of San Simeon (lat. 35°41'55" N, long. 121°11'30" W). Named on San Simeon (1958) 7.5' quadrangle.
(2) *canyon,* 8 miles long, opens into San Juan Valley 12.5 miles southeast of Shandon (lat. 35°31'05" N, long. 120°13'40" W; sec. 2, T 28 S, R 16 E). Named on Camatta Ranch (1966), Holland Canyon (1961), and La Panza Ranch (1966) 7.5' quadrangles.
(3) *canyon,* 3.25 miles long, opens into the canyon of Huasna Creek 7.5 miles northeast of the town of Nipomo (lat. 35°07'40" N, long. 120°23'50" W). Named on Caldwell Mesa (1967) and Tar Spring Ridge (1967) 7.5' quadrangles.
(4) *canyon,* drained by a stream that flows 2.5 miles to an unnamed canyon 2.5 miles north-

east of Huasna Peak (lat. 35°03'30" N, long. 120°18'50" W). Named on Huasna Peak (1967) 7.5' quadrangle.

Long Canyon [SANTA BARBARA]:
(1) *canyon,* 2.5 miles long, opens into Harris Valley 5.5 miles south of Orcutt (lat. 34°47'05" N, long. 120°25'30" W). Named on Orcutt (1959) 7.5' quadrangle.
(2) *canyon,* drained by a stream that flows 3 miles to Santa Maria Valley 1 mile southeast of the village of Sisquoc (lat. 34°51'25" N, long. 120°16'35" W; at E line sec. 18, T 9 N, R 32 W). Named on Sisquoc (1959) 7.5' quadrangle.
(3) *canyon,* drained by a stream that flows about 3 miles to La Brea Creek 3.5 miles south of Tepusquet Peak (lat. 34°51'35" N, long. 120°10'30" W). Named on Foxen Canyon (1964) and Tepusquet Canyon (1964) 7.5' quadrangles. Called Rattlesnake Canyon on Lompoc (1905) 30' quadrangle.
(4) *canyon,* 2 miles long, opens into the canyon of Jaro Creek 5.5 miles southeast of the city of Lompoc (lat. 34°35' N, long. 120° 23' W). Named on Lompoc Hills (1959) and Santa Rosa Hills (1959) 7.5' quadrangles.

Long Gulch [SAN BENITO]: *canyon,* drained by a stream that flows 2.25 miles to Pescadero Creek 9 miles west of Paicines (lat. 36°42'30" N, long. 121°26'25" W; sec. 17, T 14 S, R 5 E). Named on Mount Harlan (1968) 7.5' quadrangle.

Long Gulch: see **Aptos Creek** [SANTA CRUZ].

Long Horn Canyon [SANTA BARBARA]: *canyon,* drained by a stream that flows 2 miles to lowlands along the coast 4.5 miles southeast of Tranquillon Mountain (lat. 34°31'45" N, long. 120° 31' W). Named on Tranquillon Mountain (1959) 7.5' quadrangle.

Long Lake [SAN LUIS OBISPO]: *intermittent lake,* 900 feet long, 4.5 miles southeast of Cholame (lat. 35°40'50" N, long. 120°13'55" W; sec. 10, T 26 S, R 16 E). Named on Orchard Peak (1961) 7.5' quadrangle.

Long Ridge [MONTEREY]:
(1) *ridge,* west- to northwest-trending, 3 miles long, 3 miles south of the town of Carmel Valley (lat. 36°26'15" N, long. 121°43' W). Named on Carmel Valley (1956) and Mount Carmel (1956) 7.5' quadrangles.
(2) *ridge,* west-trending, 4 miles long, 5.5 miles north-northeast of Point Sur (lat. 36°22'30" N, long. 121°51'30" W). Named on Big Sur (1956), Mount Carmel (1956), and Point Sur (1956) 7.5' quadrangles.

Long Ridge [SAN LUIS OBISPO]: *ridge,* east-trending, 1.25 miles long, 1.5 miles southeast of Branch Mountain (lat. 35°10'05" N, long. 120°03'50" W). Named on Branch Mountain (1967) 7.5' quadrangle.

Long Ridge [SANTA CRUZ]: *ridge,* southwest-trending, 1.25 miles long, 5 miles east-north-east of Watsonville (lat. 36°57'20" N, long. 121°40'30" W). Named on Watsonville East (1955) 7.5' quadrangle. United States Board on Geographic Names (1992, p. 4) approved the name "Mill Ridge" for the feature.

Long Valley [MONTEREY]: *canyon,* 14 miles long, opens into lowlands east of San Lucas (lat. 36°07'40" N, long. 121°00'50" W). Named on Monarch Peak (1967), Nattrass Valley (1967), and San Lucas (1949) 7.5' quadrangles.

Long Valley [SAN LUIS OBISPO]: *valley,* drained by a stream that flows 1.5 miles to Graves Creek 1.5 miles west of the town of Atascadero (lat. 35°29'20" N, long. 120°41'50" W). Named on Atascadero (1965) 7.5' quadrangle.

Long Valley [SANTA CRUZ]: *canyon,* 1 mile long, opens into lowlands 3.25 miles west-northwest of Corralitos (lat. 37°00' N, long. 121°51'50" W). Named on Loma Prieta (1955) 7.5' quadrangle.

Lonnie Davis Campground [SANTA BARBARA]: *locality,* 5.5 miles south-southwest of Montgomery Potrero along South Fork Sisquoc River (lat. 34°45'20" N, long. 119°46'35" W). Named on Hurricane Deck (1964) 7.5' quadrangle. The name commemorates the head of a pioneer family that settled by Sisquoc River in the late nineteenth century ·(Gagnon, p. 89).

Lonoak [MONTEREY]: *locality,* 11 miles east-northeast of King City (lat. 36°16'35" N, long. 120°56'35" W; sec. 13, T 19 S, R 9 E). Named on Lonoak (1969) 7.5' quadrangle. Postal authorities established Lonoak post office in 1885 and discontinued it in 1954 (Frickstad, p. 136). Fairbanks (1894, p. 522) called the place Lone Oak, and Vander Leck (p. 229) called it Loanoke.

Lookout Mountain [SANTA BARBARA]: *peak,* 1.5 miles west of Zaca Lake (lat. 34°46'45" N, long. 120°03'55" W). Named on Zaca Lake (1964) 7.5' quadrangle.

Lookout Peak [SAN BENITO]: *peak,* 5.5 miles northeast of Bitterwater near the southeast end of Squire Ridge (lat. 36°25'40" N, long. 120°55'15" W; sec. 30, T 17 S, R 10 E). Altitude 2986 feet. Named on Rock Spring Peak (1969) 7.5' quadrangle.

Lookout Ridge [MONTEREY]: *ridge,* north-trending, 0.5 mile long, 6 miles southwest of Salinas (lat. 36°36'15" N, long. 121°44'20" W). Named on Spreckels (1947) 7.5' quadrangle.

Loon Point [SANTA BARBARA]: *promontory,* 3.5 miles west-northwest of Carpinteria along the coast (lat. 34°24'45" N, long. 119°34'30" W). Named on Carpinteria (1952) 7.5' quadrangle.

Lopez Campground: see **Upper Lopez Campground** [MONTEREY].

Lopez Canyon [MONTEREY]: *canyon,* drained by a stream that flows 2 miles to an unnamed canyon 10.5 miles north of Greenfield (lat. 36°28'35" N, long. 121°14'50" W; sec. 6, T 17 S, R 7 E). Named on North Chalone Peak (1969) 7.5' quadrangle.

Lopez Canyon [SAN LUIS OBISPO]: *canyon,* drained by a stream that flows 16 miles to Arroyo Grande Creek 10 miles north of the town of Nipomo (lat. 35°11'20" N, long. 120°29'05" W; sec. 33, T 31 S, R 14 E). Named on Lopez Mountain (1965), Santa Margarita Lake (1967), and Tar Spring Ridge (1967) 7.5' quadrangles. A dam on Arroyo Grande Creek near the mouth of Lopez Canyon (lat. 35°11'15" N, long. 120°29'15" W) forms a lake called Lopez Lake, or Lopez Reservoir, that extends into Lopez Canyon (United States Board on Geographic Names, 1975, p. 4).

Lopez Creek [SAN BENITO]: *stream,* flows 5.5 miles to Los Pinos Creek 4 miles northwest of Idria in Vallecitos (lat. 36°27'40" N, long. 120°43'05" W; sec. 12, T 17 S, R 11 E). Named on Hernandez Reservoir (1969) and Idria (1969) 7.5' quadrangles.

Lopez Lake: see **Lopez Canyon** [SAN LUIS OBISPO].

Lopez Mountain [SAN LUIS OBISPO]: *peak,* 5 miles east-northeast of San Luis Obispo (lat. 35°18'05" N, long. 120°34'40" W; near E line sec. 21, T 30 S, R 13 E). Altitude 2868 feet. Named on Lopez Mountain (1965) 7.5' quadrangle.

Lopez Point [MONTEREY]: *promontory,* 27 miles southeast of Point Sur along the coast (lat. 36°01'10" N, long. 121°34' W; sec. 18, T 22 S, R 4 E). Named on Lopez Point (1956) 7.5' quadrangle. Clark (1991, p. 279) attributed the name to the Lopez family, pioneers in the region.

Lopez Reservoir: see **Lopez Canyon** [SAN LUIS OBISPO].

Lopez Rock [MONTEREY]: *rock,* 150 feet long, less than 1 mile west-northwest of Lopez Point, and 0.25 mile offshore (lat. 36°01'35" N, long. 121°34'45" W). Named on Lopez Point (1956) 7.5' quadrangle.

Lorenzo: see **Boulder Creek** [SANTA CRUZ] (2).

Lorenzo Creek: see **San Lorenzo Creek** [MONTEREY-SAN BENITO].

Lorenzo Vasquez Canyon [SAN BENITO]: *canyon,* drained by a stream that flows 3.5 miles to San Benito River nearly 6 miles east of Bitterwater (lat. 36°22'45" N, long. 120°53'50" W; sec. 9, T 18 S, R 10 E). Named on Hepsedam Peak (1969), Lonoak (1969), and Rock Spring Peak (1969) 7.5' quadrangles. On Priest Valley (1915) 30' quadrangle, the stream in the canyon has the name "San Lorenzo Cr."

Loridon Canyon [MONTEREY]: *canyon,* drained by a stream that flows 1.25 miles to Espinosa Canyon (2) 7 miles south-southwest of San Lucas (lat. 36°02'25" N, long. 121°04'45" W; sec. 2, T 22 S, R 8 E). Named on Espinosa Canyon (1949) 7.5' quadrangle. The misspelled name is for Loredan Espinoza, who patented land in the canyon in 1892 (Clark, 1991, p. 28).

Los Alamos [SANTA BARBARA]:
(1) *land grant,* at and west of the town of Los Alamos. Named on Lompoc (1959), Los Alamos (1959), Orcutt (1959), and Sisquoc (1959) 7.5' quadrangles. Jose Antonio de la Guerra received the land in 1839 and claimed 48,803 acres patented in 1872 (Cowan, p. 14). According to Perez (p. 53), Jose A. Carrillo was the grantee and patentee.
(2) *town,* 12.5 miles northeast of the city of Lompoc (lat. 34°44'40" N, long. 120°15'40" W); the town is in Los Alamos Valley on Los Alamos grant. Named on Los Alamos (1959) 7.5' quadrangle. Postal authorities established Los Alamos post office in 1877 (Frickstad, p. 171). California Mining Bureau's (1917c) map shows a place called Wigmore located along the railroad about 4 miles east of Los Alamos. Postal authorities established Wickham post office, 13 miles north of Los Alamos in 1898 and discontinued it in 1899— the name was for Frederick Wickenden, first postmaster (Salley, p. 240).

Los Alamos Valley [SANTA BARBARA]: *valley,* along San Antonio Creek (1) above a point 7 miles south of Orcutt (lat. 34°46' N, long. 120°25'45" W); the valley is on Los Alamos grant. Named on Los Alamos (1959), Orcutt (1959), Sisquoc (1959), and Zaca Creek (1959) 7.5' quadrangles.

Los Alisos: see **Goleta** [SANTA BARBARA].

Los Amoles Creek [SANTA BARBARA]: *stream,* flows 4.5 miles to El Jaro Creek 7.5 miles southeast of the city of Lompoc (lat. 34°33'40" N, long. 120°21'50" W). Named on Santa Rosa Hills (1959) 7.5' quadrangle.

Los Banos Creek, South Fork [SAN BENITO]: *stream,* flows 3.25 miles to Merced County 6 miles east-southeast of Potrero Peak (lat. 36°48'15" N, long. 121°03'40" W; sec. 14, T 13 S, R 8 E). Named on Ruby Canyon (1968) 7.5' quadrangle. South Fork joins North Fork in Merced County to form Los Banos Creek.

Los Berros: see **Berros** [SAN LUIS OBISPO].

Los Berros Canyon [SAN LUIS OBISPO]: *canyon,* 8 miles long, along Los Berros Creek above a point 4.5 miles southeast of downtown Arroyo Grande (lat. 35°04'40" N, long. 120°37'30" W). Named on Nipomo (1965) and Oceano (1965) 7.5' quadrangles.

Los Berros Creek [SAN LUIS OBISPO]: *stream,* flows 12.5 miles to Arroyo Grande Valley 1.25 miles south of downtown Arroyo Grande (lat. 35°06'10" N, long. 120°34'40" W); the stream drains Los Berros Canyon. Named on Oceano (1965) 7.5' quadrangle.

Los Bueyes Creek [MONTEREY]: *stream,* flows 4 miles to Los Burros Creek 7 miles south-southwest of Jolon (lat. 35°52'35" N, long. 121°13'50" W). Named on Alder Peak (1949) and Jolon (1949) 7.5' quadrangles.

Los Burros: see **Alder Creek** [MONTEREY].

Los Burros Creek [MONTEREY]: *stream,* flows 10 miles to Nacimiento River 7 miles south-southwest of Jolon (lat. 35°52'30" N,

long. 121°13' W). Named on Alder Peak (1949), Burnett Peak (1949), Burro Mountain (1949), and Jolon (1949) 7.5' quadrangles. North Fork enters from the north 6.25 miles upstream from the mouth of the main creek; it is 4.5 miles long and is named on Alder Peak (1949) 7.5' quadrangle.

Los Carneros [MONTEREY]:
(1) *land grant,* 6 miles north-northwest of Prunedale. Named on Moss Landing (1954) and Prunedale (1954) 7.5' quadrangles. David Littlejohn received 1 league in 1834 and his heirs claimed 4482 acres patented in 1866 (Cowan, p. 24).
(2) *land grant,* 11 miles north-northeast of Salinas. Named on San Juan Bautista (1955) 7.5' quadrangle. Maria Antonia Linares received 1 league in 1842; F.A. McDougall and others claimed 1629 acres patented in 1862 (Cowan, p. 24). According to Perez (p. 61), Maria A. Anzar was the patentee.

Los Coches [MONTEREY]: *land grant,* 3.5 miles south-southeast of Soledad. Named on Paraiso Springs (1956) and Soledad (1955) 7.5' quadrangles. Josefa Soberanes received 2.25 leagues in 1841 and claimed 8794 acres patented in 1917 (Cowan, p. 28; Perez, p. 62).

Los Coches Mountain [SANTA BARBARA]: *peak,* 10.5 miles east-northeast of Santa Maria (lat. 34°59' N, long. 120°15'25" W); the peak is near the head of Cañada de los Coches (1). Altitude 3016 feet. Named on Twitchell Dam (1959) 7.5' quadrangle.

Los Corralitos [SANTA CRUZ]: *land grant,* north and northwest of Watsonville. Named on Loma Prieta (1955), Watsonville East (1955), and Watsonville West (1954) 7.5' quadrangles. Jose Amesti received 4 leagues in 1844 and his heirs claimed 15,440 acres patented in 1861 (Cowan, p. 30).

Los Dos Pueblos [SANTA BARBARA]: *land grant,* west of Goleta along the coast; includes the lower part of Dos Pueblos Canyon. Named on Dos Pueblos Canyon (1951) and Goleta (1950) 7.5' quadrangles. Nicholas A. Den received 3 leagues in 1842 and claimed 15,535 acres patented in 1877 (Cowan, p. 33).

Los Gatos [MONTEREY]: *land grant,* 4 miles north-northwest of Salinas. Named on Salinas (1947, photorevised 1968 and 1975) 7.5' quadrangle, which gives the name "Santa Rita" as an alternate. Trinidad Espinosa received 1 league in 1820 and 1837; Fermina E. Perez and Domingo Perez claimed 4424 acres patented in 1870 (Cowan, p. 37; Perez, p. 67).

Los Laureles [MONTEREY]:
(1) *land grant,* 8.5 miles east of the mouth of Carmel River on the north side of Carmel Valley (1). Named on Seaside (1947) 7.5' quadrangle. Jose Agricia received 2000 varas in 1844; L. Ransom claimed 718 acres patented in 1871 (Cowan, p. 44-45; Cowan listed the grant under the name "Rincon de los Laureles").

(2) *land grant,* 10 miles east-southeast of the mouth of Carmel River in Carmel Valley (1). Named on Carmel Valley (1956), Mount Carmel (1956), Seaside (1947), and Spreckels (1947) 7.5' quadrangles. Jose Antonio Romero received 1.5 leagues in 1835; Jose Boronda and others received the land in 1839 and claimed 6625 acres patented in 1866 (Cowan, p. 44; Cowan gave the name "Cañada de los Laureles" as an alternate).

Los Laureles Canyon [SANTA BARBARA]: *canyon,* drained by Kelly Creek, which flows 4 miles to Santa Ynez River 3 miles northwest of San Marcos Pass (lat. 34°32'35" N, long. 119° 51'30" W). Named on San Marcos Pass (1959) 7.5' quadrangle.

Los Lobos Spring [MONTEREY]: *spring,* 9 miles northwest of Bradley (lat. 35°57'35" N, long. 120°54'35" W; sec. 5, T 23 S, R 10 E). Named on Hames Valley (1949) 7.5' quadrangle.

Los Machos Creek [SAN LUIS OBISPO]: *stream,* flows 3.25 miles to Kennel Creek 4 miles west of Branch Mountain (lat. 35°11'05" N, long. 120°09'15" W). Named on Los Machos Hills (1967) 7.5' quadrangle.

Los Machos Hills [SAN LUIS OBISPO]: *ridge,* west-trending, 3 miles long, 4 miles west of Branch Mountain (lat. 35°10'40" N, long. 120°09' W); the feature is south of the confluence of Los Machos Creek and Kennel Creek. Named on Los Machos Hills (1967) 7.5' quadrangle.

Los Muertos Creek [SAN BENITO]: *stream,* flows 11 miles to Tres Pinos Creek 5 miles west of Cherry Peak (lat. 36°42' N, long. 121° 13'45" W; sec. 20, T 14 S, R 7 E); the stream heads in Los Muertos Valley. Named on Cherry Peak (1968) and Panoche Pass (1968) 7.5' quadrangles.

Los Muertos Valley [SAN BENITO]: *valley,* 9.25 miles north-northwest of Panoche Pass (lat. 36°44'45" N, long. 121°05'30" W); the valley is at the head of Los Muertos Creek. Named on Panoche Pass (1968) and Ruby Canyon (1968) 7.5' quadrangles. Pierce (p. 145) attributed the name to a story about three men found hanging from a tree in the valley in the early days—*los muertos* means "the dead ones" in Spanish.

Los Ojitos [MONTEREY]: *land grant,* 5 miles southeast of Jolon. Named on Jolon (1949) and Williams Hill (1949) 7.5' quadrangles. Mariano Soberanes received 2 leagues in 1842 and claimed 8900 acres patented in 1871 (Cowan, p. 54). The name refers to a pair of natural seepages near Quail Top that are believed to have been a watering place for mission cattle during the dry season; the seepages have the appearance of two eyes from a distance—*los ojitos* means "the little eyes" in Spanish (Howard, p. 85). Howard (p. 86) noted that a building on the grant may have housed San Antonio post office, which opened in 1858 and moved to Jolon in 1872.

According to Frickstad (p. 109), postal authorities established San Antonio post office in 1858 and discontinued it in 1887, when they moved the service to King City. Postal Route (1884) map shows San Antonio post office situated south of present King City, apparently near the mouth of present Quinado Canyon, and not on Los Ojitos grant. According to Clark (1991, p. 499), San Antonio post office was situated at the junction of Mansfield Canyon and Quinado Canyon (SE quarter sec. 18, T 21 S, R 8 E).

Los Olivos [SANTA BARBARA]: *village,* 4 miles north-northwest of Santa Ynez (lat. 34°40' N, long. 120°06'50" W; at S line sec. 23, T 7 N, R 31 W). Named on Los Olivos (1959) 7.5' quadrangle. Postal authorities established Los Olivos post office in 1887 (Frickstad, p. 171). The name is from trees left after an attempt to start an olive industry at the place (Rife, p. 78).

Los Osos [SAN LUIS OBISPO]: *town,* 4.5 miles south-southwest of Morro Rock (lat. 35°18'40" N, long. 120°49'55" W); the place is in Los Osos Valley on Cañada de los Osos y Pecho grant. Named on Morro Bay South (1965) 7.5' quadrangle. Postal authorities established Los Osos post office in 1954 and discontinued it in 1969; they combined part of Los Osos post office with Baywood Park post office in 1967 to form a new post office called Bay-Osos, which they discontinued in 1974, when they reestablished Los Osos post office (Salley, p. 16, 128).

Los Osos Creek [SAN LUIS OBISPO]: *stream,* flows 10 miles to Morro Bay 3 miles southeast of Morro Rock (lat. 35°20'20" N, long. 120°49'40" W). Named on Morro Bay South (1965) 7.5' quadrangle.

Los Osos Mountains: see **Irish Hills** [SAN LUIS OBISPO].

Los Osos Valley [SAN LUIS OBISPO]: *valley,* extends 10 miles east-southeast from Morro Bay to San Luis Obispo; partly on Cañada de los Osos y Pecho grant. Named on Morro Bay South (1965) and San Luis Obispo (1965) 7.5' quadrangles. The east part of the valley is called San Luis Valley on San Luis Obispo (1897) 15' quadrangle. According to Whitney (p. 139), the Valley of San Luis Obispo extends southeast from Estero Bay nearly to Arroyo Grande (2), and "embraces the San Luis Valley, so called, and the Cañada de los Osos." United States Board on Geographic Names (1964, p. 15) rejected the name "San Luis Valley," and later the Board (1966, p. 5) rejected the name "Valley of the Bears" for Los Osos Valley. Soldiers of the Portola expedition in 1769 named a valley, perhaps this one, Cañada de Los Osos because they had a fight with bears there; Crespi gave the same place the name "La Natividad de la Nuestra Señora" (Wagner, H.R., p. 401).

Los Padres Post Office [SAN LUIS OBISPO]: *locality,* 3.5 miles northwest of downtown San

Luis Obispo at California Mens Colony (lat. 35°19'30" N, long. 120°42' W). Named on San Luis Obispo (1965) 7.5' quadrangle. Postal authorities established the post office in 1956 and discontinued it in 1969 (Salley, p. 128).

Lospe: see **Mount Lospe** [SANTA BARBARA].

Los Pelados [SAN LUIS OBISPO]: *peak,* 6.25 miles northwest of Branch Mountain (lat. 35°14'35" N, long. 120°09'55" W). Altitude 3305 feet. Named on Los Machos Hills (1967) 7.5' quadrangle.

Lospie: see **Point Lospie**, under **Point Sal** [SANTA BARBARA].

Los Pinos Creek [SAN BENITO]: *stream,* flows 6.5 miles to Larious Creek 3.5 miles northwest of Idria in Vallecitos (lat. 36°27'30" N, long. 120°42'35" W; near S line sec. 12, T 17 S, R 11 E). Named on Hernandez Reservoir (1969) and Idria (1969) 7.5' quadrangles.

Los Prietos Campground [SANTA BARBARA]: *locality,* 2.25 miles north-northeast of San Marcos Pass (lat. 34°32'25" N, long. 119° 48' W; sec. 3, T 5 N, R 28 W). Named on San Marcos Pass (1959) 7.5' quadrangle.

Los Prietos y Najalayegua [SANTA BARBARA]: *land grant,* along the upper part of Santa Ynez River. Named on Carpinteria (1952), Hildreth Peak (1964), Little Pine Mountain (1964), Old Man Mountain (1943), San Marcos Pass (1959), and White Ledge Peak (1952) 7.5' quadrangles. Jose Dominguez received the land in 1845 and claimed 48,729 acres patented in 1875 (Cowan, p. 64).

Los Sauces: see **Willows Anchorage** [SANTA BARBARA].

Lost Knife Spring [SANTA BARBARA]: *spring,* 5 miles west-northwest of Montgomery Potrero (lat. 34°52' N, long. 119°50'05" W). Named on Hurricane Deck (1964) 7.5' quadrangle.

Los Tularcitos [MONTEREY]: *land grant,* 14 miles south of Salinas. Named on Carmel Valley (1956), Chualar (1947), Rana Creek (1956), and Spreckels (1947) 7.5' quadrangles. Rafael Gomez received 4 leagues in 1834 and his heirs claimed 26,581 acres patented in 1866 (Cowan, p. 105). The name refers to a tule-bordered lake on the grant—*los tularcitos* means "the little tules" in Spanish (Hoover, Rensch, and Rensch, p. 232).

Lost Valley [MONTEREY]: *canyon,* 1 mile long, 5.5 miles south of Tassajara Hot Springs along Higgins Creek (lat. 36°09'20" N, long. 121°34' W); the valley is near the confluence of Lost Valley Creek and Higgins Creek. Named on Tassajara Hot Springs (1956) 7.5' quadrangle.

Lost Valley Creek [MONTEREY]: *stream,* flows 6.5 miles to Arroyo Seco (1) 5 miles south-southeast of Tassajara Hot Springs (lat. 36° 10'10" N, long. 121°30'50" W; near N line sec. 27, T 20 S, R 4 E). Named on Tassajara Hot Springs (1956) 7.5' quadrangle.

Los Vaqueros Creek: see **Vaqueros Creek** [MONTEREY].

Los Vaqueros Valley: see **Vaqueros Creek** [MONTEREY].

Los Vergeles [MONTEREY-SAN BENITO]: *land grant,* 10 miles north-northeast of Salinas on Monterey-San Benito county line. Named on San Juan Bautista (1955) 7.5' quadrangle. Jose Joaquin Gomez received 2 leagues in 1835; James C. Stokes claimed 8760 acres patented in 1875 (Cowan p. 107; Cowan gave the form "Verjeles" as an alternate). *Vergel* means "flower and fruit garden" in Spanish (Gudde, 1949, p. 378).

Los Yeguas Creek: see **Yeguas Creek** [SAN LUIS OBISPO].

Loudon Gulch: see **Ellis Canyon** [MONTEREY].

Love Creek [SANTA CRUZ]: *stream,* flows nearly 4 miles to San Lorenzo River 3 miles southeast of the town of Boulder Creek at Ben Lomond (lat. 37°05'20" N, long. 122°05'10" W). Named on Castle Rock Ridge (1955) and Felton (1955) 7.5' quadrangles. The name commemorates Harry Love, who had a sawmill at the confluence of Love Creek and San Lorenzo River (Hoover, Rensch, and Rensch, p. 480).

Love Gulch: see **Aptos Creek** [SANTA CRUZ].

Lovers of Jesus Point: see **Lovers Point** [MONTEREY].

Lovers Point [MONTEREY]: *promontory,* 1.25 miles southeast of Point Pinos along the coast (lat. 36°37'35" N, long. 121°54'50" W). Named on Monterey (1947) 7.5' quadrangle. Called Pt. Aulon on Monterey (1913) 15' quadrangle, but United States Board on Geographic Names (1961b, p. 11) rejected this name for the feature. According to Fink (p. 167), the name "Lovers Point" dates from 1875, when the place was called Lovers of Jesus Point because of outdoor prayer sessions held there. Clark (1991, p. 284-285) gave evidence that this origin of the name is fanciful, and noted that the feature also had the names "Laboratory Point" for Hopkins Seaside Laboratory there, and "Organ Point" from the noise of breaking waves.

Low: see **Camp Low**, under **San Juan Bautista** [SAN BENITO].

Lowder Canyon [MONTEREY]: *canyon,* drained by a stream that flows 1.5 miles to lowlands nearly 5 miles west of Greenfield (lat. 36°18'15" N, long. 121°19'30" W). Named on Paraiso Springs (1956) 7.5' quadrangle. The name commemorates John Ellis Lowder, who patented land nearby in 1908 (Clark, 1991, p. 186).

Lowe: see **Jim Lowe's**, under **Mansfield Canyon** [MONTEREY]; **Mount Lowe** [SAN LUIS OBISPO].

Lowe Canyon [MONTEREY]: *canyon,* 3.25 miles long, opens into Long Valley from the northeast 3.5 miles east-northeast of San Lucas (lat. 36°09' N, long. 120°58' W; sec. 35, T 20 S, R 9 E). Named on Nattrass Valley

(1967) 7.5' quadrangle.

Lower Alamar Campground [SANTA BARBARA]: *locality,* about 4 miles south of Madulce Peak (lat. 34°37'55" N, long. 119°35'05" W); the place is in Alamar Canyon. Named on Madulce Peak (1964) 7.5' quadrangle.

Lower Barn Springs: see **Hot Springs** [SANTA BARBARA] (2).

Lower Bear Campground [SANTA BARBARA]: *locality,* 1 mile northeast of Big Pine Mountain along Sisquoc River (lat. 34°42'30" N, long. 119°38'25" W); the place is 0.5 mile downstream from Bear Campground. Named on Big Pine Mountain (1964) 7.5' quadrangle.

Lower Bee Camp [MONTEREY]: *locality,* 3 miles east of Slates Hot Springs along North Fork Big Creek (lat. 36°07'25" N, long. 121° 35' W; sec. 12, T 21 S, R 3 E); the place is less than 1 mile south of Bee Camp. Named on Lopez Point (1956) 7.5' quadrangle.

Lower Berry Creek Falls: see **Berry Creek Falls** [SANTA CRUZ].

Lower Grapevine Campground [SANTA BARBARA]: *locality,* nearly 4 miles west-southwest of Big Pine Mountain (lat. 34°41' N, long. 119°43'05" W); the place is along Grapevine Creek. Named on Big Pine Mountain (1964) 7.5' quadrangle.

Lower Lion Spring [SANTA BARBARA]: *spring,* 4 miles north-northwest of Salisbury Potrero (lat. 34°52'25" N long. 119°43'15" W); the spring is in Lion Canyon (4). Named on Salisbury Potrero (1964) 7.5' quadrangle.

Lower Newsome Spring [SANTA BARBARA]: *spring,* 2.5 miles north of Salisbury Potrero (lat. 34°51'25" N, long. 119°42' W); the spring is in Newsome Canyon 3600 feet north of Upper Newsome Spring. Named on Salisbury Potrero (1964) 7.5' quadrangle.

Lower Oso Campground [SANTA BARBARA]: *locality,* 3.5 miles northeast of San Marcos Pass along Santa Ynez River (lat. 34°32'50" N, long. 119°46'30" W); the place is less than 1 mile south-southwest of Upper Oso Campground near the mouth of Oso Canyon. Named on San Marcos Pass (1959) 7.5' quadrangle.

Lower Piletas Canyon [SAN LUIS OBISPO]: *canyon,* drained by a stream that heads at Upper Piletas Canyon and flows 2 miles to San Juan Creek 4 miles west-northwest of Freeborn Mountain (lat. 35° 18'15" N, long. 120°07'15" W; sec. 23, T 30 S, R 17 E). Named on California Valley (1966) 7.5' quadrangle. Upper Piletas Canyon and Lower Piletas Canyon together are called simply Piletas Canyon on La Panza (1935) 15' quadrangle, but United States Board on Geographic Names (1968c, p. 5, 7) rejected this name.

Lower Sand Spring [SANTA BARBARA]: *spring,* 3.5 miles south of Salisbury Potrero (lat. 34°46'10" N, long. 119°41'20" W). Named on Salisbury Potrero (1964) 7.5' quadrangle.

Lowes Canyon [MONTEREY-SAN LUIS OBISPO]: *canyon,* drained by San Jacinto Creek, which heads in Monterey County and flows 16 miles to Estrella Creek nearly 3 miles southeast of San Miguel in San Luis Obispo County (lat. 35°43'40" N, long. 120°39'25" W; near W line sec. 26, T 25 S, R 12 E). Named on Paso Robles (1948), Ranchito Canyon (1948), and San Miguel (1948) 7.5' quadrangles. Called San Vicente Canyon on English and Kew's (1916) map. According to Stanley (p. 112), Frank E. Lowe took a farm in 1865 in what was called San Jacinto Canyon, but which later was renamed Lowe's Canyon. Stanley (p. 18) used the name "San Vicenta Valley" for present Lowes Canyon on his map.

Lucas: see **Santa Cruz** [SANTA CRUZ].

Lucas Point [MONTEREY]: *promontory,* 0.5 mile east-southeast of Point Pinos along the coast (lat. 36°38'10" N, long. 121°55'25" W). Named on Monterey (1947) 7.5' quadrangle. Clark (1991, p. 287) suggested that the name commemorates Captain Allen Luce, keeper of the lighthouse at Point Pinos in the 1870's.

Lucia [MONTEREY]: *settlement,* 1 mile east of Lopez Point near the coast (lat. 36°01'15" N, long. 121°33' W; sec. 17, T 22 S, R 4 E). Named on Lopez Point (1956) 7.5' quadrangle. Postal authorities established Lucia post office in 1900, moved it 1 mile southwest in 1906, discontinued it in 1933, reestablished it in 1936, and discontinued it in 1938 (Salley, p. 129). The name was for the postmaster, Lucia Dani, who had been named for Santa Lucia Range (Lussier, p. 35).

Lugo Canyon [MONTEREY]: *canyon,* drained by a stream that flows 5 miles to San Antonio River 2.5 miles south-southeast of Jolon (lat. 35°56'05" N, long. 121°09'45" W). Named on Jolon (1949) 7.5' quadrangle. The name is for Antonio Lugo, who served as an altar boy for Junipero Serra (Clark, 1991, p. 288).

Lumber Canyon [MONTEREY]: *canyon,* drained by a stream that flows 5 miles to Chalone Creek 4.5 miles northeast of Greenfield (lat. 36°22'20" N, long. 121°11'20" W). Named on Greenfield (1956) and Pinalito Canyon (1969) 7.5' quadrangles.

Lyda Spring [SAN LUIS OBISPO]: *spring,* 7.5 miles east-northeast of Pozo (lat. 35°21'05" N, long. 120°15'25" W). Named on Pozo Summit (1967) 7.5' quadrangle.

Lynch: see **Tierra Redonda Mountain** [SAN LUIS OBISPO].

Lynch Canyon [MONTEREY]: *canyon,* drained by a stream that flows 10.5 miles to lowlands 9 miles north-northwest of San Ardo (lat. 35°58'35" N, long. 120°51'45" W; sec. 35, T 22 S, R 10 E). Named on Pancho Rico Valley (1967), Slack Canyon (1969), and Wunpost (1949) 7.5' quadrangles. The name commemorates Thomas Lynch, who received a patent to land in the canyon in 1892 (Clark, 1991, p. 289).

Lynch's Creek: see **Bee Rock Canyon** [MONTEREY-SAN LUIS OBISPO].

Lynch's Mountain: see **Tierra Redonda Mountain** [SAN LUIS OBISPO].

Lyon Canyon: see **Griswold Canyon** [SAN BENITO].

Lyon Spring [SAN LUIS OBISPO]: *spring*, 7 miles west-northwest of Shandon in Wolf Canyon (lat. 35°42'20" N, long. 120°28'55" W; sec. 32, T 25 S, R 14 E). Named on Shandon (1961) 7.5' quadrangle.

– M –

Machesna Mountain [SAN LUIS OBISPO]: *peak*, 2.5 miles southwest of Castle Crags (lat. 35°16'45" N, long. 120°13'50" W). Altitude 4063 feet. Named on La Panza (1967) 7.5' quadrangle. Called McChesney Mountain on La Panza (1935) 15' quadrangle, but United States Board on Geographic Names (1962a, p. 13) ruled against this name for the feature.

Machesna Potrero [SAN LUIS OBISPO]: *area*, 1.5 miles south of Castle Crags (lat. 35°16'50" N, long. 120°12'10" W); the place is 1.5 miles east of Machesna Mountain. Named on La Panza (1967) 7.5' quadrangle.

Machesna Spring [SAN LUIS OBISPO]: *spring*, 8.5 miles west-northwest of Branch Mountain (lat. 35°14'10" N, long. 120°13'05" W). Named on Los Machos Hills (1967) 7.5' quadrangle.

Machete Ridge [SAN BENITO]: *peak*, 3.5 miles north of North Chalone Peak (lat. 36°29'50" N, long. 121°12' W; sec. 34, T 16 S, R 7 E). Named on North Chalone Peak (1969) 7.5' quadrangle.

Machine Gun Flats [MONTEREY]: *area*, 5.5 miles west-southwest of Salinas (lat. 36°38'10" N, long. 121°44'30" W); the place is on Fort Ord Military Reservation. Named on Salinas (1947) 7.5' quadrangle.

Mackenzie Creek [SANTA CRUZ]: *stream*, flows 1.5 miles to Bean Creek 7 miles east-southeast of the town of Boulder Creek (lat. 37° 04'20" N, long. 122°00'55" W; sec. 7, T 10 S, R 1 W). Named on Felton (1955) 7.5' quadrangle.

Maddocks Creek [SANTA CRUZ]: *stream*, flows nearly 1 mile to Opal Creek 1 mile north of Big Basin (lat. 37°11'05" N, long. 122° 13'05" W; sec. 5, T 9 S, R 3 E). Named on Big Basin (1955) 7.5' quadrangle. The name commemorates Thomas Maddock, who arrived in the neighborhood in 1882 and built a squatter's cabin along Opal Creek (Clark, 1986, p. 194).

Madrona Canyon [MONTEREY]: *canyon*, 4 miles long, drained by Big Creek (1) above a point 2.5 miles east-northeast of Jamesburg (lat. 36°23'10" N, long. 121°33' W; near S line sec. 4, T 18 S, R 4 E). Named on Rana Creek (1956) 7.5' quadrangle.

Madulce Peak [SANTA BARBARA]: *peak*, 10.5 miles northeast of Little Pine Mountain (lat. 34°41'25" N, long. 119°35'25" W). Altitude 6536 feet. Named on Madulce Peak (1964) 7.5' quadrangle. United States Board on Geographic Names (1939, p. 23) rejected the name "Strawberry Peak" for the feature.

Magetti Flats [SAN LUIS OBISPO]: *area*, 4.25 miles northwest of Pozo in Parola Canyon (lat. 35°20'50" N, long. 120°25'50" W; sec. 1, T 30 S, R 14 E). Named on Santa Margarita Lake (1967) 7.5' quadrangle.

Magnetic Spring [SANTA CRUZ]: *locality*, 3.5 miles south-southwest of Laurel (lat. 37°04'15" N, long. 121°59'10" W). Named on Los Gatos (1919) 15' quadrangle. Clark (1986, p. 136) noted that a resort called Glenwood Magnetic Springs was at the place as early as 1875.

Mahoney Canyon [MONTEREY-SAN LUIS OBISPO]: *canyon*, drained by a stream that heads in Monterey County and flows 9.5 miles to Salinas River 1 mile north-northeast of San Miguel in San Luis Obispo County (lat. 35°45'55" N, long. 120°41'15" W; sec. 9, T 25 S, R 12 E). Named on San Miguel (1948) 7.5' quadrangle. Stanley (p. 1) called the feature Mahoney's Canyon.

Mail Camp: see **San Miguel Creek** [MONTEREY].

Mail Trail Pond [SAN BENITO]: *lake*, 850 feet long, 12 miles east-southeast of Bitterwater (lat. 36°20'40" N, long. 120°47'35" W; sec. 20, T 18 S, R 11 E). Named on Hepsedam Peak (1969) 7.5' quadrangle, which shows the lake near a route that has the label "Mail Trail."

Main Sulphur Spring: see **Paso Robles** [SAN LUIS OBISPO].

Majors [SANTA CRUZ]: *settlement*, 7 miles west-northwest of Point Santa Cruz (lat. 36°59' N, long. 122°08'40" W); the place is near the mouth of Majors Creek. Named on Santa Cruz (1954) 7.5' quadrangle. It first was called Enright (Clark, 1986, p. 195).

Majors Creek [SANTA CRUZ]: *stream*, flows 5.5 miles to the sea 6.5 miles west-northwest of Point Santa Cruz (lat. 36°58'35" N, long. 122°08'25" W). Named on Felton (1955) and Santa Cruz (1954) 7.5' quadrangles. The stream flows through Refugio grant, part of which belonged to Joseph L. Majors. Hubbard's (1943) map has the name "Coja Cr." for the stream

Mallagh Landing [SAN LUIS OBISPO]: *locality*, 1 mile east-southeast of Avila Beach at the end of a promontory that extends into San Luis Obispo Bay (lat. 35°10'25" N, long. 120°42'55" W). Named on Pismo Beach (1965) 7.5' quadrangle. The place was called Cave Landing before about 1860, when David Mallagh, an Irish sea captain, built a warehouse on the cliff there and had a wooden chute down to the water; the name "Cave Landing" is from a nearby cave called Robbers' Cave because it had been a hiding place for bandits' loot (Hoover, Rensch, and

Rensch, p. 380).

Malosky Creek [SANTA CRUZ]: *stream,* flows nearly 1 mile to San Lorenzo River near the south edge of the town of Boulder Creek (lat. 37°06'50" N, long. 122°07' W; near SE cor. sec. 30, T 9 S, R 2 W). Named on Davenport (1955) and Felton (1955) 7.5' quadrangles. Clark (1986, p. 211) used the form "Molasky Creek" for the name.

Malpaso Creek [MONTEREY]: *stream,* flows 4.25 miles to the sea nearly 1 mile south-southeast of Yankee Point (lat. 36°28'50" N, long. 121°56'15" W). Named on Mount Carmel (1956) and Soberanes Point (1956) 7.5' quadrangles. The name probably is from difficulty that horses had crossing the creek— *malpaso* means "bad crossing" in Spanish (Lussier, p. 12).

Malva Real Anchorage [SANTA BARBARA]: *anchorage,* just east of Punta Arena on the south side of Santa Cruz Island (lat. 33°57'40" N, long. 119°48'45" W). Named on Santa Cruz Island B (1943) 7.5' quadrangle. Bremner's (1932) map has the name "Cñ.. Malvareal" for a canyon that opens to the sea just west of present Malva Real Anchorage.

Manchester: see **Alder Creek** [MONTEREY].

Mangels Creek: see **Mangles Gulch** [SANTA CRUZ].

Mangels Gulch: see **Mangles Gulch** [SANTA CRUZ].

Mangles Gulch [SANTA CRUZ]: *canyon,* drained by a stream that flows 2 miles to Aptos Creek 4.25 miles east-northeast of Soquel Point (lat. 36°58'50" N, long. 121°54'10" W). Named on Laurel (1955) and Soquel (1954) 7.5' quadrangles. Called Mangels Gulch on Soquel (1954, photorevised 1968) 7.5' quadrangle. United States Board on Geographic Names (1972c, p. 3) noted that the name is for Claus Mangels, a former landowner at the place; the Board gave the name "Mangels Creek" as a variant.

Mann Canyon [MONTEREY]: *canyon,* 1.25 miles long, opens into Shirttail Gulch 7.5 miles north of Greenfield (lat. 36°25'50" N, long. 121°13'45" W; near S line sec. 20, T 17 S, R 7 E). Named on North Chalone Peak (1969) 7.5' quadrangle.

Manresa [SANTA CRUZ]: *locality,* 6.25 miles west-northwest of Watsonville at present La Selva Beach (lat. 36°56'10" N, long. 121°51'50" W). Named on Capitola (1914) 15' quadrangle. Manresa was the train station for Villa Manresa, a Catholic Church retreat named for Manresa, Spain, where Saint Ignatius of Loyola conceived the idea for the Jesuit order (Clark, 1986, p. 197). Hubbard's (1943) map shows a place called Cristo located along the railroad at about the site of present Manresa.

Manresa: see **La Selva Beach** [SANTA CRUZ].

Mansfield: see **Alder Creek** [MONTEREY].

Mansfield Canyon [MONTEREY]: *canyon,* drained by a stream that flows 2.25 miles to

Quinado Canyon 7 miles west-southwest of San Lucas (lat. 36°05'50" N, long. 121°08'50" W; near N line sec. 19, T 21 S, R 8 E). Named on Cosio Knob (1949) 7.5' quadrangle. Howard (p. 65) noted that a roadhouse called Jim Lowe's was located near the mouth of Mansfield Canyon.

Manson Creek [SANTA CRUZ]: *stream,* flows 1 mile to San Lorenzo River 4.25 miles south-southeast of the town of Boulder Creek (lat. 37°04'10" N, long. 122°05' W; near S line sec. 9, T 10 S, R 2 W). Named on Felton (1955) 7.5' quadrangle.

Manuel Peak [MONTEREY]: *peak,* 7.5 miles east-southeast of Point Sur (lat. 36°16'25" N, long. 121°46'10" W; near S line sec. 17, T 19 S, R 2 E). Named on Big Sur (1956) 7.5' quadrangle. The name is for Manuel Innocenti, a Santa Barbara mission Indian who settled in the region in the mid-nineteenth century (Lussier, p. 23; Lussier called the feature Mount Manuel).

Manzana Camp [SANTA CRUZ]: *locality,* 4 miles west-northwest of San Rafael Mountain (lat. 34°44'05" N, long. 119°52'25" W); the place is along Manzana Creek. Named on San Rafael Mountain (1959) 7.5' quadrangle.

Manzana Campground [SANTA BARBARA]: *locality,* 3.5 miles west-northwest of Bald Mountain (1) (lat. 34°49'30" N, long. 119° 59'35" W); the place is near the mouth of Manzana Creek. Named on Bald Mountain (1964) 7.5' quadrangle.

Manzana Canyon: see **Manzana Creek** [SANTA BARBARA].

Manzana Creek [SANTA BARBARA]: *stream,* flows 21 miles to Sisquoc River 3.5 miles west-northwest of Bald Mountain (1) (lat. 34°49'35" N, long. 119°59'35" W). Named on Bald Mountain (1964), Figueroa Mountain (1959), San Rafael Mountain (1959), and Zaca Lake (1964) 7.5' quadrangles. The canyon of the stream is called Manzana Canyon on Santa Ynez (1905) 30' quadrangle. The name was given in the 1870's for a large apple orchard situated near the stream—*manzana* means "apple" in Spanish (Gudde, 1949, p. 203).

Manzana Narrows Camp [SANTA BARBARA]: *locality,* 3.5 miles west-northwest of San Rafael Mountain (lat. 34°44'15" N, long. 119°51'55" W); the place is along Manzana Creek. Named on San Rafael Mountain (1959) 7.5' quadrangle.

Manzanita Canyon [MONTEREY-SAN LUIS OBISPO]: *canyon,* drained by a stream that heads in Monterey County and flows nearly 5 miles to Shimmin Canyon 6 miles north-northwest of Shandon in San Luis Obispo County (lat. 35°44'15" N, long. 120° 25'05" W; sec. 24, T 25 S, R 14 E). Named on Cholame Hills (1961) and Shandon (1961) 7.5' quadrangles.

Manzanita Mountain [SANTA BARBARA]: *peak,* 20 miles east of Santa Maria (lat.

34°53'40" N, long. 120°04'45" W). Altitude 3193 feet. Named on Manzanita Mountain (1964) 7.5' quadrangle.

Marble Peak [MONTEREY]: *peak,* 4 miles east of Partington Point (lat. 36°10'25" N, long. 121°37'35" W; sec. 22, T 20 S, R 3 E). Altitude 4031 feet. Named on Partington Ridge (1956) 7.5' quadrangle. The name is from limestone and marble at the place (Clark, 1991, p. 295).

March Rock [SANTA BARBARA]: *rock,* 5.5 miles northwest of Cardwell Point, and 200 feet offshore at the northeast end of Simonton Cove on San Miguel Island (lat. 34°04'25" N, long. 120° 22'05" W). Named on San Miguel Island East (1950) 7.5' quadrangle.

Mare Spring [SAN LUIS OBISPO]: *spring,* 9 miles northeast of Pozo (lat. 35°23'30" N, long. 120°15'50" W; sec. 21, T 29 S, R 16 E). Named on Camatta Ranch (1966) 7.5' quadrangle.

Mariana Creek [SAN LUIS OBISPO]: *stream,* flows 1.5 miles to Navajo Creek nearly 6.5 miles east-northeast of Pozo (lat. 35°21'25" N, long. 120°16'30" W; sec. 32, T 29 S, R 16 E). Named on Pozo Summit (1967) 7.5' quadrangle.

Maria Ygnacio Creek [SANTA BARBARA]: *stream,* flows nearly 7 miles to Atascadero Creek 1.25 miles southeast of downtown Goleta (lat. 34°25'30" N, long. 119°48'35" W). Named on Goleta (1950) and San Marcos Pass (1959) 7.5' quadrangles. East Fork enters from the northeast nearly 3 miles upstream from the mouth of the main creek; it is 2 miles long and is named on Goleta (1950) 7.5' quadrangle.

Marina [MONTEREY]: *town,* 8 miles west of Salinas near the coast (lat. 36°41' N, long. 121°48' W). Named on Marina (1947) 7.5' quadrangle. Postal authorities established Marina post office in 1916 (Frickstad, p. 107), and the town incorporated in 1975. William Locke-Paddon bought 1500 acres of land and had the town laid out in 1913 (Clark, 1991, p. 295).

Mariposa Peak [SAN BENITO]: *peak,* 12.5 miles east-northeast of Hollister on San Benito-Merced county line (lat. 36°57'25" N, long. 121°12'40" W; near S line sec. 21, T 11 S, R 7 E). Altitude 3448 feet. Named on Mariposa Peak (1969) 7.5' quadrangle. California Mining Bureau's (1917b) map shows a place called Lone Tree located nearly 5 miles southsouthwest of Mariposa Peak. California Mining Bureau's (1909a) map has the form "Lonetree" for the name. Postal authorities established Lonetree post office in 1900 and discontinued it in 1911 (Frickstad, p. 136).

Marmolejo Creek [SAN LUIS OBISPO]: *stream,* flows 5 miles to join Burnett Creek and form Arroyo de la Cruz 4 miles northnortheast of the village of San Simeon (lat. 35°41'55" N, long. 121° 10'15" W). Named on Pebblestone Shut-in (1959) and San

Simeon (1958) 7.5' quadrangles.

Marmolejo Flats [SAN LUIS OBISPO]: *area,* 5 miles east-northeast of the village of San Simeon (lat. 35°41'05" N, long. 121°06'55" W); the place is along Marmolejo Creek. Named on Pebblestone Shut-in (1959) 7.5' quadrangle.

Marre Canyon [SANTA BARBARA]: *canyon,* drained by a stream that flows 5.25 miles to Santa Agueda Creek 6 miles east-southeast of Los Olivos (lat. 34°37'40" N, long. 120°01'10" W). Named on Figueroa Mountain (1959) and Los Olivos (1959) 7.5' quadrangles. Figueroa Mountain (1959) 7.5' quadrangle shows Marre ranch near the head of the canyon. Called Morey Canyon on Santa Ynez (1905) 30' quadrangle, but United States Board on Geographic Names (1961b, p. 11) rejected this name for the feature.

Mars: see **Mount Mars** [MONTEREY].

Marshall Creek [SANTA CRUZ]: *stream,* flows 1.5 miles to San Lorenzo River 2.5 miles south-southeast of the town of Boulder Creek (lat. 37°05'30" N, long. 122°05'35" W; near W line sec. 4, T 10 S, R 2 W). Named on Felton (1955) 7.5' quadrangle. The name is for J.D. Marshall, who came from Texas in 1852 and settled along the stream (Rowland, p. 184).

Martin Canyon [MONTEREY]: *canyon,* drained by a stream that flows 1.5 miles to Carmel Valley (1) 2.5 miles east of the mouth of Carmel River (lat. 36°32'35" N, long. 121°53' W). Named on Monterey (1947) 7.5' quadrangle. The name commemorates John Martin, who settled in the canyon (Clark, 1991, p. 297).

Martinez Canyon [SAN LUIS OBISPO]: *canyon,* drained by a stream that flows nearly 3 miles to the canyon of San Juan Creek 4.5 miles east of Castle Crags (lat. 35°18'35" N, long. 120°07'20" W; near S line sec. 14, T 30 S, R 17 E). Named on La Panza (1967) 7.5' quadrangle. On La Panza (1935) 15' quadrangle, present Hay Canyon has the name "Martinez Canyon."

Martin Station: see **Neponset** [MONTEREY].

Martinus Corner [MONTEREY]: *locality,* 4 miles east-southeast of Jolon (lat. 35°56'25" N, long. 121°07'05" W; near E line sec. 8, T 23 S, R 8 E). Named on Williams Hill (1949) 7.5' quadrangle. The name commemorates Jan Henry Martinus, who patented land near place in 1891 (Clark, 1991, p. 298).

Mary Hill Mineral Well: see **Paso Robles** [SAN LUIS OBISPO].

Mason Canyon [MONTEREY-SAN LUIS OBISPO]: *canyon,* drained by a stream that heads in Monterey County and flows 10 miles to Estrella Creek 10 miles east-northeast of Paso Robles in San Luis Obispo County (lat. 35°41'15" N, long. 120°31'55" W; near NW cor. sec. 12, T 26 S, R 13 E). Named on Cholame Hills (1961) 7.5' quadrangle. Called Freeman Canyon on Estrella (1948) 7.5' quadrangle. On Cholame (1917) 30' quadrangle, the name "Mason Canyon" applies to present Willow Springs Canyon.

Matarana Gulch [MONTEREY]: *canyon,* drained by a stream that flows 2.5 miles to Chualar Canyon 10 miles north-northeast of Gonzales (lat. 36°38'05" N, long. 121°21'10" W; near N line sec. 18, T 15 S, R 6 E). Named on Mount Johnson (1968) and Paicines (1968) 7.5' quadrangles. The misspelled name is for Jesús Maturano, who patented land in the canyon in 1900 (Clark, 1991, p. 299).

Mattos Gulch [SANTA CRUZ]: *canyon,* 1 mile long, opens into Pajaro Valley 4.5 miles east of Watsonville (lat. 36°55'30" N, long. 121°40'15" W). Named on Watsonville East (1955) 7.5' quadrangle.

Maxwellton [SAN LUIS OBISPO]: *locality,* nearly 0.25 mile southwest of Edna along Pacific Coast Railroad and Southern Pacific Railroad (lat. 35°12' N, long. 120°37' W). Named on Arroyo Grande (1897) 15' quadrangle.

Maymens Flat [SANTA CRUZ]: *area,* 6.5 miles north of Corralitos (lat. 37°04'55" N, long. 121°49'15" W; near NE cor. sec. 11, T 10 S, R 1 E). Named on Loma Prieta (1955) 7.5' quadrangle. Charles Maymen and James Maymen homesteaded at the place in the 1890's (Young, p. 64).

McCabe Canyon [SAN BENITO]: *canyon,* drained by a stream that flows 3.25 miles to Bear Valley 4 miles northeast of North Chalone Peak (lat. 36°29'30" N, long. 121°08'55" W; sec. 31, T 16 S, R 8 E). Named on Bickmore Canyon (1968) and North Chalone Peak (1969) 7.5' quadrangles.

McCallum: see **Camp McCallum** [MONTEREY].

McChesney Mountain: see **Machesna Mountain** [SAN LUIS OBISPO].

McClappin Spring [SAN LUIS OBISPO]: *spring,* 3.5 miles southwest of Atascadero (lat. 35°26'55" N, long. 120°42'30" W). Named on Atascadero (1965) 7.5' quadrangle.

McClusky Slough [MONTEREY]: *water feature,* lakes and marsh near the coast south of the mouth of Pajaro River (lat. 36°50'25" N, long. 121°47'40" W). Named on Moss Landing (1954) 7.5' quadrangle. Capitola (1914) 15' quadrangle has the name for three connected lakes.

McConnell Canyon [MONTEREY]: *canyon,* drained by a stream that flows about 2 miles to Espinosa Canyon (2) 6 miles south-southwest of San Lucas (lat. 36°02'50" N, long. 121°03'50" W; sec. 1, T 22 S, R 8 E). Named on Espinosa Canyon (1949) 7.5' quadrangle. The name commemorates William S. McConnell, who owned land at the place (Clark, 1991, p. 301).

McCoy Canyon [MONTEREY]: *canyon,* 5.5 miles long, opens into lowlands 4.5 miles east-northeast of Gonzales (lat. 36°31'45" N, long. 121°21'45" W; near W line sec. 19, T 16 S, R 6 E); McCoy Creek drains the canyon. Named on Mount Johnson (1968) 7.5' quadrangle. The name commemorates Thomas A. McCoy, who patented land at the place in 1884 and 1892 (Clark, 1991, p. 301-302).

McCoy Canyon [SANTA BARBARA]: *canyon,* drained by a stream that flows 2.25 miles to Glen Annie Canyon 3.5 miles northwest of Goleta (lat. 34°28'15" N, long. 119°52'30" W; sec. 36, T 5 N, R 29 W). Named on Goleta (1950) 7.5' quadrangle.

McCoy Creek [MONTEREY]: *stream,* flows 8 miles before ending in lowlands 5.5 miles northwest of Soledad (lat. 36°29'35" N, long. 121°23' W; sec. 35, T 16 S, R 5 E); the stream flows through McCoy Canyon. Named on Gonzales (1955), Mount Johnson (1968), and Palo Escrito Peak (1956) 7.5' quadrangles.

McCoy Creek [SAN BENITO]: *stream,* flows nearly 7 miles to San Benito River 8.5 miles east-northeast of Bitterwater (lat. 36°24'30" N, long. 120°51' W; sec. 35, T 17 S, R 10 E). Named on Hernandez Reservoir (1969) 7.5' quadrangle.

McDonald Canyon [SAN LUIS OBISPO]: *canyon,* drained by a stream that flows 6.5 miles to San Juan Valley 4 miles south-southeast of Shandon (lat. 35°36'10" N, long. 120°21'20" W; sec. 4, T 27 S, R 15 E). Named on Camatta Canyon (1961) 7.5' quadrangle.

McDonald Gulch [SANTA CRUZ]: *canyon,* 1 mile long, along Kings Creek above a point 6.25 miles north of the town of Boulder Creek (lat. 37°13' N, long. 122°07'15" W; near S line sec. 19, T 8 S, R 2 W). Named on Castle Rock Ridge (1955) 7.5' quadrangle.

McFadden: see **Chas. McFadden**, under **One Suerte** [MONTEREY].

McGaffigan's Switch: see **San Lorenzo Park** [SANTA CRUZ].

McGinnis Creek [SAN LUIS OBISPO]: *stream,* flows nearly 3 miles to Navajo Creek 7.5 miles northeast of Pozo (lat. 35°22'50" N, long. 120°16'50" W; near S line sec. 20, T 29 S, R 16 E). Named on Camatta Ranch (1966) and Pozo Summit (1967) 7.5' quadrangles.

McGowan Canyon [MONTEREY]: *canyon,* nearly 2 miles long, opens into lowlands 8.5 miles southeast of Jolon (lat. 35°53'45" N, long. 121°03'05" W). Named on Williams Hill (1949) 7.5' quadrangle.

McKay [SAN LUIS OBISPO]: *locality,* 3.5 miles northwest of San Miguel along Southern Pacific Railroad at Camp Roberts Military Reservation (lat. 35°47' N, long. 120°43'30" W; sec. 6, T 25 S, R 12 E). Named on San Miguel (1948) 7.5' quadrangle. California Mining Bureau's (1909b) map has the name "Chanslor" for a place located at or near present McKay.

McKenna Canyon [SAN BENITO]: *canyon,* drained by a stream that flows 3.5 miles to Los Muertos Creek 2.25 miles west-northwest of Cherry Peak (lat. 36°42'05" N, long. 121°10'50" W; sec. 23, T 14 S, R 7 E). Named on Cherry Peak (1968) 7.5' quadrangle.

McKinley Mountain [SANTA BARBARA]: *peak,* 2 miles west-southwest of San Rafael Mountain (lat. 34°42'05" N, long. 119°50'40" W; at E line sec. 8, T 7 N, R 28 W). Named on San Rafael Mountain (1959) 7.5' quadrangle.

McLain Spring [SAN LUIS OBISPO]:
(1) *spring,* 5.25 miles south of Atascadero in Kathleen Valley (lat. 35°24'45" N, long. 120°40'10" W; near S line sec. 10, T 29 S, R 12 E). Named on Atascadero (1965) 7.5' quadrangle.
(2) *spring,* 5.5 miles northeast of Simmler (lat. 35°24'30" N, long. 119°54'50" W; near NW cor. sec. 14, T 29 S, R 10 E). Named on Las Yeguas Ranch (1959) 7.5' quadrangle.

McLaughlin Canyon [SAN LUIS OBISPO]: *canyon,* drained by a stream that flows 2.25 miles to Town Creek 11 miles east-northeast of the village of San Simeon (lat. 35°41' N, long. 121°00' W; sec. 9, T 26 S, R 9 E). Named on Pebblestone Shut-in (1959) 7.5' quadrangle.

McLean: see **La Panza** [SAN LUIS OBISPO].

McLeod: see **Hale McLeod Canyon** [SAN LUIS OBISPO].

McMillan Canyon [SAN LUIS OBISPO]: *canyon,* drained by a stream that flows 8 miles to Estrella River 2 miles west of Shandon (lat. 35°39'15" N, long. 120°24'40" W; sec. 24, T 26 S, R 14 E). Named on Cholame (1961), Cholame Valley (1961), and Shandon (1961) 7.5' quadrangles.

McMillan Canyon: see **Bud Canyon** [SAN LUIS OBISPO].

McMillan Spring [MONTEREY]: *spring,* 14 miles east-northeast of San Ardo along Pancho Rico Creek (lat. 36°05'15" N, long. 120° 40' W; sec. 22, T 21 S, R 12 E). Named on Slack Canyon (1969) 7.5' quadrangle.

McNeil Spring [SAN LUIS OBISPO]: *spring,* 2.5 miles southwest of Pozo (lat. 35°16'25" N, long. 120°24'10" W; near S line sec. 30, T 30 S, R 15 E). Named on Santa Margarita Lake (1967) 7.5' quadrangle.

McPhails Peak [MONTEREY-SAN BENITO]: *peak,* 11 miles north-northeast of Gonzales on Monterey-San Benito county line (lat. 36°39'25" N, long. 121°21'55" W; sec. 1, T 15 S, R 5 E). Altitude 3353 feet. Named on Paicines (1968) 7.5' quadrangle.

McPherson: see **Mount McPherson**, under **Bielawski Mountain** [SANTA CRUZ].

McPherson Peak [SANTA BARBARA]: *peak,* 33 miles north-northwest of Santa Barbara (lat. 34°53'20" N, long. 119°48'45" W). Altitude 5749 feet. Named on Peak Mountain (1964) 7.5' quadrangle.

McQuaide: see **Camp McQuaide**, under **San Andres** [SANTA CRUZ].

McWay Canyon [MONTEREY]: *canyon,* drained by a stream that flows 2.5 miles to the sea 2 miles southeast of Partington Point (lat. 36°09'30" N, long. 121°40'15" W; sec.

30, T 20 S, R 3 E). Named on Partington Ridge (1956) 7.5' quadrangle. The McWay family homesteaded in the neighborhood before 1900 (Fink, p. 210). The feature also was called Lion Gulch, and the stream in it was called Lion Creek (Clark, 1991, p. 304).

McWay Rocks [MONTEREY]: *rocks,* largest 225 feet long, 1.5 miles southeast of Partington Point, and 400 to 900 feet offshore (lat. 36° 09'45" N, long. 121°40'40" W); the rocks are 0.5 mile northwest of the mouth of McWay Canyon . Named on Partington Ridge (1956) 7.5' quadrangle.

Meadow Creek [SAN LUIS OBISPO]: *stream,* flows 2.5 miles from Pismo Lake south through marsh and lakes situated near the coast to Arroyo Grande Creek 3 miles westsouthwest of downtown Arroyo Grande (lat. 35°06' N, long. 120°37'45" W). Named on Oceano (1965) and Pismo Beach (1965) 7.5' quadrangles.

Meadows: see **James Meadows** [MONTEREY].

Meadows Canyon [MONTEREY]: *canyon,* drained by a stream that flows 2.25 miles to Carmel Valley (1) 7.5 miles east of the mouth of Carmel River (lat. 36°31'30" N, long. 121°47'35" W); the canyon is near the east edge of James Meadows grant. Named on Seaside (1947) 7.5' quadrangle.

Meadows Tract: see **James Meadows** [MONTEREY].

Meder Creek: see **Peasley Gulch** [SANTA CRUZ]; **Wilder Creek** [SANTA CRUZ].

Medford Valley [MONTEREY]: *valley,* opens into Indian Valley (3) 13 miles northeast of Bradley (lat. 35°59'50" N, long. 120°38'45" W; sec. 23, T 22 S, R 12 E). Named on Slack Canyon (1969) 7.5' quadrangle.

Meehan: see **Lompico Creek** [SANTA CRUZ].

Mehlscaw Creek: see **Mehlschau Creek** [SAN LUIS OBISPO].

Mehlschau Creek [SAN LUIS OBISPO]: *stream,* flows 2.5 miles to Nipomo Creek nearly 2 miles west-northwest of the town of Nipomo (lat. 35°03'25" N, long. 120°30' W). Named on Nipomo (1965) 7.5' quadrangle. Called Mehlscaw Creek on Nipomo (1922) 15' quadrangle.

Mercey Creek [SAN BENITO]: *stream,* heads just inside Merced County and flows 6 miles through San Benito County to Fresno County 10 miles north-northwest of Panoche (lat. 36°43'50" N, long. 121°54'25" W; near N line sec. 8, T 14 S, R 10 E). Named on Cerro Colorado (1969) and Ortigalita Peak (1969) 7.5' quadrangles. Called Mercy Creek on Panoche Valley (1944) 15' quadrangle. South Fork enters from the southwest 2.5 miles upstream from the entrance of the main creek into Fresno County; it is nearly 2 miles long and is named on Cerro Colorado (1969) 7.5' quadrangle.

Mercy Creek: see **Mercey Creek** [SAN BENITO].

Merriam: see **Camp Merriam**, under **Camp**

San Luis Obispo [SAN LUIS OBISPO].
Merrilis Hill [MONTEREY]: *peak,* 5 miles east of Seaside (lat. 36° 37'10" N, long. 121°45'45" W). Named on Seaside (1947) 7.5' quadrangle. Clark (1991, p. 306) used the form "Merrillis Hill" for the name.
Merrill Lake [SAN BENITO]: *lake,* 225 feet long, 11.5 miles east-northeast of Bitterwater (lat. 36°26'20" N, long. 120°48'25" W; sec. 19, T 17 S, R 11 E). Named on Hernandez Reservoir (1969) 7.5' quadrangle.
Merritt Lake [MONTEREY]: *valley,* drained by an artificial watercourse that reaches Tembladero Slough 4 miles west-southwest of Prunedale (lat. 36°45'05" N, long. 121°44'15" W). Named on Prunedale (1954) 7.5' quadrangle. San Juan Bautista (1917) 15' quadrangle shows marsh and lakes along the valley. This place and Espinosa Lake together are called Lagunas de la Herba de los Mansos on a diseño of Bolsa del Potrero y Moro Cojo grant (Becker, 1964). The name "Merritt" is for Josiah Merritt, who came to Monterey in 1850 (Clark, 1991, p. 307).
Mervine: see **Fort Mervine**, under **Presidio of Monterey** [MONTEREY].
Mesa: see **The Mesa** [MONTEREY]; **The Mesa**, under **Nipomo Mesa** [SAN LUIS OBISPO].
Mesa Coyote [MONTEREY]: *area,* 4.5 miles south-southwest of Jolon (lat. 35°54'25" N, long. 121°11'45" W). Named on Jolon (1949) 7.5' quadrangle.
Mesa de Ojo de Agua [SANTA CRUZ]: *land grant,* 2.25 miles north-northwest of Point Santa Cruz in Santa Cruz. Named on Santa Cruz (1954) 7.5' quadrangle.
Mesa Grande [MONTEREY]: *area,* 5 miles east-southeast of the mouth of Carmel River (lat. 36°30'25" N, long. 121°50'45" W). Named on Monterey (1913) 15' quadrangle.
Mescal Island: see **Mescalitan Island** [SANTA BARBARA].
Mescalitan Island [SANTA BARBARA]: *hill,* 1 mile south-southwest of downtown Goleta (lat. 34°25'15" N, long. 119°49'55" W). Named on Goleta (1950) 7.5' quadrangle. Called Mescal I. on Goleta (1903) 15' quadrangle, which shows the feature surrounded by water and marsh. In 1769 members of the Portola expedition gave the name "Mescalitan" to the island, a name derived from a similar island in a lake near modern Mazatlan, Mexico (Tompkins and Ruiz, p. 10).
Mescal Ridge [MONTEREY]: *ridge,* west-trending, 4 miles long, 4.5 miles northeast of Point Sur (lat. 36°21'20" N, long. 121°51' W). Named on Big Sur (1956) and Point Sur (1956) 7.5' quadrangles.
Messenger Canyon [SANTA BARBARA]: *canyon,* drained by a stream that flows 4 miles to Wells Creek 3.5 miles north-northeast of McPherson Peak (lat. 34°56'20" N, long. 119°47'50" W). Named on Peak Mountain

(1964) 7.5' quadrangle.
Messenger Canyon: see **Wells Creek** [SANTA BARBARA].
Messic Mountain [SAN BENITO]: *peak,* 9 miles northeast of Hollister (lat. 36°57' N, long. 121°17'45" W). Altitude 1814 feet. Named on Three Sisters (1954) 7.5' quadrangle.
Metz [MONTEREY]: *locality,* 3 miles northeast of Greenfield along Southern Pacific Railroad (lat. 36°21'20" N, long. 121°12'40" W; sec. 21, T 18 S, R 7 E). Named on Greenfield (1956) 7.5' quadrangle. Postal authorities established Metz post office in 1888 and discontinued it in 1933 (Frickstad, p. 107). The railroad reached the place in 1886 and the station was called Chalone, for nearby North Chalone Peak and South Chalone Peak, but when the post office opened there it was called it Metz, for W.H.H. Metz, first postmaster (Gudde, 1949, p. 213).
Meyers Peak [SAN BENITO]: *peak,* 5 miles southwest of Panoche (lat. 36°32'55" N, long. 120°54'05" W; sec. 8, T 16 S, R 10 E). Altitude 3721 feet. Named on Llanada (1969) 7.5' quadrangle.
Michaels Hill [MONTEREY]: *ridge,* northwest-trending, 1 mile long, 2.5 miles northeast of Partington Point (lat. 36°12'20" N, long. 121°40'15" W). Named on Partington Ridge (1956) 7.5' quadrangle. The feature also was known as Picks Summit (Clark, 1991, p. 310).
Midco [SANTA BARBARA]: *locality,* 2 miles southwest of downtown Santa Maria along Santa Maria Valley Railroad (lat. 34°56'10" N, long. 120°27'45" W). Named on Santa Maria (1959) 7.5' quadrangle.
Middle Anchorage [SANTA BARBARA]: *anchorage,* 3 miles southwest of San Pedro Point at the east end of Santa Cruz Island (lat. 34°00'05" N, long. 119°33' W). Named on Santa Cruz Island D (1943) 7.5' quadrangle.
Middle Canyon [SAN LUIS OBISPO]:
(1) *canyon,* drained by a stream that flows 1.5 miles to Shimmin Canyon 6.5 miles north-northwest of Shandon (lat. 35°44'40" N, long. 120°24'40" W; near N line sec. 24, T 25 S, R 14 E). Named on Cholame Hills (1961) and Shandon (1961) 7.5' quadrangles.
(2) *canyon,* drained by a stream that flows 3.5 miles to Cuyama Valley 2.5 miles north of New Cuyama [SANTA BARBARA] (lat. 34°59'10" N, long. 119°40'55" W; sec. 5, T 10 N, R 26 W). Named on New Cuyama (1964) 7.5' quadrangle.
Middle Canyon [SANTA BARBARA]: *canyon,* drained by a stream that flows 3 miles to Horse Canyon (3) 6 miles east-northeast of Santa Ynez Peak (lat. 34°34'15" N, long. 119°53' W). Named on Lake Cachuma (1959) and San Marcos Pass (1959) 7.5' quadrangles.
Middle Cove [MONTEREY]: *embayment,* at the northwest end of Point Lobos along the coast (lat. 36°31'25" N, long. 121°57'10" W). Named on Monterey (1947) 7.5' quadrangle.

Middle Fork [MONTEREY]: *stream,* flows 7.25 miles to Vineyard Canyon 12 miles east of Bradley (lat. 35°51'30" N, long. 120°35'55" W; sec. 8, T 24 S, R 13 E). Named on Ranchito Canyon (1948) and Stockdale Mountain (1948) 7.5' quadrangles.

Middle Mountain [MONTEREY]: *ridge,* northwest-trending, 8 miles long, 6 miles northwest of Parkfield (lat. 35°57'30" N, long. 120° 30' W). Named on Parkfield (1961) and Stockdale Mountain (1948) 7.5' quadrangles.

Middle Ridge [SAN LUIS OBISPO]: *ridge,* southwest-trending, 4 miles long, 5 miles east of the village of San Simeon (lat. 35°39'15" N, long. 121°06' W); the ridge is between North Fork Pico Creek and South Fork Pico Creek. Named on Pebblestone Shut-in (1959) 7.5' quadrangle.

Middle Rock [SANTA BARBARA]: *rock,* 3.5 miles northwest of Cardwell Point on the north side of San Miguel Island (lat. 34° 03'15" N, long. 120°20'40" W); the feature is in the middle of the opening to Cuyler Harbor. Named on San Miguel Island East (1950) 7.5' quadrangle.

Middle Santa Ynez Campground [SANTA BARBARA]: *locality,* 6.25 miles south-southwest of Hildreth Peak along Santa Ynez River (lat. 34°30'40" N, long. 119°34'45" W). Named on Hildreth Peak (1964) 7.5' quadrangle.

Midway Peak [SAN LUIS OBISPO]: *peak,* 25 miles east-southeast of Simmler (lat. 35°09'45" N, long. 119°37' W; sec. 4, T 32 S, R 22 E). Altitude 3662 feet. Named on Fellows (1951) 7.5' quadrangle.

Midway Point [MONTEREY]: *promontory,* 2.5 miles west-northwest of present Carmel-by-the-Sea along the coast (lat. 36°34' N, long. 121°57'45" W). Named on Monterey (1947) 7.5' quadrangle. The name is from the position of the feature about midway between Sunset Point and Pescadero Point (Clark, 1991, p. 310).

Milburn Spring [SAN LUIS OBISPO]: *spring,* 4.5 miles south of Wilson Corner (lat. 35°24'05" N, long. 120°23'30" W; sec. 17, T 29 S, R 15 E). Named on Wilson Corner (1966) 7.5' quadrangle.

Miles [SAN LUIS OBISPO]: *locality,* 1.5 miles east-northeast of Avila Beach near San Luis Obispo Creek (lat. 35°11'05" N, long. 120°42'10" W). Named on Pismo Beach (1965) 7.5' quadrangle. Arroyo Grande (1897) 15' quadrangle shows the place along Pacific Coast Railroad. California (1891) map has the label "Miles Sta. or Root P.O." at the site. Postal authorities established Root post office in 1883 and discontinued it in 1894; the name was for Oroville Root, first postmaster (Salley, p. 188).

Milindee Canyon [MONTEREY]: *canyon,* drained by a stream that flows 0.5 mile to lowlands 5 miles west of Greenfield (lat. 36°18'50" N, long. 121°19'45" W). Named

on Paraiso Springs (1956) 7.5' quadrangle.

Milkcan Spring [SAN LUIS OBISPO]: *spring,* 4.5 miles south of Wilson Corner in Wilson Canyon (lat. 35°24'15" N, long. 120°22'35" W; near N line sec. 16, T 29 S, R 15 E). Named on Wilson Corner (1966) 7.5' quadrangle.

Mill Canyon [SANTA CRUZ]: *canyon,* drained by a stream that flows 1.5 miles to Coward Creek 4.25 miles east-northeast of Watsonville (lat. 36°56'50" N, long. 121°41'15" W). Named on Watsonville East (1955) 7.5' quadrangle. United States Board on Geographic Names (1992, p. 4) approved the name "Kinky Canyon" for the feature.

Mill Canyon: see **Fern Canyon** [SANTA CRUZ].

Mill Creek [MONTEREY]:
(1) *stream,* flows 3 miles to join Turner Creek and form Bixby Creek 5.5 miles north-north-east of Point Sur (lat. 36°22'20" N, long. 121°50'35" W; near NE cor. sec. 15, T 18 S, R 1 E). Named on Big Sur (1956) 7.5' quadrangle. On Point Sur (1925) 15' quadrangle, the stream is considered part of Bixby Creek. Postal authorities established Sur post office along Mill Creek (Wall, p. 53) in 1889 and discontinued it in 1913 (Salley, p. 216).
(2) *stream,* flows 3.5 miles to the sea 6.5 miles north-northwest of Cape San Martin (lat. 35°58'55" N, long. 121°29'25" W; near S line sec. 25, T 22 S, R 4 E). Named on Cape San Martin (1949) 7.5' quadrangle. The name is from a sawmill along the stream (Clark, 1991, p. 311).

Mill Creek [SANTA CRUZ]:
(1) *stream,* flows 0.5 mile to Lompico Creek 4.25 miles east-southeast of the town of Boulder Creek (lat. 37°06'40" N, long. 122°02'50" W; sec. 35, T 9 S, R 2 W). Named on Felton (1955) 7.5' quadrangle.
(2) *stream,* flows 5 miles to Scott Creek 5.25 miles north-northwest of Davenport (lat. 37°04'35" N, long. 122°14'35" W). Named on Big Basin (1955) and Davenport (1955) 7.5' quadrangles.
(3) *stream,* flows nearly 3 miles to San Vicente Creek 2.5 miles north-northeast of Davenport (lat. 37°02'30" N, long. 122°10'25" W). Named on Davenport (1955) 7.5' quadrangle. The name is from the Glassell Brothers Mill located along the stream (Clark, 1986, p. 207).

Mill Creek: see **Bixby Creek** [MONTEREY].

Mill Creek, West Fork [SANTA BARBARA]: *stream,* flows nearly 2 miles to Manzana Creek 2.5 miles northeast of Zaca Lake (lat. 34° 48'05" N, long. 120°00' W). Named on Zaca Lake (1964) 7.5' quadrangle, which fails to show a Mill Creek.

Miller Canyon [MONTEREY]: *canyon,* drained by Miller Fork Carmel River, which flows 7.25 miles through the canyon to Carmel River 3.25 miles east-northeast of Uncle Sam Mountain (lat. 36° 21'10" N, long. 121°39' W). Named on Chews Ridge (1956) and Ventana Cones (1956) 7.5' quadrangles.

Miller Canyon [SAN BENITO]: *canyon,* 1.5 miles long, 10 miles east of Bitterwater along Laguna Creek (lat. 36°21'20" N, long. 120°49'35" W). Named on Hepsedam Peak (1969) 7.5' quadrangle.

Miller Canyon [SANTA BARBARA]: *canyon,* drained by a stream that flows nearly 3 miles to Sisquoc River 3 miles east-northeast of Bald Mountain (1) (lat. 34°49'45" N, long. 119°53'15" W). Named on Bald Mountain (1964) 7.5' quadrangle.

Miller Canyon Camp [MONTEREY]: *locality,* 4.5 miles east of Uncle Sam Mountain (lat. 36°20'20" N, long. 121°37'30" W; sec. 26, T 18 S, R 3 E); the place is along Miller Fork Carmel River. Named on Chews Ridge (1956) 7.5' quadrangle.

Miller Flat [SAN LUIS OBISPO]: *area,* 1.25 miles south-southeast of Santa Margarita (lat. 35°22'30" N, long. 120°36' W). Named on Lopez Mountain (1965) and Santa Margarita (1965) 7.5' quadrangles.

Miller Flats [SAN LUIS OBISPO]: *area,* 16 miles east-southeast of Shandon (lat. 35°36' N, long. 120°06'15" W). Named on Packwood Creek (1961) 7.5' quadrangle. Arnold and Johnson (1910, p. 21) proposed the name to commemorate James Miller, an early settler in the neighborhood.

Miller Fork: see **Carmel River** [MONTEREY].

Miller Mountain [MONTEREY]: *peak,* nearly 4 miles east-southeast of Uncle Sam Mountain (lat. 36°19'10" N, long. 121°38'40" W; sec. 34, T 18 S, R 3 E). Named on Ventana Cones (1956) 7.5' quadrangle.

Miller's Landing: see **Pajaro River** [SANTA CRUZ].

Millpond Lake [SANTA CRUZ]: *lake,* 550 feet long, 5 miles south-southeast of Laurel (lat. 37°03'05" N, long. 121°55'30" W). Named on Laurel (1955) 7.5' quadrangle.

Mill Ridge: see **Long Ridge** [SANTA CRUZ].

Milpitas [MONTEREY]: *land grant,* extends for 17 miles northwest of Jolon. Named on Alder Peak (1949), Bear Canyon (1949), Cone Peak (1949), Cosio Knob (1949), and Jolon (1949) 7.5' quadrangles. Ignacio Pastor received 3 leagues in 1838 and claimed 43,281 acres patented in 1875 (Cowan, p. 48).

Mincey Canyon [MONTEREY]: *canyon,* drained by a stream that flows 3 miles to an unnamed canyon 9.5 miles west-northwest of Bradley (lat. 35°55'10" N, long. 120°57'40" W; sec. 23, T 23 S, R 9 E). Named on Hames Valley (1949) 7.5' quadrangle. On Bradley (1929) 15' quadrangle, the name "Mincey Canyon" applies also to part of the unnamed canyon. The name is for Samuel C. Mincey, who patented land in the canyon in 1911 (Clark, 1991, p. 313).

Mine Canyon [SAN BENITO]: *canyon,* drained by a stream that flows nearly 3 miles to Moody Canyon 7.5 miles west-southwest of Panoche (lat. 36°34' N, long. 120°57'40" W; sec. 2, T 16 S, R 9 E). Named on Llanada (1969) 7.5' quadrangle.

Mine Canyon [SAN LUIS OBISPO]: *canyon,* drained by a stream that flows 2.5 miles to Harford Canyon nearly 2 miles north-northwest of Avila Beach (lat. 35°12'10" N, long. 120°44'35" W; sec. 25, T 31 S, R 11 E). Named on Port San Luis (1965) 7.5' quadrangle.

Mine Canyon [SANTA BARBARA]:
(1) *canyon,* drained by a stream that flows 4.5 miles to Peachtree Canyon 5 miles south-southwest of San Rafael Mountain (lat. 34°38'40" N, long. 119°51' W). Named on San Rafael Mountain (1959) 7.5' quadrangle. Called Peachtree Canyon on San Rafael Mountain (1943) 15' quadrangle.
(2) *canyon,* drained by a stream that flows 2 miles to San Lucas Creek 4.5 miles southeast of Santa Ynez (lat. 34°34'30" N, long. 120°00'45" W). Named on Lake Cachuma (1959) and Santa Ynez (1959) 7.5' quadrangles.
(3) *canyon,* drained by a stream that flows 5.5 miles to Sisquoc River 5 miles west-southwest of Montgomery Potrero (lat. 34°48'55" N, long. 119°50'20" W). Named on Hurricane Deck (1964) 7.5' quadrangle.

Mine Canyon Spring [SANTA BARBARA]: *spring,* 4.5 miles southwest of San Rafael Mountain (lat. 34°39'35" N, long. 119°51'35" W); the spring is near Mine Canyon (1). Named on San Rafael Mountain (1959) 7.5' quadrangle.

Mine Canyon Spring: see **East Mine Canyon Spring** [SANTA BARBARA]; **North Mine Canyon Spring** [SANTA BARBARA].

Mine Creek [SAN BENITO]: *stream,* flows 2.5 miles to James Creek 5.5 miles east-northeast of Bitterwater (lat. 36°25'10" N, long. 120° 54'40" W; sec. 29, T 17 S, R 10 E). Named on Rock Spring Peak (1969) 7.5' quadrangle, which shows Fireflex mine situated along upper reaches of the stream.

Mine Hill [SAN LUIS OBISPO]: *ridge,* northwest-trending, 1 mile long, 4 miles southwest of downtown San Luis Obispo (lat. 35°14'40" N, long. 120°42'35" W). Named on Pismo Beach (1965) 7.5' quadrangle.

Mine Mountain [MONTEREY]: *peak,* 5 miles north of Parkfield on Monterey-Fresno county line (lat. 35°58'10" N, long. 120°26' W; sec. 35, T 22 S, R 14 E). Named on Parkfield (1961) 7.5' quadrangle. The name is from mercury mines at the place (Clark, 1991, p. 313).

Miners Gulch [MONTEREY]: *canyon,* drained by a stream that flows 6.25 miles to Chalone Creek 5 miles northeast of Greenfield (lat. 36°22'35" N, long. 121°11'15" W; sec. 10, T 18 S, R 7 E). Named on North Chalone Peak (1969) 7.5' quadrangle.

Mining Ridge [MONTEREY]: *ridge,* southwest-trending, 3.5 miles long, 5 miles north of Lopez Point (lat. 36°05'30" N, long. 121°33'45" W). Named on Lopez Point (1956) 7.5' quadrangle.

Miramar [SANTA BARBARA]: *locality,* 4 miles east of downtown Santa Barbara (lat. 34°25'10" N, long. 119°37'40" W). Named on Santa Barbara (1903) 15' quadrangle.

Miranda Canyon [SANTA BARBARA]: *canyon,* drained by a stream that flows 4 miles to Cuyama Valley 3.5 miles east-northeast of Miranda Pine Mountain (lat. 35°03'30" N, long. 120°59' W). Named on Miranda Pine Mountain (1967) and Taylor Canyon (1959) 7.5' quadrangles.

Miranda Creek: see **Pine Canyon** [SANTA BARBARA] (1).

Miranda Pine Campground [SANTA BARBARA]: *locality,* 850 feet south of the top of Miranda Pine Mountain (lat. 35°02'05" N, long. 120°02'10" W). Named on Miranda Pine Mountain (1967) 7.5' quadrangle.

Miranda Pine Creek: see **Pine Canyon** [SANTA BARBARA] (1).

Miranda Pine Mountain [SANTA BARBARA]: *peak,* 23 miles east-northeast of Santa Maria (lat. 35°02'15" N, long. 120°02'10" W). Altitude 4061 feet. Named on Miranda Pine Mountain (1967) 7.5' quadrangle.

Miranda Pine Spring [SANTA BARBARA]: *spring,* 1000 feet south-southwest of the top of Miranda Pine Mountain (lat. 35°02'05" N, long. 120°02'15" W). Named on Miranda Pine Mountain (1967) 7.5' quadrangle.

Mision Nuestra Señora de la Soledad: see **Ex Mission Soledad** [MONTEREY].

Mission Canyon [SANTA BARBARA]: *canyon,* 3.5 miles long, drained by Mission Creek above a point 2 miles north-northwest of downtown Santa Barbara (lat. 34°26'45" N, long. 119°42'25" W). Named on Santa Barbara (1952) 7.5' quadrangle.

Mission Creek [MONTEREY]: *stream,* flows 10 miles to San Antonio River 5 miles northwest of Jolon (lat. 36°00'40" N, long. 121°15'10" W); the mouth of the stream is near San Antonio mission. Named on Bear Canyon (1949) and Cosio Knob (1949) 7.5' quadrangles. Howard (p. 48) noted that an aqueduct paralleled the creek from San Miguel Spring to the mission. The stream first was called Arroyo San Miguel, and later was called San Miguel Creek and Arroyo la Mission (Clark, 1991, p. 314).

Mission Creek [SANTA BARBARA]: *stream,* flows 8.5 miles to the sea less than 1 mile southeast of downtown Santa Barbara (lat. 34° 24'45" N, long. 119°41'10" W); the stream drains Mission Canyon and flows past Santa Barbara mission. Named on Santa Barbara (1952) 7.5' quadrangle. United States Board on Geographic Names (1961b, p. 12) rejected the names "Arroyo del Pedregoso" and "Pedregoso Creek" for the feature. The landing place for the mission and for the presidio at Santa Barbara was situated west of the mouth of Mission Creek, and was east of as well as on an elevation called Burton

Mound—the name "Burton" was for Lewis T. Burton, who acquired land at the landing place, including the mound, in 1860 (Hoover, Rensch, and Rensch, p. 414). Burton Mound Sulphur Springs issued along the beach there; water from one spring was utilized at a hotel that was built over it (Huguenin, p. 741).

Mission La Purisima [SANTA BARBARA]: *land grant,* north of the town of Lompoc; La Purisima Concepcion mission is on the grant. Named on Lompoc (1959) and Surf (1959) 7.5' quadrangles. Jose Ramon Malo received the land in 1845 and claimed 14,736 acres patented in 1882 (Cowan, p. 65).

Mission Pine Basin [SANTA BARBARA]: *area,* 5 miles west of Big Pine Mountain (lat. 34°42'25" N, long. 119°44'25" W). Named on Big Pine Mountain (1964) 7.5' quadrangle. The name is from the legend that pine trees at the place provided beams for the mission at Santa Barbara (Gagnon, p. 98).

Mission Pine Camp [SANTA BARBARA]: *locality,* 1 mile east-southeast of San Rafael Mountain (lat. 34°42'25" N, long. 119°47'40" W). Named on San Rafael Mountain (1959) 7.5' quadrangle.

Mission Springs [SANTA CRUZ]: *settlement,* 6.5 miles southeast of the town of Boulder Creek (lat. 37°03'50" N, long. 122°01'55" W; sec. 13, T 10 S, R 2 W). Named on Felton (1955) 7.5' quadrangle.

Mocho Camp [MONTEREY]: *locality,* 4 miles north-northeast of Partington Point (lat. 36°13'30" N, long. 121°39'45" W; sec. 5, T 20 S, R 3 E); the place is along Mocho Creek. Named on Partington Ridge (1956) 7.5' quadrangle.

Mocho Creek [MONTEREY]: *stream,* flows 1 mile to South Fork Big Sur River 4 miles north-northeast of Partington Point (lat. 36° 13'10" N, long. 121°39'45" W; sec. 5, T 20 S, R 3 E). Named on Partington Ridge (1956) 7.5' quadrangle.

Molasky Creek: see **Malosky Creek** [SANTA CRUZ].

Molino: see **Aptos Creek** [SANTA CRUZ].

Molino Creek [SANTA CRUZ]: *stream,* flows 3.5 miles to the sea 2.5 miles northwest of Davenport (lat. 37°02'10" N, long. 122°13'40" W). Named on Davenport (1955) 7.5' quadrangle. Gudde (1949, p. 220) pointed out that the stream is called Arroyo del Molino on a Mexican map of 1846—*molino* means "mill" in Spanish.

Molus [MONTEREY]: *locality,* 5 miles northwest of Soledad along Southern Pacific Railroad (lat. 36°28'05" N, long. 121°23'35" W). Named on Palo Escrito Peak (1956) 7.5' quadrangle.

Monarch Peak [MONTEREY]: *peak,* 15 miles north-northeast of San Ardo on Mustang Ridge (lat. 36°13'05" N, long. 120°48'45" W; sec. 5, T 20 S, R 11 E). Altitude 2767 feet. Named on Monarch Peak (1967) 7.5' quadrangle.

Monica Creek: see **Santa Monica Creek** [SAN BENITO].

Monjas Creek [SANTA BARBARA]: *stream,* flows 1.5 miles to Alisal Creek nearly 6 miles southeast of Buellton (lat. 34°32'45" N, long. 120°08'05" W; sec. 4, T 5 N, R 31 W). Named on Solvang (1959) 7.5' quadrangle.

Monjas Spring [SANTA BARBARA]: *spring,* 6.5 miles south-southeast of Buellton (lat. 34°31'55" N, long. 120°08'10" W; at W line sec. 9, T 5 N, R 31 W); the spring is along Monjas Creek. Named on Solvang (1959) 7.5' quadrangle.

Mono Campground [SANTA BARBARA]: *locality,* 8 miles southeast of Little Pine Mountain (lat. 34°31'45" N, long. 119°37'40" W); the place is along Mono Creek. Named on Little Pine Mountain (1964) 7.5' quadrangle. Called Mono Public Camp on Little Pine Mountain (1944) 7.5' quadrangle.

Mono Cañon: see **Mono Creek** [SANTA BARBARA].

Mono Creek [SANTA BARBARA]: *stream,* flows 25 miles to Gibraltar Reservoir 8 miles southeast of Little Pine Mountain (lat. 34°31'20" N, long. 119°37'45" W). Named on Hildreth Peak (1964), Little Pine Mountain (1964), and Madulce Peak (1964) 7.5' quadrangles. Fairbanks (1894, p. 504) referred to Mono Cañon.

Mono Creek: see **Morro Creek** [SAN LUIS OBISPO].

Mono Public Camp: see **Mono Campground** [SANTA BARBARA].

Mono Rock: see **Morro Rock** [SAN LUIS OBISPO].

Monroe Canyon [MONTEREY]: *canyon,* 4 miles long, drained by Monroe Creek, which enters lowlands 4.5 miles south-southeast of Greenfield (lat. 36°15'20" N, long. 121°13'30" W). Named on Greenfield (1956), Reliz Canyon (1949), and Thompson Canyon (1949) 7.5' quadrangles.

Monroe Creek [MONTEREY]: *stream,* flows 6.5 miles to Salinas River floodplain 5 miles southeast of Greenfield (lat. 36°16'10" N, long. 121°10'50" W); the stream drains Monroe Canyon. Named on Greenfield (1956) 7.5' quadrangle.

Monroe Lake [MONTEREY]: *intermittent lake,* 700 feet long, 3 miles west of Charley Mountain (lat. 36°08'50" N, long. 120°43'10" W; sec. 31, T 20 S, R 12 E); the feature is 0.5 mile south of Monroe Valley. Named on Priest Valley (1969) 7.5' quadrangle.

Monroe Valley [MONTEREY]: *valley,* 3.25 miles west-northwest of Charley Mountain (lat. 36°09'05" N, long. 120°43'05" W). Named on Priest Valley (1969) 7.5' quadrangle.

Monte Arido [SANTA BARBARA]: *peak,* 1.5 miles north-northwest of Old Man Mountain (1) (lat. 34°32'20" N, long. 119°27'55" W; near S line sec. 2, T 5 N, R 25 W). Altitude 6003 feet. Named on Old Man Mountain

(1943) 7.5' quadrangle. Called Montecito on Mount Pinos (1903) 30' quadrangle.

Montecito [SANTA BARBARA]: *town,* 4 miles east of downtown Santa Barbara (lat. 34°25'25" N, long. 119°37'45" W). Named on Carpinteria (1952) and Santa Barbara (1952) 7.5' quadrangles. Postal authorities established Montecito post office in 1886, discontinued it in 1914, and reestablished it in 1958 (Salley, p. 145). Santa Barbara (1903) 15' quadrangle has the name "Montecito" for a community located 1.25 miles inland from the coast, and has the same name for a site along the railroad at the coast—both places are in present Montecito.

Montecito: see **Monte Arido** [SANTA BARBARA].

Montecito Creek [SANTA BARBARA]: *stream,* flows 5.5 miles to the sea 3.5 miles east of downtown Santa Barbara (lat. 34°25' N, long. 119°38' W); the mouth of the creek is in Montecito. Named on Santa Barbara (1952) 7.5' quadrangle. The stream drains Cold Spring Canyon (2). United States Board on Geographic Names (1961b, p. 12) rejected the name "Arroyo del Montecito" for the stream.

Montecito Hot Springs: see **Hot Springs** [SANTA BARBARA] (2).

Montecito Peak [SANTA BARBARA]: *peak,* 5 miles northeast of downtown Santa Barbara (lat. 34°28'20" N, long. 119°38'15" W; at E line sec. 31, T 5 N, R 26 W); the peak is 3.25 miles north of Montecito. Altitude 3214 feet. Named on Santa Barbara (1952) 7.5' quadrangle.

Monte de Buchon: see **Irish Hills** [SAN LUIS OBISPO].

Monte Diablo Range: see **Diablo Range** [MONTEREY-SAN BENITO].

Monterey [MONTEREY]: *city,* along the coast at the south end of Monterey Bay (lat. 36°36' N, long. 121°53'30" W). Named on Monterey (1947) 7.5' quadrangle. Fremont's (1845) map has the form "Monte Rey" for the name, and Emory's (1857-1858) map has the form "Montery." Postal authorities established Monterey post office 1849 (Salley, p. 145), and the city incorporated in 1889. New Monterey, a district north of Presidio of Monterey, is named on Monterey (1947) 7.5' quadrangle. Postal authorities established New Monterey post office in 1909 and discontinued it in 1913 (Salley, p. 154).

Monterey: see **East Monterey**, under **Seaside** [MONTEREY].

Monterey Bay [MONTEREY-SANTA CRUZ]: *embayment,* along the coast north of Point Pinos; extends into Santa Cruz County. Named on Santa Cruz (1956) 1°x 2° quadrangle. Cabrillo discovered the feature in 1542 and called it Bahia de los Pinos (Wagner, H.R., p. 398). Cermeño saw it in 1595 and gave it the name "Bahia de San Pedro" to honor a martyr whose day preceded the day of

Cermeño's visit (Wagner, H.R., p. 506). Vizcaino anchored in the present harbor of Monterey in 1602 and gave the name "Puerto de Monterey" to his anchorage in honor of the Conde de Monterey, Viceroy of New Spain (Wagner, H.R., p. 398). According to Davidson (1907, p. 29), a Spanish chart made before the settlement of Monterey has the name "Po. de Monterey" for the north part of present Monterey Bay. Davidson (1887, p. 212) also noted that Vizcaino's name for the harbor was El Puerto de Monte-Rey.

Monte Toyon [SANTA CRUZ]: *locality,* 5.25 miles northeast of Soquel Point in Mangles Gulch (lat. 36°59'45" N, long. 121°53'40" W). Named on Soquel (1954) 7.5' quadrangle

Monte Vista: see **Aptos Creek** [SANTA CRUZ].

Montgomery Number 3 Spring [SANTA BARBARA]: *spring,* 5 miles southeast of McPherson Peak (lat. 34°49'55" N, long. 119°45'50" W); the spring is at Montgomery Potrero 2300 feet southwest of Montgomery Spring. Named on Hurricane Deck (1964) 7.5' quadrangle.

Montgomery Number 2 Spring [SANTA BARBARA]: *spring,* 5 miles southeast of McPherson Peak (lat. 34°49'55" N, long. 119°45'15" W); the spring is at Montgomery Potrero 1700 feet southeast of Montgomery Spring. Named on Hurricane Deck (1964) 7.5' quadrangle.

Montgomery Potrero [SANTA BARBARA]: *area,* 5 miles southeast of McPherson Peak (lat. 34°50'10" N, long. 119°45'10" W). Named on Hurricane Deck (1964) 7.5' quadrangle. Fairbanks (1894, p. 498) referred to Montgomery's Potrero.

Montgomery Spring [SANTA BARBARA]: *spring,* 5 miles southeast of McPherson Peak (lat. 34°50'10" N, long. 119°45'30" W); the spring is at Montgomery Potrero. Named on Hurricane Deck (1964) 7.5' quadrangle.

Moody Canyon [SAN BENITO]: *canyon,* drained by a stream that flows nearly 5 miles to Bitterwater Canyon 7.5 miles west of Panoche (lat. 36°35' N, long. 120°58' W; sec. 34, T 15 S, R 9 E). Named on Llanada (1969) 7.5' quadrangle.

Moody Sulphur Spring [SAN BENITO]: *spring,* 8 miles west-southwest of Panoche (lat. 36°33'05" N, long. 120°58' W; sec. 11, T 16 S, R 9 E); the spring is in Moody Canyon. Named on Llanada (1969) 7.5' quadrangle.

Moon Canyon [SANTA BARBARA]: *canyon,* drained by a stream that flows 3.5 miles to join he stream in Kelsey Canyon 10 miles northwest of McPherson Peak (lat. 34°59'45" N, long. 119°55'25" W; at W line sec. 31, T 11 N, R 28 W). Named on Bates Canyon (1964) 7.5' quadrangle.

Mooney Canyon [MONTEREY]: *canyon,* drained by a stream that flows about 4 miles to Pine Valley (2) 4.5 miles north of San Ardo (lat. 36°05'10" N, long. 120°53'55" W; sec. 21, T 21 S, R 10 E). Named on Nattrass Valley (1967) and San Ardo (1967) 7.5' quadrangles.

Moonshine Canyon [SANTA BARBARA]: *canyon,* drained by a stream that flows 2.5 miles to Nojoqui Creek 3.5 miles south of Buellton (lat. 34°33'35" N, long. 120°11'30" W). Named on Solvang (1959) 7.5' quadrangle.

Moore Creek [SANTA CRUZ]: *stream,* flows 3.5 miles, partly in a discontinuous watercourse near the coast, to the sea almost 2 miles west of Point Santa Cruz (lat. 36°57' N, long. 122°03'25" W). Named on Santa Cruz (1954) 7.5' quadrangle. The name commemorates Eli Moore, who came to Santa Cruz in 1847 and owned a ranch along the stream (Clark, 1986, p. 214). Natural Bridges Beach state park is at the mouth of Moore Creek. The first stage station on the route from Santa Cruz up the coast to San Mateo County in 1872 was called Hall's Natural Bridge (Hoover, Rensch, and Rensch, p. 478)—the name apparently referred to natural bridges at the mouth of Moore Creek.

Moores Gulch [SANTA CRUZ]: *canyon,* 1 mile long, 5.25 miles north of Soquel (lat. 37°03'45" N, long. 121°57'35" W; sec. 15, T 10 S, R 1 W). Named on Laurel (1955) 7.5' quadrangle.

Moore Spring: see **Veronica Springs** [SANTA BARBARA].

Morada: see **Rosa Morada**, under **San Joaquin** [SAN BENITO].

Morales Canyon [SAN LUIS OBISPO]: *canyon,* drained by a stream that flows 7 miles to Cuyama Valley (lat. 35°01'20" N, long. 119°50' W; sec. 23, T 11 N, R 28 W). Named on Caliente Mountain (1959) 7.5' quadrangle.

Moran Lake [SANTA CRUZ]: *lake,* 900 feet long, 1000 feet north-northwest of Soquel Point near the coast (lat. 36°57'25" N, long. 121°58'35" W). Named on Soquel (1954) 7.5' quadrangle.

Morano Creek: see **Moreno Creek** [SAN LUIS OBISPO].

Morellini Creek [SAN BENITO]: *stream,* flows nearly 3 miles to Bitterwater Creek 2.5 miles east-southeast of Bitterwater (lat. 36° 21'50" N, long. 120°57'45" W; sec. 14, T 18 S, R 9 E). Named on Lonoak (1969) and Rock Spring Peak (1969) 7.5' quadrangles.

Moreno Creek [SAN LUIS OBISPO]: *stream,* flows 4 miles in a discontinuous watercourse to Salinas River 2.5 miles east-northeast of Santa Margarita (lat. 35°24'35" N, long. 120°34'05" W; near S line sec. 10, T 29 S, R 13 E). Named on Santa Margarita (1965) 7.5' quadrangle. Called Morano Creek on San Luis Obispo (1897) 15' quadrangle, but United States Board on Geographic Names (1967c, p. 2) rejected this name for the feature.

Morey Canyon: see **Marre Canyon** [SANTA BARBARA].

Morgenson Springs [SAN LUIS OBISPO]: *springs,* two, 0.25 mile apart, 6.5 miles northwest of Shandon (lat. 35°43'25" N, long. 120° 27'15" W; sec. 27, T 25 S, R 14 E). Named on Shandon (1961) 7.5' quadrangle.

Mormon Gulch [SANTA CRUZ]: *canyon,* drained by a stream that flows 1 mile to Corralitos Creek 1.5 miles north-northwest of Corralitos (lat. 37°00'45" N, long. 121°48'40" W; at S line sec. 36, T 10 S, R 1 E). Named on Loma Prieta (1955) 7.5' quadrangle.

Moro Cojo Slough [MONTEREY]: *water feature,* 4 miles long, joins Elkhorn Slough and Old Salinas River at Moss Landing (lat. 36° 48'15" N, long. 121°47' W); the feature is on Bolsa Nueva y Moro Cojo grant. Named on Moss Landing (1954) and Prunedale (1954) 7.5' quadrangles.

Moro Creek: see **Morro Creek** [SAN LUIS OBISPO].

Moro Rock: see **Morro Rock** [SAN LUIS OBISPO].

Moro y Cayucos [SAN LUIS OBISPO]: *land grant,* along the coast between Cayucos Creek and Morro Creek. Named on Cayucos (1965) and Morro Bay North (1965) 7.5' quadrangles. Vicente Felix and Martin Olivera received 2 leagues in 1842; James McKinley claimed 8845 acres patented in 1878 (Cowan, p. 49).

Morrito: see **Point Morrito**, under **Lions Head** [SANTA BARBARA].

Morritto: see **Lions Head** [SANTA BARBARA].

Morro: see **Morro Bay** [SAN LUIS OBISPO] (2).

Morro Bay [SAN LUIS OBISPO]:
(1) *bay,* 11 miles west-northwest of San Luis Obispo (lat. 35°22'30" N, long. 120°51' W); the bay is connected to the sea by a channel near Morro Rock. Named on Morro Bay South (1965) 7.5' quadrangle. According to H.R. Wagner (p. 503), Unamuno called the place Puerto de San Lucas on October 18, 1587, the day of the saint. Captain William Shaler called the feature Bernard's Bay about 1805 (Hamilton, p. 116).
(2) *town,* 12 miles west-northwest of San Luis Obispo (lat. 35°21'45" N, long. 120°50'45" W); the town is at the north end of Morro Bay (1). Named on Morro Bay North (1965) and Morro Bay South (1965) 7.5' quadrangles. Called Morro on Cayucos (1897) 15' quadrangle. The part of the town north of Morro Creek is called Morro Beach on Cayucos (1951) 15' quadrangle. The community of Morro Bay began in 1870 when Franklin Riley bought and developed 160 acres of land facing Morro Rock (Lee and others, p. 94). Postal authorities established Morro post office in 1870 and changed the name to Morro Bay in 1923 (Frickstad, p. 165). The town incorporated in 1964. Postal authorities established Del Mar-Heights post office 2 miles north of Morro Bay post office in 1953, changed the name to Del Mar Heights in 1966, and discontinued it in 1972 (Salley, p. 57). United States Board on Geographic Names

(1983b, p. 3) approved the name "Alva Paul Creek," and rejected the name "Pauls Creek," for a stream that flows 3 miles to Estero Bay in the town of Morro Bay (lat. 35°23'50" N, long. 120°51'57" W); the name commemorates Alva Paul, who purchased land along the creek in 1882 and lived there until 1915.

Morro Beach: see **Morro Bay** [SAN LUIS OBISPO] (2).

Morro Creek [SAN LUIS OBISPO]: *stream,* flows 13 miles to the sea at the town of Morro Bay (lat. 35°22'35" N, long. 120°51'45" W). Named on Atascadero (1965) and Morro Bay North (1965) 7.5' quadrangles. United States Board on Geographic Names (1933, p. 532) rejected the names "Mono Creek," "Moro Creek," and "El Morro Creek" for the stream. East Fork enters from the east 8 miles upstream from the mouth of the main creek; it is nearly 2 miles long and is named on Atascadero (1965) and Morro Bay North (1965) 7.5' quadrangles.

Morro Creek: see **Little Morro Creek** [SAN LUIS OBISPO].

Morro Rock [SAN LUIS OBISPO]: *relief feature,* 13 miles west-northwest of San Luis Obispo along the coast (lat. 35°22'10" N, long. 120°52' W); the feature is at the entrance to Morro Bay (1). Altitude 578 feet. Named on Morro Bay South (1965) 7.5' quadrangle. Called Moro Rock on Parke's (1854-1855) map. Angel (1883, p. 323) called it El Morro. The Portola expedition applied the term "morro redondo" to the feature in 1769—*morro* is a Spanish word for a crown-shaped hill (Wagner, H.R., p. 398). Gudde (1949, p. 225) pointed out that *moro* rather than *morro* was used in the name of the nearby Moro y Caucos grant, probably because of an assumed connection with *moro,* which means "Moor" or "blue roan horse" in Spanish. United States Board on Geographic Names (1933, p. 532) rejected the forms "Mono Rock," "Moro Rock," and "El Morro Rock" for the name.

Morro Trompo: see **Point Sur** [MONTEREY].

Morro Twin: see **Hollister Peak** [SAN LUIS OBISPO].

Morse [SAN BENITO]: *locality,* 5.25 miles west-southwest of Hollister (lat. 36°50'15" N, long. 121°29'35" W). Named on Hollister (1955) 7.5' quadrangle.

Morse Creek [SANTA BARBARA]: *stream,* flows 1 mile to Alder Creek 6 miles north of Carpinteria (lat. 34°29'05" N, long. 119°30'55" W; sec. 29, T 5 N, R 25 W). Named on Carpinteria (1952) 7.5' quadrangle.

Morse Point [SANTA BARBARA]: *promontory,* 8 miles southeast of Fraser Point on the south side of Santa Cruz Island (lat. 33°58'05" N, long. 119°50'50" W). Named on Santa Cruz Island A (1943) 7.5' quadrangle.

Moses Spring [SAN BENITO]: *spring,* 2 miles north-northeast of North Chalone Peak in Bear Gulch (1) (lat. 36°28'30" N, long.

121°11'10" W; near SW cor. sec. 2, T 17 S, R 7 E). Named on North Chalone Peak (1969) 7.5' quadrangle.

Moss: see **Moss Landing** [MONTEREY].

Moss Beach [MONTEREY]: *beach,* east of Point Joe along the coast (lat. 36°36'35" N, long. 121°56'55" W). Named on Monterey (1947) 7.5' quadrangle. On Monterey (1913) 15' quadrangle, the name also applies farther north-northeast along the coast. Reinstedt (1975, p. 85) gave the name "Asilomar Beach" as an alternate.

Moss Landing [MONTEREY]: *village,* 15 miles north-northeast of Monterey at the mouth of Elkhorn Slough (lat. 36°48'15" N, long. 121°47'10" W). Named on Moss Landing (1954) 7.5' quadrangle. The name commemorates Charles Moss, who with Cato Vierra built a wharf at the site (Fink, p. 139). The place was an important whaling station in the early days (Hoover, Rensch, and Rensch, p. 235). Capitola (1914) 15' quadrangle shows a place called Moss located along Pajaro Valley Consolidated Railroad near present Moss Landing. Postal authorities established Moss post office in 1895 and changed the name to Moss Landing in 1917 (Frickstad, p. 108).

Mountain Charlie Gulch [SANTA CRUZ]: *canyon,* drained by a stream that flows 4 miles to Zayante Creek 5.5 miles east-southeast of the town of Boulder Creek (lat. 37°06'20" N, long. 122°01'15" W; at W line sec. 31, T 9 S, R 1 W). Named on Felton (1955), Laurel (1955), and Los Gatos (1953) 7.5' quadrangles. The name commemorates Charles McKiernan, who came to the area in 1850 and was known to later arrivals by the name "Mountain Charlie" (Hoover, Rensch, and Rensch, p. 476-477).

Mountain Creek: see **Soquel Creek** [SANTA CRUZ].

Mountain del Buchon: see **Irish Hills** [SAN LUIS OBISPO].

Mountain Glen Hot Springs: see **Hot Spring** [SANTA BARBARA].

Mount Bielawski: see **Bielawski Mountain** [SANTA CRUZ].

Mount Buchon: see **Irish Hills** [SAN LUIS OBISPO].

Mount Carmel [MONTEREY]: *peak,* 8.5 miles northeast of Point Sur (lat. 36°23'10" N, long. 121°47'15" W). Altitude 4417 feet. Named on Mount Carmel (1956) 7.5' quadrangle. The peak also was called Boulder Mountain for the boulders that cover it (Clark, 1991, p. 344).

Mount Chelone: see **North Chalone Peak** [MONTEREY-SAN BENITO].

Mount Cross Camp [SANTA CRUZ]: *locality,* 4 miles south-southeast of the town of Boulder Creek (lat. 37°04'20" N, long. 122°05'10" W; sec. 9, T 10 S, R 2 W). Named on Felton (1955) 7.5' quadrangle.

Mount Defiance [SAN BENITO]: *peak,* 2 miles northeast of North Chalone Peak (lat. 36°28' N, long. 121°10'15" W; near E line sec. 11, T

17 S, R 7 E). Altitude 2657 feet. Named on North Chalone Peak (1969) 7.5' quadrangle.

Mount del Buchon: see **Irish Hills** [SAN LUIS OBISPO].

Mount Diablo Range: see **Diablo Range** [MONTEREY-SAN BENITO].

Mount Hanlon: see **Mount Harlan** [SAN BENITO].

Mount Harlan [SAN BENITO]: *peak,* 7.5 miles west-southwest of Paicines (lat. 36°41'50" N, long. 121°24'15" W; sec. 22, T 14 S, R 5 E). Altitude 3274 feet. Named on Mount Harlan (1968) 7.5' quadrangle. Called Mt. Hanlon on Gonzales (1921) 15' quadrangle.

Mount Hasbrouck: see **Big Baldy** [SAN LUIS OBISPO].

Mount Hermon [SANTA CRUZ]: *settlement,* 6.25 miles southeast of the town of Boulder Creek (lat. 37°03' N, long. 122°03'30" W). Named on Felton (1955) 7.5' quadrangle. In 1905 a Christian group purchased a resort called The Tuxedo and renamed it Mount Hermon for a peak in Palestine (Gudde, 1949, p. 226). The group then proceeded to model the place after summer religious assemblies in Massachusetts and Indiana (Rowland, p. 184). Postal authorities established Mount Hermon post office in 1908 (Frickstad, p. 177). MacGregor (p. 173) noted that a railroad station called Tuxedo was 0.5 mile north of Felton at the original resort.

Mount Johnson [SAN BENITO]: *peak,* 8.5 miles south-southwest of Paicines (lat. 36°36'40" N, long. 121°18'50" W; sec. 21, T 15 S, R 6 E). Altitude 3465 feet. Named on Mount Johnson (1968) 7.5' quadrangle.

Mount Lospe [SANTA BARBARA]: *ridge,* west-trending, 1 mile long, 5.5 miles south-southwest of the town of Guadalupe (lat. 34° 53'40" N, long. 120°36'05" W). Named on Guadalupe (1959) 7.5' quadrangle.

Mount Lowe [SAN LUIS OBISPO]: *peak,* nearly 2 miles northwest of Lopez Mountain (lat. 35°19'10" N, long. 120°36' W; sec. 17, T 30 S, R 13 E). Named on Lopez Mountain (1965) 7.5' quadrangle.

Mount Manuel: see **Manuel Peak** [MONTEREY].

Mount Mars [MONTEREY]: *peak,* 9 miles southeast of Cape San Martin (lat. 35°48'45" N, long. 121°20'20" W; sec. 29, T 24 S, R 6 E). Altitude 2674 feet. Named on Burro Mountain (1949) 7.5' quadrangle.

Mount McPherson: see **Bielawski Mountain** [SANTA CRUZ].

Mount Olds [MONTEREY]: *peak,* 9.5 miles north-northeast of Gonzales (lat. 36°38'35" N, long. 121°23'55" W; on E line sec. 10, T 15 S, R 5 E). Altitude 3010 feet. Named on Mount Harlan (1968) 7.5' quadrangle.

Mount Olmstead [MONTEREY]: *peak,* 4 miles north of Partington Point (lat. 36°14' N, long. 121°41'35" W; sec. 36, T 19 S, R 2 E). Altitude 3711 feet. Named on Partington Ridge (1956) 7.5' quadrangle.

Mount Pajaro [SANTA CRUZ]: *peak,* 7 miles east of Watsonville on Santa Cruz-Santa Clara county line (lat. 36°55'25" N, long. 121° 37'40" W). Altitude 1573 feet. Named on Watsonville East (1955) 7.5' quadrangle.

Mount Reynolds [SAN BENITO]: *peak,* nearly 3 miles southeast of Mount Johnson (lat. 36°35'05" N, long. 121°16'35" W; near E line sec. 35, T 15 S, R 6 E). Altitude 3146 feet. Named on Mount Johnson (1968) 7.5' quadrangle.

Mount Roberta [SANTA CRUZ]: *peak,* 7.5 miles north-north-west of Soquel (lat. 37°05'30" N, long. 121°59'40" W; sec. 5, T 10 S, R 1 W). Named on Laurel (1955) 7.5' quadrangle.

Mount Solomon [SANTA BARBARA]: *peak,* 4 miles east-southeast of Orcutt (lat. 34°50'05" N, long. 120°22'55" W); the peak is in Solomon Hills. Altitude 1346 feet. Named on Orcutt (1959) 7.5' quadrangle. The name is for Solomon Pico, a highwayman (Gudde, 1949, p. 338).

Mount Solomon: see **Solomon Hills** [SANTA BARBARA].

Mount Toro [MONTEREY]: *peak,* 6 miles west-southwest of Chualar (lat. 36°31'35" N, long. 121°36'30" W; sec. 23, T 16 S, R 3 E). Altitude 3560 feet. Named on Chualar (1947) 7.5' quadrangle.

Mount Torro Range: see **Sierra de Salinas** [MONTEREY].

Mouse Rock [SAN LUIS OBISPO]: *rock,* nearly 2 miles east-southeast of Cayucos Point, and 0.5 mile offshore (lat. 35°26'25" N, long. 120°54'30" W). Named on Cayucos (1965) 7.5' quadrangle.

Mucho Spring [SAN LUIS OBISPO]: *spring,* 3 miles southeast of Cholame (lat. 35°41'25" N, long. 120°15'55" W; near SE cor. sec. 5, T 26 S, R 16 E). Named on Cholame (1961) 7.5' quadrangle.

Mud Creek [MONTEREY]: *stream,* flows 6.25 miles to Gabilan Creek 8.5 miles north-north-east of Salinas (lat. 36°46'55" N, long. 121°35'05" W). Named on San Juan Bautista (1955) 7.5' quadrangle. The adobe house of Don Joaquin Gomez was near the confluence of Mud Creek and Gabilan Creek; the route past the house and over highlands to the north was called Gomez's Pass (Pierce, p. 75).

Muddy Creek [MONTEREY]: *stream,* flows 3.5 miles to Chualar Canyon 7 miles north-northeast of Gonzales (lat. 36°36'10" N, long. 121°24'25" W). Named on Gonzales (1955) and Mount Johnson (1968) 7.5' quadrangles.

Mudhen Lake [MONTEREY]: *intermittent lake,* 850 feet long, 5.25 miles southwest of Salinas (lat. 36°37'40" N, long. 121°43'50" W). Named on Salinas (1947) 7.5' quadrangle.

Mud Lake [SAN LUIS OBISPO]: *marsh,* 4.25 miles south-southwest of downtown Arroyo Grande near the coast (lat. 35°03'45" N, long. 120°36'40" W). Named on Oceano (1965) 7.5' quadrangle. The marsh contains three lakes,

the largest 800 feet long.

Mud Spring [SAN BENITO]: *spring,* 7.5 miles east-northeast of Bitterwater (lat. 36°26'20" N, long. 120°53'15" W; sec. 21, T 17 S, R 10 E). Named on Rock Spring Peak (1969) 7.5' quadrangle.

Mud Spring [SANTA BARBARA]: *spring,* 5.25 miles south of San Rafael Mountain (lat. 34°38'05" N, long. 119°49'30" W). Named on San Rafael Mountain (1959) 7.5' quadrangle.

Mud Springs Canyon [MONTEREY-SAN LUIS OBISPO]: *canyon,* drained by a stream that heads in Monterey County and flows 8 miles to Mason Canyon 10 miles north-north-west of Shandon in San Luis Obispo County (lat. 35°46'45" N, long. 120°28'05" W; sec. 4, T 25 S, R 14 E). Named on Cholame Hills (1961) 7.5' quadrangle.

Muertos Canyon [SAN BENITO]: *canyon,* drained by a stream that flows 1.25 miles to an unnamed canyon 5 miles west-northwest of San Juan Bautista (lat. 36°52'15" N, long. 121°37'10" W). Named on Chittenden (1955) and San Juan Bautista (1955) 7.5' quadrangles.

Mulberry: see **Paicines** [SAN BENITO].

Mulch Spring [MONTEREY]: *spring,* 22 miles east-northeast of King City (lat. 36°18'05" N, long. 120°44'40" W; sec. 2, T 19 S, R 11 E). Named on San Benito Mountain (1969) 7.5' quadrangle.

Mule Canyon Creek [MONTEREY]: *stream,* flows 1.25 miles to the sea 3.25 miles east-southeast of Pfeiffer Point (lat. 36°13'05" N, long. 121°45'35" W; sec. 5, T 20 S, R 2 E). Named on Pfeiffer Point (1956) 7.5' quadrangle. Clark (1991, p. 346) associated the name "Mule Canyon" with the pasturing of mules.

Mulligan Hill [MONTEREY]: *hill,* 11.5 miles north-northeast of Monterey near the mouth of Salinas River (lat. 36°44'55" N, long. 121°47'55" W). Named on Marina (1947) 7.5' quadrangle. Called Cabeza de Milligan on a diseño of Bolsa del Potrero y Moro Cojo grant (Becker, 1964). The feature for a long time was called Mulligan's Head for John Milligan, an Irish sailor who arrived in California before 1819 and became part owner of the land grant that includes the hill (Gudde, 1949, p. 228).

Mulligan's Head: see **Mulligan Hill** [MONTEREY].

Munch Canyon [SANTA CRUZ]: *canyon,* drained by a stream that flows 2.5 miles to Davey Brown Creek nearly 4 miles south-southwest of Bald Mountain (1) (lat. 34°45'35" N, long. 119°57'15" W). Named on Bald Mountain (1964) and Figueroa Mountain (1959) 7.5' quadrangles.

Mungo: see **Point Sur** [MONTEREY].

Municipal Baths Springs: see **Paso Robles** [SAN LUIS OBISPO].

Murphy Crossing [MONTEREY-SANTA

CRUZ]: *locality,* 2.25 miles northwest of Aromas along Pajaro River on Monterey-Santa Cruz county line (lat. 36°54'20" N, long. 121°40'30" W). Named on Watsonville East (1955) 7.5' quadrangle.

Murphy Flat [SAN BENITO]: *area,* 7 miles west-northwest of Bitterwater (lat. 36°24'25" N, long. 121°07'15" W; sec. 32, T 17 S, R 8 E). Named on North Chalone Peak (1969) and Topo Valley (1969) 7.5' quadrangles.

Murphy Hill [SAN LUIS OBISPO]: *hill,* 2 miles west-northwest of Shandon near the mouth of McMillan Canyon (lat. 35°39'50" N, long. 120°24'35" W; sec. 13, T 26 S, R 14 E). Altitude 1268 feet. Named on Shandon (1961) 7.5' quadrangle.

Murray: see **La Salle** [SANTA BARBARA].

Murray Creek: see **Murry Creek** [MONTEREY].

Murry Creek [MONTEREY]: *stream,* flows 5 miles to Jolon Creek just east of Jolon (lat. 35°58'15" N, long. 121°10'15" W). Named on Jolon (1949) 7.5' quadrangle. On Bryson (1919) 15' quadrangle, the name "Argyle Creek" applies to present Murry Creek and to the lower part of Jolon Creek below its junction with Murry Creek. Howard (p. 75) called the stream Murray Creek, and stated that apparently it was named for brothers Carl Murray and Ernest Murray, who lived north of Jolon.

Muscio [SANTA BARBARA]: *locality,* 6 miles southeast of Santa Maria (lat. 34°54'15" N, long. 120°20'50" W; at W line sec. 34, T 10 N, R 33 W). Named on Santa Maria (1947) 15' quadrangle.

Muscle Point: see **Mussel Point** [MONTEREY].

Musick [SAN LUIS OBISPO]: *locality,* 12.5 miles north-northeast of the town of Nipomo along Arroyo Grande Creek (lat. 35°12'25" N, long. 120°23'55" W; near SW cor. sec. 20, T 31 S, R 15 E). Named on Nipomo (1922) 15' quadrangle. Postal authorities established Musick post office in 1880 and discontinued it in 1921 (Frickstad, p. 165). The name commemorates an early landowner in the neighborhood (Angel, 1883, p. 354).

Mussel Point [MONTEREY]: *promontory,* 2 miles southeast of Point Pinos along the coast (lat. 36°37'20" N, long. 121°54'15" W). Named on Monterey (1947) 7.5' quadrangle. Called Point Cabrillo on Monterey (1947, photorevised 1968) 7.5' quadrangle. Blake (1856, p. 391) referred to "Point Almeja, or Muscle Point." Davidson (1907, p. 31) mentioned that a chart of surveys made in 1851 and 1852 has the designation "Almeja or Mussel Rock" for "the principal jutting point between the presidio and Point of Pines." United States Board on Geographic Names (1936a, p. 10) approved the name "Point Cabrillo" for the feature and rejected the names "China Point" and "Mussel Point"— the name "Point Cabrillo" was given because Cabrillo is thought to have landed at the place in 1542.

Mussel Point [SANTA BARBARA]: *promon-tory,* 6 miles west-southwest of the town of Guadalupe along the coast (lat. 34°55'45" N, long. 120°40' W). Named on Point Sal (1958) 7.5' quadrangle.

Mussel Rock [SANTA BARBARA]: *rock,* 6 miles west-southwest of the town of Guadalupe (lat. 34°55'45" N, long. 120°39'55" W); the feature is at Mussel Point. Named on Point Sal (1958) 7.5' quadrangle.

Mussel Rock: see **Mussel Point** [MONTEREY].

Mustang Canyon [SANTA BARBARA]: *canyon,* drained by a stream that flows 5.5 miles to Cuyama Valley 4 miles east-northeast of Miranda Pine Mountain (lat. 35°03' N, long. 119°58' W). Named on Bates Canyon (1964) and Taylor Canyon (1959) 7.5' quadrangles.

Mustang Peak [MONTEREY]: *peak,* 5 miles north of Parkfield on Monterey-Fresno county line (lat. 35°58'30" N, long. 120°24'45" W; sec. 36, T 22 S, R 14 E). Named on Parkfield (1961) 7.5' quadrangle.

Mustang Ridge [MONTEREY]: *ridge,* northwest-trending, 16 miles long, northeast of Peach Tree Valley (lat. 36°13'30" N, long. 120° 48'30" W). Named on Hepsedam Peak (1969), Lonoak (1969), Monarch Peak (1967), and Priest Valley (1969) 7.5' quadrangles.

Mustang Spring [SAN LUIS OBISPO]: *spring,* 21 miles east-northeast of Pozo (lat. 35°24'30" N, long. 120°01'10" W; sec. 14, T 29 S, R 18 E). Named on La Panza NE (1966) 7.5' quadrangle.

Mustard Creek [SAN LUIS OBISPO]: *stream,* flows 4 miles to Salinas River 2.5 miles north of Paso Robles (lat. 35°39'55" N, long. 120°41'40" W; near E line sec. 17, T 26 S, R 12 E). Named on Paso Robles (1948) 7.5' quadrangle.

– N –

Nacimento River: see **Nacimiento River** [MONTEREY-SAN LUIS OBISPO].

Nacimiento [MONTEREY]: *locality,* 5 miles southeast of Bradley along Southern Pacific Railroad (lat. 35°48'35" N, long. 120° 45' W; sec. 26, T 24 S, R 11 E). Named on San Miguel (1948) 7.5' quadrangle. The railroad station at the place was named in 1905 for Nacimiento River (Gudde, 1949, p. 230).

Nacimiento: see **Camp Nacimiento** [MONTEREY].

Nacimiento Reservoir [SAN LUIS OBISPO]: *lake,* behind a dam on Nacimiento River 5.5 miles east of Tierra Redonda Mountain (lat. 35°45'30" N, long. 120°53' W; sec. 15, T 25 S, R 10 E). Named on Bryson (1949, photorevised 1979), Lime Mountain (1948, photorevised 1979), Pebblestone Shut-in (1959), and Tierra Redonda Mountain (1949, photorevised 1979) 7.5' quadrangles. United States Board on Geographic Names (1979a, p. 7) approved the name "Lake Nacimiento" for the feature.

Nacimiento River [MONTEREY-SAN LUIS OBISPO]: *stream,* heads in Monterey County and flows 70 miles, partly in San Luis Obispo County, to Salinas River 3.25 miles southeast of Bradley in Monterey County (lat. 35°50' N, long. 120°45'20" W; sec. 23, T 24 S, R 11 E). Named on Alder Peak (1949), Bradley (1949), Bryson (1949), Burnette Peak (1949), Cape San Martin (1949), Cone Peak (1949), Jolon (1949), Lime Mountain (1948), Pebblestone Shut-in (1959), and Tierra Redonda Mountain (1949) 7.5' quadrangles. Present Nacimiento River is called Nacismento R. on Goddard's (1857) map, and is called Sierra River on Diller and others' (1915) map. The river is identified as Rio de la Sierra on a diseño of San Miguelito de Trinidad grant made in 1841 (Becker, 1964). Whitney (p. 145) mentioned Nascimiento River, Fairbanks (1893, p. 72) noted Nacimento River, Nutter (p. 335) referred to Nacimiento Creek, and Trask (p. 21) used the name "Nacismiento River." According to Gudde (1949, p. 230), members of the Portola expedition camped by the stream in 1769 and Crespi described it as a very large arroyo whose source (*nacimiento* in Spanish) was nearby; later Anza saw the river and apparently believed that the stream had been given the name "Nacimiento," perhaps with the meaning "nativity." According to Smith (p. 3), the Portola expedition called the river Rio de las Truchas. United States Board on Geographic Names (1933, p. 540) rejected the names "Nacimento River" and "Sierra River" for the stream. Nigger Fork enters 58 miles upstream from the mouth of the river; it is 4 miles long and is named on Cape San Martin (1949) 7.5' quadrangle. Clark (1991, p. 356) associated the name of the fork with Mary L.C. Norman, known locally as Nigger Mary, who settled along the stream in 1919.

Nacimiento Summer Camp [MONTEREY]: *locality,* 5 miles west of Lopez Point (lat. 36°01'10" N, long. 121°28'30" W; sec. 13, T 22 S, R 4 E). Named on Junipero Serra (1940) 15' quadrangle.

Nacional [MONTEREY]: *land grant,* 2 miles southwest of Salinas. Named on Salinas (1947) 7.5' quadrangle. Vicente Cantua received 2 leagues in 1839 and claimed 6633 acres patented in 1866 (Cowan, p. 50-51).

Naples [SANTA BARBARA]: *locality,* 5 miles west-northwest of Coal Oil Point along Southern Pacific Railroad (lat. 34°26'25" N, long. 119°57'30" W). Named on Dos Pueblos Canyon (1951) 7.5' quadrangle. Postal authorities established Naples post office in 1890 and discontinued it in 1923 (Frickstad, p. 171).

Napoma: see **Nipomo** [SAN LUIS OBISPO] (1).

Napoma Ridge: see **Nipomo Valley** [SAN LUIS OBISPO],

Narlon [SANTA BARBARA]: *locality,* 4.25

miles west-southwest of the village of Casmalia along Southern Pacific Railroad (lat. 34°48'35" N, long. 120°35'50" W). Named on Casmalia (1959) 7.5' quadrangle.

Narrows: see **The Narrows** [MONTEREY]; **The Narrows** [SANTA BARBARA].

Narrows Campground [SANTA BARBARA]: *locality,* 4 miles south of Big Pine Mountain along Indian Creek (lat. 34°38'20" N, long. 119°39'05" W). Named on Big Pine Mountain (1964) 7.5' quadrangle.

Nashua [MONTEREY]: *locality,* 4.5 miles north-northeast of Marina along Southern Pacific Railroad (lat. 36°44'30" N, long. 121°45'50" W). Named on Marina (1947) 7.5' quadrangle.

Nasimento: see **Bradley** [MONTEREY].

Natividad [MONTEREY]: *settlement,* 5 miles northeast of Salinas (lat. 36°44' N, long. 121°35'45" W); the place is on La Natividad grant. Named on Natividad (1947) 7.5' quadrangle. Postal authorities established Natividad post office in 1855 and discontinued it in 1908 (Frickstad, p. 108). According to Clark (1991, p. 259), Natividad post office first was at a travellers stop called Gavilan House that was situated by Lagunita Lake. Natividad was a flourishing stage station in the 1850's before traffic was routed through Salinas (Hoover, Rensch, and Rensch, p. 225).

Natividad Creek [MONTEREY]: *stream,* flows 5 miles to an artificial watercourse at the northeast edge of Salinas (lat. 36°41'30" N, long. 121°37'05" W); the stream is mainly on La Natividad grant. Named on Natividad (1947) 7.5' quadrangle. Salinas (1912) 15' quadrangle shows the stream ending in a marsh.

Natoma: see **Camp Natoma** [SAN LUIS OBISPO].

Nattrass Valley [MONTEREY]: *canyon,* nearly 5 miles long, opens into Wildhorse Canyon from the east 12 miles north-northwest of San Ardo (lat. 36°11'30" N, long. 120°57'35" W; sec. 14, T 20 S, R 9 E). Named on Nattrass Valley (1967) 7.5' quadrangle. The name commemorates the Nattrass family, early landowners in the neighborhood (Clark, 1991, p. 354).

Navajo [SAN LUIS OBISPO]: *locality,* 7.5 miles northeast of Pozo (lat. 35°22'45" N, long. 120°16'50" W; sec. 29, T 29 S, R 16 E); the place is by Navajo Creek. Named on Pozo (1922) 15' quadrangle.

Navajoa Creek: see **Navajo Creek** [SAN LUIS OBISPO].

Navajo Campground [SAN LUIS OBISPO]: *locality,* nearly 6 miles northeast of Pozo along McGinnis Creek (lat. 35°22'10" N, long. 120°18'40" W; sec. 25, T 29 S, R 15 E). Named on Pozo Summit (1967) 7.5' quadrangle.

Navajo Creek [SAN LUIS OBISPO]: *stream,* flows 15 miles to San Juan Creek 10 miles east of Wilson Corner (lat. 35°30' N, long. 120°12' W; near S line sec. 12, T 28 S, R 16

E). Named on Camatta Ranch (1966), La Panza Ranch (1966), and Pozo Summit (1967) 7.5' quadrangles. Anderson and Martin (p. 49) used the name "Navajoa Creek" for the stream.

Neals Spring [SAN LUIS OBISPO]: *spring,* 4.5 miles south-southeast of Paso Robles (lat. 35°34'30" N, long. 120°38'50" W). Named on Templeton (1948) 7.5' quadrangle.

Nearys Lagoon [SANTA CRUZ]: *marsh,* nearly 1 mile north-northwest of Point Santa Cruz in Santa Cruz (lat. 36°57'50" N, long. 122°01'50" W). Named on Santa Cruz (1954) 7.5' quadrangle.

Needle Rock Point [SANTA CRUZ]: *relief feature,* 4.5 miles west of Point Santa Cruz along the coast (lat. 36°57'20" N, long. 122°06'20" W). Named on Santa Cruz (1954) 7.5' quadrangle. A slender pillar of rock stands a short distance seaward from the face of cliffs at the place (United States Coast and Geodetic Survey, p. 121).

Nelson Creek [MONTEREY]: *stream,* flows 5 miles to Big Sandy Creek 18 miles east of San Ardo (lat. 36°00'40" N, long. 120°34'55" W; sec. 16, T 22 S, R 13 E). Named on Smith Mountain (1969) and Stockdale Mountain (1948) 7.5' quadrangles. A map of Monterey County used about 1900 has the name "Nelson's Cr." for present Big Sandy Creek above the place that Big Sandy Creek enters Indian Valley.

Nelson Flat [MONTEREY]: *area,* nearly 7 miles south-southeast of Jolon (lat. 35°53'15" N, long. 121°06'45" W; sec. 33, T 23 S, R 8 E). Named on Williams Hill (1949) 7.5' quadrangle.

Neponset [MONTEREY]: *locality,* 8.5 miles west-northwest of Salinas along Southern Pacific Railroad (lat. 36°43'45" N, long. 121°47' W). Named on Marina (1947) 7.5' quadrangle. The place was called Martin Station before about 1900 (Gudde, 1949, p. 233). The name "Neponset" is an Indian one that was transferred from Massachusetts (Clark, 1991, p. 355).

New Cuyama [SANTA BARBARA]: *town,* 4.25 miles west of the village of Cuyama (lat. 34°56'50" N, long. 119°41'15" W); the place is in Cuyama Valley. Named on New Cuyama (1964) 7.5' quadrangle. Postal authorities established New Cuyama post office in 1953; Richfield Oil Company built the town in 1938 for their employees (Salley, p. 153).

Newell Creek [SANTA CRUZ]: *stream,* flows 7.5 miles to San Lorenzo River nearly 4 miles southeast of the town of Boulder Creek (lat. 37°04'50" N, long. 122°04'45" W; sec. 9, T 10 S, R 2 W). Named on Castle Rock Ridge (1955) and Felton (1955) 7.5' quadrangles. The name is for Addison Newell, who owned land along the stream in the 1860's (Clark, 1986, p. 228).

Newell Creek Reservoir: see **Loch Lomond** [SANTA CRUZ].

Newell Lake: see **Loch Lomond** [SANTA CRUZ].

New Felton: see **Felton** [SANTA CRUZ].

New Idria: see **Idria** [SAN BENITO].

Newlove Hill [SANTA BARBARA]: *peak,* 3 miles southeast of Orcutt on Graciosa Ridge (lat. 34°50'05" N, long. 120°24'10" W). Named on Orcutt (1959) 7.5' quadrangle.

New Mill Canyon [SAN BENITO]: *canyon,* drained by a stream that flows 2.5 miles to Topo Valley 5.5 miles northwest of Bitterwater (lat. 36°26'30" N, long. 121°04' W; sec. 23, T 17 S, R 8 E). Named on Topo Valley (1969) 7.5' quadrangle.

New Monterey: see **Monterey** [MONTEREY].

New Republic: see **Santa Rita** [MONTEREY].

New River [SAN LUIS OBISPO]: *stream,* flows 4.25 miles to Cuyama River 2 miles northnortheast of New Cuyama [SANTA BARBARA] (lat. 34°58'25" N, long. 119°40'15" W). Named on Cuyama (1964) and New Cuyama (1964) 7.5' quadrangles.

Newsom Canyon [SAN LUIS OBISPO]: *canyon,* drained by a stream that flows 2 miles to Guaya Canyon nearly 2 miles east of downtown Arroyo Grande (lat. 35°07'05" N, long. 120°33'05" W); the canyon is south of Newsom Ridge. Named on Arroyo Grande NE (1965) and Oceano (1965) 7.5' quadrangles.

Newsome Canyon [SANTA BARBARA]: *canyon,* drained by a stream that flows 6 miles to Branch Canyon 4.25 miles south of New Cuyama (lat. 34°53'50" N, long. 119°41'35" W; near NE cor. sec. 6, T 9 N, R 26 W). Named on New Cuyama (1964) and Salisbury Potrero (1964) 7.5' quadrangles.

Newsome Spring: see **Lower Newsome Spring** [SANTA BARBARA]; **Upper Newsome Spring** [SANTA BARBARA].

Newsom Ridge [SAN LUIS OBISPO]: *ridge,* west-trending, 7 miles long, 5.5 miles north of the town of Nipomo (lat. 35°07'15" N, long. 120°29'30" W). Named on Arroyo Grande NE (1965), Nipomo (1965), and Oceano (1965) 7.5' quadrangles.

Newsom's Arroyo Grande Springs: see **Newsom Springs** [SAN LUIS OBISPO].

Newsoms Arroyo Grande Warm Springs: see **Newsom Springs** [SAN LUIS OBISPO].

Newsom Springs [SAN LUIS OBISPO]: *spring,* 2 miles east of downtown Arroyo Grande (lat. 35°07'20" N, long. 120°32'35" W); the feature is in Newsom Canyon. Named on Oceano (1965) 7.5' quadrangle. D.F. Newsom homesteaded at the place in 1864; a resort called Newsom's Arroyo Grande Warm Springs used water from the spring (Logan, p. 694). Winslow Anderson (p. 207-208) referred to the resort as Newsom's Arroyo Grande Springs, and G.A. Waring (p. 68-69) referred to it as Newsoms Arroyo Grande Warm Spring.

New Springs: see **Iron Spring** [SAN LUIS OBISPO] (1).

New Town: see **Santa Ynez** [SANTA BARBARA].

New Year Creek: see **Año Nuevo Creek** [SANTA CRUZ].

Nifty Rock [SANTA BARBARA]: *rock,* 5 miles northwest of Cardwell Point, and 350 feet offshore on the north side of San Miguel Island (lat. 34°04'20" N, long. 120°21'35" W). Named on San Miguel Island East (1950) 7.5' quadrangle.

Nigger Fork: see **Nacimiento River** [MONTEREY].

Nigger Hill [MONTEREY]: *hill,* 12 miles northeast of San Ardo in Peachtree Valley (lat. 36°09'45" N, long. 120°46'40" W). Named on San Ardo (1956) 15' quadrangle. Clark (1991, p. 357) related the name to a Negro who was killed when he lost control of a loaded wagon on the hill.

Nimpomo: see **Nipomo** [SAN LUIS OBISPO] (1).

Nimrod Canyon [SAN BENITO]: *canyon,* drained by a stream that flows nearly 2 miles to San Benito River 7 miles south-southwest of Idria (lat. 36°19'50" N, long. 120°44'10" W; sec. 26, T 18 S, R 11 E). Named on Hepsedam Peak (1969) and San Benito Mountain (1969) 7.5' quadrangles.

Nineteen Oaks [SANTA BARBARA]: *locality,* nearly 6 miles northeast of San Marcos Pass (lat. 34°34'20" N, long. 119°45'10" W; at W line sec. 29, T 6 N, R 27 W). Named on San Marcos Pass (1959) 7.5' quadrangle.

Nipoma: see **Nipomo** [SAN LUIS OBISPO] (1) and (2).

Nipomo [SAN LUIS OBISPO]:
(1) *land grant,* at and around Nipomo Valley and Nipomo Mesa. Named on Guadalupe (1959), Huasna Peak (1967), Nipomo (1965), Oceano (1965), and Santa Maria (1959) 7.5' quadrangles. William G. Dana received 15 leagues in 1837 and claimed 37,888 acres patented in 1868 (Cowan, p. 52). Parke's (1854-1855) map has the name "Rcho. Napoma," and Whitney (p. 138) referred to Nipoma Ranch. United States Board on Geographic Names (1933, p. 554) rejected the forms "Nimpomo" and "Nipoma" for the name, which is from an Indian village (Kroeber, 1916, p. 50)—the word is said to have the meaning "foot of the mountain" (Hoover, Rensch, and Rensch, p. 386).
(2) *town,* 7.5 miles southeast of the town of Arroyo Grande (lat. 35° 02'35" N, long. 120°28'30" W); the town is in Nipomo Valley on Nipomo grant. Named on Nipomo (1965) 7.5' quadrangle. The heirs of William G. Dana had the town laid out in 1889 (Gudde, 1949, p. 237). Postal authorities established Nipoma post office in 1883, discontinued it in 1885, reestablished it in 1886, and changed the name to Nipomo in 1887 (Frickstad, p. 165).

Nipomo Creek [SAN LUIS OBISPO]: *stream,* flows 9 miles to Santa Maria River 4 miles south-southeast of the town of Nipomo (lat.

34°59'40" N, long. 120°26'20" W). Named on Nipomo (1965), Oceano (1965), and Santa Maria (1959) 7.5' quadrangles.

Nipomo Hill [SAN LUIS OBISPO]: *peak,* 1.5 miles south of downtown Arroyo Grande (lat. 35°06' N, long. 120°34'40" W); the peak is at the north end of Nipomo Mesa. Altitude 409 feet. Named on Oceano (1965) 7.5' quadrangle.

Nipomo Mesa [SAN LUIS OBISPO]: *area,* southeast of the town of Arroyo Grande between Santa Maria Valley and Nipomo Valley. Named on Nipomo (1965) and Oceano (1965) 7.5' quadrangles. Called The Mesa on Santa Maria (1959) 7.5' quadrangle, but United States Board on Geographic Names (1966, p. 5) rejected this name for the place.

Nipomo Valley [SAN LUIS OBISPO]: *valley,* at and near the town of Nipomo along Nipomo Creek. Named on Nipomo (1965) and Oceano (1965) 7.5' quadrangles. Parke (p. 6) used the name "Napoma Ridge" for the ridge situated between present Nipomo Valley and Huasna Valley; Parke's (1854-1855) map has the name "Sierra Napoma" for the same feature.

Nira Campground [SANTA BARBARA]: *locality,* 3 miles south of Bald Mountain (1) along Manzana Creek (lat. 34°46'15" N, long. 119°56'15" W). Named on Bald Mountain (1964) 7.5' quadrangle.

Noche Buena [MONTEREY]: *land grant,* at and northeast of Seaside near the coast. Named on Marina (1947) and Seaside (1947) 7.5' quadrangles. Juan Antonio Muñoz received 1 league in 1835; J. and J. de Monomany claimed 4412 acres patented in 1862 (Cowan, p. 40; Cowan gave the name "Huerta de la Nacion" as an alternate).

Nojoqui [SANTA BARBARA]: *land grant,* south of Solvang. Named on Santa Ynez 1959) and Solvang (1959) 7.5' quadrangles. Raimundo Carrillo received 3 leagues in 1843 and claimed 13,285 acres patented in 1869 (Cowan, p. 53; Cowan used the name "Nojoque" for the grant). The name seems to be of Indian origin (Kroeber, 1916, p. 50).

Nojoqui: see **Las Cruces** [SANTA BARBARA] (2).

Nojoqui Creek [SANTA BARBARA]: *stream,* flows 8.5 miles to Santa Ynez River 0.5 mile south of Buellton (lat. 34°36'20" N, long. 120°11'35" W). Named on Solvang (1959) 7.5' quadrangle. The canyon of the stream is called Cañada de Na-joa-ui on a diseño of Las Cruces grant made in 1835 (Becker, 1964).

Nojoqui Falls [SANTA BARBARA]: *waterfall,* 6 miles south of Buellton (lat. 34°31'40" N, long. 120°10'15" W; near W line sec. 7, T 5 N, R 31 W); the feature is along Nojoqui Creek. Named on Solvang (1959) 7.5' quadrangle.

Nojoqui Pass: see **Nojoqui Summit** [SANTA BARBARA].

Nojoqui Summit [SANTA BARBARA]: *pass,* 6 miles south of Buellton (lat. 34°31'40" N, long. 120°11'45" W; sec. 11, T 5 N, R 32 W). Named on Solvang (1959) 7.5' quadrangle. Called Gaviota Pass on Lompoc (1905) 30' quadrangle. Hanna (p. 213) called the feature Nojoqui Pass.

Noon Peak [SANTA BARBARA]: *peak,* 6.5 miles north of Rincon Point (lat. 34°28'10" N, long. 119°28'25" W; sec. 35, T 5 N, R 25 W). Altitude 4084 feet. Named on White Ledge Peak (1952) 7.5' quadrangle.

Norn Hill [SAN LUIS OBISPO]: *peak,* 1 mile west-northwest of downtown Paso Robles (lat. 35°38'15" N, long. 120°42'25" W). Altitude 1125 feet. Named on Paso Robles (1948) 7.5' quadrangle.

North Beach Campground [SAN LUIS OBISPO]: *locality,* 1 mile south-southeast of Pismo beach (lat. 35°07'50" N, long. 120° 38' W). Named on Pismo Beach (1965) 7.5' quadrangle.

North Canyon [SAN BENITO]: *canyon,* drained by a stream that flows 2.25 miles to Bird Creek 5.5 miles south-southwest of Hollister (lat. 36°46'25" N, long. 121°25'45" W). Named on Hollister (1955) 7.5' quadrangle.

North Chalone Peak [MONTEREY-SAN BENITO]: *peak,* 9 miles north-northeast of Greenfield on Monterey-San Benito county line (lat. 36°26'50" N, long. 121°11'40" W; sec. 15, T 17 S, R 7 E); the peak is 1 mile northwest of South Chalone Peak. Altitude 3304 feet. Named on North Chalone Peak (1969) 7.5' quadrangle. North Chalone Peak and South Chalone Peak together have the name "Chalone Mtn." on Metz (1921) 15' quadrangle. Parke's (1854-1855) map shows Mt. Chelone. The word "Chalone" is from a group of Indians who lived near the peak; an early Spanish map has the name "Cierro Chalon" (Gudde, 1949, p. 63).

North Entrance Rock [SAN LUIS OBISPO]: *rock,* 100 feet long, 0.5 mile south of the village of San Simeon, and 250 feet offshore near San Simeon Point (lat. 35°38'05" N, long. 120°11'30" W). Named on San Simeon (1958) 7.5' quadrangle.

North Grizzly Bend Creek [SAN LUIS OBISPO]: *stream,* flows 1.5 miles to present Nacimiento Reservoir 11 miles northeast of the village of San Simeon (lat. 35°45'10" N, long. 121°03'05" W; near W line sec. 18, T 25 S, R 9 E); the mouth of the creek is at Grizzly Bend. Named on Bryson (1949) 7.5' quadrangle.

North Hill [SAN BENITO]: *peak,* 1.5 miles south-southeast of Idria (lat. 36°23'50" N, long. 120°39'35" W; near N line sec. 4, T 18 S, R 12 E); the feature is 0.5 mile north-north-west of San Carlos Peak. Altitude 4658 feet. Named on Idria (1969) 7.5' quadrangle.

North Mine Canyon Spring [SANTA BARBARA]: *spring,* 2.5 miles west-northwest of Montgomery Potrero (lat. 34°51'05" N, long. 119°47'30" W); the spring is 1 mile west-northwest of East Mine Canyon Spring in a branch of Mine Canyon (3). Named on Hurricane Deck (1964) 7.5' quadrangle.

North Point: see **Cypress Cove** [MONTEREY].

North Santa Maria [SANTA BARBARA]: *locality,* in the west part of the city of Santa Maria along Santa Maria Valley Railroad (lat. 34°57'20" N, long. 120°26'35" W; sec. 10, T 10 N, R 34 W). Named on Santa Maria (1959) 7.5' quadrangle.

Northwest Anchorage [SANTA BARBARA]: *anchorage,* 1.5 miles south of Carrington Point on the north side of Santa Rosa Island in Beecher Bay (lat. 34°00'55" N, long. 120°02'50" W). Named on Santa Rosa Island North (1943) 7.5' quadrangle.

Notleys Landing [MONTEREY]: *locality,* 6.5 miles north of Point Sur near the mouth of Palo Colorado Canyon (lat. 36°23'50" N, long. 121°54'15" W; sec. 6, T 18 S, R 1 E). Named on Soberanes Point (1956) 7.5' quadrangle. A village sprang up at the place after Godfrey Notley built a landing for the shipment of tanbark and lumber (Fink, p. 210). Shipping activity at the place lasted from 1898 until 1907 (Lussier, p. 13).

Nova: see **Thyle** [SAN LUIS OBISPO].

Nuestra Señora del Refugio [SANTA BARBARA]: *land grant,* east and west of Gaviota along the coast. Named on Gaviota (1953), Point Conception (1953), Sacate (1953), Santa Rosa Hills (1959), and Tajiguas (1953) 7.5' quadrangles. Jose Francisco Ortega received 6 leagues in 1795; Antonio Maria Ortega got the land in 1834 and claimed 26,529 acres patented in 1866 (Cowan, p. 67).

– O –

Oak Canyon [SANTA BARBARA]:
(1) *canyon,* drained by a stream that flows 3.5 miles to Sisquoc River 2.5 miles northeast of Bald Mountain (1) (lat. 34°50' N, long. 119°54' W). Named on Bald Mountain (1964) 7.5' quadrangle.
(2) *canyon,* drained by a stream that flows 3.25 miles to Santa Ynez River 4.5 miles east of Surf (lat. 34°40'50" N, long. 120°31'30" W). Named on Surf (1959) 7.5' quadrangle.

Oak Creek [SANTA BARBARA]: *stream,* flows 2.5 miles to the sea 4 miles east of downtown Santa Barbara (lat. 34°25'10" N, long. 119°37'35" W). Named on Santa Barbara (1952) 7.5' quadrangle. United States Board on Geographic Names (1961b, p. 13) rejected the name "Arroyo del Tulare" for the stream.

Oak Flat [MONTEREY]: *area,* 7.5 miles south of Jolon (lat. 35°51'35" N, long. 121°11'40" W). Named on Burnett Peak (1949) 7.5' quadrangle.

Oak Flat: see **Big Oak Flat** [SAN BENITO]; **Big Sandy Creek** [MONTEREY]; **Little Oak Flat** [MONTEREY].

Oak Grove Canyon [MONTEREY]: *canyon,* 3

miles long, drained by a stream that enters California Flats 6.25 miles east-southeast of Parkfield (lat. 35°51'05" N, long. 120°20'05" W). Named on Cholame Valley (1961) 7.5' quadrangle.

Oak Knoll [SAN LUIS OBISPO]: *peak,* 3 miles west-northwest of the village of San Simeon (lat. 35°39'50" N, long. 121°14'20" W). Named on San Simeon (1958) 7.5' quadrangle.

Oak Knoll Creek [SAN LUIS OBISPO]: *stream,* flows 3.25 miles to the sea nearly 1.5 miles west-northwest of the village of San Simeon (lat. 35°39'05" N, long. 121°13'05" W). Named on San Simeon (1958) 7.5' quadrangle.

Oak Mountain [SANTA BARBARA]: *peak,* 4 miles east-southeast of Tranquillon Mountain (lat. 34°33'05" N, long. 120°30'05" W). Altitude 2014 feet. Named on Lompoc Hills (1959) and Tranquillon Mountain (1959) 7.5' quadrangles.

Oak Park [SAN LUIS OBISPO]: *district,* in the north part of Paso Robles (lat. 35°38'55" N, long. 120°41'25" W). Named on Paso Robles (1948) 7.5' quadrangle.

Oak Ridge [SAN LUIS OBISPO]: *ridge,* west-northwest-trending, nearly 1 mile long, 5 miles east-southeast of York Mountain (lat. 35°30'25" N, long. 120°45'30" W). Named on Adelaida (1961) 15' quadrangle.

Oak Ridge [SANTA CRUZ]: *ridge,* south-trending, 1.25 miles long, 6.5 miles northeast of the town of Boulder Creek (lat. 37°12' N, long. 122°03'15" W). Named on Castle Rock Ridge (1955) 7.5' quadrangle.

Oaks [SAN LUIS OBISPO]: *district,* on the west side of the town of Arroyo Grande (lat. 35°07' N, long. 120°35'45" W). Named on Oceano (1965) 7.5' quadrangle. Called Fairoaks on Arroyo Grande (1942) 15' quadrangle. Postal authorities established Oaks post office in 1949 (Salley, p. 158).

Oaks: see **The Oaks** [SAN LUIS OBISPO].

Oak Spring [SANTA BARBARA]: *spring,* 4.5 miles southeast of Salisbury Potrero (lat. 34°46'25" N, long. 119°38'55" W). Named on Salisbury Potrero (1964) 7.5' quadrangle.

Oak Tree Spring [SAN BENITO]: *spring,* 3 miles north of North Chalone Peak (lat. 36°29'20" N, long. 121°12'15" W; near SW cor. sec. 34, T 16 S, R 7 E). Named on North Chalone Peak (1969) 7.5' quadrangle.

Oat Canyon [SAN BENITO]: *canyon,* drained by a stream that flows 6 miles to Lewis Creek 16 miles southeast of Bitterwater (lat. 36°13'45" N, long. 120°47' W; sec. 33, T 19 S, R 11 E). Named on Hepsedam Peak (1969) and Monarch Peak (1967) 7.5' quadrangles. North Fork branches northwest 2.25 miles upstream from the mouth of the main canyon; it is 3 miles long and is named on Hepsedam Peak (1969) 7.5' quadrangle.

Oat Hills [MONTEREY]: *ridge,* north-trending, 1.25 miles long, 9.5 miles southwest of King

City (lat. 36°05'50" N, long. 121°13'40" W). Named on Cosio Knob (1949) 7.5' quadrangle.

Obispo Peak: see **Bishop Peak** [SAN LUIS OBISPO].

O'Brien Lake [SAN LUIS OBISPO]: *intermittent lake,* 750 feet long, 5.25 miles southeast of Cholame (lat. 35°40'25" N, long. 120°13'40" W; near SW cor. sec. 11, T 26 S, R 16 E). Named on Orchard Peak (1961) 7.5' quadrangle.

Oceano [SAN LUIS OBISPO]: *town,* 2 miles southwest of downtown Arroyo Grande near the coast (lat. 35°06'10" N, long. 120°36'30" W). Named on Oceano (1965) 7.5' quadrangle. Postal authorities established Oceano post office in 1895 (Frickstad, p. 165).

Oceano Beach [SAN LUIS OBISPO]: *locality,* 0.5 mile north of the mouth of Arroyo Grande Creek (lat. 35°06'15" N, long. 120°37'45" W); the place is west of Oceano. Named on Arroyo Grande (1942) 15' quadrangle.

Ocean View Summit [SANTA CRUZ]: *peak,* 1.5 miles north-northwest of Big Basin (lat. 37°11'25" N, long. 122°14' W; sec. 31, T 8 S, R 3 W). Altitude 1685 feet. Named on Big Basin (1955) 7.5' quadrangle.

Oil Canyon [SANTA BARBARA]:
(1) *canyon,* drained by a stream that flows 2.25 miles to Horse Canyon (3) 6.5 miles east-northeast of Santa Ynez Peak (lat. 34°34'25" N, long. 119°52'35" W). Named on San Marcos Pass (1959) 7.5' quadrangle.
(2) *canyon,* drained by a stream that flows 2.25 miles to Arroyo Paredon 3 miles north-north-west of Carpinteria (lat. 34°26'05" N, long. 119°32'55" W; near NE cor. sec. 13, T 4 N, R 26 W). Named on Carpinteria (1952) 7.5' quadrangle.

Oil Creek [SANTA CRUZ]: *stream,* flows 1.25 miles to San Mateo County 9.5 miles east-north of the town of Boulder Creek (lat. 37°15'35" N, long. 122°09'05" W; at W line sec. 1, T 8 S, R 3 W). Named on Mindego Hill (1961) 7.5' quadrangle.

Oilport: see **San Luis Obispo Bay** [SAN LUIS OBISPO].

Oil Well Canyon [SAN LUIS OBISPO]: *canyon,* drained by a stream that flows nearly 2 miles to West Corral de Piedra Creek 3 miles south of Lopez Mountain (lat. 35°15'35" N, long. 120°35'05" W). Named on Lopez Mountain (1965) 7.5' quadrangle.

Oil Well Canyon [SANTA BARBARA]: *canyon,* drained by a stream that flows 2.5 miles to the sea 4 miles west-southwest of Tranquillon Mountain (lat. 34°33'20" N, long. 120°37'25" W). Named on Tranquillon Mountain (1959) 7.5' quadrangle.

Ojeda Canyon [SAN BENITO]: *canyon,* drained by a stream that flows 1.25 miles to an unnamed branch of South Fork Los Banos Creek 9 miles east-southeast of Potrero Peak (lat. 36°46'50" N, long. 121°00'30" W; near N line sec. 29, T 13 S, R 9 E). Named on Ruby

Canyon (1968) 7.5' quadrangle.

Old Canyon [SAN LUIS OBISPO]: *canyon,* 3 miles long, opens into the canyon of San Juan Creek 5.25 miles northeast of Castle Crags (lat. 35°21'35" N, long. 120°08'15" W; sec. 34, T 29 S, R 17 E). Named on California Valley (1966) and La Panza (1967) 7.5' quadrangles.

Old Cojo: see **Cojo Bay** [SANTA BARBARA].

Old Creek [SAN LUIS OBISPO]: *stream,* flows 10 miles to the sea at Cayucos (lat. 35°26'05" N, long. 120°53'10" W). Named on Morro Bay North (1965) and York Mountain (1948) 7.5' quadrangles.

Old Creek: see **Cayucos** [SAN LUIS OBISPO].

Old Felton: see **Felton** [SANTA CRUZ].

Old Hilltown [MONTEREY]: *locality,* 3 miles south-southwest of Salinas on the north bank of Salinas River (lat. 36°37'55" N, long. 121°40'05" W). Named on Salinas (1947) 7.5' quadrangle. A ford near the site of Hill Town was called Paso del Quinto; later Hill Town had one of the first ferries on Salinas River— the ferry operated until a bridge was built in 1889 (Hoover, Rensch, and Rensch, p. 228).

Old Man Canyon [MONTEREY]: *canyon,* drained by a stream that flows 1.5 miles to Ruby Canyon 2.5 miles north-northwest of Jolon (lat. 36°00'05" N, long. 121°11'50" W). Named on Cosio Knob (1949) 7.5' quadrangle. Waring and Bradley (p. 606) used the form "Old Man's Cañon" for the name.

Old Man Mountain [SANTA BARBARA]:
(1) *peak,* 9 miles north-northeast of Carpinteria (lat. 34°31' N, long. 119°27'05" W; sec. 13, T 5 N, R 25 W). Altitude 5525 feet. Named on Old Man Mountain (1943) 7.5' quadrangle.
(2) *ridge,* west-northwest-trending, 1 mile long, 7 miles north-northeast of San Marcos Pass (lat. 34°36'20" N, long. 119°46'30" W). Named on San Marcos Pass (1959) 7.5' quadrangle.

Old Park Mill: see **Blooms Mill** [SANTA CRUZ].

Olds: see **Mount Olds** [MONTEREY].

Old Salinas River [MONTEREY]: *water feature,* extends for 5 miles from near the mouth of Salinas River to near the mouth of Elkhorn Slough at Moss Landing (lat. 36°48'15" N, long. 121°47'10" W). Named on Moss Landing (1954) 7.5' quadrangle. Salinas River followed the feature to the sea north of Moss Landing before the winter of 1909 and 1910, when the river broke through coastal dunes to reach the sea 5.5 miles farther south (Clark, 1991, p. 363).

Old Spring: see **Iron Spring** [SAN LUIS OBISPO] (1).

Old Town [SANTA BARBARA]: *locality,* less than 1 mile northwest of downtown Carpinteria (lat. 34°24'10" N, long. 119°31'50" W). Named on Carpinteria (1952) 7.5' quadrangle.

Old Wagon Cave Campground [MONTEREY]: *locality,* 4.25 miles south of

Junipero Serra Peak (lat. 36°05'05" N, long. 121°24'05" W). Named on Junipero Serra (1961) 15' quadrangle.

Old Womans Creek [SANTA CRUZ]: *stream,* flows nearly 1 mile to San Mateo County 6.25 miles north-northwest of the mouth of Waddell Creek (lat. 37°10'55" N, long. 122°18'55" W; near W line sec. 4, T 9 S, R 4 W). Named on Franklin Point (1955) 7.5' quadrangle.

O'Leary: see **Tim O'Leary Canyon** [SAN LUIS OBISPO].

Olivas Canyon [SAN BENITO]: *canyon,* drained by a stream that flows 3 miles to Wildhorse Canyon 7.5 miles west-northwest of Bitterwater (lat. 36°26'20" N, long. 121°06'55" W; near W line sec. 21, T 17 S, R 8 E). Named on Topo Valley (1969) 7.5' quadrangle.

Olive Canyon [SANTA BARBARA]: *canyon,* drained by a stream that flows nearly 4 miles to Cuyama Valley 3 miles south of the village of Cuyama (lat. 34°53'25" N, long. 119°36'30" W; sec. 1, T 9 N, R 26 W). Named on Cuyama (1964) and Fox Mountain (1964) 7.5' quadrangles.

Olivera Canyon [SANTA BARBARA]: *canyon,* drained by a stream that flows 2.25 miles to Santa Maria Valley nearly 2 miles east-southeast of the village of Sisquoc (lat. 34°51'15" N, long. 120°15'55" W; sec. 17, T 9 N, R 32 W). Named on Foxen Canyon (1964) and Sisquoc (1959) 7.5' quadrangles.

Olive Spring [SANTA BARBARA]: *spring,* 2.5 miles north of Fox Mountain (lat. 34°51'10" N, long. 119°36'05" W); the spring is in Olive Canyon. Named on Fox Mountain (1964) 7.5' quadrangle.

Olive Springs [SANTA CRUZ]: *spring,* 5.5 miles north-northeast of Soquel (lat. 37°03'30" N, long. 121°55' W). Named on Laurel (1955) 7.5' quadrangle. On Los Gatos (1919) 15' quadrangle, the name applies to a group of buildings at the confluence of Soquel Creek and Hinckley Creek, 0.25 mile west-southwest of present Olive Springs. George Olive owned the place before 1897 (Clark, 1986, p. 237). Laizure (1926, p. 88) described a small unimproved cold spring called Hinns Sulphur Spring that was located near the top of Hinckley Ridge about 1 mile east of Olive Springs.

Oliviers Mountain: see **Puerta del Diablo** [MONTEREY].

Olmstead: see **Mount Olmstead** [MONTEREY].

Olson's Cave: see **Orzaba Pictograph Cave,** under **Twin Harbors** [SANTA BARBARA].

Olympia [SANTA CRUZ]: *settlement,* 5 miles southeast of the town of Boulder Creek along Zayante Creek (lat. 37°04'15" N, long. 122°03'25" W). Named on Felton (1955) 7.5' quadrangle. Postal authorities changed the name of Eccles post office to Olympia in 1915 and discontinued it in 1942 (Frickstad, p. 177).

One Suerte [MONTEREY]: *land grant,* nearly 5 miles west of Salinas; adjacent to Two Suertes grant. Named on Salinas (1947, photorevised 1968 and 1975) 7.5' quadrangle. The grant has the name "Chas. McFadden" on Salinas (1947) 7.5' quadrangle.

Ontario Hot Springs [SAN LUIS OBISPO]: *locality,* 1.5 miles east of Avila Beach (lat. 35°10'50" N, long. 120°42'10" W). Named on Pismo Beach (1965) 7.5' quadrangle. Called Hidden Valley Hot Springs on Arroyo Grande (1952) 15' quadrangle. Logan (p. 691) described a resort at the place that was called Budan Spring for the owner, Mrs. E. Budan, and noted that water at a temperature of 178° Fahrenheit flows from an artesian well drilled there in 1908.

Opal Cliffs [SANTA CRUZ]: *district,* at and northeast of Soquel Point near the coast (lat. 36°57'45" N, long. 121°57'50" W). Named on Soquel (1954) 7.5' quadrangle.

Opal Creek [SANTA CRUZ]: *stream,* flows nearly 4 miles to join Blooms Creek and form East Waddell Creek at the south end of Big Basin (lat. 37°09'55" N, long. 122°13'25" W; near E line sec. 7, T 9 S, R 3 W). Named on Big Basin (1955) 7.5' quadrangle.

Orange Flat [SAN LUIS OBISPO]: *area,* nearly 5 miles south of Atascadero (lat. 35°25'10" N, long. 120°40' W; near E line sec. 10, T 29 S, R 12 E). Named on Atascadero (1965) 7.5' quadrangle.

Orby: see **Harris** [SANTA BARBARA]; **Santa Cruz** [SANTA CRUZ].

Orcutt [SANTA BARBARA]: *town,* 6 miles south of Santa Maria (lat. 34°51'50" N, long. 120°26'40" W; on N line sec. 15, T 9 N, R 34 W). Named on Orcutt (1959) 7.5' quadrangle. Postal authorities established Orcutt post office in 1904 (Frickstad, p. 171). Officials of Union Oil Company had the town laid out in 1903 and named it for W.W. Orcutt, geologist for the company (Gudde, 1949, p. 244). California Division of Highways' (1934) map shows a place called Ferini located 1.25 miles south of Orcutt along Pacific Coast Railroad.

Orcutt Creek [SANTA BARBARA]: *stream,* flows 12 miles to end in lowlands 6 miles southeast of the town of Guadalupe (lat. 34° 54' N, long. 120°30'55" W); the stream goes through Orcutt. Named on Guadalupe (1959), Orcutt (1959), Santa Maria (1959), and Sisquoc (1959) 7.5' quadrangles.

Ord: see **Fort Ord Military Reservation** [MONTEREY].

Ord Barracks: see **Presidio of Monterey** [MONTEREY].

Ord Village: see **Fort Ord Village** [MONTEREY].

Orejano Flat [SAN BENITO]: *area,* 15 miles east-southeast of Bitterwater (lat. 36°16'35" N, long. 120°45'10" W; sec. 15, T 19 S, R 11 E). Named on Hepsedam Peak (1969) 7.5' quadrangle.

Orejano Spring [SAN BENITO]: *spring,* 15 miles east-southeast of Bitterwater (lat. 36°16'30" N, long. 120°45'10" W; sec. 15, T 19 S, R 11 E); the spring is at Orejano Flat. Named on Hepsedam Peak (1969) 7.5' quadrangle.

Orella [SANTA BARBARA]: *locality,* 9 miles east of Gaviota along Southern Pacific Railroad (lat. 34°27'40" N, long. 120°03'30" W). Named on Lompoc (1905) 30' quadrangle.

Orford: see **Port Orford** [SANTA BARBARA].

Organ Point: see **Lovers Point** [MONTEREY].

Orizaba: see **Twin Harbors** [SANTA BARBARA].

Orizaba Pictograph Cave: see **Twin Harbors** [SANTA BARBARA].

Oro Fino Canyon [MONTEREY]: *canyon,* drained by a stream that flows 3.25 miles to San Antonio River 2 miles west of Jolon (lat. 35°57'50" N, long. 121°12'35" W). Named on Jolon (1949) 7.5' quadrangle.

Oro Fino Canyon [MONTEREY-SAN LUIS OBISPO]: *canyon,* drained by a stream that heads in San Luis Obispo County and flows 2.25 miles to San Antonio River 5.5 miles southwest of Bradley in Monterey County (lat. 35°47'40" N, long. 120°51'35" W; sec. 35, T 24 S, R 10 E). Named on Bradley (1949) 7.5' quadrangle.

Ortega [SANTA BARBARA]: *locality,* 4 miles west-northwest of Carpinteria along Southern Pacific Railroad (lat. 34°25' N, long. 119°35'05" W); the place is 1.5 miles east-southeast of Ortega Hill. Named on Carpinteria (1952, photorevised 1967) 7.5' quadrangle. Called Ortega Siding on Carpinteria (1952) 7.5' quadrangle.

Ortega Creek [SAN BENITO]: *stream,* heads in Santa Clara County and flows 4.25 miles to San Felipe Lake 9.5 miles north-northwest of Hollister (lat. 36°59'05" N, long. 121°27'15" W). Named on San Felipe (1955, photorevised 1971) 7.5' quadrangle. The name commemorates Ygnacio Ortega, original owner of San Ysidro grant in Santa Clara County (United States Board on Geographic Names, 1973, p. 3).

Ortega Hill [SANTA BARBARA]: *hill,* 5.5 miles west-northwest of Carpinteria (lat. 34°25'20" N, long. 119°36'25" W). Named on Carpinteria (1952) 7.5' quadrangle.

Ortega Siding: see **Ortega** [SANTA BARBARA].

Ortega Spring [SAN LUIS OBISPO]: *spring,* 6 miles east-southeast of Cholame (lat. 35°40'50" N, long. 120°12'10" W; sec. 12, T 26 S, R 16 E). Named on Orchard Peak (1961) 7.5' quadrangle.

Osborne Ridge [MONTEREY]: *ridge,* west-trending, nearly 2 miles long, 2.5 miles south of the town of Carmel Valley (lat. 36°26'45" N, long. 121°43'30" W). Named on Carmel Valley (1956) 7.5' quadrangle.

Oso Campground: see **Lower Oso Campground** [SANTA BARBARA]; **Upper Oso Campground** [SANTA BARBARA].

Oso Canyon [SANTA BARBARA]: *canyon,* drained by a stream that flows 6 miles to Santa Ynez River 3.5 miles northeast of San Marcos Pass (lat. 34°32'45" N, long. 119°46'30" W). Named on Little Pine Mountain (1964) and San Marcos Pass (1959) 7.5' quadrangles.

Oso Creek [SAN LUIS OBISPO]: *stream,* flows 3 miles to Arroyo Seco 15 miles northeast of the town of Nipomo (lat. 35°10'25" N, long. 120°16'50" W; near E line sec. 5, T 32 S, R 16 E). Named on Caldwell Mesa (1967) 7.5' quadrangle.

Oso Flaco Creek [SAN LUIS OBISPO]: *stream,* flows 7.25 miles to the sea nearly 7 miles south-southwest of the town of Arroyo Grande (lat. 35°01'50" N, long. 120°38' W); the stream goes through Oso Flaco Lake, Little Oso Flaco Lake, and marsh. Named on Guadalupe (1959) and Oceano (1965) 7.5' quadrangles.

Oso Flaco Lake [SAN LUIS OBISPO]: *lake,* 0.5 mile long, 6.5 miles south-southwest of the town of Arroyo Grande near the coast (lat. 35°01'50" N, long. 120°37'15" W). Named on Oceano (1965) 7.5' quadrangle. When the Portola expedition camped by the lake in 1769, Crespi gave the place the name of the Lake of the Holy Martyrs, San Juan de Perucia and San Pedro de Sacro Terrato (Hanna, p. 221-222), but the soldiers called it Oso Flaco because they killed a very lean bear on the shore of the lake—*oso flaco* means "lean bear" in Spanish (Hoover, Rensch, and Rensch, p. 379).

Oso Flaco Lake: see **Little Oso Flaco Lake** [SAN LUIS OBISPO].

Otter Harbor: see **Simonton Cove** [SANTA BARBARA].

Outer Islet: see **Piedras Blancas Point** [SAN LUIS OBISPO].

Outlaw Camp [MONTEREY]: *locality,* 5 miles north-northwest of Partington Point along Terrace Creek (lat. 36°14'30" N, long. 121°43'50" W; sec. 34, T 19 S, R 2 E). Named on Partington Ridge (1956) 7.5' quadrangle. The name is from the taking of redwood shakes from the place illegally (Clark,1991, p. 365).

Owl Canyon [SANTA BARBARA]: *canyon,* drained by a stream that flows 1.5 miles to South Fork La Brea Creek 3.5 miles east-northeast of Manzanita Mountain (lat. 34°54'35" N, long. 120°01'20" W). Named on Manzanita Mountain (1964) 7.5' quadrangle

– P –

Pacer [SANTA BARBARA]: *locality,* 3.25 miles west-southwest of Santa Maria along Santa Maria Valley Railroad (lat. 34°56'05" N, long. 120°29'20" W). Named on Santa Maria (1959) 7.5' quadrangle.

Pacheco Creek [SAN BENITO]: *stream,* heads in Santa Clara County and flows 5 miles in San Benito County to San Felipe Lake 6.25

miles north-northwest of Hollister (lat. 35°58'35" N, long. 121°27'35" W). Named on San Felipe (1955) and Three Sisters (1954) 7.5' quadrangles. Called Arroyo de S. Felipe on a diseño of San Joaquin grant made in 1836 (Becker, 1964). Hollister (1921) 15' quadrangle shows the stream ending at a marsh 2 miles southeast of San Felipe Lake. The name "Pacheco" commemorates Francisco Perez Pacheco, who had his ranch headquarters near the stream (Shumate, p. 12).

Pacific: see **Camp Pacific** [MONTEREY].

Pacific Grove [MONTEREY]: *town,* along the coast between Monterey and Point Pinos (lat. 36°37'15" N, long. 121°55' W). Named on Monterey (1947) 7.5' quadrangle. A group of Methodists founded the place in 1875 and modeled it after an encampment at Ocean Grove, New Jersey (Fink, p. 167). Postal authorities established Pacific Grove post office in 1886, discontinued it the same year, and reestablished it in 1887 (Frickstad, p. 108). The town incorporated in 1889.

Pacific Grove Acres [MONTEREY]: *district,* northwest of the main part of Pacific Grove (lat. 36°37'40" N, long. 121°55'50" W). Named on Monterey (1947) 7.5' quadrangle.

Pacific Mills: see **Ben Lomond** [SANTA CRUZ].

Pacific Valley: see **Plaskett** [MONTEREY].

Padrones Canyon [SAN LUIS OBISPO]: *canyon,* drained by a stream that flows 4 miles to Cuyama Valley 3 miles northeast of New Cuyama [SANTA BARBARA] (lat. 34°58'40" N, long. 119°38'40" W; sec. 3, T 10 N, R 26 W). Named on New Cuyama (1964) and Wells Ranch (1954) 7.5' quadrangles.

Padrones Spring [SAN LUIS OBISPO]: *spring,* 33 miles southeast of Simmler (lat. 35°00'10" N, long. 119°35'15" W; near N line sec. 31, T 11 N, R 25 W). Named on Elkhorn Hills (1954) 7.5' quadrangle. Called Pataroma Spring on Arnold and Johnson's (1910) map.

Paicines [SAN BENITO]: *village,* 11 miles southeast of Hollister near Tres Pinos Creek (lat. 36°43'40" N, long. 121°16'35" W); the village is on Cienega de los Paicines grant. Named on Paicines (1968) 7.5' quadrangle. The place first was called Tres Pinos for three pine trees there, but when in 1873 Southern Pacific Railroad built a branch line to a point 5 miles farther north-northwest, the name "Tres Pinos" was taken for the station at the end of the new rail line, and the older place was given the name "Paicines" for Cienega de los Paicines grant (Pierce, p. 126). Postal authorities established Tres Pinos post office in 1871, changed the name to Grogan in 1874, and changed the name to Paicines the same year (Frickstad, p. 136, 137). The name "Grogan" was for Alexander B. Grogan, owner of Cienega de los Paicines grant (Pierce, p. 139, 141). Kroeber (1916, p. 53) noted that Paicines is probably an Indian tribal name. California Mining Bureau's (1909a) map shows a place called Mulberry located 7 miles by stage line south-southeast of Paicines. Postal authorities established Elvina post office in 1885, changed the name to Mulberry in 1886, and discontinued it in 1917—the name "Mulberry" was from a failed scheme to plant mulberry trees for silk-worm culture (Salley, p. 69, 149).

Painted Cave [SANTA BARBARA]:
(1) *cave,* about 2.25 miles east-southeast of San Marcos Pass (lat. 34°30'15" N, long. 119°47'10" W; sec. 23, T 5 N, R 28 W). Named on San Marcos Pass (1959) 7.5' quadrangle.
(2) *cave,* 4 miles east of Fraser Point on the north side of Santa Cruz Island (lat. 34°04'15" N, long. 119°51'30" W). Named on Santa Cruz Island A (1943) 7.5' quadrangle. The name is from the heavy growths of red, yellow, and green lichens on rocks of the cave (Emery, p. 38). Gleason (p. 51) gave the Spanish equivalent "Cueva Pintada" as an alternate name.

Painted Rock [SAN LUIS OBISPO]: *relief feature,* 16 miles south-southeast of Simmler near the southwest edge of Carrizo Plain (lat. 35°08'45" N, long. 119°51'40" W; near NW cor. sec. 17, T 32 S, R 20 E). Named on Painted Rock (1959) 7.5' quadrangle. Early settlers called the feature La Piedra Pintada because of numerous Indian pictographs there—*la piedra pintada* means "the painted rock" in Spanish (Hoover, Rensch, and Rensch, p. 379). Postal authorities established Carisa post office in 1882, moved it and changed the name to Painted Rock in 1888, and discontinued it in 1895 (Salley, p. 37, 165).

Painted Rock Campground [SANTA BARBARA]: *locality,* 5 miles southeast of McPherson Peak in Montgomery Potrero (lat. 34°50'10" N, long. 119°45'10" W). Named on Hurricane Deck (1964) 7.5' quadrangle. The name is from pictographs in shallow sandstone caves near the place (Gagnon, p. 101).

Pajaro [MONTEREY]: *town,* 5 miles northeast of the mouth of Pajaro River on the south side (lat. 36°54'15" N, long. 121°44'50" W). Named on Watsonville East (1955) and Watsonville West (1954) 7.5' quadrangles. Postal authorities established Pajaro post office in 1872, discontinued it in 1873, reestablished it in 1882, and discontinued it in 1888 (Frickstad, p. 108).

Pajaro: see **Lake Pajaro**, under **Watsonville** [SANTA CRUZ]; **Mount Pajaro** [SANTA CRUZ]; **Watsonville Junction** [MONTEREY].

Pajaro Dunes: see **Palm Beach** [SANTA CRUZ].

Pajaro Gap [SAN BENITO-SANTA CRUZ]: *narrows,* nearly 2 miles north-northeast of Aromas along Pajaro River on San Benito-Santa Cruz county line (lat. 36°54'45" N, long.

121°37'30" W); the feature is the narrow part of Chittenden Pass. Named on Chittenden (1955) and Watsonville East (1955) 7.5' quadrangles.

Pajaro Landing: see **Pajaro River** [MONTEREY-SAN BENITO-SANTA CRUZ].

Pajaro River [MONTEREY-SAN BENITO-SANTA CRUZ]: *stream,* heads near San Felipe Lake and flows 30 miles to the sea 15 miles northwest of Salinas (lat. 36°51' N, long. 121°48'30" W; sec. 36, T 12 S, R 1 E); the stream marks San Benito-Santa Clara county line from near San Felipe Lake to beyond the mouth of San Benito River, and then defines San Benito-Santa Cruz county line and Monterey-Santa Cruz county line to the sea. Named on Chittenden (1955), Moss Landing (1954), San Felipe (1955), Watsonville East (1955), and Watsonville West (1954) 7.5' quadrangles. Called Sanjon de la Brea on a diseño of Llano de Tequisquita grant (Becker, 1969), called Payaro R. on Baker's (1855) map, and called R. Pajaros on Mitchell's (1856) map; on the last two maps the names apply also to present San Benito River. Some early maps from Spanish days had the name "Rio de San Antonio" for the stream (Clark, 1986, p. 307). Taylor (p. 175) called it Rio del Pajaro. Soldiers of the Portola expedition gave the name "Pajaro" to the feature in 1769 because the natives that they saw there had a huge stuffed bird (Wagner, H.R., p. 401)—*pajaro* means "bird" in Spanish. Clark (1991, p. 371) noted that the stream also had the names "Pigeon River," "Río de La Señora La Santa Ana," "Río del Paxaro," "Río de Santa Ana," "San Antonio River," and "Sanjon del Tequesquite." A landing place at the mouth of the river was called Pajaro Landing; the next landing place north along the coast, called Miller's Landing, was on land purchased by Captain C.F. Miller (Hoover, Rensch, and Rensch, p. 474). Another landing place near the mouth of the river was called Brennans Landing, for Captain James Brennan, and was used as early as 1856 (Clark, 1986, p. 45).

Pajaro Valley [MONTEREY-SANTA CRUZ]: *valley,* extends inland from the coast for 13 miles along Pajaro River on Monterey-Santa Cruz county line. Named on Moss Landing (1954), Watsonville East (1955), and Watsonville West (1954) 7.5' quadrangles.

Pala Prieta Valley: see **Palo Prieto Canyon** [SAN LUIS OBISPO].

Palisades: see **The Palisades** [MONTEREY].

Palm Beach [SANTA CRUZ]: *settlement,* 5 miles southwest of Watsonville near the coast (lat. 36°52'05" N, long. 121°49'05" W). Named on Moss Landing (1954) 7.5' quadrangle. Called Camp Goodall on Capitola (1914) 15' quadrangle. Camp Goodall, a shipping port for produce from Pajaro Valley, was named for Captain Goodall of Goodall

Perkins & Co., steamship owners; it became a popular resort area and is the location of the present development called Pajaro Dunes (Lewis, 1976, p. 144).

Palmer [SANTA BARBARA]: *locality,* nearly 3 miles south-southwest of Sisquoc (2) (lat. 34°49'40" N, long. 120°19'10" W). Named on Santa Maria (1947) 15' quadrangle.

Palmer Flats [SAN LUIS OBISPO]: *area,* 3 miles north of Cambria along San Simeon Creek (lat. 35°36'35" N, long. 121°04'20" W). Named on Cambria (1959) 7.5' quadrangle.

Palo Alto Hill [SANTA BARBARA]: *peak,* 4.5 miles northeast of Point Conception (lat. 34°29'40" N, long. 120°25' W). Altitude 1394 feet. Named on Point Conception (1953) 7.5' quadrangle.

Palo Colorado Canyon [MONTEREY]: *canyon,* drained by a stream that flows nearly 4 miles to the sea 6.5 miles north of Point Sur (lat. 36°23'55" N, long. 121°54'15" W; sec. 6, T 18 S, R 1 E). Named on Mount Carmel (1956) and Soberanes Point (1956) 7.5' quadrangles. Gudde (1949, p. 251) noted that a Spanish map of 1835 has the name "Arroyo del palo Colorado"—*palo colorado* means "redwood tree" in Spanish, and redwood trees grow in the canyon. Some old maps have the name "Soberanes Creek" for the stream in the canyon (Clark, 1991, p. 373).

Palo Corona [MONTEREY]: *peak,* 3.5 miles east of Soberanes Point (lat. 36°27'05" N, long. 121°52'05" W; near W line sec. 16, T 17 S, R 1 E). Altitude 2972 feet. Named on Mount Carmel (1956) 7.5' quadrangle.

Palo Escrito: see **Sierra de Salinas** [MONTEREY].

Palo Escrito Peak [MONTEREY]: *peak,* 9 miles west of Soledad (lat. 36°24'20" N, long. 121°29'25" W; sec. 36, T 17 S, R 4 E). Altitude 4467 feet. Named on Palo Escrito Peak (1956) 7.5' quadrangle. According to Stewart (p. 356), *palo escrito* means "tree-inscribed" in Spanish, and the name probably originated with a tree marked with symbols.

Paloma: see **Paloma Creek** [MONTEREY].

Paloma Creek [MONTEREY]: *stream,* flows 13 miles to Piney Creek 12 miles west-southwest of Greenfield (lat. 36°16'25" N, long. 121°26'55" W; near S line sec. 17, T 19 S, R 5 E). Named on Chews Ridge (1956), Palo Escrito Peak (1956), and Sycamore Flat (1956) 7.5' quadrangles. On Soledad (1915) 15' quadrangle, the lower part of present Piney Creek—below its junction with present Paloma Creek—is called Paloma Creek. Postal authorities established Paloma post office in 1923 and discontinued it in 1933 (Salley, p. 166). The post office was along Paloma Creek (NE quarter sec. 36, T 18 S, R 4 E) and was named for the stream (Clark, 1991, p. 376).

Paloma Creek [SAN LUIS OBISPO]: *stream,* flows 4.25 miles to Salinas River 2.5 miles southeast of Atascadero (lat. 35°28' N, long.

120°37'45" W). Named on Atascadero (1965) 7.5' quadrangle.

Paloma Mountain [MONTEREY]: *peak,* 9 miles west-southwest of Soledad (lat. 36°23'15" N, long. 121°28'10" W; near S line sec. 6, T 18 S, R 5 E). Altitude 3970 feet. Named on Palo Escrito Peak (1956) 7.5' quadrangle.

Paloma Ridge [MONTEREY]: *ridge,* south-southeast-trending, 5 miles long, 7 miles southwest of Soledad (lat. 36°21' N, long. 121° 24'30" W). Named on Palo Escrito Peak (1956) and Sycamore Flat (1956) 7.5' quadrangles.

Palo Parado: see **Cavern Point** [SANTA BARBARA].

Palo Prieto: see **Palo Prieto Canyon** [SAN LUIS OBISPO].

Palo Prieto Canyon [SAN LUIS OBISPO]: *canyon,* drained by a stream that flows 6 miles to Cholame Creek nearly 1 mile south-southwest of Cholame (lat. 35°42'45" N, long. 120°18'05" W; sec. 36, T 25 S, R 15 E). Named on Cholame (1961) and Orchard Peak (1961) 7.5' quadrangles. Called Prieto Canyon on Cholame (1943) 7.5' quadrangle. Angel (1890c, p. 569) called the feature Pala Prieta Valley. Postal authorities established Palo Prieto post office in 1888 and discontinued it in 1889 (Frickstad, p. 165). The post office presumably was in or near the canyon.

Palo Prieto Canyon: see **Palo Prieto Pass** [SAN LUIS OBISPO].

Palo Prieto Pass [SAN LUIS OBISPO]: *valley,* 12 miles east-southeast of Shandon on San Luis Obispo-Kern county line (lat. 35°37'30" N, long. 120°11' W). Named on Holland Canyon (1961) and Orchard Peak (1961) 7.5' quadrangles. The valley is mainly in San Luis Obispo County southeast of the head of Palo Prieto Canyon. United States Board on Geographic Names (1968a, p. 6) rejected the names "Palo Prieto Canon" and "Palo Prieto Canyon:" for the valley, and described the feature as extending for 7 miles southeast from Palo Prieto Canyon through Choice Valley.

Palos Colorados Creek [SANTA BARBARA]: *stream,* flows 2.5 miles to El Jaro Creek 6.5 miles southeast of the city of Lompoc (lat. 34°34'20" N, long. 120°22'05" W). Named on Santa Rosa Hills (1959) 7.5' quadrangle.

Palo Scrito Hills: see **Sierra de Salinas** [MONTEREY].

Palo Serito Hills: see **Sierra de Salinas** [MONTEREY].

Pancho Rico Creek [MONTEREY]: *stream,* flows 26 miles to Salinas River at San Ardo (lat. 36°00'55" N, long. 120°54'40" W). Named on Pancho Rico Valley (1967), San Ardo (1967), Slack Canyon (1969), and Smith Mountain (1969) 7.5' quadrangles. Called Poncho Rico Creek on Priest Valley (1915) 30' quadrangle, but United States Board on Geographic Names (1961b, p. 13) rejected this form of the name. Called Gaviota Cr. on

California Mining Bureau's (1917b) map. Van Winkle and Eaton (p. 75) used the names "Poncha Rica Creek" and "Gaviota Creek" for the feature. The name "Pancho Rico" commemorates Francisco Rico, who received San Lorenzo (2) grant; the stream also had the names "Galen Creek," "San Bernardo Creek," and "Williams Creek" (Clark, 1991, p. 376).

Pancho Rico Valley [MONTEREY]: *canyon,* 7.5 miles long, opens into lowlands along Salinas River at San Ardo (lat. 35°01'10" N, long. 120°53'10" W; sec. 16, T 22 S, R 10 E); Pancho Rico Creek drains the canyon. Named on Pancho Rico Valley (1967) and San Ardo (1967) 7.5' quadrangles. Kew (1920, p. 83) called the feature Pence Enrico Canyon.

Panoche [SAN BENITO]: *locality,* 15 miles east-northeast of San Benito (lat. 36°35'45" N, long. 120°50' W; sec. 25, T 15 S, R 10 E); the place is in Panoche Valley. Named on Panoche (1969) 7.5' quadrangle. Postal authorities established Panoche post office in 1870 and discontinued it in 1915 (Frickstad, p. 136). According to Hanna (p. 229), the name is a corruption of *panocha,* which is a Mexican-Spanish word for a confection of brown sugar. According to Gudde (1949, p. 252), *panoche,* or *panocha,* was the name of a sweet substance that the Indians extracted from reeds and wild fruit.

Panoche Creek [SAN BENITO]: *stream,* flows 20 miles to Fresno County 4.5 miles east of Panoche (lat. 36°36'25" N, long. 120° 45' W; sec. 22, T 15 S, R 11 E); the stream drains Panoche Valley. Named on Llanada (1969) and Panoche (1969) 7.5' quadrangles. Whitney (p. 55) referred to Big Panoche Creek, which runs through Panoche Plain.

Panoche Creek: see **Little Panoche Creek** [SAN BENITO]; **Silver Creek** [SAN BENITO].

Panoche Hills [SAN BENITO]: *range,* northeast of Panoche Valley, mainly in Fresno County. Named on Mercey Hot Springs (1969) and Panoche (1969) 7.5' quadrangles.

Panoche Pass [SAN BENITO]: *pass,* 9 miles north-northeast of San Benito (lat. 36°37'40" N, long. 121°00'45" W; sec. 17, T 15 S, R 9 E); the pass is near the head of Panoche Creek. Named on Panoche Pass (1968) 7.5' quadrangle.

Panoche Plain: see **Panoche Valley** [SAN BENITO].

Panoche Valley [SAN BENITO]: *valley,* 35 miles east-southeast of Hollister and southwest of Panoche Hills (lat. 36°37' N, long. 120° 51' W); Panoche Creek and its tributaries drain the valley. Named on Cerro Colorado (1969), Llanada (1969), Mercey Hot Springs (1969), and Panoche (1969) 7.5' quadrangles. Whitney (p. 55) referred to Panoche Plain.

Panoche Valley: see **Little Panoche Valley** [SAN BENITO].

Panochita Creek: see **Little Panoche Creek** [SAN BENITO].

Panochita Valley: see **Little Panoche Valley** [SAN BENITO].

Panorama Hills [SAN LUIS OBISPO]: *range,* 10 miles north-northeast of Caliente Mountain between Temblor Range and Carrizo Plain (lat. 35°11'30" N, long. 119°43'15" W). Named on Painted Rock (1959) and Panorama Hills (1954) 7.5' quadrangles. Arnold and Johnson (1910, p. 21) proposed the name.

Panorama Point [SAN LUIS OBISPO]: *peak,* 20 miles southeast of Simmler (lat. 35°10'45"N, long. 119°42'35" W; sec. 34, T 31 S, R 21 E); the peak is in Panorama Hills. Altitude 2521 feet. Named on Panorama Hills (1954) 7.5' quadrangle. According to Arnold and Johnson (1910, p. 22), the name was used by E.W. White, a settler in the neighborhood.

Panther Peak [SAN BENITO]: *peak,* 13 miles east-southeast of Bitterwater (lat. 36°18' N, long. 120°47'20" W; sec. 5, T 19 S, R 11 E). Altitude 4276 feet. Named on Hepsedam Peak (1969) 7.5' quadrangle.

Panza Hills: see **La Panza Range** [SAN LUIS OBISPO].

Paradise Campground [SAN LUIS OBISPO]: *locality,* 4 miles west-southwest of Branch Mountain (lat. 35°09'15" N, long. 120°08'35" W). Named on Los Machos Hills (1967) 7.5' quadrangle.

Paradise Canyon [MONTEREY]: *canyon,* 2 miles long, opens into an unnamed canyon 2.5 miles northwest of Prunedale (lat. 36°48'10" N, long. 121°42'10" W). Named on Prunedale (1954) 7.5' quadrangle.

Paradise Canyon [SANTA BARBARA]: *canyon,* drained by a stream that flows 2.5 miles to Santa Ynez River 2.25 miles north-northeast of San Marcos Pass (lat. 34°32'35" N, long. 119°48'45" W; sec. 4, T 5 N, R 28 W). Named on San Marcos Pass (1959) 7.5' quadrangle.

Paradise Park [SANTA CRUZ]: *settlement,* 9 miles south-southeast of the town of Boulder Creek along San Lorenzo River (lat. 37° 00'35" N, long. 122°02'35" W). Named on Felton (1955) 7.5' quadrangle. The settlement is at a place long known as Powder Mill Flat for a plant there that manufactured explosives from 1865 until 1916 (Hoover, Rensch, and Rensch, p. 471). A railroad siding that served the plant was called Powder Mill Siding (MacGregor, p. 130). In 1919 the place became the site of a cottage colony for members of the Masonic fraternity (Rowland, p. 216). A narrow ridge near Powder Mill Flat that is almost encircled by San Lorenzo River was called Hog's Back (Hamman, p. 85).

Paradise Valley [SAN LUIS OBISPO]: *valley,* 3 miles west of Atascadero along Graves Creek (lat. 35°29' N, long. 120°43'15" W). Named on Atascadero (1965) 7.5' quadrangle.

Paraiso Springs [MONTEREY]: *locality,* 7 miles west of Greenfield (lat. 36°19'55" N, long. 121°22' W; near E line sec. 25, T 18 S, R 5 E). Named on Paraiso Springs (1956) 7.5' quadrangle. According to Winslow Anderson (p. 219), friars at Soledad mission drank and bathed in the water, which they called Water of Paradise—*paraiso* means "paradise" in Spanish. G.A. Waring (p. 60-61) noted that at least five mineral springs rise at the place in an area of several acres where in 1908 a hotel and cottages provided accommodations for 200 guests. Postal authorities established Paraiso Springs post office in 1877, discontinued it for a time in 1899, and discontinued it finally in 1939 (Frickstad, p. 108).

Paraje de Sanchez [MONTEREY]: *land grant,* 7 miles west-northwest of Soledad. Named on Palo Escrito Peak (1956) and Rana Creek (1956) 7.5' quadrangles. Francisco Lugo received 1.5 leagues in 1839; Juana Briones de Lugo and others claimed 6584 acres patented in 1866 (Cowan, p. 58).

Parida Creek: see **Arroyo Paredon** [SANTA BARBARA].

Paris Valley [MONTEREY]: *valley,* 3.5 miles west-northwest of San Ardo (lat. 36°02'15" N, long. 120°58'10" W). Named on San Ardo (1967) 7.5' quadrangle. The name is from the large number of families of French descent that lived in the valley (Clark, 1991, p. 378).

Parker Canyon [MONTEREY]: *canyon,* drained by a stream that flows 2.5 miles to lowlands 5 miles west of Chualar (lat. 36°34'40" N, long. 121°36'20" W). Named on Chualar (1947) 7.5' quadrangle.

Parker Flats [MONTEREY]: *area,* 3.5 miles south-southeast of Marina (lat. 36°38'05" N, long. 121°47'05" W). Named on Marina (1947) 7.5' quadrangle.

Parkfield [MONTEREY]: *village,* 21 miles east of Bradley along Little Cholame Creek (lat. 35°54' N, long. 120°25'50" W; sec. 26, T 23 S, R 14 E). Named on Parkfield (1961) 7.5' quadrangle. Postal authorities established Parkfield post office in 1884 and discontinued it in 1954 (Frickstad, p. 108). According to Gudde (1949, p. 254), the place first had the name "Russelsville," but when postal officials rejected this, the postmaster selected the name "Parkfield" because the village is in a natural oak park. California Mining Bureau's (1909a) map shows a place called Imusdale located 5 miles by stage line west-northwest of Parkfield, about where Stockdale Mountain (1948) 7.5' quadrangle shows Imusdale cemetery. Postal authorities established Imusdale post office in 1875, moved it 0.5 mile north in 1899, and discontinued it in 1902; the name was for the Imus brothers, Charles, William, and Edwin, who were the first settlers in Cholame Valley (Salley, p. 103).

Park Hill [SAN BENITO]: *ridge,* north-north-west-trending, nearly 1 mile long, at the north edge of Hollister (lat. 35°51'30" N, long. 121°24'20" W). Named on Hollister (1955)

7.5' quadrangle.

Park Mills: see **Blooms Mill** [SANTA CRUZ].

Park Ridge [SAN LUIS OBISPO]: *ridge,* north-west-trending, 2 miles long, 3.5 miles east-southeast of Morro Rock (lat. 35°20'45" N, long. 120°48'30" W). Named on Morro Bay South (1965) 7.5' quadrangle.

Parks-Lead Siding [SANTA BARBARA]: *locality,* at the west edge of the city of Lompoc along Southern Pacific Railroad (lat. 34°38'40" N, long. 120°28'25" W). Named on Lompoc (1959) 7.5' quadrangle.

Parks Valley [SAN BENITO]: *canyon,* 1 mile long, 5 miles southeast of Mount Johnson (lat. 36°33'10" N, long. 121°15'25" W; on E line sec. 12, T 16 S, R 6 E). Named on Mount Johnson (1968) 7.5' quadrangle.

Parola Canyon [SAN LUIS OBISPO]: *canyon,* nearly 4 miles long, drained by Alamo Creek (1), which enters Santa Margarita Lake 4.5 miles west-northwest of Pozo (lat. 35°19'40" N, long. 120°26'20" W; sec. 11, T 30 S, R 14 E). Named on Santa Margarita Lake (1967) 7.5' quadrangle.

Parrot Spring [SAN BENITO]: *spring,* 8 miles west-southwest of Panoche (lat. 36°33'10" N, long. 120°57'50" W; sec. 11, T 16 S, R 9 E). Named on Llanada (1969) 7.5' quadrangle.

Parsons Creek [MONTEREY]: *stream,* flows 3.5 miles to Chualar Canyon 6.5 miles north of Gonzales (lat. 36°36'10" N, long. 121°25'35" W; sec. 28, T 15 S, R 5 E). Named on Gonzales (1955) and Mount Harlan (1968) 7.5' quadrangles.

Parson Spring [MONTEREY]: *spring,* 7 miles north-northeast of Soledad (lat. 36°24'50" N, long. 121°11'35" W; sec. 34, T 17 S, R 7 E). Named on North Chalone Peak (1969) 7.5' quadrangle.

Partington Cove: see **Partington Point** [MONTEREY].

Partington Creek [MONTEREY]: *stream,* flows 2.5 miles to the sea east of Partington Point (lat. 36°10'30" N, long. 121°41'45" W; sec. 24, T 20 S, R 2 E). Named on Partington Ridge (1956) 7.5' quadrangle.

Partington Landing: see **Partington Point** [MONTEREY].

Partington Point [MONTEREY]: *promontory,* 14 miles southeast of Point Sur along the coast (lat. 36°10'30" N, long. 121°41'50" W; sec. 24, T 20 S, R 2 E). Named on Partington Ridge (1956) 7.5' quadrangle. According to Lussier (p. 28), a small embayment 700 feet east of the point, and east of the cove into which Partington Creek flows, is called Partington Cove—it was the site of Partington Landing, a shipping point for tanbark, cattle, and hides in the early days. However, United States Board on Geographic Names (1992, p. 4) approved instead the name "Partington Cove" for the embayment at the mouth of Partington Creek (lat. 36°10'30" N, long, 121°41'48" W).

Partington Ridge [MONTEREY]: *ridge,* north-trending, 2.25 miles long, north of Partington Point (lat. 36°11'30" N, long. 121°41'55" W). Named on Partington Ridge (1956) 7.5' quadrangle. John Partington and Laura Partington homesteaded at the ridge in 1874 (Lussier, p. 27).

Pasa Robles: see **Paso de Robles** [SAN LUIS OBISPO].

Pasa Robles Creek: see **Paso Robles Creek** [SAN LUIS OBISPO].

Pasatiempo [SANTA CRUZ]: *settlement,* 10 miles southeast of the town of Boulder Creek (lat. 37°00'15" N, long. 122°01'30" W). Named on Felton (1955) 7.5' quadrangle.

Paso del Quinto: see **Old Hilltown** [MONTEREY].

Paso de Robles [SAN LUIS OBISPO]: *land grant,* west of Salinas River at and southwest of Paso Robles. Named on Paso Robles (1948), Templeton (1948), and York Mountain (1948) 7.5' quadrangles. Pedro Narvaez received 6 leagues in 1844; Petronilo Rios claimed 25,993 acres patented in 1866 (Cowan, p. 68). Parke's (1854-1855) map has the name "Pasa Robles," Derby (p. 4) referred to Passo de Roblas and Paso de Roblas, and Whitney (p. 145) used the name "Paso el Roble." *Paso de robles* means "passage through the oaks" in Spanish; the name was used as early as 1828 (Gudde, 1949, p. 255).

Paso el Roble: see **Paso de Robles** [SAN LUIS OBISPO].

Paso Robles [SAN LUIS OBISPO]: *town,* 24 miles north of San Luis Obispo along Salinas River (lat. 35°37'40" N, long. 120°41'25" W); the town is on Paso de Robles grant. Named on Paso Robles (1948) and Templeton (1948) 7.5' quadrangles. Promoters founded the town in 1886 and it incorporated under the name "El Paso de Robles" in 1889 (Gudde, 1949, p. 255). United States Board on Geographic Names (1933, p. 591) rejected the name "Paso de Robles" for the town, and approved the form "Paso Robles." Postal authorities established Hot Springs post office in 1867, discontinued it the same year, reestablished it in 1868, and moved it 3 miles south and changed the name to Paso Robles in 1870 (Salley, p. 100). Hot springs that occur at the original site of Hot Springs post office were well known to the Indians and were improved for use by Franciscan friars, possibly as early as 1797 (Hoover, Rensch, and Rensch, p. 386). These natural springs of warm water issue along the bank of Salinas River near the north edge of the present town, and provided water for what were known as Paso Robles Mud Bath Springs (Waring, G.A., p. 73). According to G.A. Waring (p. 72-73), by 1865 a spring of warm sulphureted water in the south part of the present town was cemented to form a swimming pool and covered by a large masonry dome; a hotel was built there about 1888, and later a bathhouse built adjoining the hotel was supplied with water at a tem-

perature of 105° Fahrenheit from an artisan well known as Main Sulphur Spring. A bathhouse called Municipal Baths Springs was supplied with hot water from another artisan well, and a well called Grand Central Sulphur Spring, drilled in the center of town in 1911, supplied water to yet another bathhouse (Logan, p. 692-693). Water from Mary Hill mineral well, located about 0.25 mile west of the center of the town, was bottled for local sale (Logan, p. 690-691).

Paso Robles Creek [SAN LUIS OBISPO]: *stream,* flows 11.5 miles to Salinas River 6.5 miles south of Paso Robles (lat. 35°31'55" N, long. 120°42'20" W); the stream is mainly on Paso de Robles grant. Named on Templeton (1948) and York Mountain (1948) 7.5' quadrangles. Parke (p. 14) referred to Pasa Robles creek.

Paso Robles Mud Bath Springs: see **Paso Robles** [SAN LUIS OBISPO].

Pass of San Lorenzo: see **San Lorenzo Creek** [MONTEREY-SAN BENITO].

Pataroma Spring: see **Padrones Spring** [SAN LUIS OBISPO].

Pato Canyon [SANTA BARBARA]: *canyon,* drained by a stream that flows nearly 5 miles to Cuyama River 12 miles southeast of the village of Cuyama (lat. 34°48'55" N, long. 119°28'25" W). Named on Cuyama Peak (1943) 7.5' quadrangle.

Patrocino: see **El Alisal** [MONTEREY] (2).

Pat Springs Camp [MONTEREY]: *locality,* 2.5 miles northwest of Uncle Sam Mountain (lat. 36°21'50" N, long. 121°44'35" W). Named on Ventana Cones (1956) 7.5' quadrangle.

Paul: see **Alva Paul Creek**, under **Morro Bay** [SAN LUIS OBISPO] (2).

Pauls Creek: see **Alva Paul Creek**, under **Morro Bay** [SAN LUIS OBISPO] (2).

Pauls Island [MONTEREY]: *island,* 1 mile long, 1 mile north of Moss Landing near the junction of Elkhorn Slough and Bennett Slough (lat. 36°59' N, long. 121°47' W; sec. 7, T 13 S, R 2 E). Named on Moss Landing (1954) 7.5' quadrangle. The name commemorates Paul Lazere, who owned the island; Lazere also owned Pauls Ferry, which operated in the 1850's across Elkhorn Slough near the mouth of the slough just north of Moss Landing—the ferry also had the names "Elkhorn Ferry" and "St. Paul's Ferry" (Clark, 1991, 384-385).

Pauls Ferry: see **Pauls Island** [MONTEREY].

Payaro River: see **Pajaro River** [MONTEREY-SAN BENITO-SANTA CRUZ].

Payne Creek [SAN BENITO]: *stream,* flows 9 miles to Tres Pinos Creek 1.5 miles northwest of Panoche Pass (lat. 36°36'45" N, long. 121°01'40" W; near N line sec. 7, T 15 S, R 9 E). Named on Panoche Pass (1968) and San Benito (1968) 7.5' quadrangles.

P-Bar Flats [SANTA BARBARA]: *area,* 6.25 miles south-southwest of Hildreth Peak along Santa Ynez River (lat. 34°30'50" N, long.

119°35'20" W). Named on Hildreth Peak (1964) 7.5' quadrangle.

P-Bar Flats Campground [SANTA BARBARA]: *locality*, 6.25 miles south-southwest of Hildreth Peak along Santa Ynez River (lat. 34° 30'50" N, long. 119°35'25" W); the place is at P-Bar Flats. Named on Hildreth Peak (1964) 7.5' quadrangle.

Peach Tree: see **Peachtree Valley** [MONTEREY].

Peachtree Canyon [MONTEREY]: *canyon*, drained by a stream that flows 4.25 miles to Pancho Rico Creek 8 miles east-northeast of San Ardo (lat. 36°04'05" N, long. 120°46'30" W; sec. 27, T 21 S, R 11 E); the canyon heads southwest of Peachtree Valley. Named on Pancho Rico Valley (1967) and Slack Canyon (1969) 7.5' quadrangles. San Ardo (1943) 15' quadrangle has the form "Peach Tree Canyon" for the name.

Peachtree Canyon [SANTA BARBARA]: *canyon*, drained by a stream that flows 5.5 miles to Santa Cruz Creek 5.5 miles south-southwest of San Rafael Mountain (lat. 34°38' N, long. 119° 51' W). Named on San Rafael Mountain (1959) 7.5' quadrangle.

Peachtree Canyon: see **Mine Canyon** [SANTA BARBARA] (1).

Peachtree Creek: see **San Lorenzo Creek** [MONTEREY-SAN BENITO].

Peach Tree Spring [SANTA BARBARA]: *spring*, 3.5 miles north of Tepusquet Peak (lat. 34°57'40" N, long. 120°10'30" W). Named on Tepusquet Canyon (1964) 7.5' quadrangle.

Peachtree Valley [MONTEREY]: *valley*, 20 miles long, 10 miles east-northeast of King City along San Lorenzo Creek (lat. 36°16'50" N, long. 120°57'45" W; sec. 14, T 19 S, R 9 E). Named on Lonoak (1969), Monarch Peak (1967), Nattrass Valley (1967), Priest Valley (1969), and Slack Canyon (1969) 7.5' quadrangles. Angel (1890a, p. 345) used the form "Peach Tree Valley" for the name. The place also was called San Lorenzo Valley (Clark, 1991, p. 386). California Mining Bureau's (1909a) map shows a place called Peach Tree located 4 miles by stage line southeast of Lonoak. Postal authorities established Peach Tree post office in 1873, discontinued it for a time the same year, changed the name to Peachtree in 1897, and discontinued it in 1909 (Salley, p. 168). Elliott and Moore (p. 76) described the village of Peach Tree as "a store, saloon and post-office in one building, a hotel, blacksmith shop and another saloon."

Peachy Canyon [SAN LUIS OBISPO]: *canyon*, drained by a stream that flows nearly 3 miles to lowlands near the south edge of Paso Robles (lat. 35°37'05" N, long. 120°41'25" W). Named on Paso Robles (1948) and Templeton (1948) 7.5' quadrangles.

Peak: see **The Peak** [SANTA CRUZ].

Peak Canyon [SAN BENITO]: *canyon*, drained by a stream that flows 3 miles to San Juan Canyon 6 miles southwest of Hollister (lat.

36°48' N, long. 121°29'15" W); the canyon heads near Fremont Peak. Named on Hollister (1955) 7.5' quadrangle.

Peak Canyon: see **Little Peak Canyon** [SAN BENITO].

Peak Mountain [SANTA BARBARA]: *peak*, nearly 3 miles west-northwest of McPherson Peak (lat. 34°54'05" N, long. 119°51'30" W). Altitude 5843 feet. Named on Peak Mountain (1964) 7.5' quadrangle.

Pear Orchard: see **Dutra Creek** [MONTEREY].

Pearson Spring [SAN LUIS OBISPO]: *spring*, 8.5 miles west-northwest of Caliente Mountain (lat. 35°05'05" N, long. 119°53'50" W; near E line sec. 31, T 12 S, R 28 W). Named on Taylor Canyon (1959) 7.5' quadrangle.

Pear Spring [SAN LUIS OBISPO]: *spring*, 5 miles west-northwest of Shandon in Shimmin Canyon (lat. 35°41'35" N, long. 120°27'10" W; sec. 3, T 26 S, R 14 E). Named on Shandon (1961) 7.5' quadrangle.

Pear Tree Spring [SAN LUIS OBISPO]: *spring*, 12.5 miles southeast of Shandon near the mouth of Long Canyon (2) (lat. 35°31'05" N, long. 120°13'40" W; near W line sec. 2, T 28 S, R 16 E). Named on Holland Canyon (1961) 7.5' quadrangle.

Peartree Spring [SAN LUIS OBISPO]: *spring*, 3.5 miles west-northwest of Branch Mountain (lat. 35°12'10" N, long. 120°08'25" W). Named on Los Machos Hills (1967) 7.5' quadrangle.

Peasley Gulch [SANTA CRUZ]: *canyon*, drained by a stream that flows 3 miles to Wilder Creek 3.25 miles west-northwest of Point Santa Cruz (lat. 36°57'50" N, long. 122°04'55" W). Named on Felton (1955) and Santa Cruz (1954) 7.5' quadrangles. On Santa Cruz (1902) 30' quadrangle, the stream in the canyon is called Meder Creek—the name "Meder" is for Moses Meder, who owned part of Refugio grant, where the stream is located (Clark, 1986, p. 203-204).

Peavine Creek [SANTA CRUZ]: *stream*, flows 1 mile to Boulder Creek (1) nearly 5 miles east-southeast of Big Basin (lat. 37°08'20" N, long. 122°08'35" W; sec. 24, T 9 S, R 3 W). Named on Big Basin (1955) 7.5' quadrangle. Berkstresser (p. A-18) listed Peavine Spring, which is located 4500 feet southwest of the mouth of Peavine Creek.

Peavine Spring: see **Peavine Creek** [SANTA CRUZ].

Pebble Beach [MONTEREY]:

(1) *beach*, on the north side of Carmel Bay (lat. 36°34' N, long. 121°56'45" W). Named on Monterey (1947) 7.5' quadrangle. The name is from the pebbly nature of the beach (Clark, 1991, p. 386).

(2) *town*, north of Carmel Bay near Pebble Beach (1) (lat. 36°34'10" N, long. 121°56'30" W). Named on Monterey (1913) 15' quadrangle. Postal authorities established Pebble Beach post office in 1909 (Frickstad, p. 108).

Pebblestone Shut-in [SAN LUIS OBISPO]:

narrows, 11 miles northeast of the village of San Simeon along Nacimiento River (lat. 35°44'45" N, long. 121°02'20" W; near N line sec. 19, T 25 S, R 9 E). Named on Pebblestone Shut-in (1959) 7.5' quadrangle.

Pebbly Beach: see **Sand Hill Cove** [MONTEREY].

Pecho Creek [SAN LUIS OBISPO]: *stream,* flows 3.25 miles to the sea 2.25 miles northwest of Point San Luis (lat. 35°10'45" N, long. 120°47'30" W); the stream is on the southeast boundary of Cañada de los Osos y Pecho y Islay grant. Named on Port San Luis (1965) 7.5' quadrangle. Called Cañada y arroyo del Pecho on the diseño of Pecho y Islay grant made in 1843 (Becker, 1969). United States Board on Geographic Names (1967a, p. 10) rejected the names "Arroyo del Pecho," and "Cañada del Pecho" for the feature. On Port Harford (1897) 15' quadrangle, Pecho Creek is shown 0.5 mile farther northwest in present Vineyard Canyon (2).

Pecho Rock [SAN LUIS OBISPO]: *rock,* 375 feet long, 3.5 miles west-northwest of Point San Luis, and 3200 feet offshore (lat. 35° 10'45" N, long. 120°48'55" W); the rock is 1.25 miles west-southwest of the mouth of Pecho Creek. Named on Port San Luis (1965) 7.5' quadrangle.

Pecho Warm Springs: see **Islay Creek** [SAN LUIS OBISPO].

Pedernales: see **Point Pedernales** [SANTA BARBARA].

Pedregoso Creek: see **Mission Creek** [SANTA BARBARA].

Pelican Bay [SANTA BARBARA]: *embayment,* nearly 1.5 miles northwest of Prisoners Harbor on the north side of Santa Cruz Island (lat. 34°02' N, long. 119°42'05" W). Named on Santa Cruz Island C (1943) 7.5' quadrangle.

Pelican Point: see **Goleta Point** [SANTA BARBARA]; **Sandy Beach** [MONTEREY].

Pelican Rock [SANTA CRUZ]: *rock,* 250 feet long, 1.5 miles south-southeast of the mouth of Waddell Creek, and 400 feet offshore (lat. 37°04'25" N, long. 122°15'50" W). Named on Año Nuevo (1955) 7.5' quadrangle.

Pence Enrico Canyon: see **Pancho Rico Valley** [MONTEREY].

Pendola Campground [SANTA BARBARA]: *locality,* 6.25 miles south of Hildreth Peak (lat. 34°30'40" N, long. 119°34'30" W). Named on Hildreth Peak (1964) 7.5' quadrangle.

Pennington Creek [SAN LUIS OBISPO]: *stream,* flows 5 miles to Chorro Creek 6 miles west-northwest of San Luis Obispo (lat. 35° 19'30" N, long. 120°45' W). Named on San Luis Obispo (1965) 7.5' quadrangle.

Penvir [MONTEREY]: *locality,* 3 miles northwest of Gonzales along Southern Pacific Railroad (lat. 36°32'20" N, long. 121°29' W). Named on Gonzales (1955) 7.5' quadrangle.

People's Wharf: see **Avila Beach** [SAN LUIS OBISPO].

Pepper Spring [SANTA BARBARA]: *spring,* nearly 3 miles south of Salisbury Potrero (lat. 34°46'50" N, long. 119°42'15" W). Named on Salisbury Potrero (1964) 7.5' quadrangle.

Percys Creek: see **Boronda Creek** [MONTEREY].

Perfumo Canyon: see **Prefumo Canyon** [SAN LUIS OBISPO].

Perry Creek [SAN LUIS OBISPO]: *stream,* flows 9 miles to Santa Rosa Creek nearly 1 mile east-northeast of Cambria (lat. 35°34'05" N, long. 121°04'10" W). Named on Cambria (1959) and Cypress Mountain (1948, photorevised 1979) 7.5' quadrangles.

Perry Ridge [MONTEREY]: *ridge,* north-trending, 0.5 mile long, 6 miles southwest of Salinas (lat. 36°37' N, long. 121°44'20" W). Named on Spreckels (1947) 7.5' quadrangle.

Pesante Canyon [MONTEREY]: *canyon,* drained by a stream that flows 3.25 miles to an unnamed canyon at Prunedale (lat. 36°46'15" N, long. 121°39'55" W). Named on Prunedale (1954) 7.5' quadrangle. The name commemorates John Pesante, an early settler (Clark, 1991, p. 388).

Pescadero Canyon [MONTEREY]: *canyon,* drained by a stream that flows 2 miles to Carmel Bay just north of Carmel-by-the-Sea (lat. 36°33'25" N, long. 121°55'50" W); the canyon is on El Pescadero grant. Named on Monterey (1947) 7.5' quadrangle.

Pescadero Creek [SAN BENITO]: *stream,* flows 14 miles to San Benito River 2.5 miles southsouthwest of Paicines (lat. 36°41'40" N, long. 121°17'10" W). Named on Mount Harlan (1968) and Paicines (1968) 7.5' quadrangles. Called Sanjon del Pescadero on a diseño of Cienega de los Paicines grant (Gudde, 1949, p. 259).

Pescadero Creek [SANTA CRUZ]: *stream,* heads in San Mateo County and flows 1 mile in Santa Cruz County before reentering San Mateo County 4 miles northeast of Big Basin (lat. 37°12'55" N, long. 122°10'40" W; at N line sec. 27, T 8 S, R 3 W). Named on Big Basin (1955) 7.5' quadrangle.

Pescadero Point [MONTEREY]: *promontory,* 2 miles southeast of Cypress Point on the north side of Carmel Bay (lat. 36°33'40" N, long. 121°57'05" W); the feature is on El Pescadero grant. Named on Monterey (1947) 7.5' quadrangle. The point and nearby rocks received the name because of fishing activity carried on there in the early days—*pescadero* means "place where fishing is done" in Spanish (Hoover, Rensch, and Rensch, p. 231). United States Board on Geographic Names (1983a, p. 6) approved the name "The Pinnacles" for a reef located 0.7 mile southwest of Pescadero Point at the north entrance to Carmel Bay (lat. 36°33'23" N, long. 121°58'03" W).

Pescadero Rocks [MONTEREY]: *rocks,* 2000 feet east of Pescadero Point (lat. 36°33'40" N, long. 121°56'35" W). Named on Monterey

(1947) 7.5' quadrangle.

Pesco [SANTA BARBARA]: *locality,* 2.25 miles south of downtown Santa Maria along Santa Maria Valley Railroad (lat. 34°55'15" N, long. 120°26'40" W; sec. 27, T 10 N, R 34 W). Named on Santa Maria (1959) 7.5' quadrangle.

Peters Creek [SANTA CRUZ]: *stream,* flows nearly 1 mile to San Mateo County 11 miles north of the town of Boulder Creek (lat. 37°16'55" N, long. 122°09'05" W; at W line sec. 36, T 7 S, R 3 W). Named on Mindego Hill (1961) 7.5' quadrangle.

Pettits Peak [MONTEREY]: *peak,* 5.5 miles southwest of Greenfield (lat. 36°15'50" N, long. 121°18'35" W; sec. 22, T 19 S, R 6 E). Altitude 2067 feet. Named on Paraiso Springs (1956) 7.5' quadrangle. The name is for Charles Pettit, who owned land near the feature (Clark, 1991, p. 391).

Pfeiffer Beach [MONTEREY]: *beach,* just north of Pfeiffer Point along the coast (lat. 36°14'20" N, long. 121°48'50" W; sec. 35, T 19 S, R 1 E). Named on Pfeiffer Point (1956) 7.5' quadrangle. The feature also had the names "Dani's Beach," from the Dani family who lived near it, and "Sycamore Beach" (Clark, 1991, p. 391).

Pfeiffer Falls [MONTEREY]: *waterfall,* along Pfeiffer-Redwood Creek 0.5 mile upstream from the mouth of the creek (lat. 36°15'25" N, long. 121°46'50" W; sec. 30, T 19 S, R 2 E). Named on Big Sur (1956) 7.5' quadrangle.

Pfeiffer Gulch [MONTEREY]: *canyon,* drained by a stream that flows nearly 1 mile to Post Creek 2.25 miles east-northeast of Pfeiffer Point (lat. 36°14'30" N, long. 121°46'20" W; near W line sec. 32, T 19 S, R 2 E). Named on Pfeiffer Point (1956) 7.5' quadrangle.

Pfeiffer Point [MONTEREY]: *promontory,* 7 miles southeast of Point Sur along the coast (lat. 36°14'05" N, long. 121°48'50" W; sec. 35, T 19 S, R 1 E). Named on Pfeiffer Point (1956) 7.5' quadrangle. United States Coast Survey personnel named the feature in 1885 to 1887 for Michael Pfeiffer, an early settler (Gudde, 1949, p. 260).

Pfeiffer-Redwood Creek [MONTEREY]: *stream,* flows 1.5 miles to Big Sur River 7.5 miles east-southeast of Point Sur (lat. 36°15'05" N, long. 121°47'10" W; sec. 30, T 19 S, R 2 E). Named on Big Sur (1956) 7.5' quadrangle.

Pfeiffer Ridge [MONTEREY]: *ridge,* northwest- to west-northwest-trending, 4 miles long, 5.5 miles east-southeast of Point Sur (lat. 36°15'45" N, long. 121°49' W). Named on Big Sur (1956) 7.5' quadrangle. United States Board on Geographic Names (1981c, p. 5) approved the name "Clear Ridge" for a feature that extends for 1.2 miles southeast from Pfeiffer Ridge (sec. 26, 35, T 19 S, R 1 E), and rejected the name "Dani Ridge" for it; the name "Clear Ridge" was given because this ridge commonly is clear when surround-

ing features are lost in fog.

Pfeiffer Rock [MONTEREY]: *rock,* 150 feet long, 0.25 mile southeast of Pfeiffer Point, and 300 feet offshore (lat. 36°13'55" N, long. 121°48'35" W). Named on Pfeiffer Point (1956) 7.5' quadrangle.

Pfost Gulch [SAN LUIS OBISPO]: *canyon,* 1 mile long, 1.5 miles east-southeast of Shandon (lat. 36°38'35" N, long. 120°21'10" W). Named on Cholame (1961) 7.5' quadrangle. Cholame (1917) 30' quadrangle shows the feature as part of Cormack Canyon.

Phelan Point: see **Point Santa Cruz** [SANTA CRUZ].

Pheneger Creek [MONTEREY]: *stream,* flows 1.25 miles to Big Sur River 5.5 miles east-southeast of Point Sur (lat. 36°16'10" N, long. 121°48'25" W; sec. 24, T 19 S, R 1 E). Named on Big Sur (1956) 7.5' quadrangle.

Phoenix Creek [SAN LUIS OBISPO]: *stream,* flows 3.25 miles to Arroyo Grande Creek 10 miles north-northeast of the town of Nipomo (lat. 35°11'05" N, long. 120°26'15" W). Named on Tar Spring Ridge (1967) 7.5' quadrangle.

Picacho [SAN LUIS OBISPO]: *peak,* nearly 3 miles east-southeast of downtown Arroyo Grande (lat. 35°06'10" N, long. 120°32'25" W; on W line sec. 36, T 32 S, R 13 E). Altitude 922 feet. Named on Oceano (1965) 7.5' quadrangle.

Picacho: see **Picacho Peak** [SAN BENITO].

Picacho Creek [SAN BENITO]: *stream,* flows nearly 3 miles to San Benito River 7 miles south-southwest of Idria (lat. 36°19'35" N, long. 120°43'15" W; at S line sec. 25, T 18 S, R 11 E); the stream heads near Picacho Peak. Named on San Benito Mountain (1969) 7.5' quadrangle.

Picacho de Gavilan: see **Fremont Peak** [MONTEREY-SAN BENITO].

Picacho del Diablo: see **Diablo Point** [SANTA BARBARA].

Picacho de Romualdo: see **Cerro Romualdo** [SAN LUIS OBISPO].

Picacho Diablo: see **Diablo Point** [SANTA BARBARA].

Picacho Peak [SAN BENITO]: *peak,* 5 miles south of Idria (lat. 36° 20'45" N, long. 120°41'15" W; sec. 20, T 18 S, R 12 E); the peak is at the southeast end of The Picachos. Altitude 4657 feet. Named on San Benito Mountain (1969) 7.5' quadrangle, which shows Picacho mine situated 1200 feet westnorthwest of the peak. This mine was discovered in 1858; a settlement near the mine was called Picacho (Hoover, Rensch, and Rensch, p. 315). Postal authorities established Picacho post office in 1869, discontinued it for a time in 1876, and discontinued it finally in 1880 (Frickstad, p. 136).

Picachos: see **The Picachos** [SAN BENITO].

Picay Creek [SANTA BARBARA]: *stream,* flows 2 miles to Romero Creek 5.25 miles west-northwest of Carpinteria (lat. 34°26'05"

N, long. 119°35'45" W). Named on Carpinteria (1952, photorevised 1967) 7.5' quadrangle. Called Ficay Cr. on Santa Barbara (1903) 15' quadrangle, but United States Board on Geographic Names (1961b, p. 13) rejected this name for the stream. On Carpinteria (1952) 7.5' quadrangle, the name applies to present Romero Creek below its junction with present Picay Creek.

Pick Creek [MONTEREY]: *stream,* flows nearly 3 miles to South Fork Big Sur River 4.25 miles northeast of Partington Point (lat. 36°12'35" N, long. 121°38' W; sec. 9, T 20 S, R 3 E). Named on Partington Ridge (1956) 7.5' quadrangle. The name commemorates Charles Pick, an early settler (Clark, 1991, p. 394).

Picks Summit: see **Michaels Hill** [MONTEREY].

Picnic Canyon [MONTEREY]: *canyon,* 0.5 mile long, 5.5 miles southwest of Salinas (lat. 36°37'15" N, long. 121°44' W). Named on Spreckels (1947) 7.5' quadrangle.

Picnic Gulch Creek: see **Bates Creek** [SANTA CRUZ].

Pico Blanco [MONTEREY]: *peak,* 5 miles east of Point Sur (lat. 36° 19'05" N, long. 121°48'40" W; sec. 36, T 18 S, R 1 E). Altitude 3709 feet. Named on Big Sur (1956) 7.5' quadrangle.

Pico Creek [SAN LUIS OBISPO]: *stream,* formed by the confluence of North Fork and South Fork, flows 1 mile to the sea 3 miles southeast of the village of San Simeon (lat. 35°36'55" N, long. 121°08'55" W). Named on Pico Creek (1959) 7.5' quadrangle. The name commemorates Jose de Jesus Pico, owner of Piedra Blanca grant where the creek is located (Gudde, 1949, p. 261). North Fork is 8 miles long and South Fork is nearly 6 miles long; both forks are named on Pebblestone Shut-in (1959), Pico Creek (1959), and San Simeon (1958) 7.5' quadrangles.

Pico Creek: see **Little Pico Creek** [SAN LUIS OBISPO].

Pico Rock [SAN LUIS OBISPO]: *rock,* poorly labeled on the quadrangle map, but apparently 4.25 miles southeast of the village of San Simeon, and about 1700 feet offshore (lat. 35°35'50" N, long. 121°08'10" W). Named on Pico Creek (1959) 7.5' quadrangle.

Pie Canyon [SANTA BARBARA]: *canyon,* drained by a stream that flows 5.5 miles to Mono Creek 4.25 miles west-southwest of Hildreth Peak (lat. 34°34'05" N, long. 119°37' W). Named on Hildreth Peak (1964) and Little Pine Mountain (1964) 7.5' quadrangles.

Piedra Blanca [SAN LUIS OBISPO]: *land grant,* along the coast between the mouths of Pico Creek and San Carpoforo Creek; the grant includes Piedras Blancas Point. Named on Burnett Peak (1949), Burro Mountain (1949), Pebblestone Shut-in (1959), Pico Creek (1959), Piedras Blancas (1959), and

San Simeon (1958) 7.5' quadrangles. Jose de Jesus Pico received the land in 1840 and claimed 48,806 acres patented in 1876 (Cowan, p. 60). Postal authorities established Piedra Blanca post office in 1870 and discontinued it in 1871 (Frickstad, p. 165). The post office was in the adobe home of Juan Castro (Hamilton, p. 136).

Piedra Creek: see **Stony Creek** [MONTEREY].

Piedra de Lobos: see **Lobos Rocks** [MONTEREY].

Piedras Atlas [MONTEREY]: *ridge,* northwest-trending, 1 mile long, 7.25 miles south-southwest of Jolon (lat. 35°52'05" N, long. 121° 12'20" W). Named on Burnett Peak (1949) 7.5' quadrangle. Hamlin (p. 12) used the term "Sierra de las Piedras" for the range that lies between San Antonio River and Nacimiento River, including present Piedras Atlas.

Piedras Blancas [SAN LUIS OBISPO]: *rocks,* two, each about 200 feet long, 1 mile east-southeast of Piedras Blancas Point, and 1500 feet offshore (lat. 35°39'35" N, long. 121°16'05" W). Named on Piedras Blancas (1959) 7.5' quadrangle. Cabrillo named the rocks for their white color—*piedras blancas* means "white rocks" in Spanish; guano covers the rocks and was gathered in the 1880's (Hamilton, p. 163, 168).

Piedras Blancas: see **Piedras Blancas Point** [SAN LUIS OBISPO].

Piedras Blancas Point [SAN LUIS OBISPO]: *promontory,* 5.5 miles west-northwest of the village of San Simeon along the coast (lat. 35°39'55" N, long. 121°17'05" W); the feature is 1 mile west-northwest of the two rocks called Piedras Blancas. Named on Piedras Blancas (1959) 7.5' quadrangle. United States Board on Geographic Names (1961b, p. 13) approved the form "Point Piedras Blancas" for the name. A lighthouse was constructed at the place in 1874 and 1875, and a post office called Piedras Blancas operated at the construction site (Hamilton, p. 164-165). Postal authorities established Piedras Blancas post office in 1875, and discontinued it the same year (Frickstad, p. 166). A large white rock located west of the point is called Outer Islet (United States Coast and Geodetic Survey, p. 116).

Piedras de los Lobos: see **Lobos Rocks** [MONTEREY].

Pigeon Point [MONTEREY]: *peak,* 5.5 miles east-southeast of Jamesburg (lat. 36°19'35" N, long. 121°30'05" W; near NW cor. sec. 36, T 18 S, R 4 E). Named on Chews Ridge (1956) 7.5' quadrangle.

Pigeon River: see **Pajaro River** [MONTEREY-SAN BENITO-SANTA CRUZ].

Pilarcitos: see **El Chamisal** [MONTEREY].

Pilarcitos Canyon [MONTEREY]: *canyon,* drained by a stream that flows 4 miles to lowlands 4 miles southwest of Salinas (lat. 36° 38' N, long. 121°42' W). Named on Salinas (1947) and Spreckels (1947) 7.5' quadrangles.

Pilarcitos Ridge [MONTEREY]: *ridge,* east- to northeast-trending, 1 mile long, 5 miles southwest of Salinas (lat. 36°37'30" N, long. 121°43'15" W); the ridge is northwest of Pilarcitos Canyon. Named on Salinas (1947) and Spreckels (1947) 7.5' quadrangles.

Piletas Canyon: see **Lower Piletas Canyon** [SAN LUIS OBISPO]; **Upper Piletas Canyon** [SAN LUIS OBISPO].

Pilitas Creek [SAN LUIS OBISPO]: *stream,* flows 5.5 miles to Salinas River 5 miles northeast of Lopez Mountain (lat. 35°21' N, long. 120°30'40" W; sec. 6, T 30 S, R 14 E). Named on Lopez Mountain (1965) and Santa Margarita Lake (1967) 7.5' quadrangles.

Pilitas Mountain [SAN LUIS OBISPO]: *peak,* 1 mile west-northwest of Branch Mountain (lat. 35°11'35" N, long. 120°06' W). Altitude 3624 feet. Named on Branch Mountain (1967) 7.5' quadrangle.

Pillar Rock [SAN LUIS OBISPO]: *rock,* 125 feet long, 50 feet off the north end of Morro Rock (lat. 35°22'30" N, long. 120°52'05" W). Named on Morro Bay South (1965) 7.5' quadrangle.

Pimental: see **The Pimental**, under **Pimental Creek** [SAN BENITO].

Pimental Creek [SAN BENITO]: *stream,* flows 8 miles to join Vallecitos Creek and form Griswold Creek 5.5 miles south of Panoche (lat. 36°30'55" N, long. 120°50' W; near N line sec. 25, T 16 S, R 10 E). Named on Llanada (1969) and Panoche (1969) 7.5' quadrangles. Preston (1893b, p. 372) referred to Primetal Cañon, and Anderson and Pack (p. 19) described a small valley called The Pimental that forms the westward continuation of The Vallecitos. United States Board on Geographic names (1933, p. 604) approved the names "Pimental Valley" and "Pimental Creek," but rejected the name "The Pimental" for the valley drained by the Creek.

Pimental Valley: see **Pimental Creek** [SAN BENITO].

Pinal Creek [MONTEREY]: *stream,* flows 5 miles to Rattlesnake Creek (2) nearly 5 miles south-southeast of Junipero Serra Peak (lat. 36°04'50" N, long. 121°23'40" W). Named on Cone Peak (1949) 7.5' quadrangle.

Pinalito Canyon [MONTEREY-SAN BENITO]: *canyon,* drained by a stream that heads in San Benito County and flows 6.5 miles to Llano Grande Canyon 8.5 miles east-southeast of Greenfield in Monterey County (lat. 36°17'20" N, long. 121°05'40" W). Named on Pinalito Canyon (1969) 7.5' quadrangle.

Pinalito Creek [MONTEREY]: *stream,* flows 3 miles to San Antonio River 6 miles south-southwest of Junipero Serra Peak (lat. 36°04'15" N, long. 121°21'45" W); the stream is 0.5 mile east of Pinal Creek. Named on Bear Canyon (1949) and Cone Peak (1949) 7.5' quadrangles.

Pine Canyon [MONTEREY]:

(1) *canyon,* drained by a stream that flows nearly 4 miles to lowlands 5 miles west-northwest of Chualar (lat. 36°35'05" N, long. 121°36'20" W). Named on Chualar (1947) and Spreckels (1947) 7.5' quadrangles.

(2) *canyon,* drained by a stream that flows 8 miles to lowlands 2 miles south-southwest of King City (lat. 36°11' N, long. 121°08'45" W). Named on Thompson Canyon (1949) 7.5' quadrangle. Called Arroyo del Pino on a diseño of Posa de los Ositos grant made in 1839 (Becker, 1969). A map of Monterey County used about 1900 has the name "Pine Cr." for the stream in the canyon.

(3) *canyon,* 4.25 miles long, opens into lowlands 6.5 miles east-southeast of Jolon (lat. 35°57' N, long. 121°03'45" W; near NW cor. sec. 12, T 23 S, R 8 E). Named on Williams Hill (1949) 7.5' quadrangle.

(4) *canyon,* drained by a stream that flows nearly 4 miles to Little Cholame Creek 4.5 miles north-northwest of Parkfield (lat. 35° 57'20" N, long. 120°28'35" W; sec. 5, T 23 S, R 14 E). Named on Parkfield (1961) 7.5' quadrangle.

Pine Canyon [MONTEREY-SAN LUIS OBISPO]: *canyon,* drained by a stream that heads in Monterey County and flows 13 miles to lowlands along Estrella River 6.54 miles west of Shandon in San Luis Obispo County (lat. 35°39'45" N, long. 120°29'30" W; sec. 17, T 26 S, R 14 E). Named on Cholame Hills (1961) and Shandon (1961) 7.5' quadrangles. The stream below the canyon is called Pine Creek on Estrella (1948) 7.5' quadrangle.

Pine Canyon [SANTA BARBARA]:

(1) *canyon,* drained by a stream that flows 12 miles to Cuyama River 9 miles west of Miranda Pine Mountain (lat. 35°01'45" N, long. 120°11'40" W). Named on Chimney Canyon (1967) and Miranda Pine Mountain (1967) 7.5' quadrangles. The stream in the canyon is called Miranda Pine Creek on Branch Mountain (1952) 15' quadrangle, but United States Board on Geographic Names (1968c, p. 6) rejected the names "Miranda Pine Creek," "Miranda Creek," and "Pine Creek" for the feature.

(2) *canyon,* drained by a stream that flows 6.5 miles to Mono Creek 4.25 miles east-southeast of Madulce Peak (lat. 34°40'10" N, long. 119°31'05" W). Named on Madulce Peak (1964) 7.5' quadrangle.

(3) *canyon,* 1 mile long, 2.5 miles southeast of Orcutt (lat. 34°50'40" N, long. 120°24'35" W; sec. 24, T 9 N, R 34 W). Named on Orcutt (1959) 7.5' quadrangle.

(4) *canyon,* 2 miles long, opens into Santa Lucia Canyon 5.5 miles east of Surf (lat. 34°41'35" N, long. 120°30'15" W). Named on Surf (1959) 7.5' quadrangle.

(5) *canyon,* drained by a stream that flows 1.25 miles to Santa Cruz Creek 7 miles northeast of Santa Ynez Peak (lat. 34°36'15" N, long. 119°54'05" W). Named on Lake Cachuma

(1959) 7.5' quadrangle.

Pine Canyon Campground [SANTA BARBARA]: *locality,* 2.5 miles east-southeast of Madulce Peak (lat. 34°40'20" N, long. 119°33'05" W); the place is in Pine Canyon (2). Named on Madulce Peak (1964) 7.5' quadrangle.

Pinecate: see **Santa Rita** [MONTEREY].

Pinecate Peak [SAN BENITO]: *peak,* 4.5 miles west-northwest of San Juan Bautista (lat. 36°51'30" N, long. 121°36'50" W). Altitude 752 feet. Named on San Juan Bautista (1955) 7.5' quadrangle.

Pine Corral Potreros [SANTA BARBARA]: *area,* 1.5 miles west of Salisbury Potrero (lat. 34°49'25" N, long. 119°43'35" W). Named on Salisbury Potrero (1944) 7.5' quadrangle.

Pine Corral Spring [SANTA BARBARA]: *spring,* 1.5 miles west of Salisbury Potrero (lat. 34°49'30" N, long. 119°43'35" W); the spring is at Pine Corral Potreros. Named on Salisbury Potrero (1964) 7.5' quadrangle, which shows a feature called Pine Corral situated 950 feet west of the spring.

Pine Creek [MONTEREY]:
(1) *stream,* flows 7 miles to Carmel River 5.5 miles south-southeast of the town of Carmel Valley (lat. 36°24'25" N, long. 121°41'25" W; near W line sec. 31, T 17 S, R 3 E). Named on Big Sur (1956), Carmel Valley (1956), and Mount Carmel (1956) 7.5' quadrangles.
(2) *stream,* flows nearly 3 miles to Little Sur River 8 miles east of Point Sur (lat. 36°19'55" N, long. 121°45'15" W). Named on Big Sur (1956) 7.5' quadrangle. United States Board on Geographic Names (1967b, p. 6) approved the name "Comings Creek" for the stream; Big Sur (1956) 7.5' quadrangle shows Comings cabin near the head of a branch of the creek. The name "Comings" is from the family that had land along the stream from 1927 until the 1950's (Clark, 1991, p. 113).
(3) *stream,* flows 8 miles to Salinas River 3.5 miles north-northwest of San Ardo (lat. 36°03'55" N, long. 120°56'10" W); the stream drains Pine Valley (2). Named on Monarch Peak (1967), Pancho Rico Valley (1967), and San Ardo (1967) 7.5' quadrangles.

Pine Creek [SAN LUIS OBISPO]:
(1) *stream,* flows 1.25 miles to Estrella Creek 10.5 miles east of Paso Robles (lat. 35°39'15" N, long. 120°30'30" W; sec. 19, T 26 S, R 14 E). Named on Estrella (1948) 7.5' quadrangle, which shows the stream draining Pine Canyon [MONTEREY-SAN LUIS OBISPO], although the stream is unnamed in the canyon on the map.
(2) *stream,* flows 5 miles to Arroyo Seco 12.5 miles northeast of the town of Nipomo (lat. 35°09'55" N, long. 120°19'10" W; near S line sec. 1, T 32 S, R 15 E). Named on Caldwell Mesa (1967) 7.5' quadrangle.

Pine Creek: see **Pine Canyon** [MONTEREY] (2); **Pine Canyon** [SANTA BARBARA] (1).

Pine Creek Camp [MONTEREY]: *locality,* 9 miles northeast of Point Sur (lat. 36°23'05" N, long. 121°46'05" W); the place is along Pine Creek (1). Named on Mount Carmel (1956) 7.5' quadrangle.

Pine Falls [MONTEREY]: *waterfall,* 2.5 miles east-northeast of Ventana Cone (lat. 36°18' N, long. 121°38'05" W; near NW cor. sec. 10, T 19 S, R 3 E); the feature is in Pine Valley (1). Named on Ventana Cones (1956) 7.5' quadrangle.

Pine Flat [SANTA BARBARA]: *area,* 1.5 miles southwest of Miranda Pine Mountain (lat. 35°01'20" N, long. 120°03'25" W); the place is at the head of Pine Canyon (1). Named on Miranda Pine Mountain (1967) 7.5' quadrangle.

Pine Mountain [SAN BENITO]: *peak,* 7 miles northeast of Bitterwater (lat. 36°27'15" N, long. 120°55'05" W; sec. 18, T 17 S, R 10 E). Altitude 3814 feet. Named on Rock Spring Peak (1969) 7.5' quadrangle.

Pine Mountain [SAN LUIS OBISPO]:
(1) *peak,* 6.5 miles east-northeast of the village of San Simeon (lat. 35°41'25" N, long. 121°05'35" W; sec. 10, T 26 S, R 8 E). Altitude 3594 feet. Named on Pebblestone Shut-in (1959) 7.5' quadrangle.
(2) *hill,* nearly 1 mile east of downtown Atascadero (lat. 35°29'35" N, long. 120°39'20" W). Altitude 1326 feet. Named on Atascadero (1965) 7.5' quadrangle.
(3) *ridge,* west-trending, 3.5 miles long, 7.5 miles east-northeast of Pozo (lat. 35°20' N, long. 120°15' W). Named on La Panza (1967) and Pozo Summit (1967) 7.5' quadrangles.

Pine Mountain [SANTA CRUZ]: *ridge,* north-northwest-trending, 1.5 miles long, 1.5 miles south-southwest of Big Basin (lat. 37°08'50" N, long. 122°13'45" W; in and near sec. 18, 19, T 9 S, R 3 W). Named on Big Basin (1955) 7.5' quadrangle. The name is from a heavy growth of knob-cone pine trees on the summit of the feature (Clark, 1986, p. 257).

Pine Mountain: see **Big Pine Mountain** [SANTA BARBARA]; **Little Pine Mountain** [SANTA BARBARA].

Pine Mountain Springs [SAN LUIS OBISPO]: *spring,* 5 miles east of Pozo (lat. 35°18'20" N, long. 120°17' W); the spring is 1.5 miles south-southwest of the west end of Pine Mountain (3). Named on Pozo Summit (1967) 7.5' quadrangle.

Pine Ridge [MONTEREY]:
(1) *ridge,* west-trending, 0.5 mile long, nearly 1 mile southeast of Point Lobos (lat. 36°30'55" N, long. 121°56'35" W). Named on Monterey (1947) 7.5' quadrangle.
(2) *ridge,* west-northwest-trending, 1 mile long, 1.5 miles east-southeast of Ventana Cone (lat. 36°16'35" N, long. 121°38'55" W). Named on Ventana Cones (1956) 7.5' quadrangle. The ridge has a fine stand of ponderosa pine trees (Clark, 1991, p. 398).

Pine Ridge [SAN BENITO]: *ridge,* northwest-trending, 2.5 miles long, 3.5 miles northeast of San Benito (lat. 36°33' N, long. 121°02'30" W). Named on San Benito (1968) 7.5' quadrangle.

Pine Ridge [SAN LUIS OBISPO]: *ridge,* northwest-trending, 6.5 miles long, 16 miles northeast of the town of Nipomo (lat. 35°12'30" N, long. 120°16'45" W). Named on Caldwell Mesa (1967) and Los Machos Hills (1967) 7.5' quadrangles.

Pine Ridge Camp [MONTEREY]: *locality,* nearly 2 miles east-southeast of Ventana Cone (lat. 36°16'25" N, long. 121°38'55" W; sec. 16, T 19 S, R 3 E); the place is on the south side of Pine Ridge (2). Named on Ventana Cones (1956) 7.5' quadrangle.

Pine Rock [SAN BENITO]: *peak,* 5 miles northwest of San Benito (lat. 36°33'50" N, long. 121°08'05" W; near SW cor. sec. 5, T 16 S, R 8 E). Named on Bickmore Canyon (1968) 7.5' quadrangle. California Mining Bureau's (1909a) map shows a place called Pinerock located near the peak. Postal authorities established Pinerock post office in 1888, discontinued it in 1893, reestablished it in 1894, and discontinued it in 1911 (Frickstad, p. 136).

Pinerock: see **Pine Rock** [SAN BENITO].

Pinery: see **East Pinery** [SANTA BARBARA].

Pines: see **Little Pines** [MONTEREY]; **Santa Margarita** [SAN LUIS OBISPO] (2).

Pines Camp: see **Little Pines Camp** [MONTEREY].

Pines Campground: see **The Pines Campground** [SANTA BARBARA].

Pine Spring [SAN LUIS OBISPO]: *spring,* 1.25 miles south-southwest of Castle Crags (lat. 35°17'20" N, long. 120°12'25" W). Named on La Panza (1967) 7.5' quadrangle. United States Board on Geographic Names (1968c, p. 6) rejected the name "Pine Spring Number 1 and 2" for the feature.

Pine Spring: see **Little Pine Spring** [SANTA BARBARA].

Pine Spring Number 1 and 2: see **Pine Spring** [SAN LUIS OBISPO].

Pine Springs [MONTEREY]: *spring,* 9 miles east-southeast of Parkfield (lat. 35°52'20" N, long. 120°16'15" W). Named on Cholame Ranch (1943) 7.5' quadrangle.

Pine Top Mountain [SAN LUIS OBISPO]: *ridge,* northwest-trending, 1.25 miles long, 5.5 miles north-northeast of Piedras Blancas Point (lat. 35°44'40" N, long. 121°15'40" W). Named on Piedras Blancas (1959) 7.5' quadrangle.

Pine Valley [MONTEREY]:

(1) *valley,* nearly 3 miles east-northeast of Ventana Cone near the head of Carmel River (lat. 36°18'05" N, long. 121°38' W). Named on Chews Ridge (1956) and Ventana Cones (1956) 7.5' quadrangles.

(2) *valley,* opens into lowlands 4 miles north-northwest of San Ardo (lat. 36°04'25" N, long. 120°55'45" W); the valley is drained by Pine Creek (3). Named on San Ardo (1967) 7.5' quadrangle.

Piney: see **Piney Creek** [MONTEREY].

Piney Creek [MONTEREY]: *stream,* flows 10.5 miles to Arroyo Seco (1) 11 miles west-southwest of Greenfield (lat. 36°15'05" N, long. 121°25'05" W; sec. 27, T 19 S, R 5 E). Named on Chews Ridge (1956) and Sycamore Flat (1956) 7.5' quadrangles. Soledad (1915) 15' quadrangle shows Piney Creek as a tributary of Paloma Creek, and shows Paloma Creek continuing along the course of present Piney Creek to Arroyo Seco (1). Postal authorities established Piney post office, located 7 miles southwest of Paraiso Springs on the east side of Piney Creek (NE quarter sec. 28, T 19 S, R 5 E), in 1897, moved it 2.5 miles east in 1904, and discontinued it in 1905 (Salley, p. 172; Clark, 1991, p. 399).

Piney Creek Campground [MONTEREY]: *locality,* 13 miles west of Greenfield (lat. 36°17'10" N, long. 121°28'45" W; at S line sec. 12, T 19 S, R 4 E); the place is along Piney Creek. Named on Sycamore Flat (1956) 7.5' quadrangle.

Piney Ridge [SAN LUIS OBISPO]: *ridge,* west-to north-northwest-trending, 0.5 mile long, 2 miles south-southeast of Lopez Mountain (lat. 35°16'40" N, long. 120°33'45" W). Named on Lopez Mountain (1965) 7.5' quadrangle.

Pinkham's Santa Barbara Mineral Springs: see **Veronica Springs** [SANTA BARBARA].

Pinnacle: see **The Pinnacle**, under **Pinnacle Point** [MONTEREY].

Pinnacle Cove [MONTEREY]: *embayment,* near the northwest end of Point Lobos along the coast (lat. 36°31'20" N, long. 121°57'10" W); the feature is just south of Pinnacle Point. Named on Monterey (1947) 7.5' quadrangle.

Pinnacle Point [MONTEREY]: *promontory,* at the northwest end of Point Lobos along the coast (lat. 36°31'25" N, long. 121°57'10" W). Named on Monterey (1947, photorevised 1968) 7.5' quadrangle. Called Carmel Point on Monterey (1947) 7.5' quadrangle, which shows Pinnacle Point as an island off Carmel Point. On California Department of Parks and Recreation's map the island has the name "The Pinnacle." Malaspina's (1791) map has the name "Punta del Carmelo" at the place, Parke's (1854-1855) map has the name "Pt. Carmel" at the south end of Carmel Bay, and Whitney (p. 157) referred to Point Carmelo. United States Board on Geographic Names (1975, p. 4-5) gave the variant names "Carmel Point" and "Pyramid Point" for the feature. At the same time, the Board (p. 4) applied the name "Carmel Point" to a promontory on the east shore of Carmel Bay just north of the mouth of Carmel River and at the southwest end of present Carmel-by-the-Sea (lat. 36°32'37" N, long. 121°55'55" W).

Pinnacle Rocks [SAN BENITO]: *relief feature,* 2.5 miles north of North Chalone Peak (lat. 36°29'15" N, long. 121°12' W; on N line sec. 3, T 17 S, R 7 E). Named on North Chalone Peak (1969) 7.5' quadrangle. The feature sometimes is called Vancouver's Pinnacles because English navigator George Vancouver supposedly visited the place in 1794 (Hoover, Rensch, and Rensch, p. 315).

Pinnacles [SAN BENITO]: *locality,* 4 miles west-northwest of San Benito in Bear Valley (lat. 36°32' N, long. 121°08'40" W; near NW cor. sec. 19, T 16 S, R 8 E). Named on Bickmore Canyon (1968) 7.5' quadrangle. San Benito (1919) 15' quadrangle has the name "Cook" at the site. Postal authorities established Cook post office in 1894, moved it and changed the name to Pinnacles in 1924, and discontinued it in 1953 (Salley, p. 49, 172).

Pinnacles: see **Little Pinnacles** [SAN BENITO]; **The Pinnacles** [MONTEREY]; **The Pinnacles**, under **Pescadero Point** [MONTEREY].

Pinole Spring [SAN LUIS OBISPO]: *spring,* 22 miles northeast of Pozo (lat. 35°29'50" N, long. 120°04'15" W; near NE cor. sec. 18, T 28 S, R 18 E). Named on La Panza NE (1966) 7.5' quadrangle.

Pinos: see **Point Pinos** [MONTEREY].

Pinto Lake [SANTA CRUZ]: *lake,* nearly 1 mile long, 3 miles north-northwest of Watsonville (lat. 36°57'20" N, long. 121°46'15" W). Named on Watsonville West (1954) 7.5' quadrangle. The name commemorates Rafael Pinto, a former Lieutenant in the Mexican army who lived near Watsonville (Rowland, p. 45).

Pinyon Peak [MONTEREY]:

(1) *peak,* 8.5 miles east-northeast of Soberanes Point (lat. 36°29'20" N, long. 121°47'10" W). Altitude 2249 feet. Named on Mount Carmel (1956) 7.5' quadrangle.

(2) *peak,* nearly 3 miles northeast of Junipero Serra Peak (lat. 36° 10'05" N, long. 121°22'50" W; sec. 25, T 20 S, R 5 E). Altitude 5264 feet. Named on Junipero Serra Peak (1949) 7.5' quadrangle. A map of Monterey County used about 1900 has the name "Vaquero Pk." for the feature, which is west of Vaqueros Creek.

Pionne Peak [SAN BENITO]: *peak,* 6.5 miles north-northwest of San Benito (lat. 36°35'10" N, long. 121°08'40" W; sec. 31, T 15 S, R 8 E). Altitude 2704 feet. Named on Bickmore Canyon (1968) 7.5' quadrangle.

Pipeline Lake [SAN LUIS OBISPO]: *lake,* 2050 feet long, 3.5 miles south-southwest of downtown Arroyo Grande near the coast (lat. 35°04'30" N, long. 120°36'25" W). Named on Oceano (1965) 7.5' quadrangle.

Pipin Corner [SAN LUIS OBISPO]: *locality,* 1.5 miles west-southwest of Pozo along Salinas River (lat. 35°17'55" N, long. 120°24'10" W; sec. 19, T 30 S, R 15 E). Named on Santa Margarita Lake (1967) 7.5' quadrangle.

Pismo [SAN LUIS OBISPO]: *land grant,* along the coast between Shell Beach and the mouth of Arroyo Grande Creek; the grant includes Pismo Beach. Named on Arroyo Grande NE (1965), Oceano (1965), and Pismo Beach

(1965) 7.5' quadrangles. Jose Ortega received 2 leagues in 1835; Isaac J. Sparks claimed 8839 acres patented in 1866 (Cowan, p. 61). Perez (p. 81) gave 1840 as the year of the grant. According to Gudde (1949, p. 264), the name is derived from an Indian word that has the meaning "tar."

Pismo: see **Pismo Beach** [SAN LUIS OBISPO].

Pismo Beach [SAN LUIS OBISPO]: *town,* 10 miles south of San Luis Obispo (lat. 35°08'30" N, long. 120°38'20" W); the town is on Pismo grant. Named on Arroyo Grande NE (1965) and Pismo Beach (1965) 7.5' quadrangles. Called Pismo on Arroyo Grande (1897) 15' quadrangle. According to Angel (1883, p. 322), in the early days the whole coast from Point Sal [SANTA BARBARA] to Point San Luis usually was called Pismo Beach. The town was founded in 1891 and incorporated in 1946 (Lee and others, p. 119). Postal authorities established Pismo post office in 1894 and changed the name to Pismo Beach in 1923 (Frickstad, p. 166). Chase (p. 142-143) described "El Pizmo, a newly exploited beach resort."

Pismo Bench [SAN LUIS OBISPO]: *area,* nearly 1 mile northeast of the mouth of Pismo Creek (lat. 35°08'30" N, long. 120°37'40" W); the place is in the town of Pismo Beach. Named on Pismo Beach (1965) 7.5' quadrangle.

Pismo Creek [SAN LUIS OBISPO]: *stream,* formed by the confluence of East Corral de Piedra Creek and West Corral de Piedra Creek, flows 5.25 miles to the sea at Pismo Beach (lat. 35°08' N, long. 120°38'25" W). Named on Arroyo Grande NE (1965) and Pismo Beach (1965) 7.5' quadrangles.

Pismo Lake [SAN LUIS OBISPO]: *marsh,* 1 mile southeast of downtown Pismo Beach (lat. 35°07'55" N, long. 120°37'40" W). Named on Pismo Beach (1965) 7.5' quadrangle.

Pit: see **The Pit** [MONTEREY].

Pitman Canyon [MONTEREY]: *canyon,* drained by a stream that flows 4 miles to Peachtree Canyon 8.5 miles east-northeast of San Ardo (lat. 36°04'55" N, long. 120°46'15" W; near S line sec. 22, T 21 S, R 11 E). Named on Monarch Peak (1967) and Pancho Rico Valley (1967) 7.5' quadrangles. The name commemorates William Luther Pitman, who homesteaded in the canyon (Clark, 1991, p. 402).

Placer Creek [SAN LUIS OBISPO]: *stream,* flows nearly 7 miles to San Juan Creek 4.5 miles northeast of Castle Crags (lat. 35°21'05" N, long. 120°08'25" W; near N line sec. 3, T 30 S, R 17 E). Named on La Panza (1967) 7.5' quadrangle. Prospectors discovered gold along the stream in 1878 (Lee and others, p. 81). This may be the feature called De la Guerra Gulch that Angel (1883, p. 248) mentioned as the site of most of the mining done in the old La Panza placer mining district.

Plaskett [MONTEREY]: *locality,* 2 miles north

155

of Cape San Martin along the coast (lat. 35°55' N, long. 121°28' W; sec. 19, T 23 S, R 5 E); the place is near the mouth of Plaskett Creek. Named on Cape San Martin (1949) 7.5' quadrangle, which shows Pacific Valley school situated north of Plaskett near the mouth of Plaskett Creek.. Crippen (p. 6) gave the name "Plaskett Point" to the first promontory along the coast south of the mouth of Plaskett Creek, and gave the name "Jade Cove" to the embayment south of the point, where nephrite jade is found. Lussier (p. 36) used the name "Pacific Valley" for a small community situated near Plaskett.

Plaskett Creek [MONTEREY]: *stream,* flows 2.5 miles to the sea 2.25 miles north-north-west of Cape San Martin (lat. 35°55'10" N, long. 121°28'15" W; sec. 19, T 23 S, R 5 E). Named on Cape San Martin (1949) 7.5' quadrangle. The name commemorates the Plaskett family, early residents in the neighborhood (Clark, 1991, p. 402-403).

Plaskett Point: see Plaskett [MONTEREY].

Plaskett Rock [MONTEREY]: *rock,* 325 feet long, 2.25 miles north-northwest of Cape San Martin, and 825 feet offshore (lat. 35°55'15" N, long. 121°28'40" W); the feature is opposite the mouth of Plaskett Creek. Named on Cape San Martin (1949) 7.5' quadrangle.

Platts Harbor [SANTA BARBARA]: *embayment,* 1.5 miles east-southeast of Diablo Point on he north side of Santa Cruz Island (lat. 34°02'50" N, long. 119°44' W). Named on Santa Cruz Island B (1943) 7.5' quadrangle. Called Dicks Harbor on Bremner's (1932) map. Doran (p. 147) referred to to the harbor as "Dick's, sometimes called Platt's."

Pleasant Valley [SANTA CRUZ]: *valley,* 1.5 miles west-northwest of Corralitos (lat. 36°59'45" N, long. 121°50' W). Named on Loma Prieta (1955) and Watsonville West (1954) 7.5' quadrangles.

Pleasant Valley: see **Hog Canyon** [MONTEREY-SAN LUIS OBISPO].

Pleito: see **Pleyto** [MONTEREY] (1) and (2).

Pleyto [MONTEREY]:

(1) *land grant,* 13 miles southeast of Jolon along San Antonio River. Named on Bryson (1949), Hames Valley (1949), Tierra Redonda Mountain (1949), and Williams Hill (1949) 7.5' quadrangles. Jose Antonio Chavez received 3 leagues in 1845; W.S. Johnson and others claimed 13,299 acres patented in 1872 (Cowan, p. 61-62; Cowan listed the grant under the names "Pleito," "Pleyto," and "San Bartolome"). The name "Pleyto" supposedly is derived from *pleito,* which means "lawsuit" in Spanish, and dates from the time that a group of Spaniards saw Indians at the place talking as if arguing legal points (Hoover, Rensch, and Rensch, p. 227).

(2) *locality,* 12.5 miles southeast of Jolon along San Antonio River (lat. 35°51'35" N, long. 120°59'35" W); the place is on Pleyto grant. Named on Tierra Redonda Mountain (1949)

7.5' quadrangle. Water of Lake San Antonio now covers the site. Postal authorities established Pleito post office in 1870, discontinued it in 1872, reestablished it in 1874, discontinued it in 1876, reestablished it in 1884, changed the name to Pleyto in 1884, and discontinued it in 1925 (Frickstad, p. 108). William Pinkerton planned the community on land he bought in 1868 (Clark, 1991, p. 404).

Plowshare Peak [SANTA BARBARA]: *peak,* 1 mile north-northwest of Miranda Pine Mountain (lat. 35°03'10" N, long. 120°02'30" W). Named on Miranda Pine Mountain (1967) 7.5' quadrangle.

Plowshare Spring [SANTA BARBARA]: *spring,* 2 miles west-northwest of Miranda Pine Mountain (lat. 35°02'45" N, long. 120° 04' W); the spring is 1.5 miles west-southwest of Plowshare Peak. Named on Miranda Pine Mountain (1967) 7.5' quadrangle. Branch Mountain (1942) 15' quadrangle shows Plowshare Spr. at the site of present Brookshire Campground.

Pocket Lake: see **Big Pocket Lake** [SAN LUIS OBISPO].

Point Almeja: see **Mussel Point** [MONTEREY].

Point Alones [MONTEREY]: *promontory,* 2.25 miles southeast of Point Pinos along the coast (lat. 37°05' N, long. 121°54' W). Named on Monterey (1947) 7.5' quadrangle. According to Clark (1991, p. 406), the name is derived from an Indian word meaning "abalone"— abalone are found at the place; the feature has the variant names "Abalone Point" and "Point Loeb," the last for Jacques Loeb, an experimental biologist who did research in the vicinity.

Point Arguelia: see **Point Arguello** [SANTA BARBARA].

Point Arguello [SANTA BARBARA]: *promontory,* 11.5 miles west-southwest of the city of Lompoc (lat. 34°34'35" N, long. 120° 39' W). Named on Point Arguello (1959) 7.5' quadrangle. United States Board on Geographic Names (1933, p. 102) rejected the name "Point Arguelia" for the feature. Vancouver named the promontory in 1792 for Jose Dario Arguello, the commandant at Monterey; soldiers of the Portola expedition called it Punta Pedernales in 1769 because they found some big flints there (Wagner, H.R., p. 373, 482)—*pedernales* means "flints" in Spanish. The name "Pedernales" now applies to a nearby promontory.

Point Aulon: see **Lovers Point** [MONTEREY].

Point Bennett [SANTA BARBARA]: *promontory,* at the westernmost tip of San Miguel Island (lat. 34°01'50" N, long. 120°27'05" W). Named on San Miguel Island West (1950) 7.5' quadrangle.

Point Buchon [SAN LUIS OBISPO]: *promontory,* 8 miles south-southwest of Morro Rock on the coast at the west extremity of Irish Hills (lat. 35°15'20" N, long. 120°53'55" W). Named on Morro Bay South (1965) 7.5' quadrangle. When members of the Portola expedition ascended present Price Canyon in 1769, they found a group of Indians whose chief had a large goiter; the soldiers called the place Buchon—*buchon* means "goiter" in Spanish—and this designation is perpetuated in the name of the point (Wagner, H.R., p. 377-378).

Point Cabrillo: see **Mussel Point** [MONTEREY].

Point Carmel: see **Pinnacle Point** [MONTEREY].

Point Carmelo: see **Pinnacle Point** [MONTEREY]; **Point Lobos** [MONTEREY].

Point Castillo [SANTA BARBARA]: *promontory,* 1.25 miles south-southeast of downtown Santa Barbara along the coast (lat. 34°24'10" N, long. 119°41'25" W). Named on Santa Barbara (1952) 7.5' quadrangle. Called Punta del Castillo on Santa Barbara (1903) 15' quadrangle, but United States Board on Geographic Names (1961b, p. 9) rejected this name for the promontory. The feature was called Punta de San Esteban in Spanish days (Wagner, H.R., p. 498).

Point Concepcion: see **Point Conception** [SANTA BARBARA].

Point Conception [SANTA BARBARA]: *promontory,* 45 miles west of Santa Barbara along the coast (lat. 34°26'55" N, long. 120°28'15" W). Named on Point Conception (1953) 7.5' quadrangle. Cabrillo called the promontory Cabo de Galera in 1542 for its galley-like shape (Wagner, H.R., p. 381). A map by Palacios that resulted from Vizcaino's voyage of 1602 has the name "Punta de la Limpia Concepcion" for the feature; Vizcaino reached the place about December 8, the day of celebration of the Purisima Concepcion (Wagner, H.R., p. 381). The promontory is called Pta. Concepcion on Parke's (1854-1855) map. United States Board on Geographic Names (1933, p. 232) rejected the form "Point Concepcion" for the name

Point Cove: see **Headland Cove** [MONTEREY].

Point Cypress: see **Cypress Point** [MONTEREY].

Point Cypress Rock: see **Cypress Point Rock** [MONTEREY].

Point Douty: see **Sunset Point** [MONTEREY].

Point Estero [SAN LUIS OBISPO]: *promontory,* 3.5 miles west-northwest of Cayucos Point along the coast (lat. 35°27'35" N, long. 121°00'05" W; sec. 33, T 28 S, R 9 E); the feature is at the north end of Estero Bay. Named on Cayucos (1965) 7.5' quadrangle. Called Punta del Estero on Costano's map that resulted from the Portola expedition (Gudde, 1949, p. 110), and called Pt. Estero on United States Coast Survey's (1854) map. Vancouver (p. 141) used the name "Punto del Esteros" in 1793. According to H.R. Wagner (p. 386), the name "Estero" evidently is from the estero at the mouth of Ellysly's Creek, or possibly from the name "Los Esteros" applied on Span-

ish maps to present Estero Bay.

Point Felipe: see **Santa Barbara Point** [SANTA BARBARA].

Point Gorda: see **Cape San Martin** [MONTEREY].

Point Harris: see **Harris Point** [SANTA BARBARA].

Point Joe [MONTEREY]: *promontory,* nearly 2.5 miles southwest of Point Pinos along the coast (lat. 36°36'35" N, long. 121°57'20" W). Named on Monterey (1947) 7.5' quadrangle. The feature first was called Pyramid Point; the name "Joe" is for a squatter who lived near the promontory for many years (Reinstedt, 1975, p. 94). The squatter was known as Chinaman Joe, but whether the point was named for Joe, or Joe for the point, is a question (Lydon, p. 152). Clark (1991, p. 407) gave Intermediate Point and Joe's Point as alternate names for the feature.

Point Lobos [MONTEREY]: *promontory,* 2.5 miles southwest of present Carmel-by-the-Sea along the coast on the south side of Carmel Bay (lat. 36°31'20" N, long. 121°57'10" W). Named on Monterey (1947) 7.5' quadrangle. Rogers and Johnston's (1857) map has the designation "Pta. de Lobos or Carmel" for the feature. On Lawson's (1893) map, the whole peninsula that includes Point Lobos has the name "Point Carmelo," and a promontory just south of present Sand Hill has the name "Pt. Lobos." California Department of Parks and Recreation's map has the name "Punta de los Lobos Marinos" for the next promontory northwest of the one called Pt. Lobos on Lawson's (1893) map; this point is between Headland Cove and Sea Lion Cove. Stewart (p. 261) identified the name "Lobos" with *lobo marino,* which means "seal" or "sea lion" in Spanish.

Point Loeb: see **Point Alones** [MONTEREY].

Point Lospie: see **Point Sal** [SANTA BARBARA].

Point Morrito: see **Lions Head** [SANTA BARBARA].

Point Pedernales [SANTA BARBARA]: *promontory,* 2 miles north-northeast of Point Arguello along the coast (lat. 34°36'15" N, long. 120°38'30" W). Named on Point Arguello (1959) 7.5' quadrangle. Soldiers of the Portola expedition gave the name "Punta Pedernales" to present Point Arguello in 1769 because they found some flints there (Wagner, H.R., p. 482)—*pedernales* means "flints" in Spanish. The name "Pedernales" applied to present Purisima Point in the 1850's, and was transferred to present Point Pedernales after 1900 (Gudde, 1949, p. 257).

Point Piedras Blancas: see **Piedras Blancas Point** [SAN LUIS OBISPO].

Point Pinos [MONTEREY]: *promontory,* northernmost point of land northwest of Monterey at the south end of Monterey Bay (lat. 36°38'15" N, long. 121°55'50" W). Named on Monterey (1947) 7.5' quadrangle. Called

Punta de los Pinos on Williamson's (1853) map. Davidson (1887, p. 212) identified present Point Pinos as the feature that Cabrillo and Ferrelo called El Cabo de San Martin and El Cabo de Martin in 1542, and that Vizcaino called La Punta de Pinos in 1602. Davidson (1907, p. 28) also noted that a map of 1646 has the name "C.S. Barbera," a map of 1672 has the name "P. de S. Barbera," and an atlas of 1709 has the name "P. de Carinde" for the promontory. The name "Pinos" is from pine trees at the place; the feature also was called Lighthouse Point (Clark, 1991, p. 410).

Point Pinos Range: see **Santa Lucia Range** [MONTEREY].

Point Sal [SANTA BARBARA]: *promontory,* 7.5 miles southwest of the town of Guadalupe along the coast (lat. 34°54'10" N, long. 120°40'15" W; sec. 34, T 10 N, R 36 W). Named on Point Sal (1958) 7.5' quadrangle. Called Pta. Sal on Parke's (1854-1855) map. Vancouver (p. 142) named the promontory to honor Hermenegildo Sal, Spanish commandant at San Francisco. Fairbanks' (1896) map has the name "Point Lospie" for a promontory 2.25 miles southeast of Point Sal.

Point Sal Landing [SANTA BARBARA]: *locality,* 1.5 miles east of Point Sal along the coast (lat. 34°53'50" N, long. 120°38'45" W). Named on Guadalupe (1905) 30' quadrangle.

Point Sal Ridge [SANTA BARBARA]: *ridge,* west-trending, 4.5 miles long, 6 miles southwest of the town of Guadalupe (lat. 34° 54'05" N, long. 120°38' W); Point Sal is at the west end of the ridge. Named on Guadalupe (1959) and Point Sal (1958) 7.5' quadrangles. Harold W. Fairbanks named the feature (Arnold and Anderson, 1907a, p. 16).

Point San Luis [SAN LUIS OBISPO]: *promontory,* 10 miles south-southwest of San Luis Obispo along the coast (lat. 35°09'35" N, long. 120°45'30" W); the feature is at the west end of San Luis Obispo Bay. Named on Port San Luis (1965) 7.5' quadrangle. Called Pta. St. Luis on Emory's (1857-1858) map.

Point Santa Cruz [SANTA CRUZ]: *promontory,* at the west end of Santa Cruz Harbor at Santa Cruz (lat. 36°57' N, long. 122°01'30" W). Named on Santa Cruz (1954) 7.5' quadrangle. Called Punta de Lobos on a Spanish map of 1796, and called Phelan Point in the 1920's; the feature acquired the unofficial name "Lighthouse Point" after a lighthouse was built there in 1869 (Clark, 1986, p. 183).

Point Sierra Nevada [SAN LUIS OBISPO]: *promontory,* 4 miles north-northwest of Piedras Blancas Point along the coast (lat. 35° 42'50" N, long. 121°18'55" W). Named on Piedras Blancas (1959) 7.5' quadrangle. The name commemorates the steamship *Sierra Nevada*, which was stranded on rocks northwest of the point (United States Coast and Geodetic Survey, p. 117).

Point Sur [MONTEREY]: *promontory,* 23 miles south of Point Pinos along the coast (lat.

36°18'25" N, long. 121°54'10" W); the feature is on El Sur grant. Named on Point Sur (1956) 7.5' quadrangle. The promontory had the name "Punta que Parece Isla" in Spanish times, although in 1769 the Portola expedition called it Morro Trompo, an allusion to the shape of the feature—*trompa* means "horn" or "trumpet" in Spanish (Wagner, H.R., p. 418, 521). A lighthouse was built at the point in 1889 (Fink, p. 215). Postal authorities established Point Sur post office 1 mile north of Bisby Creek at Bixby's Mill in 1883 and discontinued it the same year; they established Sur post office in 1889 and discontinued it in 1913; they established Mungo post office in 1895 and discontinued it in 1898, when they moved the service to Sur—the name "Mungo" was for Mungo McHolme, first postmaster (Salley, p. 149, 175, 216)

Poison Oak Hill [MONTEREY]: *peak,* 2.5 miles east of Jamesburg (lat. 36°22' N, long. 121°32'35" W; sec. 16, T 18 S, R 4 E); the peak is at the southeast end of Poison Oak Ridge. Altitude 2754 feet. Named on Chews Ridge (1956) 7.5' quadrangle.

Poison Oak Ridge [MONTEREY]: *ridge,* west-northwest-trending, 1 mile long, 2.25 miles east of Jamesburg (lat. 36°22'15" N, long. 121°33' W). Named on Chews Ridge (1956) 7.5' quadrangle.

Poison Spring [MONTEREY]: *spring,* 23 miles east-northeast of King City (lat. 36°17'15" N, long. 120°42'45" W; sec. 12, T 19 S, R 11 E). Named on San Benito Mountain (1969) 7.5' quadrangle.

Poison Water Pond [SAN LUIS OBISPO]: *lake,* 225 feet long, nearly 4 miles east-northeast of Cholame (lat. 35°44'30" N, long. 120° 14' W). Named on Annette (1943) 7.5' quadrangle.

Pole Canyon [MONTEREY]: *canyon,* drained by a stream that flows 3 miles to Jolon Valley 4.5 miles north-northeast of Jolon (lat. 36° 02' N, long. 121°09'35" W; sec. 12, T 22 S, R 7 E). Named on Cosio Knob (1949) 7.5' quadrangle.

Polonia Valley: see **Polonio Pass** [SAN LUIS OBISPO].

Polonio Pass [SAN LUIS OBISPO]: *valley,* 5.5 miles east of Cholame on San Luis Obispo-Kern county line (lat. 35°43'30" N, long. 120° 11'35" W). Named on Orchard Peak (1961) 7.5' quadrangle. Angel (1890c, p. 569) used the name "Polonia Valley."

Poncha Rica Creek: see **Pancho Rico Creek** [MONTEREY].

Poncho Rico Creek: see **Pancho Rico Creek** [MONTEREY].

Ponciano Ridge [MONTEREY]: *ridge,* west-trending, 3.5 miles long, 6 miles south of the town of Carmel Valley (lat. 36°23'45" N, long. 121°44'15" W). Named on Carmel Valley (1956) and Mount Carmel (1956) 7.5' quadrangles. The name commemorates Ponciano Manjares, a homesteader in the region (Clark,

1991, p. 413).

Poorman Canyon [SAN LUIS OBISPO]: *canyon,* drained by a stream that flows 1 mile to Corbit Canyon 5.25 miles south-southeast of Edna (lat. 35°08'05" N, long. 120°34'10" W). Named on Arroyo Grande NE (1965) 7.5' quadrangle.

Pope: see **Indian Valley** [MONTEREY] (3).

Poplar Campground [SANTA BARBARA]: *locality,* about 3.5 miles south-southeast of Big Pine Mountain along Indian Creek (lat. 34° 38'45" N, long. 119°38'10" W). Named on Big Pine Mountain (1964) 7.5' quadrangle.

Porta Suela [SAN LUIS OBISPO]: *pass,* 5.25 miles southeast of Cambria near Harmony (lat. 35°30'15" N, long. 121°01' W). Named on San Simeon (1919) 15' quadrangle.

Porter Gulch [SANTA CRUZ]: *canyon,* 1.5 miles long, opens into Tannery Gulch 4 miles northeast of Soquel Point (lat. 36°59'45" N, long. 121°55'20" W). Named on Laurel (1955) and Soquel (1954) 7.5' quadrangles. Ben Porter and his cousin George had a tannery in the canyon in the 1850's (Rowland, p. 71).

Porter Gulch: see **Aptos Creek** [SANTA CRUZ].

Porter Peak [SANTA BARBARA]: *peak,* 3.5 miles west-northwest of Miranda Pine Mountain (lat. 35°03'15" N, long. 120°05'55" W). Altitude 3384 feet. Named on Miranda Pine Mountain (1967) 7.5' quadrangle.

Porter's Landing: see **Soquel Creek** [SANTA CRUZ].

Porter Spring [SANTA BARBARA]: *spring,* 3.5 miles west-northwest of Miranda Pine Mountain (lat. 35°03'25" N, long. 120°05'45" W; sec. 1, T 11 N, R 31 W); the spring is 1700 feet northeast of present Porter Peak. Named on Branch Mountain (1952) 15' quadrangle.

Portezuelo: see **Central Valley** [SANTA BARBARA].

Port Harford: see **Port San Luis** [SAN LUIS OBISPO].

Port Hartford: see **Port San Luis** [SAN LUIS OBISPO].

Port Orford [SANTA BARBARA]: *locality,* 0.5 mile west of Gaviota along the coast at the mouth of Cañada de la Gaviota (lat. 34°28'15" N, long. 120°13'40" W). Site named on Gaviota (1953) 7.5' quadrangle. Farmers shipped their products from Gaviota Wharf, a 1000-foot-long pier at the place, from 1875 through the 1890's (Rife, p. 104).

Port Rogers: see **Port Watsonville** [SANTA CRUZ].

Port San Luis [SAN LUIS OBISPO]: *locality,* 1 mile north-northeast of Point San Luis along the coast (lat. 35°10'35" N, long. 120°45'10" W). Named on Port San Luis (1965) 7.5' quadrangle. Called Port Harford on Port Harford (1897) 15' quadrangle. Dr. John O'Farrell, one of the owners and managers of the railroad built to the site, gave the name "Port Harford" to the place to honor John Harford, the origi-

nal owner of the wharf there (Angel, 1883, p. 350). Postal authorities established Port Harford post office in 1882, changed the name to Port San Luis in 1907, and discontinued it in 1932 (Frickstad, p. 166). United States Board on Geographic Names (1933, p. 616) rejected the name "Port Hartford" for the place.

Portugee Canyon [MONTEREY]: *canyon,* drained by a stream that flows 8 miles to Pine Creek (3) 4 miles north of San Ardo (lat. 36° 04'45" N, long. 120°54'20" W). Named on Pancho Rico Valley (1967) 7.5' quadrangle. Called Redhead Canyon on San Ardo (1956) 15' quadrangle, but United States Board on Geographic Names (1968c, p. 6) rejected this name for the feature. The name "Portugee Canyon" recalls an old homesteader known as The Portugee (Clark, 1991, p. 416).

Portuguese Canyon [MONTEREY]:
(1) *canyon,* drained by a stream that flows 9 miles to Salinas River 0.5 mile east of Bradley (lat. 35°51'40" N, long. 120°47'40" W; sec. 9, T 24 S, R 11 E). Named on Bradley (1949), Valleton (1948), and Wunpost (1949) 7.5' quadrangles. The name is from the large number of Portuguese people who settled east of Bradley in the 1860's (Clark, 1991, p. 417).
(2) *canyon,* drained by a stream that flows 12 miles to Vineyard Canyon 8.5 miles east-southeast of Bradley (lat. 35°49'15" N, long. 120°39'45" W; near S line sec. 22, T 24 S, R 12 E). Named on San Miguel (1948), Stockdale Mountain (1948), and Valleton (1948) 7.5' quadrangles.

Portuguese Ridge [MONTEREY]: *ridge,* west-to southwest-trending, 2 miles long, 2 miles east-southeast of Soberanes Point (lat. 36°26'30" N, long. 121°53'20" W). Named on Soberanes Point (1956) 7.5' quadrangle.

Port Watsonville [SANTA CRUZ]: *locality,* 4.5 miles southwest of Watsonville along the coast (lat. 36°52'30" N, long. 121°49'30" W); the place is 2 miles north-northwest of the mouth of Pajaro River. Named on Capitola (1914) 15' quadrangle. Port Watsonville began in 1903 with construction of a wharf and other facilities; at first it was called Port Rogers— W.J. Rogers was one of the promoters of the enterprise (Lewis, 1976, p. 143). Beach property at the place later was offered for sale in a subdivision called Calpaco from letters in the name "California Pacific Company" (Lewis 1976, p. 148).

Posa Anchorage [SANTA BARBARA]: *anchorage,* 6.5 miles southeast of Fraser Point at the southwest end of Santa Cruz Island (lat. 33°58'45" N, long. 119°52'05" W); the anchorage is at the mouth of Cañada Posa. Named on Santa Cruz Island A (1943) 7.5' quadrangle. Called Poso Anchorage on Bremner's (1932) map.

Posa de los Ositos [MONTEREY]: *land grant,* south of Greenfield. Named on Greenfield (1956), Paraiso Springs (1956), and Thompson Canyon (1949) 7.5' quadrangles. Carlos Espinosa received 4 leagues in 1839 and claimed 16,939 acres patented in 1865 (Cowan, p. 63; Cowan listed the grant under the name "Poza de los Ositos"). California Mining Bureau's (1917b) map shows a place called Venezuela located about 4 miles southeast of Greenfield on the grant west of Salinas River.

Poso Anchorage: see **Posa Anchorage** [SANTA BARBARA].

Poso Ortega [SAN LUIS OBISPO]: *lake,* 300 feet long, 18 miles east-southeast of Shandon (lat. 35°31'15" N, long. 120°05'40" W; sec. 1, T 28 S, R 17 E). Named on Packwood Creek (1961) 7.5' quadrangle. Called Poso Ortega Lake on Packwood (1943) 7.5' quadrangle, and called Pozo Ortegta on Arnold and Johnson's (1910) map.

Poso Ortega Lake: see **Poso Ortega** [SAN LUIS OBISPO].

Post [SANTA BARBARA]: *locality,* 4.5 miles east-southeast of Surf along Southern Pacific Railroad (lat. 34°39'15" N, long. 120°32'05" W). Named on Surf (1959) 7.5' quadrangle.

Post Canyon [SAN BENITO]: *canyon,* drained by a stream that flows 1.25 miles to Byles Canyon 13 miles east of Bitterwater (lat. 36°23'20" N, long. 120°46'20" W; sec. 4, T 18 S, R 11 E). Named on Hernandez Reservoir (1969) 7.5' quadrangle.

Post Canyon [SAN LUIS OBISPO]: *canyon,* drained by a stream that flows 5 miles to Cuyama Valley 3.5 miles southwest of Caliente Mountain (lat. 35°00'30" N, long. 119°48'45" W; sec. 25, T 11 N, R 28 W). Named on Caliente Mountain (1959) 7.5' quadrangle.

Post Creek [MONTEREY]: *stream,* flows nearly 1.5 miles to Big Sur River 2.25 miles east-northeast of Pfeiffer Point (lat. 36°14'35" N, long. 121°46'25" W; at W line sec. 32, T 19 S, R 2 E). Named on Pfeiffer Point (1956) 7.5' quadrangle.

Posts [MONTEREY]: *locality,* 3 miles east-southeast of Pfeiffer Point (lat. 36°13'40" N, long. 121°45'45" W; sec. 5, T 20 S, R 2 E); the place is along Posts Creek. Named on Pfeiffer Point (1956) 7.5' quadrangle. William Brainard Post homesteaded in the neighborhood in the late 1860's and his ranch served as a stage station (Lussier, p. 24-25). Postal authorities established Posts post office in 1889, moved it 2 miles northwest in 1905, and discontinued it in 1910 (Salley, p. 177).

Post Summit [MONTEREY]: *peak,* 6 miles east of Point Sur (lat. 36° 17'20" N, long. 121°47'25" W; near SW cor. sec. 7, T 19 S, R 2 E). Altitude 3455 feet. Named on Big Sur (1956) 7.5' quadrangle.

Potato Bay: see **Potato Harbor** [SANTA BARBARA].

Potato Harbor [SANTA BARBARA]: *embayment,* 5.5 miles east-northeast of Pris-

oners Harbor on the north side of Santa Cruz Island (lat. 34°02'55" N, long. 119°35'30" W). Named on Santa Cruz Island C (1943) 7.5' quadrangle. Called Potato Bay on Bremner's (1932) map. Doran (p. 143, 150) noted that the place also was called Tyler Harbor.

Potrancas Creek: see **Anthony Creek** [MONTEREY].

Potrero Canyon [MONTEREY]: *canyon,* drained by a stream that flows 5.25 miles to Carmel River 3.5 miles east of the mouth of that river (lat. 36°32'10" N, long. 121°52'10" W); the canyon is on El Potrero de San Carlos grant. Named on Mount Carmel (1956) and Seaside (1947) 7.5' quadrangles. United States Board on Geographic Names (1977, p. 3) approved the name "Saddle Mountain" for a ridge that is between Potrero Canyon and Robinson Canyon (lat. 36°30'35" N, long. 121°49'30" W, at the east end). Milton Frumkin and his wife, Marie, owners of land on the side of the ridge, named the feature for its shape (Clark, 1991, p. 485).

Potrero Creek [SAN LUIS OBISPO]:
(1) *stream,* flows 1.5 miles to Lopez Canyon 2.25 miles east-southeast of Lopez Mountain (lat. 35°17'10" N, long. 120°32'35" W; sec. 26, T 30 S, R 13 E). Named on Lopez Mountain (1965) 7.5' quadrangle.
(2) *stream,* flows 2.5 miles to Arroyo Grande Creek 10.5 miles north-northeast of the town of Nipomo (lat. 35°11'25" N, long. 120°26' W). Named on Tar Spring Ridge (1967) 7.5' quadrangle.

Potrero de San Luis Obispo [SAN LUIS OBISPO]: *land grant,* 3 miles north of downtown San Luis Obispo. Named on San Luis Obispo (1965) 7.5' quadrangle. M. Concepcion Boronda received 1 league in 1842 and claimed 3506 acres patented in 1870 (Cowan, p. 84).

Potrero Peak [SAN BENITO]: *peak,* 14 miles east of Hollister on San Benito-Merced county line (lat. 36°51'25" N, long. 121°08'55" W; sec. 25, T 12 S, R 7 E). Altitude 3742 feet. Named on Quien Sabe Valley (1968) 7.5' quadrangle.

Potreros y Rincon de San Pedro de Reglado [SANTA CRUZ]: *land grant,* 2.5 miles north-northwest of Point Santa Cruz in Santa Cruz. Named on Santa Cruz (1954) 7.5' quadrangle. Jose Arana received the land in 1842; Thomas W. Russell claimed 92 acres patented in 1885 (Cowan, p. 87). According to Perez (p. 83), Nicolas Dordero was the patentee of 176.03 acres in 1861.

Powder Mill Flat: see **Paradise Park** [SANTA CRUZ].

Powder Mill Siding: see **Paradise Park** [SANTA CRUZ].

Powell Canyon [MONTEREY]: *canyon,* drained by a stream that flows 14 miles to Sargent Creek 7 miles north-northwest of Bradley (lat. 35°57'45" N, long. 120°50' W; near E line sec. 1, T 23 S, R 10 E). Named on Slack Canyon (1969), Valleton (1948), and Wunpost (1949)

7.5' quadrangles. Called Alexander Canyon on English and Kew's (1916) map. The name commemorates George S. Powell, an early settler in the canyon (Clark, 1991, p. 420).

Powell Canyon [SANTA BARBARA]: *canyon,* drained by a stream that flows 3.5 miles to Cuyama Valley 5.5 miles east of Miranda Pine Mountain (lat. 35°02'55" N, long. 119°56'15" W). Named on Taylor Canyon (1959) 7.5' quadrangle.

Powell Spring [MONTEREY]: *spring,* 13 miles east of San Ardo (lat. 36°01'10" N, long. 120°40'40" W; sec. 16, T 22 S, R 12 E); the spring is in Powell Canyon. Named on Slack Canyon (1969) 7.5' quadrangle.

Poza de los Ositos: see **Posa de los Ositos** [MONTEREY].

Pozo [SAN LUIS OBISPO]: *village,* 16 miles east of San Luis Obispo (lat. 35°18'15" N, long. 120°22'30" W; at N line sec. 21, T 30 S, R 15 E); the village is along Pozo Creek. Named on Pozo Summit (1967) and Santa Margarita Lake (1967) 7.5' quadrangles. Postal authorities established Pozo post office in 1878 and discontinued it in 1942 (Frickstad, p. 166). The place first was called San Jose—it lies in what was known as San Jose Valley (Angel, 1883, p. 364)—and then was called Garcia Valley for one of the early families there (Lee and others, p. 124). G.W. Lingo proposed the name "Pozo" for the post office because the village is in a holelike valley—*pozo* means "well" or "hole" in Spanish (Angel, 1883, p. 366).

Pozo Creek [SAN LUIS OBISPO]: *stream,* flows 7.5 miles to Salinas River 1 mile southwest of Pozo (lat. 35°17'45" N, long. 120°23'20" W; sec. 20, T 30 S, R 15 E). Named on Pozo Summit (1967) and Santa Margarita Lake (1967) 7.5' quadrangles. The part of the stream in present Fraser Canyon is called Sycamore Creek on Pozo (1922) 15' quadrangle, but United States Board on Geographic Names (1968b, p. 8) rejected this name for the feature.

Pozo Hondo Creek [MONTEREY]: *stream,* flows nearly 4 miles to Salmon Creek 9.5 miles south of Jolon (lat. 35°50'10" N, long. 121°12'15" W; sec. 22, T 24 S, R 7 E). Named on Burnett Peak (1949) and Burro Mountain (1949) 7.5' quadrangles.

Pozo Ortega: see **Poso Ortega** [SAN LUIS OBISPO].

Pozo Summit [SAN LUIS OBISPO]: *locality,* 5.5 miles east-northeast of Pozo (lat. 35°20'50" N, long. 120°17'40" W). Named on Pozo Summit (1967) 7.5' quadrangle.

Prader Creek: see **Gibson Creek** [MONTEREY].

Prefumo Canyon [SAN LUIS OBISPO]: *canyon,* drained by a stream that flows 3.5 miles to Los Osos Valley 2.5 miles west-southwest of San Luis Obispo (lat. 35°15'40" N, long. 120°42'10" W). Named on Morro Bay South (1965) and San Luis Obispo (1965) 7.5' quad-

rangles. Called Perfumo Canyon on Harder's (1910) map, but United States Board on Geographic Names (1964, p. 15) rejected this name for the feature.

Prefuno Creek [SAN LUIS OBISPO]: *stream,* flows 1.25 miles to San Luis Obispo Creek 3.5 miles south-southwest of downtown San Luis Obispo (lat. 35°14'40" N, long. 120°40'50" W). Named on Pismo Beach (1965) and San Luis Obispo (1965) 7.5' quadrangles.

Prescott: see **San Juan Bautista** [SAN BENITO].

Presidio de Santa Barbara Virgen y Martir: see **Santa Barbara** [SANTA BARBARA].

Presidio of Monterey [MONTEREY]: *military installation,* adjacent to the city of Monterey (lat. 35°36'20" N, long. 121°54'30" W). Named on Monterey (1947) 7.5' quadrangle. Postal authorities established Presidio of Monterey post office in 1915 (Frickstad, p. 108). Portola founded Presidio of San Carlos Borromeo de Monterey at present Monterey in 1770, and in 1822 the Mexicans built a fort about 1 mile northwest of the original presidio; after American occupation of Monterey in 1846, Colonel Richard B. Mason had a redoubt built in 1847 about 700 feet up the hill above the Mexican installation (Frazer, p. 27). The redoubt was christened Fort Stockton to honor Commodore Stockton, but the commodore ordered that it be known as Fort Mervine (*Californian*, October 3, 1846). Finally, the installation was named Fort Halleck for Lieutenant H.W. Halleck, who laid it out (Hoover, Rensch, and Rensch, p. 218). The cantonment at the place was named Ord Barracks in 1903, and this name was changed to Presidio of Monterey in 1904 (Whiting and Whiting, p. 52).

Pretty Flat [SAN BENITO]: *area,* 17 miles southeast of Bitterwater (lat. 36°14'15" N, long. 120°44'50" W; near E line sec. 34, T 19 S, R 11 E). Named on Priest Valley (1969) 7.5' quadrangle.

Prewitt Creek [MONTEREY]: *stream,* flows 3.5 miles to the sea 3.25 miles north of Cape San Martin (lat. 35°56'05" N, long. 121°28'30" W; sec. 18, T 23 S, R 5 E). Named on Cape San Martin (1949) 7.5' quadrangle. The name recalls Jim Prewitt, who had a cabin by the stream (Clark, 1991, p. 421). South Fork enters 1.25 miles upstream from the mouth of the creek; it is 2 miles long and is named on Cape San Martin (1949) 7.5' quadrangle.

Price Canyon [SAN LUIS OBISPO]: *canyon,* nearly 4 miles long, opens into lowlands along the coast at Pismo Beach (lat. 35°08'25" N, long. 120°38' W). Named on Arroyo Grande NE (1965) and Pismo Beach (1965) 7.5' quadrangles. Pismo Creek drains the canyon.

Priest Canyon [SAN LUIS OBISPO]: *canyon,* drained by a stream that flows 3.25 miles to Cuyama Valley 4 miles northwest of New Cuyama [SANTA BARBARA] (lat.

34°58'45" N, long. 119°44'25" W; sec. 2, T 10 N, R 27 W). Named on New Cuyama (1964) 7.5' quadrangle.

Priest's Ford: see **Ben Lomond** [SANTA CRUZ].

Priest Spring [SAN LUIS OBISPO]: *spring,* 4.5 miles northwest of New Cuyama [SANTA BARBARA] (lat. 34°59'40" N, long. 119°44'25" W; sec. 34, T 11 N, R 27 W); the spring is in Priest Canyon. Named on New Cuyama (1964) 7.5' quadrangle.

Priest Valley [MONTEREY]: *locality,* 3 miles north of Charley Mountain in Priest Valley [MONTEREY-SAN BENITO] (lat. 36°10'25" N, long. 120°40'20" W; sec. 21, T 20 S, R 12 E). Named on Priest Valley (1915) 30' quadrangle. Postal authorities established Priest Valley post office in 1882, moved it 1.5 miles east in 1897, discontinued it in 1909, reestablished it in 1910, and discontinued it in 1934 (Salley, p. 178).

Priest Valley [MONTEREY-SAN BENITO]: *valley,* 19 miles east-northeast of San Lucas on Monterey-San Benito county line, mainly in Monterey County (lat. 36°11'15" N, long. 120°41'45" W). Named on Priest Valley (1969) 7.5' quadrangle. Dillon (1966, p. 162) related a story about the name originating when some Americans found a padre and a hundred mission Indians rounding up wild horses in the valley; Dillon also noted that the place was known as Joaquin's Valley, for Joaquin Murieta, the Mexican outlaw.

Priest Valley Creek: see **Lewis Creek** [MONTEREY-SAN BENITO].

Prieta Point: see **Black Point** [SANTA CRUZ].

Prieto Canyon: see **Palo Prieto Canyon** [SAN LUIS OBISPO].

Primetal Cañon: see **Pimental Creek** [SAN BENITO].

Prince Island [SANTA BARBARA]: *island,* 2000 feet long, 3.25 miles northwest of Cardwell Point and 0.5 mile offshore on the north side of San Miguel Island (lat. 34°03'30" N, long. 120° 20' W). Named on San Miguel Island East (1950) 7.5' quadrangle. Called Princess Island on Bremner's (1933) map.

Princes Camp [MONTEREY]: *locality,* nearly 7 miles southeast of the town of Carmel Valley along Carmel River (lat. 36°24'05" N, long. 121°39'30" W; sec. 4, T 18 S, R 3 E). Named on Carmel Valley (1956) 7.5' quadrangle.

Princess Island: see **Prince Island** [SANTA BARBARA].

Prisoners Harbor [SANTA BARBARA]: *embayment,* 9 miles west of San Pedro Point on the north side of Santa Cruz Island (lat. 34° 01'15" N, long. 119°41' W). Named on Santa Cruz Island C (1943) 7.5' quadrangle. The name recalls the arrival at the place in 1830 of thirty convicts exiled from Mexico (Hanna, p. 244). Bremner's (1932) map has the name "Cn. del Puerto" for the canyon that opens to the sea at Prisoners Harbor.

Profile Point [SANTA BARBARA]: *promontory,* 4 miles east-northeast of Fraser Point on the north side of Santa Cruz Island (lat. 34° 04'15" N, long. 119°51'40" W). Named on Santa Cruz Island A (1943) 7.5' quadrangle.

Prunedale [MONTEREY]: *town,* 8 miles north of Salinas (lat. 36°46'45" N, long. 121°40'15" W). Named on Prunedale (1954) 7.5' quadrangle. Postal authorities established Prunedale post office in 1894, discontinued it in 1908, and reestablished it in 1953 (Salley, p. 178).

Puerta del Diablo [MONTEREY]: *peak,* nearly 2 miles east-southeast of Soberanes Point (lat. 36°26'15" N, long. 121°53'55" W; sec. 19, T 17 S, R 1 E). Altitude 1833 feet. Named on Soberanes Point (1956) 7.5' quadrangle. United States Board on Geographic Names (1960a, p. 16) rejected the name "Oliviers Mountain" for the feature.

Puerto de la Cañada del Sur: see **Valley Anchorage** [SANTA BARBARA].

Puerto de Monterey: see **Monterey Bay** [MONTEREY].

Puerto de San Lucas: see **Morro Bay** [SAN LUIS OBISPO] (2).

Puerto de Todos Santos: see **Cojo Bay** [SANTA BARBARA].

Puerto Suello Creek [MONTEREY]: *stream,* flows 2.25 miles to Little Sur River 2.5 miles west-southwest of Uncle Sam Mountain (lat. 36°19'45" N, long. 121°44'40" W). Named on Ventana Cones (1956) 7.5' quadrangle.

Punta Arena [SANTA BARBARA]: *promontory,* 7.5 miles south-southwest of Diablo Point on the south side of Santa Cruz Island (lat. 33°57'35" N, long. 119°49' W). Named on Santa Cruz Island B (1943) 7.5' quadrangle.

Punta Concepcion: see **Point Conception** [SANTA BARBARA].

Punta de Carmel: see **Point Lobos** [MONTEREY].

Punta de Echevarria: see **Government Point** [SANTA BARBARA].

Punta de la Concepcion [SANTA BARBARA]: *land grant,* at Point Conception. Named on Lompoc Hills (1959), Point Arguello (1959), Point Conception (1953), and Tranquillon Mountain (1959) 7.5' quadrangles. Anastacio Carrillo received 6 leagues in 1837 and claimed 24,992 acres patented in 1880 (Cowan, p. 29). According to Perez (p. 85), the patent was dated 1863.

Punta de la Laguna [SAN LUIS OBISPO-SANTA BARBARA]: *land grant,* west and southwest of Santa Maria; almost entirely in Santa Barbara County, but a small part extends across Santa Maria River into San Luis Obispo County. Named on Casmalia (1959), Guadalupe (1959), Orcutt (1959), and Santa Maria (1959) 7.5' quadrangles. Luis Arellanes and Emilio Miguel Ortega received 6 leagues in 1844 and claimed 26,648 acres patented in 1873 (Cowan, p. 44).

Punta de la Limpia Concepcion: see **Point Conception** [SANTA BARBARA].
Punta del Carmelo: see **Pinnacle Point** [MONTEREY].
Punta del Castillo: see **Point Castillo** [SANTA BARBARA].
Punta del Estero: see **Point Estero** [SAN LUIS OBISPO].
Punta de Lobos: see **Point Lobos** [MONTEREY]; **Point Santa Cruz** [SANTA CRUZ].
Punta de los Cipreses: see **Cypress Point** [MONTEREY].
Punta de los Lobos Marinos: see **Point Lobos** [MONTEREY].
Punta de los Pinos: see **Point Pinos** [MONTEREY].
Punta de Nuestra Señora de Los Angeles: see **Sand Point** [SANTA BARBARA].
Punta de Pantoja: see **Goleta Point** [SANTA BARBARA].
Punta de Pinos [MONTEREY]: *land grant,* south-southwest of Point Pinos on the coast. Named on Monterey (1947) 7.5' quadrangle. Jose M. Armenta and Jose Abrego received 2 leagues in 1833 and 1834; H. DeGraw and others claimed 2667 acres patented in 1880 (Cowan, p. 61). According to Perez (p. 84), Jose Abrego was the grantee in 1844.
Punta de Sanchez: see **Cojo Bay** [SANTA BARBARA].
Punta de San Esteban: see **Point Castillo** [SANTA BARBARA].
Punta de Santa Marta: see **Purisima Point** [SANTA BARBARA].
Punta de Tobar: see **Coal Oil Point** [SANTA BARBARA].
Punta de Villaverde: see **Government Point** [SANTA BARBARA].
Punta Diablo: see **Diablo Point** [SANTA BARBARA].
Punta Gorda: see **Cape San Martin** [MONTEREY].
Punta Negra: see **Black Point** [SANTA BARBARA].
Punta Pedernales: see **Point Arguello** [SANTA BARBARA].
Punta Purisima: see **Purisima Point** [SANTA BARBARA].
Punta que Parece Isla: see **Point Sur** [MONTEREY].
Punta Saint Luis: see **Point San Luis** [SAN LUIS OBISPO].
Punto del Esteros: see **Point Estero** [SAN LUIS OBISPO].
Purd Camp [MONTEREY]: *locality,* 6.5 miles southwest of Soledad (lat. 36°21'10" N, long. 121°23'50" W; sec. 23, T 18 S, R 5 E). Named on Sycamore Flat (1956) 7.5' quadrangle.
Purisima Canyon [SANTA BARBARA]: *canyon,* drained by a stream that flows 5.5 miles to lowlands 3 miles northeast of the city of Lompoc at La Purisima mission (lat. 34°40'10" N, long. 120°25'15" W). Named on Lompoc (1959) 7.5' quadrangle.

Purisima Hills [SANTA BARBARA]: *range,* extends from north of the city of Lompoc to Solvang. Named on Casmalia (1959), Lompoc (1959), Los Alamos (1959), Los Olivos (1959), Orcutt (1959), Sisquoc (1959), Solvang (1959), and Zaca Creek (1959) 7.5' quadrangles.
Purisima Point [SANTA BARBARA]: *promontory,* 8 miles southwest of the village of Casmalia along the coast (lat. 34°45'20" N, long. 120°38'10" W). Named on Casmalia (1959) 7.5' quadrangle. Called Pta. Purisima on Parke's (1854-1855) map. The Spaniards called the feature Punta de Santa Marta (Wagner, H.R., p. 512). It was known in the 1850's as Point Pedernales, a name now applied to a point located 10 miles farther south (Gudde, 1949, p. 257).
Purisima River: see **Santa Ynez River** [SANTA BARBARA].
Pyojo: see **El Piojo** [MONTEREY].
Pyramid Point: see **Pinnacle Point** [MONTEREY]; **Point Joe** [MONTEREY].

– Q –

Quail Canyon [SAN LUIS OBISPO]: *canyon,* drained by a stream that flows 3.25 miles to Cuyama Valley 3.5 miles east-northeast of Cuyama [SANTA BARBARA] (lat. 34°57'20" N, long. 119°33'30" W; sec. 16, T 10 N, R 25 W). Named on Cuyama (1964) 7.5' quadrangle.
Quail Creek [MONTEREY]: *stream,* flows 5 miles to lowlands 8.5 miles north-northwest of Gonzales (lat. 36°37'30" N, long. 121°29'25" W). Named on Chualar (1947), Gonzales (1955), and Mount Harlan (1968) 7.5' quadrangles.
Quail Flat [SAN LUIS OBISPO]: *area,* 8 miles south-southwest of Atascadero (lat. 35°23'05" N, long. 120°44'05" W; near SW cor. sec. 19, T 29 S, R 12 E). Named on Atascadero (1965) 7.5' quadrangle.
Quail Knob: see **Quail Top** [MONTEREY].
Quail Spring [SAN LUIS OBISPO]: *spring,* 4.5 miles south-southwest of Branch Mountain in Brown Canyon (lat. 35°07'20" N, long. 120°06' W). Named on Miranda Pine Mountain (1967) 7.5' quadrangle.
Quail Spring Reservoir [SAN LUIS OBISPO]: *lake,* 75 feet long, 5 miles northeast of Cuyama [SANTA BARBARA] (lat. 34°59'25" N, long. 119°33'15" W; near S line sec. 33, T 11 N, R 25 W); the lake is in Quail Canyon. Named on Cuyama (1964) 7.5' quadrangle.
Quail Top [MONTEREY]: *peak,* 6.5 miles southeast of Jolon on the south side of San Antonio River (lat. 35°53'25" N, long. 121°06'45" W; sec. 33, T 23 S, R 8 E). Altitude 1146 feet. Named on Williams Hill (1949) 7.5' quadrangle. Howard (p. 85) referred to Quail Knob.

Quail Water Creek [SAN LUIS OBISPO]: *stream,* flows 7.25 miles to Indian Creek (2) 9.5 miles south of Shandon (lat. 35°31'20" N, long. 120°23'55" W; sec. 6, T 28 S, R 15 E). Named on Shedd Canyon (1961) and Wilson Corner (1966) 7.5' quadrangles. Anderson and Martin's (1914) map has the form "Quailwater Creek" for the name.

Quarry Lake [SAN BENITO]: *lake,* 400 feet long, nearly 1.5 miles northeast of Aromas (lat. 36°54'10" N, long. 121°37'30" W). Named on Chittenden (1955) and Watsonville East (1955) 7.5' quadrangles.

Quartel: see **Quatal**, under **Santa Barbara Canyon** [SANTA BARBARA].

Quatal: see **Santa Barbara Canyon** [SANTA BARBARA].

Quatal Canyon [SANTA BARBARA]: *canyon,* mainly in Ventura County, but opens into Cuyama Valley at Santa Barbara-Ventura county line 11 miles southeast of the village of Cuyama (lat. 34° 49' N, long. 119°26'30" W; near S line sec. 33, T 9 N, R 24 W). Named on Cuyama Peak (1943) 7.5' quadrangle.

Queen Bee Campground [SAN LUIS OBISPO]: *locality,* nearly 4 miles north-northwest of Castle Crags (lat. 35°21'05" N, long. 120° 14'25" W). Named on La Panza (1967) 7.5' quadrangle. Queen Bee mine was near the place (Franke, p. 421).

Queen Canyon [SAN BENITO]: *canyon,* drained by a stream that flows 0.5 mile to San Juan Canyon 3.25 miles south-southeast of San Juan Bautista (lat. 36°48'15" N, long. 121°30'15" W). Named on San Juan Bautista (1955) 7.5' quadrangle. United States Board on Geographic Names (1994, p. 5) approved the name "Quinn Canyon" for the feature.

Quesada Spring [MONTEREY]: *spring,* 22 miles east of San Ardo (lat. 36°00'25" N, long. 120°29'55" W; sec. 19, T 22 S, R 14 E). Named on Curry Mountain (1969) 7.5' quadrangle.

Quien Sabe: see **Santa Ana y Quien Sabe** [SAN BENITO].

Quien Sabe Creek [SAN BENITO]: *stream,* flows 14 miles to Los Muertos Creek 3 miles north of Cherry Peak (lat. 36°44'10" N, long. 121°08'50" W; near NE cor. sec. 12, T 14 S, R 7 E); the stream drains Quien Sabe Valley. Named on Cherry Peak (1968), Mariposa Peak (1969), and Quien Sabe Valley (1968) 7.5' quadrangles.

Quien Sabe Valley [SAN BENITO]: *valley,* 11 miles east of Hollister (lat. 36°50' N, long. 121°11'30" W); the valley is on Santa Ana y Quien Sabe grant. Named on Mariposa Peak (1969) and Quien Sabe Valley (1968) 7.5' quadrangles.

Quien Sabe Valley: see **Little Quien Sabe Valley** [SAN BENITO].

Quinado Canyon]MONTEREY]: *canyon,* nearly 7 miles long, opens into lowlands 3 miles south of King City (lat. 36°10'15" N, long. 121°07'40" W). Named on Cosio Knob

(1949), Espinosa Canyon (1949), and Thompson Canyon (1949) 7.5' quadrangles. According to Gudde (1949, p. 277), the name is a Spanish version of an Indian word for "evil smelling," and refers to the odor of sulphur springs. On some earlier maps the feature was called Kent Canyon for John Tupper Kent, who patented land at the head of the canyon in 1884 (Clark, 1991, p. 429-431). United States Board on Geographic Names (1936a, p. 21) rejected the name Kent Canyon for the feature.

Quinn Canyon: see **Queen Canyon** [SAN BENITO].

Quiota Creek [SANTA BARBARA]: *stream,* flows 6.5 miles to Santa Ynez River 2.5 miles southwest of Santa Ynez (lat. 34°34'50" N, long. 120°06'35" W). Named on Santa Ynez (1959) 7.5' quadrangle. Called Ballard Creek on Lompoc (1905) 30' quadrangle, but United States Board on Geographic Names (1961b, p. 14) rejected the names "Ballard Creek" and "Refugio Creek" for the stream.

− R −

Rabbit Valley [SAN BENITO]: *valley,* 3 miles north of Bitterwater (lat. 36°25'15" N, long. 121°00'30" W). Named on Rock Spring Peak (1969) and Topo Valley (1969) 7.5' quadrangles. United States Board on Geographic Names (1972b, p. 4) gave the name "Little Rabbit Valley" as a variant.

Rabbit Valley: see **Little Rabbit Valley** [SAN BENITO].

Rafael Creek [SAN LUIS OBISPO]: *stream,* flows 5 miles to the canyon of San Juan Creek 4.5 miles north of Branch Mountain (lat. 35°15'05" N, long. 120°04'20" W; sec. 5, T 31 S, R 18 E). Named on Branch Mountain (1967) 7.5' quadrangle.

Ragged Point [SAN LUIS OBISPO]: *promontory,* nearly 0.5 mile south-southeast of the mouth of San Carpoforo Creek along the coast (lat. 35°45'35" N, long. 121°19'35" W). Named on Burro Mountain (1949) 7.5' quadrangle.

Railpen Canyon [SAN LUIS OBISPO]: *canyon,* drained by a stream that flows 2.5 miles to Twitchell Reservoir 2 miles northeast of Huasna Peak (lat. 35°03'35" N, long. 120°19'25" W). Named on Huasna Peak (1967) 7.5' quadrangle.

Railroad Spring: see **Chittenden's Sulphur Springs**, under **Chittenden** [SANTA CRUZ].

Rainbow Camp [MONTEREY]: *locality,* 7 miles north of Slates Hot Springs (lat. 36°13'20" N, long. 121°39'15" W; sec. 5, T 20 S, R 3 E). Named on Partington Ridge (1956) 7.5' quadrangle.

Rainbow Canyon [SANTA BARBARA]: *canyon,* drained by a stream that flows 1.25 miles to Santa Barbara Canyon 3 miles east-north-east of Fox Mountain (lat. 34°49'45" N, long.

119°33'05" W). Named on Fox Mountain (1964) 7.5' quadrangle.

Rainbow Lodge: see **Big Sur** [MONTEREY].

Rambo Spring [MONTEREY]: *spring*, 15 miles east-northeast of San Ardo in Slack Canyon (lat. 36°04'25" N, long. 120°38'55" W; sec. 26, T 21 S, R 12 E). Named on Slack Canyon (1969) 7.5' quadrangle.

Ramrod Canyon [SANTA BARBARA]: *canyon*, drained by a stream that flows 1 mile to South Fork La Brea Creek nearly 2 miles west-northwest of Manzanita Mountain (lat. 34°54' N, long. 120° 06'30" W). Named on Manzanita Mountain (1964) 7.5' quadrangle.

Ramsey Gulch [SANTA CRUZ]: *canyon*, drained by a stream that flows 2.25 miles to Browns Creek 3 miles north-northeast of Corralitos (lat. 37°01'35" N, long. 121°46'35" W; near N line sec. 32, T 10 S, R 2 E). Named on Loma Prieta (1955) 7.5' quadrangle.

Rana Creek [MONTEREY]: *stream*, flows 6.25 miles to Tularcitos Creek 6.5 miles east-south-east of the town of Carmel Valley (lat. 36°26'10" N, long. 121°37'50" W). Named on Carmel Valley (1956) and Rana Creek (1956) 7.5' quadrangles.

Ranchero Rock: see **Banchero Rock** [MONTEREY].

Ranchita: see **Arroyo Grande** [SAN LUIS OBISPO] (1).

Ranchita Canyon: see **Ranchito Canyon** [MONTEREY-SAN LUIS OBISPO].

Ranchita de Santa Fe [SAN LUIS OBISPO]: *land grant*, 3.25 miles south-southwest of downtown San Luis Obispo along San Luis Obispo Creek. Named on Pismo Beach (1965) 7.5' quadrangle. Vicente Linares received 1000 varas in 1842 and claimed 166 acres patented in 1866 (Cowan, p. 92)

Ranchita Valley: see **Ranchito Canyon** [MONTEREY-SAN LUIS OBISPO].

Ranchito Canyon [MONTEREY-SAN LUIS OBISPO]: *canyon*, drained by a stream that heads in Monterey County and flows 32 miles to Estrella Creek 4.25 miles southeast of San Miguel in San Luis Obispo County (lat. 35°42'55" N, long. 120°38'10" W; sec. 36, T 25 S, R 12 E). Named on Estrella (1948), Paso Robles (1948), Ranchito Canyon (1948) and Stockdale Mountain (1948) 7.5' quadrangles. Called Ranchita Canyon on English and Kew's (1916) map. Stanley (map on p. 18) called the feature Ranchita Valley.

Rancho del Mar: see **Aptos** [SANTA CRUZ] (2).

Rancho Nacional: see **San Julian** [SANTA BARBARA].

Rancho Nuevo Creek [SANTA BARBARA]: *stream*, flows 9 miles to Ventura County 20 miles south-southeast of the village of Cuyama (lat. 34°41'30" N, long. 119°26'35" W). Named on Madulce Peak (1964) and Rancho Nuevo Creek (1943) 7.5' quadrangles. The upper part of present Rancho Nuevo Creek is called Bear Creek on Santa Ynez

(1905) 30' quadrangle, but United States Board on Geographic Names (1950, p. 1) rejected this name for the stream.

Ranger Canyon [SAN LUIS OBISPO]: *canyon*, drained by a stream that flows 3 miles to Arroyo Seco 12.5 miles northeast of the town of Nipomo (lat. 35°10' N, long. 120°19'05" W; sec. 1, T 32 S, R 15 E). Named on Caldwell Mesa (1967) 7.5' quadrangle.

Ranger Peak [SANTA BARBARA]: *peak*, 2.5 miles southeast of Figueroa Mountain (lat. 34°43'15" N, long. 119°56'55" W; at NE cor. sec. 5, T 7 N, R 29 W). Named on Figueroa Mountain (1959) 7.5' quadrangle.

Rapetti: see **Santa Cruz** [SANTA CRUZ].

Rat Creek [MONTEREY]: *stream*, flows 1.5 miles to the sea nearly 6 miles north-north-west of Lopez Point (lat. 36°05'30" N, long. 121°37'10" W; sec. 22, T 21 S, R 3 E). Named on Lopez Point (1956) 7.5' quadrangle.

Rat Hill [MONTEREY]: *hill*, 1 mile southeast of Point Lobos (lat. 36° 30'50" N, long. 121°56'15" W). Named on Monterey (1947) 7.5' quadrangle.

Rattlesnake Canyon [SAN LUIS OBISPO]: *canyon*, drained by a stream that flows 1.5 miles to the sea 1.5 miles northwest of Point San Luis (lat. 35°10'25" N, long. 120°46'55" W). Named on Port San Luis (1965) 7.5' quadrangle.

Rattlesnake Canyon [SANTA BARBARA]:
(1) *canyon*, drained by a stream that flows 3 miles to Sisquoc River 4.5 miles northwest of Big Pine Mountain (lat. 34°44'45" N, long. 119°42'15" W). Named on Big Pine Mountain (1964) 7.5' quadrangle.
(2) *canyon*, drained by a stream that flows 4 miles to South Fork La Brea Creek 1.25 miles north of Manzanita Mountain (lat. 34°54'35" N, long. 120°04'35" W). Named on Manzanita Mountain (1964) 7.5' quadrangle.
(3) *canyon*, drained by a stream that flows 3.5 miles to Sisquoc River 5.25 mile north-north-west of Zaca Lake (lat. 34°50'35" N, long. 120°05'15" W). Named on Manzanita Mountain (1964) and Zaca Lake (1964) 7.5' quadrangles.
(4) *canyon*, drained by a stream that flows 1.5 miles to North Fork La Brea Creek 2.25 miles east of Tepusquet Peak (lat. 34°54'50" N, long. 120°08'40" W). Named on Tepusquet Canyon (1964) 7.5' quadrangle.
(5) *canyon*, drained by a stream that flows 3.5 miles to Mission Creek 2 miles north-north-west of downtown Santa Barbara (lat. 34°26'50" N, long. 119°42'30" W). Named on Santa Barbara (1952) 7.5' quadrangle.

Rattlesnake Canyon: see **Long Canyon** [SANTA BARBARA] (3).

Rattlesnake Creek [MONTEREY]:
(1) *stream*, flows 3 miles to Danish Creek nearly 3 miles north-northeast of Uncle Sam Mountain (lat. 36°22'35" N, long. 121°41'05" W; sec. 7, T 18 S, R 3 E). Named on Ventana Cones (1956) 7.5' quadrangle.

(2) *stream,* flows 4 miles to North Fork San Antonio River 5 miles south-southeast of Junipero Serra Peak (lat. 36°04'25" N, long. 121°23'50" W; sec. 26, T 21 S, R 5 E). Named on Cone Peak (1949) 7.5' quadrangle. United States Board on Geographic Names (1981a, p. 4) approved the name "Wagon Caves" for caves and bold outcrops of rock located along North Fork San Antonio River nearly 1 mile north-northwest of the mouth of Rattlesnake Creek (2) (lat. 36°04'55" N, long. 121°24'07" W); the name is from use of the shelter by pioneers in winter.

Rattlesnake Gulch [SAN BENITO]:
(1) *canyon,* drained by a stream that flows 1.5 miles to San Benito River 7 miles east of Bitterwater (lat. 36°23'40" N, long. 120° 52'40" W; sec. 3, T 18 S, R 10 E). Named on Rock Spring Peak (1969) 7.5' quadrangle.
(2) *canyon,* drained by a stream that flows 0.5 mile to Oat Canyon 14 miles east-southeast of Bitterwater (lat. 36°17'25" N, long. 120° 46'05" W; sec. 9, T 19 S, R 11 E). Named on Hepsedam Peak (1969) 7.5' quadrangle.

Rattlesnake Gulch [SANTA CRUZ]: *canyon,* drained by a stream that flows 1.5 miles to Grizzly Flat nearly 4 miles north of Corralitos (lat. 37°02'40" N, long. 121°47'35" W; sec. 19, T 10 S, R 2 E). Named on Loma Prieta (1955) 7.5' quadrangle.

Rattlesnake Spring [SANTA BARBARA]: *spring,* 1.5 miles south-southwest of Salisbury Potrero (lat. 34°48'05" N, long. 119°42'45" W). Named on Salisbury Potrero (1964) 7.5' quadrangle.

Ready: see **Aptos Creek** [SANTA CRUZ].

Real de las Aguilas [SAN BENITO]: *land grant,* 20 miles east-southeast of Hollister. Named on Cerro Colorado (1969), Cherry Peak (1968), Panoche Pass (1968), Quien Sabe Valley (1968), and Ruby Canyon (1968) 7.5' quadrangles. Francisco Arias and Saturnino Cariaga received 7 leagues in 1844; F.A. McDougal and others claimed 31,052 acres patented in 1869 (Cowan, p. 67).

Reason Mountain [MONTEREY]: *peak,* 23 miles east-southeast of San Ardo (lat. 36°00'20" N, long. 120°29'25" W; sec. 20, T 22 S, R 14 E). Altitude 3753 feet. Named on Curry Mountain (1969) 7.5' quadrangle. The name is for George Reasons, a local rancher (Clark, 1991, p. 471).

Rector Creek: see **Cottonwood Creek** [MONTEREY].

Red Corral Spring [SAN BENITO]: *spring,* 9 miles east-northeast of Bitterwater along McCoy Creek (lat. 36°26'25" N, long. 120°51'35" W; near NW cor. sec. 23, T 17 S, R 10 E). Named on Hernandez Reservoir (1969) 7.5' quadrangle, which has the name "Red Corral" at the site.

Redfield Woods: see **Cuesta-by-the Sea** [SAN LUIS OBISPO].

Redhead Canyon [MONTEREY]: *canyon,* 3.25 miles long, opens into lowlands 2 miles north

of San Ardo (lat. 36°02'55" N, long. 120° 54'40" W; sec. 5, T 22 S, R 10 E). Named on Pancho Rico Valley (1967) and San Ardo (1967) 7.5' quadrangles. Called Dutch Henry Canyon on San Ardo (1956) 15' quadrangle, and called Redwood Canyon on Priest Valley (1915) 30' quadrangle.

Redhead Canyon: see **Portugee Canyon** [MONTEREY].

Red Hill [MONTEREY]: *peak,* 4 miles east-northeast of Jamesburg (lat. 36°23'40" N, long. 121°32'50" W; sec. 4, T 18 S, R 4 E). Named on Rana Creek (1956) 7.5' quadrangle. The name is from red rocks on the peak (Clark, 1991, p. 471).

Red Hills [SAN LUIS OBISPO]: *ridge,* north-to north-northeast-trending, 3 miles long, 8 miles east-southeast of Shandon (lat. 35° 36' N, long. 120°15' W). Named on Camatta Canyon (1961) and Holland Canyon (1961) 7.5' quadrangles.

Red Mountain [SAN BENITO]: *ridge,* north-trending, 1 mile long, 7.5 miles east-north-east of Bitterwater (lat. 36°24'45" N, long. 120°52'20" W; sec. 27, 34, T 17 S, R 10 E). Named on Hernandez Reservoir (1969) 7.5' quadrangle.

Red Mountain [SAN LUIS OBISPO]: *peak,* 6.5 miles east of the village of San Simeon (lat. 35°38'35" N, long. 121°04'25" W; sec. 26, T 26 S, R 8 E). Altitude 2047 feet. Named on Pebblestone Shut-in (1959) 7.5' quadrangle.

Red Mountain Creek [SAN BENITO]: *stream,* flows almost 2 miles to Mine Creek nearly 6 miles east-northeast of Bitterwater (lat. 36°25'10" N, long. 120°54'35" W; sec. 29, T 17 S, R 10 E); the stream heads west of Red Mountain. Named on Rock Spring Peak (1969) 7.5' quadrangle.

Red Mountain Spring [SAN BENITO]: *spring,* 6.5 miles east-northeast of Bitterwater (lat. 36°25'10" N, long. 120°53'45" W; near W line sec. 28, T 17 S, R 10 E); the spring is east of Red Mountain along Red Mountain Creek. Named on Rock Spring Peak (1969) 7.5' quadrangle.

Red Rock [SAN LUIS OBISPO]: *peak,* nearly 4 miles northeast of the village of San Simeon (lat. 35°41'10" N, long. 121°08'40" W). Altitude 1653 feet. Named on San Simeon (1958) 7.5' quadrangle.

Red Rock Campground [SANTA BARBARA]: *locality,* 4.25 miles south-southeast of Little Pine Mountain along Santa Ynez River (lat. 34°32'25" N, long. 119°43'10" W; sec. 4, T 5 N, R 27 W). Named on Little Pine Mountain (1964) 7.5' quadrangle.

Red Rock Canyon [MONTEREY]: *canyon,* drained by a stream that heads in Monterey County and flows 5 miles to Cholame Valley 9.5 miles north-northeast of Shandon in San Luis Obispo County (lat. 35°45'55" N, long. 120°16'40" W). Named on Cholame Valley (1961) and Tent Hills (1942) 7.5' quadrangles. Cholame Ranch (1943) 7.5' quadrangle has the form "Redrock Canyon" for the name.

Red Rock Canyon [SAN LUIS OBISPO]: *canyon,* drained by a stream that flows 4.25 miles to Taylor Canyon 11 miles west-northwest of Caliente Mountain (lat. 35°04'20" N, long. 119°56'40" W). Named on Taylor Canyon (1959) 7.5' quadrangle. McKittrick (1912) 30' quadrangle has the form "Redrock Canyon" for the name.

Redrock Canyon [SANTA BARBARA]: *canyon,* drained by a stream that flows nearly 6 miles to Santa Ynez River 2.5 miles north of San Marcos Pass (lat. 34°32'55" N, long. 119°49'15" W). Named on San Marcos Pass (1959) 7.5' quadrangle. An outcrop of banded jasper 300 feet high, known as the Red Rock, is at the head of the canyon (Fairbanks, 1894, p. 504).

Redrock Mountain [SANTA BARBARA]: *peak,* 3.5 miles south of the town of Los Alamos (lat. 34°41'30" N, long. 120°16' W). Altitude 1984 feet. Named on Los Alamos (1959) 7.5' quadrangle. California Mining Bureau's (1917c) map has the form "Red Rock Mt." for the name. Combustion of hydrocarbons in normally white shale has altered the color of rocks at the peak to a brilliant rose or brick red (Arnold and Anderson, 1907b, p. 750, 753).

Red Roof Canyon [SANTA BARBARA]: *canyon,* 2 miles long, opens into Grey Canyon 1.5 miles northeast of Point Arguello (lat. 34°35'35" N, long. 120°38'10" W). Named on Point Arguello (1959) and Tranquillon Mountain (1959) 7.5' quadrangles.

Redwood Camp [SANTA CRUZ]: *locality,* 3.5 miles north of the town of Boulder Creek along Kings Creek (lat. 37°10'30" N, long. 122°07'05" W; sec. 6, T 9 S, R 2 W). Named on Castle Rock Ridge (1955) 7.5' quadrangle.

Redwood Canyon [SANTA CRUZ]: *canyon,* drained by a stream that flows 1.5 miles to Browns Creek 3 miles north-northeast of Corralitos (lat. 37°01'35" N, long. 121°46'50" W; near N line sec. 32, T 10 S, R 2 E). Named on Loma Prieta (1955) 7.5' quadrangle.

Redwood Canyon: see **Limekiln Creek** [MONTEREY] (2); **Redhead Canyon** [MONTEREY].

Redwood Creek [MONTEREY]: *stream,* flow 2.5 mile to North Fork Big Sur River 5 miles north-northeast of Partington Point (lat. 36° 14'50" N, long. 121°40'30" W; sec. 30, T 19 S, R 3 E). Named on Partington Ridge (1956) and Ventana Cones (1956) 7.5' quadrangles.

Redwood Creek: see **Gibson Creek** [MONTEREY]; **San Clemente Creek** [MONTEREY].

Redwood Creek Camp [MONTEREY]: *locality,* 2 miles south-southeast of Ventana Cone (lat. 36°15'20" N, long. 121°40'05" W; near W line sec. 29, T 19 S, R 3 E); the place is along Redwood Creek. Named on Ventana Cones (1956) 7.5' quadrangle.

Redwood Glen Camp [SANTA CRUZ]: *local-*

ity, 7 miles east-southeast of the town of Boulder Creek along Bean Creek (lat. 37°04'50" N, long. 122°00'25" W; sec. 7, T 10 S, R 1 W). Named on Felton (1955) 7.5' quadrangle.

Redwood Grove [SANTA CRUZ]: *settlement,* 5 miles east-southeast of Big Basin near San Lorenzo River (lat. 37°09'20" N, long. 122° 07'50" W; in and near sec. 18, T 9 S, R 2 W). Named on Big Basin (1955) 7.5' quadrangle. Ben Lomond (1946) 15' quadrangle has the name "Rices Junction" at the place.

Redwood Gulch [MONTEREY]: *canyon,* drained by a stream that flows 2.25 miles to the sea 5.5 miles southeast of Cape San Martin (lat. 35°50' N, long. 121°23'40" W; sec. 23, T 24 S, R 5 E). Named on Villa Creek (1949) 7.5' quadrangle.

Redwood Lodge [SANTA CRUZ]: *settlement,* 8.5 miles north of Soquel (lat. 37°06'30" N, long. 121°56'40" W). Named on Laurel (1955) 7.5' quadrangle. The name is from a summer resort at the place (Clark, 1986, p. 292). The resort first was called Hotel de Redwood (Hoover, Rensch, and Rensch, p. 478). Postal authorities established De Redwood post office in 1879 and discontinued it in 1882 (Frickstad, p. 176).

Redwood Park: see **Big Basin** [SANTA CRUZ].

Redwood Spring [MONTEREY]: *spring,* 9.5 miles south-southwest of Junipero Serra Peak (lat. 36°00'45" N, long. 121°27'30" W; near SE cor. sec. 18, T 22 S, R 5 E). Named on Cone Peak (1949) 7.5' quadrangle.

Redwood Springs [SANTA CRUZ]: *spring,* 6.25 miles southeast of the town of Boulder Creek at Mount Hermon (lat. 37°03'05" N, long. 122°03'10" W). Named on Felton (1955) 7.5' quadrangle.

Reeds [SAN LUIS OBISPO]: *locality,* 2.25 miles southeast of Edna along Pacific Coast Railroad (lat. 35°10'45" N, long. 120°35'20" W). Named on Arroyo Grande (1897) 15' quadrangle.

Reed's Spur: see **Brookdale** [SANTA CRUZ].

Refugio [SANTA CRUZ]: *land grant,* west of Santa Cruz along the coast, and inland into the highlands. Named on Davenport (1955), Felton (1955), and Santa Cruz (1954) 7.5' quadrangles. Three Castro sisters, Maria de los Angeles, Candida, and Jacinta, received 1 league in 1839, and Jose Bolcof received the grant in 1841; two sons of Jose Bolcoff, husband of Candida, claimed 12,147 acres patented in 1860; Joseph L. Majors, husband of Maria de los Angeles, later received one-third of the grant (Cowan, p. 67; Rowland, p. 42).

Refugio Beach [SANTA BARBARA]: *beach,* 8.5 miles east of Gaviota along the coast (lat. 34°27'45" N, long. 120°04'05" W); the beach is at the mouth of Cañada del Refugio. Named on Gaviota (1943) 15' quadrangle.

Refugio Creek: see **Quiota Creek** [SANTA BARBARA].

Refugio Pass [SANTA BARBARA]: *pass,* 5.5 miles south of Santa Ynez (lat. 34°32' N, long.

120°03'35" W; sec. 7, T 5 N, R 30 W); the pass is near the head of Cañada del Refugio. Named on Santa Ynez (1959) 7.5' quadrangle.

Reggiardo Creek [SANTA CRUZ]: *stream,* flows nearly 2 miles to Laguna Creek 3.5 miles east-northeast of Davenport (lat. 37°01'25" N, long. 122°07'50" W; near SW cor. sec. 30, T 10 S, R 2 W). Named on Davenport (1955) 7.5' quadrangle. Clark (1986, p. 293) associated the name with Filippo Regiardo, an Italian immigrant who had land along the stream in 1889.

Reinoso Peak [SAN BENITO]: *peak,* 2.5 miles south-southeast of Potrero Peak (lat. 36°49'20" N, long. 121°08'10" W; sec. 7, T 13 S, R 8 E). Altitude 3472 feet. Named on Quien Sabe Valley (1968) 7.5' quadrangle.

Release Canyon: see **Reliz Canyon** [MONTEREY].

Reliz: see **Reliz Canyon** [MONTEREY].

Reliz Canyon [MONTEREY]: *canyon,* 13 miles long, opens into lowlands 4.25 miles southwest of Greenfield (lat. 36°16'50" N, long. 121°18'05" W; sec. 15, T 19 S, R 6 E); Reliz Creek drains the canyon. Named on Paraiso Springs (1956) and Reliz Canyon (1949) 7.5' quadrangles. Goodyear (1888, p. 87) referred to Release Cañon, and Smith (p. 25) cited use of the name "Release Canyon." *Reliz* means "landslide" in Mexican Spanish (Stewart, p. 403). Postal authorities established Reliz post office in Reliz Canyon (NE quarter sec. 11, T 20 S, R 6 E) in 1899, moved it 2 miles west in 1900, and discontinued it in 1903 (Salley, p. 183).

Reliz Canyon Camp Ground [MONTEREY]: *locality,* 10 miles south-southwest of Greenfield (lat. 36°11' N, long. 121°17'45" W; near NE cor. sec. 22, T 20 S, R 6 E); the place is in Reliz Canyon. Named on Reliz Canyon (1949) 7.5' quadrangle. Called Reliz Canyon Camp on Junipero Serra (1948) 15' quadrangle.

Reliz Creek [MONTEREY]: *stream,* flows 16 miles to Arroyo Seco (1) nearly 3 miles west of Greenfield (lat. 36°18'50" N, long. 121° 17'35" W); the stream drains Reliz Canyon. Named on Paraiso Springs (1956) and Reliz Canyon (1949) 7.5' quadrangles.

Reservoir Canyon [SAN LUIS OBISPO]: *canyon,* drained by a stream that flows 2.5 miles to San Luis Obispo Creek 2 miles east-northeast of downtown San Luis Obispo (lat. 35°17'35" N, long. 120°37'50" W; near E line sec. 25, T 30 S, R 12 E). Named on Lopez Mountain (1965) 7.5' quadrangle.

Respini Creek: see **Yellow Bank Creek** [SANTA CRUZ].

Retreat [MONTEREY]: *locality,* along Southern Pacific Railroad in Seaside (lat. 36°36'10" N, long. 121°51'50" W). Named on Seaside (1947) 7.5' quadrangle.

Rex [SANTA BARBARA]: *locality,* 3.5 miles east of Santa Maria along Santa Maria Valley Railroad (lat. 34°56'40" N, long. 120°22'30"

W). Named on Santa Maria (1959) and Twitchell Dam (1959) 7.5' quadrangles.

Rex: see **Hernandez** [SAN BENITO].

Reynolds: see **Mount Reynolds** [SAN BENITO].

Rices Junction: see **Redwood Grove** [SANTA CRUZ].

Richardson Canyon [SANTA BARBARA]: *canyon,* drained by a stream that flows nearly 6 miles to Cuyama Valley 7 miles north of McPherson Peak (lat. 34°59'25" N, long. 119°48'55" W). Named on Peak Mountain (1964) 7.5' quadrangle.

Richardson Rock [SANTA BARBARA]: *rock,* 6.5 miles northwest of the westernmost tip of San Miguel Island (lat. 34°06'30" N, long. 120°31' W). Named on Santa Maria (1956) 1°x 2° quadrangle. The feature was known in Spanish times as Isla de Baxos, Isla de Lobos, or Farallon de Lobos (Wagner, H.R., p. 405).

Richardson Spring [SANTA BARBARA]: *spring,* about 5.5 miles northwest of McPherson Peak (lat. 34°55'35" N, long. 119°51' W); the spring is in Richardson Canyon. Named on Peak Mountain (1964) 7.5' quadrangle.

Rickard's Cove: see **Leffingwell Landing** [SAN LUIS OBISPO].

Rider Creek [SANTA CRUZ]: *stream,* flows nearly 2 miles to Corralitos Creek 2 miles north-northwest of Corralitos (lat. 37° 01' N, long. 121°48'55" W; sec. 36, T 10 S, R 1 E). Named on Loma Prieta (1955) 7.5' quadrangle.

Rincon [SANTA CRUZ]: *locality,* 8.5 miles south-southeast of the town of Boulder Creek along Southern Pacific Railroad (lat. 37° 00'45" N, long. 122°03'05" W); the place is on Cañada del Rincon en el Rio San Lorenzo de Santa Cruz grant. Named on Felton (1955) 7.5' quadrangle. Hamman (p. 87) noted that Rincon first had the name "Summit," but Hamman's (1980b) map shows a place called Summit situated southeast of Rincon at a railroad tunnel. The same map also shows a place called Inspiration Point located along the railroad nearly 1 mile north-northwest of Rincon.

Rinconada Creek [SAN LUIS OBISPO]: *stream,* flows 7.25 miles to Salinas River 5 miles north-northeast of Lopez Mountain (lat. 35° 21'40" N, long. 120°32' W; sec. 36, T 29 S, R 13 E). Named on Lopez Mountain (1965) and Santa Margarita Lake (1967) 7.5' quadrangles.

Rinconada del Zanjon: see **Rincon del Zanjon** [MONTEREY].

Rincon Creek [SANTA BARBARA]: *stream,* heads in Ventura County and flows 9.5 miles, mainly along Santa Barbara-Ventura county line, to the sea at Rincon Point (lat. 34°22'25" N, long. 119° 28'35" W). Named on White Ledge Peak (1952) 7.5' quadrangle.

Rincon de la Puente del Monte [MONTEREY]: *land grant,* at and near Gonzales. Named on

Gonzales (1955), Mount Johnson (1968), and Palo Escrito Peak (1956) 7.5' quadrangles. Teodoro Gonzales received 7 leagues in 1836 and claimed 15,219 acres patented in 1866 (Cowan, p. 49; Cowan used the form "Rincon de la Puenta del Monte" for the name).

Rincon de las Salinas [MONTEREY]: *land grant,* mainly south of Salinas River near the coast. Named on Marina (1947) and Moss Landing (1954) 7.5' quadrangles. Cristina Delgado received 0.5 league in 1833; Rafael Estrada claimed 2220 acres patented in 1881 (Cowan, p. 70).

Rincon de los Laureles: see **Los Laurelles** [MONTEREY] (1).

Rincon del Zanjon [MONTEREY]: *land grant,* 3 miles northwest of Salinas. Named on Salinas (1947) 7.5' quadrangle. Jose Eusebio Boronda received 1.5 leagues in 1840 and claimed 2230 acres patented in 1860 (Cowan, p. 68; Cowan, listed the grant under the designation "Rinconada (or Rincon) del Zanjon").

Rincon Point [SANTA BARBARA]: *promontory,* 3 miles east-southeast of Carpinteria along the coast at Santa Barbara-Ventura county line (lat. 34°22'55" N, long. 119°28'35" W); the feature is at the mouth of Rincon Creek on El Rincon grant. Named on White Ledge Peak (1952) 7.5' quadrangle.

Rio Buenaventura: see **Salinas River** [MONTEREY-SAN LUIS OBISPO].

Rio de la Estrella: see **Estrella Creek** [SAN LUIS OBISPO].

Rio de la Santa Inez: see **Santa Ynez River** [SANTA BARBARA].

Rio de la Santa Isabel: see **Huerhuero Creek** [SAN LUIS OBISPO].

Rio de la Santa Maria: see **Santa Maria River** [SAN LUIS OBISPO-SANTA BARBARA].

Rio de La Señora La Santa Ana: see **Pajaro River** [MONTEREY-SAN BENITO-SANTA CRUZ].

Rio de la Sierra: see **Nacimiento River** [MONTEREY-SAN LUIS OBISPO].

Rio de las Truchas: see **Nacimiento River** [MONTEREY-SAN LUIS OBISPO].

Rio Del Mar [SANTA CRUZ]: *town,* 4.5 miles east-northeast of Soquel Point near the coast (lat. 36°58' N, long. 121°53'45" W). Named on Soquel (1954) and Watsonville West (1954) 7.5' quadrangles.

Rio del Pajaro: see **Pajaro River** [MONTEREY-SAN BENITO-SANTA CRUZ].

Río del Paxaro: see **Pajaro River** [MONTEREY-SAN BENITO-SANTA CRUZ].

Rio de Monterrey: see **Salinas River** [MONTEREY].

Rio de San Antonio: see **Pajaro River** [MONTEREY-SAN BENITO-SANTA CRUZ]; **San Antonio River** [MONTEREY]; **Salinas River** [MONTEREY-SAN LUIS OBISPO].

Rio de San Bernardo: see **Santa Ynez River** [SANTA BARBARA].

Rio de San Lorenzo: see **San Lorenzo Creek** [MONTEREY-SAN BENITO].

Río de Santa Ana: see **Pajaro River** [MONTEREY-SAN BENITO-SANTA CRUZ].

Rio de Santa Rosa: see **Santa Ynez River** [SANTA BARBARA].

Rio de San Verardo: see **Santa Ynez River** [SANTA BARBARA].

Rio Estrello: see **Estrella Creek** [SAN LUIS OBISPO].

Rio Grande: see **Arroyo Grande Creek** [SAN LUIS OBISPO].

Rio Guadalupe: see **Santa Maria River** [SAN LUIS OBISPO-SANTA BARBARA].

Rioly Run [SAN LUIS OBISPO]: *stream,* flows 0.5 mile to San Simeon Creek 3.5 miles north of Cambria (lat. 35°37' N, long. 121°04' W; near W line sec. 1, T 27 S, R 8 E). Named on Cambria (1959) 7.5' quadrangle.

Rio Pajaro: see **San Benito River** [SAN BENITO].

Rio Piedras: see **Rocky Creek** [MONTEREY] (1).

Rio Sabinos: see **Salinas River** [MONTEREY-SAN LUIS OBISPO].

Rio Salinas: see **Salinas River** [MONTEREY-SAN LUIS OBISPO].

Rio Salinas de Monterey: see **Salinas River** [MONTEREY-SAN LUIS OBISPO].

Rio San Agustine: see **San Lorenzo River** [SANTA CRUZ].

Rio San Benito: see **San Benito River** [SAN BENITO].

Rio San Buenaventura: see **Salinas River** [MONTEREY-SAN LUIS OBISPO].

Rio San Elizario: see **Salinas River** [MONTEREY].

Rio Santa Maria: see **Cuyama River** [SAN LUIS OBISPO-SANTA BARBARA]; **Santa Maria River** [SAN LUIS OBISPO-SANTA BARBARA].

Rio Selina: see **Salinas River** [MONTEREY-SAN LUIS OBISPO].

Rio Wasna: see **Huasna River** [SAN LUIS OBISPO].

River Oaks [SAN BENITO]: *settlement,* 4.5 miles northwest of San Juan Bautista on the south side of Pajaro River (lat. 36°54' N, long. 121°35'30" W). Named on Chittenden (1955) 7.5' quadrangle.

Riverside Grove [SANTA CRUZ]: *settlement,* 4.5 miles east of Big Basin near San Lorenzo River (lat. 37°10'25" N, long. 122°08'30" W; sec. 1, 12, T 9 S, R 3 W). Named on Big Basin (1955) 7.5' quadrangle. Hamman's (1980b) map shows Dougherty's Mill #2 at present Riverside Grove, and shows a place called Sinnott Switch located along the railroad a short distance north of Dougherty's Mill #2.

Roach Canyon [MONTEREY]: *canyon,* drained by a stream that flows 2 miles to Carmel Valley (1) 3.25 miles east of the mouth of Carmel River (lat. 36°32'25" N, long. 121°52' W). Named on Seaside (1947) 7.5' quadrangle.

Roadamite [SANTA BARBARA]: *locality,* 2.25

miles southwest of the village of Sisquoc (lat. 34°50'40" N, long. 120°19'25" W). Named on Santa Maria (1947) 15' quadrangle.

Roadhouse Slough: see **Elkhorn Slough** [MONTEREY].

Robbers' Cave: see **Cave Landing**, under **Mallagh Landing** [SAN LUIS OBISPO].

Roberta: see **Mount Roberta** [SANTA BARBARA].

Roberts: see **Camp Robers Military Reservation** [MONTEREY-SAN LUIS OBISPO].

Robertson Creek [MONTEREY]: *stream,* flows 3.5 miles to Finch Creek 1.5 miles east-north-east of Jamesburg (lat. 36°22'40" N, long. 121°33'45" W; sec. 8, T 18 S, R 4 E). Named on Chews Ridge (1956) and Rana Creek (1956) 7.5' quadrangles. The stream was called Smith Creek before it was called Robertson Creek—both names record early residents in the neighborhood (Clark, 1991, p. 476).

Roberts Spring [SAN LUIS OBISPO]: *spring,* nearly 4 miles south-southeast of Cholame (lat. 35°40'35" N, long. 120°15'50" W; sec. 9, T 26 S, R 16 E). Named on Cholame (1961) 7.5' quadrangle.

Robinson Canyon [MONTEREY]:
(1) *canyon,* drained by a stream that flows 3.25 miles to Carmel River 6.5 miles east of the mouth of that river (lat. 36°31'05" N, long. 121°4840" W; near N line sec. 25, T 16 S, R 1 E). Named on Mount Carmel (1956) and Seaside (1947) 7.5' quadrangles. Called Robison Canyon on Monterey (1913) and Point Sur (1925) 15' quadrangles.
(2) *canyon,* 3.5 miles long, opens into lowlands 3.5 miles northeast of Jolon (lat. 36°00'40" N, long. 121°08'10" W; sec. 18, T 22 S, R 8 E). Named on Cosio Knob (1949) and Espinosa Canyon (1949) 7.5' quadrangles.

Robison Canyon: see **Robinson Canyon** [MONTEREY] (1).

Roblar Canyon [SANTA BARBARA]: *canyon,* drained by a stream that flows 5 miles to Mono Creek 1.5 miles north-northeast of Hildreth Peak (lat. 34°37'20" N, long. 119°32'35" W). Named on Hildreth Peak (1964) and Madulce Peak (1964) 7.5' quadrangles.

Roblar Valley: see **Stony Valley** [MONTEREY].

Robla Valley: see **Stony Valley** [MONTEREY].

Roble Canyon: see **Alamar Canyon** [SANTA BARBARA].

Robles del Rio [MONTEREY]: *district,* part of the town of Carmel Valley south of Carmel River (lat. 36°28'15" N, long. 121°43'30" W). Named on Carmel Valley (1956) 7.5' quadrangle. Postal authorities established Robles del Rio post office in 1941 and changed the name to Carmel Valley in 1952 (Frickstad, p. 109). Frank Porter laid out the place in 1926 (Clark, 1991, p. 478).

Rob Roy: see **La Selva Beach** [SANTA CRUZ].

Rob Roy Junction [SANTA BARBARA]: *locality,* 4 miles west-southwest of Corralitos (lat. 36°58'15" N, long. 121°52'20" W).

Named on Watsonville West (1954) 7.5' quadrangle. Rob Roy real-estate development began in 1922 at present La Selva Beach (Hamman, p. 268).

Rock Canyon: see **Hilton Canyon** [SANTA BARBARA].

Rockland: see **Rockland Landing** [MONTEREY].

Rockland Landing [MONTEREY]: *locality,* 3 miles east-southeast of Lopez Point along the coast at the mouth of Limekiln Creek (2) (lat. 36°00'30" N, long. 121°31'05" W; sec. 22, T 22 S, R 4 E). Site named on Lopez Point (1956) 7.5' quadrangle. Officials of Rockland Cement Company constructed a landing, installed three large kilns, and built houses for workmen at the place in the 1880's (Fink, p. 213). Preston (1893a, p. 260) mentioned "Rockland, on the coast," where limekilns operated formerly.

Rocks: see **The Rocks** [MONTEREY].

Rock Spring [SAN BENITO]: *spring,* 8 miles northeast of Bitterwater (lat. 36°28'20" N, long. 120°55'05" W; near NE cor. sec. 7, T 17 S, R 10 E); the spring is at the head of a tributary of Rock Springs Creek. Named on Rock Spring Peak (1969) 7.5' quadrangle.

Rock Spring [SAN LUIS OBISPO]:
(1) *spring,* 4.25 miles west of Cholame in McMillan Canyon (lat. 35°42'55" N, long. 120°22'20" W; sec. 32, T 25 S, R 15 E). Named on Cholame (1961) 7.5' quadrangle.
(2) *spring,* 4.5 miles south-southeast of Wilson Corner (lat. 35°24'20" N, long. 120°20'40" W; near SE cor. sec. 10, T 29 S, R 15 E). Named on Camatta Ranch (1966) 7.5' quadrangle.

Rock Spring Peak [SAN BENITO]: *peak,* 8 miles northeast of Bitterwater (lat. 36°28' N, long. 120°54'20" W; sec. 8, T 17 S, R 10 E); the peak is less than 1 mile east-southeast of Rock Spring. Altitude 4033 feet. Named on Rock Spring Peak (1969) 7.5' quadrangle.

Rock Springs Creek [SAN BENITO]: *stream,* flows 6 miles to San Benito River 5.5 miles north-northeast of Bitterwater (lat. 36°26'45" N, long. 120°58'40" W; sec. 15, T 17 S, R 9 E). Named on Rock Spring Peak (1969) 7.5' quadrangle.

Rocky Butte [SAN LUIS OBISPO]: *peak,* 7.5 miles east of the village of San Simeon (lat. 35°39'55" N, long. 121°03'30" W; near N line sec. 24, T 26 S, R 8 E). Altitude 3432 feet. Named on Pebblestone Shut-in (1959) 7.5' quadrangle.

Rocky Canyon [SAN LUIS OBISPO]: *canyon,* 2 miles long, opens into lowlands 5 miles north of Santa Margarita (lat. 35°27'45" N, long. 120°37'15" W). Named on Santa Margarita (1965) 7.5' quadrangle.

Rocky Canyon: see **Stephens Canyon** [SAN LUIS OBISPO].

Rocky Creek [MONTEREY]:
(1) *stream,* flows 6 miles to the sea 5 miles north of Point Sur (lat. 36°22'45" N, long.

121°54'05" W; sec. 7, T 18 S, R 1 E); the stream goes through Las Piedras Canyon. Named on Mount Carmel (1956) and Soberanes Point (1956) 7.5' quadrangles. According to Lussier (p. 13), the early Spaniards called the creek Rio Piedras, probably because of rocks in the stream—*piedras* means "stones" in Spanish.
(2) *stream,* flows 4.25 miles to Arroyo Seco (1) 7.5 miles north-northwest of Junipero Serra Peak (lat. 36°14'10" N, long. 121°29'25" W; sec. 36, T 19 S, R 4 E). Named on Chews Ridge (1956), Junipero Serra Peak (1949), and Tassajara Hot Springs (1956) 7.5' quadrangles.

Rocky Creek [SAN LUIS OBISPO]: *stream,* flows 5 miles to Santa Rita Creek 1.25 miles south of York Mountain (lat. 35°31'40" N, long. 120°50'10" W). Named on Adelaida (1961) 15' quadrangle.

Rocky Creek Camp [MONTEREY]: *locality,* 2.5 miles east-northeast of Tassajara Hot Springs (lat. 36°14'50" N, long. 121°30'15" W; sec. 26, T 19 S, R 4 E); the place is along Rocky Creek (2). Named on Tassajara Hot Springs (1956) 7.5' quadrangle.

Rocky Gorge [SAN LUIS OBISPO]: *canyon,* 1.5 miles long, 4 miles west of Atascadero along Graves Creek (lat. 35°29'20" N, long. 120°44'15" W). Named on Atascadero (1965) 7.5' quadrangle.

Rocky Point [MONTEREY]: *promontory,* 3.25 miles south-southeast of Soberanes Point along the coast (lat. 36°24'10" N, long. 121°54'50" W). Named on Soberanes Point (1956) 7.5' quadrangle.

Rocky Point [SANTA BARBARA]: *promontory,* 1 mile southeast of Point Arguello along the coast (lat. 34°33'50" N, long. 120°38'20" W). Named on Point Arguello (1959) 7.5' quadrangle.

Rocky Ridge [MONTEREY]: *ridge,* west-trending, 2 miles long, west of Fremont Peak (lat. 36°45'20" N, long. 121°31'15" W). Named on San Juan Bautista (1955) 7.5' quadrangle.

Rodeo Creek Gulch [SANTA CRUZ]: *canyon,* drained by a stream that flows 5.5 miles to Corcoran Lagoon 0.5 mile north-northwest of Soquel Point (lat. 36°57'45" N, long. 121°58'45" W); the canyon is on the west border of Arroyo del Rodeo grant. Named on Laurel (1955) and Soquel (1954) 7.5' quadrangles. Called Doyle Gulch on Los Gatos (1919) and Capitola (1914) 15' quadrangles. The name "Doyle" commemorates John Doyle, who had a farm at the place in the 1860's and 1870's (Rowland, p. 68).

Rodes Reef: see **Brockway Point** [SANTA BARBARA].

Rogers: see **Port Rogers**, under **Port Watsonville** [SANTA CRUZ].

Rogers Creek [SAN LUIS OBISPO]: *stream,* flows nearly 7 miles to San Juan Creek 2.25 miles west-southwest of Freeborn Mountain (lat. 35°16'30" N, long. 120°05'20" W; sec.

31, T 30 S, R 18 E). Named on Branch Mountain (1967) and California Valley (1966) 7.5' quadrangles.

Rogers Creek [SANTA CRUZ]: *stream,* flows less than 1 mile to Opal Creek 1.5 miles north of Big Basin (lat. 37°11'35" N, long. 122°13'05" W; sec. 32, T 8 S, R 3 W). Named on Big Basin (1955) 7.5' quadrangle. The misspelled name is for Winfield Scott Rodgers, who had tan-bark camps in the vicinity; the stream was called Lion Creek before 1895 (Clark, 1986, p. 301).

Rogue Canyon: see **Roque Canyon** [SANTA BARBARA].

Romer Canyon: see **Romero Canyon** [SANTA BARBARA].

Romero Canyon [SANTA BARBARA]: *canyon,* 2.5 miles long, along Romero Creek above a point 5.25 miles northwest of Carpinteria (lat. 34°26'40" N, long. 119°35'35" W; sec. 10, T 4 N, R 26 W). Named on Carpinteria (1952) 7.5' quadrangle. United States Board on Geographic Names (1961b, p. 14) rejected the name "Romer Canyon" for the feature.

Romero Canyon Creek [SANTA BARBARA]: see **Romero Creek** [SANTA BARBARA].

Romero Creek [SANTA BARBARA]: *stream,* flows 5 miles to the sea 6 miles west-northwest of Carpinteria and less than 1 mile west-southwest of Ortega Hill (lat. 34°25'05" N, long. 119°37'10" W); the stream drains Romero Canyon. Named on Carpinteria (1952, photorevised 1967) 7.5' quadrangle. Called Arroyo de las Ortegas on Santa Barbara (1903) 15' quadrangle, and the lower part is called Picay Creek on Carpinteria (1952) 7.5' quadrangle, but United States Board on Geographic Names (1961b, p. 14) rejected the names "Arroyo de las Ortegas," "Picay Creek," and "Romero Canyon Creek" for the stream.

Romero Reservoir [SANTA BARBARA]: *lake,* 250 feet long, 5.5 miles northwest of Carpinteria (lat. 34°26'50" N, long. 119°35'50" W). Named on Carpinteria (1952) 7.5' quadrangle.

Romero Saddle [SANTA BARBARA]: *pass,* 7 miles northwest of Carpinteria (lat. 34°28'35" N, long. 119°35'40" W); sec. 34, T 5 N, R 26 W); the pass is near the head of Romero Canyon. Named on Carpinteria (1952) 7.5' quadrangle. Called Blue Canyon Pass on Santa Barbara (1903) 15' quadrangle.

Romie: see **Fort Romie** [MONTEREY].

Roosevelt Creek [MONTEREY]: *stream,* flows 2.5 miles to Arroyo Seco (1) 3.25 miles westsouthwest of Junipero Serra Peak (lat. 36°07'25" N, long. 121°28'10" W; sec. 7, T 21 S, R 5 E). Named on Cone Peak (1949) and Junipero Serra Peak (1949) 7.5' quadrangles.

Rooster Canyon [MONTEREY]: *canyon,* drained by a stream that flows nearly 2 miles to McCoy Canyon 7.5 miles northeast of Gonzales (lat. 36°34'50" N, long. 121°20'25"

W; sec. 32, T 15 S, R 6 E). Named on Mount Johnson (1968) 7.5' quadrangle.

Root: see **Miles** [SAN LUIS OBISPO].

Rootville: see **Gabilan Range** [MONTEREY-SAN BENITO].

Roque Campground [SANTA BARBARA]: *locality,* 7 miles north-northeast of Manzanita Mountain (lat. 34°58'45" N, long. 120°00'50" W); the place is in Roque Canyon. Named on Manzanita Mountain (1964) 7.5' quadrangle.

Roque Canyon [SANTA BARBARA]: *canyon,* drained by a stream that flows nearly 4 miles to join the stream in Flores Canyon and form North Fork La Brea Creek 5.5 miles north-northeast of Manzanita Mountain (lat. 34°58'10" N, long. 120°03'05" W). Named on Manzanita Mountain (1964) 7.5' quadrangle. United States Board on Geographic Names (1967a, p. 10) rejected the name "Rogue Canyon" for the feature.

Rosa Morada: see **San Joaquin** [SAN BENITO].

Rosaria Creek: see **Tres Pinos Creek** [SAN BENITO].

Rosario del Serafin de Asculi: see **Soquel Creek** [SANTA CRUZ].

Rosas Canyon [SAN BENITO]: *canyon,* drained by a stream that flows 4 miles to an unnamed canyon nearly 3 miles east of North Chalone Peak (lat. 36°27'20" N, long. 121°08'45" W; sec. 18, T 17 S, R 8 E). Named on North Chalone Peak (1969) and Topo Valley (1969) 7.5' quadrangles.

Rosaville: see **Cambria** [SAN LUIS OBISPO].

Rose Canyon [SANTA BARBARA]: *canyon,* drained by a stream that flows 2 miles to Santa Ynez River 6.5 miles south-southwest of Hildreth Peak (lat. 34°30'50" N, long. 119°35'55" W). Named on Hildreth Peak (1964) 7.5' quadrangle.

Rosemary [SANTA BARBARA]: *locality,* 2.25 miles east of downtown Santa Maria along Santa Maria Valley Railroad (lat. 34°56'45" N, long. 120°23'35" W; sec. 18, T 10 N, R 33 W). Named on Santa Maria (1959) 7.5' quadrangle.

Rose Reservoir [SANTA CRUZ]: *lake,* 750 feet long, 3.5 miles north-northeast of Watsonville (lat. 36°58' N, long. 121°44'15" W). Named on Watsonville East (1955) 7.5' quadrangle.

Round Corral Canyon [SANTA BARBARA]: *canyon,* drained by a stream that flows 2 miles to Sisquoc River 6 miles south-southeast of Tepusquet Peak (lat. 34°49'50" N, long. 120°08'25" W). Named on Foxen Canyon (1964) and Zaca Lake (1964) 7.5' quadrangles.

Round Hill [SANTA BARBARA]: *hill,* 1.5 miles south of Tranquillon Mountain (lat. 34°33'30" N, long. 120°33'55" W). Named on Tranquillon Mountain (1959) 7.5' quadrangle.

Round Mountain [MONTEREY]: *peak,* 6.5 miles north of Charley Mountain on Monterey-Fresno county line (lat. 36°14'10"

N, long. 120°39'55" W; sec. 34, T 19 S, R 12 E). Named on Priest Valley (1969) 7.5' quadrangle.

Round Potrero [SANTA BARBARA]: *area,* 2.5 miles east-southeast of Salisbury Potrero (lat. 34°48'10" N, long. 119°39'45" W). Named on Salisbury Potrero (1964) 7.5' quadrangle.

Round Potrero Spring [SANTA BARBARA]: *spring,* 2 miles east-southeast of Salisbury Potrero (lat. 34°48'25" N, long. 119°40'05" W); the spring is less than 0.5 mile west-northwest of Round Potrero. Named on Salisbury Potrero (1964) 7.5' quadrangle.

Round Rock Camp [MONTEREY]: *locality,* nearly 2 miles north of Ventana Cone along Carmel River (lat. 36°18'35" N, long. 121°40'35" W; sec. 6, T 19 S, R 3 E). Named on Ventana Cones (1956) 7.5' quadrangle.

Round Spring [MONTEREY]: *spring,* 7.5 miles east of Cape San Martin (lat. 35°54'45" N, long. 121°20' W; near E line sec. 20, T 23 S, R 6 E). Named on Alder Peak (1949) 7.5' quadrangle.

Round Spring Valley [SAN BENITO]: *area,* 6.5 miles southeast of Fremont Peak near the head of a branch of Jamieson Creek (lat. 36°40'35" N, long. 121°26'25" W; sec. 32, T 14 S, R 5 E). Named on Mount Harlan (1968) 7.5' quadrangle.

Round Top [SAN LUIS OBISPO]: *peak,* 6.25 miles east of Edna (lat. 35°12'45" N, long. 120°31'45" W; sec. 19, T 31 S, R 14 E). Altitude 2058 feet. Named on Arroyo Grande NE (1965) 7.5' quadrangle.

Roundtree Hill: see **Twin Peak** [MONTEREY].

Ruby Canyon [MONTEREY]: *canyon,* drained by a stream that flows nearly 4 miles to lowlands 1.25 miles northwest of Jolon (lat. 35°59' N, long. 121°11'45" W). Named on Cosio Knob (1949) and Jolon (1949) 7.5' quadrangles.

Ruda Canyon [SAN LUIS OBISPO]: *canyon,* drained by a stream that flows 2 miles to Coon Creek 7.5 miles northwest of Point San Luis (lat. 35°14'35" N, long. 120°50'45" W; sec. 12, T 31 S, R 10 E). Named on Port San Luis (1965) 7.5' quadrangle. Called Ruder Canyon on Port Harford (1897) 15' quadrangle.

Ruder Canyon: see **Ruda Canyon** [SAN LUIS OBISPO].

Rude Spring [MONTEREY]: *spring,* 15 miles east-northeast of San Ardo along Pancho Rico Creek (lat. 36°04'10" N, long. 120°37'55" W; sec. 25, T 21 S, R 12 E). Named on Slack Canyon (1969) 7.5' quadrangle.

Rudolf Canyon [SAN BENITO]: *canyon,* drained by a stream that flows 1.5 miles to San Benito River 7 miles south-southwest of Idria (lat. 36°19'50" N, long. 120°43'50" W; sec. 26, T 18 S, R 11 E). Named on San Benito Mountain (1969) 7.5' quadrangle.

Ruins Creek [SANTA CRUZ]: *stream,* flows nearly 3 miles to Bean Creek 7 miles southeast of the town of Boulder Creek (lat. 37°03'25" N, long. 122°01'50" W). Named on Felton (1955) 7.5' quadrangle.

Ruiz Canyon [SANTA BARBARA]: *canyon,* drained by a stream that flows 2.5 miles to Tepusquet Canyon 2.25 miles west of Tepusquet Peak (lat. 34°54'55" N, long. 120°13'30" W). Named on Tepusquet Canyon (1964) 7.5' quadrangle.

Russels Creek: see **Cholame Creek** [MONTEREY-SAN LUIS OBISPO].

Russelsville: see **Parkfield** [MONTEREY].

Rusty Peak [SAN LUIS OBISPO]: *peak,* 6.5 miles north-northeast of the mouth of Morro Creek (lat. 35°27'50" N, long. 120°48'55" W; near N line sec. 32, T 28 S, R 11 E). Altitude 1837 feet. Named on Morro Bay North (1965) 7.5' quadrangle.

– S –

Sacate [SANTA BARBARA]: *locality,* 10.5 miles east of Point Conception along Southern Pacific Railroad (lat. 34°28'20" N, long. 120°17'35" W); the place is near the mouth of Cañada del Sacate. Named on Sacate (1953) 7.5' quadrangle.

Sacate Canyon: see **Cañada del Coyote** [SANTA BARBARA].

Saddle Mountain: see **Potrero Canyon** [MONTEREY].

Saddle Peak [SAN LUIS OBISPO]: *peak,* nearly 5 miles north-northwest of Point San Luis (lat. 35°13'20" N, long. 120°47'30" W; near SE cor. sec. 16, T 31 S, R 11 E). Altitude 1819 feet. Named on Port San Luis (1965) 7.5' quadrangle.

Sage [MONTEREY]: *locality,* 4 miles north-northeast of Salinas (lat. 36°43'45" N, long. 121°37'30" W). Named on Salinas (1947) 7.5' quadrangle.

Sage Hill [SANTA BARBARA]: *peak,* 3.5 miles north-northeast of San Marcos Pass (lat. 34°33'20" N, long. 119°47'50" W; sec. 35, T 6 N, R 28 W). Named on San Marcos Pass (1959) 7.5' quadrangle.

Sagunto: see **Santa Ynez** [SANTA BARBARA].

Saint Francis Springs: see **Chittenden's Sulphur Springs,** under **Chittenden** [SANTA CRUZ].

Saint Paul's Ferry: see **Pauls Ferry,** under **Pauls Island** [MONTEREY].

Sal: see **Point Sal** [SANTA BARBARA].

Salina Plains: see **Salinas River** [MONTEREY].

Salinas [MONTEREY]: *city,* 10 miles east-southeast of the mouth of Salinas River (lat. 36°40'30" N, long. 121°39'15" W). Named on Salinas (1947) and Natividad (1947, photorevised 1968) 7.5' quadrangles. A tavern called Halfway House opened in 1856 at the intersection of stage routes, and a village sprang up around it; the city of Salinas was laid out at the place in 1867 and incorporated in 1874 (Bancroft, p. 524). Postal authorities established Salinas post office in 1854

(Frickstad, p. 109).

Salinas: see **East Salinas,** under **Alisal** [MONTEREY].

Salinas Mountains: see **Sierra de Salinas** [MONTEREY].

Salinas Plains: see **Salinas River** [MONTEREY].

Salinas Point: see **Coal Oil Point** [SANTA BARBARA].

Salinas Range: see **Gabilan Range** [MONTEREY-SAN BENITO].

Salinas Reservoir: see **Santa Margarita Lake** [SAN LUIS OBISPO].

Salinas River [MONTEREY-SAN LUIS OBISPO]: *stream,* heads in San Luis Obispo County and flows for about 170 miles to the sea 11 miles north-northeast of Monterey in Monterey County (lat. 36° 44'45" N, long. 121°48'15" W). Named on San Luis Obispo (1956) and Santa Cruz (1956) 1° x 2° quadrangles. Marina (1947) 7.5' quadrangle shows a bar across the mouth of the stream. Members of the Portola expedition discovered the river in 1769 near present King City, and Crespi gave it the name "Rio San Elizario" in honor of the saint whose day is September 27, the day after the discovery (Wagner, H.R., p. 498). According to Davidson (1907, p. 103), the river was called Santa Delfina— Delfina was the wife of Elizario—but H.R. Wagner (p. 498) pointed out that Crespi gave her name only to a camp near the mouth of the stream. Font in 1776 used the name "Santa Delfina Valley" for the valley of Salinas River (Bolton, p. 271). The stream is called R. de Sn. Antonio on Malaspina's (1791) map, and is called Rio de Monterrey on a diseño of Guadalupe y Llanito de los Correos in 1833 (Becker, 1969). On Greenhow's (1844) map the river has the name "Buenaventura R.," on Fremont's (1845) map it has the name "Rio San Buenaventura," and on Bartlett's (1854) map it has the name "R. Sabinos or Buenaventura." Parke's (1854-1855) map has the name "Rio Salinas de Monterey," and in his text Parke (p. 1) referred to the stream by the name "Rio Salinas." Keller (p. 38) used the name "Rio Selina" in 1851. The valley of Salinas River commonly is called Salinas Valley, but that name was unknown in Spanish times, when the feature was known as Valley of Monterey (Cerruti, p. 130). During the Mexican War, Americans used the names "Salina plains" (Carson, p. 106) and "the plains of Salinaeus" (*The California Star,* August 21, 1847). Parke's (1854-1855) map has the name "Salinas Plains" along the river north of Soledad mission. Hanna (p. 264) attributed the name "Salinas" to salt marshes near the mouth of the river, Antisell (1856, p. 43) thought that the name referred to the flavor of water in the river, and Logan (p. 721) stated that the name—from the Spanish word for "salty"—was given for saline springs located along the stream and near its source. In

Spanish times two small lakes 12 miles from Monterey near the sea produced salt when they dried up (Cerruti, p. 130).

Salinas River: see **Old Salinas River** [MONTEREY].

Salinas Valley: see **Salinas River** [MONTEREY].

Salisbury Canyon [SANTA BARBARA]: *canyon,* 9 miles long, opens into Cuyama Valley 3.5 miles south-southeast of New Cuyama (lat. 34°54' N, long. 119°39'35" W); the canyon heads at Salisbury Potrero. Named on New Cuyama (1964) and Salisbury Potrero (1964) 7.5' quadrangles.

Salisbury Canyon Wash [SANTA BARBARA]: *stream,* flows 4.5 miles from the mouth of Salisbury Canyon to Branch Canyon Wash near New Cuyama (lat. 34°57'10" N, long. 119°41'40" W). Named on New Cuyama (1964) 7.5' quadrangle.

Salisbury Potrero [SANTA BARBARA]: *area,* 9 miles south-southwest of the village of Cuyama (lat. 34°49'15" N, long. 119°42' W). Named on Salisbury Potrero (1964) 7.5' quadrangle.

Salmon Cone [MONTEREY]: *peak,* 8 miles southwest of Cape San Martin (lat. 35°48'40" N, long. 121°21'50" W; sec. 30, T 24 S, R 6 E); the peak is just north of the mouth of Salmon Creek (1). Named on Burro Mountain (1949) 7.5' quadrangle. The feature also was called Salmon Peak (Clark, 1991, p. 494).

Salmon Creek [MONTEREY]:
(1) *stream,* flows 4.25 miles to the sea 8 miles southeast of Cape San Martin (lat. 35°48'30" N, long. 121°21'45" W; sec. 31, T 24 S, R 6 E). Named on Burro Mountain (1949) 7.5' quadrangle.
(2) *stream,* flows nearly 6 miles to Nacimiento River 8.5 miles south of Jolon (lat. 35°50'50" N, long. 121°11'40" W; sec. 15, T 24 S, R 7 E). Named on Burnett Peak (1949) 7.5' quadrangle. United States Board on Geographic Names (1978b, p. 5) rejected the name "Little Salmon Creek" for the stream.

Salmon Peak: see **Salmon Cone** [MONTEREY].

Salsipuedes [SANTA CRUZ]: *land grant,* north and northeast of Watsonville; extends into Santa Clara County. Named on Chittenden (1955), Loma Prieta (1955), Mount Madona (1955), Watsonville East (1955), and Watsonville West (1954) 7.5' quadrangles. Manuel Jimeno Casarin received 8 leagues in 1834 and 1840; James Blair and others claimed 31,201 acres patented in 1861 (Cowan, p. 71). The name refers to the rugged terrain on the grant—*salsipuedes* has the meaning "get out if you can" in Spanish (Arbuckle, p. 29-30).

Salsipuedes Canyon [SANTA BARBARA]: *canyon,* drained by a stream that flows 3 miles to South Fork La Brea Creek 4 miles east-northeast of Manzanita Mountain (lat. 34°55'25" N, long. 120°01'05" W). Named

on Manzanita Mountain (1964) 7.5' quadrangle. United States Board on Geographic Names (1978b, p. 5) rejected the form "Salscepudes" for the name.

Salsipuedes Creek [MONTEREY]:
(1) *stream,* flows nearly 2 miles to Las Gazas Creek 4.25 miles north-northwest of Mount Carmel (lat. 36°26'50" N, long. 121°49'10" W; near S line sec. 13, T 17 S, R 1 E). Named on Mount Carmel (1956) 7.5' quadrangle.
(2) *stream,* flows 2 miles to San Antonio River 3.5 miles east of Cone Peak (lat. 36°03'35" N, long. 121°26'05" W; sec. 33, T 21 S, R 5 E). Named on Cone Peak (1949) 7.5' quadrangle, which shows Avila ranch near the stream. According to Stewart (p. 420), *salsipuedes* means literally "jump if you can" in Spanish, and is used conventionally for difficult places. Vicente Avila took his family to an isolated valley north of San Antonio mission and gave his ranch there the name "Salsipuedes" (Fink, p. 210).

Salsipuedes Creek [SAN LUIS OBISPO]: *stream,* flows 4.5 miles to Santa Margarita Lake 5.25 miles west of Pozo (lat. 35°18'55" N, long. 120°27'55" W; sec. 15, T 30 S, R 14 E). Named on Santa Margarita Lake (1967) 7.5' quadrangle.

Salsipuedes Creek [SANTA BARBARA]: *stream,* flows 9 miles to Santa Ynez River 2.5 miles east of the city of Lompoc (lat. 34° 37'55" N, long. 120°24'40" W); the stream is partly on Cañada de Salsipuedes grant. Named on Lompoc (1959) and Lompoc Hills (1959) 7.5' quadrangles. Parke (p. 16) used the form "Sal si Puedes creek" for the name.

Salsipuedes Creek [SANTA CRUZ]: *stream,* joins Pajaro River on the east side of Watsonville (lat. 36°54'35" N, long. 121°44'40" W); part of the stream is on Salsipuedes grant. Named on Watsonville East (1955) 7.5' quadrangle. On San Juan Bautista (1917) 15 quadrangle, which does not name Salsipuedes Creek, the stream is shown as part of Corralitos Creek

Salsipuedes Number Two: see **Salsipuedes Spring Number 2** [SAN LUIS OBISPO].

Salsipuedes Spring Number 1 [SAN LUIS OBISPO]: *spring,* 4.5 miles west-southwest of Pozo (lat. 35°16'35" N, long. 120°26'50" W; sec. 26, T 30 S, R 14 E); the spring is 0.5 mile northwest of Salsipuedes Spring Number 2 along a tributary of Salsipuedes Creek . Named on Santa Margarita Lake (1967) 7.5' quadrangle. United States Board on Geographic Names (1968c, p. 6) approved the name "Salsipuedes Spring Number One" for the feature, and rejected the names "Number One Salsipuedes Springs" and "Salsipuedes Spring Number Two."

Salsipuedes Spring Number 2 [SAN LUIS OBISPO]: *spring,* 4.25 miles west-southwest of Pozo (lat. 35°16'15" N, long. 120°26'20" W; sec. 35, T 30 S, R 14 E); the spring is 0.5 mile southeast of Salsipuedes Spring Number 1 along Salsipuedes Creek. Named on Santa Margarita Lake (1967) 7.5' quadrangle. United States Board on Geographic Names (1968c, p. 6) approved the name "Salsipuedes Spring Number Two" for the feature, and rejected the names "Salsipuedes Number Two," "Salsipuedes Spring Number One," and "Salsipuedes Springs Number Two."

Salt Canyon [SAN LUIS OBISPO]: *canyon,* 1.5 miles long, opens into lowlands 15 miles eastsoutheast of Shandon (lat. 35°34'30" N, long. 120°06'55" W; sec. 14, T 27 S, R 17 E). Named on Packwood Creek (1961) 7.5' quadrangle.

Salt Creek [SAN BENITO]: *stream,* flows 9 miles to Tres Pinos Creek 3.25 miles southsoutheast of Cherry Peak (lat. 36°38'50" N, long. 121°07'35" W; sec. 8, T 15 S, R 8 E). Named on Panoche Pass (1968) and San Benito (1968) 7.5' quadrangles.

Salt Creek [SAN LUIS OBISPO]: *stream,* flows 4.5 miles to Trout Creek (2) 15 miles northnortheast of the town of Nipomo (lat. 35°13'50" N, long. 120°20'50" W; near E line sec. 15, T 31 S, R 15 E). Named on Caldwell Mesa (1967) and Tar Spring Ridge (1967) 7.5' quadrangles. According to G.A. Waring (p. 301), the stream has "notable amounts of salt that are deposited along its bed and in several other ravines near by."

Salt Lake: see **Soda Lake** [SAN LUIS OBISPO].

Saltos Canyon [SAN LUIS OBISPO]: *canyon,* drained by a stream that flows nearly 6 miles to Carrizo Canyon 14 miles west-northwest of Caliente Mountain (lat. 35°06'10" N, long. 119°59'05" W; near SW cor. sec. 30, T 32 S, R 19 E). Named on Chimineas Ranch (1959) and Taylor Canyon (1959) 7.5' quadrangles.

Sam Jones Canyon [MONTEREY]: *canyon,* drained by a stream that flows 2 miles to San Antonio River 5.25 miles south-southeast of Jolon (lat. 35°54'20" N, long. 121°07'35" W). Named on Jolon (1949) 7.5' quadrangle. The name is for an early settler in the canyon (Clark, 1991, p. 496).

Samon Peak [SANTA BARBARA]: *peak,* 2.5 miles north of Big Pine Mountain (lat. 34°44'05" N, long. 119°38'40" W). Altitude 6227 feet. Named on Big Pine Mountain (1964) 7.5' quadrangle.

Sampson Creek [SAN BENITO]: *stream,* flows 4.25 miles to Larious Creek 4 miles westnorthwest of Idria (lat. 36°25'55" N, long. 120° 44'20" W; sec. 23, T 17 S, R 11 E). Named on Idria (1969) 7.5' quadrangle.

Sampson Peak [SAN BENITO]: *peak,* nearly 2 miles west-southwest of Idria (lat. 36°24'30" N, long. 120°42'10" W; near W line sec. 31, T 17 S, R 12 E). Altitude 4663 feet. Named on Idria (1969) 7.5' quadrangle. United States Board on Geographic Names (1933, p. 663) rejected the name "Venado Peak" for the feature.

San Agustine Creek: see **San Lorenzo River** [SANTA CRUZ].

San Andreas: see **San Andres** [SANTA CRUZ].

San Andres [SANTA CRUZ]: *land grant,* west of Watsonville near the coast. Named on Moss Landing (1954) and Watsonville West (1954) 7.5' quadrangles. Joaquin Castro received 2 leagues in 1833; Guadalupe Castro and others claimed 8912 acres patented in 1876 (Cowan, p. 71). The grant also was called San Andreas in late Mexican or early American times (Rowland, p. 41). Ashley's (1894) map shows a place called San Andreas located along the railroad 3 miles west-northwest of Watsonville. Camp McQuaide, a World War I army camp, was on the grant (Hoover, Rensch, and Rensch, p. 468). Postal authorities established Camp McQuaide post office in 1941 and discontinued it in 1949; the name honored Father Joseph F. McQuaide, a World War I army chaplain (Salley, p. 35).

San Antonio: see **Los Ojitos** [MONTEREY].

San Antonio Creek [SANTA BARBARA]:

(1) *stream,* flows 31 miles to the sea 5.5 miles west-southwest of the village of Casmalia (lat. 34°47'55" N, long. 120°37'10" W). Named on Casmalia (1959), Los Alamos (1959), Orcutt (1959), Sisquoc (1959), and Zaca Creek (1959) 7.5' quadrangles. Lompoc (1905) 30' quadrangle has the name "Arroyo de los Alamos" for part of the stream, but United States Board on Geographic Names (1961a, p. 12) rejected this designation. The Board (1933, p. 664) also rejected the names "Guaymas River," "Jesus Maria River," and "Las Alamos Creek" for the stream.

(2) *stream,* flows 6.25 miles to Maria Ygnacio Creek 1.25 miles east-northeast of downtown Goleta (lat. 34°26'30" N, long. 119° 48'15" W). Named on Goleta (1950) and San Marcos Pass (1959) 7.5' quadrangles.

San Antonio Creek: see **San Antonio River** [MONTEREY].

San Antonio Hills: see **San Antonio River** [MONTEREY].

San Antonio Range: see **San Antonio River** [MONTEREY].

San Antonio Reservoir [MONTEREY]: *lake,* behind a dam on San Antonio River 6.5 miles southwest of Bradley (lat. 35°47'55" N, long. 120°53' W; sec. 34, T 24 S, R 10 E). Named on Tierra Redonda Mountain (1949, photorevised 1979) 7.5' quadrangle. United States Board on Geographic Names (1979b, p. 6) approved the name "Lake San Antonio" for the feature.

San Antonio River [MONTEREY]: *stream,* flows 58 miles to Salinas River at Bradley (lat. 35°51'30" N, long. 120°48' W; sec. 8, T 24 S, R 11 E); the stream goes past San Antonio mission. Named on Bear Canyon (1949), Bradley (1949), Bryson (1949), Cone Peak (1949), Cosio Knob (1949), Jolon (1949), Tierra Redonda Mountain (1949), and Williams Hill (1949) 7.5' quadrangles. Called Rio de S. Antonio on Parke's (1854-1855) map.

Irelan (p. 405) called the stream San Antonio Creek. According to Gudde (1949, p. 297), Junipero Serra named the river before he founded San Antonio mission. North Fork enters from the northwest 44 miles upstream from the mouth of the river; it is 6.25 miles long and is named on Cone Peak (1949) 7.5' quadrangle—North Fork has the name "Indian Creek" on a Forest Service map of 1908 (Clark, 1991, p. 229). According to Smith (p. 11), the valley of San Antonio River was known in early Spanish times as the valley of Los Robles. Eldridge (1903) called it San Antonio Valley. Antisell (1856, p. 41) and Whitney (p. 111) used the name "San Antonio Hills" for the range that lies between San Antonio River and Salinas River. Whitney (p. 151) also used the name "San Antonio Range" for the same feature.

San Antonio River: see **Pajaro River** [MONTEREY-SAN BENITO-SANTA CRUZ].

San Antonio Terrace [SANTA BARBARA]: *area,* 3.5 miles west-southwest of the village of Casmalia (lat. 34°49' N, long. 120°35'15" W); the place is north of the lower part of San Antonio Creek (1). Named on Casmalia (1959) 7.5' quadrangle.

San Antonio Valley [SANTA BARBARA]: *valley,* along San Antonio Creek (1) above a point 4.5 miles south-southwest of the village of Casmalia (lat. 34°46'30" N, long. 120°33'15" W). Named on Casmalia (1959) and Orcutt (1959) 7.5' quadrangles.

San Antonio Valley: see **San Antonio River** [MONTEREY].

San Aqueda Creek: see **Santa Agueda Creek** [SANTA BARBARA].

San Ardo [MONTEREY]: *town,* 18 miles southeast of King City at the mouth of Pancho Rico Valley (lat. 35°01'15" N, long. 120°54'15" W). Named on San Ardo (1967) 7.5' quadrangle. M.J. Brandenstein, owner of San Bernardo grant, laid out the town when the railroad reached the place in 1886; he called the community San Bernardo, but when postal authorities objected to this, he shortened the name to San Ardo (Gudde, 1949, p. 298). Postal authorities established San Bernardo post office in 1886 and changed the name to San Ardo in 1887 (Frickstad, p. 109).

San Augustin [SANTA CRUZ]: *land grant,* at Scotts Valley (1). Named on Felton (1955) and Laurel (1955) 7.5' quadrangles. Joseph L. Majors received 1 league in 1841 and claimed 4437 acres patented in 1866 (Cowan, p. 72).

San Augustin Canyon [SANTA BARBARA]: *canyon,* drained by a stream that flows 2.5 miles to the sea 4.5 miles west-southwest of East Point on Santa Rosa Island (lat. 33°55'15" N, long. 120°02'25" W). Named on Santa Rosa Island South (1943) 7.5' quadrangle.

San Augustine [SANTA BARBARA]: *locality,* nearly 7 miles east of Point Conception along Southern Pacific Railroad (lat. 34°27'35" N,

long. 120°21'25" W); the place is near the mouth of Arroyo San Augustine. Named on Sacate (1953) 7.5' quadrangle.

San Bartolome: see **Pleyto** [MONTEREY] (1).

San Benancio Gulch [MONTEREY]: *canyon,* drained by a stream that flows 5.5 miles to El Toro Creek 7 miles south-southwest of Salinas (lat. 36°34'50" N, long. 121°43' W). Named on Spreckels (1947) 7.5' quadrangle. According to Gudde (1949, p. 298), a map of 1834 has the name "Cañada de San Benancio."

San Benito [MONTEREY]: *land grant,* along Salinas River at San Lucas. Named on Espinosa Canyon (1949) and San Lucas (1949) 7.5' quadrangles. Francisco Garcia received 1.5 leagues in 1842; James Watson claimed 6671 acres patented in 1869 (Cowan, p. 73).

San Benito [SAN BENITO]: *locality,* 18 miles southeast of Paicines (lat. 36°30'35" N, long. 121°04'50" W; on W line sec. 26, T 16 S, R 8 E); the place is near San Benito River. Named on San Benito (1968) 7.5' quadrangle. Postal authorities established San Benito post office in 1869, moved it 1 mile southeast in 1940, and discontinued it in 1968 (Salley, p. 192).

San Benito Hill [SAN BENITO]: *locality,* 5.25 miles south of Idria (lat. 36°20'35" N, long. 120°39'50" W; sec. 21, T 18 S, R 12 E); the place is along San Benito River. Site named on San Benito Mountain (1969) 7.5' quadrangle.

San Benito Mountain [SAN BENITO]: *peak,* 3.5 miles south-southeast of Idria (lat. 36°22'10" N, long. 120°38'35" W; on N line sec. 15, T 18 S, R 12 E). Altitude 5241 feet. Named on San Benito Mountain (1969) 7.5' quadrangle.

San Benito River [SAN BENITO]: *stream,* flows 105 miles to Pajaro River nearly 4 miles north-northwest of San Juan Bautista (lat. 36°53'45" N, long. 121°33'45" W). Named on Santa Cruz (1956) 1°x 2° quadrangle. Called Rio San Benito on Parke's (1854-1855) map, called R. Pajaro on Eddy's (1854) map, and called San Juan Riv. on Holt's (1863) map. Goddard's (1857) map has the name "Cañada Benito" along upper reaches of the river. Crespi gave the name "San Benedicto" to the stream in 1772 to honor Saint Benedict, but the name later was contracted to San Benito (Bradley and Logan, p. 616). Elliott and Moore (p. 163) mentioned that Cinnabar post office was located 22 miles from Hollister on the right bank of San Benito River. Salley (p. 44) noted that postal authorities established Cinnabar post office 5 miles north of San Benito post office in 1875 and discontinued it in 1882.

San Benito Valley: see **San Juan Valley** [SAN BENITO].

San Benvenuto: see **Santa Rosa Creek** [SAN LUIS OBISPO].

San Bernabe [MONTEREY]: *land grant,* along Salinas River south and southeast of King

City. Named on San Lucas (1949) and Thompson Canyon (1949) 7.5' quadrangles. Jesus Molina and Petronilo Rios received 3 leagues in 1841 and 1842; Henry Cocks claimed 13,297 acres patented in 1873 (Cowan, p. 73; Perez, p. 88). Cocks was an English marine on United States Man-of-War *Dale*; he deserted at Monterey in 1846, married a daughter of Francisco Garcia, and moved in 1853 to San Bernabe grant, where his adobe house was known as Cocks'Station (Howard, p. 90).

San Bernardino: see **San Bernardo** [MONTEREY].

San Bernardo [MONTEREY]: *land grant,* along Salinas River at San Ardo. Named on Espinosa Canyon (1949), Hames Valley (1949), San Ardo (1967), and Wunpost (1949) 7.5' quadrangles. Mariano Soberanes and Jose Soberanes received 3 leagues in 1841; Mariano Soberanes claimed 13,346 acres patented in 1874 (Cowan, p. 73—Cowan listed the grant under the name "San Bernardino"; Perez, p. 89).

San Bernardo [SAN LUIS OBISPO]: *land grant,* near the coast at the town of Morro Bay. Named on Morro Bay North (1965) and Morro Bay South (1965) 7.5' quadrangles. Vicente Cane received 1 league in 1840 and claimed 4379 acres patented in 1865 (Cowan, p. 73).

San Bernardo: see **San Ardo** [MONTEREY].

San Bernardo Creek [SAN LUIS OBISPO]: *stream,* flows nearly 7 miles to Chorro Creek 3.25 miles east-southeast of Morro Rock (lat. 35°21'25" N, long. 120°48'40" W). Named on Atascadero (1965), Morro Bay North (1965), and Morro Bay South (1965) 7.5' quadrangles.

San Bernardo Creek: see **Pancho Rico Creek** [MONTEREY].

San Buenaventura: see **Santa Rosa Creek** [SAN LUIS OBISPO].

San Carlos Bolsa [SAN BENITO]: *area,* 3 miles east of Idria (lat. 36° 24'55" N, long. 120°37'15" W); the place is on upper reaches of East Fork San Carlos Creek. Named on Ciervo Mountain (1969) and Idria (1969) 7.5' quadrangles. According to Anderson and Pack (p. 20), *bolsa* means "pocket" or "purse" in Spanish, and applies to a topographic basin.

San Carlos Canyon [MONTEREY]: *canyon,* drained by a stream that flows 1.5 miles to lowlands 3 miles east-northeast of Greenfield (lat. 36°20'05" N, long. 121°11'20" W). Named on Greenfield (1956) 7.5' quadrangle.

San Carlos Creek [SAN BENITO]: *stream,* flows 9 miles to join Larious Creek and form Silver Creek 3.5 miles north of Idria (lat. 36°28'05" N, long. 120°41'05" W; near N line sec. 8, T 17 S, R 12 E); the stream heads southeast of San Carlos Peak. Named on Idria (1969) 7.5' quadrangle. East Fork enters from the east 3 miles upstream from the mouth of the main stream; it is 9 miles long and is

named on Ciervo Mountain (1969) and Idria (1969) 7.5' quadrangles.

San Carlos de Jonata [SANTA BARBARA]: *land grant,* at and north of Buellton. Named on Los Alamos (1959), Los Olivos (1959), Santa Ynez (1959), Solvang (1959), and Zaca Creek (1959) 7.5' quadrangles. Joaquin Carrillo and others received 6 leagues in 1846 and claimed 26,634 acres patented in 1872 (Cowan, p. 74). According to Perez (p. 89), Joaquin Carillo and Jose Covarrubias were the grantees in 1845 and the patentees in 1872.

San Carlos Peak [SAN BENITO]: *peak,* 2 miles south-southeast of Idria (lat. 36°23'30" N, long. 120°39'20" W; sec. 4, T 18 S, R 12 E); the peak is near San Carlos Creek and San Carlos mine. Altitude 4845 feet. Named on Idria (1969) 7.5' quadrangle.

San Carlos River: see **Carmel River** [MONTEREY].

San Carpoforo Creek [MONTEREY-SAN LUIS OBISPO]: *stream,* heads in Monterey County and flows 10.5 miles to the sea 11 miles northwest of the village of San Simeon in San Luis Obispo County (lat. 35°45'50" N, long. 121°19'25" W). Named on Burro Mountain (1949) 7.5' quadrangle. Crespi gave the name "Santa Humiliana" to the stream when the Portola expedition reached it in 1769 (Wagner, H.R., p. 511). United States Board on Geographic Names (1933, p. 664) rejected the names "San Carpojaro Creek," "San Carpojo Creek," and "San Carpovoro Creek." for the stream, and later the Board (1943, p. 12) rejected the names "Arroyo San Carpoforo," "Arroyo San Carpojo," "San Carpoforo Valley," and "San Carpojoro Creek."

San Carpoforo Valley: see **San Carpoforo Creek** [MONTEREY-SAN LUIS OBISPO].

San Carpojaro Creek: see **San Carpoforo Creek** [MONTEREY-SAN LUIS OBISPO].

San Carpojo Creek: see **San Carpoforo Creek** [MONTEREY-SAN LUIS OBISPO].

San Carpojoro Creek: see **San Carpoforo Creek** [MONTEREY-SAN LUIS OBISPO].

San Carpovoro Creek: see **San Carpoforo Creek** [MONTEREY-SAN LUIS OBISPO].

San Clemente Creek [MONTEREY]: *stream,* flows 7.5 miles to a lake 3.5 miles southeast of the town of Carmel Valley along Carmel River (lat. 36°25'55" N, long. 121°42'45" W; near S line sec. 23, T 17 S, R 2 E). Named on Carmel Valley (1956) and Mount Carmel (1956) 7.5' quadrangles. The stream first was called Redwood Creek (Clark, 1991, p. 505).

San Clemente Ridge [MONTEREY]: *ridge,* west-trending, nearly 2 miles long, 4.25 miles south-southwest of the town of Carmel Valley (lat. 36°25'15" N, long. 121°45'30" W); the ridge is south of San Clemente Creek. Named on Carmel Valley (1956) and Mount Carmel (1956) 7.5' quadrangles.

Sand Canyon: see **Sandy Canyon** [SAN LUIS OBISPO].

Sand City [MONTEREY]: *village,* 2 miles northeast of Monterey near the coast (lat. 36°37' N, long. 121°50'50" W). Named on Seaside (1947, photorevised 1983) 7.5' quadrangle. Postal authorities established Sand City post office in 1961 (Salley, p. 193). Sand City occupies an area 2.5 miles long and 0.5 mile wide; it incorporated in 1960 with the backing of sand companies, and is almost entirely industrial (Grant Harden in *San Jose Mercury News,* February 15, 1981).

Sand Creek [MONTEREY]: *stream,* flows 8 miles to Piney Creek 11 miles west-southwest of Greenfield (lat. 36°15'50" N, long. 121°25'50" W; sec. 21, T 19 S, R 5 E). Named on Sycamore Flat (1956) 7.5' quadrangle.

Sand Creek: see **Big Sand Creek** [MONTEREY]; **Bracken Brae Creek** [SANTA CRUZ]; **Little Sand Creek** [MONTEREY]; **Sandy Canyon** [SAN LUIS OBISPO].

Sand Cut: see **Aromas** [MONTEREY-SAN BENITO].

Sand Hill [MONTEREY]: *hill,* 0.25 mile south of Point Lobos near the coast (lat. 36°31'05" N, long. 121°57' W). Named on Monterey (1947) 7.5' quadrangle.

Sand Hill Bluff [SANTA CRUZ]: *relief feature,* 7 miles west-northwest of Point Santa Cruz along the coast (lat. 36°58'40" N, long. 122°09' W). Named on Santa Cruz (1954) 7.5' quadrangle.

Sand Hill Cove [MONTEREY]: *embayment,* nearly 1 mile south-southeast of Point Lobos along the coast (lat. 36°31' N, long. 121°56'55" W); the embayment is southeast of Sand Hill. Named on Monterey (1947) 7.5' quadrangle. California Department of Parks and Recreation's map shows a feature called Pebbly Beach situated 0.5 mile southeast of Sand Hill Cove, about halfway between Sand Hill Cove and China Cove; United States Board on Geographic Names (1980, p. 4) approved the name "Weston Beach" for this feature to honor photographer Edward Weston, noted for his photographs of Point Lobos and vicinity.

San Diego Creek [SAN LUIS OBISPO]: *stream,* heads in Kern County and flows 3.5 miles to Carrizo Plain 8 miles east-southeast of Simmler (lat. 35°19'20" N, long. 119°51'05" W; near N line sec. 17, T 30 S, R 20 E). Named on McKittrick Summit (1959) 7.5' quadrangle. McKittrick (1912) 30' quadrangle has the form "Sandiego Creek" for the name. United States Board on Geographic Names (1933, p. 665) first approved the form "Sandiego Creek," but later (1978d, p. 3) decided in favor of the form "San Diego Creek."

San Diego Joe's [SAN LUIS OBISPO]: *locality,* 8 miles east-southeast of Simmler along Sandiego Creek (present San Diego Creek) (lat. 35°19'45" N, long. 119°50'40" W; near E line sec. 8, T 30 S, R 20 E). Named on McKittrick (1912) 30' quadrangle.

Sand Point [SANTA BARBARA]: *promontory,* 1 mile west of downtown Carpinteria along the coast (lat. 34°23'45" N, long. 119°32'10" W). Named on Carpinteria (1952) 7.5' quadrangle. Esteban Jose Martinez gave the name "Punta de Nuestra Señora de los Angeles" to the feature in 1782 (Wagner, H.R., p. 478).

Sands: Henry Sands Canyon [MONTEREY].

Sand Spring: see **Lower Sand Spring** [SANTA BARBARA].

Sandstone Point [SANTA BARBARA]: *promontory,* 3.5 miles southeast of San Pedro Point at the east end of Santa Cruz Island (lat. 33°59'40" N, long. 119°33'45" W). Named on Santa Cruz Island D (1943) 7.5' quadrangle. Goodyear (1890, map following p. 156) showed Shaw Anch. [Anchorage] off present Sandstone Point. The name "Shaw" recalls Dr. Shaw, who was superintendent of Santa Cruz Island Company (Doran, p. 151).

Sandstone Ridge [MONTEREY]: *ridge,* east-northeast-trending, 1.5 miles long, 5 miles southwest of Salinas (lat. 36°38' N, long. 121°43'30" W). Named on Salinas (1947) 7.5' quadrangle.

Sandy Beach [MONTEREY]: *beach,* 1.25 miles southeast of Point Lobos along the coast (lat. 36°30'25" N, long. 121°56'20" W). Named on Monterey (1947) 7.5' quadrangle. Called Gibson Beach on California Department of Parks and Recreation's map—the beach is by the mouth of Gibson Creek; the map has the name "Pelican Point" for the promontory at the west end of the beach.

Sandy Canyon [SAN LUIS OBISPO]: *canyon,* drained by a stream that flows 8 miles to San Juan Valley 15 miles southeast of Shandon (lat. 35°30'20" N, long. 120°11'30" W; near W line sec. 7, T 28 S, R 17 E). Named on La Panza NE (1966) and La Panza Ranch (1966) 7.5' quadrangles. Called Sand Canyon on Holland Canyon (1961) 7.5' quadrangle. The stream in the canyon is called Sand Creek on La Panza (1935) 15' quadrangle, and on Packwood Creek (1961) 7.5' quadrangle, but United States Board on Geographic Names (1968b, p. 9) rejected the names "Sand Canyon" and "Sand Creek" for the feature.

Sandy Creek: see **Big Sandy Creek** [MONTEREY].

Sandy Flat Gulch [SANTA CRUZ]: *canyon,* drained by a stream that flows 1.25 miles to the sea 3.5 miles west of Point Santa Cruz (lat. 36°57'15" N, long. 122°05'25" W). Named on Santa Cruz (1954) 7.5' quadrangle.

Sandyland [SANTA BARBARA]: *settlement,* nearly 2 miles west-northwest of Carpinteria along the coast (lat. 34°24'20" N, long. 119°32'45" W). Named on Carpinteria (1952) 7.5' quadrangle.

Sandyland Cove [SANTA BARBARA]: *embayment,* 1 mile west of downtown Carpinteria along the coast (lat. 34°23'45" N, long. 119°32' W); the feature is 1 mile southeast of Sandyland. Named on Carpinteria (1952) 7.5' quadrangle.

Sandy Point [SANTA BARBARA]: *promontory,* at the westernmost tip of Santa Rosa Island (lat. 34°00'05" N, long. 120°14'55" W). Named on Santa Rosa Island West (1943) 7.5' quadrangle. Doran (p. 190) called the feature West Point. United States Coast and Geodetic Survey (p. 111) described Talcott Shoal, which is 1.5 miles north-northeast of Sandy Point.

San Felipe Lake [SAN BENITO]: *lake,* 3300 feet long, 9.5 miles north-northwest of Hollister (lat. 36°58'55" N, long. 121°27'35" W); the lake is connected to the head of Pajaro River by an artificial watercourse. Named on San Felipe (1955) 7.5' quadrangle. The feature also was called Soap Lake because Jose Maria Sanchez and Thomas O. Larkin had a soap-making operation there until 1848 (Hoover, Rensch, and Rensch, p. 312).

San Francisco Canyon [SAN LUIS OBISPO]: *canyon,* 1.25 miles long, drained by a stream that enters Dover Canyon 2.5 miles northwest of York Mountain (lat. 35°34'15" N, long. 120°51'45" W; sec. 23, T 27 S, R 10 E). Named on Adelaida (1961) 15' quadrangle.

San Francisco Mountain: see **Sugarloaf Mountain** [SANTA CRUZ].

San Francisquito [MONTEREY]: *land grant,* south of Carmel Valley (1) 7.5' miles east-southeast of the mouth of Carmel River. Named on Mount Carmel (1956) and Seaside (1947) 7.5' quadrangles. Catalina Manzaneli de Munras received 2 leagues in 1835; Jose Abrego and others claimed 8814 acres patented in 1862 (Cowan, p. 77).

San Francisquito Flat [MONTEREY]: *valley,* 7 miles east of Soberanes Point (lat. 36°27'25" N, long. 121°48'15" W); the valley is on San Francisquito grant. Named on Mount Carmel (1956) 7.5' quadrangle. According to Gudde (1949, p. 304), the place was mentioned as early as 1822 under the name "el llanito de San Francisquito."

San Geronimo [SAN LUIS OBISPO]: *land grant,* northwest of Cayucos near the coast. Named on Cambria (1959), Cayucos (1965), and Cypress Mountain (1948) 7.5' quadrangles. Rafael Villavicencio received 2 leagues in 1842 and claimed 8893 acres patented in 1876 (Cowan, p. 78). Postal authorities established Villa Creek post office on the grant in 1879 and discontinued it the same year (Salley, p. 231).

San Jacinto Canyon: see **Lowes Canyon** [MONTEREY-SAN LUIS OBISPO].

San Jacinto Creek [MONTEREY-SAN LUIS OBISPO]: *stream,* heads in Monterey County and flows 16 miles to Estrella Creek 3 miles southeast of San Miguel in San Luis Obispo County (lat. 35°43'40" N, long. 120°39'25" W; near W line sec. 26, T 25 S, R 12 E). Named on Paso Robles (1948) and San Miguel (1948) 7.5' quadrangles. The stream drains Lowes Canyon.

Sanja Cota Creek: see **Zanja de Cota Creek** [SANTA BARBARA].

San Joaquin [SAN BENITO]: *land grant,* 4.5 miles northeast of Hollister. Named on San Felipe (1955) and Three Sisters (1954) 7.5' quadrangles. Cruz Cervantes received 2 leagues in 1836 and claimed 7425 acres patented in 1874 (Cowan, p. 69; Cowan gave the alternate name "Rosa Morada" for the grant).

San Joaquin Peak [SAN BENITO]: *peak,* 8.5 miles east-northeast of Hollister (lat. 36°54'15" N, long. 121°15'40" W; sec. 12, T 12 S, R 6 E); the peak is east of San Joaquin grant. Altitude 2918 feet. Named on Three Sisters (1954) 7.5' quadrangle.

Sanjon de Borregas: see **Borregas Creek** [SANTA CRUZ].

Sanjon de la Brea: see **Pajaro River** [MONTEREY-SAN BENITO].

Sanjon del Pescadero: see **Pescadero Creek** [SAN BENITO].

Sanjon del Tembladera: see **Tembladero Slough** [MONTEREY].

Sanjon del Tequesquite: see **Pajaro River** [MONTEREY-SAN BENITO-SANTA CRUZ]; **Tequisquita Slough** [SAN BENITO].

San Jose: see **Pozo** [SAN LUIS OBISPO].

San Jose Creek [MONTEREY]: *stream,* flows 8.5 miles to Carmel Bay nearly 1 mile south of the mouth of Carmel River (lat. 36°31'35" N, long. 121°55'25" W); the stream is on San Jose y Sur Chiquito grant. Named on Monterey (1947) and Mount Carmel (1956) 7.5' quadrangles. According to Howard (p. 32), the name of the stream probably came from an Indian village called San Jose by the Spaniards and located west of the mouth of the creek. North Fork enters 1.25 miles upstream from the mouth of the creek; it is 2.25 miles long and is named on Monterey (1947) 7.5' quadrangle.

San Jose Creek [SANTA BARBARA]: *stream,* flows 10 miles to San Pedro Creek 1 mile south of downtown Goleta (lat. 34°25'15" N, long. 119°49'45" W). Named on Goleta (1950) and San Marcos Pass (1959) 7.5' quadrangles.

San Jose Mountains: see **La Panza Range** [SAN LUIS OBISPO].

San Jose Range: see **La Panza Range** [SAN LUIS OBISPO].

San Jose Valley: see **Pozo** [SAN LUIS OBISPO].

San Jose y Sur Chiquito [MONTEREY]: *land grant,* between Carmel River and Palo Colorado Canyon near the coast. Named on Monterey (1947) and Soberanes Point (1956) 7.5' quadrangles. Teodoro Gonzales received 2 leagues in 1835, and Marcelino Escobar received the land in 1839; Jose Castro claimed 8876 acres patented in 1888 (Cowan, p. 80—Cowan used the form "Chiquita" in the name; Perez, p. 92).

San Juan: see **San Juan Bautista** [SAN BENITO].

San Juan Bautista [SAN BENITO]: *town,* 7.5 miles west of Hollister (lat. 36°50'40" N, long. 121°32'10" W); the town is in San Juan Valley. Named on San Juan Bautista (1955) 7.5' quadrangle. Called S. Juan Baptista on Farnham's (1845) map, and called San Juan on Goddard's (1857) map. The town grew around San Juan Bautista mission, founded in 1797 on the feast day of Saint John the Baptist, and named for that saint (Hoover, Rensch, and Rensch, p. 309). Jose Tiburcio Castro became the civil administrator of the mission after secularization, and for a short time the town was known as San Juan de Castro (Pierce, p. 29). Postal authorities established San Juan post office in 1851 and changed the name to San Juan Bautista in 1905 (Frickstad, p. 137). The town incorporated in 1896. A military establishment at the place during the Civil War was called Camp Low for California Governor Frederick F. Low (Hoover, Rensch, and Rensch, p. 311). San Juan Bautista (1917) 15' quadrangle shows California Central Railroad extending southeast from Southern Pacific Railroad at Pajaro River and through the valley east of San Juan Bautista before continuing on up present San Juan Canyon for 3 miles. California Mining Bureau's (1917b) map shows two stations on this rail line: Prescott, located less than 2 miles north of San Juan Bautista, and Canfield, situated about halfway from Prescott to the junction with Southern Pacific Railroad.

San Juan Canyon [SAN BENITO]: *canyon,* drained by a stream that flows 4.5 miles to San Juan Valley less than 1 mile south-southeast of San Juan Bautista (lat. 36°50'05" N, long. 121°31'40" W; sec. 4, T 13 S, R 4 E). Named on Hollister (1955) and San Juan Bautista (1955) 7.5' quadrangles. The stream in the canyon is called San Juan Creek on San Juan Bautista (1917) 15' quadrangle.

San Juan Creek [SAN LUIS OBISPO]: *stream,* flows 45 miles to join Cholame Creek and form Estrella River at Shandon (lat. 35°39'35" N, long. 120°22'10" W; near NW cor. sec. 21, T 26 S, R 15 E). Named on Branch Mountain (1967), California Valley (1966), Camatta Canyon (1961), Cholame (1961), Holland Canyon (1961), La Panza (1967), La Panza Ranch (1966), and Shandon (1967) 7.5' quadrangles. Called San Juan River on Cholame (1917) 30' quadrangle. Antisell (1856, p. 93) considered San Juan Creek and Estrella Creek as one stream, referred to "San Juan or Estrella river," and stated that the upper part of this combined stream is called Carrizo Creek.

San Juan Creek: see **San Juan Canyon** [SAN BENITO].

San Juan Range: see **Gabilan Range** [MONTEREY-SAN BENITO].

San Juan River: see **San Benito River** [SAN BENITO]; **San Juan Creek** [SAN LUIS OBISPO].

San Juan Valley [SAN BENITO]: *valley,* along San Benito River from west of Hollister to Pajaro River; San Juan Bautista is in the valley. Named on Chittenden (1955), Hollister (1955), and San Juan Bautista (1955) 7.5' quadrangles. Called San Benito Valley on San Juan Bautista (1917) 15' quadrangle.

San Juan Valley [SAN LUIS OBISPO]: *valley,* opens into lowlands 2.5 miles south-southeast of Shandon (lat. 35°37' N, long. 120° 21' W); the valley is along the lower course of San Juan Creek. Named on Camatta Canyon (1961) and Holland Canyon (1961) 7.5' quadrangles.

San Julian [SANTA BARBARA]: *land grant,* southeast of the city of Lompoc. Named on Gaviota (1953), Lompoc Hills (1959), Point Conception (1953), Sacate (1953), Santa Rosa Hills (1959), and Solvang (1959) 7.5' quadrangles. George Rock, acting for Jose de la Guerra y Noriega, received 6 leagues in 1837; Jose de la Guerra y Noriega claimed 48,221 acres patented in 1873 (Cowan, p. 82). The place was called Rancho Nacional when it was established in 1817 to provide meat for soldiers at Santa Barbara (Dibblee, p. 11).

San Justo [SAN BENITO]: *land grant,* at and around Hollister. Named on Hollister (1955), San Felipe (1955), San Juan Bautista (1955), and Tres Pinos (1955) 7.5' quadrangles. Jose Castro received 4 leagues in 1839; Francisco Perez Pacheco claimed 34,620 acres patented in 1865 (Cowan, p. 82).

San Lawrence Terrace [SAN LUIS OBISPO]: *settlement,* 1 mile east-southeast of San Miguel on the east side of Salinas River (lat. 35°44'45" N, long. 120°41' W; sec. 21, T 25 S, R 12 E). Named on Paso Robles (1948) 7.5' quadrangle.

San Lorenzo [MONTEREY]:
(1) *land grant,* at and north of King City. Named on Greenfield (1956), Pinalito Canyon (1969), San Lucas (1949), and Thompson Canyon (1949) 7.5' quadrangles. Feliciano Soberanes received 5 leagues in 1841 and claimed 21,884 acres patented in 1866 (Cowan, p. 83).
(2) *land grant,* 18 miles east of King City, where it covers part of Peachtree Valley. Named on Monarch Peak (1967), Nattrass Valley (1967), and Priest Valley (1969) 7.5' quadrangles. Francisco Rico received 5 leagues in 1842; the heirs of Andrew Randall claimed 22,264 acres patented in 1870 (Cowan, p. 83).

San Lorenzo [MONTEREY-SAN BENITO]: *land grant,* 10 miles east-northeast of Greenfield on Monterey-San Benito county line. Named on Greenfield (1956), North Chalone Peak (1969), and Pinalito Canyon (1969), Rock Spring Peak (1969), and Topo Valley (1969) 7.5' quadrangles. Rafael Sanchez received 11 leagues in 1846 and claimed 48,286 acres patented in 1870 (Cowan, p. 83).

San Lorenzo Creek [MONTEREY-SAN BENITO]: *stream,* heads near Priest Valley and flows 45 miles, partly along Monterey-San Benito county line, to Salinas River at King City (lat. 36°11'50" N, long. 121°07'30" W). Named on Santa Cruz (1956) 1°x 2° quadrangle. Called Rio de San Lorenzo on Parke's (1854-1855) map. Parke (p. 13) also used the name "San Lorenzo creek" for the feature, which he stated "forms what is known as the San Lorenzo Pass" to Tulare plain. Derby's (1850) map has the name "Pass of San Lorenzo" along the creek. Gabb (p. 106) referred to San Lorenzo Valley, and Fairbanks (1894, p. 522) mentioned Lorenzo Creek. On Eldridge's (1901) map and on Hamlin's (1904) map, the part of present San Lorenzo Creek in Peachtree Valley has the name "Peachtree Cr."

San Lorenzo Creek: see **Lorenzo Vasquez Canyon** [SAN BENITO].

San Lorenzo Park [SANTA CRUZ]: *settlement,* 4.5 miles east-northeast of Big Basin near San Lorenzo River (lat. 37°11'45" N, long. 122°08'35" W; sec. 36, T 8 S, R 3 W). Named on Big Basin (1955) 7.5' quadrangle. The place also is called San Lorenzo River Park (Clark, 1986, p. 310). Hamman's (1980b) map shows a place called McGaffigan's Switch located along a railroad at about present San Lorenzo Park; it was named for Patrick J. McGaffigan, a lumber company superintendent (Hamman, p. 118). The same map shows a place called Waterman Switch located 1.5 miles up the river from present San Lorenzo Park along a railroad; it was at the end of a mile-long skid road built to bring lumber over Waterman Gap (Hamman, p. 123). The same map also shows a stream called Feeder Creek that joins San Lorenzo River 1 mile south of present San Lorenzo Park; the name is from use of water from the stream to augment the water in a V-flume that carried lumber down the canyon of San Lorenzo River to Felton (Hoover, Rensch, and Rensch, p. 479).

San Lorenzo Pass: see **San Lorenzo Creek** [MONTEREY-SAN BENITO].

San Lorenzo River [SANTA CRUZ]: *stream,* flows 30 miles to the sea 1.25 miles northeast of Point Santa Cruz in Santa Cruz (lat. 36° 57'50" N, long. 122°00'40" W). Named on Big Basin (1955), Castle Rock Ridge (1955), Cupertino (1961), Felton (1955), Mindego Hill (1961), and Santa Cruz (1954) 7.5' quadrangles. Members of the Portola expedition named the stream in 1769 (Wagner, H.R., p. 410). Goddard's (1857) map has the name "San Agustine C." for what appears to be present San Lorenzo River, and Trask (p. 24) mentioned Rio San Augustine in 1854.

San Lorenzo River Park: see **San Lorenzo Park** [SANTA BARBARA].

San Lorenzo Valley: see **Peachtree Valley** [MONTEREY]; **San Lorenzo Creek** [MONTEREY].

San Louis Pass: see **Cuesta Pass** [SAN LUIS OBISPO].

San Lucas [MONTEREY]:
(1) *land grant,* south of the village of San Lucas near Salinas River. Named on Espinosa Canyon (1949) and San Ardo (1967) 7.5' quadrangles. Rafael Estrada received 2 leagues in 1842; James McKinley claimed 8875 acres patented in 1872 (Cowan, p. 83).
(2) *village,* 8 miles southeast of King City along Salinas River (lat. 36°07'45" N, long. 121°01'10" W). Named on San Lucas (1949) 7.5' quadrangle. Officials of Southern Pacific Railroad named the place in 1886 for nearby San Lucas grant (Gudde, 1949, p. 308). Postal authorities established Griswold post office, named for William Griswold, first postmaster, in Long Valley (NE quarter sec. 27, T 20 N, R 10 E) in 1884; they moved it 8.5 miles west and changed the name to San Lucas in 1887 (Salley, p. 90; Clark, 1991, p. 198). Southern Pacific Railroad's (1890) map shows a place called Upland located along the railroad less than halfway from San Lucas to San Ardo.

San Lucas Canyon [MONTEREY]: *canyon,* 4.25 miles long, opens into lowlands 2.5 miles north of Lockwood (lat. 35°58'30" N, long. 121°05' W; sec. 34, T 22 S, R 8 E). Named on Espinosa Canyon (1949) and Williams Hill (1949) 7.5' quadrangles.

San Lucas Creek [SANTA BARBARA]: *stream,* flows 5 miles to Santa Ynez River 4 miles east-southeast of Santa Ynez (lat. 34° 35'30" N, long. 120°00'55" W). Named on Santa Ynez (1959) 7.5' quadrangle. Called Wons Creek on Los Olivos (1943) 15' quadrangle, but United States Board on Geographic Names (1961b, p. 14) rejected this name for the stream.

San Lucas Creek: see **Calabazal Creek** [SANTA BARBARA].

San Luis: see **Point San Luis** [SAN LUIS OBISPO]: **Port San Luis** [SAN LUIS OBISPO].

San Luis Canyon [SAN LUIS OBISPO]: *canyon,* drained by a stream that flows nearly 4 miles to Wilkinson Canyon 13 miles southeast of Shandon (lat. 35°32' N, long. 120°11'50" W; sec. 36, T 27 S, R 16 E). Named on Holland Canyon (1961) 7.5' quadrangle.

San Luis Hill [SAN LUIS OBISPO]: *peak,* 0.5 mile north-northwest of Point San Luis (lat. 35°10'05" N, long. 120°45'50" W). Altitude 705 feet. Named on Port San Luis (1965) 7.5' quadrangle.

San Luis Hot Spring: see **Sycamore Springs** [SAN LUIS OBISPO].

San Luisito [SAN LUIS OBISPO]: *land grant,* 7 miles northwest of San Luis Obispo along San Luisito Creek and Chorro Creek. Named on Morro Bay South (1965) and San Luis Obispo (1965) 7.5' quadrangles. Guadalupe Cantua received the land in 1841 and claimed 4390 acres patented in 1860 (Cowan, p. 84).

San Luisito Creek [SAN LUIS OBISPO]:

stream, flows 6.25 miles to Chorro Creek 4.5 miles east-southeast of Morro Rock (lat. 35°21'15" N, long. 120°47'30" W); the stream is partly on San Luisito grant. Named on Atascadero (1965), Morro Bay South (1965), and San Luis Obispo (1965) 7.5' quadrangles.

San Luisito Creek: see **Chorro Creek** [SAN LUIS OBISPO].

San Luis Obispo [SAN LUIS OBISPO]: *city,* 9 miles from the coast along San Luis Obispo Creek (lat. 35°16'45" N, long. 120°39'30" W). Named on Arroyo Grande NE (1965), Lopez Mountain (1965), Pismo Beach (1965), and San Luis Obispo (1965) 7.5' quadrangles. The mission at the place was founded in 1772 and named for Saint Louis, Bishop of Toulouse; W.R. Hutton laid out and named the city in 1850 (Gudde, 1949, p. 309). Postal authorities established San Luis Obispo post office in 1851 (Frickstad, p. 166), and the city incorporated in 1856.

San Luis Obispo: see **Camp San Luis Obispo** [SAN LUIS OBISPO].

San Luis Obispo Bay [SAN LUIS OBISPO]: *embayment,* 9 miles south-southwest of San Luis Obispo (lat. 35°10' N, long. 120° 44' W); the feature is east of Point San Luis. Named on Pismo Beach (1965) and Port San Luis (1965) 7.5' quadrangles. According to Gleason (p. 128), Cabrillo discovered the embayment and named it Todos Santos. H.R. Wagner (p. 378) noted that at one time it was called Ensenada de Buchon, and he (p. 411) identified it also as the place called Ensenada de Abrigo where Vizcaino stopped and traded with Indians. Whitney (p. 139) called the feature Bay of San Luis. Chase (p. 143) mentioned a place on the shore of the embayment called Oilport, where oil pipelines reached the coast. Postal authorities established Oilport post office in 1907 and discontinued it in 1908 (Frickstad, p. 165).

San Luis Obispo Creek [SAN LUIS OBISPO]: *stream,* flows 17 miles to San Luis Obispo Bay at the west end of Avila Beach (lat. 35°10'45" N, long. 120°44'15" W); the stream goes through San Luis Obispo. Named on Lopez Mountain (1965), Pismo Beach (1965), and San Luis Obispo (1965) 7.5' quadrangles. Soldiers of the Portola expedition gave the name "Cañada Angosta" to the valley of the creek in 1769 (Wagner, H.R. p. 426).

San Luis Pass: see **Cuesta Pass** [SAN LUIS OBISPO].

San Luis Peak: see **Cerro San Luis Obispo** [SAN LUIS OBISPO],

San Luis Range: see **Irish Hills** [SAN LUIS OBISPO].

San Luis Valley: see **Los Osos Valley** [SAN LUIS OBISPO].

San Marcos [SANTA BARBARA]: *land grant,* north of San Marcos Pass along and north of Santa Ynez River. Named on Figueroa Mountain (1959), Lake Cachuma (1959), San Marcos Pass (1959), and San Rafael Mountain (1959) 7.5' quadrangles. Richard S. Den

bought the land in 1846, and Nicholas A. Den claimed 35,573 acres patented in 1869; the property was part of Santa Barbara mission lands (Cowan, p. 84). Perez (p. 94) listed Nicolas A. Den and Richard Den as both grantees and patentees.

San Marcos: see **San Miguel** [SAN LUIS OBISPO].

San Marcos Creek [SAN LUIS OBISPO]: *stream,* flows 13 miles to Salinas River 6 miles north of Paso Robles (lat. 35°43'15" N, long. 120°41'40" W; sec. 29, T 25 S, R 12 E). Named on Adelaida (1948) and Paso Robles (1948) 7.5' quadrangles. According to Gudde (1949, p. 309), the stream was mentioned under the name "El arroyo de San Marcos" as early as 1795.

San Marcos Hot Springs: see **Hot Spring** [SANTA BARBARA].

San Marcos Pass [SANTA BARBARA]: *pass,* 10 miles northwest of Santa Barbara (lat. 34°30'45" N, long. 119°49'30" W; near W line sec. 16, T 5 N, R 28 W). Named on San Marcos Pass (1959) 7.5' quadrangle.

San Marcos Trout Club [SANTA BARBARA]: *locality,* 4 miles north-northeast of Goleta (lat. 34°29'25" N, long. 119°47'55" W; sec. 27, T 5 N, R 28 W). Named on Goleta (1950) 7.5' quadrangle.

San Martin: see **Cape San Martin** [MONTEREY].

San Martin Rocks: see **Cape San Martin** [MONTEREY].

San Martin Top [MONTEREY]: *peak,* 3.25 miles east-southeast of Cape San Martin (lat. 35°52'30" N, long. 121°24'25" W; sec. 3, T 24 S, R 5 E). Named on Cape San Martin (1949) 7.5' quadrangle. The name is from Cape San Martin (Clark, 1991, p. 509).

San Miguel [SAN LUIS OBISPO]: *town,* 8.5 miles north of Paso Robles on the west side of Salinas River (lat. 35°45'20" N, long. 120°41'45" W). Named on Paso Robles (1948) and San Miguel (1948) 7.5' quadrangles. The Franciscans founded San Miguel Arcangel mission at the place in 1797; the site was known as Las Pozas in Spanish times (Gudde, 1949, p. 272, 310). The town was started south of the mission about 1846, but it was relocated north of the mission after a fire in 1887 (Lee and others, p. 136). Postal authorities established San Miguel post office in 1860, discontinued it the same year, reestablished it in 1861, and discontinued it in 1862; they established San Marcos post office in 1864, discontinued it in 1865, reestablished it in 1869, and moved it 3 miles north when they renamed it San Miguel in 1881 (Salley, p. 196). They established Cruessville post office 8 miles north of San Miguel in Monterey County near Big Sandy Creek (NE quarter sec. 8, T 24 S, R 12 E) in 1888 and discontinued it in 1891; the name was for Frank Cruess, first postmaster (Clark, 1991, p. 123).

San Miguel: see **Bolsa de las Escorpinas** [MONTEREY].

San Miguel Canyon [MONTEREY]: *canyon,* drained by a stream that flows 5 miles to Merritt Lake 0.5 mile south of Prunedale (lat. 36°46' N, long. 121°40'10" W). Named on Prunedale (1954) 7.5' quadrangle.

San Miguel Canyon [SAN LUIS OBISPO]: *canyon,* 1.25 miles long, opens into lowlands at the south edge of San Miguel (lat. 35°44'45" N, long. 120°42' W; near N line sec. 20, T 25 S, R 12 E). Named on Paso Robles (1919) 15' quadrangle.

San Miguel Creek [MONTEREY]: *stream,* flows 8 miles to Nacimiento River 10 miles east-northeast of Cape San Martin (lat. 35°56'50" N, long. 121°18' W; sec. 10, T 23 S, R 6 E). Named on Alder Peak (1949) and Cape San Martin (1949) 7.5' quadrangles. Clark (1991, p. 291) noted that a place called Mail Camp was situated near the confluence of San Miguel Creek and Nacimiento River; a stage brought mail from King City to the place, where pack animals were kept to carry the mail on to residents along the coast.

San Miguel Creek: see **Mission Creek** [MONTEREY].

San Miguel Island [SANTA BARBARA]: *island,* 9 miles long, 45 miles southwest of Santa Barbara (lat. 34°02'30" N, long. 120°22'30" W). Named on San Miguel Island East (1950) and San Miguel Island West (1950) 7.5' quadrangles. Cabrillo discovered the island in 1542 and gave the name "Islas de San Lucas" to it and neighboring islands (Wagner, H.R., p. 503). Cabrillo later called present San Miguel Island by the name "Isla Posesion," and after Cabrillo's death the island was called Isla de Juan Rodrigues and Isla Capitana to honor him (Wagner, H.R., p. 465, 486).

San Miguelito [MONTEREY]: *land grant,* 5 miles west-southwest of Jolon. Named on Alder Peak (1949), Bear Canyon (1949), and Jolon (1949) 7.5' quadrangles. Rafael Gonzales received 5 leagues in 1841; Mariana Gonzales claimed 22,136 acres patented in 1867 (Cowan, p. 86; Cowan listed the grant under the name "San Miguelito de Trinidad"). Perez (p. 94) listed Jose R. Gonzales as both grantee and patentee.

San Miguelito [SAN LUIS OBISPO]: *land grant,* near the coast on lower reaches of San Luis Obispo Creek and at Point San Luis. Named on Pismo Beach (1965) and Port San Luis (1965) 7.5' quadrangles. Miguel Avila received 2 leagues in 1842 and 1846; he claimed 14,198 acres patented in 1877 (Cowan, p. 85-86). Perez (p. 94) gave 1839 as the date of the grant.

San Miguelito Creek [SANTA BARBARA]: *stream,* flows 6.5 miles to the valley of Santa Ynez River 0.5 mile south-southwest of downtown Lompoc (lat. 34°37'50" N, long. 120°27'35" W). Named on Lompoc (1959),

Lompoc Hills (1959), and Tranquillon Mountain (1959) 7.5' quadrangles.

San Miguelito de Trinidad: see **San Miguelito** [MONTEREY].

San Miguel Passage [SANTA BARBARA]: *water feature,* strait between San Miguel Island and Santa Rosa Island (lat. 34°01' N, long. 120°16' W). Named on San Miguel Island East (1950) and Santa Rosa Island West (1943) 7.5' quadrangles.

San Miguel Spring: see **Mission Creek** [MONTEREY].

San Pedro Alcantara: see **Scott Creek** [SANTA CRUZ].

San Pedro Canyon [SANTA BARBARA]: *canyon,* 3.5 miles long, along San Pedro Creek above a point 1.5 miles northwest of downtown Goleta (lat. 34°27'15" N, long. 119°50'35" W). Named on Goleta (1950) 7.5' quadrangle.

San Pedro Creek [SANTA BARBARA]: *stream,* flows 6.5 miles to the sea 1.25 miles south of downtown Goleta (lat. 34°25'05" N, long. 119°49'45" W). Named on Goleta (1950) 7.5' quadrangle.

San Pedro Point [SANTA BARBARA]: *promontory,* at the extreme east end of Santa Cruz Island (lat. 34°02'05" N, long. 119°31'10" W). Named on Santa Cruz Island D (1943) 7.5' quadrangle.

San Rafael Mountain [SANTA BARBARA]: *peak,* 21 miles north-northwest of Santa Barbara (lat. 34°42'40" N, long. 119°48'45" W; sec. 3, T 7 N, R 28 W); the peak is in San Rafael Mountains. Altitude 6593 feet. Named on San Rafael Mountain (1959) 7.5' quadrangle.

San Rafael Mountains [SANTA BARBARA]: *range,* south of Sisquoc River. Named on Bald Mountain (1964), Big Pine Mountain (1964), Figueroa Mountain (1959), Foxen Canyon (1964), Hurricane Deck (1964), San Rafael Mountain (1959), Twitchell Dam (1959), and Zaca Lake (1964) 7.5' quadrangles. Called Sierra de San Rafael on Parke's (1854-1855) map, but United States Board on Geographic Names (1965b, p. 15) rejected the names "Sierra de San Rafael" and "Sierra Madre Mountains" for the range.

San Rafael Mountains: see **Sierra Madre Mountains** [SANTA BARBARA].

San Ramon: see **Arroyo Grande** [SAN LUIS OBISPO] (1).

San Roque Canyon [SANTA BARBARA]: *canyon,* 4 miles long, along San Roque Creek above a point 3 miles northwest of downtown Santa Barbara (lat. 34°27' N, long. 119°44' W). Named on Santa Barbara (1952) 7.5' quadrangle. United States Board on Geographic Names (1961b, p. 15) rejected the name "San Rouke Canyon" for the feature.

San Roque Creek [SANTA BARBARA]: *stream,* flows 5.25 miles to Arroyo Burro (3) 3 miles west-northwest of downtown Santa Barbara (lat. 34°26'20" N, long. 119°44'45"

W). Named on Santa Barbara (1952) 7.5' quadrangle.

San Roque Creek: see **Arroyo Burro** [SANTA BARBARA] (3).

San Rouke Canyon: see **San Roque Canyon** [SANTA BARBARA].

Sans [MONTEREY]: *locality,* 9 miles northeast of Cape San Martin (lat. 35°58'25" N, long. 121°20'20" W; sec. 32, T 22 S, R 6 E). Named on Cape San Martin (1921) 15' quadrangle, where the name applies to buildings situated near Nacimiento River, including one with the label "Nacimiento School."

San Simeon [SAN LUIS OBISPO]:
(1) *land grant,* on the coast between San Simeon Creek and Pico Creek. Named on Cambria (1959), Pebblestone Shut-in (1959), Pico Creek (1959), and San Simeon (1958) 7.5' quadrangles. Jose Ramon Estrada received 1 league in 1842; Jose Miguel Gomez claimed 4469 acres patented in 1865 (Cowan, p. 88).
(2) *village,* 38 miles northwest of San Luis Obispo near the coast (lat. 35°38'40" N, long. 121°11'20" W). Named on San Simeon (1958) 7.5' quadrangle. Leopold Frankl founded and named the village in the mid-1870's (Gudde, 1949, p. 313). Postal authorities established San Simeon post office in 1873, discontinued it in 1876, and reestablished it in 1878 (Frickstad, p. 166). The place was a whaling station (Bancroft, p. 523).

San Simeon: see **Cambria** [SAN LUIS OBISPO].

San Simeon Bay [SAN LUIS OBISPO]: *embayment,* along the coast at the village of San Simeon (lat. 35°38'25" N, long. 121°11'15" W). Named on San Simeon (1958) 7.5' quadrangle. Called Harbor of St. Simeon on Colton's (1855) map. According to Hamilton (p. 150), records of San Miguel mission for 1830 record Bay of San Simeon.

San Simeon Creek [SAN LUIS OBISPO]: *stream,* formed by the confluence of North Fork and South Fork, flows 5.5 miles to the sea 3.25 miles northwest of Cambria (lat. 35°35'40" N, long. 121°07'35" W). Named on Cambria (1959) 7.5' quadrangle. North Fork is 3.5 miles long and is named on Pebblestone Shut-in (1959) 7.5' quadrangle. South Fork is 4.5 miles long and is named on Cambria (1959) and Pebblestone Shut-in (1959) 7.5' quadrangles. Crespi called the stream Arroyo de San Nicolas when the Portola expedition reached the place in 1769; soldiers of the expedition called it El Cantil, probably because of steep cliffs there—*el cantil* means "a steep rock" in Spanish (Wagner, H.R., p. 439, 506).

San Simeon Point [SAN LUIS OBISPO]: *promontory,* 0.5 mile south-southwest of the village of San Simeon along the coast (lat. 35°38'05" N, long. 121°11'35" W); the feature is at San Simeon Bay. Named on San Simeon (1958) 7.5' quadrangle.

Santa Agueda Creek [SANTA BARBARA]: *stream,* flows 12 miles to Santa Ynez River 3.25 miles east-southeast of Santa Ynez (lat. 34°35'15" N, long. 120°01'55" W). Named on Los Olivos (1959) and Santa Ynez (1959) 7.5' quadrangles. United States Board on Geographic Names (1961b, p. 15) rejected the names "San Aqueda Creek" and "Santa Aqueda Creek" for the stream.

Santa Ana Creek [SAN BENITO]: *stream,* flows 20 miles to Tequisquita Slough 5.25 miles north of Hollister (lat. 36°55'40" N, long. 121°24'50" W); the upper part of the stream is on Santa Ana y Quien Sabe grant. Named on Hollister (1955), Quien Sabe Valley (1968), San Felipe (1955), and Tres Pinos (1955) 7.5' quadrangles.

Santa Ana Mountain [SAN BENITO]: *peak,* 8 miles east-northeast of Hollister (lat. 36°52'40" N, long. 121°15'45" W); the peak is on Santa Ana y Quien Sabe grant. Altitude 3112 feet. Named on Three Sisters (1954) 7.5' quadrangle.

Santa Ana Valley [SAN BENITO]: *valley,* 6 miles east of Hollister (lat. 36°50'30" N, long. 121°17'30" W); the valley is along Santa Ana Creek on Santa Ana y Quien Sabe grant. Named on Tres Pinos (1955) 7.5' quadrangle.

Santa Ana y Quien Sabe [SAN BENITO]: *land grant,* east of Hollister Valley in Diablo Range. Named on Mariposa Peak (1969), Quien Sabe Valley (1968), Three Sisters (1954), and Tres Pinos (1955) 7.5' quadrangles. Francisco Javier Castillo Negrete received 7 leagues in 1836; the land was regranted in 1839 to Manuel Larios and Juan Maria Anzar, who claimed 48,823 acres patented in 1860 (Cowan, p. 90). According to Gudde (1949, p. 277), *quien sabe* means "who knows?" in Spanish, and probably was applied to the grant in jest when the phrase came in answer to the question of the extent or ownership of the land.

Santa Anita: see **Drake** [SANTA BARBARA].

Santa Aqueda Creek: see **Santa Agueda Creek** [SANTA BARBARA].

Santa Barbara [SANTA BARBARA]: *city,* in the southeast part of Santa Barbara County (lat. 34°25'15" N, long. 119°41'50" W); the city is along Santa Barbara Channel. Named on Santa Barbara (1952) 7.5' quadrangle. Postal authorities established Santa Barbara post office in 1850 (Frickstad, p. 171), and the city incorporated the same year. Spaniards established Presidio de Santa Barbara Virgen y Martir at the place in 1782 (Frazer, p. 31); they founded Santa Barbara mission there in 1783 and named it for Santa Barbara Channel (Wagner, H.R., p. 413). Travelers landed at Santa Barbara by boat through the surf before a pier was built in 1865 (Gleason, p. 127).

Santa Barbara Canyon [SANTA BARBARA]: *canyon,* drained by a stream that flows 15 miles to Cuyama Valley 6 miles northeast of Fox Mountain (lat. 34°52'10" N, long.

119°31'05" W). Named on Fox Mountain (1964) and Madulce Peak (1964) 7.5' quadrangles. Huguenin (p. 737) noted that a gypsum deposit was located on the east side of Santa Barbara Canyon 5 miles south of Quartel post office in Cuyama Valley—the post office apparently was near the mouth of Santa Barbara Canyon; Huguenin must have meant Quatal post office, which postal authorities established in 1896, moved 4 miles south in 1899, and discontinued in 1904 (Salley, p. 179).

Santa Barbara Channel [SANTA BARBARA]: *water feature,* between the sea coast and the islands of San Miguel, Santa Rosa, Santa Cruz, and Anacapa (Anacapa is in Ventura County). Named on Los Angeles (1955) and Santa Maria (1956) 1°x 2° quadrangles. Vizcaino gave the name "Canal de Santa Barbara" to the feature when he sailed through it in 1602 on December 4, the day of the saint (Wagner, H.R., p. 118, 413). The four islands—Anacapa, Santa Cruz, Santa Rosa, and San Miguel—located on the south side of Santa Barbara Channel are called Santa Barbara Islands, and are part of the larger group called Channel Islands (United States Coast and Geodetic Survey, p. 106).

Santa Barbara Hot Springs: see **Hot Springs** [SANTA BARBARA] (2).

Santa Barbara Hot Sulphur Springs: see **Hot Springs** [SANTA BARBARA] (2).

Santa Barbara Island [SANTA BARBARA]: *island,* 9000 feet long, 75 miles south-southeast of Santa Barbara (lat. 33°28'35" N, long. 119°02' W). Named on United States Geological Survey's (1973) map. Vizcaino named the island in 1602 (Wagner, H.R., p. 413).

Santa Barbara Islands: see **Santa Barbara Channel** [SANTA BARBARA].

Santa Barbara Mountains: see **Santa Lucia Range** [MONTEREY-SAN LUIS OBISPO]; **Santa Ynez Mountains** [SANTA BARBARA].

Santa Barbara Point [SANTA BARBARA]: *promontory,* 1.5 miles south of downtown Santa Barbara along the coast (lat. 34°23'50" N, long. 119°42'05" W). Named on Santa Barbara (1952) 7.5' quadrangle. Vancouver (p. 161) called the feature Point Felipe in 1793 to honor the commandant of Santa Barbara.

Santa Barbara Potrero [SANTA BARBARA]: *area,* 4.25 miles southeast of Salisbury Potrero (lat. 34°46'25" N, long. 119°38'25" W). Named on Salisbury Potrero (1964) 7.5' quadrangle.

Santa Barbara Reservoir: see **Gibralter Reservoir** [SANTA BARBARA].

Santa Barbara Springs: see **Veronica Springs** [SANTA BARBARA].

Santa Clara Valley [SAN BENITO]: *valley,* almost entirely in Santa Clara County, but the southeasternmost end extends into northern San Benito County northwest of Hollister. Named on Santa Cruz (1956) 1°x 2° quadrangle.

Santa Cora Creek: see **Zanja de Cota Creek** [SANTA BARBARA].

Santa Cota Creek: see **Zanja de Cota Creek** [SANTA BARBARA].

Santa Cruz [SANTA CRUZ]: *city,* on the coast around the mouth of San Lorenzo River (lat. 36°58'30" N, long. 122°01'45" W). Named on Santa Cruz (1954) and Soquel (1954) 7.5' quadrangles. Members of the Portola expedition gave the name "Santa Cruz" to a stream near the present city in 1768 (Rowland, p. 95), and the name was perpetuated by Santa Cruz mission (Hanna, p. 289), built west of the San Lorenzo River in 1791. A pueblo called Branciforte was started in 1797 across the river from the mission; the name honored the Marquis de Branciforte, Viceroy of Mexico (Hoover, Rensch, and Rensch, p. 466). After secularization of the mission, a community that grew up around the mission plaza was called Santa Cruz; the state legislature granted it a charter in 1866, and it incorporated in 1876 (Hoover, Rensch, and Rensch, p. 467). Farnham's (1845) map has both the names "S. Cruz" and "Ville de Francfort" at the site. Postal authorities established Santa Cruz post office in 1850 (Frickstad, p. 177). Branciforte became part of the city of Santa Cruz by a special election in 1907 (Hoover, Rensch, and Rensch, p. 467). Postal authorities established Rapetti post office as a branch of Santa Cruz post office in 1911 and discontinued it in 1912 (Salley, p. 181). Hamman's (1980b) map shows a place called Eblis located along the railroad 2 miles north of Point Santa Cruz in Santa Cruz. Rowland (p. 148) noted a place called Four Corners in the 1860's was located at the intersection of present Bay Street and Mission Street in Santa Cruz. California Mining Bureau's (1917a) map shows a place called Seabright located east of Santa Cruz along the railroad—United States Coast and Geodetic Survey (p. 121) referred to Seabright as a suburb of Santa Cruz. Postal authorities established Seabright post office in 1899; the place was named in 1880 after Seabright, New Jersey (Salley, p. 200). California Mining Bureau's (1909d) map shows a place called Orby located along the railroad near the west edge of present Santa Cruz, probably about 0.5 mile east of the railroad crossing of Moore Creek. Postal authorities established Coast post office 9 miles northwest of Santa Cruz in 1889 and discontinued it in 1905 (Salley, p. 46). They established Lucas post office in 1885 and discontinued it in 1886, when they moved the service to Santa Cruz; the name was for Jonathan Lucas, lumberman and pioneer of 1838 (Salley, p. 129).

Santa Cruz: see **Point Santa Cruz** [SANTA CRUZ].

Santa Cruz Bay [SANTA BARBARA]: *embayment,* 5 miles northeast of Santa Ynez Peak along the north side of Lake Cachuma (lat. 34° 34'55" N, long. 119°55'20" W); the feature is at the mouth of Santa Cruz Creek. Named on Lake Cachuma (1959) 7.5' quadrangle.

Santa Cruz Beach [SANTA CRUZ]: *beach,* 1 mile north-northeast of Point Santa Cruz and west of the mouth of San Lorenzo River (lat. 36°57'50" N, long. 122°01' W); the beach is in Santa Cruz. Named on Santa Cruz (1954) 7.5' quadrangle.

Santa Cruz Channel [SANTA BARBARA]: *water feature,* strait between Santa Cruz Island and Santa Rosa Island (lat. 33°59' N, long. 119°56' W). Named on Santa Cruz Island A (1943) and Santa Rosa Island East (1943) 7.5' quadrangles.

Santa Cruz Creek [SANTA BARBARA]: *stream,* formed by the confluence of East Fork and West Fork, flows 13 miles to Lake Cachuma 5.5 miles northeast of Santa Ynez Peak at Santa Cruz Bay (lat. 34°35'30" N, long. 119°54'50" W). Named on Lake Cachuma (1959), San Marcos Pass (1959), and San Rafael Mountain (1959) 7.5' quadrangles. East Fork is 7.25 miles long and is named on Big Pine Mountain (1964) 7.5' quadrangle. West Fork is 5.5 miles long and is named on San Rafael Mountain (1959) 7.5' quadrangle.

Santa Cruz Harbor [SANTA CRUZ]: *embayment,* along the coast between Point Santa Cruz and Black Point (lat. 36°57'30" N, long. 122°00' W). Named on Santa Cruz (1954) and Soquel (1954) 7.5' quadrangles.

Santa Cruz Island [SANTA BARBARA]: *island,* 23 miles long, 25 miles south of Santa Barbara across Santa Barbara Channel. Named on Santa Cruz Island A (1943), Santa Cruz Island B (1943), Santa Cruz Island C (1943), and Santa Cruz Island D (1943) 7.5' quadrangles. Cabrillo discovered the island in 1542 and gave the name "Islas de San Lucas" to it and neighboring islands (Wagner, H.R., p. 503). Ferrer called it Isla San Sebastian in 1543 on the day of the saint, and Vizcaino called it Isla de Gente Barbudo because one of the members of the expedition claimed that he saw bearded men there; the present name stems from an incident in 1769, when one of the friars on the ship *San Antonio* left a staff with a cross on it at the island, and Indians returned the staff (Wagner, H.R., p. 414).

Santa Cruz Mountains [SANTA CRUZ]: *range,* extends northwest from Pajaro River into San Mateo County; the east boundary of Santa Cruz County is along the crest of the range. Named on San Francisco (1956), San Jose (1962), and Santa Cruz (1956) 1°x 2° quadrangles. Called Sierra de la Santa Cruz on Parke's (1854-1855) map. Fremont (p. 30) used the designation "cuesta de los gatos (wild-cat ridge)" for the feature, and Blake (1856, p. 378) called it Santa Cruz range.

Santa Cruz Peak [SANTA BARBARA]: *peak,* 3 miles south of San Rafael Mountain (lat. 34°40'10" N, long. 119°48'40" W; near E line

sec. 22, T 7 N, R 28 W); the peak is north of Santa Cruz Creek. Altitude 5570 feet. Named on San Rafael Mountain (1959) 7.5' quadrangle.

Santa Cruz Point [SANTA BARBARA]: *promontory,* 4 miles northeast of Santa Ynez Peak on the north side of Lake Cachuma (lat. 34°34'25" N, long. 119°55'55" W); the feature is at the mouth of Santa Cruz Bay. Named on Lake Cachuma (1959) 7.5' quadrangle.

Santa Cruz Range: see **Santa Cruz Mountains** [SANTA CRUZ].

Santa Delfina Valley: see **Salinas River** [MONTEREY-SAN LUIS OBISPO].

Santa Humiliana: see **San Carpoforo Creek** [MONTEREY-SAN LUIS OBISPO].

Santa Inez: see **Cañada de los Pinos or College Rancho** [SANTA BARBARA].

Santa Inez Range: see **Santa Ynez Mountains** [SANTA BARBARA].

Santa Inez River: see **Santa Ynez River** [SANTA BARBARA].

Santa Inez Valley: see **Santa Ynez Valley** [SANTA BARBARA].

Santa Isabel: see **Santa Ysabel** [SAN LUIS OBISPO].

Santa Lucia Canyon [SANTA BARBARA]: *canyon,* drained by a stream that flows 6.5 miles to Santa Ynez River 5 miles east of Surf (lat. 34°40'50" N, long. 120°31'05" W). Named on Lompoc (1959) and Surf (1959) 7.5' quadrangles.

Santa Lucia Creek [MONTEREY]:
(1) *stream,* flows 10 miles to Arroyo Seco (1) 7 miles northwest of Junipero Serra Peak (lat. 36°13'20" N, long. 121°29'45" W; sec. 2, T 20 S, R 4 E); the stream is in Santa Lucia Range. Named on Junipero Serra Peak (1949) 7.5' quadrangle. South Fork enters from the south-southeast nearly 3 miles upstream from the mouth of the main stream; it is 3 miles long and is named on Junipero Serra Peak (1949) 7.5' quadrangle.
(2) *stream,* flows 3.5 miles to North Fork San Antonio River 4.25 miles south of Junipero Serra Peak (lat. 36°05'05" N, long. 121°25'05" W); the stream is in Santa Lucia Range. Named on Cone Peak (1949) 7.5' quadrangle. Called Sycamore Creek on Junipero Serra (1948) 15' quadrangle.

Santa Lucia Mountain: see **Junipero Serra Peak** [MONTEREY].

Santa Lucia Mountains: see **Santa Lucia Range** [MONTEREY-SAN LUIS OBISPO].

Santa Lucia Peak: see **Junipero Serra Peak** [MONTEREY].

Santa Lucia Range [MONTEREY-SAN LUIS OBISPO]: *range,* extends southeast from Monterey Bay along and near the coast in Monterey and San Luis Obispo Counties. Named on San Luis Obispo (1956) and Santa Cruz (1956) 1°x 2° quadrangles. According to Davidson (1887, p. 210-211), Cabrillo and Ferrelo gave the range the name "Las Sierras de San Martin" in 1542, and Vizcaino gave it the name "Sierra de Santa Lucia" in 1602. According to H.R. Wagner (p. 414), Cabrillo used the name "Sierra Nevadas" for the range, and Vizcaino applied the name "Santa Lucia" to the north part only to honor the saint whose day is December 13, the day before Vizcaino sighted the range from northwest of Point Sur. Greenhow's (1844) map has the name "Sta. Barbara Mountains" along the coast, and Parke's (1854-1855) map has the name "Sierra de la Santa Lucia" for coastal mountains all the way from Monterey Bay to present Ventura County. Parke's (1854-1855) map also has the name "Sierra Wasna" for the part of the present Santa Lucia Range at the head of Rio Wasna (present Huasna River). Antisell (1856, p. 47) used the name "Point Pinos Range" for the north part of present Santa Lucia Range, and (p. 58) used the name "Santa Lucia Mountains" for the rest. Whitney (p. 111) used the names "Sierra Santa Lucia" and "Santa Lucia chain" for the entire range.

Santa Manuela [SAN LUIS OBISPO]: *land grant,* 5 miles east of the town of Arroyo Grande. Named on Arroyo Grande NE (1965), Nipomo (1965), Oceano (1965), and Tar Spring Ridge (1967) 7.5' quadrangles. Francis Z. Branch received the land in 1837 and claimed 16,955 acres patented in 1869 (Cowan, p. 93). Perez (p. 97) gave 1868 as the date of the patent. Branch named the grant for his wife, Manuela (Nicholson, p. 12).

Santa Margarita [SAN LUIS OBISPO]:
(1) *land grant,* around the town of Santa Margarita. Named on Atascadero (1965), Lopez Mountain (1965), San Luis Obispo (1965), Santa Margarita (1965), and Santa Margarita Lake (1967) 7.5' quadrangles. Joaquin Estrada received 4 leagues in 1841 and claimed 17,735 acres patented in 1861 (Cowan, p. 93). Rogers and Johnston's (1857) map has the name "Sta. Margarite."
(2) *town,* 8 miles north-northeast of San Luis Obispo (lat. 35°23'30" N, long. 120°36'20" W); the town is on Santa Margarita grant. Named on Santa Margarita (1965) 7.5' quadrangle. The town was laid out when Southern Pacific Railroad reached the place in 1889 (Lee and others, p. 137). Postal authorities established Santa Margarita post office in 1867, discontinued it in 1881, and reestablished it in 1889 (Frickstad, p. 166). They established Pines post office 17 miles southeast of Santa Margarita in 1893 and discontinued it the same year (Salley, p. 172).

Santa Margarita Creek [SAN LUIS OBISPO]: *stream,* flows 9 miles to Salinas River 3.5 miles north of the town of Santa Margarita (lat. 35°26'40" N, long. 120°36'20" W; sec. 31, T 28 S, R 13 E). Named on Atascadero (1965), San Luis Obispo (1965), and Santa Margarita (1965) 7.5' quadrangles.

Santa Margarita Lake [SAN LUIS OBISPO]: *lake,* behind a dam on Salinas River 5 miles east-northeast of Lopez Mountain (lat.

35°20'15" N, long. 120°30'05" W; near NW cor. sec. 8, T 30 S, R 14 E). Named on Santa Margarita Lake (1967) 7.5' quadrangle. Called Salinas Reservoir on Lopez Mountain (1965) 7.5' quadrangle, but United States Board on Geographic Names (1968c, p. 6) rejected this name for the lake.

Santa Maria [SANTA BARBARA]: *city,* 55 miles northwest of Santa Barbara (lat. 34°57'10" N, long. 120°26'05" W; around NE cor. sec. 15, T 10 N, R 34 W); the city is in Santa Maria Valley. Named on Santa Maria (1959) 7.5' quadrangle. Postal authorities established Santa Maria post office in 1869, discontinued it in 1871, and reestablished it in 1875 (Frickstad, p. 171). The city incorporated in 1905. The place first was called Grangeville and later Central City (Hoover, Rensch, and Rensch, p. 423). California Division of Highways' (1934) map shows a place called Suey Junction located along Pacific Coast Railroad 1.5 miles south-southwest of downtown Santa Maria (sec. 22, T 10 N, R 34 E), and a place called Suey situated along the railroad 4 miles east of Suey Junction (sec. 20, T 10 N, R 33 W).

Santa Maria: see **North Santa Maria** [SANTA BARBARA]; **Tepusquet** [SANTA BARBARA].

Santa Maria Canyon [SANTA BARBARA]: *canyon,* drained by a stream that flows 2.5 miles to Santa Maria Valley 11 miles east-southeast of Santa Maria (lat. 34°53'05" N, long. 120°16'15" W). Named on Twitchell Dam (1959) 7.5' quadrangle.

Santa Maria Plain: see **Santa Maria Valley** [SANTA BARBARA].

Santa Maria Point: see **Black Point** [SANTA CRUZ].

Santa Maria River [SAN LUIS OBISPO-SANTA BARBARA]: *stream,* formed by the confluence of Cuyama River and Sisquoc River, flows 24 miles along and near San Luis Obispo-Santa Barbara county line to the sea 4.5 miles west of the town of Guadalupe (lat. 34°58'15" N, long. 120°38'55" W). Named on Guadalupe (1959), Point Sal (1958), Santa Maria (1959), and Twitchell Dam (1959) 7.5' quadrangles. Called R. Guadalupe on Wilkes' (1849) map, and called Rio de la Sta. Maria on Parke's (1854-1855) map, which has the name "Rio S. Maria" for present Cuyama River. Parke (p. 2) also used the name "Rio Santa Maria" for present Santa Maria River. Present Cuyama River is called Santa Maria River on California Mining Bureau's (1909c) map, and present Sisquoc River has the name "Santa Maria R." on Goddard's (1857) map.

Santa Maria Valley [SAN LUIS OBISPO-SANTA BARBARA]: *valley,* along Santa Maria River on San Luis Obispo-Santa Barbara county line, and extends eastward along Sisquoc River in Santa Barbara County. Named on Foxen Canyon (1964), Guadalupe (1959), Nipomo (1965), Oceano (1965), Point

Sal (1958), Santa Maria (1959), Sisquoc (1959), and Twitchell Dam (1959) 7.5' quadrangles. Called Guadalupe Largo on Parke's (1854-1855) map. Fairbanks (1894, p. 501) called it Santa Maria Plain.

Santa Monica Canyon [SANTA BARBARA]: *canyon,* 3.5 miles long, along Santa Monica Creek above a point 1.5 miles north-north-west of Carpinteria (lat. 34°25'10" N, long. 119°31'35" W; sec. 20, T 4 N, R 25 W). Named on Carpinteria (1952) 7.5' quadrangle.

Santa Monica Creek [SANTA BARBARA]: *stream,* flows nearly 5 miles to El Estero 0.5 mile west-northwest of downtown Carpinteria (lat. 34°24' N, long. 119°31'45" W); the stream drains Santa Monica Canyon. Named on Carpinteria (1952) 7.5' quadrangle. United States Board on Geographic Names (1978b, p. 5) rejected the name "Monica Creek" for the stream.

Santa Rita [MONTEREY]: *town,* 3.5 miles north of Salinas (lat. 36° 43'30" N, long. 121°39'15" W); the town is on Los Gatos or Santa Rita grant. Named on Salinas (1947) 7.5' quadrangle. Jose Manuel Soto bought the grant and set aside 1 square mile for a townsite that he named New Republic (Newhall, p. 31-32). Postal authorities established New Republic post office in 1870, changed the name to Santa Rita in 1874, and discontinued it in 1907 (Salley, p. 154, 198). The place also was known as Sotoville for Jose Manuel Soto, and as Pinecate for nearby Pinecate Peak [SAN BENITO] (Clark, 1991, p. 513).

Santa Rita [SANTA BARBARA]:
(1) *land grant,* east and northeast of the city of Lompoc. Named on Lompoc (1959), Lompoc Hills (1959), Los Alamos (1959), and Santa Rosa Hills (1959) 7.5' quadrangles. Jose Ramon Malo received 3 leagues in 1845 and claimed 13,316 acres patented in 1875 (Cowan, p. 94).
(2) *settlement,* 7.5 miles east of the town of Lompoc (lat. 34°40' N, long. 120°19'40" W); the place is in Santa Rita Valley. Named on Lompoc (1905) 30' quadrangle. Postal authorities established Santa Rita post office in 1909 and discontinued it in 1914 (Frickstad, p. 172).

Santa Rita: see **Los Gatos** [MONTEREY].

Santa Rita Creek [SAN LUIS OBISPO]: *stream,* flows 9 miles to Paso Robles Creek 4.5 miles east of York Mountain (lat. 35°32'10" N, long. 120°45'05" W). Named on York Mountain (1948) 7.5' quadrangle. South Fork enters from the south 4 miles upstream from the mouth of the main stream; it is 4.25 miles long and is named on Morro Bay North (1965) and York Mountain (1948) 7.5' quadrangles.

Santa Rita Hills [SANTA BARBARA]: *range,* east of the city of Lompoc between Santa Ynez River and Santa Rita Valley, on and near Santa Rita grant. Named on Lompoc (1959), Los Alamos (1959), and Santa Rosa Hills (1959)

7.5' quadrangles. Called Serro de Santa Rita on a diseño of Santa Rosa grant made in the mid-1830's (Becker, 1964).

Santa Rita Peak [SAN BENITO]: *peak,* 6.25 miles southeast of Idria (lat. 36°20'50" N, long. 120°36'05" W; sec. 24, T 18 S, R 12 E). Altitude 5165 feet. Named on Santa Rita Peak (1969) 7.5' quadrangle.

Santa Rita Valley [SANTA BARBARA]: *valley,* 6.5 miles south-southwest of the town of Los Alamos (lat. 34°39'40" N, long. 120° 20'30" W); the valley is on Santa Rita grant. Named on Los Alamos (1959) 7.5' quadrangle.

Santa Rosa [SAN LUIS OBISPO]: *land grant,* on the coast south and southeast of Cambria. Named on Cambria (1959) and Cypress Mountain (1948) 7.5' quadrangles. Julian Estrada received 3 leagues in 1841 and claimed 13,184 acres patented in 1865 (Cowan, p. 95).

Santa Rosa [SANTA BARBARA]: *land grant,* west of Buellton along Santa Ynez River. Named on Los Alamos (1959), Santa Rosa Hills (1959), Solvang (1959), and Zaca Creek (1959) 7.5' quadrangles. Francisco Cota received 3.5 leagues in 1839; M.J. Olivera de Cota and others claimed 15,526 acres patented in 1872 (Cowan, p. 95). Perez (p. 98) gave 1845 as the date of the grant.

Santa Rosa: see **Cambria** [SAN LUIS OBISPO].

Santa Rosa Creek [SAN LUIS OBISPO]: *stream,* flows 14 miles to the sea at Cambria (lat. 35°34'05" N, long. 121°06'35" W). Named on Cambria (1959) and Cypress Mountain (1948) 7.5' quadrangles. Crespi gave the name "San Benvenuto" to the stream, or to its valley, when the Portola expedition reached the place in 1769; soldiers of the expedition called it Cañada del Osito, and on the return trip Crespi referred to the site as San Buenaventura (Wagner, H.R., p. 480, 497). Angel (1883, p. 340) used the name "Santa Rosa Valley" for the valley of the stream.

Santa Rosa Creek [SANTA BARBARA]: *stream,* flows 7.5 miles to Santa Ynez River 10 miles east-southeast of the city of Lompoc (lat. 34°36'30" N, long. 120°17'15" W); the creek is on and near Santa Rosa grant. Named on Los Alamos (1959) and Santa Rosa Hills (1959) 7.5' quadrangles.

Santa Rosa de Chualar: see **Chualar** [MONTEREY] (1).

Santa Rosa Hills [SANTA BARBARA]: *range,* 10.5 miles east-southeast of the city of Lompoc (lat. 34°34'30" N, long. 120°17'30" W); the range is south of Santa Rosa grant. Named on Santa Rosa Hills (1959) 7.5' quadrangle.

Santa Rosa Island [SANTA BARBARA]: *island,* 16 miles long, 39 miles south-southwest of Santa Barbara (lat. 33°58' N, long. 120°06' W). Named on Santa Rosa Island East (1943),

Santa Rosa Island North (1943), Santa Rosa Island South (1943), and Santa Rosa Island West (1943) 7.5' quadrangles. Cabrillo discovered the island in 1542 and gave the name "Islas de San Lucas" to it and neighboring islands; later he restricted the name to present Santa Rosa Island (Wagner, H.R., p. 503). Vizcaino called the feature Isla San Ambrosio in 1602 for the saint whose day is December 7 (Wagner, H.R., p. 495).

Santa Rosalia Mountain [SANTA CRUZ]: *peak,* 6.5 miles north-northwest of Corralitos (lat. 37°04'20" N, long. 121°51'25" W). Named on Loma Prieta (1955) 7.5' quadrangle. Hamman's (1980a) map shows a place called Camp No. 3 situated about 0.5 mile north-northwest of Santa Rosalia Mountain. Hamman (p. 70) noted that Camp No. 3 also was called Sheep Camp because the meadow surrounding the place was leased for sheep grazing.

Santa Rosa Reef [SAN LUIS OBISPO]: *shoal,* 1.5 miles west of Point San Luis and 1 mile offshore (lat. 35°09'20" N, long. 120°47'20" W). Named on Port San Luis (1965) 7.5' quadrangle.

Santa Rosa Valley: see **Santa Rosa Creek** [SAN LUIS OBISPO].

Santa Ynez [SANTA BARBARA]: *town,* 6.5 miles east of Buellton on Cañada de los Pinos or College Rancho grant (lat. 34°36'45" N, long. 120°04'50" W); the town is in Santa Ynez Valley. Named on Santa Ynez (1959) 7.5' quadrangle. Postal authorities established Santa Ynez post office in 1863, discontinued it in 1868, and reestablished it in 1883 (Frickstad, p. 172). Bishop Francisco Mora opened the Church's Cañada de los Pinos grant for subdivision in 1881, and the community that started there was called New Town by residents of nearby Ballard; for a short time the community was called Sagunto, for the Spanish village where Bishop Mora was born, but it took the name "Santa Ynez" when the post office opened (Tompkins and Ruiz, p. 79). Postal Route (1884) map shows a place called Childs located 8.5 miles west of Santa Ynez. Postal authorities established Childs post office in 1881 and discontinued it in 1888—the name was for Augustus F. Childs, first postmaster (Salley, p. 42).

Santa Ynez Campground [SANTA BARBARA]: *locality,* 4.25 miles south of Little Pine Mountain (lat. 34°32'15" N, long. 119°44'30" W; near SE cor. sec. 6, T 5 N, R 27 W); the place is along Santa Ynez River. Named on Little Pine Mountain (1964) 7.5' quadrangle.

Santa Ynez Campground: see **Middle Santa Ynez Campground** [SANTA BARBARA]; **Upper Santa Ynez Campground** [SANTA BARBARA].

Santa Ynez Mountains [SANTA BARBARA]: *range,* between Santa Ynez River and the coast. Named on Los Angeles (1955) and Santa Maria (1956) 1°x 2° quadrangles. Called Sierra de la Santa Inez on Parke's (1854-1855) map. Blake (1857, p. 137) called the feature Santa Inez range, Antisell (1856, p. 65) called it Santa Barbara Mountains, and Whitney (p. 111) called it Sierra Santa Iñez.

Santa Ynez Peak [SANTA BARBARA]: *peak,* 9 miles west of San Marcos Pass (lat. 34°31'35" N, long. 119°58'40" W); the peak is in Santa Ynez Mountains. Altitude 4298 feet. Named on Lake Cachuma (1959) 7.5' quadrangle.

Santa Ynez Point [SANTA BARBARA]: *promontory,* 5 miles northeast of Santa Ynez Peak on the south side of Lake Cachuma (lat. 34°34'05" N, long. 119°54'15" W). Named on Lake Cachuma (1959) 7.5' quadrangle.

Santa Ynez River [SANTA BARBARA]: *stream,* heads just inside Ventura County and flows 90 miles to the sea 0.5 mile north of Surf (lat. 34°41'30" N, long. 120°36'10" W). Named on Los Angeles (1955) and Santa Maria (1956) 1°x 2° quadrangles. Called Rio de la Sta. Inez on Parke's (1854-1855) map, and called Santa Inez River on Ransom and Doolittle's (1863) map. H.R. Wagner (p. 403, 414) gave the names "Purisima River," "Rio de San Bernardo," "Rio de San Verardo," and "Rio de Santa Rosa" as early designations for the stream.

Santa Ynez Valley [SANTA BARBARA]: *valley,* at and north of Santa Ynez (lat. 34°38' N, long. 120°04' W). Named on Los Olivos (1959) and Santa Ynez (1959) 7.5' quadrangles. Parke (p. 9) referred to Santa Inez valley.

Santa Ysabel [SAN LUIS OBISPO]: *land grant,* east of Salinas River and southeast of Paso Robles. Named on Creston (1948), Estrella (1948), Paso Robles (1948), and Templeton (1948) 7.5' quadrangles. Francisco C. Arce received 4 leagues in 1844 and claimed 17,774 acres patented in 1866 (Cowan, p. 93; Cowan used the form "Santa Isabel" for the name).

Santa Ysabel Springs: see **Sulphur Spring** [SAN LUIS OBISPO] (1).

San Vicenta Valley: see **Lowes Canyon** [MONTEREY-SAN LUIS OBISPO].

San Vicente [MONTEREY]: *land grant,* at and northwest of Soledad. Named on Gonzales (1955), Palo Escrito Peak (1956), and Soledad (1955) 7.5' quadrangles. Francisco Esteban Munras received 2 leagues in 1835; Concepcion Munras and others claimed 19,979 acres patented in 1865 (Cowan, p. 89). According to Perez (p. 95), Stephen Munras was the grantee in 1842.

San Vicente [SANTA CRUZ]: *land grant,* extends from the coast north of Davenport into Santa Cruz Mountains. Named on Big Basin (1955) and Davenport (1955) 7.5' quadrangles. Antonio Rodriguez received 2 leagues in 1839; Blas A. Escamilla received the land in 1846 and claimed 10,803 acres patented in 1870 (Cowan, p. 89).

San Vicente Canyon: see **Lowes Canyon** [MONTEREY-SAN LUIS OBISPO].

San Vicente Creek [SANTA CRUZ]: *stream,* flows 9 miles to the sea at Davenport (lat. 37°00'35" N, long. 122°11'35" W); the stream forms the east boundary of San Vicente grant. Named on Davenport (1955) 7.5' quadrangle. The stream also was called Arroyo de San Vicente and Blas Creek; the name "Blas" was for Blas A. Escamilla, who received San Vicente grant (Clark, 1986, p. 33). Hamman's (1980c) map shows West Fork and Middle Fork entering the main creek 2 miles northwest of present Bonnie Doon; the map has the name "East Fork" for the present main stream above Middle Fork, and has the name "Bear Trap Gulch" for the canyon of Middle Fork. In the 1850's, lumber was loaded on schooners at Williams Landing, which was located at the mouth of San Vicente Creek on the edge of Arroyo de la Laguna grant; the place also was a stage station and was named for the owners of the grant (Hoover, Rensch, and Rensch, p. 473, 478). Hamman's (1980c) map shows a place called Buena Vista located along San Vicente Creek near the mouth of Mill Creek. This was a company town started by Santa Cruz Portland Cement Company about 1920 and destroyed by a landslide in 1961 (Clark, 1986, p. 50).

San Vicente Junction: see **Swanton** [SANTA CRUZ].

San Ysidro Canyon [SANTA BARBARA]: *canyon,* 2.5 miles long, along San Ysidro Creek above a point nearly 7 miles west-northwest of Carpinteria (lat. 34°26'50" N, long. 119°37'15" W). Named on Carpinteria (1952) 7.5' quadrangle. United States Board on Geographic Names (1961b, p. 15) rejected the name "Dinsmore Canyon" for the feature.

San Ysidro Creek [SANTA BARBARA]: *stream,* flows 4.5 miles to the sea 6 miles west-northwest of Carpinteria (lat. 34°25'10" N, long. 119°37'10" W); the stream drains San Ysidro Canyon. Named on Carpinteria (1952) 7.5' quadrangle. United States Board on Geographic Names (1961b, p. 15) rejected the name "Arroyo San Ysidro" for the stream.

Sapaque: see **Bryson** [MONTEREY].

Sapaque Creek [MONTEREY-SAN LUIS OBISPO]: *stream,* heads in Monterey County and flows 4 miles to Nacimiento River 11 miles north-northeast of the village of San Simeon in San Luis Obispo County (lat. 35°47'20" N, long. 121°05'25" W; sec. 3, T 25 S, R 8 E); the stream goes through Sapaque Valley. Named on Bryson (1949) 7.5' quadrangle. The stream first was called Woods Creek, for Job Wood, an early settler (Clark, 1991, p. 514).

Sapaque Valley [MONTEREY]: *valley,* 12 miles south-southeast of Jolon (lat. 35°48'20" N, long. 121°05'25" W). Named on Bryson (1949) 7.5' quadrangle. The place also was

called Woods Valley, for Job Wood, a landowner there (Clark, 1991, p. 514).

Saquel: see **Soquel** [SANTA CRUZ].

Saquel Cove: see **Soquel Cove** [SANTA CRUZ].

Saquel Creek: see **Soquel Creek** [SANTA CRUZ].

Saquel Point: see **Soquel Point** [SANTA CRUZ].

Sarah Canyon [MONTEREY]: *canyon,* drained by a stream that flows 6 miles to Salinas River 2.5 miles northwest of Bradley (lat. 35°53'20" N, long. 120°50'05" W; sec. 36, T 23 S, R 10 E). Named on Wunpost (1949) 7.5' quadrangle.

Saratoga Gap [SANTA CRUZ]: *pass,* 9 miles north of the town of Boulder Creek on Santa Cruz-Santa Clara county line (lat. 37°15'30" N, long. 122°07'10" W; near S line sec. 6, T 8 S, R 2 W). Named on Cupertino (1961) 7.5' quadrangle.

Sargent Canyon [MONTEREY]: *canyon,* drained by Sargent Creek, which flows 14 miles to lowlands 7 miles north-northwest of Bradley (lat. 35°57'05" N, long. 120°51'40" W; near S line sec. 2, T 23 S, R 10 E). Named on Pancho Rico Valley (1967), Slack Canyon (1969), and Wunpost (1949) 7.5' quadrangles. Called Sargent Gulch on a map of Monterey County used about 1900. The name is for Bradley V. Sargent, who owned land at the place (Clark, 1991, p. 515).

Sargent Creek [MONTEREY]: *stream,* flows 14 miles to lowlands 7 miles north-northwest of Bradley (lat. 35°57'05" N, long. 120°51'40" W; near S line sec. 2, T 23 S, R 10 E); the stream goes through Sargent Canyon. Named on Wunpost (1949) 7.5' quadrangle.

Sargent Gulch: see **Sargent Canyon** [MONTEREY].

Saucelito Creek [SAN LUIS OBISPO]: *stream,* flows nearly 4 miles to Arroyo Grande Creek 11.5 miles north-northeast of the town of Nipomo (lat. 35°12'15" N, long. 120°25'15" W). Named on Tar Spring Ridge (1967) 7.5' quadrangle.

Saucelito Ridge [SAN LUIS OBISPO]: *ridge,* north-northwest- to northwest-trending, 2.5 miles long, 11 miles east-northeast of the town of Nipomo (lat. 35°11'30" N, long. 120°24'30" W); the ridge is southwest of Saucelito Creek. Named on Tar Spring Ridge (1967) 7.5' quadrangle.

Saucito [MONTEREY]: *land grant,* 2.5 miles south-southeast of Seaside. Named on Seaside (1947) 7.5' quadrangle. Graciano Manjares received 1.5 leagues in 1833; John Wilson and others claimed 2212 acres patented in 1862 (Cowan, p. 96).

Saucito Canyon [MONTEREY]: *canyon,* drained by a stream that flows 2.25 miles to the canyon of Chalone Creek 3.25 miles northeast of Greenfield (lat. 36°21'15" N, long. 121°12'05" W). Named on Greenfield (1956) 7.5' quadrangle.

Sauguil: see **Soquel** [SANTA CRUZ].

Sauquel: see **Soquel** [SANTA CRUZ].

Sauquel Cove: see **Soquel Cove** [SANTA CRUZ].

Sauquel Creek: see **Soquel Creek** [SANTA CRUZ].

Sauquel Point: see **Soquel Point** [SANTA CRUZ].

Sausal [MONTEREY]: *land grant,* north and northeast of Salinas. Named on Natividad (1947) and Salinas (1947) 7.5' quadrangles. Agustin Soberanes received 2 leagues in 1823, and the land was regranted to Jose Tiburcio Castro in 1834 and 1845; Jacob P. Leese claimed 10,242 acres patented in 1859 (Cowan, p. 96; Cowan listed the grant under the name "Sauzal").

Sauzal: see **Sausal** [MONTEREY].

Sawmill Basin [SANTA BARBARA]: *area,* less than 1 mile southwest of Figueroa Mountain (lat. 34°44'05" N, long. 119°59'40" W; on S line sec. 25, T 8 N, R 30 W). Named on Figueroa Mountain (1959) 7.5' quadrangle.

Sawmill Canyon [MONTEREY]: *canyon,* drained by a stream that flows 2 miles to Stone Canyon 6.5 miles southeast of Smith Mountain (lat. 36°00'35" N, long. 120°30'45" W; near E line sec. 13, T 22 S, R 13 E). Named on Curry Mountain (1969) and Smith Mountain (1969) 7.5' quadrangles. Priest Valley (1915) 30' quadrangle has the label "Old Sawmill" for a building near the mouth of the canyon.

Sawmill Creek [SAN BENITO]: *stream,* flows 3.5 miles to San Benito River 5.25 miles south of Idria (lat. 36°20'35" N, long. 120° 39'30" W; near SE cor. sec. 21, T 18 S, R 12 E). Named on San Benito Mountain (1969) and Santa Rita Peak (1969) 7.5' quadrangles.

Sawmill Flat Campground [MONTEREY]: *locality,* about 2.25 miles east-northeast of Pfeiffer Point (lat. 36°14'55" N, long. 121° 46'45" W; sec. 30, T 19 S, R 2 E). Named on Pfeiffer Point (1956) 7.5' quadrangle.

Sawmill Gulch [MONTEREY]: *canyon,* drained by a stream that flows 2 miles to the sea 2.25 miles south-southwest of Point Pinos (lat. 35°36'30" N, long. 121°57' W). Named on Monterey (1947) 7.5' quadrangle.

Sayante: see **Zayanta** [SANTA CRUZ].

Schau Peak [SAN LUIS OBISPO]: *peak,* 3 miles north of the town of Nipomo on Temettate Ridge (lat. 35°05'20" N, long. 120°28'20" W). Named on Nipomo (1965) 7.5' quadrangle.

Schillings Camp: see **Aptos Creek** [SANTA CRUZ].

Schneider Hill [MONTEREY]: *peak,* 1.25 miles south-southeast of Prunedale (lat. 36°45'40" N, long. 121°39'35" W). Named on Prunedale (1954) 7.5' quadrangle.

School Hill [MONTEREY]: *hill,* 2.25 miles east-northeast of Jamesburg (lat. 36°22'50" N, long. 121°33' W; sec. 9, T 18 S, R 4 E). Altitude 2158 feet. Named on Rana Creek (1956)

7.5' quadrangle. The name is from a private school established in 1929 and closed in 1941 (Clark, 1991, p. 517).

Schoolhouse Canyon [SANTA BARBARA]:

(1) *canyon,* drained by a stream that flows 8 miles to Cuyama River 12 miles east of Miranda Pine Mountain (lat. 35°00'15" N, long. 119°49'35" W). Named on Caliente Mountain (1959) and Peak Mountain (1964) 7.5' quadrangles.

(2) *canyon,* 2 miles long, opens into the canyon of Asphaltum Creek 8 miles south-southeast of Tepusquet Peak (lat. 34°48' N, long. 120°07'50" W). Named on Foxen Canyon (1964) and Zaca Lake (1964) 7.5' quadrangles.

Schoolhouse Ridge [SAN BENITO]: *ridge,* north-northwest-trending, about 2 miles long, 3.5 miles southwest of Potrero Peak (lat. 36°49'30" N, long. 121°11'45" W). Named on Quien Sabe Valley (1968) 7.5' quadrangle. Quien Sabe (1922) 15' quadrangle shows Quien Sabe school situated at the east base of the ridge in Quien Sabe Valley.

School Spring [SAN LUIS OBISPO]: *spring,* 4 miles east of the mouth of San Carpoforo Creek (lat. 35°46'40" N, long. 121°15'10" W; sec. 7, T 25 S, R 7 E). Named on Burro Mountain (1949) 7.5' quadrangle.

Schumann: see **Shuman** [SANTA BARBARA].

Schumann Canyon: see **Shuman Canyon** [SANTA BARBARA].

Schwan Lake: see **Schwans Lagoon** [SANTA CRUZ].

Schwans Lagoon [SANTA CRUZ]: *lake,* 0.5 mile long, 1.25 miles west-northwest of Soquel Point near the coast (lat. 36°57'55" N, long. 121°59'40" W). Named on Soquel (1954) 7.5' quadrangle. According to Clark (1986, p. 329), who called the feature Schwan Lake, the name commemorates Jacob Schwan, who came to the neighborhood before 1862; this lake and Woods Lagoon together are known as Twin Lakes. United States Board on Geographic Names (1994, p. 5) approved the name "Schwan Lagoon" for the feature, and rejected the forms "Schwan Lake," "Schwans Lagoon," "Schwans Lake," and "Swan Lake" for the name.

Scorpion: see **Little Scorpion**, under **Scorpion Anchorage** [SANTA BARBARA].

Scorpion Anchorage [SANTA BARBARA]: *embayment,* 2.25 miles west-northwest of San Pedro Point on the north side of Santa Cruz Island (lat. 34°02'55" N, long. 119°33'15" W). Named on Santa Cruz Island D (1943) 7.5' quadrangle. Called Scorpion Harbor on Bremner's (1932) map. United States Board on Geographic Names (1934, p. 16) rejected the name "East End Anchorage" for the feature. Two bold rocks near shore just east of Scorpion Anchorage form a protected place called Little Scorpion (Gleason, p. 49).

Scorpion Harbor: see **Scorpion Anchorage** [SANTA BARBARA].

Scott Creek [SANTA CRUZ]: *stream,* flows 10.5 miles to the sea nearly 3 miles northwest of Davenport (lat. 37°02'25" N, long. 122°13'40" W). Named on Año Nuevo (1955), Big Basin (1955), and Davenport (1955) 7.5' quadrangles. According to H.R. Wagner (p. 506), Crespi gave the name "San Pedro Alcantara" in 1769 to a camping place of the Portola expedition that probably was near Scott Creek. California Mining Bureau's (1909d) map shows a place called Scott Jn. located along the railroad where the line turns inland along Scott Creek to Swanton.

Scott Junction: see **Scott Creek** [SANTA CRUZ].

Scott Rock [SAN LUIS OBISPO]: *peak,* 1 mile north-northeast of Cambria (lat. 35°34'35" N, long. 121°04'25" W; sec. 23, T 27 S, R 8 E). Altitude 660 feet. Named on Cambria (1959) 7.5' quadrangle.

Scotts Valley [SANTA CRUZ]:
(1) *valley,* 7.5 miles southeast of the town of Boulder Creek along Carbonera Creek (lat. 37°03'45" N, long. 122°00'15" W). Named on Felton (1955) and Laurel (1955) 7.5' quadrangles. Called Scott Valley on Los Gatos (1919) 15' quadrangle. The name commemorates Hiram Daniel Scott, who in 1852 bought San Augustin grant where the valley is situated (Hoover, Rensch, and Rensch, p. 471).
(2) *town,* 7.5 miles southeast of the town of Boulder Creek (lat. 37° 03' N, long. 122°00'50" W); the town is in Scotts Valley (1). Named on Felton (1955) 7.5' quadrangle. Called Scott Valley on Ben Lomond (1946) 15' quadrangle. Postal authorities established Scotts Valley post office in 1951 (Salley, p. 199), and the town incorporated in 1966.

Scott Valley: see **Scotts Valley** [SANTA CRUZ] (1) and (2).

Scout Peak [SAN BENITO]: *peak,* 2.25 miles north of North Chalone Peak (lat. 26°28'45" N, long. 121°11'55" W; sec. 3, T 17 S, R 7 E). Named on North Chalone Peak (1969) 7.5' quadrangle.

Script Canyon Number 1 [SANTA BARBARA]: *canyon,* drained by a stream that flows 2 miles to South Fork La Brea Creek 1.5 miles northwest of Manzanita Mountain (lat. 34°54'30" N, long. 120°05'55" W); the feature is west of Script Canyon Number 2. Named on Manzanita Mountain (1964) 7.5' quadrangle.

Script Canyon Number 2 [SANTA BARBARA]: *canyon,* drained by a stream that flows 2.5 miles to South Fork La Brea Creek 1.25 miles north-northwest of Manzanita Mountain (lat. 34°54'35" N, long. 120°05'30" W); the feature is east of Script Canyon Number 1. Named on Manzanita Mountain (1964) 7.5' quadrangle.

Seabright: see **Santa Cruz** [SANTA CRUZ].

Seagirt: see **Gaviota** [SANTA BARBARA].

Seagull Canyon [SANTA BARBARA]: *canyon,* drained by a stream that flows 3 miles to Redrock Canyon 4.5 miles north of San Marcos Pass (lat. 34°34'40" N, long. 119°48'30" W). Named on San Marcos Pass (1959) 7.5' quadrangle.

Sea Lion Cove [MONTEREY]: *embayment,* 0.25 mile south of Point Lobos (lat. 36°31'05" N, long. 121°57'05" W). Named on Monterey (1947) 7.5' quadrangle.

Sea Lion Rocks: see **Seal Rocks** [MONTEREY].

Seal Rock [MONTEREY]: *rock,* 150 feet long, nearly 1 mile northeast of Cypress Point, and 500 feet offshore (lat. 36°35'20" N, long. 121°57'55" W). Named on Monterey (1947) 7.5' quadrangle.

Seal Rock: see **Lion Rock** [SANTA BARBARA].

Seal Rock Creek [MONTEREY]: *stream,* flows 2.25 miles to the sea 2.5 miles northeast of Cypress Point (lat. 36°35'20" N, long. 121°57'50" W); the mouth of the stream is opposite Seal Rock. Named on Monterey (1947) 7.5' quadrangle.

Seal Rocks [MONTEREY]: *rocks,* 0.5 mile southwest of Point Lobos, and 0.25 mile offshore (lat. 36°31' N, long. 121°57'20" W). Named on Monterey (1947) 7.5' quadrangle. Called Sea Lion Rocks on California Department of Parks and Recreation's map. Monterey (1913) 15' quadrangle has the name "Whalers Rock" near present Seal Rocks.

Seaside [MONTEREY]: *city,* 2.25 miles east-northeast of Monterey near the coast (lat. 36°36'30" N, long. 121°51' W). Named on Seaside (1947) 7.5' quadrangle. Dr. J.L.D. Roberts laid out the community in 1888 and called it East Monterey; when postal authorities rejected this name, Roberts gave the place the name "Seaside" (Gudde, 1949, p. 323). Postal authorities established Seaside post office in 1891 (Salley, p. 200), and the city incorporated in 1954. According to Johnston (p. 117), an Indian named White Wolf came to Seaside about 1900, married a wealthy woman, and built Grey Eagle Terrace, a home for elderly Indians; the structure burned in 1917, but the district around the site still is known as Grey Eagle Terrace.

Seaside: see **Arroyo las Trancas** [SANTA CRUZ].

See Canyon [SAN LUIS OBISPO]: *canyon,* drained by a stream that flows nearly 6 miles to San Luis Obispo Creek 1.25 miles east-northeast of Avila Beach (lat. 35°11'15" N, long. 120°42'45" W). Named on Pismo Beach (1965) and Port San Luis (1965) 7.5' quadrangles. The name commemorates Joseph See, who came to the neighborhood in 1857 (Hanna, p. 299).

Sellars Potrero [SAN LUIS OBISPO]: *area,* 5 miles southeast of Pozo (lat. 35°15'35" N, long. 120°18'10" W). Named on Pozo Summit (1967) 7.5' quadrangle. United States Board on Geographic Names (1968b, p. 9) rejected the form "Sellers Potrero" for the name.

Semas Mountain [MONTEREY]: *peak,* nearly 2 miles northwest of Bradley (lat. 35°52'55" N, long. 120°49'15" W; sec. 31, T 23 S, R 11 E). Altitude 1225 feet. Named on Wunpost (1949) 7.5' quadrangle.

Semper Spring [SAN LUIS OBISPO]: *spring,* 27 miles southeast of Simmler (lat. 35°02'20" N, long. 119°41'45" W; sec. 18, T 11 N, R 26 W). Named on Wells Ranch (1954) 7.5' quadrangle.

Sempervirens Creek [SANTA CRUZ]: *stream,* flows 2 miles to Blooms Creek near the east end of Big Basin (lat. 37°10'05" N, long. 122°12'45" W; sec. 8, T 9 S, R 3 W). Named on Big Basin (1955) 7.5' quadrangle.

Sempervirens Reservoir [SANTA CRUZ]: *lake,* 950 feet long, behind a dam on Sempervirens Creek 1.5 miles north-northeast of Big Basin (lat. 37°11'25" N, long. 122°12'25" W; near E line sec. 32, T 8 S, R 3 W). Named on Big Basin (1955) 7.5' quadrangle.

Seneca Creek [MONTEREY]: *stream,* flows nearly 3 miles to San Jose Creek 3.5 miles southeast of the mouth of Carmel River (lat. 36°30'05" N, long. 121°52'50" W; sec. 32, T 16 S, R 1 E). Named on Mount Carmel (1956) and Soberanes Point (1956) 7.5' quadrangles.

Serena [SANTA BARBARA]: *settlement,* 2.5 miles west-northwest of Carpinteria (lat. 34°24'45" N, long. 119°33'20" W). Named on Carpinteria (1952) 7.5' quadrangle. Postal authorities established Serena post office in 1889 and discontinued it in 1900 (Frickstad, p. 172). Santa Barbara (1903) 15' quadrangle shows Carpinteria Landing at the site.

Serena Park [SANTA BARBARA]: *settlement,* 3.5 miles west-northwest of Carpinteria (lat. 34°25'05" N, long. 119°34'15" W); the place is less than 1 mile west-northwest of Serena. Named on Carpinteria (1952) 7.5' quadrangle.

Serra: see **Junipero Serra Peak** [MONTEREY].

Serra Hill: see **Sierra Hill** [MONTEREY].

Serrano [SAN LUIS OBISPO]: *locality,* 3.5 miles north of San Luis Obispo along Southern Pacific Railroad (lat. 35°20'05" N, long. 120°39'10" W). Named on San Luis Obispo (1965) 7.5' quadrangle. Postal authorities established Serrano post office in 1907 and discontinued it in 1908 (Frickstad, p. 166). Railroad officials named the place in 1893 for the Serrano family, from whom the right of way there was obtained (Gudde, 1949, p. 326).

Seven Well Canyon [MONTEREY]: *canyon,* drained by a stream that flows 2.5 miles to lowlands 4.5 miles west-southwest of San Lucas (lat. 36°05'55" N, long. 121°05'30" W; sec. 15, T 21 S, R 8 E). Named on Espinosa Canyon (1949) 7.5' quadrangle. The name reportedly is from seven wells drilled for water before the last was successful (Clark, 1991, p. 522).

Shady Lane Canyon [MONTEREY]: *canyon,*

drained by a stream that flows 2.25 miles to McCoy Canyon 5.5 miles east-northeast of Gonzales (lat. 36°32'25" N, long. 121°21'05" W; sec. 18, T 16 S, R 6 E). Named on Mount Johnson (1968) 7.5' quadrangle.

Shag Rock [SANTA BARBARA]: *island,* 400 feet long, 350 feet off the north side of Santa Barbara Island (lat. 33°29'15" N, long. 119° 02'05" W). Named on United States Geological Survey's (1973) map.

Shale Sulphur Springs: see **Chittenden's Sulphur Springs**, under **Chittenden** [SANTA CRUZ].

Shandon [SAN LUIS OBISPO]: *village,* 18 miles east of Paso Robles (lat. 35°39'20" N, long. 120°22'30" W; sec. 20, T 26 S, R 15 E). Named on Cholame (1961) and Shandon (1961) 7.5' quadrangles. According to Salley (p. 202, 212), postal authorities established Starkey post office in 1885, moved it 1.5 miles northeast in 1888, and moved it 1.5 miles northeast again in 1891, when they changed the name to Shandon; the post office names were for Starkey Shandon, a pioneer settler. According to Stanley (p. 46), the townsite, first called Sunset, was surveyed in 1890 and developed by West Coast Land Company; the name was changed from Sunset to Shandon in 1891 at the suggestion of Dr. John Hughes, after Dr. Hughes had read a story called "Shandon Belle" published in *Harper's* in 1882.

Shandon Flat [SAN LUIS OBISPO]: *area,* 1.5 miles southwest of Shandon (lat. 35°38'10" N, long. 120°23'40" W). Named on Shandon (1961) 7.5' quadrangle.

Shaw Anchorage: see **Sandstone Point** [SANTA BARBARA].

Shaw Canyon [SAN LUIS OBISPO]: *canyon,* drained by a stream that flows 3.25 miles to Alamo Creek 8 miles west-southwest of Branch Mountain (lat. 35°07'30" N, long. 120°12'25" W; sec. 24, T 32 S, R 16 E). Named on Chimney Canyon (1967) 7.5' quadrangle.

Shear Creek [SANTA CRUZ]: *stream,* flows nearly 2 miles to Bear Creek 5.5 miles northeast of the town of Boulder Creek (lat. 37°11'05" N, long. 122°03'20" W; near S line sec. 35, T 8 S, R 2 W). Named on Castle Rock Ridge (1955) 7.5' quadrangle.

Shedd Canyon [SAN LUIS OBISPO]: *canyon,* 9 miles long, opens into lowlands nearly 4 miles west of Shandon (lat. 35°39'15" N, long. 120°26'30" W; sec. 23, T 26 S, R 14 E). Named on Shandon (1961) and Shedd Canyon (1961) 7.5' quadrangles.

Sheehee Spring [MONTEREY]: *spring,* 5.5 miles southwest of Smith Mountain (lat. 36°01'50" N, long. 120°40'15" W; sec. 10, T 22 S, R 12 E). Named on Slack Canyon (1969) 7.5' quadrangle.

Sheep Camp [SAN LUIS OBISPO]: *locality,* 12 miles south-southeast of Simmler (lat. 35°12' N, long. 119°52' W; sec. 30, T 31 S, R 20 E).

Named on Painted Rock (1959) 7.5' quadrangle.

Sheep Camp: see **Camp No. 3**, under **Santa Rosalia Mountain** [SANTA CRUZ].

Sheep Camp Canyon [SAN LUIS OBISPO]: *canyon,* drained by a stream that flows 5 miles to lowlands along Estrella Creek 11 miles east-northeast of Paso Robles (lat. 35°41' N, long. 120°30'40" W; sec. 7, T 26 S, R 14 E). Named on Shandon (1961) 7.5' quadrangle.

Sheep Camp Creek [SANTA BARBARA]: *stream,* flows 2.5 miles to Aliso Creek 5 miles west of Miranda Pine Mountain (lat. 35°02'05" N, long. 120°07'15" W). Named on Miranda Pine Mountain (1967) 7.5' quadrangle.

Sheepcamp Creek [SAN LUIS OBISPO]: *stream,* flows nearly 6 miles to Paso Robles Creek 3.25 miles east of York Mountain (lat. 35°33'05" N, long. 120°46'30" W). Named on York Mountain (1948) 7.5' quadrangle. Adelaida (1947) 15' quadrangle has the form "Sheep Camp Creek" for the name.

Sheep Canyon [MONTEREY]: *canyon,* drained by a stream that flows 3.5 miles to Powell Canyon 5.5 miles north of Bradley (lat. 35°56'45" N, long. 120°48'10" W; sec. 8, T 23 S, R 11 E). Named on Wunpost (1949) 7.5' quadrangle.

Sheep Creek [SAN LUIS OBISPO]: *stream,* flows 4.5 miles to Alamo Creek 5.5 miles west of Branch Mountain (lat. 35°11'05" N, long. 120°10'45" W). Named on Los Machos Hills (1967) 7.5' quadrangle.

Sheffield Reservoir [SANTA BARBARA]: *lake,* 950 feet long, 1.5 miles north of downtown Santa Barbara (lat. 34°26'40" N, long. 119°41'30" W; sec. 10, T 4 N, R 27 W). Named on Santa Barbara (1952) 7.5' quadrangle.

Shell Beach [SAN LUIS OBISPO]: *district,* 2 miles west-northwest of downtown Pismo Beach along the coast (lat. 35°09'20" N, long. 120°40'15" W). Named on Pismo Beach (1965) 7.5' quadrangle. Postal authorities established Shell Beach post office in 1939 (Frickstad, p. 166). Floyd Calvert laid out the community on 41 acres of land that he bought in 1926 (Lee and others, p. 139). The place now is part of Pismo Beach.

Shell Creek [SAN LUIS OBISPO]: *stream,* flows 7.5 miles to Camatta Canyon 3 miles east-northeast of Wilson Corner (lat. 35°29' N, long. 120°19'40" W; near N line sec. 23, T 28 S, R 15 E). Named on Camatta Ranch (1966) 7.5' quadrangle.

Shell Peak [SAN LUIS OBISPO]: *peak,* 10 miles southwest of Branch Mountain (lat. 35°04'20" N, long. 120°11'20" W; near W line sec. 31, T 12 N, R 31 W). Altitude 2460 feet. Named on Chimney Canyon (1967) 7.5' quadrangle.

Shepard Mesa [SANTA BARBARA]: *ridge,* west-trending, 0.5 mile long, 2 miles north-northeast of Rincon Point (lat. 34°23'55" N, long. 119°27'55" W). Named on White Ledge Peak (1952) 7.5' quadrangle. Ventura (1941) 15' quadrangle has the name "Shepard Park" on the ridge.

Shepard Park: see **Shepard Mesa** [SANTA BARBARA].

Shepards [SANTA BARBARA]: *locality,* 2.25 miles northeast of Rincon Point (lat. 34°23'50" N, long. 119°27'10" W); the place is east of present Shepard Mesa. Named on Ventura (1904) 15' quadrangle.

Shields Canyon [SAN BENITO]: *canyon,* drained by a stream that flows nearly 4 miles to San Benito River 2.5 miles north-northwest of San Benito (lat. 36°32'30" N, long. 121°06'05" W). Named on San Benito (1968) 7.5' quadrangle.

Shimmin Canyon [SAN LUIS OBISPO]: *canyon,* drained by a stream that flows 12 miles to Estrella River 5.5 miles west of Shandon (lat. 35°39'10" N, long. 120°28'05" W; sec. 21, T 26 S, R 14 E). Named on Cholame Hills (1961) and Shandon (1961) 7.5' quadrangles. Called Simmons Canyon on Cholame (1917) 30' quadrangle.

Shingle Mill Creek [SANTA CRUZ]: *stream,* flows 1.5 miles to San Lorenzo River 6.25 miles south-southeast of the town of Boulder Creek (lat. 37°02'35" N, long. 122°04'15" W). Named on Felton (1955) 7.5' quadrangle.

Shingle Mill Gulch [SANTA CRUZ]: *canyon,* nearly 1 mile long, branches east from Eureka Canyon 4 miles north of Corralitos (lat. 37°02'40" N, long. 121°48'50" W; sec. 24, T 10 S, R 1 E). Named on Loma Prieta (1955) 7.5' quadrangle.

Shingle Springs: see **Ben Lomond** [SANTA CRUZ].

Shirttail Gulch [MONTEREY]: *canyon,* 3.5 miles long, opens into lowlands 3.5 miles east-southeast of Soledad (lat. 36°24'50" N, long. 121°15'45" W; sec. 36, T 17 S, R 6 E). Named on North Chalone Peak (1969) and Soledad (1955) 7.5' quadrangles.

Shoquel [SANTA CRUZ]: *land grant,* at and east of Soquel near the coast. Named on Soquel (1954) 7.5' quadrangle. Martina Castro received 0.5 league in 1833 and claimed 1668 acres patented in 1860 (Rowland, p. 39; Rowland listed the grant under the name "Soquel"). The name is from an Indian village (Kroeber, 1916, p. 59)

Shoquel: see **Soquel** [SANTA CRUZ].

Shoquel Augmentation [SANTA CRUZ]: *land grant,* along and east of Soquel Creek; extends a short distance over the crest of Santa Cruz Mountains into Santa Clara County. Named on Laurel (1955), Loma Prieta (1955), Los Gatos (1953), Soquel (1954), and Watsonville West (1954) 7.5' quadrangles. Arbuckle (p. 35) listed the grant under the name "Soquel Augmentacion," and noted that Martina Castro, who received the land in 1844 as an addition to her Shoquel grant, claimed 32,702 acres patented in 1860.

Shoquel Cove: see Soquel Cove [SANTA CRUZ].

Shoquel Creek: see Soquel Creek [SANTA CRUZ].

Shoquel Point: see Soquel Point [SANTA CRUZ].

Shovel Handle Creek [MONTEREY]: *stream,* flows nearly 1 mile to Zigzag Creek 3.25 miles southwest of Tassajara Hot Springs (lat. 36°11'45" N, long. 121°34'55" W; sec. 13, T 20 S, R 3 E). Named on Tassajara Hot Springs (1956) 7.5' quadrangle.

Shuman [SANTA BARBARA]: *locality,* 2 miles north-northeast of the village of Casmalia along Southern Pacific Railroad (lat. 34°52' N, long. 120°31'20" W); the place is near the head of Shuman Canyon. Named on Casmalia (1959) 7.5' quadrangle. Called Schumann on Guadalupe (1905) 30' quadrangle, but United States Board on Geographic Names (1949, p. 4) rejected the forms "Schumann" and "Schuman" for the name.

Shuman Canyon [SANTA BARBARA]: *canyon,* drained by a stream that flows 7.5 miles to lowlands along the coast 3.5 miles west of the village of Casmalia (lat. 34°50'45" N, long. 120°35'40" W). Named on Casmalia (1959) 7.5' quadrangle. Called Schumann Canyon on Guadalupe (1905) 30' quadrangle, but United States Board on Geographic Names (1949, p. 4) rejected this form of the name.

Shut-in: see The Shut-in [MONTEREY].

Sienega del Gabilan: see Cienega del Gabilan [MONTEREY-SAN BENITO].

Sierra Blanca [SANTA BARBARA]: *ridge,* south-southwest-trending, 0.5 mile long, 1.25 miles north of Punta Arena on Santa Cruz Island (lat. 33°58'50" N, long. 119°49'10" W). Named on Santa Cruz Island B (1943) 7.5' quadrangle.

Sierra Creek [MONTEREY]: *stream,* flows 3.25 miles to Bixby Creek 4.25 miles north-northeast of Point Sur (lat. 36°21'55" N, long. 121°53'10" W; sec. 17, T 18 S, R 1 E); the stream is northeast of Sierra Hill. Named on Big Sur (1956) and Point Sur (1956) 7.5' quadrangles.

Sierra de Buchon: see Irish Hills [SAN LUIS OBISPO].

Sierra de Gavilan: see Gabilan Range [MONTEREY-SAN BENITO].

Sierra de la Santa Cruz: see Santa Cruz Mountains [SANTA CRUZ].

Sierra de la Santa Inez: see Santa Ynez Mountains [SANTA BARBARA].

Sierra de la Santa Lucia: see Santa Lucia Range [MONTEREY-SAN LUIS OBISPO].

Sierra de las Piedras: see Piedras Atlas [MONTEREY].

Sierra del Monte Diablo: see Diablo Range [MONTEREY-SAN BENITO].

Sierra de Salinas [MONTEREY]: *range,* extends along the southwest side of Salinas River from near Salinas to Greenfield. Named on Santa Cruz (1956) 1°x 2° quadrangle.

Whitney (p. 111) used the name "Palo Scrito Hills" for the range, Fairbanks (1894, p. 520) used the name "Soledad Hills" for the feature, Angel (1890a, p. 568) used the name "Palo Serito Hills" for it, and Reed (p. 44) mentioned the names "Palo Escrito" and "Mount Torro Range." Parke's (1854-1855) map has the name "Sierra Salinas" for highlands west of Salinas River as far south as San Antonio River, and in his text Parke (p. 6) used the name "Salinas mountains" for the same highlands.

Sierra de San Rafael: see San Rafael Mountains [SANTA BARBARA].

Sierra de Santa Lucia: see Santa Lucia Range [MONTEREY-SAN LUIS OBISPO].

Sierra Hill [MONTEREY]: *ridge,* northwest-trending, 2 miles long, 3.25 miles north-north-east of Point Sur (lat. 36°21' N, long. 121° 53' W); the ridge is southwest of Sierra Creek. Named on Point Sur (1956) 7.5' quadrangle. According to Clark (1991, p. 520-521), the feature should have the name "Serra Hill."

Sierra Madre Mountains [SANTA BARBARA]: *range,* between Cuyama Valley and Sisquoc River. Named on Los Angeles (1955) and San Luis Obispo (1956) 1°x 2° quadrangles. Called San Rafael Mountains on San Luis Obispo (1948) and Santa Maria (1956) 1°x 2° quadrangles, but United States Board on Geographic Names (1965b, p. 15) rejected this name for the feature. Parke (p. 6) called the range Cuyama mountains, Whitney (p. 112) called it Cuyamas Range, and Fairbanks (1894, p. 498) called it Cuyama range.

Sierra Madre Mountains: see San Rafael Mountains [SANTA BARBARA].

Sierra Napoma: see Nipomo Valley [SAN LUIS OBISPO].

Sierra Nevada: see Point Sierra Nevada [SAN LUIS OBISPO].

Sierra Nevadas: see Santa Lucia Range [MONTEREY-SAN LUIS OBISPO].

Sierra Pablo [SANTA BARBARA]: *ridge,* east-northeast-trending, less than 1 mile long, 3.5 miles west of East Point on Santa Rosa Island (lat. 33°56'35" N, long. 120°01'40" W). Named on Santa Rosa Island East (1943) 7.5' quadrangle.

Sierra River: see Nacimiento River [MONTEREY-SAN LUIS OBISPO].

Sierra Salinas: see Sierra de Salinas [MONTEREY].

Sierra San Jose: see La Panza Range [SAN LUIS OBISPO].

Sierra Santa Iñez: see Santa Ynez Mountains [SANTA BARBARA].

Sierra Santa Lucia: see Santa Lucia Range [MONTEREY-SAN LUIS OBISPO].

Sierra Wasna: see Santa Lucia Range [SAN LUIS OBISPO].

Silver Creek [SAN BENITO]: *stream,* formed by the confluence of San Carlos Creek and Larious Creek, flows 10 miles to Fresno County 7 miles east-southeast of Panoche (lat.

36°34'05" N, long. 120°42'05" W; sec. 6, T 16 S, R 12 E). Named on Idria (1969) and Tumey Hills (1956) 7.5' quadrangles. United States Board on Geographic Names (1933, p. 693) rejected the name "Panoche Creek" for the stream.

Silver Creek [SANTA CRUZ]: *stream,* flows 0.5 mile to Boulder Creek (1) 5 miles east-south-east of Big Basin (lat. 37°08' N, long. 122°08'20" W; sec. 24, T 9 S, R 3 W). Named on Big Basin (1955) quadrangle.

Silver Lake [SAN LUIS OBISPO]: *intermittent lake,* 500 feet long, 8 miles northeast of Santa Margarita (lat. 35°28'50" N, long. 120°31'20" W). Named on Santa Margarita (1965) 7.5' quadrangle.

Silver Peak [MONTEREY]: *peak,* 6.5 miles east-southeast of Cape San Martin (lat. 35°50'50" N, long. 121°21'30" N; sec. 18, T 24 S, R 6 E). Altitude 3590 feet. Named on Burro Mountain (1949) 7.5' quadrangle.

Simas Lake [SANTA CRUZ]: *lake,* 950 feet long, 5.5 miles north of Watsonville (lat. 36°59'50" N, long. 121°44'20" W). Named on Watsonville East (1955) 7.5' quadrangle.

Simmler [SAN LUIS OBISPO]: *settlement,* 38 miles east of San Luis Obispo in the north part of Carrizo Plain (lat. 35°21'05" N, long. 119°59'10" W; near SW cor. sec. 31, T 29 S, R 19 E). Named on Simmler (1959) 7.5' quad-rangle. Postal authorities established Simmler post office in 1887 and discontinued it in 1930 (Frickstad, p. 166). The name commemorates the John J. Simmler family, who came to California in 1853 (Gudde, 1949, p. 333).

Simmons Canyon: see **Shimmin Canyon** [SAN LUIS OBISPO].

Simonton Cove [SANTA BARBARA]: *embayment,* 4 miles east-northeast of Point Bennett on the north side of San Miguel Island (lat. 34°03'20" N, long. 120°23'15" W). Named on San Miguel Island East (1950) and San Miguel Island West (1950) 7.5' quad-angles. Bremner's (1933) map has the name "Otter Harbor" at the west end of the embayment.

Sinnott Switch: see **Riverside Grove** [SANTA CRUZ].

Sisquoc [SANTA BARBARA]:
(1) *land grant,* east-southeast of Santa Maria along and near Sisquoc River. Named on Foxen Canyon (1964), Manzanita Mountain (1964), Tepusquet Canyon (1964), and Zaca Lake (1964) 7.5' quadrangles. Maria Antonio Caballero received the land in 1833; James B. Huie and others claimed 35,486 acres patented in 1866 (Cowan, p. 98). Perez (p. 99) gave 1845 as the date of the grant.
(2) *village,* 10 miles southeast of Santa Maria (lat. 34°51'55" N, long. 120°17'30" W; at SW cor. sec. 7, T 9 N, R 32 W); the village is near Sisquoc River. Named on Sisquoc (1959) 7.5' quadrangle.
(3) *locality,* 6.5 miles northeast of Los Alamos in Foxen Canyon (lat. 34°47'45" N, long.

120°11'05" W). Named on Lompoc (1905) 30' quadrangle. Postal authorities established Sis Quoc post office in 1881, discontinued it in 1898, and reestablished it with the name "Sisquoc" the same year; they moved the post office 3 miles southeast in 1902, discontin-ued it in 1910, reestablished it in 1911, and discontinued it in 1931 (Salley, p. 205). Cali-fornia Mining Bureau's (1917c) map shows a place called Foxen located about 2.5 miles northwest of Sisquoc. Postal authorities es-tablished Foxen post office in 1910, when they moved Sisquoc post office to the place, and discontinued it in 1914 (Salley, p. 79). They established Asphaltea post office in 1897 and discontinued it in 1898, when they moved it 10 miles northwest to Sisquoc; the name was from nearby deposits of asphaltum (Salley, p. 11).

Sisquoc Falls [SANTA BARBARA]: *waterfall,* 5.5 miles northwest of Big Pine Mountain (lat. 34°44'35" N, long. 119°43'50" W); the fea-ture is along a tributary of Sisquoc River. Named on Big Pine Mountain (1964) 7.5' quadrangle.

Sisquoc Grange [SANTA BARBARA]: *local-ity,* nearly 2 miles east-southeast of the vil-lage of Sisquoc (lat. 34°51'15" N, long. 120°15'50" W; sec. 17, T 9 N, R 32 W). Named on Sisquoc (1959) 7.5' quadrangle.

Sisquoc River [SANTA BARBARA]: *stream,* flows 55 miles to join Cuyama River and form Santa Maria River 8 miles east-southeast of Santa Maria (lat. 34°54'10" N, long. 120°18'40" W; at E line sec. 36, T 10 N, R 33 W). Named on Bald Mountain (1964), Big Pine Mountain (1964), Foxen Canyon (1964), Hurricane Deck (1964), Salisbury Potrero (1964), Sisquoc (1959), Twitchell Dam (1959), and Zaca Lake (1964) 7.5' quad-rangles. Called Santa Maria R. on Goddard's (1857) map. South Fork enters from the south 5.25 miles south-southwest of Montgomery Potrero; it is 4.25 miles long and is named on Hurricane Deck (1964) and San Rafael Moun-tain (1959) 7.5' quadrangles.

Sixteen Spring [SAN LUIS OBISPO]: *spring,* 14 miles east-northeast of Pozo along San Juan Creek (lat. 35°24'15" N, long. 120°09'35" W; sec. 16, T 29 S, R 17 E). Named on La Panza Ranch (1966) 7.5' quad-rangle.

Skinner Creek [MONTEREY]: *stream,* flows 3.5 miles to Little Sur River 6.25 miles east-northeast of Point Sur (lat. 36°19'40" N, long. 121°47'35" W); the stream is east of Skinner Ridge. Named on Big Sur (1956) 7.5' quad-rangle.

Skinner Ridge [MONTEREY]: *ridge,* south-east- to south-trending, 3 miles long, 7 miles east-northeast of Point Sur (lat. 36°21'30" N, long. 121°47'30" W); the ridge is west of Skin-ner Creek. Named on Big Sur (1956) 7.5' quadrangle.

Skull Gulch: see **Cañada Tecolote** [SANTA BARBARA].

Skunk Campground [SANTA BARBARA]: *locality,* 5.25 miles south-southwest of Salisbury Potrero along Sisquoc River (lat. 34° 45'10" N, long. 119°44'25" W). Named on Salisbury Potrero (1964) 7.5' quadrangle.

Skunk Point [SANTA BARBARA]: *promontory,* nearly 3 mile north-northwest of East Point (lat. 33°59' N, long. 119°58'40" W). Named on Santa Rosa Island East (1943) 7.5' quadrangle.

Skyland: see **Skyland Ridge** [SANTA CRUZ].

Skyland Ridge [SANTA CRUZ]: *ridge,* east- to southeast-trending, 3 miles long, 8.5 miles north-northeast of Soquel (lat. 37°06'30" N, long. 121°55'15" W). Named on Laurel (1955) 7.5' quadrangle. California Mining Bureau's (1917a) map shows a place called Skyland located 2.5 miles east of Laurel on or near present Skyland Ridge. Postal authorities established Skyland post office in 1884, discontinued it in 1886, reestablished it in 1893, and discontinued it in 1912 (Salley, p. 206).

Slabtown: see **Cambria** [SAN LUIS OBISPO].

Slack Canyon [MONTEREY]: *valley,* 3 miles west-southwest of Smith Mountain (lat. 36°03'30" N, long. 120°38' W). Named on Slack Canyon (1969) and Smith Mountain (1969) 7.5' quadrangles. The valley is drained by Pancho Rico Creek and a tributary of that creek. J.W. Slack came to California in the 1850's and took up range land in the canyon that bears his name (Stanley, p. 126-127). Fairbanks (1894, p. 522) referred to Slack's Cañon. Postal authorities established Slack Canyon post office in 1873 about 15 miles north of Valleton (NE quarter sec. 27, T 21 S, R 12 E) and discontinued it in 1902 (Salley, p. 206).

Slacks Valley [SAN BENITO]: *valley,* drained by a stream that flows 4 miles to Las Aguilas Creek (1) 6.25 miles north-northwest of Panoche Pass (lat. 36°42'55" N, long. 121°02'20" W). Named on Cerro Colorado (1969) and Panoche Pass (1968) 7.5' quadrangles.

Slate Canyon [MONTEREY]: *canyon,* drained by a stream that flows 3.25 miles to Robertson Creek 4.25 miles east of Jamesburg (lat. 36°21'55" N, long. 121°31' W; sec. 14, T 18 S, R 4 E). Named on Chews Ridge (1956), Palo Escrito Peak (1956), and Rana Creek (1956) 7.5' quadrangles.

Slate Rock [MONTEREY]: *rock,* 125 feet long, less than 1 mile west-northwest of Slates Hot Spring, and 0.25 mile offshore (lat. 36°07'35" N, long. 121°38'55" W). Named on Partington Ridge (1956) 7.5' quadrangle.

Slate Rock: see **Little Slate Rock** [MONTEREY].

Slates Hot Springs [MONTEREY]: *spring,* 8 miles north-northwest of Lopez Point (lat. 36°07'20" N, long. 121°38'10" W; sec. 9, T 21 S, R 3 E). Named on Lopez Point (1956) 7.5' quadrangle. On Lucia (1921) 15' quadrangle, the name "Slate's Hot Springs" applies to a building. Irelan (p. 411) referred to Slate's Springs, Crawford (1894, p. 341) described Slate's Hot Sulphur Springs, and Berkstresser (p. A-9) listed the feature under the name "Big Sur Hot Springs." Thomas B. Slate settled at the place in 1868 after water from the spring there apparently cured him of arthritis; later a small resort developed at the site (Waring, G.A., p. 56; Fink, p. 209, 230). Esalen Institute is at the place now (Wall, p. 75, 142).

Sleeper Gulch [SANTA CRUZ]: *canyon,* drained by a stream that flows 1 mile to Kings Creek 5.5 miles north of the town of Boulder Creek (lat. 37°12'20" N, long. 122°07' W; sec. 30, T 8 S, R 2 W). Named on Castle Rock Ridge (1955) 7.5' quadrangle.

Sleepy Hollow [MONTEREY]: *locality,* 2.5 miles south-southeast of the town of Carmel Valley at a wide place in the canyon of Carmel River (lat. 36°26'40" N, long. 121°42'50" W; sec. 23, T 17 S, R 2 E). Named on Carmel Valley (1956) 7.5' quadrangle.

Slickrock Creek [MONTEREY]: *stream,* flows 2 miles to Nacimiento River 9 miles northeast of Cape San Martin (lat. 35°58'45" N, long. 121°21'05" W; sec. 31, T 22 S, R 6 E). Named on Alder Peak (1949) 7.5' quadrangle. Cape San Martin (1921) 15' quadrangle has the form "Slick Rock Creek" for the name.

Slide Hill [SAN LUIS OBISPO]: *peak,* nearly 6 miles east-northeast of Edna (lat. 35°13'20" N, long. 120°31'55" W; sec. 13, T 31 S, R 13 E). Altitude 2168 feet. Named on Arroyo Grande NE (1965) 7.5' quadrangle.

Sloans Canyon [SANTA BARBARA]: *canyon,* drained by a stream that flows 3.5 miles to lowlands along Santa Ynez River 6.5 miles east-southeast of Surf (lat. 34°38'10" N, long. 120°30'10" W). Named on Lompoc (1959), Surf (1959), and Tranquillon Mountain (1959) 7.5' quadrangles.

Slocum Canyon [SAN LUIS OBISPO]: *canyon,* drained by a stream that flows 3.5 miles to San Juan Valley 3 miles south-southeast of Shandon (lat. 35°37' N, long. 120°20'55" W; near S line sec. 34, T 26 S, R 15 E). Named on Camatta Canyon (1961) and Cholame (1961) 7.5' quadrangles.

Small Twin Lake [SAN LUIS OBISPO]: *lake,* 1000 feet long, nearly 4 miles south-southwest of downtown Arroyo Grande near the coast (lat. 35°04'10" N, long. 120°36'15" W); the feature is east of Big Twin Lake. Named on Oceano (1965) 7.5' quadrangle.

Smith Canyon [SANTA BARBARA]: *canyon,* drained by a stream that flows 4.5 miles to Manzanita Mountain (lat. 34°57'30" N, long, 120°05'45" W). Named on Manzanita Mountain (1964) and Miranda Pine Mountain (1967) 7.5' quadrangles.

Smith Creek [SAN LUIS OBISPO]: *stream,* flows nearly 2 miles to Toro Creek 4 miles north-northeast of the town of Morro Bay (lat. 35°26'30" N, long. 120°49'50" W). Named on Morro Bay North (1965) 7.5' quadrangle.

Smith Creek [SANTA CRUZ]: *stream,* flows nearly 1 mile to Love Creek 2.5 miles southeast of the town of Boulder Creek (lat. 37° 05'55" N, long. 122°05'05" W; at S line sec. 33, T 9 S, R 2 W). Named on Felton (1955) 7.5' quadrangle.

Smith Creek: see **Robertson Creek** [MONTEREY].

Smith Island [SAN LUIS OBISPO]: *island,* 250 feet long, 0.5 mile east-northeast of Point San Luis and 250 feet offshore (lat. 35°09'45" N, long. 120°45'15" W). Named on Port San Luis (1965) 7.5' quadrangle. The name, given in the 1880's, commemorates Joe Smith and Mattie Smith, who lived on the island (Lee and others, p. 123).

Smith Mountain [MONTEREY]: *peak,* 18 miles east-northeast of San Ardo on Monterey-Fresno county line (lat. 36°04'45" N, long. 120°35'55" W; sec. 29, T 21 S, R 13 E). Altitude 3947 feet. Named on Smith Mountain (1969) 7.5' quadrangle.

Smoker Canyon [SAN BENITO]: *canyon,* drained by a stream that flows 5.25 miles to San Benito River 8 miles north-northwest of Bitterwater (lat. 36°29'30" N, long. 121°01'45" W; sec. 31, T 16 S, R 9 E). Named on Llanada (1969), San Benito (1968), and Topo Valley (1969) 7.5' quadrangles.

Smugglers Cove [SANTA BARBARA]: *embayment,* 1.5 miles southwest of San Pedro Point at the east end of Santa Cruz Island (lat. 34°01'10" N, long. 119°32'20" W). Named on Santa Cruz Island D (1943) 7.5' quadrangle.

Snake Creek [SAN LUIS OBISPO]: *stream,* flows 7 miles to Nacimiento River 7 miles northeast of Lime Mountain (lat. 35°44'25" N, long. 120°54'25" W; near W line sec. 21, T 25 S, R 10 E). Named on Adelaida (1948) and Lime Mountain (1948) 7.5' quadrangles. The stream now enters an arm of Nacimiento Reservoir.

Snivleys Ridge [MONTEREY]: *ridge,* north- to northwest-trending, 2 miles long, 8 miles east-southeast of the mouth of Carmel River and south of Carmel Valley (1) (lat. 36°30'15" N, long. 121°47'20" W). Named on Mount Carmel (1956) and Seaside (1947) 7.5' quadrangles. The misspelled name commemorates Richard Collier Snively, who had a fruit farm and dairy near the mouth of Robinson Canyon (1) (Clark, 1991, p. 531).

Snowball Mountain [SANTA BARBARA]: *peak,* 4 miles north of Rincon Point (lat. 34°25'45" N, long. 119°28'55" W; sec. 15, T 4 N, R 25 W). Altitude 1680 feet. Named on White Ledge Peak (1952) 7.5' quadrangle.

Soap Lake: see **San Felipe Lake** [SAN BENITO].

Soberanes Creek [MONTEREY]: *stream,* flows 3.5 miles to the sea north of Soberanes Point (lat. 36°27'20" N, long. 121°55'25" W). Named on Soberanes Point (1956) 7.5' quadrangle.

Soberanes Creek: see **Palo Colorado Canyon** [MONTEREY].

Soberanes Point [MONTEREY]: *promontory,* 10 miles north of Point Sur along the coast (lat. 36°27' N, long. 121°55'40" W). Named on Soberanes Point (1956) 7.5' quadrangle. The name commemorates early settlers who homesteaded near the feature (Lussier, p. 12).

Soda Lake [SAN LUIS OBISPO]: *intermittent lake,* 5 miles long, 10 miles southeast of Simmler in Carrizo Plain (lat. 35°14' N, long. 119°53'30" W). Named on Chimineas Ranch (1959), Painted Rock (1959), and Simmler (1959) 7.5' quadrangles. According to Arnold and Johnson (1909, p. 3), the feature was known locally as Soda Lake or Salt Lake. Logan (p. 721) referred to "Soda Lake, or Dry Lake, as it is often called." United States Board on Geographic Names (1933, p. 704) rejected the name "Salt Lake" for the feature.

Soda Lake [SANTA CRUZ]: *lake,* 1600 feet long, 8 miles east of Watsonville (lat. 36°54'30" N, long. 121°36'25" W). Named on Chittenden (1955) 7.5' quadrangle. Shown as an intermittent lake on Chittenden (1955, photorevised 1968 and 1973) 7.5' quadrangle.

Soda Spring Creek [MONTEREY]: *stream,* flows nearly 1.5 miles to the sea 7 miles southeast of Cape San Martin (lat. 35°49' N, long. 121°22'35" W; sec. 25, T 24 S, R 5 E). Named on Burro Mountain (1949) 7.5' quadrangle. The name is from a soda spring found near the feature (Clark, 1991, p. 533).

Soldiers Home Spring: see **Goat Rock** [SANTA BARBARA].

Soledad [MONTEREY]: *town,* 25 miles southeast of Salinas near Salinas River (lat. 36°25'30" N, long. 121°19' W). Named on Soledad (1955) 7.5' quadrangle. Postal authorities established Soledad post office in 1869 (Frickstad, p. 109), and the town incorporated in 1921. When the Portola expedition passed the place in 1769, an Indian there responded to a question with a word that sounded like *soledad,* which means "solitude" in Spanish; later a nearby mission took the name "La Mision de Nuestra Señora de la Soledad" (Gudde, 1949, p. 338).

Soledad Hills: see **Sierra de Salinas** [MONTEREY].

Solomon: see **Mount Solomon** [SANTA BARBARA]; **Mount Solomon**, under **Solomon Hills** [SANTA BARBARA].

Solomon Canyon [SANTA BARBARA]: *canyon,* 3 miles long, along Orcutt Creek above a point 3.25 miles east-southeast of Orcutt (lat. 34°51'10" N, long. 120°23'05" W); the canyon is in Solomon Hills. Named on Orcutt (1959) and Sisquoc (1959) 7.5' quadrangles. The name commemorates Solomon Pico, a highway robber who used the canyon as a base in the 1850's (Gudde, 1949, p. 338).

Solomon Hills [SANTA BARBARA]: *range,* south of Santa Maria Valley and Sisquoc River between Graciosa Canyon and Zaca Creek.

Named on Foxen Canyon (1964), Los Olivos (1959), Orcutt (1959), Sisquoc (1959), and Zaca Creek (1959) 7.5' quadrangles. United States Board on Geographic Names (1965d, p. 12) rejected the name "Mount Solomon" for the range.

Solvang [SANTA BARBARA]: *town*, 3.25 miles east-southeast of Buellton along Santa Ynez River (lat. 34°35'45" N, long. 120°08'25" W). Named on Solvang (1959) 7.5' quadrangle. Postal authorities established Solvang post office in 1912 (Frickstad, p. 172). Danish-American Corporation founded a colony at the place in 1911—*solvang* means "sun meadow" in Danish (Gudde, 1949, p. 338). Postal authorities established Ionata post office near present Solvang (SW quarter sec. 21, T 6 N, R 31 W) in 1874 and discontinued it in 1876; the name was from San Carlos de Jonata grant (Salley, p. 105).

Soqual: see **Soquel** [SANTA CRUZ].

Soque: see **Soquel** [SANTA CRUZ].

Soque Cove: see **Soquel Cove** [SANTA CRUZ].

Soque Creek: see **Soquel Creek** [SANTA CRUZ].

Soquel [SANTA CRUZ]: *town*, 2.5 miles north-northeast of Soquel Point (lat. 36°59'15" N, long. 121°57'20" W); the town is along Soquel Creek and partly on Shoquel grant. Named on Soquel (1954) 7.5' quadrangle. Called Sauguil on Rogers and Johnston's (1857) map, and called Soqual on Bancroft's (1864) map. United States Board on Geographic Names (1933, p. 706) rejected the forms "Saquel," "Sauquel," "Shoquel," and "Soque" for the name. The first general store at the place opened in 1853 (Lewis, 1977, p. 80), and postal authorities established Soquel post office in 1857 (Frickstad, p. 177).

Soquel: see **Shoquel** [SANTA CRUZ].

Soquel Augmentacion: see **Shoquel Augmentation** [SANTA CRUZ].

Soquel Cove [SANTA CRUZ]: *embayment*, east of Soquel Point (lat. 36°58' N, long. 121°56' W). Named on Soquel (1954) 7.5' quadrangle. United States Board on Geographic Names (1933, p. 706) rejected the forms "Saquel Cove," "Sauquel Cove," "Shoquel Cove," and "Soque Cove" for the name.

Soquel Creek [SANTA CRUZ]: *stream*, flows 18 miles to the sea 1.5 miles northeast of Soquel Point (lat. 36°58'20" N, long. 121°57'05" W). Named on Laurel (1955), Loma Prieta (1955), and Soquel (1954) 7.5' quadrangles. Trask (p. 24) mentioned the arroya Sogell in 1854. United States Board on Geographic Names (1933, p. 706) rejected the forms "Saquel Creek," "Sauquel Creek," "Shoquel Creek," and "Soque Creek" for the name. Members of the Portola expedition called the valley of the stream Rosario del Serafin de Asculi in 1769 because they found wild roses there that reminded them of the roses of Spain (Rowland, p. 95). West Branch enters from the north 6.5 miles upstream from the mouth of the main stream; it is formed by the confluence of Burns Creek and Laurel Creek, is 6 miles long, and is named on Laurel (1955) 7.5' quadrangle. Alexander (fig. 5) used the name "Mtn. Cr." for the next tributary to Soquel Creek south of West Branch (lat. 37°01'50" N, long. 121°56'45" W; near E line sec. 27, T 10 S, R 1 W)—Laurel (1955) 7.5' quadrangle shows Mountain school near the mouth of this tributary. A place called Porter's Landing was situated on the coast at the mouth of Soquel Creek in the early days (Hoover, Rensch, and Rensch, p. 474).

Soquel Landing: see **Capitola** [SANTA BARBARA].

Soquel Point [SANTA CRUZ]: *promontory*, 3 miles east of Point Santa Cruz along the coast (lat. 36°57'15" N, long. 121°58'30" W). Named on Soquel (1954) 7.5' quadrangle. United States Board on Geographic Names (1933, p. 706) rejected the forms "Saquel Point," "Sauquel Point," "Shoquel Point," and Soque Point" for the name.

Soque Point: see **Soquel Point** [SANTA CRUZ].

Soto Canyon [SAN LUIS OBISPO]: *canyon*, drained by a stream that flows 4 miles to Salinas River 3 miles east-southeast of Pozo (lat. 35°17'10" N, long. 120°19'20" W; near NW cor. sec. 25, T 30 S, R 15 E). Named on Pozo Summit (1967) 7.5' quadrangle.

Soto Spring [SAN LUIS OBISPO]: *spring*, 5 miles southwest of Branch Mountain along Branch Creek (lat. 35°08'20" N, long. 120°08'50" W). Named on Los Machos Hills (1967) 7.5' quadrangle.

Sotoville: see **Santa Rita** [MONTEREY].

South Campground [MONTEREY]: *locality*, 2.25 miles east-northeast of Pfeiffer Point (lat. 36°14'35" N, long. 121°46'30" W; sec. 31, T 19 S, R 2 E). Named on Pfeiffer Point (1956) 7.5' quadrangle.

South Chalone Peak [MONTEREY]: *peak*, 8.5 miles north-northeast of Greenfield (lat. 36°26'10" N, long. 121°11'05" W; sec. 23, T 17 S, R 7 E); the peak is 1 mile southeast of North Chalone Peak. Altitude 3269 feet. Named on North Chalone Peak (1969) 7.5' quadrangle. On Metz (1921) 15' quadrangle, South Chalone Peak and North Chalone Peak together have the name "Chalone Mtn."

Southeast Anchorage [SANTA BARBARA]: *embayment*, 3.5 miles northwest of East Point on the north side of Santa Rosa Island (lat. 33°58'50" N, long. 120°00'20" W). Named on Santa Rosa Island East (1943) 7.5' quadrangle.

South Fall Creek [SANTA CRUZ]: *stream*, flows 1.5 miles to Fall Creek 5 miles south-southeast of the town of Boulder Creek (lat. 37°03'25" N, long. 122°05'30" W; sec. 16, T 10 S, R 2 W). Named on Felton (1955) 7.5' quadrangle.

South Point [MONTEREY]: *promontory*, on the west side of Point Lobos between Pinnacle Cove and Headland Cove (lat. 36°31'20" N, long. 121°57'15" W). Named on Monterey (1947, photorevised 1968) 7.5' quadrangle.

South Point [SAN LUIS OBISPO]: *promontory,* 3.5 miles east-southeast of Avila Beach along the coast at Shell Beach (lat. 35°09'10" N, long. 120°40'25" W). Named on Pismo Beach (1965) 7.5' quadrangle

South Point [SANTA BARBARA]: *promontory,* at southernmost tip of Santa Rosa Island (lat. 33°53'40" N, long. 120°07' W). Named on Santa Rosa Island South (1943) 7.5' quadrangle.

South Ventana: see **South Ventana Cone** [MONTEREY].

South Ventana Cone [MONTEREY]: *peak,* 2.5 miles east-southeast of Ventana Cone (lat. 36°16'30" N, long. 121°38'10" W; on E line sec. 16, T 19 S, R 3 E). Altitude 4965 feet. Named on Ventana Cones (1956) 7.5' quadrangle. United States Board on Geographic Names (1962a, p. 16) rejected the name "South Ventana" for the peak.

Souza Rock [SAN LUIS OBISPO]: *shoal,* 3.25 miles south of Avila Beach in San Luis Obispo Bay (lat. 35°07'50" N, long. 120°44'15" W). Named on Pismo Beach (1965) 7.5' quadrangle.

Sozers Creek: see **Doud Creek** [MONTEREY].

Spanish Bay [MONTEREY]: *embayment,* 1.5 miles south-southwest of Point Pinos along the coast (lat. 36°37' N, long. 121°56'30" W). Named on Monterey (1947) 7.5' quadrangle.

Spanish Cabin Creek [SAN LUIS OBISPO]: *stream,* flows 2 miles to Burnett Creek 5.25 miles north-northeast of San Simeon (lat. 35° 42'55" N, long. 121°09'45" W). Named on San Simeon (1958) 7.5' quadrangle.

Spanish Flats [SAN BENITO]: *area,* 9.5 miles southeast of Bitterwater (lat. 36°18' N, long. 120°51'35" N; on S line sec. 2, T 19 S, R 10 E). Named on Hepsedam Peak (1969) 7.5' quadrangle.

Spence [MONTEREY]: *locality,* 7 miles southeast of Salinas along Southern Pacific Railroad (lat. 36°36'45" N, long. 121°34' W). Named on Chualar (1947) 7.5' quadrangle. Railroad officials named the station at the place in the 1870's for David Spence, owner of Encinal y Buena Esperanza grant, where the station is situated (Gudde, 1949, p. 340).

Split Oak Spring [SAN BENITO]: *spring,* 15 miles east-southeast of Bitterwater (lat. 36°17'10" N, long. 120°45'30" W; near S line sec. 10, T 19 S, R 11 E). Named on Hepsedam Peak (1969) 7.5' quadrangle.

Split Rock [SAN BENITO]: *relief feature,* 13 miles east-southeast of Bitterwater on the east side of Horsethief Canyon (2) (lat. 36°19'05" N, long. 120°46'05" W). Named on Hepsedam Peak (1969) 7.5' quadrangle.

Splitrock Canyon [MONTEREY]: *canyon,* drained by a stream that flows 4 miles to Sargent Canyon 10 miles west-southwest of Smith Mountain (lat. 36°00'20" N, long. 120°44'55" W; sec. 23, T 22 S, R 11 E).

Named on Slack Canyon (1969) 7.5' quadrangle.

Splitrock Spring [MONTEREY]: *spring,* 4.25 miles west-northwest of Smith Mountain (lat. 36°05'30" N, long. 120°40'05" W; sec. 22, T 21 S, R 12 E). Named on Slack Canyon (1969) 7.5' quadrangle.

Spoor Canyon [SANTA BARBARA]: *canyon,* drained by a stream that flows 5 miles to Kelly Canyon (1) 6 miles east of Miranda Pine Mountain (lat. 35°01' N, long. 119°56'15" W). Named on Bates Canyon (1964) and Taylor Canyon (1959) 7.5' quadrangles.

Sprague Camp [SAN LUIS OBISPO]: *locality,* 10 miles south of Shandon in Commatti (present Camatta) Canyon (lat. 35°31'10" N, long. 120°19'40" W). Named on Commatti Canyon (1943) 7.5' quadrangle.

Spreckels [MONTEREY]: *town,* 3 miles south of Salinas (lat. 36°37'25" N, long. 121°38'40" W). Named on Salinas (1947) and Spreckels (1947) 7.5' quadrangles. The name commemorates Claus Spreckels, who built a sugar refinery at the place in 1899 (Gudde, 1949, p. 341). Postal authorities established Spreckels post office in 1898 (Frickstad, p. 109).

Spreckels Junction [MONTEREY]: *locality,* in the southeast part of Salinas along Southern Pacific Railroad (lat. 36°39'30" N, long. 121°37'45" W); a rail line to Spreckels branches off at the place. Named on Salinas (1947) 7.5' quadrangle.

Spreckels Lagoon: see **Valencia Lagoon** [SANTA CRUZ].

Spring Canyon [MONTEREY]: *canyon,* drained by a stream that flows 4.5 miles to Sweetwater Canyon 6.25 miles north of San Lucas (lat. 36°13'15" N, long. 121°00'30" W; sec. 4, T 20 S, R 9 E). Named on Nattrass Valley (1967) 7.5' quadrangle.

Spring Canyon [SANTA BARBARA]: *canyon,* drained by a stream that flows 1.25 miles to lowlands along the coast 3.5 miles south of Surf (lat. 34°37'55" N, long. 120°37' W). Named on Surf (1959) and Tranquillon Mountain (1959) 7.5' quadrangles.

Spring Canyon: see **Little Spring Canyon** [SANTA BARBARA].

Spring Creek [SANTA CRUZ]: *stream,* flows 0.5 mile to San Lorenzo River 5 miles east-southeast of Big Basin (lat. 37°08'55" N, long. 122°08'10" W; sec. 13, T 9 S, R 3 W). Named on Big Basin (1955) 7.5' quadrangle.

Spring Creek: see **Aptos Creek** [SANTA CRUZ].

Spring Creek Gulch [SANTA CRUZ]: *canyon,* drained by a stream that flows 0.5 mile to San Lorenzo River near the south edge of the town of Boulder Creek (lat. 37°07' N, long. 122°06'50" W; near W line sec. 29, T 9 S, R 2 W). Named on Felton (1955) 7.5' quadrangle.

Springer: see **Betteravia Stockyards** [SANTA BARBARA].

Spring in Bush [MONTEREY]: *spring,* 8 miles

east of Parkfield (lat. 35°53'35" N, long. 120°17'20" W; near S line sec. 30, T 23 S, R 16 E). Named on The Dark Hole (1961) 7.5' quadrangle.

Springs: see **Sycamore Springs** [SAN LUIS OBISPO].

Springtown: see **Confederate Corners** [MONTEREY].

Spruce Creek [MONTEREY]: *stream*, flows 1 mile to the sea 2.25 miles southeast of Cape San Martin (lat. 35°52'05" N, long. 121° 26'20" W; near SW cor. sec. 4, T 24 S, R 5 E). Named on Villa Creek (1949) 7.5' quadrangle.

Square Black Rock [MONTEREY]: *rock*, 125 feet long, nearly 2 miles northwest of Gamboa Point, and 1000 feet offshore (lat. 36° 04'20" N, long. 121°36'35" W). Named on Lopez Point (1956) 7.5' quadrangle.

Square Corral Spring [SAN LUIS OBISPO]: *spring*, 10 miles north-northwest of Shandon in Mason Canyon (lat. 35°47' N, long. 120° 27'45" W; near E line sec. 4, T 25 S, R 14 E). Named on Cholame Hills (1961) 7.5' quadrangle.

Squaw Peak [MONTEREY]: *peak*, 16 miles east of San Lucas (lat. 36°03'30" N, long. 120°36'15" W; near E line sec. 13, T 21 S, R 13 E). Altitude 2924 feet. Named on Smith Mountain (1969) 7.5' quadrangle.

Squire Canyon [SAN LUIS OBISPO]: *canyon*, drained by a stream that flows 1.5 miles to the canyon of San Luis Obispo Creek 2.25 miles east-northeast of Avila Beach (lat. 35°11'35" N, long. 120° 41'35" W). Named on Pismo Beach (1965) 7.5' quadrangle.

Squire Ridge [SAN BENITO]: *ridge*, northwest-to west-northwest-trending, 2 miles long, 5.25 miles northeast of Bitterwater (lat. 36° 26' N, long. 120°55'50" W). Named on Rock Spring Peak (1969) 7.5' quadrangle.

Squirrel Spring [MONTEREY]: *spring*, 13 miles east-northeast of Cape San Martin (lat. 35°58'25" N, long. 121°15'30" W). Named on Cape San Martin (1921) 15' quadrangle.

Stag Canyon [SANTA BARBARA]: *canyon*, drained by a stream that flows 3.25 miles to Roque Canyon 5.25 miles north-northeast of Manzanita Mountain (lat. 34°57'55" N, long. 120°02'45" W). Named on Manzanita Mountain (1964) 7.5' quadrangle.

Stanley Mountain [SAN LUIS OBISPO]: *peak*, 6 miles east-northeast of Huasna Peak (lat. 35°04'25" N, long. 120°15' W; sec. 33, T 12 N, R 32 W). Altitude 2490 feet. Named on Chimney Canyon (1967) and Huasna Peak (1967) 7.5' quadrangles.

Star Flat [MONTEREY-SAN BENITO]: *area*, 4.5 miles southeast of North Chalone Peak on Monterey-San Benito county line (lat. 36° 23'55" N, long. 121°08' W). Named on North Chalone Peak (1969) 7.5' quadrangle.

Starkey: see **Shandon** [SAN LUIS OBISPO].

Steele [SAN LUIS OBISPO]: *locality*, 1 mile north-northwest of Edna along the railroad (lat. 35°12'50" N, long. 120°37' W). Named

on Arroyo Grande (1897, reprinted 1903) 15' quadrangle. Called Steeles on California Mining Bureau's (1917c) map.

Steer Creek [SANTA BARBARA]: *stream*, flows 4 miles to join El Dorado Creek and form Gobernador Creek 3.5 miles north of Rincon Point (lat. 34°25'30" N, long. 119°28'25" W; sec. 14, T 4 N, R 25 E). Named on White Ledge Peak (1952) 7.5' quadrangle.

Steinbach Canyon: see **Steinback Canyon** [SAN BENITO].

Steinback Canyon [SAN BENITO]: *canyon*, drained by a stream that flows 1.5 miles to San Juan Canyon 6.5 miles southwest of Hollister (lat. 36°48'05" N, long. 121°29'50" W). Named on Hollister (1955) 7.5' quadrangle. Called Steinbach Canyon on San Juan Bautista (1955) 7.5' quadrangle. United States Board on Geographic Names (1994, p. 5) approved the name "Steinbeck Canyon" for the feature, and rejected the forms "Steinbach Canyon" and "Steinback Canyon" for the name.

Steiner Creek [SAN LUIS OBISPO]: *stream*, flows 8 miles to San Simeon Creek 3.25 miles north of Cambria (lat. 35°36'35" N, long. 121°04'20" W). Named on Cambria (1959) and Cypress Mountain (1948) 7.5' quadrangles.

Stenner Creek [SAN LUIS OBISPO]: *stream*, flows nearly 7.25 miles to San Luis Obispo Creek 0.5 mile west-southwest of downtown San Luis Obispo (lat. 35°16'35" N, long. 120°40'05" W; sec. 34, T 30 S, R 12 E). Named on San Luis Obispo (1965) 7.5' quadrangle.

Stephani: see **Camp Stephani** [MONTEREY].

Stephens Canyon [SAN LUIS OBISPO]: *canyon*, drained by a stream that flows 5.5 miles to Carrie Creek 4 miles north of Huasna Peak (lat. 35°05'40" N, long. 120°20'05" W; sec. 35, T 32 S, R 15 E). Named on Huasna Peak (1967) 7.5' quadrangle. Called Rocky Canyon on Nipomo (1922) 15' quadrangle, but United States Board on Geographic Names (1963b, p. 15) rejected this name.

Steve Creek [MONTEREY]: *stream*, flows 3 miles to Salmon Creek 8 miles south-southwest of Jolon (lat. 35°50'40" N, long. 121°11'55" W; sec. 15, T 24 S, R 7 E). Named on Burnett Peak (1949) 7.5' quadrangle. The stream first was called Cobblestone Creek; Serafin Steve patented land near the creek in 1886 (Clark, 1991, p. 544).

Stillwater Cove [MONTEREY]: *embayment*, west of Arrowhead Point on the north side of Carmel Bay (lat. 36°33'55" N, long. 121°56'30" W). Named on Monterey (1947) 7.5' quadrangle.

Stockdale Mountain [MONTEREY]: *peak*, 15 miles northeast of Bradley (lat. 35°59'15" N, long. 120°34'50" W; near W line sec. 28, T 22 S, R 13 E). Altitude 2593 feet. Named on Stockdale Mountain (1948) 7.5' quadrangle. The name is for a member of the Stockdale family, early residents of Cholame Valley (Clark, 1991, p. 545).

Stockton [MONTEREY]: see **Fort Stockton**, under **Presidio of Monterey** [MONTEREY].

Stone Canyon [MONTEREY]:

(1) *canyon*, 5 miles long, 5 miles south-southeast of Smith Mountain along upper reaches of Big Sandy Creek (lat. 36°01' N, long. 120°33' W). Named on Smith Mountain (1969) 7.5' quadrangle. Fairbanks (1894, p. 520) used the name "Stone's Cañon." F.M. Stone discovered coal at the place in 1870, and a coal mine operated there intermittently until 1935; a railroad built along Big Sandy Creek reached the mine in 1907 (Mosier, p. 7).

(2) *locality*, at the end of the rail line to the coal mine in Stone Canyon (1) (lat. 36°00'50" N, long. 120°32'30" W; sec. 14, T 22 S, R 13 E). Named on Priest Valley (1915) 30' quadrangle, where the name has the form "Stone Canon." Postal authorities established Stone Canon post office in 1900 and discontinued it in 1932 (Frickstad, p. 109).

Stone Canyon [SAN BENITO]: *canyon*, drained by Stone Creek, which flows 10 miles to San Benito River 6.5 miles southwest of Cherry Peak (lat. 36°38'20" N, long. 121°14'10" W; near SE cor. sec. 7, T 15 S, R 7 E). Named on Cherry Peak (1968) and Paicines (1968) 7.5' quadrangles, where the name may apply only to the part of the canyon along lower reaches of Stone Creek.

Stone Corral Canyon [MONTEREY-SAN LUIS OBISPO]: *canyon*, nearly 2 miles long, on Monterey-San Luis Obispo county line; opens into Cholame Valley 11 miles southeast of Parkfield (lat. 35° 47' N, long. 120°17'35" W). Named on Cholame Valley (1961) 7.5' quadrangle.

Stone Corral Flats [MONTEREY]: *area*, 10.5 miles southeast of Parkfield (lat. 35°48'30" N, long. 120°16'30" W). Named on Cholame Valley (1961) 7.5' quadrangle.

Stone Creek [SAN BENITO]: *stream*, flows 10 miles to San Benito River 6.5 miles southwest of Cherry Peak (lat. 36°38'20" N, long. 121°14'10" W; near SE cor. sec. 7, T 15 S, R 7 E). Named on Mount Johnson (1968) and Paicines (1968) 7.5' quadrangles.

Stonewall Canyon [MONTEREY]: *canyon*, 6 miles long, opens into lowlands 2 miles east-northeast of Soledad (lat. 36°26'25" N, long. 121°30' W; sec. 23, T 17 S, R 6 E). Named on North Chalone Peak (1969) and Soledad (1955) 7.5' quadrangles. The name is from the steep rocky sides of the canyon (Gudde, 1949, p. 344).

Stonewall Creek [MONTEREY]: *stream*, flows 8.5 miles to Salinas River 1.5 miles southeast of Soledad (lat. 36°24'30" N, long. 121° 18'20" W); the stream drains Stonewall Canyon. Named on Soledad (1955) 7.5' quadrangle.

Stony Creek [MONTEREY]: *stream*, flows 11 miles to Nacimiento River 11 miles east-northeast of Cape San Martin (lat. 35°55'40" N, long. 121°16'35" W). Named on Alder Peak (1949) and Bear Canyon (1949) 7.5' quadrangles. The stream is identified as Arroyo de las Piedras on a diseño of San Miguelito de Trinidad grant made in 1841 (Becker, 1964; Becker noted the alternate name "Piedra Creek" for the stream).

Stony Creek [SAN LUIS OBISPO]: *stream*, flows 10 miles to join Trout Creek (2) and form Huasna River 13 miles northeast of the town of Nipomo (lat. 35°12'05" N, long. 120°21' W; sec. 27, T 31 S, R 15 E). Named on Caldwell Mesa (1967) and Los Machos Hills (1967) 7.5' quadrangles.

Stony Creek Campground [SAN LUIS OBISPO]: *locality*, 17 miles northeast of the town of Nipomo (lat. 35°12'35" N, long. 120°15'30" W); the place is along Stony Creek. Named on Caldwell Mesa (1967) 7.5' quadrangle.

Stony Valley [MONTEREY]: *valley*, 11.5 miles east-northeast of Cape San Martin (lat. 35°59' N, long. 121°18' W); Stony Creek drains the valley. Named on Alder Peak (1949) 7.5' quadrangle. The place is identified as Cañon de las Piedras on a diseño of San Miguelito de Trinidad grant made in 1841 (Becker, 1964). Cozzens and Davies' (1927) map has the name "Robla Valley" along Nacimiento River for the first valley southwest of Stony Valley. Smith (p. 63) mentioned a feature called Roblar Valley located along Nacimiento River;

Stovall Canyon [SANTA BARBARA]: *canyon*, drained by a stream that flows 2 miles to Schoolhouse Canyon (1) 4.5 miles northwest of McPherson Peak (lat. 34°56'25" N, long. 119°52' W). Named on Peak Mountain (1964) 7.5' quadrangle.

Strawberry Camp [MONTEREY]: *locality*, 3.5 miles southwest of Tassajara Hot Springs (lat. 36°12'15" N, long. 121°36'05" W; sec. 11, T 20 S, R 3 E); the place is in Strawberry Valley, and Clark (1991, p. 548) called it Strawberry Valley Camp. Named on Tassajara Hot Springs (1956) 7.5' quadrangle.

Strawberry Canyon [MONTEREY]: *canyon*, drained by a stream that flows 2.5 miles to marsh along Elkhorn Slough 5 miles northwest of Prunedale (lat. 36°49'45" N, long. 121°44' W). Named on Prunedale (1954) 7.5' quadrangle.

Strawberry Peak: see **Madulce Peak** [SANTA BARBARA].

Strawberry Valley [MONTEREY]: *canyon*, 1 mile long, drained by Zigzag Creek above the confluence of Zigzag Creek and Tan Oak Creek nearly 4 miles southwest of Tassajara Hot Springs (lat. 36° 11'45" N, long. 121°35'55" W; near E line sec. 14, T 20 S, R 3 E). Named on Tassajara Hot Springs (1956) 7.5' quadrangle.

Strawberry Valley Camp: see **Strawberry**

Camp [MONTEREY].

Struve Slough [SANTA CRUZ]: *stream,* flows nearly 3 miles, mainly in an artificial watercourse, to Watsonville Slough 2 miles southwest of Watsonville (lat. 36°54' N, long. 121°47' W). Named on Watsonville West (1954) 7.5' quadrangle. The name is for Hans Christian Struve, a Danish farmer who came to California in 1855 (Clark, 1986, p. 356). West Branch enters from the north-northwest 0.5 mile above the mouth of the main stream; it is 2 miles long, is partly in an artificial watercourse, and is named on Watsonville West (1954) 7.5' quadrangle.

Stuart: see **Lompoc** [SANTA BARBARA] (2).

Stuke Canyon [SANTA BARBARA]: *canyon,* drained by a stream that flows 3.5 miles to Santa Cruz Creek 8 miles northeast of Santa Ynez Mountain (lat. 34°37' N, long. 119°52'40" W). Named on Figueroa Mountain (1959), Lake Cachuma (1959), and San Rafael Mountain (1959) 7.5' quadrangles.

Sudden [SANTA BARBARA]: *locality,* 3.25 miles south-southeast of Tranquillon Mountain along Southern Pacific Railroad (lat. 34°32'25" N, long. 120°32'20" W); the place is near the mouth of Sudden Canyon. Named on Tranquillon Mountain (1959) 7.5' quadrangle. Postal authorities established Sudden post office in 1901, discontinued it for a time in 1908, and discontinued it finally in 1914 (Frickstad, p. 172). The name commemorates Robert Sudden, a ship's master who came to California in 1850 and later owned property at the site (Hanna, p. 319).

Sudden Canyon [SANTA BARBARA]: *canyon,* drained by a stream that flows 1.25 miles to the sea 3 miles south-southeast of Tranquillon Mountain (lat. 34°32'25" N, long. 120°32'35" W). Named on Tranquillon Mountain (1959) 7.5' quadrangle.

Sudden Flats [SANTA BARBARA]: *area,* 2 miles south-southwest of Tranquillon Mountain along the coast (lat. 34°33' N, long. 120°34'45" W); the place is 2.5 miles westnorthwest of the mouth of Sudden Canyon. Named on Tranquillon Mountain (1959) 7.5' quadrangle.

Sudden Peak [SANTA BARBARA]: *peak,* 3.5 miles east-southeast of Tranquillon Mountain (lat. 34°33'55" N, long. 120°30' W); the peak is 3 miles northeast of the mouth of Sudden Canyon. Altitude 2122 feet. Named on Lompoc Hills (1959) and Tranquillon Mountain (1959) 7.5' quadrangles.

Suey [SAN LUIS OBISPO-SANTA BARBARA]: *land grant,* mainly east of Santa Maria along Cuyama River on San Luis Obispo-Santa Barbara county line. Named on Chimney Canyon (1967), Huasna Peak (1967), Nipomo (1965), Santa Maria (1959), Tepusquet Canyon (1964), and Twitchell Dam (1959) 7.5' quadrangles. Ramona Carrillo received the land in 1837; Ramona Carrillo de Wilson claimed 48,834 acres patented in 1865

(Cowan, p. 100). Postal authorities established Suey post office on the grant at the ranch headquarters in 1870 and discontinued it in 1875; the post office was in Santa Barbara County until a county-line change in 1872 placed it in San Luis Obispo County (Salley, p. 214).

Suey [SANTA BARBARA]: *locality,* 1.25 mile east-southeast of downtown Santa Maria along Santa Maria Valley Railroad (lat. 34° 56'45" N, long. 120°24'45" W); the place is near the boundary of Suey grant. Named on Santa Maria (1959) 7.5' quadrangle.

Suey: see **Santa Maria** [SANTA BARBARA].

Suey Canyon [SANTA BARBARA]: *canyon,* drained by a stream that flows 4 miles to Tepusquet Canyon 3.5 miles northwest of Tepusquet Peak (lat. 34°56'40" N, long. 120°13'40" W); the canyon is on Suey grant. Named on Tepusquet Canyon (1964) 7.5' quadrangle.

Suey Creek [SAN LUIS OBISPO]: *stream,* flows 9.5 miles to Santa Maria River 6.5 miles southeast of the town of Nipomo (lat. 34°58'15" N, long. 120°24' W); the stream is on Suey grant. Named on Huasna Peak (1967), Nipomo (1965), Santa Maria (1959), and Twitchell Dam (1959) 7.5' quadrangles.

Suey Junction: see **Santa Maria** [SANTA BARBARA].

Sugarloaf [MONTEREY]: *peak,* about 11 miles west-southwest of Soledad (lat. 36°21'05" N, long. 121°31'15" W; near W line sec. 23, T 18 S, R 4 E). Altitude 2706 feet. Named on Chews Ridge (1956) 7.5' quadrangle.

Sugarloaf [SAN BENITO]: *peak,* 8 miles northwest of Panoche Pass (lat. 36°42'35" N, long. 121°07' W). Altitude 2840 feet. Named on Panoche Pass (1968) 7.5' quadrangle. This may be the feature called Cerro del Venado on California Mining Bureau's (1917b) map.

Sugarloaf Mountain [SANTA CRUZ]: *peak,* 5.5 miles north-northeast of Soquel (lat. 37°03'55" N, long. 121°55'55" W). Altitude 1268 feet. Named on Laurel (1955) 7.5' quadrangle. The feature formerly was called San Francisco Mountain (Clark, 1986, p. 310).

Sugarloaf Peak [MONTEREY]: *hill,* 7.5 miles north-northeast of Salinas (lat. 36°46'05" N, long. 121°35'40" W). Altitude 954 feet. Named on San Juan Bautista (1955) 7.5' quadrangle.

Sugar Tail Spring [MONTEREY]: *spring,* 9.5 miles east of Parkfield (lat. 35°53'20" N, long. 120°15'35" W; sec. 32, T 23 S, R 16 E). Named on The Dark Hole (1961) 7.5' quadrangle.

Sullivan Canyon [MONTEREY]: *canyon,* drained by a stream that flows nearly 3 miles to lowlands 4.5 miles east of Gonzales (lat. 36°30'55" N, long. 121°21'30" W; sec. 30, T 16 S, R 6 E). Named on Mount Johnson (1968) 7.5' quadrangle. Daniel Sullivan patented land in the lower part of the canyon in 1889 (Clark, 1991, p. 549).

Sulphur Canyon [MONTEREY-SAN LUIS OBISPO]: *canyon,* drained by a stream that heads in San Luis Obispo County and flows 2.5 miles to San Antonio River 6.25 miles southwest of Bradley in Monterey County (lat. 35°47'40" N, long. 120°52'20" W; sec. 34, T 24 S, R 10 E). Named on Bradley (1949) and Tierra Redonda Mountain (1949) 7.5' quadrangles.

Sulphur Canyon [SAN BENITO]:
(1) *canyon,* drained by a stream that flows nearly 4 miles to San Benito River 3 miles west-northwest of Paicines (lat. 36°44'30" N, long. 121°19'40" W; sec. 5, T 14 S, R 6 E). Named on Paicines (1968) 7.5' quadrangle.
(2) *canyon,* 2.25 miles long, 11 miles east-southeast of Bitterwater along Laguna Creek (lat. 36°19'30" N, long. 120°49'15" W). Named on Hepsedam Peak (1969) 7.5' quadrangle.

Sulphur Canyon [SAN LUIS OBISPO]: *canyon,* drained by a stream that flows 5.5 miles to Cuyama Valley 3.5 miles northwest of New Cuyama [SANTA BARBARA] (lat. 34°58'45" N, long. 119°43'55" W; sec. 2, T 10 N, R 27 W); Sulphur Spring (3) is in the canyon. Named on New Cuyama (1964) 7.5' quadrangle.

Sulphur Creek [SAN BENITO]:
(1) *stream,* flows 3 miles to San Benito River 5.5 miles north-northwest of San Benito (lat. 36°34'25" N, long. 121°07'55" W; sec. 5, T 16 S, R 8 E). Named on Bickmore Canyon (1968) and San Benito (1968) 7.5' quadrangles.
(2) *stream,* heads in Santa Clara County and flows nearly 3 miles to Arroyo de las Vibaoras 8 miles north-northeast of Hollister (lat. 36°57'20" N, long. 121°20'25" W). Named on Three Sisters (1954) 7.5' quadrangle.

Sulphur Creek [SANTA BARBARA]: *stream,* flows 1 mile to Dry Creek (1) 2.25 miles northeast of Zaca Lake (lat. 34°48'05" N, long. 120°00'30" W); the stream heads near Sulphur Spring (2). Named on Zaca Lake (1964) 7.5' quadrangle.

Sulphuritos Creek [SAN BENITO]: *stream,* flows nearly 4 miles to Tres Pinos Creek 3.5 miles northwest of Panoche Pass (lat. 36°39'20" N, long. 121°03'50" W; sec. 2, T 15 S, R 8 E). Named on Panoche Pass (1968) 7.5' quadrangle.

Sulphur Pots [SAN LUIS OBISPO]: *springs,* 1.5 miles east-southeast of Lopez Mountain in Lopez Canyon (lat. 35°17'40" N, long. 120°33'10" W; near S line sec. 23, T 30 S, R 13 E). Named on Lopez Mountain (1965) 7.5' quadrangle.

Sulphur Spring [MONTEREY]:
(1) *spring,* 2.5 miles east of Uncle Sam Mountain (lat. 36°20'50" N, long. 121°39'35" W; sec. 21, T 18 S, R 3 E). Named on Jamesburg (1939) 15' quadrangle.
(2) *spring,* 0.5 mile north-northwest of Smith Mountain (lat. 36°05'15" N, long. 120°36' W;

sec. 20, T 21 S, R 13 E). Named on Smith Mountain (1969) 7.5' quadrangle.

Sulphur Spring [SAN BENITO]:
(1) *spring,* 6.5 miles east-southeast of Bitterwater (lat. 36°20'50" N, long. 120°53'20" W; sec. 21, T 18 S, R 10 E). Named on Lonoak (1969) 7.5' quadrangle.
(2) *spring,* 14 miles east-southeast of Bitterwater (lat. 36°17'50" N, long. 120°46'20" W; near N line sec. 9, T 19 S, R 11 E). Named on Hepsedam Peak (1969) 7.5' quadrangle.

Sulphur Spring [SAN LUIS OBISPO]:
(1) *spring,* 3.5 miles south-southeast of Paso Robles (lat. 35°34'55" N, long. 120°39'50" W). Named on Templeton (1948) 7.5' quadrangle. Berkstresser (p. A-15) identified this feature as Santa Ysabel Springs—it is on Santa Ysabel grant. According to Winslow Anderson (p. 235), Santa Ysabel Spring was used by Indians and Spaniards, who came from afar to seek cures by drinking the water and bathing in it. A resort was started at the spring in the late 1880's, but by 1908 there was only a small private bathhouse (Waring, G.A., p. 76).
(2) *spring,* 2.5 miles east-southeast of Branch Mountain (lat. 35°10'25" N, long. 120°02'30" W). Named on Branch Mountain (1967) 7.5' quadrangle.
(3) *spring,* 4.5 miles northwest of New Cuyama [SANTA BARBARA] (lat. 34°59'50" N, long. 119°44' W; sec. 35, T 11 N, R 27 W); the spring is in Sulphur Canyon. Named on New Cuyama (1964) 7.5' quadrangle.
(4) *spring,* 4.5 miles north-northwest of Caliente Mountain (lat. 35°05'40" N, long. 119°47'10" W; sec. 36, T 32 S, R 20 E). Named on Caliente Mountain (1959) 7.5' quadrangle. On Caliente Mountain (1941) 15' quadrangle, the name applies to a spring located 0.5 mile farther northwest.

Sulphur Spring [SANTA BARBARA]:
(1) *spring,* 6 miles south of the city of Lompoc along Espada Creek (lat. 34°33'10" N, long. 120°28'35" W). Named on Lompoc Hills (1959) 7.5' quadrangle.
(2) *spring,* 1.5 miles east-northeast of Zaca Lake (lat. 34°47'10" N, long. 120°00'40" W); the spring is near the head of Sulphur Creek. Named on Zaca Lake (1964) 7.5' quadrangle.
(3) *spring,* 4 miles east-southeast of Salisbury Potrero (lat. 34° 48' N, long. 119°38' W); the spring is in Sulphur Spring Canyon (1). Named on Salisbury Potrero (1964) 7.5' quadrangle.

Sulphur Spring: see **Little Sulphur Spring** [SANTA BARBARA]; **Sulphur Spring Canyon** [MONTEREY].

Sulphur Spring Canyon [MONTEREY]: *canyon,* drained by a stream that flows 6.5 miles to lowlands 4.5 miles northwest of Jolon (lat. 36°00'30" N, long. 121°14'25" W). Named on Cosio Knob (1949) 7.5' quadrangle. According to Berkstresser (p. A-9), a spring called Sulphur Spring is located less than 3 miles above the mouth of Sulphur Spring Canyon (lat. 36°02'28" long. 121°13'15" W).

Sulphur Spring Canyon [SANTA BARBARA]: (1) *canyon,* drained by a stream that flows 5 miles to Salisbury Canyon 2 miles east-north-east of Salisbury Potrero (lat. 34°49'40" N, long. 119°40' W); Sulphur Spring (3) is in the canyon. Named on Salisbury Potrero (1964) 7.5' quadrangle.

(2) *canyon,* drained by a stream that flows 4.5 miles to Manzana Creek 4.25 miles south-southeast of Bald Mountain (1) (lat. 34°45'30" N, long. 119°53'40" W). Named on Bald Mountain (1964) and Hurricane Deck (1964) 7.5' quadrangles.

Sulphur Springs [MONTEREY]: *spring,* 7 miles north-northwest of Parkfield (lat. 35°59'45" N, long. 120°28'40" W; sec. 20, T 22 S, R 14 E). Named on Parkfield (1961) 7.5' quadrangle.

Sulphur Springs [SAN BENITO]: *springs,* 6 miles south of Bitterwater near San Lorenzo Creek (lat. 36°17'40" N, long. 120°59'05" W; sec. 10, T 19 S, R 9 E). Named on Lonoak (1969) 7.5' quadrangle.

Sulphur Springs [SANTA CRUZ]: *spring,* 8 miles north-northeast of Soquel (lat. 37°05'10" N, long. 121°53'20" W). Named on Laurel (1955) 7.5' quadrangle. On Los Gatos (1919) 15' quadrangle, the name has the singular form "Sulphur Spring."

Sulphur Springs: see **Willow Spring** [MONTEREY] (3).

Sulphur Springs Camp [MONTEREY]: *locality,* 2.5 miles east of Uncle Sam Mountain (lat. 36°20'50" N, long. 121°39'35" W; sec. 21, T 18 S, R 3 E). Named on Ventana Cones (1956) 7.5' quadrangle. Jamesburg (1939) 15' quadrangle shows Sulphur Spring (1) at the place.

Summerland [SANTA BARBARA]: *town,* 5 miles west-northwest of Carpinteria (lat. 34°25'20" N, long. 119°35'45" W). Named on Carpinteria (1952) 7.5' quadrangle. Postal authorities established Summerland post office in 1889 (Frickstad, p. 172).

Summit [SAN LUIS OBISPO]: *locality,* 3 miles northwest of the town of Nipomo along Pacific Coast Railroad (lat. 35°04'05" N, long. 120°30'40" W). Named on Arroyo Grande (1897) 15' quadrangle. Arroyo Grande (1952) 15' quadrangle has the name "Summit" at the place, although it does not show the railroad.

Summit: see **Rincon** [SANTA CRUZ].

Summit Canyon [SAN LUIS OBISPO]: *canyon,* 3.5 miles long, 5 miles north-northeast of York Mountain (lat. 35°36'45" N, long. 120°48'10" W). Named on York Mountain (1948) 7.5' quadrangle.

Summit Creek [SAN LUIS OBISPO]: *stream,* flows 5.25 miles to a branch of Jack Creek nearly 3 miles north of York Mountain (lat. 35°35'10" N, long. 120°49'55" W); the stream drains Summit Canyon. Named on Adelaida (1948) and York Mountain (1948) 7.5' quadrangles.

Sunium Point: see **Arrowhead Point** [MONTEREY].

Sunset: see **Shandon** [SAN LUIS OBISPO].

Sunset Point [MONTEREY]: *promontory,* nearly 1 mile south-southeast of Cypress Point along the coast (lat. 36°34'10" N, long. 121°58'10" W). Named on Monterey (1947) 7.5' quadrangle. Called Pt. Douty on Monterey (1913) 15' quadrangle, but United States Board on Geographic Names (1936a, p. 23) rejected this name for the feature.

Sunset Valley [SANTA BARBARA]: *valley,* 4 miles south of Bald Mountain (1) (lat. 34°45'10" N, long. 119°56' W). Named on Bald Mountain (1964) and Figueroa Mountain (1959) 7.5' quadrangles. McPherson Peak (1943) 15' quadrangle shows the feature located about 1.5 miles farther east along Fish Creek.

Sur: see **Mill Creek** [MONTEREY] (1); **Point Sur** [MONTEREY].

Sur Breakers [MONTEREY]: *shoal,* 1.25 miles south-southeast of Point Sur and less than 1 mile offshore (lat. 36°17'20" N, long. 121°53'20" W). Named on Point Sur (1956) 7.5' quadrangle.

Sur Chiquito: see **San Jose y Sur Chiquuito** [MONREREY].

Surf [SANTA BARBARA]: *locality,* 9 miles west-northwest of the city of Lompoc along Southern Pacific Railroad near the coast (lat. 34°41'05" N, long. 120°36'10" W). Named on Surf (1959) 7.5' quadrangle. Postal authorities established Surf post office in 1897 and discontinued it in 1957 (Salley, p. 216). The place first was called Lompoc Junction (Hanna, p. 320). Crespi, while with the Portola expedition in 1769, gave the name "Cañada de Santa Rosalia" to a dry creek just south of present Surf, and soldiers of the expedition called the same feature Cañada Seca (Wagner, H.R., p. 513, 515). The beach at Surf has been called Lompoc Beach (Diller and others, p. 111). California Division of Highways' (1934) map shows a place called Ajax located 1.5 miles north-northeast of Surf along Southern Pacific Railroad.

Sur River: see **Big Sur River** [MONTEREY]; **Little Sur River** [MONTEREY].

Sur Rock [MONTEREY]: *rock,* less than 2 miles south-southwest of Point Sur, and 4500 feet offshore (lat. 36°16'55" N, long. 121°53'15" W). Named on Point Sur (1956) 7.5' quadrangle. Point Sur (1925) 15' quadrangle shows the feature located much closer to shore.

Susie Spring [MONTEREY]: *spring,* 16 miles east-northeast of King City near Lewis Creek (lat. 36°17'15" N, long. 120°51'30" W; sec. 11, T 19 S, R 10 E). Named on Hepsedam Peak (1969) 7.5' quadrangle.

Sutil Island [SANTA BARBARA]: *island,* 1250 feet long, 1900 feet off the southwest end of Santa Barbara Island (lat. 33°27'50" N, long. 119°02'50" W). Named on United States Geological Survey's (1973) map. United States

Board on Geographic Names (1939, p. 34) rejected the name "Gull Island" for the feature, and noted that the name "Sutil" is for one of Vizcaino's ships.

Sutton Canyon [SANTA BARBARA]: *canyon,* drained by a stream that flows 3.5 miles to Carpinteria Creek 4 miles north-northwest of Rincon Point (lat. 34°25'45" N, long. 119°29'25" W; sec. 15, T 4 N, R 25 W). Named on Carpinteria (1952) and White Ledge Peak (1952) 7.5' quadrangles.

Swain's Canyon: see **Swain Valley** [MONTEREY].

Swain Valley [MONTEREY]: *canyon,* 3.25 miles long, opens into lowlands 3 miles northwest of Bradley (lat. 35°53'30" N, long. 120°50'30" W; near N line sec. 36, T 23 S, R 10 E). Named on Hames Valley (1949) and Wunpost (1949) 7.5' quadrangles. English (p. 237) referred to Swains Canyon, and Kew (1920, p. 104) mentioned Swain's Canyon. Charles Swain and George H. Swain took up land at the place in 1891 (Clark, 1991, p. 552-553).

Swallow Rock [SAN LUIS OBISPO]: *peak,* 3 miles south-southeast of Cambria (near lat. 35°31'25" N, long. 121°03'45" W). Named on San Simeon (1919) 15' quadrangle, where the exact location is uncertain.

Swamp Creek [MONTEREY]: *stream,* flows nearly 2 miles through a series of lakes to Gabilan Creek 16 miles north of Gonzales (lat. 36°44'20" N, long. 121°28'25" W). Named on Mount Harlan (1968) 7.5' quadrangle.

Swan Lake: see **Schwans Lagoon** [SANTA CRUZ].

Swanson Bluff [SAN BENITO]: *escarpment,* northwest-trending, 3.25 miles long, 9 miles southeast of Hollister on the southwest side of Tres Pinos Creek (lat. 36°45' N, long. 121°18' W). Named on Paicines (1968) and Tres Pinos (1955) 7.5' quadrangles.

Swanton [SANTA CRUZ]: *locality,* 4 miles north-northwest of Davenport along Scott Creek (lat. 37°03'50" N, long. 122°13'35" W). Named on Davenport (1955) 7.5' quadrangle. Postal authorities established Swanton post office in 1897 and discontinued it in 1930 (Frickstad, p. 177). The name commemorates one of the builders of a power house on Big Creek; the place earlier was the site of a stage station called Laurel Grove (Hoover, Rensch, and Rensch, p. 473). Ingalls Station was a stage stop located along Scott Creek near the mouth of Big Creek in what later became Swanton; the name was for Nathan P. Ingalls, who took over Santa Cruz-Pescadero stage line in 1874 (Clark, 1986, p. 164-165). Hamman's (1980c) map shows a place called Folger Wye located along the railroad 1.25 miles south of Swanton. J.R. Wagner (p. 61) mentioned a small settlement called Folger, situated near Swanton, that served as a center for the lumber industry. The name "Folger" was for J.A. Folger, a San Francisco coffee

merchant and first vice-president of Ocean Shore Railroad (Clark, 1986, p. 121). Hamman's (1980c) map also shows a place called San Vicente Junction located along the railroad just south of Swanton, where a rail line of San Vicente Lumber Company starts up Little Creek.

Sweetwater Canyon [MONTEREY]: *canyon,* 10 miles long, opens into lowlands 2.5 miles east-northeast of King City (lat. 36°13' N, long. 121°04'35" W). Named on Nattrass Valley (1967) and San Lucas (1949) 7.5' quadrangles.

Sweetwater Canyon [SANTA BARBARA]: *canyon,* drained by a stream that flows 6.5 miles to Sisquoc River 5 miles south-southwest of Montgomery Potrero (lat. 34°46'05" N, long. 119°46'55" W). Named on Hurricane Deck (1964) and Salisbury Potrero (1964) 7.5' quadrangles.

Sweetwater Creek [MONTEREY]: *stream,* flows 5.5 miles to Arroyo Seco (1) 7.5 miles west-southwest of Greenfield (lat. 36°15'45" N, long. 121°21'15" W; sec. 19, T 19 S, R 6 E). Named on Paraiso Springs (1956) and Reliz Canyon (1949) 7.5' quadrangles.

Sweetwater Creek [SANTA BARBARA]: *stream,* flows 1 mile to Lake Cachuma 3.5 miles north of Santa Ynez Peak (lat. 34°34'40" N, long. 119°58'20" W). Named on Lake Cachuma (1959) 7.5' quadrangle.

Sweetwater Spring [SAN BENITO]: *spring,* 8.5 miles east-southeast of Bitterwater (lat. 36°21'15" N, long. 120°54'05" W; near NE cor. sec. 23, T 18 S, R 10 E). Named on Hepsedam Peak (1969) 7.5' quadrangle.

Swiss Canyon [MONTEREY]:
(1) *canyon,* drained by a stream that flows nearly 2 miles to marsh along Elkhorn Slough 5 miles northwest of Salinas (lat. 36°49'45" N, long. 121°43'40" W). Named on Prunedale (1954) 7.5' quadrangle.
(2) *canyon,* drained by a stream that flows nearly 2 miles to the sea 2.25 miles southeast of Point Sur (lat. 36°17'10" N, long. 121° 52' W). Named on Big Sur (1956) 7.5' quadrangle.

Swope Canyon [MONTEREY]: *canyon,* drained by a stream that flows 2 miles to Chualar Canyon 9.5 miles north-northeast of Gonzales (lat. 36°37'50" N, long. 121°21'35" W; sec. 18, T 15 S, R 6 E). Named on Paicines (1968) 7.5' quadrangle.

Sycamore Beach: see **Pfeiffer Beach** [MONTEREY].

Sycamore Campground [SANTA BARBARA]: *locality,* 3.5 miles west-southwest of Montgomery Potrero along Sisquoc River (lat. 34°48'30" N, long. 119°48'15" W). Named on Hurricane Deck (1964) 7.5' quadrangle.

Sycamore Canyon [MONTEREY]: *canyon,* drained by a stream that flows 2 miles to the sea just north of Pfeiffer Point (lat. 36°14'15" N, long. 121°48'50" W; sec. 35, T 19 S, R 1 E). Named on Pfeiffer Point (1956) 7.5' quadrangle.

Sycamore Canyon [SAN LUIS OBISPO]:
(1) *canyon*, drained by a stream that flows 1.25 miles to Toro Creek 9 miles north-northeast of the mouth of Morro Creek (lat. 35°28'55" N, long. 120°47'05" W). Named on Morro Bay North (1965) 7.5' quadrangle.
(2) *canyon*, drained by a stream that flows 2.5 miles to Los Osos Valley 3 miles west of San Luis Obispo (lat. 35°16'25" N, long. 120°42'55" W). Named on San Luis Obispo (1965) 7.5' quadrangle.
(3) *canyon*, 1 mile long, opens into Miller Flat 4 miles north of Lopez Mountain (lat. 35°21'45" N, long. 120°35'10" W). Named on Lopez Mountain (1965) 7.5' quadrangle.
(4) *canyon*, drained by a stream that flows 2 miles to Los Berros Canyon nearly 4 miles north of the town of Nipomo (lat. 35°05'50" N, long. 120°28'20" W; sec. 33, T 32 S, R 14 E). Named on Nipomo (1965) 7.5' quadrangle.
(5) *canyon*, drained by a stream that flows nearly 2 miles to Suey Creek 5.5 miles east of the town of Nipomo (lat. 35°02'10" N, long. 120°22'25" W). Named on Nipomo (1965) 7.5' quadrangle.

Sycamore Canyon [SANTA BARBARA]:
(1) *canyon*, drained by a stream that flows 5.5 miles to Alamo Pintado Creek 3.5 miles north of Los Olivos (lat. 34°43'05" N, long. 120°06'35" W). Named on Los Olivos (1959) and Zaca Lake (1964) 7.5' quadrangles.
(2) *canyon*, 2.5 miles long, along Sycamore Creek above a point 1.25 miles east-northeast of downtown Santa Barbara (lat. 34°25'45" N, long. 119°40'35" W). Named on Santa Barbara (1952) 7.5' quadrangle. United States Board on Geographic Names (1961b, p. 17) rejected the name "Valley of Los Alisos" for the canyon.

Sycamore Canyon Creek: see **Sycamore Creek** [SANTA BARBARA].

Sycamore Creek [MONTEREY]: *stream,* flows 2.5 miles to El Piojo Creek 9 miles south of Jolon (lat. 35°50'25" N, long. 121°09'20" W; sec. 13, T 24 S, R 7 E). Named on Burnett Peak (1949) 7.5' quadrangle.

Sycamore Creek [SAN LUIS OBISPO]: *stream,* flows 3 miles to Cuyama River 7.25 miles south-southeast of Branch Mountain (lat. 35°05'20" N, long. 120°02'20" W); the creek heads on Sycamore Ridge. Named on Miranda Pine Mountain (1967) 7.5' quadrangle.

Sycamore Creek [SANTA BARBARA]: *stream,* flows nearly 4 miles to the sea 2 miles east of downtown Santa Barbara (lat. 34°25' N, long. 119°39'55" W); the stream drains Sycamore Canyon (2). Named on Santa Barbara (1952) 7.5' quadrangle. United States Board on Geographic Names (1961b, p. 17) rejected the name "Sycamore Canyon Creek" for the stream.

Sycamore Creek: see **Pozo Creek** [SAN LUIS OBISPO]; **Santa Lucia Creek** [MONTEREY] (2).

Sycamore Flat [MONTEREY]: *settlement,* 9 miles west-southwest of Greenfield along Arroyo Seco (1) (lat. 36°15'50" N, long. 121°23'30" W; sec. 23, T 19 S, R 5 E). Named on Sycamore Flat (1956) 7.5' quadrangle.

Sycamore Gulch [MONTEREY]: *canyon,* drained by a stream that flows 2.5 miles to the canyon of Tularcitos Creek 5 miles east-southeast of the town of Carmel Valley (lat. 36°26'50" N, long. 121°38'50" W). Named on Carmel Valley (1956) 7.5' quadrangle.

Sycamore Hot Sulphur Spring: see **Sycamore Springs** [SAN LUIS OBISPO].

Sycamore Ridge [SAN LUIS OBISPO]: *ridge,* northwest-trending, 3.5 miles long, 6 miles southeast of Branch Mountain (lat. 35°07'15" N, long. 120°00'15" W). Named on Branch Mountain (1967), Chimineas Ranch (1959), Miranda Pine Mountain (1967), and Taylor Canyon (1959) 7.5' quadrangles.

Sycamore Spring [MONTEREY]: *spring,* 9 miles east of Cape San Martin (lat. 35°55'10" N, long. 121°18'15" W; sec. 22, T 23 S, R 6 E). Named on Alder Peak (1949) 7.5' quadrangle.

Sycamore Spring [SAN LUIS OBISPO]: *spring,* 8 miles northeast of the town of Morro Bay (lat. 35°29'15" N, long. 120°46'35" W); the spring is on the east side of Sycamore Canyon (1). Named on Morro Bay North (1965) 7.5' quadrangle.

Sycamore Springs [SAN LUIS OBISPO]: *locality,* 1.25 miles east-northeast of Avila Beach along San Luis Obispo Creek (lat. 35°11'10" N, long. 120°42'50" W). Named on Pismo Beach (1965) 7.5' quadrangle. Sycamore Hot Sulphur Spring, a health and pleasure resort at the place, used warm water from an artesian well drilled from 1885 to 1887 (Crawford, 1896, p. 517). G.A. Waring (p. 70) called the resort San Luis Hot Spring. Postal authorities established Springs post office, named for Sycamore Hot Springs, in 1900 and discontinued it the same year (Salley, p. 210).

Sykes Camp [MONTEREY]: *locality,* 5 miles north of Partington Point along Big Sur River (lat. 36°14'55" N, long. 121°41'05" W; sec. 30, T 19 S, R 3 E). Named on Partington Ridge (1956) 7.5' quadrangle. The name is from Sykes Hot Springs, which are situated 400 yards downstream from the camp (Clark, 1991, p. 555).

Sykes Hot Springs: see **Sykes Camp** [MONTEREY].

Sylvester Spring [SAN BENITO]: *spring,* 6.25 miles south of Idria (lat. 36°19'45" N, long. 120°41'40" W; sec. 30, T 18 S, R 12 E). Named on San Benito Mountain (1969) 7.5' quadrangle.

Syncline Divide [SAN BENITO]: *pass,* about 14 miles east-northeast of Bitterwater near the head of Vallecitos Creek (lat. 36°28'55" N, long. 120°47'25" W; sec. 5, T 17 S, R 11 E). Named on Hernandez Reservoir (1969) 7.5' quadrangle.

Syncline Hill [SAN LUIS OBISPO]: *ridge,* west-northwest-trending, 1.5 miles long, 6 miles north-northwest of Freeborn Mountain (lat. 35°21'50" N, long. 120°06'15" W). Named on California Valley (1966) 7.5' quadrangle. Arnold and Johnson (1910, p. 22) proposed the name because rocks at the place form a syncline.

– T –

Table Mountain [MONTEREY]: *ridge,* west-to northwest-trending, 10 miles long, 6 miles east of Parkfield, where Monterey County, Fresno County, and Kings County meet (lat. 35°54'30" N, long. 120°19' W). Named on Garza Peak (1953), Parkfield (1961), and The Dark Hole (1961) 7.5' quadrangles.

Table Rock [SANTA CRUZ]: *promontory,* 6 miles west of Point Santa Cruz along the coast (lat. 36°58'05" N, long. 122°08'05" W). Named on Santa Cruz (1954) 7.5' quadrangle.

Tajea Flat [SAN LUIS OBISPO]: *area,* 2 miles east-southeast of Branch Mountain (lat. 35°10'15" N, long. 120°03'10" W). Named on Branch Mountain (1967) 7.5' quadrangle.

Tajea Spring [SAN LUIS OBISPO]: *spring,* 2.5 miles southeast of Branch Mountain (lat. 35°09'45" N, long. 120°02'55" W); the spring is near the south end of Tajea Flat. Named on Branch Mountain (1967) 7.5' quadrangle.

Tajiguas [SANTA BARBARA]: *locality,* 6.25 miles east of Gaviota along Southern Pacific Railroad (lat. 34°28' N, long. 120°06'20" W); the place is west of the mouth of Tajiguas Creek. Named on Tajiguas (1953) 7.5' quadrangle.

Tajiguas Creek [SANTA BARBARA]: *stream,* flows 5.25 miles to the sea nearly 7 miles east of Gaviota (lat. 34°27'20" N, long. 120° 06' W). Named on Santa Ynez (1959) and Tajiguas (1953) 7.5' quadrangles. The name is from an Indian village (Kroeber, 1916, p. 61).

Talaki: see **Camp Talaki** [SAN LUIS OBISPO].

Talcott Shoal: see **Sandy Point** [SANTA BARBARA].

Tangair [SANTA BARBARA]: *locality,* 7.25 miles southwest of the village of Casmalia along Southern Pacific Railroad (lat. 34°45'15" N, long. 120°36'35" W). Named on Casmalia (1959) 7.5' quadrangle.

Tanganyika: see **Lake Tanganyika** [SAN BENITO].

Tank Siding: see **Clems** [SANTA BARBARA].

Tannery Gulch [SANTA CRUZ]: *canyon,* drained by a stream that flows 2.5 miles to the sea 2.5 miles northeast of Soquel Point (lat. 36°58'40" N, long. 121°56'15" W). Named on Laurel (1955) and Soquel (1954) 7.5' quadrangles. The name is from tanneries operated in the canyon as early as 1854 (Clark, 1986, p. 364).

Tan Oak Camp [MONTEREY]: *locality,* nearly 4 miles southwest of Tassajara Hot Springs (lat. 36°11'50" N, long. 121°35'55" W; sec. 14, T 20 S, R 3 E); the place is near the mouth of Tan Oak Creek. Named on Tassajara Hot Springs (1956) 7.5' quadrangle.

Tan Oak Creek [MONTEREY]: *stream,* flows nearly 1 mile to Zigzag Creek 4 miles southwest of Tassajara Hot Springs (lat. 36° 11'45" N, long. 121°35'55" W; sec. 14, T 20 S, R 3 E). Named on Tassajara Hot Springs (1956) 7.5' quadrangle.

Taro Creek: see **Toro Creek** [SAN LUIS OBISPO] (2).

Tar Spring Creek [SAN LUIS OBISPO]: *stream,* flows 9 miles to Arroyo Grande Creek 6 miles southeast of Edna (lat. 35°08' N, long. 120°33' W); the stream heads at Tar Spring Ridge. Named on Arroyo Grande NE (1965) and Tar Spring Ridge (1967) 7.5' quadrangles. Natural deposits of tar occur along the stream.

Tar Spring Ridge [SAN LUIS OBISPO]: *ridge,* east-southeast- to southeast-trending, 4.5 miles long, 8 miles north-northeast of the town of Nipomo (lat. 35°09' N, long. 120°26'30" W); the ridge is north of Tar Spring Creek. Named on Tar Spring Ridge (1967) 7.5' quadrangle.

Tash Creek [MONTEREY]: *stream,* flows 6 miles to Paloma Creek 13 miles west of Greenfield (lat. 36°18'05" N, long. 121°28'25" W; sec. 6, T 19 S, R 5 E). Named on Sycamore Flat (1956) 7.5' quadrangle. The name is from the Tash family, early residents of the neighborhood (Clark, 1991, p. 558).

Tassajara: see **Tassajara Hot Springs** [MONTEREY].

Tassajara Creek [MONTEREY]: *stream,* flows 11 miles to Arroyo Seco (1) 10 miles northeast of Slates Hot Springs (lat. 36°13'10" N, long. 121°30'05" W; sec. 2, T 20 S, R 4 E). Named on Chews Ridge (1956), Tassajara Hot Springs (1956), and Ventana Cones (1956) 7.5' quadrangles. The name is from Tassajara Hot Springs (Clark, 1991, p. 559).

Tassajara Hot Springs [MONTEREY]: *locality,* 9 miles east-northeast of Partington Point (lat. 36°14' N, long. 121°32'55" W; sec. 32, T 19 S, R 4 E); the place is along Tassajara Creek. Named on Tassajara Hot Springs (1956) 7.5' quadrangle. Postal authorities established Tassajara post office in 1892 and discontinued it in 1894; they established Tassajara Hot Springs post office in 1912 and discontinued it in 1944 (Frickstad, p. 109). A hotel was built at the springs in 1893 and 1894 (Johnston, p. 118). According to G.A. Waring (p. 57-58), about 17 thermal springs occur at the place; the name, which dates from early days of the cattle industry, is from an Indian or Mexican word that means "the place where meat is cured by drying."

Tassajera Creek [SAN LUIS OBISPO]: *stream,* flows 4 miles to Santa Margarita Creek 2 miles west-southwest of the town of Santa Margarita (lat. 35°22'45" N, long. 120°38'25" W).

Named on Atascadero (1965) 7.5' quadrangle.

Taylor Canyon [MONTEREY-SAN LUIS OBISPO]: *canyon,* drained by a stream that heads in Monterey County and flows 7 miles to Shimmin Canyon 5 miles northwest of Shandon in San Luis Obispo County (lat. 35°42'25" N, long. 120°26'05" W; sec. 35, T 25 S, R 14 E). Named on Cholame Hills (1961) and Shandon (1961) 7.5' quadrangles.

Taylor Canyon [SAN LUIS OBISPO]: *canyon,* drained by a stream that flows 8 miles to Cuyama River 11 miles west of Caliente Mountain (lat. 35°03'20" N, long. 119°57'15" W). Named on Taylor Canyon (1959) 7.5' quadrangle.

Taylor Spring [MONTEREY]: *spring,* nearly 1 mile west-northwest of Smith Mountain along Pancho Rico Creek (lat. 36°04'55" N, long. 120°36'25" W; sec. 19, T 21 S, E 13 E). Named on Smith Mountain (1969) 7.5' quadrangle.

Taylor Spring [SAN LUIS OBISPO]: *spring,* 11 miles west-northwest of Caliente Mountain (lat. 35°05'40" N, long. 119°54'55" W; near W line sec. 35, T 32 S, R 19 E); the spring is in Taylor Canyon (2). Named on Taylor Canyon (1959) 7.5' quadrangle.

Taylor Well [SAN LUIS OBISPO]: *well,* 3.5 miles southeast of Branch Mountain along San Juan Creek (lat. 35°10' N, long. 120° 01'30" W). Named on Branch Mountain (1967) 7.5' quadrangle.

Tecolito Creek: see **Tecolotito Creek** [SANTA BARBARA].

Tecolote Canyon [SANTA BARBARA]: *canyon,* drained by a stream that flows 6.5 miles to the sea 3 miles northwest of Coal Oil Point (lat. 34°25'50" N, long. 119°55' W). Named on Dos Pueblos Canyon (1951) and Lake Cachuma (1959) 7.5' quadrangles. *Tecolote* means "small owl" in Mexican Spanish (Gudde, 1949, p. 355).

Tecolotito Canyon: see **Glen Annie Canyon** [SANTA BARBARA].

Tecolotito Creek [SANTA BARBARA]: *stream,* flows 4.5 miles to Goleta Slough 1.5 miles west-southwest of downtown Goleta (lat. 34°25'35" N, long. 119°50'55" W). Named on Goleta (1950) 7.5' quadrangle. United States Board on Geographic Names (1978b, p. 5) rejected the name "Tecolito Creek" for the stream.

Tembladero Slough [MONTEREY]: *stream,* heads at a ditch that drains Merritt Lake and flows nearly 4 miles to Old Salinas River 2 miles south of Moss Landing (lat. 36°46'25" N, long. 121°47'15" W). Named on Moss Landing (1954) and Prunedale (1954) 7.5' quadrangles. Called Sanjon del Tembladera in a diseño of Bolsa del Potrero y Moro Cojo grant (Becker, 1964). United States Board on Geographic Names (1943, p. 14) rejected the name "Cooper Slough" for the feature.

Temblor Range [SAN LUIS OBISPO]: *range,* northeast of Carrizo Plain and San Juan Val-ley along San Luis Obispo-Kern county line. Named on Bakersfield (1962) and San Luis Obispo (1956) 1°x 2° quadrangles. Arnold and Anderson (1908, p. 13) named the feature and stated that *temblor* means "earthquake" in Spanish and is particularly suited for the range "because the great California fault line [San Andreas fault], along which earthquakes have repeatedly originated, follows the range from one end to the other," and because the well-known old Temblor ranch is on its west flank. United States Board on Geographic Names (1933, p. 748) rejected the form "Temploa Range" for the name.

Temettate Creek [SAN LUIS OBISPO]: *stream,* flows 2.25 miles to Los Berros Canyon 3.5 miles northeast of the town of Nipomo (lat. 35°04'40" N, long. 120°25'50" W); the stream heads on Temettate Ridge. Named on Nipomo (1965) 7.5' quadrangle. Gudde (1949, p. 358) traced the name to *temetate,* a Mexican word for a curved stone used as a mortar for grinding corn.

Temettate Ridge [SAN LUIS OBISPO]: *ridge,* northwest-trending, 9 miles long, 2.5 miles east-northeast of the town of Nipomo on the northeast side of Nipomo Valley (lat. 35°03'30" N, long. 120° 26' W). Named on Huasna Peak (1967) and Nipomo (1965) 7.5' quadrangles.

Templeton [SAN LUIS OBISPO]: *town,* 5.5 miles south of Paso Robles (lat. 35°33' N, long. 120°42'15" W). Named on Templeton (1948) 7.5' quadrangle. Postal authorities established Templeton post office in 1886 (Frickstad, p. 166). The town was laid out in 1886 when the railroad reached the place; first it was called Crocker and then Templeton, perhaps for Templeton Crocker, grandson of Charles Crocker of Central Pacific Railroad (Gudde, 1949, p. 358). The Templeton neighborhood was called Bethel District (Lee and others, p. 147)—Templeton (1948) 7.5' quadrangle shows the abandoned Bethel school situated 2.25 miles north-northwest of Templeton.

Temploa Range: see **Temblor Range** [SAN LUIS OBISPO].

Tennison Canyon [SANTA BARBARA]: *canyon,* drained by a stream that flows nearly 6 miles to Cuyama Valley 4.5 miles southeast of the village of Cuyama (lat. 34°53'20" N, long. 119°33'20" W). Named on Cuyama (1964) and Fox Mountain (1964) 7.5' quadrangles.

Tennison Spring [SANTA BARBARA]: *spring,* 2.25 miles north-northeast of Fox Mountain (lat. 34°50'30" N, long. 119°34'35" W); the spring is in Tennison Canyon. Named on Fox Mountain (1964) 7.5' quadrangle.

Tepusquet [SANTA BARBARA]: *land grant,* east of the confluence of Cuyama River and Sisquoc River. Named on Foxen Canyon (1964), Sisquoc (1959), Tepusquet Canyon (1964), and Twitchell Dam (1959) 7.5' quadrangles. Tomas Olivera received 2 leagues in 1837; Antonia Maria Cota and others claimed 8901 acres patented in 1871 (Cowan, p. 102). Angel (1883, p. 215) gave the alternate name "Santa Maria" for the grant.

Tepusquet Canyon [SANTA BARBARA]: *canyon,* 9 miles long, opens into Santa Maria Valley 4.5 miles southwest of Tepusquet Peak (lat. 34°52'05" N, long. 120°14'40" W); Tepusquet Creek drains the canyon. Named on Tepusquet Canyon (1964) 7.5' quadrangle. Called Arroyo de Tepusque on a diseño of Tepusquet grant made in 1837 (Becker, 1969).

Tepusquet Creek [SANTA BARBARA]: *stream,* flows 10 miles to Sisquoc River 2 miles east of the village of Sisquoc (lat. 34°51'45" N, long. 120°15'15" W). Named on Foxen Canyon (1964), Sisquoc (1959), and Tepusquet Canyon (1964) 7.5' quadrangles.

Tepusquet Peak [SANTA BARBARA]: *peak,* 15 miles east of Santa Maria (lat. 34°54'35" N, long. 120°11'05" W); the peak is east of Tepusquet Canyon. Altitude 3253 feet. Named on Tepusquet Canyon (1964) 7.5' quadrangle.

Tequepis [SANTA BARBARA]: *land grant,* along Santa Ynez River at the mouth of Cachuma Creek. Named on Lake Cachuma (1959) 7.5' quadrangle. Joaquin Villa received 2 leagues in 1843; Antonio M. Villa claimed 8919 acres patented in 1869 (Cowan, p. 102). According to Perez (p. 101), Antonio M. Villa was the grantee in 1845. The name is from an Indian village (Kroeber, 1916, p. 62).

Tequepis Canyon [SANTA BARBARA]: *canyon,* drained by a stream that flows 3.25 miles to Lake Cachuma 3.25 miles north-northeast of Santa Ynez Peak (lat. 34°34'10" N, long. 119°56'55" W); the mouth of the canyon is on Tequepis grant. Named on Lake Cachuma (1959) 7.5' quadrangle. Called Cañada de Tequepis on a diseño of Tequepis grant (Becker, 1969).

Tequepis Point [SANTA BARBARA]: *promontory,* 4 miles north-northeast of Santa Ynez Peak on the south side of Lake Cachuma (lat. 34°35'05" N, long. 119°57'25" W); the feature is on Tequepis grant. Named on Lake Cachuma (1959) 7.5' quadrangle.

Tequisquita Slough [SAN BENITO]: *stream,* formed by the confluence of Arroyo de las Viboras and Arroyo Dos Picachoes, flows nearly 7 miles, partly in an artificial watercourse, to San Felipe Lake 9 miles north-northeast of Hollister (lat. 36°58'45" N, long. 121°27'45" W). Named on San Felipe (1955) 7.5' quadrangle. Called Sanjon del Tequesquite on a diseño of Llano de Tequisquita grant made in 1834 (Becker, 1969)—the stream is partly on the grant.

Tequisquite: see **Llano del Tequisquita** [SAN BENITO].

Terminal Rock: see **Big Dome Cove** [MONTEREY].

Terrace Creek [MONTEREY]: *stream,* flows 1 mile to Big Sur River 5.25 miles north-

northwest of Partington Point (lat. 36°14'55" N, long. 121°43'35" W; sec. 27, T 19 S, R 2 E). Named on Partington Ridge (1956) 7.5' quadrangle.

Terrace Creek Camp [MONTEREY]: *locality,* 5.25 miles north-northwest of Partington Point (lat. 36°14'45" N, long. 121°43'45" W; sec. 27, T 19 S, R 2 E); the place is along Terrace Creek. Named on Partington Ridge (1956) 7.5' quadrangle.

Terrace Hill [SAN LUIS OBISPO]: *hill,* 0.5 mile southeast of downtown San Luis Obispo (lat. 35°16'25" N, long. 120°39' W; near E line sec. 35, T 30 S, R 12 E). Named on San Luis Obispo (1965) 7.5' quadrangle.

Terrace Point [SANTA CRUZ]: *promontory,* 2.25 miles west of Point Santa Cruz along the coast (lat. 36°56'55" N, long. 122°03'55" W). Named on Santa Cruz (1954) 7.5' quadrangle.

The Basin [MONTEREY]: *relief feature,* 9.5 miles west of Greenfield (lat. 36°19'10" N, long. 121°24'40" W; sec. 34, T 18 S, R 5 E); the feature is on upper reaches of Basin Creek, where the canyon of the creek widens and the stream divides into four major branches. Named on Sycamore Flat (1956) 7.5' quadrangle.

The Bear Trap [MONTEREY]: *ridge,* northnorthwest-trending, 1.5 miles long, 3 miles southeast of Jamesburg (lat. 36°19'45" N, long. 121°33'15" W). Named on Chews Ridge (1956) 7.5' quadrangle.

The Bluff [SAN BENITO]: *escarpment,* northeast-trending, 0.25 mile long, 5.5 miles northeast of Bitterwater (lat. 36°26'05" N, long. 120°55'40" W; sec. 19, T 17 S, R 10 E). Named on Rock Spring Peak (1969) 7.5' quadrangle.

The Cantinas [SAN LUIS OBISPO]: *relief feature,* 13 miles northeast of the village of San Simeon (lat. 35°45'55" N, long. 121°00'50" W; near W line sec. 9, T 25 S, R 9 E); the feature is along Cantinas Creek. Named on Bryson (1949) 7.5' quadrangle. On Bryson (1919) 15' quadrangle, the name applies to three small ponds situated 0.5 mile farther north-northeast in narrows along Cantinas Creek.

The Caves [MONTEREY]: *locality,* 6.5 miles south of Jamesburg (lat. 36°16'25" N, long. 121°35'05" W; sec. 13, T 19 S, R 3 E). Named on Chews Ridge (1956) 7.5' quadrangle. The name is from caves and rockshelters in sandstone at the place, which has the variant name "Church Creek Rockshelter" (Clark, 1991, p. 564).

The Chalks [SANTA CRUZ]: *area,* 5.5 miles north of the mouth of Waddell Creek (lat. 37°10'30" N, long. 122°17' W); the place is north-northeast of Chalk Mountain. Named on Franklin Point (1955) 7.5' quadrangle.

The City of King: see **King City** [MONTEREY].

The Dry Lake [MONTEREY]: *intermittent lake,* 400 feet long, 10.5 miles west-southwest of Greenfield (lat. 36°16'25" N, long. 121° 25'25" W; sec. 16, T 19 S, R 5 E). Named on Sycamore Flat (1956) 7.5' quadrangle.

The Espada [SANTA BARBARA]: *relief feature,* 4.25 miles southeast of Tranquillon Mountain (lat. 34°32' N, long. 120°31' W). Named on Tranquillon Mountain (1959) 7.5' quadrangle.

The Falls [MONTEREY]: *waterfall,* 10.5 miles northeast of Bradley in Walters Canyon (lat. 35°59'20" N, long. 120°41'50" W; sec. 29, T 22 S, R 12 E). Named on San Miguel (1919) 15' quadrangle.

The Fingers [SAN BENITO]: *relief feature,* 2.5 miles north-northwest of North Chalone Peak (lat. 36°29' N, long. 121°12'20" W; on E line sec. 4, T 17 S, R 7 E). Named on North Chalone Peak (1969) 7.5' quadrangle.

The Gorge [SAN BENITO]: *canyon,* 1 mile long, 10.5 miles east-southeast of Bitterwater along Laguna Creek (lat. 36°20'45" N, long. 120°49'15" W; sec. 19, T 18 S, R 11 E). Named on Hepsedam Peak (1969) 7.5' quadrangle.

The Hole [SAN BENITO]: *canyon,* 0.5 mile long, 7 miles north of San Benito (lat. 36°36'35" N, long. 121°05'20" W; sec. 22, T 15 S, R 8 E). Named on San Benito (1968) 7.5' quadrangle.

The Indians [MONTEREY]: *locality,* 3 miles south-southwest of Junipero Serra Peak (lat. 36°06'20" N, long. 121°26'05" W). Named on Cone Peak (1949) 7.5' quadrangle. The name is from neophytes of San Antonio mission who settled at the place after secularization of the mission (Clark, 1991, p. 566).

The Island: see **Aptos Creek** [SANTA CRUZ].

The Lakes [MONTEREY]: *lakes,* two, largest 1650 feet long, 7 miles north-northwest of Junipero Serra Peak near Arroyo Seco (1) (lat. 36°14' N, long. 121°28'55" W; near S line sec. 36, T 19 S, R 4 E). Named on Junipero Serra Peak (1949) 7.5' quadrangle.

The Mesa [MONTEREY]: *area,* nearly 6 miles east of Ventana Cone (lat. 36°16'10" N, long. 121°34'45" W; sec. 19, T 19 S, R 4 E). Named on Chews Ridge (1956) 7.5' quadrangle.

The Mesa: see **Nipomo Mesa** [SAN LUIS OBISPO].

The Narrows [MONTEREY]: *narrows,* 5.5 miles south of Stockdale Mountain along a branch of Middle Fork (lat. 35°54'35" N, long. 120°34'15" W; sec. 21, T 23 S, R 13 E). Named on Stockdale Mountain (1948) 7.5' quadrangle.

The Narrows [SANTA BARBARA]: *narrows,* 2 miles west-northwest of Hildreth Peak (lat. 34°36'45" N, long. 119°34'45" W). Named on Hildreth Peak (1964) 7.5' quadrangle.

The Oaks [SAN LUIS OBISPO]: *locality,* 4 miles southeast of San Simeon (lat. 35°36'10" N, long. 121°08'10" W). Named on Pico Creek (1959) 7.5' quadrangle.

The Palisades [MONTEREY]: *ridge,* north-northwest-trending, 1.5 miles long, 8 miles

south-southwest of Jolon (lat. 35°51'55" N, long. 121°12'40" W). Named on Burnett Peak (1949) 7.5' quadrangle.

The Peak [SANTA CRUZ]: *peak,* 7 miles north-northeast of the town of Boulder Creek on Castle Rock Ridge (lat. 37°13'10" N, long. 122°04'15" W; sec. 22, T 8 S, R 2 W). Altitude 2886 feet. Named on Castle Rock Ridge (1955) 7.5' quadrangle.

The Picachos [SAN BENITO]: *ridge,* northwest-trending, 1.25 miles long, 4.5 miles south-southwest of Idria (lat. 36°21'10" N, long. 120°41'40" W); the ridge extends northwest from Picacho Peak. Named on San Benito Mountain (1969) 7.5' quadrangle.

The Pimental: see **Pimental Creek** [SAN BENITO].

The Pines Campground [SANTA BARBARA]: *locality,* 5 miles southwest of Big Pine Mountain (lat. 34°38'30" N, long. 119°42'35" W). Named on Big Pine Mountain (1964) 7.5' quadrangle.

The Pinnacle: see **Pinnacle Point** [MONTEREY];

The Pinnacles [MONTEREY]: *peak,* 1.5 miles southeast of Smith Mountain on Monterey-Fresno county line (lat. 36°03'40" N, long. 120°34'45" W; sec. 33, T 21 S, R 13 E). Named on Smith Mountain (1969) 7.5' quadrangle.

The Pinnacles: see **Pescadero Point** [MONTEREY].

The Pit [MONTEREY]: *embayment,* less than 1 mile east of Point Lobos along the coast on the south side of Carmel Bay (lat. 36°31'15" N, long. 121°56'10" W). Named on Monterey (1947) 7.5' quadrangle. The name is from a gravel pit that was operated at the place from 1920 until 1926 (Clark, 1991, p. 569).

The Rocks [MONTEREY]: *relief feature,* bold northwest-trending sandstone outcrops 6.5 miles east of Junipero Serra Peak between Reliz Creek and Vaqueros Creek (lat. 36°09'50" N, long. 121°18'15" W; sec. 27, T 20 S, R 6 E). Named on Reliz Canyon (1949) 7.5' quadrangle.

The Shut-in [MONTEREY]: *narrows,* 10 miles south of Jolon along Nacimiento River (lat. 35°49'50" N, long. 121°09' W; sec. 19, T 24 S, R 8 E). Named on Burnett Peak (1949) 7.5' quadrangle.

The Tules [SAN BENITO]: *water feature,* three springs and two small spring-fed lakes 7.25 miles northeast of Bitterwater (lat. 36°27'25" N, long. 120°54'45" W; near NW cor. sec. 17, T 17 S, R 10 E). Named on Rock Spring Peak (1969) 7.5' quadrangle.

The Tuxedo: see **Mount Hermon** [SANTA CRUZ].

The Vallecitos: see **Vallecitos** [SAN BENITO].

The Wash [SAN LUIS OBISPO]: *stream,* flows 4.5 miles to New River 1.5 miles north-northeast of Cuyama [SANTA BARBARA] (lat. 34°57'15" N, long. 119°36'15" W). Named on Cuyama (1964) 7.5' quadrangle.

The Willows [SANTA CRUZ]: *settlement, 8 miles north-northeast of Soquel (lat. 37°06'10" N, long. 121°55'25" W). Named on Laurel (1955) 7.5' quadrangle.

Thirtyfive Canyon [SAN LUIS OBISPO]: *canyon,* drained by a stream that flows 4.5 miles to Branch Creek 4.5 miles southwest of Branch Mountain (lat. 35°08'20" N, long. 120°08'25" W). Named on Branch Mountain (1967) and Los Machos Hills (1967) 7.5' quadrangles.

Thompson Canyon [MONTEREY]: *canyon,* drained by a stream that flows 8 miles to lowlands 3.25 miles west-southwest of King City (lat. 36°13'30" N, long. 121°10'45" W; sec. 2, T 20 S, R 7 E). Named on Thompson Canyon (1949) 7.5' quadrangle. The name commemorates Pleasant Thompson, who settled in the neighborhood in 1872 (Clark, 1991, p. 571).

Thompson Creek [SAN BENITO]: *stream,* flows 6 miles to Pescadero Creek 3 miles southwest of Paicines (lat. 36°42'05" N, long. 121°19'10" W). Named on Mount Harlan (1968) and Paicines (1968) 7.5' quadrangles. Irelan (p. 488) discussed lime manufacturing carried out at a place called Cienega that was located near present Thompson Creek (sec. 30, T 14 S, R 6 E). Paicines (1968) 7.5' quadrangle shows Limekiln Road along the creek.

Thompson Spring [SAN LUIS OBISPO]:
(1) *spring,* about 1.5 miles east of Branch Mountain (lat. 35°11'20" N, long. 120°03'25" W; sec. 33, T 31 S, R 18 E). Named on Branch Mountain (1967) 7.5' quadrangle.
(2) *spring,* nearly 1 mile northeast of Simmler (lat. 35°21'40" N, long. 119°58'40" W; sec. 31, T 29 S, R 19 E). Named on Simmler (1959) 7.5' quadrangle.

Thompson Valley [SAN BENITO]: *valley,* 8 miles southwest of Paicines (lat. 36°39'55" N, long. 121°23'20" W; on S line sec. 35, T 14 S, R 5 E); the valley is along a branch of Thompson Creek. Named on Mount Harlan (1968) 7.5' quadrangle.

Three Corners [SAN BENITO]: *locality,* 7.5 miles northeast of Bitterwater, where three ridges meet (lat. 36°27'35" N, long. 121° 54'10" W; near S line sec. 8, T 17 S, R 10 E). Named on Rock Spring Peak (1969) 7.5' quadrangle.

Three Corners Creek [SAN BENITO]: *stream,* flows nearly 2 miles to James Creek 6 miles northeast of Bitterwater (lat. 36°26'05" N, long. 120°54'50" W; near W line sec. 20, T 17 S, R 10 E); the stream heads near Three Corners. Named on Rock Spring Peak (1969) 7.5' quadrangle.

Three Mile Flat: see **Arroyo Seco** [MONTEREY] (2).

Three Peaks [MONTEREY]: *peaks,* 9 miles east-southeast of Cape San Martin (lat. 35°51' N, long. 121°18'25" W; sec. 15, T 24 S, R 6 E). Named on Burro Mountain (1949) 7.5' quadrangle.

Three Sisters [SAN BENITO]: *peaks,* on an east-trending ridge 1 mile long situated 8 miles east-northeast of Hollister (lat. 36°53'35" N, long. 121°15'45" W; sec. 13, T 12 S, R 6 E). Named on Three Sisters (1954) 7.5' quadrangle.

Three Sisters: see **La Carpa Potrero** [SANTA BARBARA].

Three Troughs [SAN LUIS OBISPO]: *water feature,* 3 miles northeast of the village of San Simeon (lat. 35°40'30" N, long. 121° 09' W). Named on San Simeon (1958) 7.5' quadrangle.

Three Troughs Canyon [SAN BENITO]: *canyon,* drained by a stream that flows nearly 2 miles to Stone Canyon 6 miles south of Paicines (lat. 36°38'45" N, long. 121°17'05" W; sec. 11, T 15 S, R 6 E). Named on Paicines (1968) 7.5' quadrangle.

Thyle [SAN LUIS OBISPO]: *locality,* 4.5 miles north-northeast of San Luis Obispo along Southern Pacific Railroad (lat. 35°20'25" N, long. 120°37'55" W). Named on San Luis Obispo (1965) 7.5' quadrangle. California Mining Bureau's (1917c) map shows a place called Nova located along the railroad about 1.5 miles south-southeast of present Thyle.

Tiber [SAN LUIS OBISPO]: *locality,* 1.5 miles south of Edna along Southern Pacific Railroad (lat. 35°10'40" N, long. 120°37'05" W); the place is near the mouth of Tiber Canyon. Named on Arroyo Grande NE (1965) 7.5' quadrangle.

Tiber Canyon [SAN LUIS OBISPO]: *canyon,* drained by a stream that flows 1 mile to Pismo Creek 1.5 miles south-southwest of Edna (lat. 35°10'45" N, long. 120°37'05" W). Named on Arroyo Grande NE (1965) 7.5' quadrangle.

Tickner Canyon [MONTEREY]: *canyon,* 1.5 miles long, opens into the valley of Pine Creek (3) 8 miles north-northeast of San Ardo (lat. 36°08'15" N, long. 120°51'45" W; sec. 2, T 21 S, R 10 E). Named on Monarch Peak (1967) 7.5' quadrangle. The name is for members of the Tickner family who had land in the neighborhood (Clark, 1991, p. 572).

Tide Rock: see **Cape San Martin** [MONTEREY].

Tie Gulch [SANTA CRUZ]: *canyon,* drained by a stream that flows nearly 1 mile to Branciforte Creek 4.5 miles north-northwest of Soquel (lat. 37°03' N, long. 121°58'50" W; sec. 21, T 10 S, R 1 W). Named on Laurel (1955) 7.5' quadrangle.

Tierra Redonda Mountain [SAN LUIS OBISPO]: *mountain,* 19 miles west-northwest of Paso Robles (lat. 35°46'15" N, long. 120°59'05" W; sec. 10, 11, T 25 S, R 9 E). Altitude 2051 feet. Named on Tierra Redonda Mountain (1949) 7.5' quadrangle. Arnold (p. 18, 70) called the feature Lynch's Mountain and Lynchs Mountain for James Lynch, who came to California in 1846 with Stevenson's New York Volunteers, and later lived near the mountain (Lynch, p. 65). Loel and Corey (p.

121) called it Tierra Redondo Mountain. California Mining Bureau's (1909b) map shows a place called Lynch located 7 miles by stage line south of Pleyto [MONTEREY] at the north base of Tierra Redonda Mountain, where James Lynch lived. Postal authorities established Lynch post office in 1894, moved it 4 miles northeast in 1910, and discontinued it in 1912; the name was for Alice C. Lynch, first postmaster (Salley, p. 129).

Tiger Spring [MONTEREY]: *spring,* 10 miles east of Parkfield (lat. 35°5245" N, long. 120°14'50" W; sec. 33, T 23 S, R 16 E). Named on Garza Peak (1953) 7.5' quadrangle.

Tiger Spring: see **Little Tiger Spring** [MONTEREY].

Timber Peak [SANTA BARBARA]: *peak,* 2 miles southeast of Miranda Pine Mountain (lat. 35°00'50" N, long. 120°00'45" W). Altitude 4764 feet. Named on Miranda Pine Mountain (1967) 7.5' quadrangle.

Timber Top [MONTEREY]: *peak,* 3 miles north-northwest of Partington Point (lat. 36°13'05" N, long. 121°42'45" W; sec. 2, T 20 S, R 2 E). Named on Partington Ridge (1956) 7.5' quadrangle.

Tim O'Leary Canyon [SAN LUIS OBISPO]: *canyon,* drained by a stream that flows 2.25 miles to Huasna Creek 6.5 miles east-northeast of the town of Nipomo (lat. 35°04'35" N, long. 120°22'10" W). Named on Nipomo (1965) 7.5' quadrangle.

Tims Creek [SANTA CRUZ]: *stream,* flows 0.5 mile to West Waddell Creek nearly 2 miles west-northwest of Big Basin (lat. 37°10'40" N, long. 122°15'05" W; sec. 1, T 9 S, R 4 W). Named on Big Basin (1955) 7.5' quadrangle. Clark (1986, p. 373) used the form "Timms" for the name, and noted that George Timm was an early resident of the neighborhood.

Tinaquaic [SANTA BARBARA]: *land grant,* at and near the west part of Foxen Canyon. Named on Foxen Canyon (1964) and Sisquoc (1959) 7.5' quadrangles. Victor Linares received 2 leagues in 1837; William D. Foxen claimed 8875 acres patented in 1872 (Cowan, p. 103; Cowan used the form "Tinaguaic" for the name, and gave the form "Tinaquaic" as an alternate).

Tin Can Canyon: see **Tin Pan Canyon** [SAN LUIS OBISPO].

Tinker's Cove: see **Twin Harbors** [SANTA BARBARA].

Tinkers Harbor: see **Twin Harbors** [SANTA BARBARA].

Tin Pan Canyon [SAN LUIS OBISPO]: *canyon,* 4 miles long, branches south-southwest from San Juan Valley 10 miles southeast of Shandon (lat. 35°32'45" N, long. 120°15'30" W; sec. 28, T 27 S, R 16 E). Named on Camatta Canyon (1961) and Camatta Ranch (1966) 7.5' quadrangles. Called Tin Can Canyon on Commatti Canyon (1943) 7.5' quadrangle.

Tinta Creek [SANTA BARBARA]: *stream,* flows 5.25 miles to Ventura County 17 miles southeast of the village of Cuyama (lat. 34°44'20" N, long. 119°26'35" W). Named on Madulce Peak (1964) and Rancho Nuevo Creek (1943) 7.5' quadrangles.

Tobacco Creek [SAN LUIS OBISPO]: *stream,* flows 5 miles to Little Burnett Creek 8.5 miles northeast of the village of San Simeon (lat. 35°44'35" N, long. 121°05'45" W; sec. 22, T 25 S, R 8 E). Named on Pebblestone Shut-in (1959) 7.5' quadrangle.

Todds Spring [MONTEREY]: *spring,* 3.5 miles south-southwest of Parkfield (lat. 35°50'55" N, long. 120°27'10" W; near S line sec. 10, T 24 S, R 14 E). Named on Cholame Hills (1961) 7.5' quadrangle. The name commemorates William Lewis Todd, who raised stock in the neighborhood in the 1870's (Clark, 1991, p. 574).

Todds Spring Canyon [MONTEREY]: *canyon,* drained by a stream that flows nearly 4 miles to Cholame Creek 3 miles south-southeast of Parkfield (lat. 35°51'45" N, long 120°24'20" W; near NE cor. sec. 12, T 24 S, R 14 E); Todds Spring is in a branch of the canyon. Named on Cholame Hills (1961) 7.5' quadrangle.

Todos Santos: see **San Luis Obispo Bay** [SAN LUIS OBISPO].

Todos Santos y San Antonio [SANTA BARBARA]: *land grant,* 10 miles south-southwest of Santa Maria. Named on Casmalia (1959), Lompoc (1959), and Orcutt (1959) 7.5' quadrangles. Salvador Osio received 5 leagues in 1841; the heirs of William E.P. Hartnell claimed 20,772 acres patented in 1876 (Cowan, p. 103). According to Perez (p. 102), Hartnell was the grantee in 1841.

Tomasini Canyon [MONTEREY]: *canyon,* drained by a stream that flows 1 mile to Carmel River 8.5 miles east of the mouth of that river (lat. 36°30'50" N, long. 121°46'25" W; sec. 29, T 16 S, R 2 E). Named on Seaside (1947) 7.5' quadrangle.

Tom Valley [MONTEREY]: *valley,* drained by a stream that flows 4.5 miles to Wildhorse Canyon 5.5 miles northeast of San Lucas (lat. 36°11'30" N, long. 120°57'35" W; sec. 14, T 20 S, R 9 E). Named on Nattrass Valley (1967) 7.5' quadrangle.

Tongue Ridge [MONTEREY]: *ridge,* east- to east-northeast-trending, nearly 1 mile long, 5.25 miles east of Seaside (lat. 36°37'10" N, long. 121°45'15" W). Named on Seaside (1947) 7.5' quadrangle.

Toomey Gulch: see **Tumey Gulch** [SAN BENITO].

Topo Creek [MONTEREY-SAN BENITO]: *stream,* heads in San Benito County and flows 12 miles to Chalone Creek 6.5 miles northeast of Greenfield in Monterey County (lat. 36°23'20" N, long. 121°09'50" W); the stream drains Topo Valley. Named on North Chalone Peak (1969) and Topo Valley (1969) 7.5' quadrangles.

Topo Valley [SAN BENITO]: *valley,* 4.5 miles northwest of Bitterwater near the southeast end of Gabilan Range (lat. 36°24'45" N, long. 121°04'15" W). Named on Topo Valley (1969) 7.5' quadrangle.

Toro: see **Mount Toro** [MONTEREY].

Toro Canyon [SANTA BARBARA]: *canyon,* 2 miles long, along Toro Canyon Creek above a point 4 miles northwest of Carpinteria (lat. 34°26' N, long. 119°34'15" W; sec. 14, T 4 N, R 26 W). Named on Carpinteria (1952, photorevised 1967) 7.5' quadrangle.

Toro Canyon Creek [SANTA BARBARA]: *stream,* flows 3.5 miles to the sea 3 miles west-northwest of Carpinteria (lat. 34°24'55" N, long. 119°33'55" W). Named on Carpinteria (1952, photorevised 1967) 7.5' quadrangle. Called Garrapata Creek on Carpinteria (1952) 7.5' quadrangle, but United States Board on Geographic Names (1962a, p. 18) rejected this name.

Toro Creek [SAN LUIS OBISPO]:

(1) *stream,* flows 11 miles to the sea 2.5 miles north-northwest of the mouth of Morro Creek (lat. 35°24'45" N, long. 120°52'20" W). Named on Morro Bay North (1965) 7.5' quadrangle.

(2) *stream,* flows 5 miles to Salinas River 3 miles west-northwest of Pozo (lat. 35°19'20" N, long. 120°25'25" W; sec. 12, T 30 S, R 14 E). Named on Pozo Summit (1967) and Santa Margarita Lake (1967) 7.5' quadrangles. United States Board on Geographic Names (1968b, p. 10) rejected the name "Taro Creek" for the stream.

Toro Creek: see **El Toro Creek** [MONTEREY].

Torre Canyon [MONTEREY]: *canyon,* drained by a stream that flows 1.5 miles to the sea 1.5 miles northwest of Partington Point (lat. 36°11'30" N, long. 121°42'50" W; sec. 14, T 20 S, R 2 E). Named on Partington Ridge (1956) 7.5' quadrangle. The name commemorates the de la Torre family, early residents of the neighborhood (Lussier, p. 27).

Town Creek [SAN LUIS OBISPO]: *stream,* flows 9 miles to Las Tablas Creek 4 miles north-northwest of Lime Mountain (lat. 35° 43'10" N, long. 120°57'20" W; near N line sec. 36, T 25 S, R 9 E). Named on Lime Mountain (1948) and Pebblestone Shut-in (1959) 7.5' quadrangles. The stream now enters an arm of Nacimiento Reservoir.

Towne Creek [MONTEREY-SAN BENITO]: *stream,* heads in San Benito County and flows nearly 4 miles to Mud Creek 10 miles north-northeast of Salinas in Monterey County (lat. 36°47'50" N, long. 121°34'05" W). Named on San Juan Bautista (1955) 7.5' quadrangle.

Town Spring [SAN LUIS OBISPO]: *spring,* 10.5 miles east-northeast of the village of San Simeon (lat. 35°40'45" N, long. 121°00'30" W; at N line sec. 16, T 26 S, R 9 E); the spring is near Town Creek. Named on Pebblestone Shut-in (1959) 7.5' quadrangle.

Trail Spring Camp [MONTEREY]: *locality,*

about 4.5 miles northeast of Lopez Point (lat. 36°03'30" N, long. 121°30'05" W; sec. 35, T 21 S, R 4 E). Named on Lopez Point (1956) 7.5' quadrangle.

Trampa Canyon [MONTEREY]: *canyon,* drained by a stream that flows 2 miles to Cachagua Creek 8.5 miles southeast of the town of Carmel Valley (lat. 36°23'30" N, long. 121°37'25" W; sec. 2, T 18 S, R 13 E). Named on Carmel Valley (1956) and Rana Creek (1956) 7.5' quadrangles.

Tranquillon Mountain [SANTA BARBARA]: *peak,* 7 miles southwest of the city of Lompoc (lat. 34°34'55" N, long. 120°33'40" W). Altitude 2159 feet. Named on Tranquillon Mountain (1959) 7.5' quadrangle. Called El Tranquillon on Guadalupe (1905) 30' quadrangle, but United States Board on Geographic Names (1962a, p. 18) rejected the names "El Tranquillon," "El Tranquillon Mountain," "Arguello," and "Arguello Mountain" for the peak. William Eimbeck of United States Coast Survey named the peak formally in 1873; the name had been used locally and is of Indian origin (Gudde, 1969, p. 343).

Tranquillon Ridge [SANTA BARBARA]: *ridge,* extends for 4.5 miles west-northwest from Tranquillon Mountain (center near lat. 34°35'15" N, long. 120°35'30" W). Named on Point Arguello (1959) and Tranquillon Mountain (1959) 7.5' quadrangles.

Treasure Island: see **The Island**, under **Aptos Creek** [SANTA CRUZ].

Treplett Mountain [SANTA BARBARA]: *peak,* 2.5 miles southwest of Miranda Pine Mountain (lat. 35°00'55" N, long. 120°04'20" W). Altitude 3828 feet. Named on Miranda Pine Mountain (1967) 7.5' quadrangle.

Tres Ojos de Agua [SANTA CRUZ]: *land grant,* 2 miles north-northwest of Point Santa Cruz in Santa Cruz. Named on Santa Cruz (1954) 7.5' quadrangle. Nicolas Dodero received 1300 varas in 1844 and claimed 176 acres patented in 1866 (Cowan, p. 104-105). *Tres ojos de agua* means "three eyes of water" in Spanish, and refers to springs (Hoover, Rensch, and Rensch, p. 474).

Tres Pinos [SAN BENITO]: *village,* 6.5 miles southeast of Hollister (lat. 36°47'25" N, long. 121°19'15" W); the village is on the east side of Tres Pinos Creek. Named on Tres Pinos (1955) 7.5' quadrangle. When Southern Pacific Railroad reached the site in 1873, the name "Tres Pinos" was appropriated from present Paicines and applied to the new station (Pierce, p. 126). Postal authorities established Tres Pinos post office at the place in 1874 (Frickstad, p. 137).

Tres Pinos Creek [SAN BENITO]: *stream,* flows 30 miles to San Benito River 5 miles south-southeast of Hollister (lat. 36°47'05" N, long. 121°21'45" W; near E line sec. 24, T 13 S, R 5 E). Named on Cherry Peak (1968), Paicines (1968), Panoche Pass (1968), and Tres Pinos (1955) 7.5' quadrangles. Called

Rosaria Creek on California Mining Bureau's (1917b) map. Gudde (1949, p. 368) noted that on old maps the stream has the names "Arroyo del puerto del Rosario" and "Arroyo del Rosario." Whitney (p. 53) used the name "Arroyo Joaquin Soto" for what probably is present Tres Pinos Creek.

Trough Canyon [SANTA BARBARA]: *canyon,* drained by a stream that flows 2.25 miles to Branch Canyon 4.25 miles northwest of Salisbury Potrero (lat. 34°52'20" N, long. 119°44'35" W). Named on Hurricane Deck (1964) and Salisbury Potrero (1964) 7.5' quadrangles.

Trough Canyon Spring: see **Upper Trough Canyon Spring** [SANTA BARBARA].

Trough Spring [SAN BENITO]: *spring,* 6 miles east-southeast of Bitterwater (lat. 36°20'55" N, long. 120°53'55" W; sec. 21, T 18 S, R 10 E). Named on Lonoak (1969) 7.5' quadrangle.

Trout Creek [SAN LUIS OBISPO]:
(1) *stream,* flows 10 miles to Santa Margarita Creek 3.5 miles north of Santa Margarita (lat. 35°26'30" N, long. 120°36'25" W). Named on Lopez Mountain (1965) and Santa Margarita (1965) 7.5' quadrangles.
(2) *stream,* flows 8 miles to join Stony Creek and form Huasna River 13 miles northeast of the town of Nipomo (lat. 35°12'05" N, long. 120°21' W; sec. 27, T 31 S, R 15 E). Named on Caldwell Mesa (1967), Pozo Summit (1967), and Santa Margarita (1965) 7.5' quadrangles.

Trout Creek: see **Trout Creek Gulch** [SANTA CRUZ].

Trout Creek Gulch [SANTA CRUZ]: *canyon,* drained by a stream that flows 4 miles to Valencia Creek 4.5 miles east-northeast of Soquel Point at Aptos (lat. 36°58'35" N, long. 121°53'45" W). Named on Laurel (1955) and Soquel (1954) 7.5' quadrangles. Capitola (1914) and Los Gatos (1919) 15' quadrangles show Trout Creek in the canyon.

Trujillo Creek [SAN LUIS OBISPO]: *stream,* flows nearly 4 miles to Pozo Creek 1.5 miles east-northeast of Pozo (lat. 35°18'45" N, long. 120°20'55" W; sec. 15, T 30 S, R 15 E). Named on Pozo Summit (1967) 7.5' quadrangle.

Tucker Canyon [SAN LUIS OBISPO]: *canyon,* drained by a stream that flows 7 miles to San Juan Creek 3.5 miles south-southeast of Shandon (lat. 35°36'30" N, long. 120°21' W; sec. 3, T 27 S, R 15 E). Named on Camatta Canyon (1961) and Cholame (1961) 7.5' quadrangles.

Tucker Gulch [SAN BENITO]: *canyon,* drained by a stream that flows nearly 3 miles to San Benito River 11 miles east of Bitterwater (lat. 36°22'15" N, long. 120°48'10" W; sec. 7, T 18 S, R 11 E). Named on Hepsedam Peak (1969) and Hernandez Reservoir (1969) 7.5' quadrangles.

Tucker Mountain [SAN BENITO]: *peak,* 12.5 miles east of Bitterwater (lat. 36°24'50" N,

long. 120°46'50" W; near SE cor. sec. 29, T 17 S, R 11 E). Altitude 4092 feet. Named on Hernandez Reservoir (1969) 7.5' quadrangle. Called Cane Mtn. on Hernandez Valley (1943) 15' quadrangle.

Tularcitos Creek [MONTEREY]: *stream,* flows 14 miles to Carmel River 1.5 miles southeast of the town of Carmel Valley (lat. 36°27'50" N, long. 121°42'50" W); the stream is mainly on Los Tularcitos grant. Named on Carmel Valley (1956) and Rana Creek (1956) 7.5' quadrangles.

Tularcitos Ridge [MONTEREY]: *ridge,* west-northwest-trending, 7 miles long, 6 miles southeast of the town of Carmel valley (lat. 36° 25'30" N, long. 121°39'30" W); the ridge is south of Tularcitos Creek. Named on Carmel Valley (1956) and Rana Creek (1956) 7.5' quadrangles.

Tule Canyon [MONTEREY]: *canyon,* nearly 1.5 miles long, opens into the canyon of San Antonio River 7 miles southeast of Jolon (lat. 35°54'10" N, long. 121°05'10" W). Named on Williams Hill (1949) 7.5' quadrangle.

Tules: see **The Tules** [SAN BENITO].

Tuley Springs: see **East Tuley Springs** [SAN LUIS OBISPO]: **West Tuley Springs** [SAN LUIS OBISPO].

Tully Creek [SAN BENITO]: *stream,* flows nearly 3 miles to Bitterwater Creek 4 miles southeast of Bitterwater (lat. 36°20'35" N, long. 120°56'55" W; near S line sec. 24, T 18 S, R 9 E). Named on Lonoak (1969) 7.5' quadrangle. Called Alvarez Cr. on Priest Valley (1915) 30' quadrangle.

Tully Mountain [SAN BENITO]: *peak,* 6 miles east-southeast of Bitterwater (lat. 36°21'25" N, long. 120°53'50" W; on N line sec. 21, T 18 S, R 10 E). Named on Lonoak (1969) 7.5' quadrangle.

Tumey Gulch [SAN BENITO]: *canyon,* drained by a stream that flows nearly 7 miles to Fresno County 12.5 miles east-southeast of Panoche (lat. 36°30'40" N, long. 120°37'55" W; sec. 26, T 16 S, R 12 E); the canyon is east of Tumey Hills. Named on Idria (1969) and Tumey Hills (1956) 7.5' quadrangles. According to Gudde (1969, p. 347), the name also had the form "Toomey."

Tumey Hills [SANTA BARBARA]: *range,* 9 miles east-southeast of Panoche and east of Silver Creek on San Benito-Fresno county line (lat. 36°32'30" N, long. 120°40' W). Named on Idria (1969) and Tumey Hills (1956) 7.5' quadrangles.

Tunnel Canyon [MONTEREY]: *canyon,* drained by a stream that flows 5 miles to Deer Canyon 8.5 miles east of Bradley (lat. 35° 52'20" N, long. 120°39'15" W; near E line sec. 3, T 24 S, R 12 E). Named on Valleton (1948) 7.5' quadrangle.

Tunnel Canyon [SANTA BARBARA]: *canyon,* drained by a stream that flows 4.25 miles to Sisquoc River 5 miles north of Zaca Lake (lat. 34°50'55" N, long. 120°03'20" W). Named on Manzanita Mountain (1964) and Zaca Lake (1964) 7.5' quadrangles.

Tunnel Flat [SAN LUIS OBISPO]: *area,* 2.5 miles east-southeast of Huasna Peak near the mouth of Alamo Creek (lat. 35°01'05" N, long. 120°18'30" W). Named on Huasna Peak (1967) 7.5' quadrangle. Water of Twitchell Reservoir now covers the place.

Tunnel Point [SAN LUIS OBISPO]: *promontory,* 1.25 miles north-northeast of Point San Luis along the coast near Port Harford (lat. 35°10'30" N, long. 120°45'10" W). Named on Port Harford (1897) 15' quadrangle.

Tunnel Spring [SAN LUIS OBISPO]: *spring,* 10 miles east-southeast of Shandon in Holland Canyon (lat. 35°36'05" N, long. 120°12'25" W; sec. 1, T 27 S, R 16 E). Named on Holland Canyon (1961) 7.5' quadrangle.

Tunnel Spring [SANTA BARBARA]: *spring,* nearly 6 miles north of Zaca Lake (lat. 34°51'40" N, long. 120°02'55" W); the spring is in Tunnel Canyon. Named on Zaca Lake (1964) 7.5' quadrangle.

Turkey Camp [SAN LUIS OBISPO]: *locality,* 10.5 miles south of Simmler (lat. 35°12'05" N, long. 119°58'05" W; near W line sec. 29, T 31 S, R 19 E). Named on Chimineas Ranch (1959) 7.5' quadrangle.

Turkey Camp Well [SAN LUIS OBISPO]: *well,* 10.5 miles south-southeast of Simmler (lat. 35°12'05" N, long. 119°57'05" W; near W line sec. 28, T 31 S, R 19 E); the well is 1 mile east of Turkey Camp. Named on Chimineas Ranch (1959) 7.5' quadrangle. McKittrick (1912) 30' quadrangle has the form "Turkeycamp Well" for the name.

Turkey Flat [MONTEREY]: *area,* 4.5 miles east-southeast of Parkfield (lat. 35°53' N, long,. 120°21'30" W). Named on Cholame Valley (1961), Parkfield (1961), and The Dark Hole (1961) 7.5' quadrangles. The name reportedly is from turkeys raised at the place in the early days (Clark, 1991, p. 581).

Turkey Foot: see **Boulder Creek** [SANTA CRUZ] (2).

Turkey Trap Ridge [SANTA BARBARA]: *ridge,* west-northwest-trending, 1 mile long, 1.25 miles east-northeast of New Cuyama in Cuyama Valley (lat. 34°57'25" N, long. 119°40' W). Named on New Cuyama (1964) 7.5' quadrangle.

Turner Creek [MONTEREY]: *stream,* flows nearly 3 miles to join Hill Creek (1) and form Bixby Creek 5.5 miles north-northeast of Point Sur (lat. 36°22'20" N, long. 121°50'35" W; near NE cor. sec. 15, T 18 S, R 1 E). Named on Big Sur (1956) and Mount Carmel (1956) 7.5' quadrangles.

Turner Creek Camp [MONTEREY]: *locality,* 7 miles northeast of Point Sur (lat. 36°22'40" N, long. 121°48'35" W; sec. 12, T 18 S, R 1 E); the place is along Turner Creek. Named on Mount Carmel (1956) 7.5' quadrangle. Clark (1991, p. 17) listed a place called Apple Tree Camp located along Turner Creek about

1.5 miles southeast of Turner Creek Camp (SW quarter sec. 7, T 18 S, R 2 E).

Turtle Creek [MONTEREY]: *stream,* flows nearly 4.5 miles to Nacimiento River 12.5 miles south-southeast of Jolon (lat. 35°47'55" N, long. 121°06'20" W; sec. 33, T 24 S, R 8 E). Named on Bryson (1949) 7.5' quadrangle.

Tuxedo: see **Mount Hermon** [SANTA CRUZ].

Twin Harbors [SANTA BARBARA]: *embayments,* 2.5 miles east-southeast of Diablo Point on the north side of Santa Cruz Island (lat. 34°02'35" N, long. 119°42'55" W). Named on Santa Cruz Island B (1943) 7.5' quadrangle. Goodyear (1890, map following p. 156) called the feature Tinkers Hbr., but United States Board on Geographic Names (1936b, p. 42) rejected this name for the place. Doran (p. 147) noted that the names "Twin Harbors," "Tinker's Cove," and "Orizaba" have been used interchangeably, and that Orizaba Pictograph Cave—also called Olson's Cave—is in the first draw west of the west embayment of Twin Harbors.

Twin Lake: see **Big Twin Lake** [SAN LUIS OBISPO]; **Small Twin Lake** [SAN LUIS OBISPPO].

Twin Lakes [SANTA CRUZ]: *town,* 1.5 miles west-northwest of Soquel Point near the coast (lat. 36°57'55" N, long. 121°59'50" W); the town is mainly between Woods Lagoon and Schwans Lagoon. Named on Soquel (1954) 7.5' quadrangle. The name is from the two lagoons, which are called Twin Lakes (Clark, 1986, p. 329). Ashley (plate 23) showed a place called Fairview located along the railroad at or near present Twin Lakes.

Twin Lakes: see **Schwans Lagoon** [SANTA CRUZ].

Twin Lakes Beach [SANTA CRUZ]: *beach,* 1.5 miles west-northwest of Soquel Point (lat. 36°57'45" N, long. 121°59'55" W); the beach is at the town of Twin Lakes. Named on Santa Cruz (1954) and Soquel (1954) 7.5' quadrangles.

Twin Peak [MONTEREY]: *peak,* 4 miles northeast of Lopez Point (lat. 36°03'10" N, long. 121°30'25" W; sec. 2, T 22 S, R 4 E). Altitude 4843 feet. Named on Lopez Point (1956) 7.5' quadrangle. This appears to be the feature called Roundtree Hill on Hamlin's (1904) map.

Twin Peaks [MONTEREY]:
(1) *peak,* 8 miles north-northeast of Point Sur (lat. 36°24'05" N, long. 121°49'25" W; sec. 2, T 18 S, R 1 E). Altitude 3568 feet. Named on Mount Carmel (1956) 7.5' quadrangle.
(2) *peaks,* two, 900 feet apart, 7 miles southwest of Soledad (lat. 36°22'15" N, long. 121°25'40" W; near N line sec. 16, T 18 S, R 5 E). Named on Sycamore Flat (1956) 7.5' quadrangle.
(3) *peaks,* two, 5.5 miles north of Charley Mountain on Monterey-Fresno county line (lat. 36°13'15" N, long. 120°38'40" W; sec. 2, T 20 S, R 12 E). Named on Priest Valley (1969) 7.5' quadrangle.

216

Twin Rocks [SAN LUIS OBISPO]: *peaks,* two, 5.5 miles south-southwest of Branch Mountain (lat. 35°06'45" N, long. 120°07'15" W; near E line sec. 26, T 32 S, R 17 E). Named on Miranda Pine Mountain (1967) 7.5' quadrangle.

Twin Seal Rocks: see **Lobos Rocks** [MONTEREY].

Twin Valley Creek [MONTEREY]: *stream,* flows 2.5 miles to El Piojo Creek 7 miles south of Jolon (lat. 35°52'10" N, long. 121°10'20" W). Named on Burnett Peak (1949) 7.5' quadrangle. The name was given because the stream heads in two separate valleys (Clark, 1991, p. 583).

Twisselmann Lake [SAN LUIS OBISPO]: *intermittent lake,* 450 feet long, 6 miles eastsoutheast of Cholame (lat. 35°39'40" N, long. 120°12'50" W; sec. 14, T 26 S, R 16 E). Named on Orchard Peak (1961) 7.5' quadrangle.

Twitchell Reservoir [SAN LUIS OBISPO-SANTA BARBARA]: *lake,* 8 miles long, behind a dam on Cuyama River 7 miles eastnortheast of Santa Maria on San Luis Obispo-Santa Barbara county line (lat. 34°59'10" N, long. 120°19'20" W). Named on Huasna Peak (1967), Nipomo (1965), and Twitchell Dam (1959) 7.5' quadrangles. United States Board on Geographic Names (1959, p. 3) rejected the name "Vaquero Reservoir" for the lake, and noted that the name "Twitchell" honors T.A. Twitchell for his efforts in behalf of water conservation in the region.

Two Bar Creek [SANTA BARBARA]: *stream,* flows nearly 4 miles to San Lorenzo River 5.25 miles east-southeast of Big Basin (lat. 37°08'30" N, long. 122°07'55" W; near NW cor. sec. 19, T 9 S, R 2 W). Named on Big Basin (1955) and Castle Rock Ridge (1955) 7.5' quadrangles.

Two Suertes [MONTEREY]: *land grant,* 5 miles west of Salinas. Named on Salinas (1947) 7.5' quadrangle. Gregory and Williams claimed 38 acres patented in 1872 (Cowan, p. 106).

Tyler Bight [SANTA BARBARA]: *embayment,* on the south side of San Miguel Island 2.25 miles east of Point Bennett (lat. 34°01'50" N, long. 120°24'40" W). Named on San Miguel Island West (1950) 7.5' quadrangle.

Tyler Canyon [SANTA BARBARA]: *canyon,* drained by a stream that flows 2 miles to Colson Canyon 2.25 miles north-northwest of Tepusquet Peak (lat. 34°56'30" N, long. 120°11'50" W). Named on Tepusquet Canyon (1964) 7.5' quadrangle.

Tyler Harbor: see **Potato Harbor** [SANTA BARBARA].

Tynan: see **Lake Tynan** [SANTA CRUZ].

– U –

Uncle Sam Mountain [MONTEREY]: *peak,* 4.5 miles north-northwest of Ventana Cone (lat. 36°20'30" N, long. 121°42'20" W). Altitude 4766 feet. Named on Ventana Cones (1956) 7.5' quadrangle. The name is from an early Mexican resident of the neighborhood who had the nickname "Uncle Sam" (Clark, 1991, p. 585).

Union [SAN LUIS OBISPO]: *locality,* 7.5 miles east of Paso Robles near Dry Creek (1) (lat. 35°38'15" N, long. 120°33'35" W; sec. 27, T 26 S, R 13 E). Named on Paso Robles (1919) 15' quadrangle. Postal authorities established Union post office in 1900 and discontinued it in 1924 (Frickstad, p. 166).

Union: see **Lake View** [SANTA BARBARA].

Union Creek [SANTA CRUZ]: *stream,* flows 1.5 miles to Sempervirens Creek nearly 1 mile northeast of Big Basin (lat. 37°10'30" N, long. 122°12'30" W; near NE cor. sec. 8, T 9 S, R 3 E). Named on Big Basin (1955) 7.5' quadrangle. The name is from Union Mill, built in 1895 (Clark, 1986, p. 382).

Upland: see **San Lucas** [MONTEREY] (2).

Upper Barn Springs: see **Hot Springs** [SANTA BARBARA] (2).

Upper Bee Camp: see **Bee Camp** [MONTEREY].

Upper Branch Canyon Spring [SANTA BARBARA]: *spring,* 0.5 mile north-northwest of Montgomery Potrero (lat. 34°50'45" N, long. 119°45'20" W); the spring is in Branch Canyon. Named on Hurricane Deck (1964) 7.5' quadrangle.

Upper Hog Pen Spring [SANTA BARBARA]: *spring,* 1 mile east-southeast of McPherson Peak (lat. 34°52'55" N, long. 119°47'30" W); the spring is 1300 feet northwest of Hog Pen Spring. Named on Peak Mountain (1964) 7.5' quadrangle.

Upper Horse Canyon [SANTA BARBARA]: *canyon,* drained by a stream that flows 1.5 miles to Horse Canyon (3) 6.5 miles northnorthwest of San Marcos Pass (lat. 34°36'25" N, long. 119°50'55" W). Named on San Marcos Pass (1959) 7.5' quadrangle.

Upper Lopez Campground [SAN LUIS OBISPO]: *locality,* nearly 1 mile east-northeast of Lopez Mountain (lat. 35°18'20" N, long. 120°34' W; sec. 22, T 30 S, R 13 E); the place is in Lopez Canyon. Named on Lopez Mountain (1965) 7.5' quadrangle.

Upper Newsome Spring [SANTA BARBARA]: *spring,* nearly 2 miles north of Salisbury Potrero (lat. 34°50'50" N, long. 119°42' W); the spring is 3600 feet south of Lower Newsome Spring in Newsome Canyon. Named on Salisbury Potrero (1964) 7.5' quadrangle.

Upper Oso Campground [SANTA BARBARA]: *locality,* 4.5 miles northeast of San Marcos Pass (lat. 34°33'25" N, long. 119°45'10" W); the place is less than 1 mile north-northeast of Lower Oso Campground in Oso Canyon. Named on San Marcos Pass (1959) 7.5' quadrangle.

Upper Piletas Canyon [SAN LUIS OBISPO]:

canyon, drained by a stream that flows nearly 2 miles to Lower Piletas Canyon 4.5 miles east-southeast of Castle Crags (lat. 35°16'40" N, long. 120°07'45" W; near NE cor. sec. 34, T 30 S, R 17 E). Named on La Panza (1967) 7.5' quadrangle. Upper Piletas Canyon and Lower Piletas Canyon together are called Piletas Canyon on La Panza (1935) 15' quadrangle, but United States Board on Geographic Names (1968c, p. 5) rejected the name "Piletas Canyon" for the combined features.

Upper Santa Ynez Campground [SANTA BARBARA]: *locality,* 8 miles north of Rincon Point (lat. 34°29'30" N, long. 119°27'05" W; sec. 25, T 5 N, R 25 W); the place is near the head of Santa Ynez River. Named on White Ledge Peak (1952) 7.5' quadrangle.

Upper Trough Canyon Spring [SANTA BARBARA]: *spring,* 2.5 miles north-northwest of Montgomery Potrero (lat. 34°52'15" N, long. 119°46'05" W); the spring is in Trough Canyon. Named on Hurricane Deck (1964) 7.5' quadrangle.

Upton Canyon [SAN LUIS OBISPO]: *canyon,* 6.25 miles long, opens into Shedd Canyon 9 miles south of Shandon (lat. 35°31'55" N, long. 120°24'10" W; sec. 31, T 27 S, R 15 E). Named on Camatta Canyon (1961), Camatta Ranch (1966), and Shedd Canyon (1961) 7.5' quadrangles.

— V —

Vaca Flat [SAN LUIS OBISPO]: *area,* 5.5 miles west-northwest of Pozo (lat. 35°19'25" N, long. 120°28'05" W; near W line sec. 10, T 30 S, R 14 E). Named on Santa Margarita Lake (1967) 7.5' quadrangle.

Valdez Harbor: see **Cueva Valdaze** [SANTA BARBARA].

Valencia: see **Valencia Creek** [SANTA CRUZ].

Valencia Creek [SANTA CRUZ]: *stream,* flows 7.25 miles to Aptos Creek 4.25 miles east-northeast of Soquel Point at Aptos (lat. 36°58'30" N, long. 121°54'05" W). Named on Loma Prieta (1955) Soquel (1954), and Watsonville West (1954) 7.5' quadrangles. Hamman's (1980a) map shows a place called Valencia Creek Mill situated along the stream 2 miles east-northeast of Aptos, and a tributary called Cox Creek that joins Valencia Creek near the mill. California Mining Bureau's (1909d) map shows a place called Valencia located 3 miles by road east-north-east of Aptos. Postal authorities established Valencia post office in 1893 and discontinued it in 1909 (Frickstad, p. 177).

Valencia Creek: see **Coon Creek** [SAN LUIS OBISPO].

Valencia Creek Mill: see **Valencia Creek** [SANTA CRUZ].

Valencia Lagoon [SANTA CRUZ]: *marsh,* 5.25 miles east-northeast of Soquel Point (lat. 36°58'25" N, long. 121°52'55" W); the fea-

ture is near Valencia Creek. Named on Soquel (1954) 7.5' quadrangle. Capitola (1914) 15' quadrangle has the name for a lake. The feature was called Spreckels Lagoon in the 1880's (Clark, 1986, p. 384).

Valencia Peak [SAN LUIS OBISPO]: *peak,* 7.25 miles south of Morro Rock (lat. 35°15'50" N, long. 120°52'15" W). Altitude 1347 feet. Named on Morro Bay South (1965) 7.5' quadrangle.

Vallecitos [SAN BENITO]: *valley,* center 9 miles south-southeast of Panoche (lat. 36°29' N, long. 120°46' W); the northwest part of the valley is drained by Vallecitos Creek. Named on Hernandez Reservoir (1969), Idria (1969), and Panoche (1969) 7.5' quadrangles. Called The Vallecitos on Priest Valley (1915) 30' quadrangle.

Vallecitos Creek [SAN BENITO]: *stream,* flows 4.25 miles to join Pimental Creek and form Griswold Creek 5.5 miles south of Panoche (lat. 36°30'55" N, long. 120°50' W; near N line sec. 25, T 16 S, R 10 E); the stream drains part of Vallecitos. Named on Hernandez Reservoir (1969) and Panoche (1969) 7.5' quadrangles. Called Griswold Creek on Santa Cruz (1956) 1°x 2° quadrangle, and United States Board on Geographic Names (1972a, p. 1) listed this name as a variant.

Vallejo Slough: see **Elkhorn Slough** [MONTEREY].

Valleton [MONTEREY]: *locality,* 6 miles east-northeast of Bradley in Indian Valley (3) (lat. 35°53'20" N, long. 120°42'15" W; sec. 32, T 23 S, R 12 E). Named on Valleton (1948) 7.5' quadrangle. Postal authorities established Valleton post office in 1887, moved it 4 miles southwest in 1901, and discontinued it in 1918 (Salley, p. 229). San Miguel (1919) 15' quadrangle shows the place along Stone Canyon Railroad. California Mining Bureau's (1917b) map shows a place called Eagle located along the railroad 2.5 miles north-northeast of Valleton—San Miguel (1919) 15' quadrangle shows Eagle school in the same neighborhood.

Valley Anchorage [SANTA BARBARA]: *embayment,* nearly 3 miles south-southeast of Prisoners Harbor on the south side of Santa Cruz Island (lat. 33°59'05" N, long. 119°39'45" W); the embayment is east of the east end of Central Valley. Named on Santa Cruz Island C (1943) 7.5' quadrangle. Called Puerto de la Cañada del Sur on Rand's (1931) map. Bremner's (1932) map has the name "Blue Bank" at the place, and has the name "Cñ. Pomona" for the canyon that opens to the sea there.

Valley of Los Alisos: see **Sycamore Canyon** [SANTA BARBARA] (2).

Valley of Los Robles: see **San Antonio River** [MONTEREY].

Valley of Monterey: see **Salinas Valley**, under **Salinas River** [MONTEREY-SAN LUIS OBISPO].

Valley of San Luis Obispo: see **Los Osos Valley** [SAN LUIS OBISPO].

Valley of the Bears: see **Los Osos Valley** [SAN LUIS OBISPO].

Valley of the Coxo: see **Cañada del Cojo** [SANTA BARBARA].

Van Allen Ridge [SANTA CRUZ]: *ridge,* south-southwest-trending, 1.25 miles long, 4.5 miles east-southeast of the town of Boulder Creek (lat. 37°06'15" N, long. 122°02'30" W). Named on Felton (1955) 7.5' quadrangle.

Van Cliff Canyon [SAN BENITO]: *canyon,* drained by a stream that flows 3.25 miles to Pimental Creek 6.25 miles south-southwest of Panoche (lat. 36°30'55" N, long. 120°52'45" W; sec. 28, T 16 S, R 10 E). Named on Llanada (1969) and Rock Spring Peak (1969) 7.5' quadrangles.

Vancouver's Pinnacles: see **Pinnacle Rocks** [SAN BENITO].

Vandenberg Air Force Base [SANTA BARBARA]: *military installation,* northwest of the city of Lompoc along the coast. Named on Casmalia (1959), Guadalupe (1959), Lompoc (1959), Orcutt (1959), Point Sal (1958), and Surf (1959) 7.5' quadrangles. Called Camp Cooke Military Reservation on Point Sal (1947) 15' quadrangle, which shows Camp Cooke on the reservation. The name "Cooke" commemorated Philip St. George Cooke, who led the Mormon Battalion to California during the Mexican War (Gudde, 1949, p. 78). The name "Vandenberg" honors General H.S. Vandenberg, who was chief of staff for United States Air Force from 1948 until 1953 (Hart, J.D., p. 461).

Van Gordon Creek [SAN LUIS OBISPO]:
(1) *stream,* flows 3.5 miles to Burnett Creek 6 miles north of the village of San Simeon (lat. 35°43'40" N, long. 121°10'25" W). Named on San Simeon (1958) 7.5' quadrangle.
(2) *stream,* flows 4.5 miles to San Simeon Creek 3 miles northwest of Cambria (lat. 35°35'40" N, long. 121°07'10" W; near NW cor. sec. 16, T 27 S, R 8 E). Named on Cambria (1959) and Pebblestone Shut-in (1959) 7.5' quadrangles.

Vanoni Peak: see **Atherton Peak** [SANTA CRUZ].

Van Winkleys Canyon [MONTEREY]: *canyon,* drained by a stream that flows 2 miles to San Jose Creek 4.5 miles northeast of Soberanes Point (lat. 36°29'10" N, long. 121°51'40" W; sec. 4, T 17 S, R 1 E). Named on Mount Carmel (1956) 7.5' quadrangle.

Vaquero Cañon: see **Vaqueros Creek** [MONTEREY].

Vaquero Creek: see **Vaqueros Creek** [MONTEREY].

Vaquero Flat [SAN LUIS OBISPO]: *area,* 1.5 miles south-southeast of Huasna Peak (lat. 35°00'50" N, long. 120°20'25" W). Named on Huasna Peak (1967) 7.5' quadrangle.

Vaquero Peak: see **Pinyon Peak** [MONTEREY] (2).

Vaquero Reservoir: see **Twitchell Reservoir** [SAN LUIS OBISPO-SANTA BARBARA].

Vaqueros Canyon: see **Vaqueros Creek** [MONTEREY].

Vaqueros Creek [MONTEREY]: *stream,* flows 10 miles to Arroyo Seco (1) 6.5 miles southwest of Greenfield (lat. 36°15'50" N, long. 121°20'10" W; sec. 20, T 19 S, R 6 E). Named on Paraiso Springs (1956) and Reliz Canyon (1949) 7.5' quadrangles. Called Vaquero Creek on Soledad (1915) 15' quadrangle. Hamlin (p. 14) used the name "Los Vaqueros Valley" for the valley along the upper part of the stream, which he (fig 11) called Los Vaqueros Cr. Goodyear (1888, p. 87) called the same valley Vaquero Cañon, and Wiedey (p. 99) called it Vaqueros Canyon.

Vasques Creek: see **Vasquez Creek** [SAN LUIS OBISPO].

Vasquez: see **Lorenzo Vasquez Canyon** [SAN BENITO].

Vasquez Creek [SAN BENITO]: *stream,* flows 5.25 miles to Fresno County 8.5 miles north-northwest of Panoche (lat. 36°42'45" N, long. 120°53' W; sec. 16, T 14 S, R 10 E). Named on Cerro Colorado (1969) 7.5' quadrangle.

Vasquez Creek [SAN LUIS OBISPO]: *stream,* flows nearly 6 miles to Lopez Canyon 11.5 miles north of the town of Nipomo (lat. 35°12'25" N, long. 120°28'55" W; sec. 21, T 31 S, R 14 E). Named on Arroyo Grande NE (1965) and Tar Spring Ridge (1967) 7.5' quadrangles. Called Basquez Creek on Arroyo Grande (1897) 15' quadrangle, but United States Board on Geographic Names (1967a, p. 10) rejected the names "Basquez Creek" and "Vasques Creek" for the stream.

Vasquez Crossing [SAN BENITO]: *locality,* 9.5 miles east-southeast of Bitterwater along Hepsedam Creek (lat. 36°19'05" N, long. 120°51'15" W; sec. 35, T 18 S, R 10 E); the place is 1 mile southeast of Vasquez Rock. Named on Hepsedam Peak (1969) 7.5' quadrangle.

Vasquez Knob [MONTEREY]: *peak,* 9.5 miles east of Soberanes Point (lat. 36°28'10" N, long. 121°45'40" W; sec. 9, T 17 S, R 2 E). Named on Mount Carmel (1956) 7.5' quadrangle.

Vasquez Rock [SAN BENITO]: *peak,* 8 miles east-southeast of Bitterwater (lat. 36°19'35" N, long. 120°52'05" W; near NE cor. sec. 34, T 18 S, R 10 E). Altitude 3884 feet. Named on Hepsedam Peak (1969) 7.5' quadrangle.

Vega [MONTEREY]: *locality,* 2.5 miles west-northwest of Aromas along Southern Pacific Railroad (lat. 36°53'55" N, long. 121°41'20" W). Named on San Juan Bautista (1917) 15' quadrangle. The station name, given in 1871, is from Vega del Rio del Pajaro grant, where the place was located (Gudde, 1969, p. 352).

Vega del Rio del Pajaro [MONTEREY]: *land grant,* west of Aromas along Pajaro River. Named on Prunedale (1954) and Watsonville East (1955) 7.5' quadrangles. Antonio Maria Castro received the land in 1820; F.A.

McDougal and others claimed 4310 acres patented in 1864 (Cowan, p. 56). Perez (p. 104) gave 1833 as the date of the grant.

Venado Peak: see **Sampson Peak** [SAN BENITO].

Venezuela: see **Posa de los Ositos** [MONTEREY].

Ventana Camp [MONTEREY]: *locality,* 4 miles west-southwest of Ventana Cone along Big Sur River (lat. 36°15'35" N, long. 121°44'30" W; sec. 21, T 19 S, R 2 E); the place is near the confluence of Big Sur River with Ventana Creek (2). Named on Ventana Cones (1956) 7.5' quadrangle.

Ventana Cone [MONTEREY]: *peak,* 12.5 miles east of Point Sur (lat. 36°17'05" N, long. 121°40'35" W; sec. 18, T 19 S, R 3 E). Altitude 4727 feet. Named on Ventana Cones (1956) 7.5' quadrangle. According to Lussier (p. 13), the name is from a windowlike gap between two peaks—*ventana* means "window" in Spanish.

Ventana Cone: see **South Ventana Cone** [MONTEREY].

Ventana Creek [MONTEREY]:
(1) *stream,* flows 2.25 miles to Little Sur River 7.5 miles east of Point Sur (lat. 36°19'35" N, long. 121°46'05" W); the stream heads near Ventana Double Cone. Named on Big Sur (1956) and Ventana Cones (1956) 7.5' quadrangles. United States Board on Geographic Names (1967b, p. 7) approved the name "Jackson Creek" for the stream. The junction of the creek with Little Sur River is 1 mile east of Jackson Camp.
(2) *stream,* flows nearly 4 miles to Big Sur River 4.25 miles west-southwest of Ventana Cone (lat. 36°15'30" N, long. 121°44'40" W; near S line sec. 21, T 19 S, R 2 E); the stream heads near Ventana Double Cone. Named on Ventana Cones (1956) 7.5' quadrangle.

Ventana Double Cone [MONTEREY]: *peaks,* two, 2.25 miles west-northwest of Ventana Cone (lat. 36°17'55" N, long. 121°42'50" W; sec. 11, T 19 S, R 2 E). Named on Ventana Cones (1956) 7.5' quadrangle. United States Board on Geographic Names (1962a, p. 18) rejected the names "Double Summit" and "Ventana Double Summit" for the peaks.

Ventana Double Summit: see **Ventana Double Cone** [MONTEREY].

Ventana Mesa Creek [MONTEREY]: *stream,* flows 2.25 miles to Carmel River 2 miles north of Ventana Cone (lat. 36°18'50" N, long. 121°40'50" W; sec. 32, T 18 S, R 3 E); the stream heads near Ventana Double Cone. Named on Ventana Cones (1956) 7.5' quadrangle.

Ventucopa [SANTA BARBARA]: *locality,* 11.5 miles southeast of the village of Cuyama (lat. 34°49'45" N, long. 119°28' W). Named on Cuyama Peak (1943) 7.5' quadrangle. Postal authorities established Ventucopa post office in 1935 and discontinued it in 1954; the coined name is from the words "Ventura" and

"Mari<u>copa</u>" (Salley, p. 230).

Ventura Rocks [MONTEREY]: *rocks,* two, largest 75 feet long, 3.5 miles north of Point Sur, and 3000 feet offshore (lat. 36°20'35" N, long. 121°54'20" W). Named on Point Sur (1956) 7.5' quadrangle. The name commemorates the steamship *Ventura,* which was wrecked on the rocks in 1875 (Reinstedt, 1975, p. 109).

Veratina: see **Nasimento**, under **Bradley** [MONTEREY].

Verde [SAN LUIS OBISPO]: *locality,* 3.5 miles southeast of Edna in the upper part of Corbit Canyon (lat. 35°10'15" N, long. 120°33'25" W); the place is above the head of Cañada Verde. Named on Arroyo Grande NE (1965) 7.5' quadrangle. Arroyo Grande (1897) 15' quadrangle shows the place along Pacific Coast Railroad.

Veronica Springs [SANTA BARBARA]: *spring,* 2.5 miles west-southwest of downtown Santa Barbara (lat. 34°24'40" N, long. 119°44'30" W). Named on Santa Barbara (1952) 7.5' quadrangle. Huguenin (p. 743) mentioned that the springs occur on the west side of Veronica Valley. Huguenin (p. 741-742) also noted that Bythenia Springs are situated 0.5 mile northwest of Veronica Springs, Moore Spring is in Veronica Valley opposite Veronica Springs, and Pinkham's Santa Barbara Mineral Springs are near the top of a low mesa that overlooks Veronica Valley. G.A. Waring (p. 295) listed Santa Barbara Springs, which were located about 0.75 mile northeast of Veronica Springs.

Veronica Valley: see **Veronica Springs** [SANTA BARBARA].

Viboras Creek: see **Arroyo de las Viboras** [SAN BENITO].

Vicente Camp [MONTEREY]: *locality,* 1.5 miles south-southeast of Cone Peak (lat. 36°01'45" N, long. 121°29'15" W; sec. 12, T 22 S, R 4 E). Named on Cone Peak (1949) 7.5' quadrangle. Called Vicente Flat Campground on Junipero Serra (1961) 15' quadrangle. United States Board on Geographic Names (1978b, p. 5) approved the name "Vicente Flat" for the place, and rejected the names "Vicente Camp" and "Vincente Flat." The name is from Vicente Avila, who kept stock at the place and had a cabin there (Clark, 1991, p. 592).

Vicente Creek [MONTEREY]: *stream,* flows 3.25 miles to the sea 2 miles north-northwest of Lopez Point (lat. 36°02'40" N, long. 121°35'05" W; sec. 1, T 22 S, R 3 E). Named on Lopez Point (1956) 7.5' quadrangle. The name is for Vicente Avila (Clark, 1991, p. 592).

Vicente Flat: see **Vicente Camp** [MONTEREY].

Vicente Flat Campground: see **Vicente Camp** [MONTEREY].

Vierra Canyon [MONTEREY]:
(1) *canyon,* drained by a stream that flows 2.25 miles to San Miguel Canyon at Prunedale (lat. 36°47'30" N, long. 121°40' W). Named on

Prunedale (1954) 7.5' quadrangle. The name is for Roleno José Vierra, who had a summer place in the canyon (Clark, 1991, p. 594).

(2) *canyon,* drained by a stream that flows 3.25 miles to Mud Creek 8 miles north-northeast of Salinas (lat. 36°46'55" N, long. 121°35'05" W). Named on San Juan Bautista (1955) 7.5' quadrangle.

Vierras Knoll [MONTEREY]: *hill,* 1.25 miles southeast of Point Lobos (lat. 36°30'30" N, long. 121°56'20" W). Named on Monterey (1947) 7.5' quadrangle. The name commemorates Juan Vierra Pre (Clark, 1991, p. 594).

Villa Creek [MONTEREY]: *stream,* flows 4.25 miles to the sea 4 miles southeast of Cape San Martin (lat. 35°51' N, long. 121°24'30" W; sec. 17, T 24 S, R 5 E). Named on Burro Mountain (1949) and Villa Creek (1949) 7.5' quadrangles.

Villa Creek [SAN LUIS OBISPO]:
(1) *stream,* flows 12 miles to the sea nearly 2 miles east of Point Estero (lat. 35°27'35" N, long. 120°58'10" W; sec. 35, T 28 S, R 9 E). Named on Cayucos (1965) and Cypress Mountain (1948) 7.5' quadrangles.
(2) *stream,* flows 3.5 miles to East Corral de Piedra Creek 4 miles northeast of Edna (lat. 35°14'05" N, long. 120°33'20" W). Named on Arroyo Grande NE (1965) and Lopez Mountain (1965) 7.5' quadrangles.

Villa Creek: see **San Geronimo** [SAN LUIS OBISPO].

Ville de Francfort: see **Santa Cruz** [SANTA CRUZ].

Vilo: see **Ellwood** [SANTA BARBARA].

Vincente Flat: see **Vicente Camp** [MONTEREY].

Vineyard Canyon [MONTEREY-SAN LUIS OBISPO]: *canyon,* drained by a stream that heads in Monterey County and flows 16 miles to Salinas River in 1.5 miles north-northwest of San Miguel San Luis Obispo County (lat. 35°46'30" N, long. long. 120°42'10" W; sec. 8, T 25 S, R 12 E). Named on Ranchito Canyon (1948), San Miguel (1948), and Stockdale Mountain (1948) 7.5' quadrangles. Nomland (p. 215) used the name "Vineyard Creek" for the stream in the canyon. Stanley (p. 124) mentioned Vineyard Springs that were situated "about four miles up the canyon." California Mining Bureau's (1909a) map shows a place called Apricot located in Monterey County 10 miles by stage line southwest of Imusdale. Postal authorities established Apricot post office in Vineyard Canyon 9 miles northeast of San Miguel in 1887 and discontinued it in 1900 (Salley, p. 8).

Vineyard Canyon [SAN LUIS OBISPO]: *canyon,* drained by a stream that flows 3.25 miles to the sea nearly 3 miles northwest of Point San Luis (lat. 35°11' N, long. 120°48' W). Named on Port San Luis (1965) 7.5' quadrangle. Port Harford (1897) 15' quadrangle shows Pecho Creek in the canyon. United States Board on Geographic Names (1967c,

p. 2) adopted the name "Irish Canyon" for the feature, and rejected the names "Vineyard Canyon" and "Pecho Creek."

Vineyard Creek: see **Vineyard Canyon** [MONTEREY-SAN LUIS OBISPO].

Vineyard Springs: see **Vineyard Canyon** [MONTEREY]:

Vinyard [SAN BENITO]: *locality,* 7 miles south of Hollister (lat. 36° 45' N, long. 121°23'05" W). Named on Hollister (1921) 15' quadrangle. Hollister (1955) 7.5' quadrangle shows a winery at the place.

Viscaino Hill: see **Bluefish Cove** [MONTEREY].

Von Helm Rock [SAN LUIS OBISPO]: *rock,* 2.5 miles southwest of Cambria (lat. 35°32'20" N, long. 121°06'40" W). Named on Cambria (1959) 7.5' quadrangle.

Vulture Rock [SAN LUIS OBISPO]: *peak,* 9.5 miles east of the village of San Simeon (lat. 35°38'40" N, long. 121°01'05" W; sec. 29, T 26 S, R 9 E). Altitude 2849 feet. Named on Pebblestone Shut-in (1959) 7.5' quadrangle.

– W –

Waddell: see **Bonnie Doon** [SANTA CRUZ].

Waddell Creek [SANTA CRUZ]: *stream,* formed by the confluence of East Waddell Creek and West Waddell Creek, flows 3.5 miles to the sea 16 miles west-northwest of Santa Cruz (lat. 37°05'35" N, long. 122°16'30" W; near W line sec. 2, T 10 S, R 4 W). Named on Año Nuevo (1955) and Franklin Point (1955) 7.5' quadrangles. Crespi gave the name "La Cañada de San Luis Beltran" to a campsite that the Portola expedition had by the stream in 1769, but the soldiers, who rested there to recover from sickness, called the place Cañada de la Salude— *salude* means "health" in Spanish; the canyon of the stream was called Big Gulch in the early days of lumbering in the region, but the stream itself was named for William W. Waddell after he built a sawmill along it in 1862 (Hoover, Rensch, and Rensch, p. 475-476).

Waddell Creek: see **East Waddell Creek** [SANTA CRUZ]; **West Waddell Creek** [SANTA CRUZ].

Waddell Gulch: see **Granite Creek** [SANTA CRUZ].

Wagner Creek [MONTEREY]: *stream,* flows 2.5 miles to San Carpoforo Creek 12 miles east-southeast of Cape San Martin (lat. 35° 49'20" N, long. 121°16'10" W; sec. 25, T 24 S, R 6 E). Named on Burnett Peak (1949) and Burro Mountain (1949) 7.5' quadrangles.

Wagon Cave Campground: see **Old Wagon Cave Campground** [MONTEREY].

Wagon Caves: see **Rattlesnake Creek** [MONTEREY] (2).

Wagon Flat Campground [SANTA BARBARA]: *locality,* 4.5 miles north-northwest of Manzanita Mountain along North Fork La

Brea Creek (lat. 34°57'25" N, long. 120°05'45" W). Named on Manzanita Mountain (1964) 7.5' quadrangle.

Waldo: see **Waldorf** [SANTA BARBARA].

Waldorf [SANTA BARBARA]: *locality,* 4.25 miles south-southeast of the town of Guadalupe along Southern Pacific Railroad (lat. 34°54'40" N, long. 120°33'15" W). Named on Guadalupe (1959) 7.5' quadrangle. Called Waldo on California Mining Bureau's (1917c) map.

Walker Canyon [MONTEREY]: *canyon,* drained by a stream that flows 7.5 miles to Sargent Creek 8 miles north of Bradley (lat. 35° 58'30" N, long. 120°47'50" W; sec. 32, T 22 S, R 11 E). Named on Slack Canyon (1969), Valleton (1948), and Wunpost (1949) 7.5' quadrangles. Members of the Walker family lived in and near the canyon (Clark, 1991, p. 598).

Walker Peak [SAN BENITO]: *peak,* 8 miles west of Panoche (lat. 36°35'50" N, long. 120°58'15" W; sec. 27, T 15 S, R 9 E). Altitude 2835 feet. Named on Llanada (1969) 7.5' quadrangle.

Waller Creek [MONTEREY]: *stream,* flows 3 miles to El Piojo Creek 9.5 miles south of Jolon (lat. 35°50'10" N, long. 121°09'10" W; near NW cor. sec. 19, T 24 S, R 8 E). Named on Bryson (1949) and Burnett Peak (1949) 7.5' quadrangles. Edward Waller patented land along the stream in 1889 (Clark, 1991, p. 598). South Fork enters 1 mile upstream from the mouth of the main stream; it is 3.25 miles long and is named on Bryson (1949) and Burnett Peak (1949) 7.5' quadrangles.

Walnut Creek [SAN LUIS OBISPO]: *stream,* heads in Kern County and flows 1 mile in San Luis Obispo County to join Yeguas Creek and form Bitterwater Creek 25 miles southeast of Shandon (lat. 35°27'30" N, long. 120°00'45" W; sec. 26, T 28 S, R 18 E). Named on La Panza NE (1966) 7.5' quadrangle.

Walters Camp [SAN LUIS OBISPO]: *locality,* 11.5 miles south-southwest of Shandon (lat. 35°30'35" N, long. 120°27'50" W). Named on Shedd Canyon (1961) 7.5' quadrangle.

Walters Canyon [MONTEREY]: *canyon,* drained by a stream that flows 5 miles to Powell Canyon 7 miles north-northeast of Bradley (lat. 35°57' N, long. 120°44'50" W; sec. 11, T 23 S, R 11 E). Named on Slack Canyon (1969) and Valleton (1948) 7.5' quadrangles.

Warden Lake [SAN LUIS OBISPO]: *marsh,* 1 mile wide, 5.5 miles southeast of Morro Rock in Los Osos Valley (lat. 35°18'40" N, long. 120°47'45" W). Named on Morro Bay South (1965) 7.5' quadrangle. Cayucos (1951) 15' quadrangle shows a lake, 4300 feet long, at the place.

Warner Lake [MONTEREY]: *lake,* 1200 feet long, 5.5 miles west of Aromas in marsh (lat. 36°52'50" N, long. 121°44'30" W). Named on Watsonville East (1955) 7.5' quadrangle.

Wash: see **The Wash** [SAN LUIS OBISPO].

Washington Flat [SAN LUIS OBISPO]: *valley,* 8 miles northeast of the town of Nipomo (lat. 35°08' N, long. 120°23'30" W). Named on Nipomo (1922) 15' quadrangle.

Wasibo: see **Camp Wasibo** [SANTA CRUZ].

Wasioja [SANTA BARBARA]: *locality,* 4.5 miles north-northwest of McPherson Peak (lat. 34°56'50" N, long. 119°50'30" W). Named on Santa Ynez (1905) 30' quadrangle. Postal authorities established Wasioja post office in 1893, moved it 2 miles west in 1898, moved it 1 mile northwest in 1901, moved it 8 miles east in 1902, and discontinued it in 1933; the name is from a place in Minnesota (Salley, p. 235).

Wasna Creek: see **Huasna River** [SAN LUIS OBISPO].

Water Canyon [SAN LUIS OBISPO]: *canyon,* drained by a stream that flow nearly 3 miles to Trout Creek (1) 2.5 miles north-northwest of Lopez Mountain (lat. 35°20'20" N, long. 120°35'10" W; near S line sec. 4, T 30 S, R 13 E). Named on Lopez Mountain (1965) 7.5' quadrangle.

Water Canyon [SANTA BARBARA]:
(1) *canyon,* drained by a stream that flows 6.5 miles to Sisquoc River 2 miles north-northwest of Bald Mountain (1) (lat. 34°50'25" N, long. 119°56'35" W). Named on Bald Mountain (1964) and Bates Canyon (1964) 7.5' quadrangles. Called Wellman Canyon on Santa Ynez (1905) 30' quadrangle.
(2) *canyon,* drained by a stream that flows 2.25 miles to the sea 2.5 miles south of Tranquillon Mountain (lat. 34°32'35" N, long. 120° 33'35" W). Named on Tranquillon Mountain (1959) 7.5' quadrangle.

Water Canyon Campground [SANTA BARBARA]: *locality,* about 2.25 miles north of Bald Mountain (1) along Sisquoc River (lat. 34°50'40" N, long. 119°56'30" W); the place is near the mouth of Water Canyon (1). Named on Bald Mountain (1964) 7.5' quadrangle.

Waterdog Creek [MONTEREY]: *stream,* flows nearly 4 miles to Nacimiento River 12 miles south-southeast of Jolon (lat. 35°47'45" N, long. 121°06'15" W; sec. 33, T 24 S, R 8 E). Named on Bryson (1949) and Burnett Peak (1949) 7.5' quadrangles.

Waterman Gap [SANTA CRUZ]: *pass,* 4.5 miles northeast of Big Basin (lat. 37°12'40" N, long. 122°09'20" W; sec. 26, T 8 S, R 3 W). Named on Big Basin (1955) 7.5' quadrangle.

Waterman Switch: see **San Lorenzo Park** [SANTA CRUZ].

Watson Creek [MONTEREY]: *stream,* flows 6.5 miles to El Toro Creek 9.5 miles southsouthwest of Salinas (lat. 36°33' N, long. 121°43'55" W); the stream drains Corral de Tierra Valley. Named on Spreckels (1947) 7.5' quadrangle.

Watsonville [SANTA CRUZ]: *town,* 15 miles east-southeast of Santa Cruz on the northwest side of Pajaro River (lat. 36°54'55" N, long. 121°45'10" W). Named on Watsonville East (1955) and Watsonville West (1954) 7.5' quadrangles. J.H. Watson and D.S. Gregory laid out the town in 1852 (Bancroft, p. 525). Postal authorities established Watsonville post office in 1853 (Frickstad, p. 177), and the town incorporated in 1868. Lewis (1976, p. 163) noted that a dam on Pajaro River at Watsonville formed a lake in 1907 that first was called Lake Pajaro and later was called Lake Watsonville.

Watsonville: see **Lake Watsonville**, under **Watsonville** [SANTA CRUZ]; **Port Watsonville** [SANTA CRUZ].

Watsonville Junction [MONTEREY]: *locality,* 5.5 miles west of Aromas along Southern Pacific Railroad, where the line to Watsonville branches from the main line (lat. 36°53'40" N, long. 121°44'40" W). Named on Watsonville East (1955) 7.5' quadrangle. The place first was called Pajaro (Clark, 1991, p. 601).

Watsonville Slough [SANTA CRUZ]: *stream,* flows 7.25 miles, mainly in an artificial watercourse, to Pajaro River 5.5 miles southwest of Watsonville (lat. 36°51'10" N, long. 121°58'30" W). Named on Moss Landing (1954) and Watsonville West (1954) 7.5' quadrangles.

Wave [SANTA BARBARA]: *locality,* 1 mile northwest of Rincon Point along Southern Pacific Railroad (lat. 34°22'55" N, long. 119° 29'15" W). Named on White Ledge Peak (1952) 7.5' quadrangle.

Wayland Creek [MONTEREY]: *stream,* flows 4.5 miles to Big Sandy Creek 4.25 miles south of Smith Mountain (lat. 36°01' N, long. 120°35'25" W; sec. 17, T 22 S, R 13 E). Named on Smith Mountain (1969) 7.5' quadrangle. The name is from members of the Wayland family, landowners in the neighborhood (Clark, 1991, p. 602). California Mining Bureau's (1917b) map shows a place called Hill situated near the confluence of Wayland Creek and Big Sandy Creek along the railroad that follows Big Sandy Creek to Stone Canyon.

Weferling Canyon [MONTEREY]: *canyon,* 3 miles long, opens into lowlands nearly 6 miles east of Jolon (lat. 35°57'55" N, long. 121° 04'30" W; near W line sec. 2, T 23 S, R 8 E). Named on Williams Hill (1949) 7.5' quadrangle. The name commemorates William Weferling, who claimed 160 acres at Lockwood in the 1880's (Clark, 1991, p. 602).

Welby [MONTEREY]: *locality,* 3.5 miles eastsoutheast of King City along Southern Pacific Railroad (lat. 36°11'20" N, long. 121°04'15" W). Named on San Lucas (1949) 7.5' quadrangle.

Welch Ridge [MONTEREY]: *ridge,* northwest-trending, 0.5 mile long, 3.25 miles south of Marina (lat. 36°38'10" N, long. 121° 48' W). Named on Marina (1947) 7.5' quadrangle.

Wellman Canyon [SANTA BARBARA]: *canyon,* drained by a stream that flows 6.25 miles to Sisquoc River nearly 2 miles north-north-east of Bald Mountain (1) (lat. 34°50'10" N, long. 119°55'15" W). Named on Bald Mountain (1964), Bates Canyon (1964), and Peak Mountain (1964) 7.5' quadrangles.

Wellman Canyon: see **Water Canyon** [SANTA BARBARA] (1).

Wells Canyon [SAN LUIS OBISPO]: *canyon,* drained by a stream that flows 3 miles to Cuyama Valley 3 miles north-northeast of New Cuyama [SANTA BARBARA] (lat. 34°59'10" N, long. 119°40'05" W; sec. 4, T 10 N, R 26 W). Named on New Cuyama (1964) 7.5' quadrangle.

Wells Creek [SANTA BARBARA]: *stream,* flows 4.25 miles to Aliso Canyon (1) 5.5 miles north-northeast of McPherson Peak (lat. 34° 57'45" N, long. 119°46'30" W). Named on Peak Mountain (1964) 7.5' quadrangle. United States Board on Geographic Names (1965c, p. 13) rejected the name "Messenger Canyon" for the feature.

Wells Creek: see **Coyote Gulch** [SANTA BARBARA].

Wellsonia [SAN LUIS OBISPO]: *locality,* 4.5 miles north of Paso Robles (lat. 35°41'50" N, long. 120°41'35" W; sec. 4, 5, T 26 S, R 12 E). Named on Paso Robles (1948) 7.5' quadrangle. Paso Robles (1919) 15' quadrangle shows the place along Southern Pacific Railroad. Postal authorities established Wellsona post office in 1898 and discontinued it the same year (Salley, p. 236).

Wells Spring [SAN LUIS OBISPO]: *spring,* 28 miles southeast of Simmler (lat. 35°01'55" N, long. 119°41' W; near NW cor. sec. 20, T 11 N, R 26 W). Named on Wells Ranch (1954) 7.5' quadrangle.

Wescott Shoal: see **Castle Rock** [SANTA BARBARA].

Weser Spur [SANTA BARBARA]: *locality,* 1.5 miles south of Surf along Southern Pacific Railroad (lat. 34°39'40" N, long. 120°36'35" W). Named on Surf (1947) 7.5' quadrangle.

West Beach [SANTA BARBARA]: *beach,* 1.25 miles south of downtown Santa Barbara along the coast (lat. 34°24'05" N, long. 119°41'55" W). Named on Santa Barbara (1952) 7.5' quadrangle.

West Branciforte Creek: see **Carbonera Creek** [SANTA CRUZ].

West Browns Creek: see **Carbonera Creek** [SANTA CRUZ].

West Canyon [SANTA BARBARA]: *canyon,* drained by a stream that flows less than 0.5 mile to Windmill Canyon 4 miles east-north-east of McPherson Peak (lat. 34°54'45" N, long. 119°45' W; near N line sec. 34, T 10 N, R 27 W). Named on Peak Mountain (1964) 7.5' quadrangle.

West Corral de Piedra Creek [SAN LUIS OBISPO]: *stream,* flows 7 miles to join East Corral de Piedra Creek and form Pismo Creek nearly 0.5 mile south-southeast of Edna (lat. 35°11'50" N, long. 120°36'35" W); the stream is on Corral de Piedra grant. Named on Arroyo Grande NE (1965) and Lopez Mountain (1965) 7.5' quadrangles.

Westdahl Rock [SAN LUIS OBISPO]: *shoal,* 1.5 miles southwest of Point San Luis, and 1.5 miles offshore (lat. 35°08'50" N, long. 120° 46'55" W). Named on Port San Luis (1965) 7.5' quadrangle.

West Liddell Creek [SANTA CRUZ]: *stream,* flows 2.5 miles to Liddell Creek 1 mile east-southeast of Davenport (lat. 37°00'10" N, long. 122°10'35" W). Named on Davenport (1955) 7.5' quadrangle.

Weston Beach: see **Sand Hill Cove** [MONTEREY].

West Point [SANTA BARBARA]: *promontory,* 1.25 miles north-northeast of Fraser Point at the west end of Santa Cruz Island (lat. 34°04'40" N, long. 119°55'05" W). Named on Santa Cruz Island A (1943) 7.5' quadrangle.

West Point: see **Sandy Point** [SANTA BARBARA].

West Rock: see **Wilson Rock**, under **Harris Point** [SANTA BARBARA].

West Tuley Springs [SAN LUIS OBISPO]: *springs,* two, 400 feet apart, 5.5 miles northwest of Shandon (lat. 35°43'10" N, long. 120° 25'55" W; sec. 26, T 25 S, R 14 E); the springs are 0.5 mile west of East Tuley Springs. Named on Shandon (1961) 7.5' quadrangle.

West Waddell Creek [SANTA CRUZ]: *stream,* heads just inside San Mateo County and flows 6 miles to join East Waddell Creek and form Waddell Creek 2.5 miles north-northeast of the mouth of Waddell Creek (lat. 36°08' N, long. 122°16' W; near S line sec. 23, T 9 S, R 4 W). Named on Big Basin (1955) and Franklin Point (1955) 7.5' quadrangles.

Weyland Camp [MONTEREY]: *locality,* 2.5 miles east-northeast of Pfeiffer Point along Big Sur River (lat. 36°14'40" N, long. 121°46'20" W; near SW cor. sec. 29, T 19 S, R 2 E). Named on Pfeiffer Point (1956) 7.5' quadrangle. The misspelled name commemorates Dr. Charles Wayland, who started a private campground at the place in 1906 (Clark, 1991, p. 601).

Whaleboat Rock: see **Bird Rock** [MONTEREY] (2).

Whaler Island: see **Whalers Island** [SAN LUIS OBISPO].

Whale Rock [SAN LUIS OBISPO]: *rock,* 3 miles east-southeast of Cayucos Point, and 650 feet offshore (lat. 35°26'05" N, long. 120° 53'30" W). Named on Cayucos (1965) 7.5' quadrangle.

Whale Rock Reservoir [SAN LUIS OBISPO]: *lake,* 2.25 miles long, behind a dam on Old Creek 0.5 mile east-northeast of Cayucos (lat. 35°26'50" N, long. 120°53'05" W); the mouth of Old Creek is near Whale Rock. Named on Cayucos (1965) and Morro Bay North (1965) 7.5' quadrangles.

Whalers Cove: see **Carmel Cove** [MONTEREY].

Whalers Island [SAN LUIS OBISPO]: *island,* 300 feet long, 500 feet offshore at Point San Luis (lat. 35°09'35" N, long. 120°45'15" W). Named on Port San Luis (1965) 7.5' quadrangle, which shows a breakwater connecting the feature to shore. Called Whaler Id. on Port Harford (1897) 15' quadrangle, but United States Board on Geographic Names (1991, p. 7) rejected this form of the name. The place was known as Whaler's Island about 1887 because of a short-lived whaling station there that employed 29 men (Lee and others, p. 123).

Whalers Knoll [MONTEREY]: *hill,* 0.25 mile east of Point Lobos on the south side of Carmel Bay (lat. 36°31'15" N, long. 121°56'45" W). Named on Monterey (1947) 7.5' quadrangle. Whalers in the 1880's used the hill to sight whales (Clark, 1991, p. 605).

Whalers Rock: see **Seal Rocks** [MONTEREY].

Wheat Peak [SANTA BARBARA]: *peak,* 3 miles west-northwest of Bald Mountain (1) (lat. 34°49'55" N, long. 119°59' W). Altitude 2436 feet. Named on Bald Mountain (1964) 7.5' quadrangle. Hiram Preserved Wheat homesteaded near Sisquoc River in 1885 (Rife, p. 110).

Whiskey Hill: see **Freedom** [SANTA CRUZ].

Whiskey Spring [SAN LUIS OBISPO]: *spring,* 6 miles north-northwest of San Luis Obispo (lat. 35°21'45" N, long. 120°41'45" W; sec. 33, T 29 S, R 12 E). Named on San Luis Obispo (1965) 7.5' quadrangle.

White Canyon [SAN LUIS OBISPO]: *canyon,* drained by a stream that flows 5.5 miles to Cholame Creek 1 mile south-southwest of Cholame (lat. 35°42'35" N, long. 120°18'15" W; sec. 36, T 25 S, R 15 E). Named on Cholame (1961) and Cholame Valley (1961) 7.5' quadrangles.

White Hills [SANTA BARBARA]: *range,* 2.5 miles south-southeast of the city of Lompoc (lat. 34°36'15" N, long. 120°26' W). Named on Lompoc Hills (1959) 7.5' quadrangle. White strata are conspicuous in the range.

White Hills Siding [SANTA BARBARA]: *locality,* near the east edge of the city of Lompoc along Southern Pacific Railroad (lat. 34°38'35" N, long. 120°26'45" W). Named on Lompoc (1959) 7.5' quadrangle.

Whitehouse Camp [SANTA CRUZ]: *locality,* 5.5 miles north-northwest of the mouth of Waddell Creek (lat. 37°10'10" N, long. 122° 18'15" W); the place is along Whitehouse Creek. Named on Año Nuevo (1943) 15' quadrangle.

Whitehouse Creek [SANTA CRUZ]: *stream,* flows nearly 2 miles to San Mateo County 5.5 miles north-northwest of the mouth of Waddell Creek (lat. 37°10'15" N, long. 122°18'50" W; sec. 9, T 9 S, R 4 W). Named on Franklin Point (1955) 7.5' quadrangle. The name is for a white prefabricated building that was shipped around the Horn and erected near the stream in 1852; the creek was called Arroyo de Soto in the 1840's for Eugenio Soto, who lived near it, and later it had the Spanish name "Arroyo de la Casa Blanca" (Brown, p. 100-101; Brown used the form "White House Creek" for the name).

White Lake [SAN LUIS OBISPO]: *lake,* 3000 feet long, 4 miles south-southwest of downtown Arroyo Grande near the coast (lat. 35°03'55" N, long. 120°36'30" W). Named on Oceano (1965) 7.5' quadrangle.

White Lake: see **Kelly Lake** [SANTA CRUZ].

White Ledge Canyon [SANTA BARBARA]: *canyon,* drained by a stream that flows nearly 5 miles to South Fork Sisquoc River 5.5 miles south-southwest of Montgomery Potrero (lat. 34°45'25" N, long. 119°46'40" W). Named on Hurricane Deck (1964) 7.5' quadrangle.

White Oaks Camp [MONTEREY]: *locality,* 3 miles south-southeast of Jamesburg (lat. 36°19'35" N, long. 121°34'25" W; near NW cor. sec. 32, T 18 S, R 4 E). Named on Chews Ridge (1956) 7.5' quadrangle.

White Point [SAN LUIS OBISPO]: *promontory,* 2 miles southeast of Morro Rock on the east side of Morro Bay (lat. 35°20'50" N, long. 120°50'35" W). Named on Morro Bay South (1965) 7.5' quadrangle.

White Rock [SAN LUIS OBISPO]:
(1) *rock,* 2.25 miles south of Cambria, and 750 feet offshore (lat. 35°32' N, long. 121°05'15" W). Named on Cambria (1959) 7.5' quadrangle.
(2) *rock,* 100 feet long, 1.5 miles southeast of Avila Beach in San Luis Obispo Bay, and nearly 1 mile offshore (lat. 35°09'50" N, long. 120°42'30" W). Named on Pismo Beach (1965) 7.5' quadrangle.

White Rock [SANTA CRUZ]: *relief feature,* 5.5 miles east-northeast of the town of Boulder Creek (lat. 37°09'20" N, long. 122°01'35" W). Named on Castle Rock Ridge (1955) 7.5' quadrangle.

White Rock: see **White Rock Number 1** [MONTEREY].

Whiterock Bluff [SAN LUIS OBISPO]: *escarpment,* 4 miles west-southwest of Caliente Mountain on the north side of Cuyama Valley (lat. 35°00'30" N, long. 119°49'15" W; sec. 25, T 11 N, R 28 W). Named on Caliente Mountain (1959) 7.5' quadrangle.

White Rock Canyon [SANTA BARBARA]: *canyon,* drained by a stream that flows 2 miles to Fish Creek 3.25 miles east of Figueroa Mountain (lat. 34°44'20" N, long. 119°55'35" W; sec. 27, T 8 N, R 29 W). Named on Figueroa Mountain (1959) 7.5' quadrangle.

White Rock Lake [MONTEREY]: *lake,* 700 feet long, 10 miles northeast of Point Sur (lat. 36°24'40" N, long. 121°46'20" W; sec. 32, T 17 S, R 2 E); the lake is at the east end of White Rock Ridge. Named on Mount Carmel (1956) 7.5' quadrangle.

White Rock Number 1 [MONTEREY]: *rock,* 7.5 miles southeast of Cape San Martin, and 2200 feet offshore (lat. 35°48'25" N, long. 121°22'35" W). Named on Cape San Martin (1921) 15' quadrangle. Called White Rock on Cape San Martin (1949) 15' quadrangle.

White Rock Number 2 [MONTEREY]: *rock,* 5.5 miles southeast of Cape San Martin, and 200 feet offshore (lat. 35°49'55" N, long. 121°23'50" W). Named on Cape San Martin (1921) 15' quadrangle.

White Rock Ridge [MONTEREY]: *ridge,* east-trending, 3 miles long, 9 miles north-northeast of Point Sur (lat. 36°25' N, long. 121°48'30" W). Named on Mount Carmel (1956) 7.5' quadrangle.

White's [SAN LUIS OBISPO]: *locality,* 18 miles southeast of Simmler in Elkhorn Plain (lat. 35°11'50" N, long. 119°42'50" W; sec. 27, T 31 S, R 21 E). Named on McKittrick (1912) 30' quadrangle. California Mining Bureau's (1917c) map has the form "Whites" for the name.

Whites Lagoon [SANTA CRUZ]: *lake,* 500 feet long, 6 miles northeast of Soquel on China Ridge (lat. 37°02'50" N, long. 121°52'40" W). Named on Laurel (1955) 7.5' quadrangle.

White Spring [SAN LUIS OBISPO]: *spring,* 2.5 miles west of Cholame (lat. 35°43'50" N, long. 120°20'20" W; sec. 27, T 25 S, R 15 E). Named on Cholame (1961) 7.5' quadrangle.

White Sulphur Springs: see **Chittenden's Sulphur Springs**, under **Chittenden** [SANTA CRUZ].

White Well [SAN LUIS OBISPO]: *well,* 2.5 miles west of Cholame (lat. 35°43'35" N, long. 120°20'20" W; sec. 27, T 25 S, R 15 E). Named on Cholame (1961) 7.5' quadrangle.

Whitley Gardens [SAN LUIS OBISPO]: *settlement,* 11 miles east of Paso Robles (lat. 35°39'30" N, long. 120°30'15" W). Named on Estrella (1948) and Shandon (1961) 7.5' quadrangles.

Whoop Canyon [SANTA BARBARA]: *canyon,* drained by a stream that flows 2 miles to Foxen Canyon 7 miles south of Tepusquet Peak (lat. 34°48'40" N, long. 120°12'35" W). Named on Foxen Canyon (1964) 7.5' quadrangle.

Wickham: see **Los Alamos** [SANTA BARBARA] (2).

Wigmore: see **Los Alamos** [SANTA BARBARA] (2).

Wilcox Canyon [SAN LUIS OBISPO]: *canyon,* drained by a stream that flows 2 miles to Branch Creek 4.5 miles southwest of Branch Mountain (lat. 35°08'20" N, long. 120°08'40" W). Named on Los Machos Hills (1967) 7.5' quadrangle.

Wildcat Canyon [MONTEREY]:
(1) *canyon,* drained by a stream that flows 1 mile to Impossible Canyon 5.5 miles east of Seaside (lat. 36°37'05" N, long. 121°45'10" W); the canyon is north and west of Wildcat Ridge. Named on Seaside (1947) 7.5' quadrangle.

(2) *canyon,* drained by a stream that flows nearly 4 miles to Garrapata Creek 4 miles southeast of Soberanes Point (lat. 36°24'15" N, long. 121°53'05" W; sec. 32, T 17 S, R 1 E). Named on Mount Carmel (1956) and Soberanes Point (1956) 7.5' quadrangles.

(3) *canyon,* 4 miles long, opens into lowlands 6.25 miles east of Jolon (lat. 35°57'15" N, long. 121°04'15" W; sec. 2, T 23 S, R 8 E). Named on Williams Hill (1949) 7.5' quadrangle.

Wildcat Canyon [SAN BENITO]: *canyon,* drained by a stream that flows 2 miles to Santa Clara County nearly 2 miles west of Mariposa Peak (lat. 36°57'35" N, long. 121°14'30" W; sec. 19, T 11 S, R 7 E). Named on Mariposa Peak (1969) 7.5' quadrangle.

Wildcat Creek [MONTEREY]: *stream,* flows 1.5 miles to the sea 3.5 miles north of Soberanes Point (lat. 36°29'50" N, long. 121°56'10" W). Named on Soberanes Point (1956) 7.5' quadrangle.

Wildcat Ridge [MONTEREY]: *ridge,* north-trending, 1.25 miles long, 7 miles southwest of Salinas (lat. 36°36'20" N, long. 121° 45' W). Named on Seaside (1947) and Spreckels (1947) 7.5' quadrangles.

Wild Cattle Creek [MONTEREY]: *stream,* flows nearly 2 miles to the sea 5.5 miles north-northwest of Cape San Martin (lat. 35°58'05" N, long. 121°29'05" W; near N line sec. 1, T 23 S, R 4 E). Named on Cape San Martin (1949) 7.5' quadrangle. United States Board on Geographic Names (1978b, p. 6) rejected the name "Wild Creek" for the stream.

Wild Cherry Canyon [SAN LUIS OBISPO]: *canyon,* drained by a stream that flows 3 miles to the sea nearly 1 mile west of Avila Beach (lat. 35°10'40" N, long. 120°44'45" W). Named on Pismo Beach (1965) and Port San Luis (1965) 7.5' quadrangles.

Wild Creek: see **Wild Cattle Creek** [MONTEREY].

Wilder Beach: see **Wilder Creek** [SANTA CRUZ].

Wilder Creek [SANTA CRUZ]: *stream,* flows 5 miles to the sea 3 miles west of Point Santa Cruz (lat. 36°57'10" N, long. 122°04'35" W). Named on Felton (1955) and Santa Cruz (1954) 7.5' quadrangles. The name commemorates the Wilder family, owners of land along the stream, which also was called Bolcoff Creek and Meder Creek for earlier owners of land along it; the creek reaches the sea at Wilder Beach (Clark, 1986, p. 402). Hubbard's (1943) map shows a place called Wilder Spur located along the railroad nearly 1 mile west of present Wilder Creek. California Mining Bureau's (1917a) map shows a place called Wilders situated along the coast, apparently just east of the mouth of present Wilder Creek.

Wilders: see **Wilder Creek** [SANTA CRUZ].

Wilder Spur: see **Wilder Creek** [SANTA CRUZ].

Wild Hog Creek [SAN LUIS OBISPO]: *stream,* flows nearly 3 miles to San Juan Creek 3.25 miles northeast of Branch Mountain (lat. 35°13'15" N, long. 120°02'40" W; at N line sec. 21, T 31 S, R 18 E). Named on Branch Mountain (1967) 7.5' quadrangle.

Wild Horse Canyon [SAN LUIS OBISPO]: *canyon,* drained by a stream that flows nearly 6 miles to Freeman Canyon 12 miles east-northeast of Paso Robles (lat. 35°43'20" N, long. 120°30'40" W; sec. 30, T 25 S, R 14 E). Named on Cholame Hills (1961) and Shandon (1961) 7.5' quadrangles. Estrella (1948) 7.5' quadrangle has the form "Wildhorse Canyon" for the name.

Wildhorse Canyon [MONTEREY]: *canyon,* 10 miles long, opens into lowlands 4 miles north-northwest of San Lucas (lat. 36°11'15" N, long. 121°02'30" W; sec. 18, T 20 S, R 9 E). Named on Nattrass Valley (1967) and San Lucas (1949) 7.5' quadrangle.

Wildhorse Canyon [SAN BENITO]: *canyon,* drained by a stream that flows 6 miles to Chalone Creek 3.5 miles southeast of North Chalone Peak (lat. 36°24'40" N, long. 121°08'50" W; sec. 31, T 17 S, R 8 E). Named on North Chalone Peak (1969) and Topo Valley (1969) 7.5' quadrangles.

Wildhorse Canyon [SANTA BARBARA]: *canyon,* drained by a stream that flows 4 miles to Sisquoc River 5 miles north-northwest of Zaca Lake (lat. 34°50'45" N, long. 120°04'15" W). Named on Zaca Lake (1964) 7.5' quadrangle.

Wild Horse Flat [SANTA BARBARA]: *area,* 1.5 miles west of Tranquillon Mountain (lat. 34°35'05" N, long. 120°35'25" W); the place is 0.25 mile west-southwest of Wild Horse Peak. Named on Tranquillon Mountain (1959) 7.5' quadrangle.

Wild Horse Peak [SANTA BARBARA]: *peak,* 1.5 miles west of Tranquillon Mountain (lat. 34°35'10" N, long. 120°35'05" W). Named on Tranquillon Mountain (1959) 7.5' quadrangle.

Wild Horse Spring [SAN LUIS OBISPO]: *spring,* 7 miles north of Pozo (lat. 35°24'10" N, long. 120°21'25" W; sec. 15, T 29 S, R 15 E). Named on Camatta Ranch (1966) 7.5' quadrangle.

Wild Oat Creek [SAN BENITO]: *stream,* flows 1.25 miles to Mine Creek 6.5 miles northeast of Bitterwater (lat. 36°26' N, long. 120° 54' W; sec. 20, T 17 S, R 10 E); the stream heads at Wild Oat Springs. Named on Rock Spring Peak (1969) 7.5' quadrangle.

Wild Oat Peak [SAN BENITO]: *peak,* 8 miles northeast of Bitterwater (lat. 36°27'10" N, long. 120°53'35" W; sec. 16, T 17 S, R 10 E). Altitude 3992 feet. Named on Rock Spring Peak (1969) 7.5' quadrangle.

Wild Oat Springs [SAN BENITO]: *springs,* 7.5 miles northeast of Bitterwater (lat. 36°27' N, long. 120°53'50" W; on W line sec. 16, T 17 S, R 10 E); the springs are 0.25 mile south-west of Wild Oat Peak at the head of Wild

Oat Creek. Named on Rock Spring Peak (1969) 7.5' quadrangle.

Wildwood [SANTA CRUZ]: *settlement,* 5 miles east-southeast of Big Basin near San Lorenzo River (lat. 37°09'05" N, long. 122°08'05" W; near E line sec. 13, T 9 S, R 3 W). Named on Big Basin (1955) 7.5' quadrangle.

Wilkins Canyon [MONTEREY]: *canyon,* drained by a stream that flows 1.5 miles to Quinado Canyon 7.5 miles south of King City (lat. 36°06'10" N, long. 121°08'40" W; sec. 18, T 21 S, R 8 E). Named on Cosio Knob (1949) 7.5' quadrangle. The name commemorates Edward H. Wilkins, who received a patent for land at the canyon in 1892 (Clark, 1991, p. 608).

Wilkinson Canyon [SAN LUIS OBISPO]: *canyon,* drained by a stream that flows nearly 5 miles to San Juan Valley 13 miles southeast of Shandon (lat. 35°31'25" N, long. 120°12'35" W; near W line sec. 1, T 28 S, R 16 E). Named on Holland Canyon (1961) 7.5' quadrangle.

Williams Canyon [MONTEREY]:

(1) *canyon,* drained by a stream that flows 2.5 miles to San Jose Creek 4.5 miles east-northeast of Soberanes Point (lat. 36°28'50" N, long. 121°51'20" W; sec. 4, T 17 S, R 1 E). Named on Mount Carmel (1956) 7.5' quadrangle. The name commemorates Shadrack Williams, who received a patent on land at the head of the canyon in 1904 (Clark, 1991, p. 609).

(2) *canyon,* 3 miles long, opens into lowlands 9 miles east-southeast of Jolon (lat. 35°55'35" N, long. 121°01'55" W; sec. 18, T 23 S, R 9 E); the canyon heads near Williams Hill. Named on Williams Hill (1949) 7.5' quadrangle. The name commemorates Wait Williams, who had a homestead in the canyon (Clark, 1991, p. 609).

Williams Creek: see **Pancho Rico Creek** [MONTEREY].

Williams Hill [MONTEREY]: *peak,* 10 miles east of Jolon (lat. 35° 57'05" N, long. 121°00'05" W; near S line sec. 4, T 23 S, R 9 E). Named on Williams Hill (1949) 7.5' quadrangle. The name is from Williams Canyon (2) (Clark, 1991, p. 609).

Williams Hollow [SAN BENITO]: *canyon,* drained by a stream that flows 2.5 miles to San Benito River 8 miles south of Idria (lat. 36° 17'55" N, long. 120°41'35" W; near SE cor. sec. 6, T 19 S, R 12 E). Named on San Benito Mountain (1969) 7.5' quadrangle.

Williams Landing: see **San Vicente Creek** [SANTA CRUZ].

Williams Mountain [SAN BENITO]: *peak,* 11 miles south-southwest of Idria (lat. 36°15'55" N, long. 120°44'30" W; sec. 23, T 19 S, R 11 E). Altitude 4124 feet. Named on San Benito Mountain (1969) 7.5' quadrangle.

Williamson Spring [SAN LUIS OBISPO]: *spring,* 9 miles east-southeast of Shandon (lat. 35°36'10" N, long. 120°13'45" W; near E line

sec. 3, T 27 S, R 16 E). Named on Holland Canyon (1961) 7.5' quadrangle

Williamson Valley [SAN BENITO]: *valley,* 5 miles south-southeast of Mount Johnson (lat. 36°32'30" N, long. 121°17'15" W). Named on Mount Johnson (1968) 7.5' quadrangle.

Willow Campground [SANTA BARBARA]: *locality,* 3 miles south-southeast of Fox Mountain in Santa Barbara Canyon (lat. 34°46'30" N, long. 119°34'20" W). Named on Fox Mountain (1964) 7.5' quadrangle.

Willow Canyon [SAN LUIS OBISPO]: *canyon,* 0.5 mile long, opens into the canyon of San Juan Creek 4 miles northeast of Castle Crags (lat. 35°20'25" N, long. 120°08'50" W; near E line sec. 4, T 30 S, R 17 E). Named on La Panza (1967) 7.5' quadrangle. The canyon divides at the head into North Fork and South Fork. North Fork is 5.25 miles long and South Fork is nearly 4 miles long; both forks are named on La Panza (1967) 7.5' quadrangle. United States Board on Geographic Names (1968c, p. 6, 7) rejected the name "Hay Canyon" for Willow Canyon, North Fork Willow Canyon, and South Fork Willow Canyon; the Board also rejected the name "Willow Canyon" for North Fork Willow Canyon.

Willow Creek [MONTEREY]:

(1) *stream,* flows 3 miles to Tassajara Creek nearly 2 miles southeast of Tassajara Hot Springs (lat. 36°12'55" N, long. 121°31'45" W; near SE cor. sec. 4, T 20 S, R 4 E). Named on Tassajara Hot Springs (1956) 7.5' quadrangle.

(2) *stream,* flows 6 miles to the sea nearly 0.5 mile north-northeast of Cape San Martin (lat. 35°53'35" N, long. 121°27'40" W; sec. 31, T 23 S, R 5 E). Named on Cape San Martin (1949) 7.5' quadrangle. North Fork enters from the northeast nearly 3 miles upstream from the mouth of the main stream, and is 4.25 miles long. South Fork enters from the southeast 1 mile upstream from the mouth of the main stream, and is 3.5 miles long. Both forks are named on Cape San Martin (1949) 7.5' quadrangle.

Willow Creek [SAN BENITO]: *stream,* flows 10 miles to San Benito River 9 miles northwest of San Benito (lat. 36°35'50" N, long. 121° 11'30" W; sec. 27, T 15 S, R 7 E). Named on Bickmore Canyon (1968) and Mount Johnson (1968) 7.5' quadrangles. South Fork enters from the south 1.25 miles upstream from the mouth of the main creek; it is 8 miles long and is named on Bickmore Canyon (1968) and Mount Johnson (1968) 7.5' quadrangles.

Willow Creek [SAN LUIS OBISPO]:

(1) *stream,* flows 4.25 miles to the sea 3.5 miles east-southeast of Cayucos Point (lat. 35°25'40" N, long. 120°52'55" W). Named on Cayucos (1965) and Morro Bay North (1965) 7.5' quadrangles.

(2) *stream,* flows nearly 5 miles to Paso Robles Creek 3.25 miles east of York Mountain (lat.

35°33'05" N, long. 120°46'25" W). Named on York Mountain (1948) 7.5' quadrangle.

Willow Creek Camp [MONTEREY]: *locality,* 2 miles south-southwest of Tassajara Hot Springs (lat. 36°12'25" N, long. 121°33'25" W; sec. 8, T 20 S, R 4 E); the place is along Willow Creek (1). Named on Tassajara Hot Springs (1956) 7.5' quadrangle.

Willow Creek Peak [SAN BENITO]: *peak,* 9.5 miles northwest of San Benito (lat. 36°35'10" N, long. 121°13'15" W; sec. 32, T 15 S, R 7 E); the peak is less than 1 mile southwest of the confluence of Willow Creek and South Fork Willow Creek. Altitude 2437 feet. Named on Bickmore Canyon (1968) 7.5' quadrangle.

Willow Lake [SAN LUIS OBISPO]: *lake,* 550 feet long, 3.5 miles south-southwest of downtown Arroyo Grande near the coast (lat. 35°04'45" N, long. 120°36'50" W). Named on Oceano (1965) 7.5' quadrangle. On Arroyo Grande (1952) 15' quadrangle, this lake, a nearby lake, and some associated marsh have the name "Willow Lake."

Willows: see **The Willows** [SANTA CRUZ].

Willows Anchorage [SANTA BARBARA]: *embayment,* 4 miles east of Punta Arena on the south side of Santa Cruz Island (lat. 33°57'45" N, long. 119°44'50" W). Named on Santa Cruz Island B (1943) 7.5' quadrangle. Bremner's (1932) map has the name "Cñ. las Sauces de los Colorados" for a canyon that opens to the sea at the west edge of present Willows Anchorage. Rand's (1931) map has the name "Los Sauces" at present Willows Anchorage.

Willow Spring [MONTEREY]:
(1) *spring,* 10 miles north-northwest of Charley Mountain (lat. 36° 16'45" N, long. 120°42'45" W; sec. 13, T 19 S, R 11 E). Named on San Benito Mountain (1969) 7.5' quadrangle.
(2) *spring,* 6.25 miles south-southwest of Parkfield (lat. 35°48'45" N, long. 120°27'55" W; sec. 28, T 24 S, R 14 E); the spring is in a branch of Willow Springs Canyon. Named on Cholame Hills (1961) 7.5' quadrangle.
(3) *spring,* 8.5 miles east-southeast of Parkfield (lat. 35°52'05" N, long. 120°17' W; sec. 6, T 24 S, R 16 E). Named on Cholame Valley (1961) 7.5' quadrangle. Called Sulphur Springs on Cholame Ranch (1943) 7.5' quadrangle, but United States Board on Geographic Names (1963a, p. 7) rejected this name.

Willow Spring [SAN BENITO]:
(1) *spring,* 5.5 miles west of San Benito (lat. 36°30'35" N, long. 121°10'50" W; sec. 26, T 16 S, R 7 E). Named on Bickmore Canyon (1968) 7.5' quadrangle.
(2) *spring,* 7 miles north-northeast of Bitterwater (lat. 36°28'05" N, long. 120°56'10" W; near NW cor. sec. 7, T 17 S, R 10 E). Named on Rock Spring Peak (1969) 7.5' quadrangle.

(3) *spring,* 5.5 miles east-southeast of Bitterwater (lat. 36°20'25" N, long. 120°54'55" W; sec. 29, T 18 S, R 10 E). Named on Lonoak (1969) 7.5' quadrangle.
(4) *spring,* 7.5 miles south of Idria (lat. 36°18'20" N, long. 120°40'35" W; near E line sec. 5, T 19 S, R 12 E). Named on San Benito Mountain (1969) 7.5' quadrangle.

Willow Spring [SAN LUIS OBISPO]:
(1) *spring,* 4.5 miles west-southwest of Atascadero (2) (lat. 35°28'20" N, long. 120°44'35" W). Named on Atascadero (1965) 7.5' quadrangle.
(2) *spring,* 4.5 miles south of Wilson Corner (lat. 35°24'05" N, long. 120°22'20" W; sec. 16, T 29 S, R 15 E). Named on Camatta Ranch (1966) 7.5' quadrangle.
(3) *spring,* 18 miles northeast of Simmler (lat. 35°29'40" N, long. 120°08'50" W; sec. 16, T 28 S, R 17 E). Named on La Panza Ranch (1966) 7.5' quadrangle.
(4) *spring,* 3.5 miles north of Cuyama [SANTA BARBARA] (lat. 34° 59'10" N, long. 119°36'05" W; near NE cor. sec. 1, T 10 N, R 26 W). Named on Cuyama (1964) 7.5' quadrangle.

Willow Spring [SANTA BARBARA]:
(1) *spring,* nearly 6 miles west-northwest of Miranda Pine Mountain (lat. 35°03'35" N, long. 120°08' W). Named on Chimney Canyon (1967) 7.5' quadrangle.
(2) *spring,* 0.5 mile east-northeast of Figueroa Mountain (lat. 34° 44'50" N, long. 119°58'25" W; near N line sec. 30, T 8 N, R 29 W. Named on Figueroa Mountain (1959) 7.5' quadrangle. On McPherson Peak (1943) 15' quadrangle, the name applies to a spring situated nearly 0.5 mile farther north.
(3) *spring,* 3.5 miles northeast of Point Conception (lat. 34°28'30" N, long. 120°24'55" W). Named on Point Conception (1953) 7.5' quadrangle.
(4) *spring,* 3.5 miles north of San Marcos Pass (lat. 34°33'50" N, long. 119°50' W). Named on San Marcos Pass (1959) 7.5' quadrangle.

Willow Spring Canyon [SANTA BARBARA]: *canyon,* drained by a stream that flows 1 mile to Fir Canyon 4.5 miles south-southwest of Bald Mountain (1) (lat. 34°45'10" N, long. 119°57'55" W); Willow Spring (2) is in the canyon. Named on Bald Mountain (1964) and Figueroa Mountain (1959) 7.5' quadrangles.

Willow Spring Creek [SAN BENITO]: *stream,* flows nearly 2 miles to Tres Pinos Creek 2.5 miles northwest of Panoche Pass (lat. 36° 39'10" N, long. 121°02'35" W; sec. 1, T 15 S, R 8 E). Named on Panoche Pass (1968) 7.5' quadrangle.

Willow Springs Canyon [MONTEREY-SAN LUIS OBISPO]: *canyon,* drained by a stream that heads in Monterey County and flows 5.25 miles to Mason Canyon 9.5 miles northwest of Shandon in San Luis Obispo County (lat. 35°46'10" N, long. 120°28'50" W; near E line. sec. 8, T 25 S, R 14 E); Willow Spring

[MONTEREY] (2) is in a branch of the canyon. Named on Cholame Hills (1961) 7.5' quadrangle. Called Mason Canyon on Cholame (1917) 30' quadrangle.

Wilson Canyon [SAN LUIS OBISPO]: *canyon*, drained by a stream that flows 3.5 miles to an unnamed valley 5.25 miles south-southwest of Wilson Corner (lat. 35°23'40" N, long. 120°24'25" W; sec. 18, T 29 S, R 15 E). Named on Camatta Ranch (1966) and Wilson Corner (1966) 7.5' quadrangles.

Wilson Corner [SAN LUIS OBISPO]: *locality*, 16 miles east of Atascadero (lat. 35°28'05" N, long. 120°22'40" W; near N line sec. 29, T 28 S, R 15 E). Named on Wilson Corner (1966) 7.5' quadrangle.

Wilson Gulch [SANTA CRUZ]: *canyon*, drained by a stream that flows 0.5 mile to the sea 1.25 miles northwest of the mouth of Waddell Creek at Santa Cruz-San Mateo county line (lat. 37°06'25" N, long. 122°17'30" W; sec. 34, T 9 S, R 4 W). Named on Año Nuevo (1955) 7.5' quadrangle.

Wilson Rock: see **Harris Point** [SANTA BARBARA].

Winchester Canyon [SANTA BARBARA]: *canyon*, drained by a stream that flows 3.5 miles to Bell Canyon 3 miles north-northwest of Coal Oil Point (lat. 34°26'30" N, long. 119°54'15" W). Named on Dos Pueblos Canyon (1951) 7.5' quadrangle. The name commemorates Dr. Robert Fulton Winchester, who lived in the canyon (Tompkins and Ruiz, p. 111).

Windmill Canyon [MONTEREY]: *canyon*, drained by a stream that flows nearly 2 miles to Chavoya Canyon 8 miles east-northeast of San Ardo (lat. 36°04'45" N, long. 120°46'35" W; sec. 27, T 21 S, R 11 E). Named on Pancho Rico Valley (1967) 7.5' quadrangle.

Windmill Canyon [SANTA BARBARA]: *canyon*, drained by a stream that flows 1.25 miles to Bitter Creek 3.5 miles southwest of New Cuyama (lat. 34°54'40" N, long. 119°44'10" W; near N line sec. 35, T 10 N, R 27 W). Named on New Cuyama (1964) and Peak Mountain (1964) 7.5' quadrangles.

Windmill Creek [SAN LUIS OBISPO]: *stream*, flows 3 miles to Navajo Creek 12 miles northeast of Pozo (lat. 35°25'35" N, long. 120°13'30" W; near S line sec. 2, T 29 S, R 16 E). Named on La Panza Ranch (1966) 7.5' quadrangle.

Windsor Canyon [SANTA BARBARA]: *canyon*, drained by a stream that flows 2.5 miles to Santa Ynez River 2.5 miles north-north-west of San Marcos Pass (lat. 34°32'45" N, long. 119°50'45" W). Named on San Marcos Pass (1959) 7.5' quadrangle.

Windy Point [SAN LUIS OBISPO]: *locality*, 3.25 miles east-northeast of the mouth of San Carpoforo Creek (lat. 35°46'55" N, long. 121° 16'20" W; sec. 1, T 25 S, R 6 E). Named on Burro Mountain (1949) 7.5' quadrangle.

Winter Creek: see **Archibald Creek** [SANTA CRUZ].

Wittenberg Creek [SAN LUIS OBISPO]: *stream*, flows nearly 6 miles to Arroyo Grande Creek 11 miles north of the town of Nipomo (lat. 35°11'45" N, long. 120°28'05" W; near W line sec. 27, T 31 S, R 14 E). Named on Santa Margarita Lake (1967) and Tar Spring Ridge (1967) 7.5' quadrangles.

Wizard Gulch [MONTEREY]: *canyon*, drained by a stream that flows nearly 5 miles to San Antonio River 6 miles south of Junipero Serra Peak (lat. 36°03'35" N, long. 121°23'50" W; sec. 35, T 21 S, R 5 E). Named on Bear Canyon (1949) and Cone Peak (1949) 7.5' quadrangles.

Wolf Canyon [SAN LUIS OBISPO]: *canyon*, drained by a stream that flows 6 miles to Clarke Canyon 7 miles west-northwest of Shandon (lat. 35°41'05" N, long. 120°29'40" W; sec. 8, T 26 S, R 14 E). Named on Shandon (1961) 7.5' quadrangle.

Wolf Hill [MONTEREY]: *hill*, 5.5 miles east-southeast of Seaside (lat. 36°35'15" N, long. 121°45'30" W). Named on Seaside (1947) 7.5' quadrangle.

Wolfort's [SAN LUIS OBISPO]: *locality*, nearly 4 miles east-northeast of Simmler at the southwest base of Temblor Range (lat. 35°22'40" N, long. 119°55'40" W; sec. 27, T 29 S, R 19 E). Named on McKittrick (1912) 30' quadrangle.

Wons Creek: see **San Lucas Creek** [SANTA BARBARA].

Wood Canyon [MONTEREY]: *canyon*, drained by a stream that flows nearly 1.25 miles to lowlands 13 miles southeast of Parkfield (lat. 35°47'25" N, long. 120°14'15" W; near SE cor. sec. 33, T 24 S, R 16 E). Named on Tent Hills (1942) 7.5' quadrangle.

Wood Canyon [SAN LUIS OBISPO]: *canyon*, drained by a stream that flows 6 miles to Estrella River 2.5 miles west of Shandon (lat. 35°39'15" N, long. 120°25'15" W; sec. 24, T 26 S, R 14 E). Named on Shandon (1961) and Shedd Canyon (1961) 7.5' quadrangles.

Wood Canyon [SANTA BARBARA]: *canyon*, drained by a stream that flows 3.5 miles to the sea 1.5 miles east of Point Conception (lat. 34°27'05" N, long. 120°26'30" W). Named on Point Conception (1953) 7.5' quadrangle.

Woods Creek: see **Sapaque Creek** [MONTEREY-SAN LUIS OBISPO].

Woods Lagoon [SANTA CRUZ]: *lake*, nearly 1 mile long, 1.5 miles northeast of Point Santa Cruz near the coast (lat. 36°58' N, long. 122°00'05" W). Named on Santa Cruz (1954) and Soquel (1954) 7.5' quadrangles. The name commemorates John Woods, who had property by the lake; this lake and Schwans Lagoon together are known as Twin Lakes (Clark, 1986, p. 329, 406).

Woods Valley: see **Sapaque Valley** [MONTEREY].

Woodtick Canyon [MONTEREY]: *canyon*, drained by a stream that flows 3 miles to Arroyo Seco (1) 6.5 miles north-northwest of

Junipero Serra Peak (lat. 36°14'20" N, long. 121°26'35" W; sec. 32, T 19 S, R 5 E). Named on Junipero Serra Peak (1949) 7.5' quadrangle.

Workfield Siding [MONTEREY]: *locality,* 3 miles south-southwest of Marina along Southern Pacific Railroad (lat. 36°38'40" N, long. 121°49'20" W). Named on Marina (1947) 7.5' quadrangle.

Wreck Beach [MONTEREY]: *beach,* 1 mile east of Pfeiffer Point along the coast (lat. 36°14'05" N, long. 120°47'50" W; sec. 36, T 19 S, R 1 E). Named on Pfeiffer Point (1956) 7.5' quadrangle. The name recalls shipwrecks that occurred at the place in 1909, 1916, and 1922 (Clark, 1991, p. 613).

Wreck Canyon [SANTA BARBARA]: *canyon,* drained by a stream that flows 3.5 miles to the sea nearly 3.25 miles east-northeast of South Point on Santa Rosa Island (lat. 33°54'45" N, long. 120°03'40" W). Named on Santa Rosa Island South (1943) 7.5' quadrangle. The name is from the wreck of the ship *Crown of England* near the mouth of the canyon; the feature first was called Cañada La Jolla (Doran, p. 190).

Wunpost [MONTEREY]: *locality,* 5.5 miles northwest of Bradley along Southern Pacific Railroad (lat. 35°55'45" N, long. 120°51'40" W; sec. 14, T 23 S, R 10 E). Named on Wunpost (1949) 7.5' quadrangle. According to local tradition, the name commemorates a Chinese workman killed near the place during construction of the railroad (Bruce Montgomery, personal communication, 1970).

Wyckoff Ledge: see **Crook Point** [SANTA BARBARA].

Wylie Canyon [SANTA BARBARA]: *canyon,* drained by a stream that flows nearly 1 mile to San Pedro Canyon 2.5 miles north-north-west of downtown Goleta (lat. 34°28'15" N, long. 119°50'35" W; at E line sec. 31, T 5 N, R 28 W). Named on Goleta (1950) 7.5' quadrangle.

— X - Y —

Yankee Point [MONTEREY]: *promontory,* 3 miles north-northwest of Soberanes Point along the coast (lat. 35°29'30" N, long. 121°56'40" W). Named on Soberanes Point (1956) 7.5' quadrangle.

Yankee Point Rock [MONTEREY]: *rock,* 100 feet long, 325 feet offshore at Yankee Point (lat. 36°29'25" N, long. 121°56'50" W). Named on Soberanes Point (1956) 7.5' quadrangle.

Yaqui Canyon [MONTEREY]: *canyon,* drained by a stream that flows 3.5 miles to Lewis Creek 14 miles east-northeast of King City (lat. 36°18'05" N, long. 120°54'15" W; near E line sec. 5, T 19 S, R 10 E). Named on Hepsedam Peak (1969) and Lonoak (1969) 7.5' quadrangles.

Yaro Creek [SAN LUIS OBISPO]: *stream,* flows 4.5 miles to Toro Creek (2) 3 miles north-northwest of Pozo (lat. 35°20'35" N, long. 120°23'50" W; at E line sec. 6, T 30 S, R 15 E). Named on Camatta Ranch (1966), Santa Margarita Lake (1967), and Wilson Corner (1966) 7.5' quadrangles.

Ybarra Spring [SAN LUIS OBISPO]: *spring,* 1.5 miles south-southeast of Cholame in Palo Prieto Canyon (lat. 35°42'15" N, long. 120°17'05" W; sec. 31, T 25 S, R 16 E). Named on Cholame (1961) 7.5' quadrangle.

Yeguas Creek [SAN LUIS OBISPO]: *stream,* heads in Kern County and flows 1.25 miles in San Luis Obispo County to join Walnut Creek and form Bitterwater Creek 25 miles southeast of Shandon (lat. 35°27'30" N, long. 120°00'45" W; sec. 26, T 28 S, R 18 E). Named on La Panza NE (1966) 7.5' quadrangle. The name "Los Yeguas Creek" was applied to the stream because many brood mares were pastured about its head—*yeguas* means "mares" in Spanish (Arnold and Johnson, 1910, p. 21).

Yellow Bank: see **Yellowbanks Anchorage** [SANTA BARBARA].

Yellow Bank Creek [SANTA CRUZ]: *stream,* flows nearly 3 miles to the sea 8.5 miles west-northwest of Point Santa Cruz (lat. 36°59'35" N, long. 122°10'10" W). Named on Davenport (1955) and Santa Cruz (1954) 7.5' quadrangles. Called Respini Creek on Ben Lomond (1946) 15' quadrangle. A Swiss settler named Respini lived along the stream (Hoover, Rensch, and Rensch, p. 473).

Yellowbanks Anchorage [SANTA BARBARA]: *embayment,* 2 miles southwest of San Pedro Point at the east end of Santa Cruz Island (lat. 34°00'40" N, long. 119°32'35" W). Named on Santa Cruz Island D (1943) 7.5' quadrangle. Bremner's (1932) map has the name "Yellow Bank" at the place.

Yellow Hill [SAN LUIS OBISPO]: *peak,* 4.25 miles north-northwest of Piedras Blancas Point (lat. 35°43'30" N, long. 121°18'05" W). Altitude 481 feet. Named on Piedras Blancas (1959) 7.5' quadrangle.

Yerba Buena Creek [SAN LUIS OBISPO]: *stream,* flows 5.5 miles to Santa Margarita Creek 1.5 miles north of Santa Margarita (lat. 35° 24'40" N, long. 120°36'20" W). Named on Lopez Mountain (1965) and Santa Margarita (1965) 7.5' quadrangles.

Ygnacio: see **Maria Ygnacio Creek** [SANTA BARBARA].

Yokum Bend [SAN LUIS OBISPO]: *bend,* 6.5 miles west-southwest of Shandon along Estrella River (lat. 35°38'15" N, long. 120°29'15" W; sec. 29, T 26 S, R 14 E). Named on Shandon (1961) 7.5' quadrangle.

York Mountain [SAN LUIS OBISPO]: *peak,* 9.5 miles southwest of Paso Robles (lat. 35°32'45" N, long. 120°50' W; near SW cor. sec. 30, T 27 S, R 11 E). Altitude 1658 feet. Named on York Mountain (1948) 7.5' quadrangle.

Yost Canyon [MONTEREY]: *canyon,* 5 miles long, opens into Hames Valley 8.5 miles west-northwest of Bradley (lat. 35°55' N, long. 120°56'20" W; near W line sec. 24, T 23 S, R 9 E). Named on Bradley (1961) 15' quadrangle. Hames Creek drains the lower part of the canyon.

Yridisis Creek [SANTA BARBARA]: *stream,* flows 3.25 miles to El Jaro Creek 12.5 miles southeast of the city of Lompoc (lat. 34°31'30" N, long. 120°17'50" W). Named on Santa Rosa Hills (1959) 7.5' quadrangle.

Ysabel: see **Lake Ysabel** [SAN LUIS OBISPO].

Ytias Creek [SANTA BARBARA]: *stream,* flows 4.25 miles to El Jaro Creek 8.5 miles southeast of the city of Lompoc (lat. 34°32'50" N, long. 120°21'25" W). Named on Santa Rosa Hills (1959) 7.5' quadrangle.

– Z –

Zaca [SANTA BARBARA]: *locality,* 2.5 miles northwest of Los Olivos along Pacific Coast Railroad (lat. 34°41'10" N, long. 120° 09'15" W); the place is along La Zaca (present Zaca) Creek. Named on Lompoc (1905) 30' quadrangle.

Zaca Creek [SANTA BARBARA]: *stream,* flows 18 miles to Santa Ynez River less than 1 mile southwest of Buellton (lat. 34°36'30" N, long. 120°12'15" W); the stream heads near Zaca Lake and crosses La Zaca grant. Named on Los Olivos (1959), Solvang (1959), Zaca Creek (1959), and Zaca Lake (1964) 7.5' quadrangles. Called La Zaca Creek on Lompoc (1905) 30' quadrangle, but United States Board on Geographic Names (1961b, p. 18) rejected this name for the feature, although the Board recognized that the stream is named for La Zaca grant.

Zaca Lake [SANTA BARBARA]: *lake,* 1150 feet long, 12 miles southeast of Tepusquet Peak (lat. 34°46'40" N, long. 120°02'20" W); the lake is near the head of Zaca Creek. Named on Zaca Lake (1964) 7.5' quadrangle.

Zaca Peak [SANTA BARBARA]: *peak,* 1 mile southeast of Zaca Lake (lat. 34°46'05" N, long. 120°01'20" W); the peak is on Zaca Ridge. Altitude 4341 feet. Named on Zaca Lake (1964) 7.5' quadrangle.

Zaca Ridge [SANTA BARBARA]: *ridge,* west-to northwest-trending, 4 miles long, center 0.5 mile south of Zaca Lake (lat. 34°46'05" N,

long. 120°02'15" W). Named on Zaca Lake (1964) 7.5' quadrangle.

Zanja Cota Creek: see **Zanja de Cota Creek** [SANTA BARBARA].

Zanja de Cota Creek [SANTA BARBARA]: *stream,* flows 4 miles to Santa Ynez River 2.25 miles south-southwest of Santa Ynez (lat. 34°35' N, long. 120°05'45" W). Named on Los Olivos (1959) and Santa Ynez (1959) 7.5' quadrangles. Called Santa Cota Cr. on Lompoc (1905) 30' quadrangle, but United States Board on Geographic Names (1961a, p. 13) rejected the names "Santa Cota Creek," "Sanja Cota Creek," "Santa Cora Creek," and "Zanja Cota Creek" for the stream.

Zanjon de Borregas: see **Borregas Creek** [SANTA CRUZ].

Zanjones [MONTEREY]: *land grant,* south of Chualar. Named on Chualar (1947) and Gonzales (1955) 7.5' quadrangles. Gabriel de la Torre received 1.5 leagues in 1839; Mariano Malarin, executor, claimed 6714 acres patented in 1866 (Cowan, p. 109).

Zayanta [SANTA CRUZ]: *land grant,* at and north of Felton and Mount Hermon. Named on Felton (1955) 7.5' quadrangle. Joseph L. Majors received 1 league in 1841; Isaac Graham and others claimed 2658 acres patented in 1870 (Cowan, p. 97—Cowan listed the grant under the designation "Sayante (or Zayante)"; Perez, p. 104). Colton's (1863) map has the name "Grahams" for a place located within the grant.

Zayante [SANTA CRUZ]: *settlement,* 5 miles east-southeast of the town of Boulder Creek (lat. 37°05'20" N, long. 122°02'40" W; sec. 2, T 10 S, R 2 W); the place is along Zayante Creek. Named on Felton (1955) 7.5' quadrangle. Postal authorities established Zayante post office in 1916 and discontinued it in 1938 (Salley, p. 246).

Zayante: see **Zayanta** [SANTA CRUZ].

Zayante Creek [SANTA CRUZ]: *stream,* flows 10 miles to San Lorenzo River 6 miles south-southeast of the town of Boulder Creek (lat. 37°02'55" N, long. 122°04' W). Named on Castle Rock Ridge (1955) and Felton (1955) 7.5' quadrangles. According to Stewart (p. 548), the name "Zayante" is of Indian origin.

Zigzag Creek [MONTEREY]: *stream,* flows 5.5 miles to Lost Valley Creek 4.5 miles south of Tassajara Hot Springs (lat. 36°10'10" N, long. 121°32'45" W; near NE cor. sec. 29, T 20 S, R 4 E). Named on Tassajara Hot Springs (1956) 7.5' quadrangle.

REFERENCES CITED

BOOKS AND ARTICLES

Alexander, C.S. 1953. "The marine and stream terraces of the Capitola-Watsonville area." *University of California Publications in Geography*, v. 10, no. 1, p. 1-44.

Anderson, Frank M. 1905. "A stratigraphic study in the Mount Diablo Range of California." *Proceedings of the California Academy of Sciences* (series 3), v. II, no. 2, p. 156-248.

Anderson, Frank M., and Martin, Bruce. 1914. "Neocene record in the Temblor basin, California, and Neocene deposits of the San Juan district, San Luis Obispo County." *Proceedings of the California Academy of Sciences* (series 4), v. 4, p. 15-112.

Anderson, Robert, and Pack, Robert W. 1915. *Geology and oil resources of the west border of the San Joaquin Valley north of Coalinga, California*. (United States Geological Survey Bulletin 603.) Washington: Government Printing Office, 220 p.

Anderson, Winslow. 1892. *Mineral springs and health resorts of California*. San Francisco: The Bancroft Company, 347 p.

Angel, Myron. 1883. *History of San Luis Obispo County, California, with illustrations and biographical sketches of its prominent men and pioneers*. Oakland, California: Thompson & West, 391 p.

_____1890a. "Monterey County." *Tenth annual report of the State Mineralogist, for the year ending December 1, 1890*. Sacramento: California State Mining Bureau, p. 345-348.

_____1890b. "San Benito County." *Tenth annual report of the State Mineralogist, for the year ending December 1, 1890*. Sacramento: California State Mining Bureau, p. 515-517.

_____1890c. "San Luis Obispo County." *Tenth annual report of the State Mineralogist, for the year ending December 1, 1890*. Sacramento: California State Mining Bureau, p. 567-585.

Antisell, Thomas. 1855. [On fossiliferous beds in San Luis Obispo County, California.] *California Academy of Natural Sciences Proceedings*, v. 1, p. 34-35.

_____1856. "Geological report." *Reports of explorations and surveys, to ascertain the most practicable and economical route for a railroad from the Mississippi River to the Pacific Ocean*. Volume VII, Part II. (33d Cong., 2d Sess., Sen. Ex. Doc. No. 78.) Washington: Beverley Tucker, Printer, 204 p.

Arbuckle, Clyde. 1968. *Santa Clara Co.*

Ranchos. San Jose, California: The Rosicrucian Press, Ltd., 46 p.

Arnold, Ralph. 1906. *The Tertiary and Quaternary pectens of California*. (United States Geological Survey Professional Paper 47.) Washington: Government Printing Office, 264 p.

Arnold, Ralph, and Anderson, Robert. 1907a. *Geology and oil resources of the Santa Maria oil district, Santa Barbara County, California*. (United States Geological Survey Bulletin 322.) Washington: Government Printing Office, 161 p.

_____1907b. "Metamorphism by combustion of the hydrocarbons in the oil-bearing shale of California." *Journal of Geology*, v. 15, no. 8, p. 750-758.

_____1908. *Preliminary report on the Coalinga oil district, Fresno and Kings Counties, California*. (United States Geological Survey Bulletin 357.) Washington: Government Printing Office, 142 p.

Arnold, Ralph, and Johnson, Harry R. 1909. *Sodium sulphate in Soda Lake, Carriso Plain, San Luis Obispo County, California*. (United States Geological Survey Bulletin 380-L.) Washington: Government Printing Office, 5 p.

_____1910. *Preliminary report on the McKittrick-Sunset oil region, Kern and San Luis Obispo Counties, California*. (United States Geological Survey Bulletin 406.) Washington: Government Printing Office, 225 p.

Ashley, George Hall. 1895. "The Neocene of the Santa Cruz Mountains: I—Stratigraphy." *Proceedings of the California Academy of Sciences* (series 2), v. 5, p. 273-367.

Bancroft, Hubert Howe. 1888. *History of California, Volume VI, 1848-1859*. San Francisco; The History Company, Publishers, 787 p.

Becker, Robert H. 1964. *Diseños of California ranchos*. San Francisco: The Book Club of California, (no pagination).

_____1969. *Designs on the land*. San Francisco: The Book Club of California, (no pagination).

Berkstresser, C.F., Jr. 1968. *Data for springs in the Southern Coast, Transverse, and Peninsular Ranges of California*. (United States Geological Survey, Water Resources Division, Open-file report.) Menlo Park, California, 21 p. + appendices.

Blake, William P. 1856. "Observations on the physical geography and geology of the coast of California, from Bodega bay to San Diego." *United States Coast Survey, Report of the Superintendent 1855.* (34th Cong., 1st Sess., Sen. Ex. Doc. No. 22.) Appendix 65, p. 376-398.

_____1857. "Geological report." *Reports of explorations and surveys, to ascertain the most practicable and economical route for a railroad from the Mississippi River to the Pacific Ocean.* Volume V, Part II. (33d Cong., 2d Sess., Sen. Ex. Doc. No. 78.) Washington: Beverley Tucker, Printer, 370 p.

Bolton, Herbert Eugene. 1931. *Outpost of empire.* New York: Alfred A Knopf, 334 p.

Bradley, Walter W., and Logan, C.A. 1919. "San Benito County." *Report XV of the State Mineralogist.* Sacramento: California State Mining Bureau, p. 617-673.

Bremner, Carl St. J. 1932. *Geology of Santa Cruz Island, Santa Barbara County, California.* (Occasional Papers Number 1.) Santa Barbara, California: Santa Barbara Museum of Natural History, 33 p.

_____1933. *Geology of San Miguel Island, Santa Barbara County, California.* (Occasional Papers Number 2.) Santa Barbara, California: Santa Barbara Museum of Natural History, 23 p.

Brewer, William H. 1949. *Up and down California in 1860-1864.* Berkeley and Los Angeles: University of California Press, 583 p.

Brown, Alan K. 1975. *Place names of San Mateo County.* San Mateo, California: San Mateo County Historical Association, 118 p.

Burgess, Sherwood D. 1962. "Lumbering in Hispanic California." *The California Historical Society Quarterly,* v. 41, no. 3, p. 237-248.

California Division of Highways. 1934. *California highway transportation survey, 1934.* Sacramento: Department of Public Works, Division of Highways, 130 p. + appendices.

Carson, James H. 1950. *Recollections of the California mines.* Oakland, California: Biobooks, 113 p.

Cerruti, Henry. 1954. *Ramblings in California, The adventures of Henry Cerruti.* Berkeley, California: Friends of the Bancroft Library, 143 p.

Chase, J. Smeaton. 1913. *California coast trails.* Boston and New York: Houghton Mifflin Company, 326 p.

Clark, Donald Thomas. 1986. *Santa Cruz County place names.* Santa Cruz: Santa Cruz Historical Society, 552 p.

_____1991. *Monterey County place names.* Carmel Valley, California: Kestrel Press, 737 p.

Cowan, Robert G. 1956. *Ranchos of California.* Fresno, California: Academy Library Guild, 151 p.

Coy, Owen C. 1923. *California county boundaries.* Berkeley: California Historical Survey Commission, 335 p.

Crawford, J.J. 1894. "Report of the State Mineralogist." *Twelfth report of the State Mineralogist, (Second Biennial,) two years ending September 15, 1894.* Sacramento: California State Mining Bureau, p. 8-412.

_____1896. "Report of the State Mineralogist." *Thirteenth report (Third Biennial) of the State Mineralogist for the two years ending September 15, 1896.* Sacramento: California State Mining Bureau, p. 10-646.

Crippen, Richard A., Jr. 1951. *Nephrite jade and associated rocks of the Cape San Martin region, Monterey County, California.* (California Division of Mines Special Report 10-A.) San Francisco: Division of Mines, 14 p.

Davidson, George. 1887. "An examination of some of the early voyages of discovery and exploration on the northwest coast of America, from 1539 to 1603." *Report of the Superintendent of the U.S. Coast and Geodetic Survey, showing progress of the work during the fiscal year ending with June, 1886.* Appendix No. 7. Washington: Government Printing Office, p. 155-247.

_____1907. "The discovery of the Bay of San Francisco and the rediscovery of the Port of Monterey." *Transactions and Proceedings of the Geographical Society of the Pacific* (series II), v. IV, p, 1-153.

Davis, Charles H. 1912. "The Los Burros mining district." *Mining and Scientific Press,* v. 104, no. 20, p. 696-698.

Derby, Geo. H. 1852. "A report of the Tulare valley." *Report of the Secretary of War.* (32d Cong., 1st Sess., Sen. Ex. Doc. 110.) 17 p.

Dibblee, T.W., Jr. 1950. *Geology of southwestern Santa Barbara County, California.* (California Division of Mines Bulletin 150.) San Francisco: Division of Mines, 95 p.

Diller, J.S., and others. 1915. *Guidebook of the Western United States, Part D. The Shasta Route and Coast Line.* (United States Geological Survey Bulletin 614.) Washington: Government Printing Office, 142 p.

Dillon, Richard H. 1960. *La Panza.* San Francisco: Printed for private circulation by the Grabhorn Press, 12 p.

_____1966. *The legend of Grizzly Adams: California's greatest mountain man.* New York: Coward-McCann, Inc., 223 p.

Doran, Adelaide LeMert. 1980. *Pieces of eight Channel Islands, A bibliographical guide and source book.* Glendale, California: The Arthur H. Clark Company, 340 p.

Eldridge, George H. 1901. "The asphalt and bituminous rock deposits of the United States." *Twenty-second annual report of the United States Geological Survey to the Secretary of the Interior, 1900-01.* Part. I. Washington: Government Printing Office, p. 209-452.

_____1903. "Origin and distribution of asphalt and bituminous rock deposits in the United States." *Contributions to economic geology, 1902.* (United States Geological Survey Bulletin 213.) Washington: Government Printing Office, p. 296-305.

Elliott and Moore. 1881. *History of Monterey County, California.* San Francisco, California: Elliott and Moore, Publishers, 197 p.

Emery, K.O. 1954. "The Painted Cave, Santa Cruz Island." *Sea and Pacific Motorboat,* v. 46, p. 38-39, 91-92.

English, Walter A. 1918. "Geology and oil prospects of the Salinas Valley-Parkfield area, California." *Contributions to economic geology, 1918, Part II.—Mineral fuels.* (United States Geological Survey Bulletin 691-H.) Washington: Government Printing Office, p. 219-250.

Fagan, Brian M. 1981. *California coastal passages.* Santa Barbara and Anaheim, California: Capra Press and CharGuide Ltd., 159 p.

Fairbanks, Harold W. 1893. "Notes on a farther study of the pre-Cretaceous rocks of the California Coast Ranges." *American Geologist,* v. 11, no. 2, p. 69-84.

_____1894. "Geology of northern Ventura, Santa Barbara, San Luis Obispo, Monterey, and San Benito Counties." *Twelfth report of the State Mineralogist, (Second Biennial,) two years ending September 15, 1894.* Sacramento: California State Mining Bureau, p. 493-526.

_____1895. "On analcite diabase from San Luis Obispo County, California." *University, of California, Bulletin of the Department of Geology,* v. 1, no. 9, p. 273-300.

_____1896. "The geology of Point Sal." *University of California, Bulletin of the Department of Geology,* v. 2, no. 1, p. 1-92.

Farnham, Thomas Jefferson. 1947. *Travels in California.* Oakland, California: Biobooks, 166 p.

Fink, Augusta. 1972. *Monterey, The presence of the past.* San Francisco: Chronicle Books, 254 p.

Forbes, Alexander. 1839. *California, A history of Upper and Lower California, from their first discovery to the present time.* London: Smith, Elder and Co., Cornhill, 352 p.

Franke, Herbert A. 1935. "Mines and mineral resources of San Luis Obispo County." *California Journal of Mines and Geology,* v. 31, no. 4, p. 402-464.

Frazer, Robert W. 1965. *Forts of the West.* Norman: University of Oklahoma Press, 246 p.

Fremont, John Charles. 1964. *Geographical memoir upon Upper California in illustration of his map of Oregon and California, newly reprinted from the edition of 1848.* San Francisco: The Book Club of California, 65 p.

Frickstad, Walter N. 1955. *A century of California post offices, 1848 to 1954.* Oakland, California: Philatelic Research Society, 395 p.

Gabb, W.M. 1869. *Cretaceous and Tertiary fossils.* (Geological Survey of California. Palæontology, Volume II.) Published by authority of the Legislature of California, 299 p.

Gagnon, Dennis R. 1981. *Exploring the Santa Barbara backcountry.* Santa Cruz: Western Tanager Press, 151 p.

Gleason, Duncan. 1958. *The islands and ports of California.* New York: The Devin-Adair Company, 201 p.

Goodyear, W.A. 1888. "Petroleum, asphaltum, and natural gas." *Seventh annual report of the State Mineralogist, for the year ending October 1, 1887.* Sacramento: California State Mining Bureau, p. 63-114.

_____1890. "Santa Cruz Island." *Ninth Annual Report of the State Mineralogist, for the year ending December 1, 1889.* Sacramento: California State Mining Bureau, p. 155-170.

Greenhow, Robert. 1844. *The history of Oregon and California, and the other territories on the North-west coast of North America.* Boston: Charles C. Little and James Brown, 482 p.

Gudde, Erwin G. 1949. *California place names.* Berkeley and Los Angeles: University of California Press, 431 p.

_____1969. *California place names.* Berkeley and Los Angeles: University of California Press, 416 p.

Hamilton, Geneva. 1974. *Where the highway ends—Cambria, San Simeon and the ranchos.* San Luis Obispo, California: Padre Productions, 219 p.

Hamlin, Homer. 1904. *Water resources of the Salinas Valley, California.* (United States Geological Survey Water-Supply and Irrigation Paper No. 89.) Washington: Government Printing Office, 91 p.

Hamman, Rick. 1980. *California central coast railways.* Boulder, Colorado: Pruett Publishing Company, 309 p.

Hanna, Phil Towsend. 1951. *The dictionary of California land names.* Los Angeles: The Automobile Club of Southern California, 392 p.

Harder, E.C. 1910 "Some chromite deposits in western and central California." *Contributions to economic geology, 1909, Part I.—Metals and nonmetals, except fuels. Rare Metals.* (United States Geological Survey Bulletin 430-D.) Washington: Government Printing Office, p. 19-35.

Hart, Earl W. 1978. *Limestone, dolomite, and shell resources of the Coast Range Province, California.* (California Division of Mines and Geology Bulletin 197.) Sacramento, California: California Division of Mines and Geology, 103 p.

Hart, James D. 1978. *A companion to California.* New York: Oxford University Press, 504 p.

Hobson, J.B. 1890. "The Santa Maria River." *Tenth annual report of the State Mineralogist, for the year ending December 1, 1890.* Sacramento: California State Mining Bureau, p. 600-601.

Hoover, Mildred Brooke, Rensch, Hero Eugene, and Rensch, Ethel Grace. 1966. *Historic spots in California.* (Third edition, revised by William N. Abeloe.) Stanford, California: Stanford University Press, 642 p.

Howard, Don. 1973. *Lost adobes of Monterey County.* Carmel, California: Monterey County Archæological Society, 105 p.

Hubbard, Henry G. 1943. "Mines and mineral

resources of Santa Cruz County." *California Journal of Mines and Geology,* v. 39, no. 1, p. 11-52.

Huguenin, Emile. 1919. "Santa Barbara County." *Report XV of the State Mineralogist.* Sacramento: California State Mining Bureau, p. 727-750.

Irelan, William, Jr. 1888. "Report of the State Mineralogist." *Eighth annual report of the State Mineralogist. For the year ending October 1, 1888.* Sacramento, California State Mining Bureau, p. 12-695.

Johnston, Robert B. 1970. *Old Monterey County, A pictorial history.* (No place): Monterey Savings and Loan Association, 119 p.

Keller, George. 1955. *A trip across the plains and life in California.* Oakland, California: Biobooks, 44 p.

Kew, William S.W. 1920. "Cretaceous and Cenozoic Echinoidea of the Pacific Coast of North America." *University of California Publications in Geology,* v. 12, no. 2, p. 23-236.

_____1927. "Geologic sketch of Santa Rosa Island, Santa Barbara County, California." *Bulletin of the Geological Society of America,* v. 38, no. 4, p. 645-653.

Kroeber, A.L. 1916. "California place names of Indian origin." *University of California Publications in American Archæology and Ethnology,* v. 12, no. 2, p. 31-69.

_____1925. *Handbook of the Indians of California.* (Smithsonian Institution, Bureau of American Ethnology Bulletin 78.) Washington: Government Printing Office, 995 p.

Laizure, C. McK. 1925. "San Francisco field division (Monterey County)." *Mining in California,* v. 21, no. 1, p. 23-57.

_____1926. "San Francisco field division (Santa Cruz County)." *Mining in California,* v. 22, no. 1, p. 68-93.

Lawson, Andrew C. 1893. "The geology of Carmelo Bay." *University of California, Bulletin of the Department of Geology,* v. 1, no. 1, p. 1-59.

Lee, Georgia, and others. 1977. *An uncommon guide to San Luis Obispo County, California.* San Luis Obispo, California: Padre Productions, 160 p.

Lewis, Betty. 1976. *Watsonville, Memories that linger.* Fresno: Valley Publishers, 220 p.

_____1977. *Monterey Bay yesterday.* Fresno: Valley Publishers, 124 p.

Loel, Wayne, and Corey, W.H. 1932. "The Vaqueros Formation, lower Miocene of California; I, Paleontology." *University of California Publications, Bulletin of the Department of Geological Sciences,* v. 22, no. 3, p. 31-410.

Loew, Oscar. 1876. "Report on the physical and agricultural features of southern California, and especially of the Mohave Desert." *Annual report upon the geographical surveys west of the one hundredth meridian, in California, Nevada, Utah, Colorado, Wyoming, New Mexico, Arizona, and Montana.* (Appendix JJ of *The Annual Report of the Chief of Engineers for 1876.*) Washington: Government Printing Office, p. 214-222.

Logan, C.A. 1917. "San Luis Obispo County." *Report XV of the State Mineralogist.* Sacramento: California State Mining Bureau, p. 674-726.

Lussier, Tomi Kay. 1979. *Big Sur, A complete history and guide.* Monterey, California: Big Sur Publications, 59 p.

Lydon, Sandy. 1985. *Chinese gold, The Chinese in the Monterey Bay region.* Capitola, California: Capitola Book Company, 550 p.

Lydon, Sandy, and Swift, Carolyn. 1978. *Soquel Landing to Capitola-by-the-Sea.* California History Center, DeAnza College, 99 p.

Lynch, James. 1970. "With Stevenson to California, 1846-1848." *The New York Volunteers in California.* Glorieta, New Mexico: The Rio Grande Press, Inc., 65 p.

MacGregor, Bruce A. 1968. *South Pacific Coast, An illustrated history of the narrow gauge South Pacific Coast Railroad.* Berkeley, California: Howell-North Books, 280 p.

Mendenhall, Walter C. 1908. *Preliminary report on the ground waters of San Joaquin Valley, California.* (United States Geological Survey Water-Supply Paper 222.) Washington: Government Printing Office, 52 p.

Mosier, Dan L. 1979. *California coal towns, coaling stations, & landings.* San Leandro, California: Mines Road Books, 8 p.

Newhall, Ruth Waldo. 1958. *The Newhall ranch.* San Marino, California: The Huntington Library, 120 p.

Nicholson, Loren. 1980. *Rails across the ranchos.* Fresno, California: Valley Publishers, 197 p.

Nomland, Jorgen O. 1917. "The Etchegoin Pliocene of middle California." *University of California Publications, Bulletin of the Department of Geology,* v. 10, no. 14, p. 191-254.

Nutter, Edward Hoit. 1901. "Sketch of the geology of the Salinas Valley, California." *Journal of Geology,* v. 9, no. 4, p. 330-336.

Orr, Phil C. 1960. *Radiocarbon dates from Santa Rosa Island, II.* (Bulletin No. 3, Department of Anthropology.) Santa Barbara: Santa Barbara Museum of Natural History, 10 p.

Parke, John G. 1857. "General report." *Reports of explorations and surveys, to ascertain the most practicable and economical route for a railroad from the Mississippi River to the Pacific Ocean.* Volume VII. (33d Cong., 2d Sess., Sen. Ex. Doc. No. 78.) Washington: Beverley Tucker, Printer, 42 p.

Perez, Crisostomo N. 1996. *Land grants in Alta California.* Rancho Cordova, California: Landmark Enterprises, 264 p.

Pierce, Marjorie. 1977. *East of the Gabilans.* Fresno: Valley Publishers, 194 p.

Preston, E.B. 1893a. "Monterey County." *Elev-*

enth report of the State Mineralogist, (First Biennial,) Two years ending September 15, 1892. Sacramento: California State Mining Bureau, p. 259-262.

_____1893b. "San Benito County." Eleventh report of the State Mineralogist, (First Biennial,) Two years ending September 15, 1892. Sacramento: California State Mining Bureau, p. 370-373.

Rambo, F. Ralph. 1964. Almost forgotten. (Author), 48 p.

Rand, William W. 1931. "Preliminary report of the geology of Santa Cruz Island, Santa Barbara County, California." Mining in California, v. 27, no. 2, p. 214-219.

Reed, Ralph D. 1933. Geology of California. Tulsa, Oklahoma: American Association of Petroleum Geologists, 355 p.

Reinstedt, Randall A. 1973. Gold in the Santa Lucias. Carmel, California: Ghost Town Publications, 96 p.

_____1975. Shipwrecks & sea monsters of California's central coast. Carmel, California: Ghost Town Publications, 168 p.

Rife, Joanne. 1977. Where the light turns gold, The story of the Santa Ynez Valley. Fresno: Valley Publishers, 167 p.

Rintoul, William. 1978. Oildorado. Santa Cruz, California: Valley Publishers, 241 p.

Rowland, Leon. 1980. Santa Cruz, The early years. Santa Cruz, California: Paper Vision Press, 273 p.

Salley, H.E. 1977. History of California post offices, 1849-1976. La Mesa, California: Postal History Associates, Inc., 300 p.

Shumate, Albert. 1977. Francisco Pacheco of Pacheco Pass. Stockton, California: University of the Pacific, 47 p.

Smith, Frances Rand. 1932. The mission of San Antonio de Padua. Stanford University, California: Stanford University Press, 108 p.

Spence, Mary Lee, and Jackson, Donald (editors). 1973. The expeditions of John Charles Frémont, Volume 2, The Bear Flag revolt and the court-martial. Urbana, Chicago, and London: University of Illinois Press, 519 p.

Stanley, Leo L. 1976. San Miguel at the turn of the century. Fresno: Valley Publishers, 148 p.

Stewart, George R. 1970. American place-names, A concise and selective dictionary for the continental United States of America. New York: Oxford University Press, 550 p.

Talbot, Theodore. 1972. Soldier in the West, Letters of Theodore Talbot during his services in California, Mexico and Oregon, 1845-53. Norman: University of Oklahoma Press, 210 p.

Taylor, Bayard. 1850. Eldorado, or Adventures in the path of empire. New York: George P. Putnam, (two volumes) 251 p. + 255 p.

Tompkins, Walker A., and Ruiz, Russell A. 1970. Historical high lights of Santa Barbara. (No place): Santa Barbara National Bank, 136 p.

Townsend, E.D. 1970. The California diary of General E.D. Townsend. Los Angeles: The Ward Ritchie Press, 184 p.

Trask, John B. 1854. Report on the geology of the Coast Mountains, and part of the Sierra Nevada: embracing their industrial resources in agriculture and mining. (Sen., Sess. of 1854, Doc. No. 9.) Sacramento: State Printer, 95 p.

United States Board on Geographic Names (under name "United States Geographic Board"). 1933. Sixth report of the United States Geographic Board, 1890 to 1932. Washington: Government Printing Office, 834 p.

_____(under name "United States Geographic Board"). 1934. Decisions of the United States Geographic Board, No. 34—Decisions June 1933-March 1934. Washington: Government Printing Office, 20 p.

_____(under name "United States Board on Geographical Names"). 1936a. Decisions of the United States Board on Geographical Names, Decisions rendered between July 1, 1934, and June 30, 1935. Washington: Government Printing Office, 26 p.

_____(under name "United States Board on Geographical Names"). 1936b. Decisions of the United States Board on Geographical Names, Decisions rendered between July 1, 1935, and June 30, 1936. Washington: Government Printing Office, 44 p.

_____(under name "United States Board on Geographical Names"). 1938. Decisions of the United States Board on Geographical Names, Decisions rendered between July 1, 1937, and June 30, 1938. Washington: Government Printing Office, 62 p.

_____(under name "United States Board on Geographical Names"). 1939. Decisions of the United States Board on Geographical Names, Decisions rendered between July 1, 1938, and June 30, 1939. Washington: Government Printing Office, 41 p.

_____(under name "Board on Geographical Names"). 1943. Decisions rendered between July 1, 1941, and June 30, 1943. Washington: Department of the Interior, 104 p.

_____1949. Decision lists nos. 4905, 4906, May, June, 1949. Washington: Department of the Interior, 10 p.

_____1950. Decision lists nos. 4910, 4911, 4912, October, November, December, 1949. Washington: Department of the Interior, 10 p.

_____1959. Decisions on names in the United States, Puerto Rico and the Virgin Islands, Decisions rendered from April 1957 through December 1958. (Decision list no. 5901.) Washington: Department of the Interior, 100 p.

_____1960a. Decisions on names in the United States and Puerto Rico, Decisions rendered in May, June, July, and August, 1959. (Decision list no. 5903.) Washington: Department of the Interior, 79 p.

_____1960b. Decisions on names in the United States, Decisions rendered from September 1959 through December 1959. (Decision list no. 5904.) Washington: Department of the Interior, 68 p.

_____1960c. *Decisions on names in the United States, Puerto Rico and the Virgin Islands, Decisions rendered from January through April 1960.* (Decision list no. 6001.) Washington: Department of the Interior, 79 p.

_____1961a. *Decisions on names in the United States, Decisions rendered from January through April 1961.* (Decision list no. 6101.) Washington: Department of the Interior, 74 p.

_____1961b. *Decisions on names in the United States, Decisions rendered from May through August 1961.* (Decision list no. 6102.) Washington: Department of the Interior, 81 p.

_____1962a. *Decisions on names in the United States, Decisions rendered from September through December 1961.* (Decision list no. 6103.) Washington: Department of the Interior, 75 p.

_____1962b. *Decisions on names in the United States, Decisions rendered from January through April 1962.* (Decision list no. 6201.) Washington: Department of the Interior, 72p.

_____1962c. *Decisions on names in the United States, Decisions rendered from May through August 1962.* (Decision list no. 6202.) Washington: Department of the Interior, 81 p.

_____1963a. *Decisions on names in the United States, Decisions rendered from September through December 1962.* (Decision list no. 6203.) Washington: Department of the Interior, 59 p.

_____1963b. *Decisions on geographic names in the United States, May through August 1963.* (Decision list no. 6302.) Washington: Department of the Interior, 81 p.

_____1964. *Decisions on geographic names in the United States, May through August 1964.* (Decision List No. 6402.) Washington: Department of the Interior, 85 p.

_____1965a. *Decisions on geographic names in the United States, September through December 1964.* (Decision list no. 6403.) Washington: Department of the Interior, 66 p.

_____1965b. *Decisions on geographic names in the United States, January through March 1965.* (Decision list no. 6501.) Washington: Department of the Interior, 85 p.

_____1965c. *Decisions on geographic names in the United States, April through June 1965.* (Decision list no. 6502.) Washington: Department of the Interior, 39 p.

_____1965d. *Decisions on geographic names in the United States, July through September 1965.* (Decision list no. 6503.) Washington: Department of the Interior, 74 p.

_____1966. *Decisions on geographic names in the United States, April through June 1966.* (Decision list no. 6602.) Washington: Department of the Interior, 36 p.

_____1967a. *Decisions on geographic names in the United States, July through September 1966.* (Decision list no. 6603.) Washington: Department of the Interior, 38 p.

_____1967b. *Decisions on geographic names in the United States, October through December 1966.* (Decision list no. 6604.) Washington: Department of the Interior, 36 p.

_____1967c. *Decisions on geographic names in the United States, January through March 1967.* (Decision list no. 6701.) Washington: Department of the Interior, 20 p.

_____1967d. *Decisions on geographic names in the United States, July through September 1967.* (Decision list no. 6703.) Washington: Department of the Interior, 29 p.

_____1968a. *Decisions on geographic names in the United States, October through December 1967.* (Decision list no. 6704.) Washington: Department of the Interior, 46 p.

_____1968b. *Decisions on geographic names in the United States, January through March 1968.* (Decision list no. 6801.) Washington: Department of the Interior, 51 p.

_____1968c. *Decisions on geographic names in the United States, April through June 1968.* (Decision list no. 6802.) Washington: Department of the Interior, 42 p.

_____1972a. *Decisions on geographic names in the United States, October through December 1971.* (Decision list no. 7104.) Washington: Department of the Interior, 20 p.

_____1972b. *Decisions on geographic names in the United States, January through March 1972.* (Decision list no. 7201.) Washington: Department of the Interior, 32 p.

_____1972c. *Decisions on geographic names in the United States, July through September 1972.* (Decision list no. 7203.) Washington: Department of the Interior, 17 p.

_____1973. *Decisions on geographic names in the United States, October through December 1972.* (Decision list no. 7204.) Washington: Department of the Interior, 15 p.

_____1974a. *Decisions on geographic names in the United States, January through March 1974.* (Decision list no. 7401.) Washington: Department of the Interior, 27 p.

_____1974b. *Decisions on geographic names in the United States, July through September 1974.* (Decision list no. 7403.) Washington: Department of the Interior, 34 p.

_____1975. *Decisions on geographic names in the United States, July through September 1975.* (Decision list no. 7503.) Washington: Department of the Interior, 33 p.

_____1977. *Decisions on geographic names in the United States, July through September 1977.* (Decision list no. 7703.) Washington: Department of the Interior, 25 p.

_____1978a. *Decisions on geographic names in the United States, January through March 1978.* (Decision list no. 7801.) Washington: Department of the Interior, 18 p.

_____1978b. *Decisions on geographic names in the United States, April through June 1978.* (Decision list no. 7802.) Washington: Department of the Interior, 30 p.

_____1978c. *Decisions on geographic names in*

the United States, July through September 1978. (Decision list no. 7803.) Washington: Department of the Interior, 32 p.

_____1978d. *Decisions on geographic names in the United States, October through December 1978.* (Decision list no. 7804.) Washington: Department of the Interior, 48 p.

_____1979a. *Decisions on geographic names in the United States, April through June 1979,* (Decision list no. 7902.) Washington: Department of the Interior, 33 p.

_____1979b. *Decisions on geographic names in the United States, July through September 1979.* (Decision list no. 7903.) Washington: Department of the Interior, 38 p.

_____1980. *Decisions on geographic names in the United States, October through December 1979.* (Decision list no. 7904.) Washington: Department of the Interior, 26 p.

_____1981a. *Decisions on geographic names in the United States, January through March 1981.* (Decision list no. 8101.) Washington: Department of the Interior, 23 p.

_____1981b. *Decisions on geographic names in the United States, April through June 1981.* (Decision list no. 8102.) Washington: Department of the Interior, 28 p.

_____1981c. *Decisions on geographic names in the United States, July through September 1981.* (Decision list no. 8103.) Washington: Department of the Interior, 20 p.

_____1983a. *Decisions on geographic names in the United States, January through March 1983.* (Decision list no. 8301.) Washington: Department of the Interior, 33 p.

_____1983b. *Decisions on geographic names in the United States, July through September 1983.* (Decision list no. 8303.) Washington: Department of the Interior, 26 p.

_____1988. *Decisions on geographic names in the United States, July through September 1988.* (Decision list no. 8803.) Washington: Department of the Interior, 19 p.

_____1991. *Decisions on geographic names in the United States.* (Decision list no. 1991.) Washington: Department of the Interior, 40 p.

_____1992. *Decisions on geographic names in the United States.* (Decision list no. 1992.) Washington: Department of the Interior, 21 p.

_____1994. *Decisions on geographic names in the United States.* (Decision list no. 1994.) Washington: Department of the Interior, 17 p.

_____1995. *Decisions on geographic names in the United States.* (Decision list no. 1995.) Washington: Department of the Interior, 19 p.

United States Coast and Geodetic Survey. 1963. *United States Coast Pilot 7, Pacific Coast, California, Oregon, Washington, and Hawaii.* (Ninth edition.) Washington: United States Government Printing Office, 336 p.

United States Coast Survey. 1855. *Report of the Superintendent of the Coast Survey, showing the progress of the Survey during the year 1854.* Washington: Beverley Tucker, Public Printer.

Vancouver, George. 1953. *Vancouver in California, 1792-1794.* (The original account edited and annotated by Marguerite Eyer Wilbur.) Los Angeles: Glen Dawson, 274 p.

Vander Leck, Lawrence. 1922. "Memoranda on asphalt and bituminous sand deposits of California." *Mining in California,* v. 18, no. 5, p. 228-230.

Van Winkle, Walton, and Eaton, Frederick M. 1910. *The quality of the surface waters of California.* (United States Geological Survey Water-Supply Paper 237.) Washington: Government Printing Office, 142 p.

Wagner, Henry R. 1968. *The cartography of the Northwest coast of America to the year 1800.* (One-volume reprint of the 1937 edition.) Amsterdam: N. Israel, 543 p.

Wagner, Jack R. 1974. *The last whistle (Ocean Shore Railroad).* Berkeley, California: Howell-North Books, 135 p.

Wall, Rosalind Sharpe. 1987. *When the coast was wild and lonely, Early settlers of The Sur.* Pacific Grove, California: The Boxwood Press, 190 p.

Waring, Clarence A., and Bradley, Walter W. 1917. "Monterey County." *Report XV of the State Mineralogist.* Sacramento: California Mining Bureau, p. 595-615.

Waring, Gerald A. 1915. *Springs of California.* (United States Geological Survey Water-Supply Paper 338.) Washington: Government Printing Office, 410 p.

Whiting, J.S., and Whiting, Richard J. 1960. *Forts of the State of California.* Seattle, Washington: (Authors), 90 p.

Whitney, J.D. 1865. *Report of progress and synopsis of the field-work from 1860 to 1864.* (Geological Survey of California, Geology, Volume I.) Published by authority of the Legislature of California, 498 p.

Wiedey, Lionel William. 1928. "Notes on the Vaqueros and Temblor Formations of the California Miocene, with descriptions of new species." *Transactions of the San Diego Society of Natural History,* v. 5, no. 10, p. 95-182.

Young, John V. 1979. *Ghost towns of the Santa Cruz Mountains.* Santa Cruz, California: Paper Vision Press, 156 p.

MISCELLANEOUS MAPS

Alexander. 1953. (Untitled map, fig. 5 *in* Alexander.)

Anderson and Martin. 1914. "Geologic map of the San Juan district, northeastern San Luis Obispo County, California." (Plate X *in* Anderson and Martin.)

Arnold and Johnson. 1910. "Preliminary geologic and structural map of the McKittrick-Sunset oil region, California." (Plate I *in* Arnold and Johnson, 1910.)

Ashley. 1894. "Sketch map of the area of the Santa Cruz Mountains." (Plate XXIII *in* Ashley.)

Baker. 1855. "Map of the mining region, of California." Drawn by Geo A. Baker.

Bancroft. 1864. "Bancroft's map of the Pacific States." Compiled by Wm. H. Knight. Published by H.H. Bancroft & Co., Booksellers and Stationers, San Francisco, Cal..

Bartlett. 1854. "General map showing the countries explored & surveyed by the United States & Mexican Boundary Commission in the years 1850, 51, 52, & 53, under the direction of John R. Bartlett, U.S. Commissioner."

Blake. 1857. "Geological map of a part of the State of California explored in 1855 by Lieut. R.S. Williamson, U.S. Top. Engr." (*Accompanies* Blake, 1857.)

Bremner. 1932. "Geologic map, Santa Cruz Island, Santa Barbara County, California." (Plate IV *in* Bremner, 1932.)

_____1933. "Geologic map, San Miguel Island, Santa Barbara County, California." (Plate IV *in* Bremner, 1933.)

California. 1891. (Map reproduced in *Early California, Southern Edition.* Corvalis, Oregon: Western Guide Publishers, p. 44-45.)

California Department of Parks and Recreation. (No date.) (Map of Point Lobos State Reserve.)

California Division of Highways. 1934. (Appendix "A" *of* California Division of Highways.)

California Mining Bureau. 1909a. "San Benito and Monterey Counties." (*In* California Mining Bureau Bulletin 56.)

_____1909b. "San Luis Obispo County." (*In* California Mining Bureau Bulletin 56.)

_____1909c. "Santa Barbara and Ventura Counties." (*In* California Mining Bureau Bulletin 56.)

_____1909d. "San Francisco, San Mateo, Contra Costa, Alameda, Santa Clara, and Santa Cruz Counties." (*In* California Mining Bureau Bulletin 56.)

_____1917a. (Untitled map *in* California Mining Bureau Bulletin 74, p. 166.)

_____1917b. (Untitled map *in* California Mining Bureau Bulletin 74, p. 172.)

_____1917c. (Untitled map *in* California Mining Bureau Bulletin 74, p. 173.)

Colton. 1855. "California." J.H. Colton & Co., New York.

_____1863. "Colton's map of California, Nevada, Utah, Colorado, Arizona, & New Mexico." Published by J.H. Colton, 172 William St., New York.

Cozzens and Davies. 1927. "Map showing location of Mission San Antonio de Padua." Compiled by H.F. Cozzens and Wm. Davies. (Plate II *in* Smith.)

Derby. 1850. "Reconnaissance of the Tulares Valley." Lieut. G.H. Derby, Topl. Engrs., April and May, 1850.

Diller and others. 1915. "Geologic and topographic map of the Coast Route from Los Angeles, California, to San Francisco, California." (*In* Diller and others.)

Eddy. 1854. "Approved and declared to be the official map of the State of California by an act of the Legislature passed March 25th 1853." Compiled by W.M. Eddy, State Surveyor General. Published for R.A. Eddy, Marysville, California, by J.H. Colton, New York.

Eldridge. 1901. "Region of San Lorenzo Creek, Cal." (Figure 45 *in* Eldridge, 1901.)

Emory. 1857-1858. "Map of the United States and their territories between the Mississippi and the Pacific Ocean, and part of Mexico." Compiled from Surveys made under the order of W.H. Emory.

English and Kew. 1916. "Geologic map of middle Salinas Valley, Cal." (Plate 27 *in* English.)

Fairbanks. 1896. "Geological map of Point Sal." (Plate I *in* Fairbanks, 1896.)

Farnham. 1845. "Map of the Californias." (*Accompanies* Farnham.)

Forbes. 1839. "The coasts of Guatimala and Mexico from Panama to Cape Mendocino, with the principal harbors in California." (*Accompanies* Forbes.)

Fremont. 1845. "Map of an exploring expedition to the Rocky Mountains in the year 1842 and to Oregon & North California in the years 1843-44." By Brevet Capt. J.C. Frémont.

Goddard. 1857. "Britton & Rey's map of the State of California." By George H. Goddard.

Greenhow. 1844. "Map of the western and middle portions of North America, to illustrate the history of California, Oregon, and other countries on the north-west coast of America." By Robert Greenhow.

Hamlin. 1904. "Map of the drainage basin of the Salinas River, showing hydrographic features." (Plate I *in* Hamlin.)

Hamman. 1980a. "Aptos Creek." (*In* Hamman, p. 38.)

_____1980b. "Santa Cruz to Los Gatos & the San Lorenzo River basin railroads." (*In* Hamman, p. 82.)

_____1980c. "Ocean Shore Southern Pacific San Vicinte Lumber Co. railroads. " (*In* Hamman, p. 168.)

Harder. 1910. "Map showing the distribution of serpentine areas and chromite mines in the San Luis Obispo district, California." (Plate I *in* Harder.)

Holt. 1863. "A new map of the State of California and Nevada Territory." Published by W. Holt, San Francisco.

Hubbard. 1943. "Map of Santa Cruz County." (Plate II *in* Hubbard.)

Kew. 1927. "Geologic map of Santa Rosa Island, Santa Barbara County, California." (Figure 1 *in* Kew, 1927).

Lawson. 1893. "Geological map of Carmelo Bay." (Plate I *in* Lawson.).

Malaspina. 1791. "Plano del Puerto y Bahie de Monterey, situado en la costa de Californ."

Mendenhall. 1908. "Artesian areas and groundwater levels in the San Joaquin Valley, California." (Plate I *in* Mendenhall.)

Mitchell. 1856. "Mitchell's new national map."

Published by S. Augustus Mitchell, Philadelphia.

Parke. 1854-1855. "Map No. 1, San Francisco Bay to the plains of Los Angeles." From explorations and surveys made by Lieut. John G. Parke. Constructed and drawn by H. Custer. (In *Reports of explorations and surveys, to ascertain the most practicable and economical route for a railroad from the Mississippi River to the Pacific Ocean.* Volume XI. 1861.)

Postal Route. 1884. (Map reproduced in *Early California, Southern Edition.* Corvalis, Oregon: Western Guide Publishers, p. 34-43.)

Railway. 1903. "Commissioners official railway map of California." Approved by the Board of Railroad Commissioners, November 1st, 1903. (Map reproduced in *Early California, Southern Edition.* Corvalis, Oregon: Western Guide Publishers, p. 46-47.)

Rand. 1931. "Geologic map of Santa Cruz Island, California." (*Accompanies* Rand.)

Ransom and Doolittle. 1863. "A new map of the State of California and Nevada Territory." By Lander Ransom and A.J. Doolittle. Published by W. Holt, San Francisco.

Rogers and Johnston. 1857. "State of California." By Prof. H.D. Rogers & A. Keith Johnston.

Southern Pacific Railroad. 1890. "Map of Coast Line from San Francisco to San Luis Obispo." (Reproduced *in* Nicholson, p. 176.)

United States Coast Survey. 1854. "Sketch J, showing progress of the survey on the western coast of the United States, sections X & XI, from 1850 to 1854." (*In* United States Coast Survey.)

United States Geological Survey. 1973. "Channel Island National Monument."

Wilkes. 1849. "Map of Upper California." By the best authorities.

Williamson. 1853. "General map of explorations and surveys in California." By Lieut. R.S. Williamson, Topl. Engr., assisted by Lieut. J.G. Parke, Topl. Engr., and Mr. Isaac William Smith, Civ. Engr. (In *Reports of explorations and surveys, to ascertain the most practicable and economical route for a railroad from the Mississippi River to the Pacific Ocean.* Volume XI. 1861.)

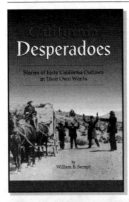

CALIFORNIA DESPERADOES

Stories of Early California Outlaws in Their Own Words
by William B. Secrest

> *"Fascinating..."*
> — John Boessenecker,
> author of *Gold Dust and Gunsmoke*

$15.95
Printed two-color throughout
Many rare photographs & illustrations
Bibliography • Index
272 pages • 6" x 9" • ISBN 1-884995-19-5

FROM MUD-FLAT COVE TO GOLD TO STATEHOOD

California 1840-1850
By Irving Stone
With a foreword by Jean Stone

> Irving Stone *"...one of America's foremost
> literary figures and its greatest story teller."*

> *"...a fascinating book for high school students and adults."*
> —The Bookhandler

$12.95
176 pages • 6" x 9" • ISBN 1-884995-17-9

THE NEWHALL INCIDENT

America's Worst Uniformed Cop Massacre
by Chief John Anderson with Marsh Cassady

> *"Not since Truman Capote's* In Cold Blood *has there been a
> true crime story that so intimately captures the lives of
> killers, victims and police."*
> — Ted Schwarz, author of *The Hillside Strangler*

$14.95
With never-before published CHP photographs
192 pages • 6" x 9" • ISBN 1-884956-01-7

SAN JUAN BAUTISTA

The Town, The Mission & The Park
by Charles W. Clough

> *"Highly recommended."*
> —The Bookwatch

$18.95
175 historic photos, maps and other illustrations
Bibliography • Index
144 pages • 8½" x 11" • ISBN 1-884995-07-1

Available from bookstores, on-line bookstores or by calling 1-800-497-4909